Praise for *The Irish Republican Brotherhood*

'This tersely argued study of the IRB's last years, deploying a remarkable source base, should become required reading on the organization's part in the Irish revolution.'

Charles Townshend, Professor Emeritus of International History,
Keele University

'A masterpiece! John O'Beirne Ranelagh's path-breaking history of the Irish Republican Brotherhood shows that, without it, there would have been no Easter Rising, no IRA and no War of Independence. Provocatively but persuasively, he also forces us to reconsider the role of terror in modern Irish history.'

Christopher Andrew, Emeritus Professor of Modern and
Contemporary History at Cambridge University

'John O'Beirne Ranelagh's landmark study of the IRB shines new light into the darkest and most clandestine recesses of the Irish revolutionary movement. His book is a glowing vindication of painstaking, detailed and judicious historical scholarship. Long will it remain an indispensable reference work for students of Irish state formation.'

John M. Regan, University of Dundee

THE IRISH REPUBLICAN BROTHERHOOD
1914–1924

JOHN O'BEIRNE RANELAGH

IRISH ACADEMIC PRESS

First published in 2024 by
Irish Academic Press
10 George's Street
Newbridge
Co. Kildare
Ireland
www.iap.ie

© John O'Beirne Ranelagh, 2024

978 1 78537 494 4 (Cloth)
978 1 78537 495 1 (Ebook)
978 1 78855 176 2 (PDF)

A CIP catalogue record for this book is available from the British Library.

All rights reserved. No part of this publication may be reproduced, stored in a retrieval system, or transmitted, in any form or by any means (electronic, mechanical, photocopying, recording or otherwise), without the prior written permission of both the copyright owner and the publisher of this book.

Typeset in Adobe Garamond Pro 11/15 pt

Cover design by riverdesignbooks.com

Irish Academic Press is a member of Publishing Ireland.

For my father,

Jim O'Beirne

In the presence of God, I ... do solemnly swear that I will do my utmost to establish the national independence of Ireland, and that I will bear true allegiance to the Supreme Council of the Irish Republican Brotherhood and Government of the Irish Republic and implicitly obey the constitution of the Irish Republican Brotherhood and all my superior officers and that I will preserve inviolable the secrets of the Organisation.

IRB Oath, 1873–1920

CONTENTS

Glossary		ix
Biographies		xv
Preface		xxvii
	Introduction	1
1	Politics and Ideals	11
2	Conspirators	22
3	Infamy	31
4	1873–1917 Constitution	43
5	Members	54
6	Supreme Council	63
7	Infiltration	76
8	Principals: Hobson, Clarke, MacDermott	89
9	Guns and Plans	106
10	Disorganisation	116
11	Rising	124
12	Post Mortem	132
13	Reorganisation	143
14	Collins Emerges	152
15	Elections	170
16	1917–22 Constitution	177
17	The Candidate	182
18	GHQ	193
19	1918 Election	203
20	Killing	212
21	Relationships	220

22	Brugha	235
23	Truce	241
24	Talking	256
25	Three Days in December	269
26	Divides	278
27	1922 Constitution	287
28	Civil War	290
29	1923 Constitution	302
30	Mutiny	306
31	'That's That'	311

Appendix I	Interviews	319
Appendix II	IRB Constitution 1869–73	328
Appendix III	1894: Rules and Regulations	333
Appendix IV	IRB Constitution 1873–1917	340
Appendix V	IRB Constitution 1917–22	346
Appendix VI	IRB Constitution Amendments 1919–21	357
Appendix VII	IRB Constitution 1922	358
Appendix VIII	IRB Constitution 1923	366
Appendix IX	IRB Supreme Council Circular March 1921	375
Appendix X	Michael Collins' Note of the March 1922 IRB Meeting with County Centres and Supreme Council Members on 'The Post-Treaty Situation'	379
Appendix XI	IRB Supreme Council Members 1907–22	382
Appendix XII	IRB Members in Senior Positions 1916–22	389
Appendix XIII	IRB Participation in the 1916 Rising	392

Endnotes	396
Sources and Select Bibliography	498
Acknowledgements	520
Index	523

GLOSSARY

Abstentionism: The policy, formulated by Arthur Griffith and espoused by Sinn Féin, of not taking Westminster parliamentary seats. Sinn Féin MPs elected to Westminster in 1918 formed Dáil Éireann as an Irish parliament instead.

Ancient Order of Hibernians (AOH): The Catholic support organisation of the Irish Parliamentary Party (IPP). Especially strong in Ulster where it protected Catholics from unionist attacks.

Army Mutiny (1924): Disgruntled officers in the Free State's National Army plotted a mutiny asserting that the Free State government was not seeking greater independence from Britain. Most of those involved were to be demobilised or reduced in rank, and this acted as a spur. They were broken up before a mutiny actually took place.

Auxiliaries (1920–21): A feared and effective counter-insurgency unit, nominally a part of the Royal Irish Constabulary (RIC) but effectively independent. About 2,300 ex-British officers in total joined, including three who had won the Victoria Cross. Because of the dreadful attrition of British officers on the Western Front during the First World War, by November 1918 many officers had been promoted from the ranks.

Black and Tans (1920–21): In total, 7,684 men recruited from among ex-British soldiers to reinforce the RIC. Arrived in Ireland in March 1920. At first they wore a combination RIC ('black' – actually dark green) and British Army (tan) uniform, giving them their name. By mid-1921 their uniforms were indistinguishable from those of the RIC. They are often described as having been released from prisons in England to terrorise Ireland. This was not true. Very few had criminal records (perhaps 0.6 per cent), and those who did seem to have largely been charged with non-violent crimes.[1]

Bureau of Military History (BMH): Established by the government in 1947. Recorded 1,773 interviews with participants in the period up to 1921 and in some cases beyond that. Also collected documents. Together with the Military Archives established in 1924 (that include the Military Pensions records), an invaluable resource.

Glossary

Centre: The elected head of an Irish Republican Brotherhood (IRB) Circle.

Circle: The membership unit of the IRB.

Clan na Gael: The American sister organisation of the IRB and a source of finance. Organised a 'Fenian' terror bombing campaign in England in the 1880s.

County Board: Consisting of the Centres of a County.

County Centre: The Centre elected by the Centres of Circles in a County to represent them on the Divisional Board.

Cumann na mBan (the Irish Women's Council): Established in Dublin on 2 April 1914 as an independent republican women's organisation. Some of its members – notably Constance Markievicz – fought during the Rising. After 1916 it was directed by the Irish Volunteers Executive, and later, the Irish Republican Army (IRA) Executive. Its members often acted as couriers for the IRA and IRB and most took the Republican side in the Civil War. Its emblem was a rifle with 'C na mb' superimposed on it – and from 1916 it was an auxiliary unit of the Volunteers/IRA. The Cumann membership was countrywide and provided intelligence, support of all kinds, couriers and smugglers (women were not usually searched). It was a crucial and integrated element in Volunteer/IRA activity. For the IRB it was an effective secret communication channel. Petie Joe McDonnell, officer commanding (O/C), West Connemara Brigade, provided a typical example of Cumann's everyday usefulness to the Volunteers/IRA: 'There was a sister of Paddy Kelly's in the Dublin Co-op Clothing Company who could get in touch with GHQ [Volunteer/IRA General Headquarters Staff], and our reports were sent to her for GHQ'.[2]

Dáil Éireann: The nationalist Irish Parliament composed of all the Sinn Féin MPs elected in the 1918 and 1922 general elections. Since 1922 the Dáil has been the Irish Parliament. Dáil was the Irish for 'Assembly'.

Divisional Board: Consisting of the County Centres of an IRB Division – in Ireland the divisions were the four provinces – who elected one of their number to be the Divisional representative on the Supreme Council. Frequently referred to as 'Leinster Board' or 'Munster Board', etc.

Divisional Centre: The elected head of an IRB Division, usually a member of the IRB Supreme Council.

Dominion: The semi-independent states of the British Empire that, after the First World War, pressed for full independence. The exact nature of Dominion status was not defined until the 1926 Balfour Report, which established that

Glossary

they were 'autonomous Communities within the British Empire, equal in status, in no way subordinate one to another in any aspect of their domestic or external affairs, though united by a common allegiance to the Crown, and freely associated as members of the British Commonwealth of Nations'. In 1926 the Dominions were Canada, Newfoundland, South Africa, Australia, New Zealand and the Irish Free State.

Dublin Castle: The seat of British administration in Ireland.

Dublin Metropolitan Police (DMP) (1836–1925): The unarmed Dublin city police force. Its armed plain-clothes detectives were a particular target for IRA assassination.

Fenian Brotherhood: The American counterpart to the IRB founded in 1858 by John O'Mahony, a Young Irelander. The precursor to Clan na Gael.

Fenians: The name popularly given to the IRB and Clan na Gael. Between 1881 and 1886 a Fenian bombing campaign in Britain, conducted by Irish-American Fenians, prompted journalists to refer to members of both organisations as 'Fenians'.

Fianna Éireann: First established in 1902 by Bulmer Hobson in Belfast, and then recreated in 1909 with Constance Markievicz, as a boys' nationalist organisation modelled on the Boy Scouts but with military training.

Free State Army: The unofficial name of the National Army.

Gaelic Athletic Association (GAA): Founded in 1884 with IRB support. Devoted to Gaelic sports.

Gaelic League: Irish-language and cultural organisation founded in 1893, a prime recruiting ground for the IRB.

General Headquarters Staff (GHQ): Formed in March 1918 by the Volunteer/IRA Executive to direct Volunteer/IRA activities. Its letterhead referred to it as 'General Headquarters' of 'Óglaigh na hÉireann', thus remaining consciously ambivalent about 'Irish Volunteers' and the 'IRA'.

German Plot (1918): Alleged conspiracy by Sinn Féin and Germany to launch another uprising that was used as an excuse to intern Irish republicans.

Irish Citizen Army (ICA) (1913–16): Created by James Connolly to defend demonstrating workers on strike from police attacks. Merged together with the Irish Volunteers into the IRA in 1916.

Irish Convention (1917): Called by Prime Minster David Lloyd George to negotiate agreement between nationalists and unionists on the nature of Home Rule. It met from July 1917 to March 1918 at Trinity College Dublin (TCD). It was boycotted by Sinn Féin and broke up without result.

xii   Glossary

Irish hierarchy: The organised Roman Catholic priesthood from cardinals to parish priests.

Irish Parliamentary Party (IPP): The nationalist constitutionalist political party committed to traditional democratic procedures.

Irish Republican Army (IRA): Created in 1916 as the army of the Republic proclaimed at the start of the Rising. Confusingly, usually called Volunteers until officially renamed IRA in 1921, when there were a theoretical 115,550 members of whom about 1,600 had arms and ammunition.

IRA Executive: The governing body of the IRA from late 1921, the renamed Irish Volunteer Executive.

Irish National Aid and Volunteers' Dependants' Fund (INAVDF) (1917): The amalgamated Irish Republican Prisoners' Dependants' Fund (IRPDF) and National Aid Fund with Kathleen Clarke as president.

Irish Republican Brotherhood (IRB): The secret society responsible for the 1916 Rising and the IRA.

Irish Republican Prisoners' Dependants' Fund (IRPDF) (1916): Established by Kathleen Clarke in May 1916 with money from Clan na Gael and the IRB to support rebels' families.

Irish Volunteers/Óglaigh na hÉireann: Created in 1913 on the IRB's initiative to defend the introduction of Home Rule being opposed by Ulster unionists and the Conservative and Unionist Party. Became the IRA officially in 1921.

Irish Volunteer Executive: The governing body of the Irish Volunteers from 1917. Became the IRA Executive in 1921.

Irish Volunteer Provisional Committee: The governing body of the Volunteers until 1916.

Liberty Clubs (1917): Abstentionist clubs formed by Count Plunkett as the basis of a new political party, but rapidly merged with Sinn Féin.

Mansion House Convention (1917): Arranged by Count Plunkett in an unsuccessful effort to unify the different nationalist political groups. Boycotted by the IPP.

Mansion House Conference (1918): A coming together of the IPP, Sinn Féin, and the Roman Catholic Church opposed to conscription. It signalled the rise of Sinn Féin at the expense of the IPP.

Military Committee: The small and very secret IRB group that planned and organised the 1916 Rising.

National Aid Fund (NAF) (1916): Started by the IPP to help families

Glossary

distressed by the 1916 Rising. Amalgamated with the IRPDF to form the INAVDF.

National Army/Óglaigh na hÉireann (1922–24): The army of the Irish Provisional Government and then of the Irish Free State. Commanded by Michael Collins and then by Richard Mulcahy. Successfully fought against the Republican IRA (also terming themselves Óglaigh na hÉireann) in the 1922–23 Civil War.

O/C: Officer Commanding.

Óglaigh na hÉireann: The Irish name for the Irish Volunteers, the IRA, the National Army and today's Irish Defence Forces. 'The use of the term Óglaigh na hÉireann has been contested since the start of the Civil War when a split in the forces occurred. Official anti-Treaty IRA records captured by the National Army during the Civil War and held in Military Archives (Captured Documents Collection) show the anti-Treaty forces using the term on their headed paper. The use of the term Óglaigh na hÉireann for the National Army continues to this day and was enshrined in the 1954 Defence Act.'[3]

Parliament of Southern Ireland: Created in 1920. First met in January 1922. Named Dáil Éireann after the 1922 general election.

Provisional Irish Republican Army: The breakaway IRA group responsible for most of the republican violence in Northern Ireland since 1969.

Republic, The: A theoretical affair, never fully formulated. Unambiguously rejected by Britain from 1916 to 1923. The Irish Republic was finally established in 1947.

Republicans: A term I have adopted for members of the various IRAs opposed to the 1921 Treaty who fought against the National Army during the 1922–23 Civil War. They were 'Republicans' on the grounds that they were the grouping that continued to recognise the Irish Republic as opposed to the pro-Treaty grouping that accepted the supremacy of the Crown. The Free State was not a republic and was not what Republicans had fought for. This was the cause of the 1922–23 Civil War.

Royal Irish Constabulary (RIC) (1822–1922): An armed constabulary and police force organised on military lines under the control of the Dublin Castle administration. It bore the brunt of the 1919–21 fight with the IRA. Seán Gibbons, a Mayo IRB member, described them: 'Generally speaking, from a physique point of view, they were the most perfect police force in the world and in ordinary times were highly disciplined. Socially, until

xiv Glossary

1916, they had a very good place in the community and generally they married very fine types of womanhood. The results could be seen in their families who were usually of a high degree of intelligence and generally very national.'[4] The force was succeeded by the Royal Ulster Constabulary in Northern Ireland and by An Garda Síochána in the Irish Free State.

Separatism: Seeking independence from Britain. Arthur Griffith advocated an Austro-Hungarian type of dual monarchy. Militant separatists – the IRB – sought complete independence.

Sinn Féin: Founded in 1905. Political party advocating the boycott of Westminster and the creation of an Irish parliament in Dublin. Became the republican party after 1916 but was, in Michael Collins' words, 'the union of all the various sects and leagues' of Irish nationalism.[5] In October 1917, effectively acknowledging that support for a republic might not command a majority, the party allowed for a non-republican settlement.

Supreme Council: The governing body of the IRB consisting of the Divisional Centres and co-opted members.

Teachta Dála (TD): A member of Dáil Éireann.

Treaty, The: Anglo-Irish agreement signed on 6 December 1921 establishing a never fully defined 'not-quite-Dominion' status for Southern Ireland and confirming partition whereby six Ulster counties remained within the United Kingdom. Disagreement about the Treaty was the cause of the 1922–23 Civil War.

Truce, The: Started on 11 July 1921, between the IRA and British forces in Ireland, presaging the Treaty.

Ulster Volunteer Force (UVF) (1912–22): Organised by Unionists to prevent the introduction of Home Rule to Unionist-dominated Ulster. Inspired the creation of the Irish Volunteers a year later.

Young Ireland: A movement in the 1840s dedicated to Irish independence, led by a group of Trinity College graduates who wrote for *The Nation* weekly journal. Made furious by the Great Famine, in 1848 some of its members attempted a rebellion in Tipperary that was easily suppressed and termed 'The Battle of Widow McCormack's Cabbage Patch'. Several Young Irelanders later joined the IRB, and some went to the United States and formed the Fenian Brotherhood and Clan na Gael.

BIOGRAPHIES

Ernest Blythe (1889–1975): Born in Lisburn, Co. Antrim, the son of a Church of Ireland farmer. In 1905, aged 16, he was employed as a boy clerk in Dublin at the Department of Agriculture. He joined the Gaelic League and the GAA. Two years later he was sworn into the IRB Teeling Circle by George Irvine. He joined the Orange Order in 1910 and remained a member for two years; later, this raised questions about his loyalties. He became a recruiter for the IRB, was deported to England and imprisoned, thus not participating in the 1916 Rising. He took no part in the IRB subsequently. He was elected Sinn Féin TD for Monaghan North in 1918 and was appointed Minister for Trade and Commerce in the Dáil of 1919–22. He supported the Treaty and was Minister for Local Government (1922–23), Minister for Finance (1923–32) and then simultaneously Minister for Posts and Telegraphs (1927–32) and Vice-President of the Free State government (1927–32). In 1933 he was a founding member of the Irish fascist organisation, the Blueshirts. In 1935 he became a director of the Abbey Theatre, remaining on the board until 1972. From 1941 to 1967 he was managing director of the theatre.

Úna Brennan (née Bolger) (1888–1958): Born in Co. Wexford. Journalist and republican activist. In 1909 she married Robert Brennan, an Irish-language teacher and member of the IRB, who insisted that the IRB accept his wife as a member.

Cathal Brugha (1874–1922): See Chapter 22. Born Charles William St John Burgess. His father was an English Protestant, his mother a Roman Catholic. He changed his name officially to an Irish form in 1899, influenced by the Irish Ireland movement of the late nineteenth century. His brothers and sisters (of whom there were thirteen) did not change their names. A Gaelic League enthusiast – and a useful cricketer (as Robert Barton told me). IRB organiser. Passionate, brave and a simplistic republican. Joined the Gaelic League (1899) and taught himself Irish, becoming fluent. Joined the IRB (1908). A founder and travelling salesman of Lalor & Co., candle makers (1909), using it as a cover for IRB recruitment around the country. Joined the Irish Volunteers (1913) and took part in the Howth gunrunning (1914). Severely wounded during the 1916 Rising. Rejected the IRB after 1916 on the grounds that its members had not fully taken part in the Rising, and that there was no longer a need for a secret society. IRA Chief of Staff (1917–18). President of Dáil Éireann (1919). Dáil Minister for Defence (1919–22). He refused to take a salary, remitting it to Richard Mulcahy who succeeded him as IRA Chief of Staff and was Deputy Minister for Defence. He opposed the Treaty. He was killed in a shoot-out with National Army forces at the start of the 1922–23 Civil War.

Sir Roger Casement, CMG (1864–1916): Humanitarian and Irish nationalist. Born in Co. Dublin and brought up in Maherintemple, Co. Antrim. 'He was an ardent Home-Ruler and was actually more than that. He was a follower of Arthur Griffith and a separatist. He was one of the pioneers of the Gaelic League.'[1] He joined the British Consular Service and was appointed British Consul in the Belgian Congo where he reported on atrocities committed against the native population. In 1904 his findings were published by the British government to outrage at the exploitation of the country and its people by the Belgian King Leopold. His next appointment was British Consul in Brazil where he again investigated atrocities and his report again caused outrage. He was knighted in 1911 for his investigations. In 1913 he joined the Irish Volunteers' Provisional Committee and was involved in the purchase of rifles and ammunition that were landed at Howth and Kilcoole in 1914. Two months after the start of the First World War, he went to Germany to seek support for an Irish rebellion. He returned to Ireland in 1916 just before the Rising and was arrested shortly after landing from a German submarine at Banna Strand in Co. Kerry, about seven miles north-west of Tralee. Diaries detailing his homosexual exploits were used to dissuade influential friends from interceding on his behalf. He was convicted of treason and hanged in London's Pentonville Prison on 3 August 1916.

Kathleen Clarke (née Daly) (1878–1972): Born in Limerick. Seamstress and dressmaker. Her uncle, John Daly, introduced her to Tom Clarke in 1898. Emigrated to New York in 1901 where she married Clarke. Returned with Clarke to Ireland in 1907 and became fully engaged in his IRB work. Joined Cumann na mBan at its inauguration and later was elected president of its

Dublin central branch. Arrested and imprisoned after the 1916 Rising. Her brother, Edward, and husband were executed for their parts in the Rising. Instrumental in reviving the IRB in 1916–17. She established the IRPDF in 1916, later amalgamated with the National Aid Fund to form the INAVDF of which she was president. Elected to the Executive of Sinn Féin in 1917 and as vice-president of Cumann na mBan. She was arrested and imprisoned in 1918–19 for eleven months in Holloway Prison during the 'German Plot' scare. Elected to Dáil Éireann in 1921. She opposed the Treaty and remained in Irish politics until she emigrated to Liverpool in 1965. Elected the first woman lord mayor of Dublin (1939–41).

Tom Clarke (1857–1916): See Chapter 8. Probably born in Tipperary and brought up on the Isle of Wight where his father, a Co. Leitrim Protestant Bombardier in the Royal Artillery, served; mother a Tipperary Catholic. Joined the IRB (1877). Went to New York and joined Clan na Gael (1878). He took part in the Fenian bombing campaign in England organised by Clan na Gael (1883). Arrested and sentenced to life imprisonment. Released (1898). Returned to New York (1899). Married Kathleen Daly in New York (1901). He became an American citizen on 2 November 1905. Returned to Ireland (1907) determined to prepare a rebellion with a revived IRB supported by Clan na Gael. Opened a tobacconist shop in Dublin. He was the principal contact between the IRB and the Clan (1907–16). Co-founder of *Irish Freedom* newspaper (1910). Treasurer, IRB Supreme Council (1911–16). President of the 1916 Irish Provisional Government. Executed (1916).

Michael Collins (1890–1922): The leading Irish figure of the 1916–22 period, although for most of the period did not occupy the foremost public positions. Born near Clonakilty in west Cork. Worked in London Post Office Bank (1905–10), at Horne & Co. stockbrokers (1910–14), and at the London office of the Guaranty Trust Company of New York (1914–15). Joined the IRB in London (1908). Fought in the 1916 Rising, was interned, then released. Faced the rivalrous antagonism of Cathal Brugha after 1916. President of the IRB (1919–22). IRA Director of Intelligence (1918–22). Dáil Minister for Finance (1919–22). Plenipotentiary during 1921 Treaty negotiations. Leader of the pro-Treaty faction in the Dáil and IRA. Chairman of the Irish Provisional Government (1922). Commander-in-Chief of the National Army (1922). Killed in an ambush in Cork, August 1922.

xviii   Biographies

James Connolly (1868–1916): See Chapter 8. Labour leader. Born in Edinburgh. Formed the ICA. A signatory of the Proclamation of an Irish Republic in 1916. Wounded during the Rising, he was executed tied to a chair.

Sir Alfred Cope (1877–1954): Born in London. A Quaker and a civil servant: he was a detective in HM Customs and Excise. In May 1920 he was appointed Assistant Under Secretary in Ireland, becoming Lloyd George's secret emissary to Michael Collins in particular. Cope was 'ruthless, determined, unorthodox in his official life. In his private life he was gentle, he was loving, he was kind. He was unmarried, but he had a sister who was full of rheumatoid arthritis and couldn't move … she played a remarkable part in helping her brother. She insisted, indeed, on going to live in Ireland … And there, one night, sitting in her chair, immovable, with no one there, totally alone, the rebels burst in – threatened her because she wouldn't give information. So much so that they threatened to light a fire under her chair. They got no information, but they didn't light the fire.'[2]

Cardinal Dr Paul Cullen (1803–1878): Ireland's first cardinal and strongly opposed to the IRB.

Éamon de Valera (1882–1975): See Chapter 17. Born in New York. He became an embodiment of the great Irish nationalist issues as the senior surviving 1916 Rising officer. In 1926 he founded Fianna Fáil and in 1927 entered the Free State Dáil, thus being seen by Republicans as selling out. He was the dominant Irish politician after 1933: Taoiseach for all but six years between 1933 and 1959 and then President of Ireland for sixteen more years (1959–75). Mathematics teacher. Joined the IRB in 1915, but rejected it after 1916, arguing that open organisations offered the best hope for independence. He spent a good deal of 1917 and 1918 in prison, escaping in early 1919 and smuggled soon after to the United States by the IRB where he campaigned unsuccessfully for official American support for Irish independence (1919–20). This took him away from events in Ireland and contributed to the rise of Michael Collins. Often in absentia, he was President of the notional Irish Republic (1921–22), of the Irish Volunteers/IRA (1917–22), of Sinn Féin (1917–26), of Dáil Éireann (1919–22). Taoiseach, Dáil government (1919–22). Leader of the anti-Treaty faction in the Dáil (1921–22).

Biographies

John Devoy (1842–1928): Revolutionary and journalist. The principal Irish-American republican. He was of central importance in the IRB and Clan na Gael 1870–1900 and was the principal figure in Irish-American support for the IRB and Volunteers/IRA after 1916. Born in Co. Kildare. Joined the IRB (1861). In the French Foreign Legion (1861–62). Responsible for recruiting for the IRB within the British Army (1862–66). Arrested and imprisoned (1866–71). Released in 1871 and went to the US, where he founded two newspapers, the *Irish Nation* (1882) and *Gaelic American* (1903) while advancing to the leadership of Clan na Gael. Provided the majority of funding for the IRB. Broke with de Valera over how best to campaign for American recognition of the Republic in the United States (1919–20). Supported the Treaty.

Arthur Griffith (1871–1922): Nationalist journalist and politician. Anglophobe. Born in Dublin. An active member of the Gaelic League and the IRB (1893–*c*. 1910). Founder and editor of *United Irishman* newspaper (1899). His *The Resurrection of Hungary: A Parallel for Ireland* (1904) advocated a dual monarchy solution for Ireland's independent relationship with Britain. A founder of Sinn Féin (1905). James Joyce, writing in September 1906 to his brother, Stanislaus, opined that Griffith 'was the first person in Ireland to revive the separatist idea on modern lines … [He] is educating the people of Ireland on the old pap of racial hatred whereas anyone can see that if the Irish question exists, it exists for the Irish proletariat chiefly.'[3] Griffith opposed Home Rule as not giving Ireland sufficient fiscal independence. Arrested after the 1916 Rising although he had not taken part. Stood aside in favour of de Valera as President of Sinn Féin (1917). Elected Sinn Féin MP for East Cavan (1918). Acting President, Dáil Éireann (1919). Leader of the Irish plenipotentiaries negotiating the Anglo-Irish Treaty (October–December, 1921). Succeeded de Valera as President of the Republic, President of the Dáil, and Taoiseach (January–June 1922). Provisional Government Minister for Foreign Affairs (July–August 1922). Died of a brain haemorrhage (12 August 1922). The strong political move of forming an Irish parliament, the Dáil, whose members refused to take their seats at Westminster, was his achievement. His flexibility about the form that government might take enabled Sinn Féin to be many things to many men – it opened separatism to patriots, and simultaneously diluted it. His rejection of IRB absolutism was in tune with majority opinion generally. By 1922 he did not seem to care what form of government existed in Ireland as long as it possessed a fiscal independence.

Biographies

Bulmer Hobson (1883–1969): See Chapter 8. The reviver of the IRB (1904–14) and principal IRB opponent of Clarke and MacDermott (1914–16). Born in Belfast as a Quaker. Joined the Gaelic League in 1901 and the IRB in 1904. A co-founder of the Dungannon Clubs (1905) to promote republican policies, and of Fianna Éireann (1909), the nationalist boy scouts. Editor, *Irish Freedom* (1910–14). Elected to IRB Supreme Council representing Leinster (1913). Secretary of Irish Volunteers' Provisional Committee (1914–16). Organised the Howth gunrunning (1914). Supported Redmond's demand for half the seats on the Provisional Committee, broke with Clarke and MacDermott, and resigned from the Supreme Council (1914). Opposed the 1916 Rising and withdrew from public affairs.

Douglas Hyde (1860–1949): An academic linguist and the son of a Church of Ireland minister. The Gaelic League's first president. He wanted the League simply to be a cultural organisation but was thwarted by the IRB. First President of the Irish Free State (1938–45).

Charles Kickham (1828–82): Poet and journalist. A founding member of the IRB and regular contributor to *The Irish People*. Generally regarded as the leading IRB intellectual. Arrested in 1865 for plotting rebellion, he was sentenced to fourteen years' penal servitude but released on grounds of ill health in 1869 when he became head of the IRB. In 1873 he drafted a new IRB constitution wherein the Brotherhood claimed to be the government of the Irish Republic, thus providing a counter to the Church's opposition to it as a secret society.

David Lloyd George (1863–1945): Prime Minister of the United Kingdom 1916–22. A Welsh nationalist, genuinely friendly to Irish aspirations, he led the British Empire to victory in the First World War. A great reforming politician. He introduced the basic elements of the welfare state; legislated women's emancipation; oversaw the 1911 Parliament Act that ended the veto power of the House of Lords; introduced the 1920 Government of Ireland Act that partitioned Ireland; and negotiated the 1921 Anglo-Irish Treaty creating the Irish Free State.

Diarmuid Lynch (1878–1950): An agricultural supplier salesman. Born in Cork, he emigrated to the United States in 1896 where he became president of the New York City Gaelic League. In 1907 he returned to Cork, moving to Dublin a year

Biographies   xxi

later, joining the IRB Bartholomew Teeling Circle. In 1911 he was appointed the Munster representative on the IRB Supreme Council. He fought in the General Post Office (GPO) in 1916. Released from prison in June 1917, he worked on reorganising the IRB. In June 1918 he was deported to the United States. He returned to Cork in 1933 and was actively involved in establishing the BMH.

Liam Lynch (1893–1923): IRA Chief of Staff (1922–23), leading the Republican side against the Treaty in the 1922–23 Civil War. O/C First Southern Division (1921–22). Joined the IRB in 1918; member of IRB Supreme Council (1921–22). Killed fleeing National Army troops in 1923.

Maud Gonne MacBride (1866–1953): Born in Hampshire, England. Idolised by W.B. Yeats. Devoted to republican, socialist and women's causes. A founder member of Cumann na mBan. Sworn into the IRB *c.* 1900 but resigned in 1903.[4] Converted to Roman Catholicism in 1902 and in 1903 married Major John MacBride, who had commanded an Irish group fighting for the Boers and who was executed in 1916. Mother of Seán MacBride.

Seán MacBride (1904–88): Barrister. IRA Chief of Staff (1936–37). Worked closely with Michael Collins in 1921. Minister for External Affairs (1948–51). Chairman, Amnesty International (1961–75). Secretary-General, International Commission of Jurists (1963–71). Winner of the Nobel Peace Prize (1974) and the Lenin Peace Prize (1976).

Seán MacDermott (1884–1916): See Chapter 8. Principal organiser of the 1916 Rising. Born in Co. Leitrim. Worked as a gardener and bartender in Scotland (1900–5). Tram conductor in Belfast (1906). Joined the Gaelic League and IRB (1906) and became a full-time revolutionary organiser. Co-founder of the *Irish Freedom* newspaper, he became a close collaborator of Tom Clarke (1910). Made lame by polio (1911). Elected to the Provisional Committee of Irish Volunteers (1913). Arrested and jailed for sedition in 1915; released the same year and joined IRB Military Committee. A signatory of the 1916 Proclamation of a Republic. Executed after the Rising. His name was often spelled McDermott by contemporaries.

John (Eoin) MacNeill (1867–1945): Academic nationalist. President and Chief of Staff of the Irish Volunteers (1913–16). A founding member of the

Gaelic League (1893). Professor of Early and Medieval Irish History, University College Dublin (UCD) (1909–16; 1918–42). With IRB backing started the Irish Volunteers in 1913. Issued the countermand order preventing the Easter Sunday 1916 Volunteer manoeuvres that were intended to start a nationwide rising. Dáil Minister for Industries (1919–21). Speaker of Second Dáil (1921–22). Minister for Education in the Irish Free State (1922–25) and Irish Free State member of the Northern Ireland Border Commission determining the extent of Northern Ireland.

Samuel (Sam) Maguire (1877–1927): Born to a Church of Ireland farming family near Dunmanway in West Cork. In 1897 he passed the British civil service examination and went to London for a job in the post office. There he joined the IRB and the GAA, becoming a champion Gaelic footballer, reportedly captaining the London Hibernians team to several All-Ireland finals. He became IRB London District Centre and South of England Divisional Secretary. Recommended Michael Collins for membership in 1909, becoming his close colleague and the key IRB man in England. Co-opted onto the Supreme Council in 1921. He was suspected of involvement in the 1922 assassination of Field Marshal Sir Henry Wilson. He returned from London in 1923 to a job in the Irish post office. In 1924 he was implicated in the Army Mutiny and dismissed. He died three years later of tuberculosis. The Sam Maguire Cup, commissioned in his honour in 1928, is presented to this day to the winner of the All-Ireland GAA Football Championship.

Constance 'Countess' Markievicz (1868–1927): Born Constance Gore-Booth, eldest daughter of Sir Henry Gore-Booth, Bt, a Co. Sligo landowner. She studied art at the Slade in London. In 1900 she married Casimir Markievicz, who styled himself 'Count' without justification. They moved to Ireland in 1903 and five years later Constance started her involvement in politics, joining Sinn Féin. In 1909 she co-founded Fianna Éireann with Bulmer Hobson. In 1913 Casimir moved to Poland and Constance joined James Connolly's workers' protection force, the ICA, rising to be its third in command and causing startled comment: 'The Countess was a prominent figure at the Soup Kitchen, dressed in trousers and smoking cigarettes, both of which were regarded as astonishing things for women to do in those days.'[5] She took an active part in the 1916 Rising. In 1918 she became the first woman elected to the British Parliament. She opposed the 1921 Treaty.

Biographies   xxiii

Seán McGarry 1886–1958: President of the IRB (1917–18). A councillor and then alderman on the Dublin Corporation (1920–24). Sinn Féin TD for Mid Dublin (1921–23). He supported the Treaty. A captain in the National Army during the Civil War, he was targeted by the IRA (because of his IRB importance) who set his home on fire (10 December 1922), killing his seven-year-old son, Emmet. In January 1923 his electrical fittings shop was bombed. He was TD for Dublin North (1923–24). He was one of the nine 'National Group' TDs who ceased supporting the Free State government in protest at the its handling of the 1924 Army Mutiny. He retired from politics and joined the Irish Hospitals Trust.

Right Rev. Dr David Moriarty (1814–1877): Roman Catholic Bishop of Kerry. Condemned the IRB.

Richard Mulcahy (1886–1971): IRA Chief of Staff (1918–22). Born in Waterford. Joined the Gaelic League (1902). He worked as a post office engineer in Dublin and joined the IRB (1908). Joined the Irish Volunteers (1913). Fought a successful action against the RIC at Ashbourne, Co. Meath, in 1916. National Army Chief of Staff and Provisional Government Minister for Defence (1922). Succeeded Michael Collins as Commander-in-Chief (1922–23). Irish Free State Minister for Defence (1923–24). Resigned from the government following the 1924 Army Mutiny. Minister for Local Government and Public Health (1927–32). Leader of Fine Gael (1944–59). Minister for Education (1948–51; 1954–57). Retired from politics in 1961.

Bartholomew (Batt) O'Connor (1870–1935): Builder. Member of the IRB and Irish Volunteers. Did not take part in the Rising but was interned in 1916. A Collins confidant. Built secret rooms and hideaways. Took the Free State side in the Civil War, but never revealed his secret rooms where Republicans often hid. TD for Dublin County (1923–35).

Jeremiah O'Donovan Rossa (1831–1915): A determined nationalist, in 1856 he formed the Phoenix National Literary Society, a precursor of the IRB with which it merged. He was an active recruiter for the IRB and manager of the IRB newspaper, *The Irish People*. He was arrested in 1865 for plotting rebellion and sentenced to penal servitude. He was elected MP for Tipperary in 1869, but as a prisoner his election was ruled invalid. In 1870 he was released from prison together with John Devoy and sailed to the United States. In New York he joined Clan na Gael and there established the *United Irishman* newspaper, campaigning for Irish independence. He was an organiser of the Fenian bombing campaign in Britain during the 1880s. In later life he turned against Fenianism. His funeral in Dublin, organised by the IRB, provided a platform for extreme nationalist sentiment, voiced famously by Patrick Pearse in his oration: 'The fools, the fools, the fools! – they have left us our Fenian dead, and while Ireland holds these graves, Ireland unfree shall never be at peace.'

Patrick Pearse (1879–1916): Commander-in-Chief of the 1916 IRA. Romantic nationalist, barrister, journalist and orator. Headmaster of St Enda's, a nationalist Irish-language school in Dublin that he founded in 1908. Joined the Gaelic League (1896). Qualified as a barrister (1901). Joined the Irish Volunteers and the IRB (1913). Irish Volunteer Press Secretary and then Director of Organisation; member of the IRB Military Committee (1915). His mobilisation order for the Easter Sunday 1916 Volunteer manoeuvres was to be the cover for a national uprising, but it was countermanded by Eoin MacNeill, the Volunteer President and Chief of Staff, causing confusion and a much smaller rising than had been planned. A signatory of the 1916 Proclamation of an Irish Republic. Often incorrectly referred to as President of the 1916 Republic, which was Tom Clarke. Executed (1916).

George Noble, Count Plunkett (1851–1948): Born in Dublin. A wealthy builder. Created a Papal Count in 1884 for donations to a nursing order. Father of seven children including Geraldine, Joseph (d. 1916, a principal planner of the 1916 Rising and signatory of the 1916 Proclamation, who was executed afterwards) and George (d. 1944, who became IRA Chief of Staff in 1943). His home in Kimmage, south of Dublin, was the base for men from England who took part in the Rising and because of this was known as the 'Kimmage Garrison'. In February 1917 as an Independent he won the North Roscommon parliamentary seat in a by-election and then refused to take his seat, inaugurating the policy of abstentionism advocated by Arthur Griffith. He founded the Liberty Clubs to be the core of an abstentionist party that merged with Sinn Féin in October 1917. He convened the April 1917 Mansion House Convention in an effort to unite nationalists. He was elected the first Ceann Comhairle (Speaker) of Dáil Éireann in January 1919. Dáil Minister for Foreign

Affairs (1919–21). Dáil Minister for Fine Arts (1921–22). In December 1938, he was one of the members of the Second Dáil who transferred their claims to sole republican legitimacy to the IRA Army Council. To the present day, the various IRAs have claimed this legitimacy.

Geraldine Plunkett (1891–1986): Born in Dublin, the fourth child of Count Plunkett. She married Thomas Dillon, a lecturer in chemistry at UCD, on Easter Sunday 1916. She was a republican and an Irish-language activist couriering messages for Michael Collins and weapons and explosives for the Volunteers/IRA. She was sworn into the IRB in 1921. Her memoir covering the lead up to and the Rising itself provides a detailed account of the thinking and plans about which her brother Joseph told her. Her account, *All in the Blood*, edited by her granddaughter, was published in 2006.

John Redmond (1856–1918): Born in Wexford into a leading banking and political family. A barrister. Elected MP for New Ross in 1891 and subsequently for North Wexford (1891–95) and Waterford City (1891–1918). He led the minority IPP MPs loyal to Charles Stewart Parnell after Parnell's death in 1891 and succeeded in reuniting the party with Parnell's opponents. This, and the passage of the 1914 Government of Ireland Act establishing British agreement to Irish Home Rule, were the two great achievements of his political career. Upon the outbreak of war in 1914, Redmond, in a speech at Woodenbridge, Co. Wicklow on 20 September, called on the Irish Volunteers to enlist and support the British war effort. The vast majority of Volunteers responded positively, leading to a split between the Redmondite National Volunteers and the rump of the Irish Volunteers. He died in March 1918, nine months before his party collapsed at the polls.

Austin Stack (1879–1929): Born in Tralee. Solicitor's clerk. Captain of the Kerry Gaelic football team that won the 1904 All-Ireland final. President of the Kerry GAA. TD (1918–27). Joined the IRB in 1908. Commandant of the Kerry Irish Volunteers (1916). He was arrested on Good Friday evening when he walked into an RIC barracks in Tralee where a colleague was being held. He never explained this action. He was released in November 1917 but rearrested in April 1918. Escaped from jail in 1919, having been elected Sinn Féin MP/TD for Kerry West in the December 1918 general election. Minister for Justice (1920) and then Minister for Home Affairs (1921–22) in the Dáil government. Successfully set up the Dáil courts. He was less successful setting up a republican police force. Nominally Volunteer/IRA Deputy Chief of Staff (1918–21). Wrangled with Michael Collins, who called his efforts as a Minister a 'joke'. Took the anti-Treaty side. Arrested in 1923, he went on hunger strike for forty-one days but was released in July 1924. He never fully recovered. Refused to join de Valera's Fianna Fáil party and remained a Sinn Féin TD until 1927 when he retired.

PREFACE

> The I.R.B. was at the heart of the matter, and the complacent assurances of the [government officials in Dublin] Castle were fatally wrong. A determined effort to stamp out this dangerous body, versed as it has always been in murder and intrigue, might have cost many lives but would have freed Ireland from a terror whence no good thing can come ...[1]
>
> *Arthur Norway, head of the Irish post office, 1916*

Without the IRB, there would not have been a Rising in 1916, or an IRA, let alone a War of Independence.

The IRB was a consciously small and elite secret society. It created the IRA. In particular, the IRB launched the 1916 Rising and its Irish Republic; it was in effect the 1916–21 Volunteers/IRA; it dominated the IRA GHQ; it successfully influenced and manipulated the Sinn Féin party, the GAA, the Gaelic League and the 1918 election – thus undermining democracy and capturing nationalist leadership. The IRA assassination squad that hunted British agents and the Dublin Metropolitan Police (DMP) was formed by IRB members, and Michael Collins, the IRA's effective leader and Britain's principal opponent, gave his foremost loyalty to the IRB.

The history of the IRB in 1914–24 is a hidden history, buried within the political and military chronology of the time. It was, of course, part of the overall history, but was not in the historical mainstream and was not documented. J. Bowyer Bell in the third edition of his ground-breaking history of the IRA, *The Secret Army* (2017), remarked on the lack of knowledge about the IRB, that it had disappeared 'amid flickers of rumors, faint, fading, and gone without trumpets'.[2] The IRB's story after 1916 is generally unknown as the major edited histories reveal: volume IV of *The Cambridge History of Ireland: 1880 to the Present* (2018) indexes the IRB only twice after 1916; *The Oxford History of Ireland* (2001) three times, and *The Princeton History of Modern Ireland* (2016) not once. Volumes VI (1989) and VII (2010) of

xxviii   Preface

Oxford's *A New History of Ireland* between them have fourteen post-1916 references.[3]

Telling the story of any secret society is especially complicated, not simply because of the difficulty of establishing facts that were intended to remain secret, but because secret society themes are entwined with, but not synchronous with, the political chronology, and consequently are hard to disentangle. Accordingly, in order to appreciate the IRB's influence, it is necessary to weave its story into the wider world within which it operated and to place it in its time. Chapters 23 to 26 cover the political swirl of 1921–22 where the IRB per se, with some exceptions, remained in the background but where the principal actors with few exceptions were all respectful IRB members. Michael Collins, from 1919 onwards until his death, personified the IRB, as his colleagues perceived. His path in those years was the IRB's path.

My research into the IRB, beginning in 1970, was prompted by the awareness that, through my father (who had been a member of the IRB – some of his experience is told in *Bloody Sunday* (1962) by James Gleeson) and his friends, I had special access to the 1914–24 generation that was then dying. Soon after starting, it became clear to me that the IRB was the one element that held the various nationalist organisations together in common purpose up to 1922. I found that the IRB story provides a different narrative to the popularly accepted version of events in the 1916–22 War of Independence.

Moss Twomey, Chief of Staff of the IRA (1927–36), had been a member of the IRB and a senior officer in the IRA's First Southern Division in 1919–23. When I spoke to him in 1972 about the IRB, he said:

> Well now, you're going to find it terrible difficult. You have put your finger on something. When [Florence] O'Donoghue was doing his book [*No Other Law*, 1954], 'I'll tell you, Florrie', I said, 'what I'd like you to do: we could have a best seller if we could work up the IRB.' He was in it himself and, dammit, when we went to do it, we had some considerable difficulty. Even if we met people, they couldn't remember the names![4]

The IRB was dedicated to violence to achieve its objective of an independent thirty-two-county Irish republic. Violence became terrorism, defined in the *Oxford English Dictionary* as 'A policy intended to strike with terror those against whom it is adopted; the employment of methods of intimidation; the fact of terrorising or condition of being terrorised'. This was a development

Preface

that Britain shared: British violence and then terror in 1919–21 equalled if not exceeded the IRB's and IRA's terror. Jeremiah O'Donovan Rossa, instrumental in the 1880s' Fenian Brotherhood (the Irish-American sister society of the IRB) bombing campaign in England, described the IRB as a murder organisation, 'preaching the doctrine of assassination in Ireland's fight for Home Rule'.[5] Michael Collins, IRB president from 1919 until his death in 1922, knew the usefulness of terror from his experience of the IRB. Joseph Connell, in his book *The Terror War* (2021), reports Collins as saying, 'Careful application of terrorism is also an excellent form of total communication.'[6] In July 1919 Collins formed his IRA assassination 'Squad'.[7] Máire Comerford, a leading member of Cumann na mBan, the Volunteers'/IRA's women's auxiliary organisation, described them thus: 'The Special Squad – Collins's men, based in pubs not homes; men who were tragically young; the gun men, the hunters of spies, the hunted. They were the IRB.'[8]

They targeted the DMP, Royal Irish Constabulary (RIC), spies and British Intelligence operatives, successfully nullifying the DMP intelligence officers, killing them unless they ceased to investigate Collins' and the IRA's activities.

Collins attempted the same with the British Secret Service in Dublin on Bloody Sunday, 21 November 1920. The IRA, in turn, used terror against the Provisional Government during the 1922–23 Civil War in an unsuccessful effort to prevent the functioning of an Irish government, established by Britain, that they did not recognise. That government, formed by many erstwhile members of the IRB and IRA, also successfully used terror to defeat the IRA. Since 1922, British and Irish armies have been necessary in Ireland, not because of a danger of invasion, but because of 'loyalist' terror and the terror of the IRB's creation: the IRA.

My father introduced me to the IRB story and encouraged me to research it. He had taken part in the 1916 Rising, in the subsequent War of Independence, and had then fought on the Republican side during the Civil War.[9] Nevertheless, Michael Collins, who led the Free State forces against the Republicans at the start of the Civil War was, for him, the great loss of the conflict. He came to see Collins as a practical nationalist who would not have indulged the romantic views of Éamon de Valera, the post-1916 republican political leader, who, when in power after 1932, did not ameliorate the condition of two generations in a Catholic-dominated and impoverished country.[10] My father had not fought, he said, to see RTÉ refuse to employ Frank O'Connor because he 'lived in sin' or Edna O'Brien's and John McGahern's books banned in deference to Catholic xxx

Preface

sensibilities,[11] or to maintain the slums of Dublin and Limerick, and he believed Collins would have come to the same conclusion and done something about living conditions and Catholic influence. Collins' distant relationship with the Catholic Church was another recommendation.[12]

When I was a boy, my father told the story of the escape from Dublin Castle in January 1592 of the rebels Art and Henry O'Neill and Red Hugh O'Donnell, and how they struggled through snow to safety (Art O'Neill died on the way) with our putative forebear Fiach McHugh O'Byrne in his 'Ranelagh' fastness in the Wicklow mountains. The O'Neills and O'Byrnes fostered each other's children in the Celtic tradition as a way of cementing alliances, which was why the escapees headed to Wicklow. My father took me to the cave above Glenmalure where they hid and to the forbidding grey looming tower in Dublin Castle whence they escaped. This memory and my pride in these rebels and in Fiach remain with me. I feel a pulse of family engagement in the history of Ireland going back more than 1,000 years: we Byrnes trace our ancestry to the sixth century AD.[13]

Ancestral memory was also strong in Joseph O'Doherty when I interviewed him in 1972. He told the story of sitting on his grandfather's knee as a boy and hearing how, as a young man in 1798, his great uncle had been gathering the harvest in a field:

> The password at the time was 'Are ye up?' If you met a fellow who was breathing nationalism but you were not quite sure if he was one of the boys or not, then this was the password to find out. But the yeomanry had apparently got to know this password and this uncle of mine was loading the corn and it seems he was a very strong man and he had backed down to lay a sack of corn on his shoulders to lift up to a waiting vehicle, a cart or something, and when he was down he saw the high boots of a yeoman behind him, and the yeoman whispered in his ear, 'Are ye up?' and he said, 'I'm rising.'[14]

He knew it was a yeoman: those who would be 'up' could not afford boots.

More than 200 years later, through Joe, I find myself one life away from '98. It is a lesson in the force of memory.

The emotional pull of ancestral voices can also be strong, as is particularly the case with unionists in Northern Ireland today. They, too, are harbingers of old causes.

Preface

xxxi

My father's status and contacts gave me a tremendous opportunity, probably unique, to interview people who had been in the IRB – many of whom had refused other interview requests – and to be accepted by them as an 'insider' they could trust. Between 1971 and 1975 and again in 1979–80 I travelled extensively in Ireland interviewing men and women who had taken part in the events of 1914–24. Memorable encounters were with Éamon de Valera, President of Ireland; Emmet Dalton, who had been with Michael Collins when he was killed; Nora Connolly O'Brien, a daughter of James Connolly, a 1916 Rising leader, who was sent to Belfast by the IRB Military Committee to chivvy northern separatists to take part in the Rising; Peadar O'Donnell, on the 1922–23 IRA's governing body, the Army Executive; Seán MacEoin, who in 1921–22 had been a member of the IRB's governing body, the Supreme Council; Alec McCabe, who had been on the 1916 Supreme Council and knew the 1916 Rising leaders personally; Dr Emmet Clarke, Tom and Katherine Clarke's son; Lawrence (Larry) de Lacey, who shared rooms with Leon Trotsky in New York and obtained the first Thompson sub-machine guns smuggled to Ireland; Sighle Humphries, who had been secretary and vice-president of Cumann na mBan; Vinnie Byrne, a member of Collins' assassination Squad, who recounted killing British undercover officers on Bloody Sunday, saying, 'I put them up against the wall and said "May God have mercy on your souls", and then I plugged them.'[15] And Joe O'Doherty, whose brother in 1916–17 was President of the IRB.

In the early 1970s terrorism in Northern Ireland that also reached into the South and into England was at its height and inevitably engaged the memories and thoughts of those I spoke to. References to contemporary events were made and parallels at times drawn. I have included some of these reflections in various interview quotes. My feeling then and now is that this did not affect memories of the IRB. Civil War divisions were strong, but the IRB represented an idealism that both Republicans and Free Staters could, for the most part, discuss without animosity. I tried to meet the trust that I was given by not using personal remarks and accusations in writing up my research. Hundreds of men and women who took part in the 1914–24 events were still alive, and families still felt the heat of Civil War conflict. Publishing continuing animosity then could only cause hurt. I feel that caution no longer applies.

It is not often that a study of Irish history in the 1914–24 period does not discuss the Black and Tans or the Auxiliaries and does not deal with many of the events that caused international sensation at the time. That is because the IRB played little or no part in these events, and its members encountered the Tans and Auxies as members of other organisations. The hunger strike and death of the Lord Mayor of Cork, Terence MacSwiney, an IRB member, is one such example. The fascinating British political progress from agreeing Home Rule to enacting Dominion status and partition is another.[16] My focus, however, is the role of the IRB during the years 1914 to 1924, establishing the extent of IRB influence and control that revolutionised Irish national movements.

Introduction

> To subvert the tyranny of our execrable government, to break the connection with England, the never-failing source of all our political evils and to assert the independence of my country – these were my objectives. To unite the whole people of Ireland, to abolish the memory of all past dissensions, and to substitute the common name of Irishman in place of the denominations of Protestant, Catholic and Dissenter – these were my means.[1]
>
> *Wolfe Tone, Memoirs*

The intricate tapestry of the 1914–24 period begins with the origins of the IRB and Theobald Wolfe Tone (1763–98). Tone was a leader of the 1798 Irish rebellion, the most serious rebellion in Ireland since 1641, with France as an ally. A member of the Church of Ireland, he was inspired by the American and French Revolutions, and was motivated by the condition of the impoverished Catholic Irish. Tone believed that only violence would expel England from Ireland. He influenced all future Irish revolutionaries and is venerated by republicans to the present day.[2]

Tone represented political non-sectarian nationalism, which is always open to compromise. Irish Catholic nationalism was cultural and thus more absolute. The IRB, however, like Tone, was not sectarian. Indeed, several of its leaders were Protestants. The men and women of 1916 fought for an idea of Irish culture that they saw fading in the face of an anglophone cultural, economic and political attack.[3] At all times the IRB concentrated on influencing cultural organisations. It dismissed the Irish Parliamentary Party (IPP) as craven at the feet of England – of 'the foreigner'.[4] For the IRB, cultural nationality was paramount.

The IRB was created in 1858 and was at first known as the Irish Revolutionary Brotherhood (see Chapter 1). Its goal was complete Irish independence. It named its membership 'Circles' – its basic organisational unit – after leaders of the 1798 rebellion. In 1964 the IRB's remaining funds paid in part for Tone's statue, sculpted and cast by Edward Delaney and erected in St Stephen's Green in a granite monolith setting designed by Noel Keating and unveiled on 18 November 1967 by President de Valera.[5] Tone was the IRB's inspiration and, as we shall see in Chapter 31, he also marked its end.

The IRB had international reach and membership: the Irish diaspora was substantial within the British Empire, South America and the United States. From its formation in 1858 until 1922 it maintained an identity separate from all other organisations, although during 1920–21 passively within the IRA. It was intellectually substantial. It thought beyond blood and excitement. It was an organisation designed to expend itself in rebellion, not to live forever. It wanted to establish a state governed by Irishmen and prosperous in the long term. Italy and Greece had been established in the nineteenth century by the determination of a handful of people in secret societies: the IRB positioned itself to achieve the same for Ireland.[6] Its leaders did not really think of being the government of an Irish state. They thought of themselves as awakeners of the oppressed nation whose language and culture had been destroyed by England. They also thought that the Church had been won over to side with Britain.[7] The Church, itself an imperial organisation, understood that Ireland within the United Kingdom gave it influence within the British Empire, principally through Irish MPs: it was not surprising that the Church generally sided with the government in Ireland and condemned membership of a secret society – the IRB – as sinful. In 1919, for example, a priest who gave evidence in court on behalf of a Volunteer/IRA man was transferred within a week to the United States.[8]

The use of the term 'Irish Republican Army' rather than 'Volunteers' became more general in 1921. Interviewees and memoirs slide between the two names. I have chosen to use 'Volunteers/IRA' from 1916 up to August 1921 when the Dáil – the Irish Parliament established by Sinn Féin abstentionist MPs in 1919 – formally adopted the 'Irish Republican Army', and then 'IRA' alone after that. The nomenclature was the most obvious illustration of the differences between the more extreme nationalist groupings. It signifies the distinction between the IRB – whose 'army' initially was the secret IRA – and the somewhat more moderate extremists, who looked to Sinn Féin and the openly formed Irish Volunteers. Both wanted to carry independence to success, but the IRB's effort was dedicated to force, not debate, to achieve it.[9] Richard

Mulcahy, Volunteer/IRA Chief of Staff (1918–22), summed up the IRB as 'something that infused its idea and its spirit of service in all directions'.[10] Larry de Lacey, a journalist member, saw it as a driving force:

> It was that curious live core; it was the power cell. Because the people that were in it were of a pretty good standard … But there were a good many very able men, and there were men with influence in queer, far-reaching ways: very important. They were influencing public bodies; they were preventing votes of flattery to the Queen and the King; they were preventing this, that and the other.[11]

The IRB voiced liberal generalisations but was not really interested in social issues. In October 1865 a Ladies' Committee was established, mainly by wives and relatives of IRB leaders, to support IRB prisoners' families.[12] Yet in the twentieth century only three women, Maud Gonne MacBride, Geraldine Plunkett and Úna Brennan, were ever members of the IRB itself.[13] From 1873 it had a constitution that through omission made its lack of interest in social matters clear. Being Irish was its entry requirement, as clause 1 of the constitution stated: 'The IRB is and shall be composed of Irishmen, irrespective of class or creed resident in Ireland, England, Scotland, America, Australia, and in all other lands where Irishmen live, who are willing to labour for the establishment of a free and independent Republican Government in Ireland.'

In common with many secret societies, the IRB's existence was known from its start; exactly what it was doing was unknown until it burst out in revolt. But there was no secret about its objective, its nature or its leaders, all of whom were known to the DMP and the RIC. 'They were a conspiratorial mob,' said David Neligan when I interviewed him in 1973. He had been in the DMP Detective Division in 1919 and 1920 where he had read IRB files: 'They were a secret society. Started by a parson's son and a Catholic. They had no religious affiliations … They kept the thing alive. They're all having more or less cold water thrown on them now, but I wouldn't throw cold water on them because they kept the whole thing alive for dozens of years anyway. That's a fact, do you see? It was nationalism gone mad: that's just what it is now too.'[14]

They were rebels and terrorists. Such people are conspiratorial and invariably have a simple black and white view of the world, often sustained by historical misrepresentation. Terror and rebellion were the IRB's defining elements and, through the IRA, its legacy to modern Ireland.

4   The Irish Republican Brotherhood, 1914–1924

Secret societies protect themselves with conspiracies underpinned with deceit and propaganda. They also have a mystique that can attract members and may have objectives that are attractive too. They use initiation ceremonies as an entry point to a belief system with the comradeship and exclusivity of membership acting as powerful attractions.[15] A formal oath-taking was the IRB's ceremony. When rebellions are the purpose of these societies, fear is added to the mix: rebellions are intended to be unnoticed until unleashed and so call forth murderous policing of secrecy. Revolutionary conspirators are imprisoned by the deceits that also protect them: self-delusion is a necessity as they prepare to kill and to die for their cause.

Ignorance and secrecy were intended within the IRB. It did not have mechanisms for feedback from below. It did not want debate. This was a reaction to an overwhelming enemy presence: only an extreme organisation could make itself felt. Its leaders thought – wrongly as 1916 demonstrated – that a suicide charge would inflame Ireland; that in the long term they would achieve a united, armed independent country that would ally with Britain's many enemies.

The IRB was not a force for democracy (although democracy and violence are not mutually exclusive), and its members did not respect democracy. Identifying men of ability with strong nationalist feelings and binding them to fight for an independent republic was its modus vivendi. 'They were the "saved",' said Joe O'Doherty, 'and they were going to see that everybody was in line with their idea of salvation.'[16] Infiltration of nationalist bodies, exercising influence rather than command and control, was its modus operandi. Thomas Malone, in the IRB from 1914, observed: 'On the quiet, when it was a question of some one fellow instead of another fellow being put in as O/C or something or other, the IRB influence was used.'[17] It was a doorway to what the IRB termed 'physical force' that, once taken, saw its members absorbed by the Volunteers/IRA after 1919. Tom McEllistrim, Vice-O/C Volunteer/IRA Second Kerry Brigade, put it simply: 'the Volunteers ate up the I.R.B.'[18]

Looking back in 1973, Tom Maguire, a senior IRB member and O/C Volunteer/IRA Second Western Division in 1921, saw the IRB as the guardian of Irish republicanism: 'If everybody else failed the IRB would hold for the republican tradition.'[19] Patrick Mullaney, the Co. Kildare IRB leader, was definite: 'We knew the IRB was the highest thing behind the actions of the IRA and I considered that unless I was a member of the IRB I couldn't consider myself a real republican soldier.'[20]

Introduction 5

The IRB itself, after its inception, experienced a generation of depression verging on obsolescence. From the 1880s, despite being pledged to rebellion, it collaborated with the constitutionalist IPP's drive for Home Rule: in 1909 at least one in four IPP MPs were or had been members of the IRB.[21] It was revived after 1907 by a small group of dedicated nationalists, most of whom came from Ulster, one of the most dynamic being Bulmer Hobson. Their activities are covered in Chapter 8.

After 1914 the IRB had two peaks of achievement: launching the 1916 Rising and then as the carrier of Collins' career after 1916 when, as Denis McCullough, IRB President (1915–16), observed, 'The thread that ran through [the IRB membership] holding them together were the Intelligence strings from Collins's hands.'[22] Patrick O'Daly, North of England representative on the Supreme Council from November 1920, from his experience put it simply: 'Collins controlled everything by virtue of the I.R.B.'[23] Richard Mulcahy considered that the Brotherhood was central to Collins' success:

> The secret organisation remained as a kind of humus in the political ground on the one hand, and on the other was the core of the kernel of the intelligence organisation effectively built up by Collins and controlled by him, that disrupted and outwitted the secret service, destroyed its murder arm, and on the other hand, manipulated the machinery that so controlled the 'water ways' that de Valera could be brought from Lincoln to Ireland and then to the United States and then back home again, and was the basis of the security which prevented the country ever having to feel that either its parliament or its executive government had been destroyed by enemy action.[24]

The IRA theoretically existed as the IRB's army in the 1870s when land ownership agitation was at a high. It was recreated on Easter Monday 1916 by the Rising leaders. 'Our army was in existence again,' declared Michael Collins, distinguishing between the Irish Volunteers and the IRA. 'It was not brought into being, as is wrongfully supposed, by the example of Carson's recruiting in North-East Ulster. It needed no such example. It was already in being – the old Irish Republican Brotherhood in fuller force.'[25] 'We had become the Irish Republican Army,' said a 1916 rebel, Robert Evans.[26]

As 'Volunteers/IRA' indicates, there was a conscious confusion of the two nationalist strands by their participants, both claiming the 1916 Rising as their inspirational spark. Calling the second Parliament of Southern Ireland and its successors Dáil Éireann was another example. This has led to permanent uneasiness in Irish politics that, on the one hand, seeks to honour the men and women of 1916–21 and thus inferentially the IRA, and on the other insists on the legitimacy of constitutional democracy established in 1922. The two do not march together. The confusion came from the understandable desire in 1916–21 to present a united nationalist front, submerging the differences between the revolutionary-minded IRB/IRA and the constitutionalist-minded Sinn Féin. Terminological exactitude was avoided so as to hide differences.[27] Subsequently, this has supported the assertion that Irish independence was won and not given. It has given room for the IRA and its variants to justify themselves to the present day: they are – as they claim – the lineal descendants of the IRB and of the fighting men and women of 1916–21. '1916 is unjustifiable unless one also justifies the present IRA campaign,' stated a pamphlet supporting the Provisional IRA in February 1974. 'One cannot condemn one and condone the other.'[28] Unfortunately, this is correct.

To understand the inevitable tensions within the IRB, the Volunteers/IRA and Sinn Féin, we need to return to 1916 and the currents of Irish nationalism. The seven signatories of the 1916 independence proclamation and their close colleagues believed that their cause justified whatever they did. They believed in Irish culture, English wickedness (not always untrue) and a tradition of revolt. They were in a small world of their own creation. Indeed, theirs was a secret within the secret of the IRB. They were absolutely determined to stage a rebellion during the First World War on the traditional premise that 'England's difficulty is Ireland's opportunity'.[29] The result, however, was failure and the deaths of 504 people, more than half – 276 – being civilians and most being Irish.[30] The next nationalist 'opportunity' came in 1917 and 1918 with the reaction against threats of conscription, and not as a result of the Rising.

There were two currents in Irish nationalist consciousness. First, a surface one of a defeated Ireland with occasional murders and expressed bitterness, where people felt that they had been beaten again and again, did not think of armed struggle and had come to accept that they were part of British imperium. Deaths during the mid-nineteenth-century Great Famine and resulting emigration, when perhaps 1 million people died and 2–3 million emigrated, followed by land reform that quietened peasant resistance, had achieved this acceptance. *The Irish RM* books written by Edith Somerville and Violet Ross, published between 1899 and 1915, described a colonial-type

Introduction

resident magistrate who was accepted along with his function (replacing juries that would not convict for offences against landlords). Acceptance of British administration and values was seen by the IRB and passionate nationalists as reflecting Irish subjugation and weary defeatism. The 1916 Rising was in part a reaction to the fact that most people in Ireland had supported Britain's war effort.[31] Francis McQuillan, an IRB member in Dundalk, looking back on the years before 1916, simply observed, 'The general body of the people were not friendly to the policy of the I.R.B.'[32] The Rising leaders were determined to ignore popular support for Britain and instead stand for a desperate attempt to pull Irish people back to an historical, revolutionary nationalism.

The British administration in Ireland – mostly consisting of Irish officials – headquartered at Dublin Castle, became confident that nationalist Irish rebellion was dead, and in any case was in the process of arranging to hand government over to the IPP at the end of the World War. Even Tom Clarke, the man within the IRB leadership who constantly pressed for a rising, thought that Home Rule would make self-government his focus. 'When the Home Rule Bill was passed [in 1914] my mother asked my father about his plans for a rising if the Bill was implemented,' recorded Dr Emmet Clarke, Tom's son. 'He remarked that their plans would be halted for the moment but that they would try to get every ounce of good for Ireland out of its operation.'[33] Understandably, the British administration in Ireland was surprised when perhaps about 1,600 men and women who took part in the 1916 Rising proved their assumptions wrong. The ideals of these men and women, rejected at the time by the vast majority of their countrymen, nevertheless brought the second current to the surface.

This second current was a hidden emotional, idealistic resolve to roll back the anglicisation of Ireland. The French Revolution and the independence of Greece and Italy showed that dramatic change was possible and gave nationalism in Europe a powerful popular element that was expressed in Ireland in ballads and in oral story/history telling – as we have already seen with Joe O'Doherty. The memory of the Great Famine and assumptions as well as memories of British devilry gave this current an even deeper power.[34] It had not always been submerged: it generated uprisings into the mid-nineteenth century but then declined as living conditions and opportunities improved, and as the IPP at Westminster successfully worked to secure Home Rule. But the ancestral voices remained strong. Eamon Broy, brought up on a farm in Co. Kildare, found them dramatically expressed:

There was a belief in phantom horsemen being heard galloping across the pasture land near the bog. An old man told me he often heard them and that he could hear the leather of the saddles creaking as they sped past. He said they were the Geraldines[35] who would one day return to drive the English out of Ireland. The people were always confident that one day the invaders would be driven out. Some believed that it would be through the Irish Party winning Home Rule; others that only force would avail and that sooner or later force would be adopted and would be successful.[36]

James McElligott, a young civil servant in 1913, remembered about himself: 'Then the nationalist streak that had always been more or less dormant woke up and I joined the Volunteers.'[37] John Chartres,[38] a thoroughly anglicised Anglo-Irish barrister and journalist in London, had a similar epiphany after the 1916 Rising: 'something woke inside me which had been dormant for a long time … I realised I was not an Englishman but an Irishman. All my sympathy was with Ireland, and I decided that I would have to fight for her.'[39] Mary MacSwiney, sister of Terence MacSwiney, argued that Ireland's cause was 'essentially a spiritual fight; it has been a fight of right against wrong, a fight of a small people struggling for a spiritual ideal against a mighty, rapacious and material Empire'.[40] Interestingly, many of the 1916 and later rebels, including Éamon de Valera and Michael Collins, acted in nationalistic plays in the early years of the twentieth century: it was a way of expressing passion without violence.

The ideal of indomitable resistance in a nationalist cultural struggle is what motivated the IRB men who led the 1916 Rising. 'All we can do is have a scrap and send it on to the next generation,' said John MacBride, executed for his part in the Rising.[41] They thought of themselves as the awakeners of an oppressed nation. The drumbeat assertion that each generation had rebelled against Britain was never correct: insurrections had occurred regularly since the fourteenth century, but they never involved a whole generation and, after 1798, had attracted less and less support. The assertion nevertheless became a truism to physical-force nationalists who repeated it, mantra-like, to justify their intentions, and to appeal to that deep emotional nationalist undercurrent that was ever-present in the Irish subconscious.

Liam Ó Briain was involved in printing the 1916 Proclamation of an Irish Republic and also took part in the Rising. A year later he was appointed Professor of Romance languages at University College Galway – a post he held for forty-two years. In a statement recollecting his experience, he said:

Introduction

I have often thought that 1920–21 is the real justification of the Easter Week leaders, and that their real greatness was the intensity of vision and faith which foresaw the possibility of such a campaign, at a time when Ireland was profoundly at peace, when 'physical force' as it used be called had passed into romantic dreamland out of practical politics, when modern weapons had made such action or methods seem absurd and when there was no example of such 'resistance' methods against regular troops anywhere in the world of the day.[42]

When I spoke to him in 1971 he noted how the memory of the Fenians, as the IRB was often called in the nineteenth century, motivated the 1916 leaders: 'They got so beset by this idea of the Fenians and that the Fenians had not fought. Pearse's famous angle was "The failure of the last generation. All previous generations had fought or had tried to fight but the last generation had dropped the idea altogether and had become constitutional agitators in Parliament".'[43] Pearse had in mind the lack of rebellious activity in Ireland since 1867 and the subsequent weakening of the IRB. He and his colleagues did not expect immediate victory. Famously, as Pearse put it, they wanted to die, to be a 'blood sacrifice'.[44] They believed that a hopeless rebellion would reinvigorate resistance to anglicisation: 'The old heart of the earth needed to be warmed with the red wine of the battlefields.'[45] Their followers thought they too would die. 'I thought I was finished, you know,' said Fergus O'Kelly, who fought in 1916. 'I thought we wouldn't get out of this. When I saw how the caper was going, "We're going to cop it this time!" When I found myself afterwards out of the whole thing, I thought "This is a bonus!": I was living on borrowed time!'[46]

The emotional rendering of Irish history, not the factual, provided the justifications for the Rising and the War of Independence that followed. A veneration of ancestral resistance overpowered rational assessment. Ernie O'Malley, a member of the IRB and O/C of the Volunteer/IRA's Second Southern Division in 1921–22, was emblematic of this spirit. As Diarmuid Ferriter observed, O'Malley 'held democracy in contempt and believed that people should be coerced if necessary, or in his words, "clear out and support the Empire".'[47] The 1919–21 period was the most intense experience of his life; several times he mentions that he did not expect to live through it. He had absorbed a myth in youth and was 'prepared to follow it, like a single flame, no matter what the cost was to himself or others'.[48]

The brief but bloody 1922–23 Civil War that the Republicans lost militarily and electorally was a nasty corrective as Britain's settlement was enforced by Irish governments that saw no alternative other than to kill Republican idealists in the interests of peace, law and democracy – and of course their own self-interest.

A republic was seen by many nationalists as simply the clearest expression of independence. Patrick Pearse and Joseph Plunkett, for example, signatories of the 1916 Proclamation of a Republic, thought Prince Joachim of Prussia might become their king in Ireland;[49] Arthur Griffith, the founder of Sinn Féin, was a monarchist; Éamon de Valera said he was willing to accept whatever form of government the Irish electorate wanted;[50] Michael Collins was focused on the realities of independence, not the forms. This ambivalence about a republic was reflected in a decision by Sinn Féin in 1919 that once a republic was achieved, it would then be left to the electorate to decide whether they wanted it or not.[51]

There was a passion for a republic enshrined in the IRB, inspired by the French and American Revolutions, which wanted to be rid of monarchies. An oath of allegiance to the King was a serious matter for many – if not a majority – of the Volunteers/IRA. France had supported Wolfe Tone in 1798, and French secret societies had played a part in inspiring the IRB. Ireland's strong link with the United States came with the massive emigration there after the Great Famine and later with Irish-American financing of the IRB.

Charles Townshend has phrased the central question of the period thus:

> The argument that the essence of the Treaty settlement [that gave effective independence] could have been achieved without 'the bloody catalogue of assassination and war', as Roy Foster put it in *Modern Ireland*, was posed from the start by Sinn Féiners and has never gone away. But was a non-violent revolution on the original Sinn Féin model possible, or was the application of military force inescapable?[52]

For the IRB the answer was simple: only force would achieve their goal.

CHAPTER 1

Politics and Ideals

As early, perhaps, as 1912, and certainly since 1917, [Lloyd George's] Irish policy was guided by the conviction that he must first resolve the Ulster question, and then make the best terms that could be made with nationalist Ireland.[1]

D.G. Boyce, 'How to Settle the Irish Question: Lloyd George and Ireland, 1916–21'

The backdrop against which Irish affairs took place in 1914–24 was a swirling torrent of major social, technological, engineering and political transformations. Yet, while change in most areas of life was dramatic and must have influenced the attitudes and politics of a majority of people, apart from President Wilson's Fourteen Points and the Paris Peace Conference, little – if any – mention of changes and events was made at the time by Irish nationalist activists in letters, articles, books, documents and debates, altogether emphasising a narrow historical and cultural focus. 'We lived in dreams always; we never enjoyed them,' sombrely reflected Denis McCullough. 'I dreamt of an Ireland that never existed and never could exist. I dreamt of the people of Ireland as a heroic people, a Gaelic people.'[2]

The massive military and economic effort of the First World War with its horrific slaughter, and the advent of fascism and international communism were outstanding in contemporary political consciousness. Then, in no particular order, were: President Wilson's Fourteen Points that encouraged national aspirations; the Paris Peace Conference; W.B. Yeats being awarded the Noble Prize for Literature; the end of the Ottoman Empire and creation of modern Turkey; Mahatma Gandhi's campaign for Indian independence; the

'Roaring Twenties' of jazz and the Charleston; the adoption of proportional representation in Ireland; the debilitating 1918–20 Spanish flu pandemic that infected about one-third of the world's population; Prohibition in the United States; Pope Benedict XV's encyclical *Alcohol Paraclitus*; the advent of commercial air travel; the canonisation of Joan of Arc; the establishment of the League of Nations and the International Court of Justice; the opening of Tutankhamun's tomb; the banning of James Joyce's *Ulysses* in the United States as 'obscene, lewd, or lascivious'; the inauguration of transcontinental United States air mail flights; the formation of the modern Middle East signalling inter alia Britain's gradual withdrawal from empire; the formation of the British Commonwealth; women's suffrage; Bessie Coleman, the first African-American aviatrix; the opening in New York of the first African-American musical comedy, *Shuffle Along*; the first transatlantic radio broadcast; the declarations of independence by Georgia, Estonia, Latvia, Lithuania, Ukraine, Mongolia, Mirdita; the murderous slaughter in Russia conducted by Lenin and Trotsky; the creation of the USSR; formation of Tel Aviv as a Jewish municipality; the release of Charlie Chaplin's *The Kid* (1921).

There were few families in Britain and Ireland not touched by war death or injury. War and the dominating fear of Bolshevik subversion pushed Ireland down the list of British concerns, even after the 1916 Rising. Ireland affected relations with the United States, but it was never central to British war-making or politics until the last six months of 1921. Britain's settlement of a partitioned semi-independent country and a devolved United Kingdom province was agreed by the Dáil in January 1922 and then accepted by the Irish electorates, North and South.

Until the outbreak of war in 1914, the dominating political issue in Ireland had been unionist opposition to Irish Home Rule, which had been proposed in 1912 and enacted but postponed in 1914.[3] Out of this came the Ulster Volunteer Force (UVF) in 1912, armed and trained by retired army officers and non-commissioned officers in order forcibly to prevent Protestant unionist Northern Ireland becoming part of a Catholic home-ruled Ireland. And then the Irish Volunteers were formed in 1913, far less well-armed and trained, to defend the expected implementation of Home Rule. Nevertheless, Prime Ministers Herbert Asquith and then David Lloyd George resolved to give Ireland self-government whenever the war ended. To pacify unionists, the Home Rule Act was amended to enable unionist Ulster to be separate. Partition was now part of the settlement. Achieving Home Rule on these terms was the

Politics and Ideals

13

objective of the government's 1914–22 Irish policies: it wanted Irishmen to deal with Irish problems.[4] It also wanted to reduce historically disruptive Irish representation at Westminster.

After 1918 Lloyd George had a battle not only in Ireland but also in Britain with the Conservative and Unionist Party, the majority partners in his 1916–22 coalition government, about when and how much – if any – self-government to give. Political and popular opposition in Britain to Home Rule was very strong and threatened to defeat a British government that did not proceed carefully.[5] The Liberal Party's delay in implementing Home Rule, from Gladstone's support of it in 1885 to its enactment in 1914, was a measure of the domestic and imperial political difficulties involved for Britain.

In 1912–14 Unionists, some parts of the army, and elements of the Conservative and Unionist Party had threatened treason and civil war. In March 1914, five months before the war began, the Curragh Mutiny saw British officers threaten to resign rather than move against armed Ulster Unionists opposed to Home Rule. The government gave in to them. This gave a fillip to a reinvigorated IRB seeking a republic through its commitment to 'force of arms'. Extra-parliamentary agitation and armed militias were seen to be the winning game of political power in Ireland, not least because it was recognised that the British Army might well refuse to enforce Home Rule. As Nicholas Mansergh observed, 'force, or the threat of it, delivered the goods, or most of them, where constitutionalism, after long trial, had not'.[6] When the First World War started, Lloyd George, then Chancellor of the Exchequer, set out the government's dilemma clearly:

> How could action be taken against the Irish Volunteers unless corresponding action were also taken against the Ulster Volunteers, who were also armed to resist the Government and oppose the Act now on the Statute Book? How could we defend the rights of Belgium and in the same breath coerce Ireland for arming to secure for herself a measure of independence which the majority of the House of Commons had admitted to be just? How could we resort to coercion in Ireland – unless events made it inevitable – and maintain with America the friendly relations which were essential to our success in the War?[7]

Irish nationalist loss of confidence in the parliamentary process to achieve Home Rule underpinned the period. Arthur Norway, head of the Irish post

14   The Irish Republican Brotherhood, 1914–1924

office, noted the growing unrest in 1912–14: 'There was however beginning to emerge, both North and South, a conviction that loyalty to political ends must override all other loyalties.'[8] Lloyd George, in his *Memoirs*, considered that Irish antagonisms went beyond this:

> The long-drawn-out and wearisome tragedy of the relations between Great Britain and Ireland played an important part in the World War [and] was one of the considerations which encouraged Germany to guarantee Austria unconditional support in her Serbian adventure ... Had there been no Irish grievance, it is by no means improbable that America would have come much earlier into the War, and by so much shortened its duration ... The paradox of the situation was that Ulster's rebellion was acclaimed by a powerful section of British opinion as loyalty, while Southern Ireland's preparations to defend the decision of the Imperial Parliament were denounced as sedition ... There seemed plenty of excellent reasons for doing nothing. There always are. So nothing was done.[9]

The First World War probably prevented armed violence if not civil war in 1914, but the preoccupying fear of the government was that there would be revolt in Ulster and beyond: in 1912–14 mass demonstrations in support of Ulster unionists or 'loyalists' were held in Canada, Australia and New Zealand.[10] In South Africa, Rhodesia and Kenya British settlers agitated on their behalf. They all saw themselves as servants of Empire who had settled in part to maintain British rule in British colonies, if necessary in the face of indigenous opposition. The prospect of Home Rule seemed to them a betrayal by a Britain prepared to leave its colonists alone and unsupported. As Donal Lowry has observed, 'not only Ulstermen but Empire loyalists generally witnessed what they regarded as the unfolding of an emergency of supreme importance to the survival of their Empire'.[11] Ulster discontent threatened the integrity of the Empire: this was the perceived danger in 1914.

After August 1921, the IRB, entrenched in the Volunteers/IRA, surrendered its claims to political leadership to the Dáil, the nationalist Parliament formed in 1919 by Irish MPs who refused to take their Westminster seats. Significantly, however, the Volunteers/IRA never came fully under Dáil control, not least because of the Dáil's unwillingness to be associated with Volunteer/IRA violence. The IRB, which was dominated by Collins, itself dominated the Volunteer/IRA's governing body, the Executive, and kept the armed side of

Politics and Ideals

the independence movement independent of Sinn Féin and the Dáil. It was suspicious of politicians perceived generally as willing to compromise.[12] In November 1921, Éamon de Valera, President of the Dáil Republic, and Cathal Brugha, Dáil Minister for Defence, very conscious of Collins' influence and authority, tried to replace the IRA with a new army to secure Dáil control, but nothing came of this.

From March 1918 the Volunteers/IRA, first on local IRB initiative and then directed by its IRB-dominated GHQ, carried out attacks on the RIC. From June 1919, they also began attacking the DMP, starting the War of Independence, which led to the creation by the British government of the Black and Tans, recruited from ex-rank-and-file soldiers – an estimated 882 of the total force of 7,684 were Irish born[13] – and the Auxiliaries, recruited from ex-officers, to supplement the RIC. From 1918 until 1921 the War of Independence was effectively a civil war between the RIC, augmented by Black and Tans and Auxiliaries, and the Volunteers/IRA, rather than a war against the British Army. Close co-operation between the British military and the RIC only began in early 1921, six months before the end of fighting.[14] In 1917–21, 491 IRA men, 523 RIC/DMP (including 143 Tans and 43 Auxiliaries) and 261 British military were killed.[15] In proportion to the armed members of each organisation in Ireland, IRA deaths were approximately 30 per cent; RIC deaths approximately 4 per cent, and British military less than 0.5 per cent. Attrition at the level the IRA experienced (30 per cent casualties, not simply deaths, can be taken as devastating to any war making) made most unlikely the chance of ever achieving victory.

After 1916 there was not a widespread popular insurrection. Insurrections occur when people are less afraid of dying than of subjection, as in Hungary in 1956. In Ireland people had contemporary democracy, freedom and increasing prosperity. Democracies like peace and quiet, and Ireland was not an exception. The 1916 Rising was not supported by the Irish electorate, as Michael Collins pointed out: 'The Republic of Easter Week had not lived on, as is supposed, supported afresh at each election, and endorsed finally in the General Election of 1918.'[16] A terrorist war was fought between a small minority and the armed forces of the Crown.[17] Large sections of the country had little if any IRA activity[18] – something that Collins frequently complained about – suggesting limited popular support for violence or, when taken with later election results, for a republic and separation from Britain. During the 1921 Treaty negotiations, Collins admitted that there was a 'general wish to settle'.[19] In 1921, far from fighting British forces to a standstill, the IRA had only about 1,600 armed men. Richard Mulcahy declared that the IRA had been defeated[20] and – as Republicans accurately insisted – the War of Independence was not won. Nor was there a revolution in Ireland after 1921.[21] Personnel changed but there was no political or social change: the British parliamentary system, the civil service, banking and education remained the same, as did the law.

In 1918 the IPP, seen as lacking influence at Westminster, collapsed at the ballot box, ensuring a delay in implementing Home Rule. Sinn Féin slowly emerged as a viable replacement. Throughout, Lloyd George pushed ahead with handing over power on British terms, in 1920 legislating to set up two parliaments in Ireland, one for a six-county Northern Ireland, the second for the other twenty-six counties in the South. Who would inhabit the Southern Parliament was an open question. Éamon de Valera, the nominal Southern leader, had a romantic nationalist view of Ireland and its future. However, Michael Collins, the de facto head of the IRA, emerged as the necessary hard-headed realist.

Collins, who so effectively followed the 1916 leaders, used IRB mystique and organisation to gain influence and power. He had taken part in the 1916 Rising, subsequently becoming a Scarlet Pimpernel figure who carried hope for a benevolent independence, and a bogey man possessing the capacity for cold ruthlessness, actively engaged in arranging murders. The IRB's strength came from Collins' association with it; its weakness came from Collins too. He habitually cut through the hierarchy of the organisation to deal directly with members at all levels, reducing its coherence and discipline, ultimately making it dependent upon him.

Collins wanted the IRB to be 'a force on practical lines and headed by realists'.[22] He understood that a republic would not be allowed by Britain at that time: British political parties would not even consider it. He kept this awareness to himself. He also stayed away from nationalist politics, immersing himself in IRB and IRA activity and thus remaining 'pure' in the eyes of republicans – and powerful with them – until he signed the 1921 Treaty conceding partition and a republic. He may have distanced himself from politics, but there is no doubt that he was an effective political operator. Over Christmas in 1920 he openly visited friends and associates and sent gifts with personal messages to practically everyone who had assisted him during the year. He understood the cult of the leader and that these gifts and messages would be cherished.[23]

Politics and Ideals

A British agent, John Byrnes (1885–1920) who used the cover name 'John Jameson', in early December 1919 identified Collins as 'the Chief Director of all active movement amongst the Sinn Féiners ... [who] has now taken the place of De Valera'.[24] Lloyd George knew from Byrnes and subsequently from Alfred Cope, Assistant Under Secretary for Ireland, that Collins was the man to deal with and in 1920–21 over a fourteen-month period conducted secret discussions with him through intermediaries, especially Cope.[25]

In the press and through Cope, Lloyd George was explicit that there would be no negotiation if Sinn Féin insisted on a republic. Knowing this, in 1921 de Valera nevertheless agreed to negotiate a settlement, thus inferentially acknowledging that a republic was not obtainable. Collins made this point when they disagreed about the eventual settlement, the 1921 Treaty that confirmed British objectives: a devolved Northern Ireland, a Dominion-type settlement for Southern Ireland and a Southern government that would enforce law and order, effectively protecting the North. Everything was dictated by British imperial needs, British political party needs and British economic needs. The Treaty gave more independence than the 1914 Home Rule Act did but at the cost of partition, the loss of British Exchequer benefits as a consequence of fiscal autonomy, two generations of falling living standards and vast emigration. This was the achievement of IRA/IRB violence. Paralleling the 'Cuban model' that de Valera had proposed in 1920, where Cuba had agreed not to pursue a foreign policy antagonistic to the United States, there was no question of allowing Ireland to have the freedom to make treaties with other powers, but short of that most other freedoms were given.[26]

Northern Ireland was allowed to opt to remain a devolved part of the United Kingdom. This it did in January and again in December 1922, but with a Boundary Commission to decide its borders.[27] The Commission consisted of three men: one was an English Unionist; a second – the chairman – was a South African imperialist; the Free State was represented by Eoin MacNeill. Unlikely as it was, Alfred Cope 'was positive that on the Border question a Commission could be set up that would give Ireland complete unity'.[28] His thinking, and that of Collins and probably Lloyd George, was that the Border Commission would separate the predominantly Protestant four north-eastern counties of Ulster as the new Northern Ireland province and this would make it economically unviable and would eventually force it to find an accommodation with the Dublin government, both perhaps helped to compromise by being under the umbrella of the Imperial Parliament.[29]

The Treaty was a step to an Irish republic, as Collins argued and as Conservatives and Unionists in Britain and the North understood. But Republicans did not agree, refusing to accept that they could not win immediate British recognition of an all-Ireland republic. Collins and his colleagues, thinking that Northern Ireland would not last, did not confront partition openly. Collins tried to use the IRB, *the* republican organisation, to convince Republicans that a republic would be achieved, just not right away. He proposed that the IRB should be the guardian of the republic, and the arbiter of its fulfilment. He failed on both counts.

Some Republicans were prepared to give Collins the benefit of the doubt, but a majority were not. The essential difference between the supporters of the Treaty and its opponents was that Republicans were prepared to fight on for a republic and risk British resolve to defeat them, while Treaty supporters might not be fully content, but were prepared to accept the settlement and the powers and patronage of self-government. A majority of Sinn Féin, of the IRA's leadership and of the IRB's Supreme Council, when offered Dominion status, not a republic, followed Collins' lead and accepted formal allegiance to the Crown in exchange for the real independence that a Dominion would have. A problem for Collins was that while he dominated the IRB and the IRA leadership in Dublin, elsewhere in the country local loyalties and leaders undermined and challenged his authority. Overall, a majority of IRA and IRB members refused to accept the Treaty terms.

Collins formed the so-called Provisional Government in January 1922 to implement the 1921 Treaty agreement, supported by a large majority of the Irish electorate who had never been wedded to the idea of a republic, simply wanting peace. The June 1922 election in the South, the first to be fully proportional, gave pro-Treaty candidates 80 per cent of the vote.[30] In the six counties of Northern Ireland another majority accepted that devolution. The IRB, IRA and Sinn Féin split pro- and anti-Treaty. Collins tried hard to prevent civil war by giving personal assurances that he regarded agreement to the Treaty as a tactic that would lead to a republic. Once civil war started at the end of June 1922, he took dramatic steps to prove his republicanism to his Republican opponents, notably supplying weapons to the IRA in Northern Ireland so that they could defend nationalist civilians against unionist attacks and themselves attack the police and British military forces. On 22 August 1922 Collins was killed in a Republican ambush in Co. Cork. He had been hoping to meet Republican leaders, using IRB contacts, to see if he could convince them to stop fighting.

Politics and Ideals

For many of the men and women who had fought in 1916 and later during the 1919–21 War of Independence, the Treaty, the Provisional Government and Dominion status represented defeat, not victory. They had fought for a completely independent, united Irish republic, and they had sworn oaths to this effect. Today it is, perhaps, difficult to appreciate the power of the Church and how seriously IRB and IRA men took their oaths, not least because they were protective: the assertion of their Republic provided them with – in their minds – an effective counter to the risk of excommunication. They considered themselves soldiers of a legitimate government and that they were therefore legitimate in the eyes of the Church. If they reneged, they would be acknowledging that they had been part of a sinful illegitimate undertaking. Peadar O'Donnell noted the ferocity with which some Republicans held to their oaths:

> There was an element in the Republican side that I think couldn't be brought out at all by any historical documents, and that is there were men like Michael Kilroy [O/C West Mayo Brigade], Liam Pilkington [O/C Third Western Division], Tom Maguire of Mayo [O/C Second Western Division] and to some degree Liam Lynch [O/C First Southern Division], and they had taken an oath to the Republic almost like a clerical, a priest's vow, and they weren't capable of coming down from the high ground of the Republic to the low level of the Treaty. And they were the kind of men that in any case would have to be fired on: they were the stuff that makes martyrs but don't make revolutions.[31]

Men like these were committed to their ideal of national resurgence and independence, preferring to die for it rather than accept a settlement other than of their own making. They were not interested in what Lloyd George might give; they wanted the complete independence that they considered was rightfully theirs. In 1911, when King George V was visiting Ireland, Tom Clarke put up a poster in his Dublin tobacconist shop window: 'Damn your concessions, England, we want our country!' IRB Republicans insisted on taking for themselves and not being given anything.

By May 1923 the Free State had defeated the Republicans in the Civil War. Senior IRB members in the Free State attempted to re-form the IRB in an effort to provide Republicans with an organisation to which they could submit honourably. Nothing came of this, as we shall see in Chapter 29.

Republicans decided to end their IRB connections, hide their arms, and melt away. Disaffected Collins loyalists in the Free State National Army attempted a mutiny in 1924 in protest at their reductions in rank and loss of jobs, the elevation of ex-British officers and at what they saw as the Free State government's willingness to accept its Dominion status and not work towards achieving a republic – something they were convinced had been Collins' purpose. The consequence was an end to what remained of the IRB and the resignations of several senior Free State Army officers, two government ministers – defence and industry and commerce – and eight TDs (Chapter 30 deals with this).

The Irish government established the Bureau of Military History (BMH) in 1947 to collect statements and documents from participants ('witnesses') in the events up to 1922. On 3 January 1951 Sir Alfred Cope, knighted in 1923, wrote to Elizabeth Foxe, Private Secretary to the Irish Ambassador in London, with a brilliant, anguished refusal to give a witness statement to Michael McDunphy, Director of the Bureau, on the grounds that a false history of the 1916–21 period had overwhelmed any disagreement. His implication was that the willingness of the British government to meet Irish national aspirations, and the efforts of Lloyd George to achieve peaceful settlement, had been ignored in favour of an Irish narrative that elevated violence and fighting:

> It is not possible for this history to be truthful although I am sure Mr McDunphy will do his utmost to make it so – the job is beyond human skill. The I.R.A. must be shown as national heroes and the British Forces as brutal oppressors. Accordingly, the Truce and Treaty will have been brought about by the defeat of the British by the valour of small and ill-equipped groups of irregulars. And so on. What a travesty it will be and must be. Read by future generations of Irish children, it will simply perpetuate the long standing hatred of England and continue the miserable work of self-seeking politicians who, for their own aggrandisement, have not permitted the Christian virtues of Forgiveness and Brotherhood to take its place. Ireland has too many histories; she deserves a rest. Her present need is a missioner to teach her that Love, not Hate, is still the only password both to Earthly Happiness and the Heavenly Kingdom.[32]

The straightforward facts of the period tend to support Cope's view. In 1914, while the strong possibility of partition was in the air, Home Rule for a united

Ireland was nevertheless enacted by Britain; in 1921 it was implemented with partition and, in Southern Ireland, approaching full Dominion status. Between 1914 and 1922 there was fighting and terror that did not stop the British settlement and did not win it. For all their bravery and idealism, what did 1916 and the 1918–21 guerrilla campaign really achieve? A partitioned country; great dislocation; bloodshed; tremendous anti-British propaganda and the maintenance of hatreds that extended into the next century, fuelling the IRA. British and Northern unionists had a good deal to answer for too, not least in starting the new cycle of violence in 1912 with the creation of the UVF.

The Brotherhood cast a long shadow. De Valera and others ascribed dark machinations to it. Ordinary members of the Volunteers and the IRA regarded it with a certain awe. The worldwide interest in the romantic figure of Michael Collins, so engaged with the secret society, projected its reputation far into the twentieth century. In the 1940s the Jewish terrorist groups Irgun Zvai Leumi and the breakaway Lohamei Herut Israel (also called the Stern Gang) looked to Ireland, the IRB and the IRA for lessons in how to fight the British. Avraham Stern translated P.S. O'Hegarty's *The Victory of Sinn Féin* (1924) into Hebrew so that his followers could emulate the Irish.[33] One of Stern's lieutenants, Yitzhak Shamir, Prime Minister of Israel (1983–4 and 1986–92), while on the run in the 1940s took the codename Michael in a salute to Michael Collins for the contribution he made to their thinking and strategy.

The IRB was a powerful, extremist force and a master of secrecy. After 1916, in the hands of Michael Collins, it became more prominent and provided most of the IRA's leaders. With Collins' death the IRB effectively came to an end. He had dominated it to the exclusion of his colleagues, who understood their powerlessness without him and within four months of his death had decided to wind up the organisation, as we shall see in Chapter 31.

CHAPTER 2

Conspirators

Insurrectionary committees were embedded in the secret societies, and in the offices of republican journals. We are ignorant of what went on. They were no doubt more involved in discussion than in action. Conspirators are limited and have only a small number of colleagues to rely on, only having influence when in tune with a current idea or an age-old passion.[1]

Alphonse de Lamartine, Histoire de la Révolution de 1848

The IRB was founded in Dublin by James Stephens on St Patrick's Day, 1858. In the previous eighteen months, by his own account, he had walked 3,000 miles around Ireland seeking revolutionary-minded men.[2] He had joined the Young Irelanders, a nationalist cultural and political movement, and participated in their disorganised attack in 1848 on forty-six RIC men who took refuge in a stone house in Tipperary, in what became known derisively as 'The Battle of Widow McCormack's Cabbage Patch'. He avoided arrest and fled to France where he learned about the early nineteenth-century anti-clerical, nationalist Carbonari, which was organised in small 'circles' of members to counteract informers.[3] Informers were a bête noire for Irish rebels. Every Irish rebellion had been (and would be) infiltrated by government informers. The failure of Irish rebellions was invariably blamed, in part, on informers. Stephens returned to Ireland in 1856 and when he started the IRB his security model was the Carbonari,[4] while his ideas came from Wolfe Tone.

In 1858 other Young Irelanders who had escaped to the United States formed the Fenian Brotherhood, the forerunner of Clan na Gael, which became the principal Irish nationalist organisation in the United States and

Conspirators

lent its name to the IRB. They prompted Stephens to start the IRB as a sister organisation which they paid for – a relationship that continued with Clan na Gael until 1920–21.[5]

James Stephens solidified post-Tone nationalism. He set the IRB to foment rebellion and to infiltrate every nationalist organisation. In its 1869 Constitution and in a 1873 'Address of the I.R.B. Supreme Council to the Officers and Men of the I.R.A.',[6] the IRB referred to the IRA – its creation – as 'the army of the Irish Republic'.[7] When the IRB launched its 1916 Rising and proclaimed its Irish Republic, the Republic's army was the IRA – formed principally from IRB members of the Irish Volunteers and the ICA, but also from Cumann na mBan, the women's arch-nationalist organisation,[8] and some members of the Ancient Order of Hibernians (AOH), the IPP's activists.[9] In January 1919, when the Dáil affirmed itself as the Parliament of the IRB's 1916 Republic, technically the IRA, not the Irish Volunteers, continued as the Republic's army.[10]

The principal IRB constitution, operating from 1873 to 1917, adopted Tone's separatism. The men of no property, however, did not form the core of the IRB: it drew its countryside membership not from the very poor, but mostly from tenant and small farmers, teachers and tradesmen. In towns and cities its members principally came from the trades – drapers, cobblers, carpenters, etc. – and clerks. The Dublin membership alone accounted for about half the IRB's total.[11] Its leadership came from men who had not suffered dramatic economic changes.[12]

In the United States, the Fenians were powerful and determined. From 1866 to 1871, they launched military attacks on Canada, seeking international recognition of Irish national claims. Stephens had prevaricated about a rebellion in Ireland in 1865 and again in 1866, and consequently had been ousted as head of the IRB. Fearing for his life at the hands of his erstwhile colleagues, he once more escaped to Paris. In February 1867 his successors made an abortive raid on a British arms depot at Chester Castle and in March launched another disorganised and ineffective rebellion in Ireland that was speedily put down. The leaders were arrested, but on 18 September, while being transported from court to Belle Vue Prison in Manchester, were rescued by an IRB team who killed Police Sergeant Brett in the process. Three of the rescuers – William Allen, Michael Larkin and Michael O'Brien – were captured, tried and hanged for Brett's murder, becoming the Manchester Martyrs in Irish nationalist expression. One of the accused[13] cried 'God save Ireland!' from the dock which was immediately taken up as a catchphrase and was the title of a ballad that became the marching song of the IRB and the unofficial national anthem. The evidence against the 'martyrs' was flimsy, generating demonstrations and church services in Ireland in their support, reducing faith in British justice, and bolstering an IRB legend. In December 1867 another IRB team exploded a bomb at Clerkenwell Prison in London in an attempt to free some prisoners. The effort failed but resulted in the outright deaths of twelve people, with another eighteen dying later and 120 wounded. In the last public hanging in England, one of the bombers, Michael Barrett, was executed for the Clerkenwell affair. Stephens returned to Ireland from France in 1886, no longer engaged with the IRB.

In 1916 the IRB Rising leaders were resolved not to emulate Stephens' escapes, considering them desertion, as Geraldine Plunkett related about her brother, Joseph Plunkett, the chief planner of the Rising: 'I asked Joe what was going to happen, and he said that they had discussed all the possibilities. Under no circumstances would the leaders do the same as James Stephens, and run away, leaving the rank and file.'[14]

The Fenians (the name continued to be used popularly to describe both the IRB and Clan na Gael when it replaced the Fenian Brotherhood in 1867) remained active. The Clan commissioned the first modern armed submarine, the *Fenian Ram*, launched in 1881 in New York but never used: there were arguments about money with the designer, John Holland, an Irish émigré engineer, and on its first outing it sank, but the crew survived.[15] Later it was retrieved and made functional. For four years from 1881, the Clan and the IRB carried out a Fenian bombing terror campaign in England. More than eighty people were injured in the attacks; one young boy was killed. In 1885 two bombs exploded at Westminster, one in the House of Commons and another in Westminster Hall. The campaign led to the creation in 1883 of the London Metropolitan Police Special Irish Branch (later simply the Special Branch), as an undercover counterterror unit.

In 1882 the Irish National Invincibles, an assassination unit within the IRB (and a precursor of Michael Collins' assassination Squad), using twelve-inch surgical knives slashed to death the Chief Secretary for Ireland, Lord Frederick Cavendish, and the Permanent Under Secretary for Ireland, Thomas Burke, as they walked in Dublin's Phoenix Park. These men were fearsome.

In 1912, when Arthur Norway first came to Dublin, he thought the country was peaceful:

Conspirators

> In all quarters I found the same light complacency. The country was quiet. Why should it not remain so? But ere long I began to get an occasional police report indicating that a member of my staff was suspected of belonging to the Irish Republican Brotherhood, of which I had not heard before ... I asked a Resident Magistrate, one O'Sullivan, whether he knew anything of the Brotherhood. He looked startled and answered, 'Not now. Formerly of course I did.' 'And what was it, when you knew it?' I continued. 'A black murder Society,' he rapped out, 'and never anything else.' 'Does it exist now?' I went on. 'I hope to God it doesn't,' he replied. 'You would be alarmed?' 'Very much indeed,' he said ... I told him of my police reports, and he became grave, and warned me that the reports were probably indications of coming trouble.[16]

The centenary of 1798 and the funerals of Stephens (1901) and other Young Ireland and Fenian leaders provided opportunities for nationalist demonstrations honouring insurrections, reminding people that rebellious coals still smouldered. The IPP, representing most of Ireland at Westminster, successfully battled against the violent, murderous and rebellious tradition of the IRB, and in 1914 secured Home Rule, although its implementation was delayed until the end of the First World War. This delay enabled the Rising, the disruption of the IPP, and the 1918–21 War of Independence. Thomas Taylor, since 1908 a Dublin IRB member, echoed contemporary opinion: 'If the Home Rule Bill had gone through, there would never have been any struggle. Never. That would have settled the whole thing, and we'd have been in the British Empire. But there was delay and delay before that. Even in Gladstone's time there was delay. And the younger generation, the IRB men, had no hope at all; only a rising.'[17]

Following the Easter Rising, ruthless retribution by the British military authorities,[18] followed by threats to impose conscription, alienated Irish nationalist voters who over the next two and a half years eventually switched their support from the IPP to Sinn Féin. Days after the Rising, Lloyd George, then Minister for Munitions, was charged by Prime Minister Herbert Asquith with responsibility for settling Ireland.[19] He tried to implement Home Rule in the southern twenty-six counties immediately. He was supported in this by the Ulster Unionists who, after the Rising, had been promised their own six Ulster counties but was ultimately prevented by British Unionists who felt that unionists in the south would be left unprotected, deserted both by the British government and by their colleagues in the north.[20]

In Ireland, 1917 and 1918 were spent by an IRB group of Rising survivors electioneering and shaping the IRB to be the core of the Volunteers/IRA and selecting IRB men to be Sinn Féin parliamentary candidates.

The IRB had a network of members throughout Britain, and close relations with Clan na Gael. It was experienced in arms procurement and smuggling. It provided an excellent courier service; it had members in the post office, on ships and at ports, among hotel staff, in the railways, in the civil service and in the police and RIC.[21] From 1918, police, RIC, military and government messages were routinely intercepted and delivered to Michael Collins, enabling him to warn colleagues of impending arrests and to inform Volunteer/IRA units of military and police plans. It provided him with intelligence about all the other nationalist organisations. He managed several prison escapes in England using the IRB network there and smuggled several people to and from the United States. Michael O'Leary in Liverpool described Collins' direct involvement:

> Michael Collins always outlined the plans. From our side, these plans were carefully examined and studied in detail. When all hitches were removed, the all-clear was given, that is, we sent word back to Dublin that we were ready ... It must be remembered that those acts were carried out in the enemy's country, where the greatest secrecy was important, but the I.R.A. and I.R.B. men in charge knew their work.[22]

The IRB was the principal supplier of arms and ammunition for the Volunteers/IRA, very often through Liverpool and always through Collins. These IRB channels and usefulness built up Collins and the IRB in the imaginations of practically everyone and gave him more real power and influence than any of his colleagues.

There were differing retrospective views of the IRB among junior members and non-members unaware of its intelligence, access to American money, arms procurement abroad and smuggling activity. Some, such as Arthur Greene in Dundalk, while remaining in their Circles, thought the IRB was pointless: 'The activities of the I.R.B. were devoted mostly to meetings of the Circle. I could see little use in it. We were constantly "hatching" and nothing came out of our plans. A lot of the I.R.B. were old men and were useless as a physical-force body.'[23] Upon joining the IRB in 1913, Rory Haskins in Belfast also thought that 'The activities of the I.R.B. after I joined looked to

Conspirators 27

me as rather futile.'[24] However, Val Jackson, a Dublin Deputy Centre, noted a change in 1913:

> After the formation of the Volunteers, late in 1913, the work of the Circles began to liven up considerably. Instructions were issued that all members who were anyway fit were to join the Volunteers and to attend drill regularly and that every effort should be made by the Centres and others to get on to the working committees of the Volunteers.[25]

Post-1916, attitudes to the Brotherhood were more divided and clear-cut, reflecting the way in which the Volunteers/IRA were doing what until then the IRB alone had done – actual rebellion. Members in Dublin tended to prefer the Volunteers/IRA to the IRB. Jim Slattery, in Collins' Squad, said of the IRB: 'It never meant much to me at all … The whole thing was bloody ridiculous in our day … they were a lot of gombeens! Thought a lot about themselves … I took very little interest in it. It was only a bloody talking shop.'[26] Seán MacBride, who worked with Collins in Volunteer/IRA Intelligence, agreed: 'I was a member of the IRB for a time. But I always thought it was a pretty useless organisation … I regarded it as an awful waste of time to go to meetings in Parnell Square and listen to Old Fogies!'[27] Michael Hayes, a leading member of Sinn Féin, thought so too: 'I was never asked to join the IRB which is taken that at some time I probably said I thought it was a cod.'[28] Moss Twomey, a commandant in the First Southern Division, thought it unnecessary and ominous:

> I was sworn in to the IRB in 1919. But I had no regard for it at all. I thought it should have stopped at the time of the Volunteers [1916]. It was sort of an underground, spooky sort of thing which Collins and others used to their own advantage … I had a high position in the IRA and if I didn't join they'd probably object to me.[29]

Conversely, Liam O'Dwyer, a Battalion O/C in West Cork, thought the IRB was of great importance:

> The extent of the IRB and their superiority is not [recorded] in history … [the important jobs] were carried out by the IRA but really by the IRB members within it … [The IRB] was in fact superior to the IRA as well as preceding it … The IRB didn't interfere if things were going

right … In Dublin things were different but in the country we had less IRB control. Our company thought a certain girl was a spy and giving information to an English officer, when she was getting information from him. They wanted to shave her head and a request was sent for permission to shoot her. The IRB had to step in there. The IRB were merely watchdogs.[30]

Looking back in 1954, Seán Gibbons, who had been a member of the Westport IRB Circle and adjutant of the West Mayo Brigade, considered that the importance of the IRB lay in its republican resolve:

There is no doubt in my mind after the years that the I.R.B. did a good job of work and there was no danger of things falling asunder while they stood behind the scenes in one organisation and participated in, ruled and controlled the other national organisations … There is no doubt in my mind that the Sinn Féin organisation and the I.R.A. organisation in our Brigade area were definitely animated and made living things originally by the Irish Republican Brotherhood.[31]

The IRB was never omniscient. Apart from the post-1916 Volunteers/IRA, it did not have a commanding grip on all the organisations it infiltrated[32] or created, and even with the Volunteers/IRA outside Dublin its control was loose. Nor were some of its members as wedded to secrecy as its constitutions demanded. Liam O'Doherty, a Dublin IRB member, was taken aback when he found less rigorous observance away from the capital: 'There is one thing I noticed as I went down the country: they spoke about the IRB which you daren't mention in Dublin.'[33] For the British Army, however, IRB secrecy was effective. Arthur Percival, when a major serving with the Essex Regiment in Kinsale, noted:

With regard to the plans of the I.R.A. it was very difficult to get any information about these in time to take action. This was on account of the very strict oath taken by members of the I.R.B. who alone knew the details of any approaching operations. The ordinary members of the I.R.A. were simply told to parade at a certain place at a certain time and did not know the nature of the operations until they got there.[34]

Conspirators

Time and again the IRB concentrated on packing the executive committees of organisations while paying less attention – to its cost – to lower echelons. This was a mistake made apparent by the confusion surrounding the launch of the 1916 Rising and made apparent again by the inability of the IRB to cohere in 1921–22 when faced with disagreement presaging civil war. Its organisation was speckled, not uniform. This was also the case with Volunteer/IRA formations, as they were usually based on IRB membership. In Dublin discipline was good, but outside Dublin local Volunteer/IRA leaders, most of whom were members of the IRB, were not averse to independent action and often had little contact with headquarters in Dublin. When Mrs Maria Lindsay and her chauffeur, James Clarke, were shot as spies by the IRA in Co. Cork in March 1921, for example, Collins wrote that 'they should have referred it to me for decision, but did not do so'.[35] All too often what was decided in Dublin by the IRB and the Volunteers/IRA was assumed by their leaderships to be accepted throughout their membership, and this was not the case. Charles Townshend summed up Volunteer/IRA command and control:

> What the evidence suggests ... is that right up to the Truce most IRA units were weakly organized, marginally effective, and by no means in full sympathy, or even contact, with the ordinary people. The overall structure of the army was marked by wild inconsistencies in strength, standards, and control. Its military position was in many ways, and especially in relation to its own ambitions, far worse than most commentators have thought. Psychologically and politically its position was better, but one must question whether many of its members understood themselves to be waging a political war. The sort of arguments employed by opponents of the Treaty in 1922 suggest that a belief in the possibility of purely physical victory persisted to the end.[36]

Idealogues have a tenuous relationship with reality.

Tom Maguire, a senior Volunteer/IRA commander in Mayo and a member of the IRB attended a meeting with the IRB President, Michael Collins, only once, and that was in January 1922 when fighting with the RIC and British military was over.[37] Some parts of the country produced strong membership; others produced scanty membership.[38] In Kildare, where the bulk of British military forces were based, Tom Harris explained: 'We did not consider it wise to take too many into the organisation down there. Our object was to have a couple in each place or district. There were a few in Naas and a few in Kilcock and Newbridge – just one or two in each – but it was never fully developed in the county.'[39]

The majority of members of the IRB were also members of the Volunteers/IRA. From 1916 onwards members of the Supreme Council were on the Volunteer/IRA Executive and GHQ; the single most important and influential being Michael Collins.

CHAPTER 3

Infamy

Oh, God's heaviest curse, His withering blighting, blasting curse on them
… When we look down into the fathomless depth of this infamy of the
leaders of the Fenian conspiracy, we must acknowledge that eternity is
not long enough, nor hell hot enough, to punish such miscreants.[1]

Right Rev. Dr David Moriarty, Bishop of Kerry, 17 February 1867

The attitude of the Roman Catholic Church to the IRB and its members
had a deleterious effect on IRB recruitment and forced its leaders to adjust
the organisation's constitutions accordingly. The Church's stand was basic and
straightforward: killing and disruption were generally condemned, as were
political creeds that did not accept the centrality of Christianity. In addition,
the physical-force nature of the Brotherhood 'combined with its secret
organisation was the basis of the charge frequently made against the Fenians,
especially by the Catholic clergy, that they were communists'.[2] Or, nearly as
bad, socialists.

In the twenty-six counties of the present Republic, the 1911 census
indicated that 89.6 per cent of the population was Catholic, the large majority
practising members of their faith.[3] Yet despite this, as John Whyte observed in
1971, the Church had 'never been able to count on the obedience of their flocks
on all issues. Religious loyalties are strong, but other forces have sometimes
proved stronger still'.[4] National feeling provided the strongest opposition to the
Church, and for a minority of Irishmen the IRB's complete dedication to Irish
independence provided a more dynamic conception of Irish identity than any
endorsed by the Church.[5] This did not mean that they rejected the Catholic
faith. Many members were deeply religious: Tomás MacCurtain, a member

of the IRB and of the Volunteers/IRA, and Lord Mayor of Cork, murdered by RIC men in 1920, was described by a priest who knew him as 'an ardent Catholic and a member of the Third Order of St. Francis'.[6] Tom Clarke, a practising Catholic and President of the 1916 Irish Republic, would not admit the Rising was sinful, and so was refused absolution before his execution in 1916. He explained to his wife, 'I was not going to face my God with a lie on my tongue.'[7] During the 1922–23 Civil War, two Republican IRA men went to Rome to seek an audience with Pope Benedict XV, hoping for support. Patrick Ruttledge, then on the IRA's governing Army Council, recalled, 'The Pope wouldn't see them unless they were prepared to accept his laws as laid down by the Bishops.'[8] The bishops had issued a joint pastoral letter in October 1922 condemning the Republican IRA. Seán MacDermott placed the Church as one of the principal 'Blocks in the Way' of the IRB together with the 'Hibernians, the Parliamentary Party, Clergy, Spy System, Want of Employment, Want of Money.'[9]

In the two generations before 1924, there were three episodes when the force of national feeling proved strong enough to lead men to defy the Church: the Fenian/IRB terror campaigns in England in the 1880s, the Republican side during the 1922–23 Civil War, and Charles Stewart Parnell being cited as the co-respondent in a divorce case. This was the most divisive event. Parnell for ten years had been pressing the case for Home Rule at Westminster, but as a result of the divorce case the Liberal Party made clear it could not continue to support Home Rule while Parnell remained leader. The Standing Committee of the Irish hierarchy declared that the proceedings in the divorce case made Parnell unfit for leadership. Notwithstanding this, as subsequent elections showed, a substantial number of Catholics remained loyal to Parnell and ignored the opposition of the Church to their hero.[10]

The hostility of the Church to the IRB was particularly clear in the 1860s and 1870s. It came directly from the fact that it was a secret society. To join a secret society or to swear blind obedience to strangers was sinful. A series of papal bulls, *In eminenti* (1738), *Providas* (1751), *Ecclesiam* (1821) and *Quo Graviora* (1825) clearly condemned secret societies. *Apostolicae Sedis Moderationi* (1869) went into some detail, naming the Carbonari and Freemasons. The encyclical *Quanta Cura* (1864) condemned opposition to the separation of Church and State, a principal IRB objective. The IRB was pledged to rebellion and this resulted in even more conflict with the Church. Four conditions for justifiable rebellion were laid down by the Church, and it was usually pointed out that one or more had not been met when Fenian/IRB rebellions were discussed. First, the government must be habitually and intolerably oppressive. Second, rebellion must be a last resort after other means of opposition have been tried and have failed. Third, there must be a reasonable prospect of success and of not making matters worse. Fourth, the resistance must enjoy approval by a popular majority.[11]

In 1861, three years after its formation, IRB members were excommunicated ipso facto by the Archbishop of Dublin, Dr Paul Cullen, who was Ireland's leading churchman and in 1866 was appointed the country's first ever cardinal.[12] The Archbishop's diktat was taken by the Bishop of Cork to include membership of the Volunteers/IRA when he issued a blanket excommunication of members in his diocese on 12 December 1920. Ecclesiastical hostility to the IRB reached a climax in 1870 when the Sacred Congregation of the Holy See, otherwise known as the Inquisition, with the authority of Pope Pius IX, reaffirmed Cullen's action.[13] Still, the IRB numbered an estimated 80,000 in the early 1860s and launched an abortive rising in 1867 that culminated in the RIC firing on and dispersing a column of rebels at Tallaght in south Co. Dublin.[14]

The rising in 1867 failed not only because it was badly organised and led (since 1865 many IRB leaders had been arrested), but also because the IRB never enjoyed widespread popular support. This was always a source of worry to them, and they directly attributed it to their condemnation by the Church. John O'Mahony, in 1858 one of the founders of the Fenian Brotherhood in the United States, foresaw this difficulty from the outset. As a secret society avowedly determined to pursue the cause of Irish independence by force of arms, the IRB was bound to antagonise the Church. Writing in 1859, O'Mahony set out the initial tactics of the IRB in dealing with the Church:

> We must calculate upon a certain amount of opposition from some of the priests. I do not, however, consider it judicious to come into collision with them openly. Those who denounce us go beyond their duties as clergymen. They are either bad Irishmen, who do not wish to see Ireland a nation, or stupid and ignorant zealots ... Our association is neither anti-Catholic nor irreligious. We are an Irish army, not a secret society.[15]

This argument was advanced by the IRB throughout its life. It was refined in the columns of the IRB's newspaper, *The Irish People*, founded by James

34 The Irish Republican Brotherhood, 1914–1924

Stephens in 1863, resulting in a clear call for the separation of Church and State: 'We saw from the first that ecclesiastical authority in temporal affairs should be shivered to atoms before we could advance a single step towards the liberation of our suffering country.'[16]

This call, together with their dedication to force, was the essence of the IRB.[17] But it did not hold water with the Church. The hierarchy, at a general meeting in Dublin on 4 August 1863, condemned Fenianism in toto.[18] Immediately following the 1867 rising, Bishop Moriarty of Kerry delivered his furious condemnation of the IRB from the pulpit of Killarney Cathedral on 17 February (quoted at the head of this chapter).[19]

Yet, while the hierarchy, the Pope and the Inquisition vehemently opposed the IRB, many priests did not. The execution of the IRB's Manchester Martyrs in November 1867 provided the strongest evidence of the sympathy between many priests and the secret society. Prayers were said at Mass for the three hanged men. Requiem Masses were held for them throughout Ireland. A procession was held for them in Killarney, despite the fierce opposition of Bishop Moriarty.[20] Cullen allowed private Masses for them; Archbishop McHale of Tuam took part in a High Mass for them.

In 1873 the IRB was reorganised by Charles Kickham. He masterminded the IRB's reply to the attacks of the Church during the 1860s and 1870s. Under his influence, the IRB's governing body, the Supreme Council, approved a constitution for the society in which it was declared that the president of the IRB was the president of the (self-declared) Irish Republic and together with the Supreme Council provided the Republic with its government. By creating their own republic, the IRB argued that its relations with the Church were the same as with any other government. For IRB men, the only legitimate authority in Ireland was their own, and thus they gave themselves all the moral authority which, as good Catholics, they needed. The constitution was framed to take account of Catholic teaching, including a clause requiring public support as a requirement for an insurrection. It also firmly asserted the separation of Church and State.[21]

In the face of the explicit 1870 papal ban, the IRB's membership declined from several tens of thousands in the 1860s to about 1,500 in 1911.[22] Despite the fact that at least one priest was a member of the IRB at the time of the 1916 Rising,[23] Diarmuid Lynch, who did a great deal of recruiting for the Brotherhood between 1908 and 1918, testified to the powerful effect of the Church's ban upon potential recruits: 'Often when after tedious investigation a man was deemed fit in every respect, the inquisitor found himself "up against a stone wall" – that of religious scruples in the matter of joining a "secret organisation". This was a stumbling block in the matter of numerical progress.'[24]

This wall was of real concern to the IRB. The reality was that the Church had a strong hold on the average Irishman.[25] Even after being sworn in as a member of the IRB, religious qualms had effect. Joe McGarrity, a leading member of Clan na Gael (he was Treasurer and then President of the Clan), visited Circles in Scotland sometime in 1911–12. Daniel Kelly, Centre of the Greenock and Port Glasgow Circle, met him there:

> He told us some of his experiences in America. There was a mission or retreat on in Philadelphia one time and he wanted to go to confession to one of the three priests giving the mission. He went into the confessional and the first thing the missioner asked him was, 'Are you a member of any organisation?' He said, 'I am a member of St. Vincent's.' 'Oh!', he said, 'I don't mean that. Are you a member of the Irish Republican Brotherhood or this Clan na Gael?' He told him, 'I am.' 'Well,' he said, 'I won't hear your confession.' So McGarrity went to the other two missioners and they said the same.

For Kelly, the battle lines with the Church were firm, and confessing to a priest was tantamount to fraternising with the enemy: 'At one meeting I remember an Irish engineer got up and informed us that he had informed the priest in confession that he was a member of the I.R.B. I had to propose this man's expulsion from the organisation.'[26] Yet fear of the Church, even with men who did not confess their membership, remained a constant concern. Thomas Barry, a long-standing IRB member, described one of the IRB's attempts to allay members' fear of hellfire:

> In 1908 in Dublin the men were being asked in Confession if they belonged to the I.R.B. This was causing a certain amount of embarrassment and Reverend Father Sheehy visited all the Circles and spoke to the men. After that in 1909 or 1910 a general meeting of the Dublin men was held at Clontarf Town Hall … and the meeting was addressed by Father Denis O'Sullivan.[27]

Francis Daly was at this meeting and remembered what Fr O'Sullivan said:

> [T]he trend of his address [was] that the organisation had somewhat deteriorated, that although there had been good men carrying it on, there were others who had somehow developed it into a sort of debating society – he did not use those words – but that new blood had come into it and would strike a more effective blow than in '67. He spoke about the oath. The people spoke against secret societies but he gave us his word that we were quite justified in taking the oath to defend our country.[28]

The result of Fr O'Sullivan's lecture quietened members' concerns, but there was a persistent worry on the part of many that they risked damnation and the loss of jobs because of IRB membership. Michael McGinn, who was the caretaker at Clontarf Town Hall where the Supreme Council met in January 1916, experienced both condemnation from the altar and losing his previous job in Omagh because of his IRB membership:

> The local priest in Omagh preached one Sunday against the Fenians. After that, Dan Hackett asked McGinn was he at Mass that day, and he said he was, at first Mass. He asked, 'Did you hear what the priest said?' Mick said he did. Then Dan asked him, 'Did you know what it was all about?' Mick said, 'No', he did not know. 'Well,' he said, 'you are the only man in Omagh who did not know what it was about.' Then he said to him, 'You had better clear out. I don't want you any more.' The priest had almost pointed to McGinn during his sermon. Mick could not get any other job there, and so he came to Dublin.[29]

The IRB's public reply to the Church's condemnation was set out in an article entitled 'The faith of a Fenian' in the February 1911 edition of the IRB's new newspaper, *Irish Freedom*, launched in November 1910. It maintained that the Church had been influenced by British diplomacy in its condemnation of Fenianism,[30] that Irish patriotism was at the heart of Fenianism, and that there was nothing morally wrong in Irishmen banding together to free their country.

As with the Manchester Martyrs, there were always priests like Fr O'Sullivan who supported the IRB. Patrick McCartan in Tyrone was able to enlist two priests to calm IRB members' fears:

Infamy
37

I think one of these priests said in the course of his talk, 'When you go to confession, you go to confess your sins, not your virtues.' I had got in touch with Fr O'Daly to give this talk because he [and the other priest, Fr Coyle, had agreed to join the IRB]. I told the two of them that it was an oath-bound organisation and that perhaps it would be unfair to them if they were asked by their Bishop did they ever take an oath and they would have to admit that they did ... We took them into the I.R.B. without administering any oath, and that was how they came to speak to the young men in my father's barn.[31]

Joseph Barrett, an IRB Centre and an early Volunteer, noted how important the IRB's stance towards the Church was in maintaining not only IRB membership, but also Volunteers:

As is well known, the I.R.B. was banned by the Catholic Church, and that ban would have had a serious effect on the Volunteer organisation as well as the I.R.B., had not the I.R.B. members been advised that any action taken by men for the freedom of their country was no sin. They were told that the clergy were bound to take such action and propound such views as the hierarchy might direct, but that, where men were satisfied – and it was pointed out to them how they could satisfy their own consciences – that their actions were good and legitimate, they need not disclose their membership of the organisation to their confessor.[32]

The contest with the Church was never-ending. Special steps were taken around 1913 to combat the effect of the Church's ban of the IRB at another Clontarf meeting, with Fr O'Sullivan again being used to reassure members as he had three or four years earlier. Diarmuid Lynch recalled the importance of O'Sullivan's intervention:

The [ban], to my personal knowledge, prevented many men from joining. Even some enrolled members occasionally developed uneasiness on that point. I believe it was to meet this situation that a visit to Ireland by the Rev. Denis O'Sullivan of Valentia was availed of in getting him to address the men of the Dublin district on the theological aspect. A 'general meeting' of these was held in the Clontarf Town Hall for that purpose.[33]

The Irish Republican Brotherhood, 1914–1924

Ernest Blythe, brought up as a Quaker in Belfast and somewhat dismissive of religious concerns, was at this Clontarf meeting:

> If anybody said in Confession he was in the IRB, the priest said he couldn't give him absolution until he'd resigned. We were always losing members. The Church was against secret societies, and of course the IRB reply was that it wasn't a secret society: it was an army in hiding … Sunday morning someone came round to my house to tell me there'd be a meeting in Clontarf Town Hall that night with the priest to address them. I thought he'd give a theological argument, but of course all he said was 'I am a member'.[34]

Reassurance from O'Sullivan and some other priests and monks was sufficient for many IRB members who were sincere rebels and sincere Catholics. Some priests went further. In Athlone, just before the 1916 Rising, Henry O'Brien, a captain in the Athlone Irish Volunteer Brigade, credited a priest with procuring guns for his men: 'About a week or so before the Rebellion Father O'Reilly procured arms for the Tang [village] section of our company. This armament consisted of about 12 rifles – service pattern long Lee Enfields, and some .303 ammunition which was the service ammunition for such rifles.'[35]

Immediately before the Rising, James Daly found himself surrounded by Volunteers: 'On Saturday I went into town early. I went to Marlborough St. I went to Confession. I wasn't at all surprised to find Marlborough St. filled with young men – mostly Volunteers – dozens of whom I knew, all the one thing, going to confession.'[36] James Lalor during Easter Week 1916 had a late lunch at Kelly's Hotel, Maryborough (now Portlaoise):

> We had been out all night and were very hungry as we had no breakfast. When we got to the hotel it was too early for dinner so we ordered tea with steak and onions for the three of us. The waiter stared at us in a strange manner, but passed no remark. He served the meal to which we did justice, but still we noticed that he continued to stare at us in a strange way. Subsequently it dawned on us that the day was Spy Wednesday and, of course, a fast day. Our ordering and eating steak on that day must have shocked the poor waiter.[37]

Batt O'Connor recorded the devotion of many of the men interned after taking part in the 1916 Rising:

> When I say that each day closed with a song, that is not quite true; it closed with prayer. Our last act at night was to go down on our knees and repeat the Rosary and the Litany of the Blessed Virgin. The Rosary was said every night in every hut in Frongoch camp, not at the command of the camp leader, but out of the impulse to prayer which was in the heart of each of us. Nearly everyone had one or other of the holy images hanging over his bed.[38]

After the Rising, the Church wisely took its time to decide upon its attitude to the rebellion,[39] and in the following years took an ambivalent attitude to the Volunteers/IRA and Sinn Féin. Both organisations wanted to avoid confrontation with the Church, so there was tacit accommodation on all sides. Priests were on the Sinn Féin Executive. Many reports appear in the memoirs of Volunteers/IRA and IRB men of priests and nuns helping them after 1916. Patrick McCartan, evading arrest after the Rising, was offered help from monks: 'I could be smuggled out [to America] too. Some of the Church Street [Dublin] priests, the Capuchins, were arranging this, I think.'[40] In Ennis, Co. Clare, on Armistice Day 1919, Michael Brennan, an IRB Volunteer/IRA member, publicly burned a Union Jack. Then:

> I was talking in the garden with Canon O'Kennedy and some other members of the Clare Sinn Féin Executive when a shrieking and apparently drunken mob of soldiers and civilians arrived. Somebody slammed and bolted the high garden door, but they started to climb over it. I fired three shots over their heads and they disappeared hurriedly. It was, of course, obvious at this stage that official action would follow and I made a 'strategic retreat' being guided over various walls until I reached the convent where the nuns kept me until it was dark. Two of the local priests called then in a motor car and I went with them to St. Flannan's College.[41]

In Belfast in 1920 and 1921 when there was severe sectarian fighting, Manus O'Boyle, an IRB captain of a Volunteer/IRA company, spoke of the support he and his men received from nuns:

During all the fighting our headquarters were in the Cross and Passion Convent in Bryson Street. The nuns were magnificent. Mother Teresa, Sister Ethna, Sister Peter Paul and Sister Bridget are four that I remember particularly. This continued all through 1920 and up to and after the Truce ... Mother Teresa could always present us with hundreds of rounds of .45 ammunition which she received from [RIC District Inspector McConnell who was an IRA informant].[42]

Church opposition to the IRB was muted after the Rising, but it is fair to say that the Church always maintained its specific opposition to the society.[43] The effect on even some of the toughest IRB and Volunteer/IRA men was substantial, as Richard Mulcahy related:

> On one occasion, for instance, three men going along on the duty of shooting a particular detective came into a situation as follows: moving in O'Connell Street, naturally a little bit away from one another in order to cover one another if necessary, one of the three dropped back and linked up with the person who was in charge of the work. The latter was an officer of the Second Battalion whose Company had contributed to a lot of activity in the city. His colleague came to him and said he had a difficulty that he would like to talk about. He said, 'I'm going to be married in a fortnight's time and I am wondering if we shoot this man, could it bring any affliction on the children of the marriage?'[44]

In 1917 the Church found a supporter of its condemnation of the Brotherhood in Éamon de Valera, after 1917 President of Sinn Féin, President of the Volunteers/IRA, after 1919 President of the Dáil government, and in late 1921 finally declared President of the Republic. He had been a member of the IRB for about a year in 1915–16 and theoretically until mid-1917 when he simply announced he had left. He argued in favour of Eoin MacNeill's actions in 1916 against the IRB and the Rising,[45] having concluded that the organisation was no longer justified, and in any case, he disliked it on religious grounds.

There was one public condemnation by Bishop Daniel Cohalan of Cork. On 12 December 1920 he excommunicated members of the Volunteers/IRA in his diocese, but he had no more than a momentary effect.[46] He was alone in his stand amongst the bishops and was not supported by Cardinal

Logue or Archbishop Walsh, Ireland's leading clerics. Fr Dominic O'Connor, a Franciscan monk, styled as the chaplain of the Third Cork Brigade, Volunteers/IRA, rejected Cohalan's decree in a circular, using the Kickham argument:

> Now kidnapping, ambushing and killing ordinarily would be grave sins or violations of Law. And if these acts were being performed by the I[rish] V[olunteers] as private persons (whether physical or moral) would fall under the excommunication. But they are doing them by and with the authority of the State and the Republic of Ireland. And the State has the right and duty to defend the lives and property of its citizens and to punish even with death those who are aiming at the destruction of the lives or property of its citizens or itself.[47]

Fr O'Connor provided Catholics in the Cork Volunteers/IRA with the reassurance they needed. This was reinforced by Fr O'Flanagan, who had been on the Volunteer Executive, in the GPO in 1916, and then graced the leadership of Sinn Féin and found no difficulty in supporting the rebels.

Michael Collins reflected IRB intransigence and hostility to the Church, recognising the force of excommunication. He met one of his agents, Séamas Ó Maoileoin, late in 1920 and complained about Bishop Cohalan:

> 'Séamas', he said, 'if I had my way that so-and-so of a bishop would be shot. There is neither sense nor reason in shooting ignorant, uneducated idiots as spies and letting people like the Bishop of Cork get away with it. According to the rules of warfare, any civilian aiding the enemy is a spy. But I suppose our political friends would never agree to it.' We discussed many other things that night, but the Excommunication had priority.[48]

After their Civil War defeat in 1923, the IRA of necessity became a secret society, and its members had to deal with ecclesiastical condemnation, as members of the IRB had before them.[49] Republicans sought to remain within the Church and only if forced placed their dedication to an Irish republic before their Catholicism. Again and again the argument Fr O'Connor explained in 1920 and the IRB put forward in 1873 was employed: they act with the authority of the State – their State.

The appeal of force to deeply rooted Irish nationalism was a constant undercurrent to Irish politics. Bishop Moriarty of Kerry, after consigning the Fenians to somewhere hotter than hell in February 1867, some weeks later showed himself well aware of the Fenian appeal: 'Fenianism, with all its fraud and falsehood, with all its braggart cowardice, and with that hatred of religion which marked its every utterance, found sympathy and raised strong hopes in the Irish poor. And unfortunately, the Irish poor means the Irish people.'[50]

Moriarty was correct about the Irish people being poor. Until the later nineteenth-century land ownership reform, culminating in the 1903 Wyndham Act, Ireland had been the United Kingdom's very own Third World.

CHAPTER 4

1873–1917 Constitution

'We always referred to the I.R.B. as "The Organisation"'.[1]

Christopher Byrne, 19 December 1948

The 1873 Constitution provided the IRB with a purpose that subsequent constitutions did not fundamentally change. It stated the objective of the IRB: 'overthrowing of English power in Ireland, and of establishing an independent Irish Republic ... by force of arms.'[2] No other way of securing a republic was considered. Its organisational structure did not arrange separate electoral or administrative divisions of Ireland but accepted the county demarcations established by Britain. Its general concern was with unity, nationalism and revolution. It contained the advantages and disadvantages of authoritarianism: concentrated power at the top, no feedback from below, and no debate about Supreme Council decisions. The authority of the Supreme Council and its Executive Committee was firmly established. The Supreme Council had the power to act without reference to the IRB's membership: 'The Supreme Council of the Irish Republican Brotherhood is hereby declared in fact, as well as by right, the sole Government of the Irish Republic.'[3] Where there is real secrecy, of necessity there is simplicity with lines of communication that are difficult to penetrate. The IRB achieved this, keeping members in small discrete Circles, and giving information on a 'need to know' basis that was generally observed.

The constitution was framed with the Church's opposition firmly in mind and sought to deflect it. The first clause declared the IRB's disinterest in class and creed.[4] One complete clause was devoted to a declaration that: 'In the Irish Republic there shall be no State religion but every citizen shall be free to worship God according to his conscience, and perfect freedom of worship shall be guaranteed as a right and not granted as a privilege.'[5]

This non-sectarian stance and firm division between Church and State was at the heart of the IRB programme and remained a central objective up to 1922.[6] By its resistance to ecclesiastical censure and its rigorous attempt to separate Church and State, the IRB proclaimed that the independence for which it fought was intellectual, even spiritual, as much as political.[7]

Perhaps the most important result of the IRB confrontation with the Church was that in maintaining the principle of separation of Church and State the IRB contributed to the development of Irish nationalism.[8] However, notwithstanding its declaration that 'The military authority shall at all times be and remain subject to the Civil Government', the IRB was dedicated to force to obtain its objective. Its concern with government was more than balanced by its attention to the practicalities of securing weapons and ammunition. The constitution's uneasy blend of civil authority with violence remained unreconciled. The IRB oaths that members swore had an implicit commitment to force. James Stephens' original 1858 IRB oath ran:

> I, A.B., do solemnly swear in the presence of almighty God that I will do my utmost at every risk while life lasts, to make Ireland an independent democratic republic; that I will yield implicit obedience in all things not contrary to the law of God to the commands of my superior officers, and that I shall preserve inviolable secrecy regarding all the transactions of this secret society that may be confided in me. So help me God. Amen.[9]

In 1859 Stephens asked Thomas Clarke Luby, a fellow conspirator, to revise the oath to counteract Church opposition. 'Henceforth,' wrote Luby, 'we denied that we were technically a secret body. We called ourselves a military organisation, with, so to speak, a legionary oath like all soldiers.'[10] In order to achieve this, the new oath declared that the Irish Republic was virtually established, implying that the IRB provided the Republic with its government and its army:

> I, A.B., in the presence of Almighty God, do solemnly swear allegiance to the Irish Republic, now virtually established; and that I will do my very utmost at every risk, while life lasts, to defend its independence and integrity; and finally, that I will yield implicit obedience in all things not

1873–1917 Constitution

contrary to the laws of God to the commands of my superior officers. So help me God. Amen.[11]

Following the disastrous attempt at a rising in 1867, the IRB was drastically overhauled and a new constitution and yet another oath were adopted. This oath lasted until November 1920:

> In the presence of God, I … do solemnly swear that I will do my utmost to establish the national independence of Ireland, and that I will bear true allegiance to the Supreme Council of the Irish Republican Brotherhood and Government of the Irish Republic and implicitly obey the constitution of the Irish Republican Brotherhood and all my superior officers, and that I will preserve inviolable the secrets of the Organisation.[12]

The power of these oaths was very real. In 1950, Val Jackson felt he was in some way breaking his oath when he agreed to be interviewed for the Bureau of Military History:

> In making this statement to the Bureau of Military History, I feel satisfied that I am no longer bound by the terms of the oath I then took, as the matters on which I propose to speak are now ancient history and cannot in any way be a cause of injury or annoyance to persons named who are still living. Neither can my remarks now affect the objects for which the I.R.B. laboured.[13]

The commitment to secrecy came more forcefully from Seán MacEoin, who served as Chief of Staff of the Irish Defence Forces (1929), Minister for Justice (1948–51) and Minister for Defence (1951, 1954–57), saying when I interviewed him in 1973:

> It's doubtful again if I'm free to say who was who – who was president or who was not. The presidentship was so secret. He was never to be mentioned by anybody except at a Supreme Council meeting. The Supreme Council meeting was the very identical same as the Parish [Circle] one: the last thing you did was to swear that you would never divulge any of the secrets.[14]

The 1873 Constitution cemented James Stephens' Circles of members as the base of the IRB's hierarchy. These Circles varied in size, some growing to over fifty members while others had fewer than ten. 'Prior to 1916 the Circles could be as large as 50 – there could be 50 members in a Parish Circle,' noted Seán MacEoin, but after 1916 'the largest a Circle could be was nine'.[15] However, it is unlikely that nine was the absolute for Circle membership: Michael Collins' Dublin Circle had 35 members in 1919[16] when the Dublin city Circles accounted for about 20 per cent of all the members.[17]

The members of each Circle elected one of their number as Centre, the head of the Circle. Val Jackson described a Centre's role: 'The routine duty of a Centre was first of all to preside over his own Circle. Secondly, to attend the meeting of the Centres Board at which meeting, amongst other things, Centres were appointed to visit other Circles.'[18] The Centres Board was formed by the Circle Centres in a District.[19] Centres had the principal responsibility for recruiting members, as Diarmuid Lynch explained: 'Recruiting for the individual Circles was the business of the respective local Centres – who had an intimate knowledge of men in their respective localities and thus were the best judges of suitability for induction into the IRB.'[20]

A high level of dedication to the national ideal was required, and Centres were depended upon to recruit only those who satisfied these requirements.[21] Circle meetings varied, but recruitment was a constant priority. In Dublin, James Daly joined the James Fintan Lalor Circle in 1903 or 1904:

> We used to meet once a month and after about six months I thought the meetings of the circle were very often boring and a waste of time. The chief matter always discussed at these meetings was proposals to take new members. A name would be proposed and this would be debated on by everybody who gave his opinion for or against ... One of the first proposals I heard within the circle was one put forward by Seán O'Casey for the election to membership of James Larkin, the well-known Labour leader. This proposal created much discussion and most of the members were against it. O'Casey was asked to withdraw his proposal but he refused as he was a stubborn disruptive character. The proposal was sent on to the Supreme Council and every month O'Casey used raise it afresh. Eventually we were given to understand the whole thing was turned down and we heard no more about it.[22]

1873–1917 Constitution   47

Around 1906, nineteen-year-old Gilbert Morrissey became a member of the IRB in Galway. His Circle had about thirty-five members and met every two months. 'The thing I remember most distinctly about those meetings,' he said, 'is that [the Centre] always impressed on us that another fight for freedom was impending and that our big aim should be to be prepared for it.'[23] Joseph Furlong joined the IRB in Wexford in 1908. Recruitment and high jinks occupied them:

> On joining we took the Oath of the I.R.B. and paid a subscription of one shilling per month towards expenses. We did no drilling or training of any sort. We held debates and discussions and read a lot of literature and the writings of James Fintan Lalor. We recruited further members for the centre. Our only other activity at that time was the posting up of anti-recruiting pamphlets. This was against recruiting for the British Army. When King Edward of England died [6 May 1910], the 'Union Jack' was flown on the Custom house in Wexford at 'half mast'. We cut down the flag and hid it under the woodwork on the quays. There was great police activity following this, the whole Harbour was dredged, but they failed to find it. A Police officer named Scully told me he knew who cut down the flag but could not produce the evidence. He swore he would find the flag. He never did. On King George's coronation [22 June 1911] we black-flagged the Town. This was done at night.[24]

In Clare, Circles were more practical, as Joseph Barrett detailed:

> We took an active part in the local agitation for the acquisition of ranches by the Land Commission and, in the division of such lands, we tried to ensure that our members would get preference. These large estates had been in the hands of landlords against whom there was a traditional hostility; they were mostly of planter stock and invariably were opposed to every Irish national movement ... The question of recruits occupied a good deal of the time at those meetings, and another matter which generally came up for discussion was the number of guns of all sorts, particularly those in the houses of the ascendancy class, which were immediately available in the neighbourhood if the occasion should arise to acquire them. In actual fact, the Circle did come into possession of

four or five rifles of the Winchester type by purchase from gamekeepers in the employment of landlords for whom they had no great love.[25]

Val Jackson's Circle also worked to obtain weapons: '[Subscription] money was paid in to the C[entres] B[oard] and as it accrued, rifles were purchased and balloted for by the subscribers.'[26]

In 1894 the Supreme Council detailed the governance of the organisation in 'Laws, Rules and Regulations for the Government of the I.R.B.' It was a classic piece of terminological and bureaucratic entwinement establishing 'Vigilance Committees' 'to keep a watch upon all members of the Circle'; whose members 'shall be known to no member or officer of the Circle save the Centre' and 'shall be unknown to each other'. The particular focus of these committees was to prevent the stealing of Circle subscriptions and 'to report to the Vigilance C all cases of drunkenness, violation of secrecy, etc.'[27] These committees and the detailed rules of conduct seem not to have lasted very long. In any case, the arrangements were far too complicated to be practical. They reflect intra-IRB divisions and struggles of the 1890s that were resolved by the beginning of the twentieth century. There is no mention of Vigilance Committees in the memoirs and statements of IRB members active after 1900.

With the creation of the Irish Volunteers, IRB members had a much clearer sense of purpose and use for their guns. Weapons, of course, were for rebellions, always the IRB's raison d'être.

Counties and cities were divided into 'Districts'. Centres in each District formed a 'Centres Board' and elected a 'District Centre'. District Centres were responsible to the 'County Centre'. County Centres were elected for each county or city by all the local Centres. 'Each [County Centre] was presented with the little book to study and memorise,' remembered Patrick Mullaney. 'It was only about two or three pages, and the rules of the Constitution were there. They were never discussed. You simply read them and gave back the book. There was only a limited number in existence.'[28] The County Centres formed the 'Divisional Boards' of each of the seven 'Divisions' of the IRB: Leinster, Ulster, Munster, Connacht, North of England, South of England and Scotland.[29] The Divisional Boards elected a 'Civil Secretary' and a 'Military Secretary':

[T]he duty of the Civil Secretary shall be to act in all respects as Deputy of the member of the Supreme Council of his Division and in the event of removal of said member by the act of the enemy, disability or death the Civil Secretary shall exercise authority in the Division until a new member of the Supreme Council shall have been elected in the manner provided for in the Constitution of the Supreme Council; and the duties of the Military Secretary shall be to execute all orders received by him in relation to the procuring, distribution and safe keeping of arms and ammunition.[30]

In Dublin, Cork, Limerick, Belfast, London and Glasgow a Committee of Five, elected by the Centres in each city, directed local organisation 'subject to the supervision and control of the County or District Centres'.[31] The County and District Centres had the purely organisational function of overseeing such committees and Circles in their areas, electing civil and military secretaries, and sending monthly reports to their civil secretaries.

In each of the seven Divisions, a convention of the County and District Centres also elected a Committee of Five, which, sworn to secrecy, was responsible for the return of one member from each Division to the Supreme Council. The Council was the ultimate authority in the organisation. The seven Divisional members together elected – 'co-opted' – four more members whose names were only to be known to the Supreme Council. The ensuing eleven members of the Supreme Council elected a president, secretary and treasurer from amongst their number. These three men acted as the Executive Committee of the Supreme Council, 'the decision of any two of whom shall be binding on all'.[32] When the Council was not in session, power was exercised by the Executive. Since Supreme Councils met only from two to four times a year, the Executive in practice dominated.

The effect of this system was that members of Circles in theory only knew their Centre and other members of the Circle. Centres in turn knew only their Circle members, the other Centres in their county or town, and the County or District Centre. The County or District Centres knew the Circle Centres in their areas, the other County and District Centres in their Division, the civil and military secretaries of their Division, and the Committee of Five that elected the Divisional representative to the Supreme Council. But, unless a District or County Centre was elected to the Committee of Five, they should not know the name of their representative on the Supreme Council.

Despite these precautions, the RIC and DMP may not have known exact plans but usually knew or suspected who were the leaders of the IRB in their districts and, as occasion demanded, arrested them. James Stephens' 1867 insurrection attempt was foiled by early arrests of IRB leaders around the country. After the surprise of the 1916 Rising, IRB leaders were immediately identified and arrested by police and constabulary.

Civil secretaries were deputies to Divisional members of the Supreme Council and were senior to military secretaries. The Divisional officers (i.e. the civil and military secretaries and the Supreme Council representative in each Division) 'shall have power to make all bye-laws framed in accordance with the spirit of the Constitution – which they may deem necessary for the purpose of local organisation'.[33] These regional triumvirates in each of the seven IRB Divisions administered the organisation. Civil secretaries also had responsibility for collecting monthly reports from their Divisional, County and District Centres which they forwarded to the secretary of the Supreme Council.[34]

Funds were raised by members' subscriptions: 'Each member of the I.R.B. shall contribute according to his means for the production of war materials and also towards the expense of keeping up communication in the different Divisions of the I.R.B. and for maintaining the efficiency of the Supreme Council.'[35]

The treasurer kept an eye on the receipts and expenditures of the organisation: 'At each meeting of the Supreme Council the members thereof shall hand in a summarised statement of the receipts and expenditure of the respective Divisions.'[36]

There was again an emphasis on securing weapons, with the whole of clause 7 of the constitution devoted to the subject.[37] Having a military secretary in each Division, and the nature of the IRB's organisation and chain of command, emphasised force over politics.

The most important element in the 1873 Constitution, however, was the IRB's claim that the Supreme Council was 'declared in fact as well as by right the sole government of the Irish Republic',[38] and the president of the Supreme Council was similarly declared to be 'in fact as well as by right, President of the Irish Republic'.[39] This was, of course, to counter Church opposition.[40] The IRB never really thought of itself as an embryonic government of an Irish State. Its constitutional claims were for internal coherence, not for public testing. 'Nobody regarded ourselves as the government,' said Alec McCabe, Connacht representative on the Supreme Council 1915–16. '[It] was propagandist more than anything else.'[41] Nevertheless, this notional republic provided the members of the IRB with all the authority they believed that they required to conspire and to fight for Irish independence while remaining, if Catholic, good Catholics.

The authority claimed by the Supreme Council was absolute (while in practice impossible to enforce): 'The Supreme Council of the Irish Republican Brotherhood and Government of the Irish Republic ... and enactments of the Government so constituted shall be the laws of the Irish Republic until the territory thereof shall have been recovered from the English Enemy and a permanent Government established.'[42]

The Council could 'levy taxes, negotiate loans, make war and peace and do all other acts necessary for the protection of the Irish Republic'[43] and it reserved to itself 'the right of dealing with all friendly powers on all matters concerning the welfare of Ireland and the advancement of the cause of Irish independence'.[44] Furthermore:

> The Supreme Council shall have power to award Capital Punishment only in cases of treason and the crime of treason is hereby defined as any wilful act or word on the part of any member of the I.R.B. or of the Supreme Council calculated to betray the cause of Irish Independence and subserve the interest of the British or any other foreign Government in Ireland to the detriment of Irish Independence.[45]

The Council could appoint secret courts 'for the trial of all members charged with the commission of treason or grave misdemeanours'[46] and it undertook the punishment of all minor offences committed by members of the IRB,[47] giving special attention to the punishment of those members who 'unlawfully appropriate moneys entrusted to them for national purposes'.[48] The last clause of the constitution reserved to the Council the right to alter it.[49]

The function of the eleven members of the Supreme Council was to direct the policies and activities of the IRB and 'the exercise of moral influences – the cultivation of union and brotherly love amongst Irishmen – the propagation of Republican Principles and a spreading of a knowledge of the national rights of Ireland'.[50] However, they had to 'await the decision of the Irish Nation as expressed by a majority of the Irish people as to the fit hour of inaugurating a war against England'.[51] The reason for this clause, which ran counter to the IRB's purpose of armed rebellion, was to avoid doomed and unpopular revolts (as in 1848 and 1867) and to deal with Church teaching on legitimate rebellions.

How a majority of Irish people could or would show that they wanted a war with England was left to the imagination. Because of this lack of clarity, this clause was to become central to arguments for and against the 1916 Rising: did the Supreme Council's powers override this constitutional requirement? In the event, the answer was that in practice they did.

The president was *primus inter pares*: 'The duty of the President of the Supreme Council shall be to direct the working of the Irish Republican Brotherhood in all its departments, subject to the control of the Supreme Council.'[52]

The duties of the secretary and the treasurer were not explained in the constitution beyond their forming, with the president, the Executive Committee of the Supreme Council. However, the secretary kept himself, the Council and the Executive informed about organisational developments in the same way as County and District Centres were meant to keep the civil secretaries informed. The civil secretaries were in turn required to report to the secretary at monthly intervals.[53] When the Supreme Council was not in session the Executive exercised its authority, and non-Executive members of the Council along with all other IRB members were subject to the Executive: 'Every member of the I.R.B., and every member of the Supreme Council owes Civil and Military obedience to the Executive of the Supreme Council.'[54]

This clause may well have been regarded as giving the Executive the authority to organise the 1916 Rising without informing the other members of the Council. And while the constitution contained no provision for the formation of the Military Committee that planned and organised the Rising, the Executive clearly had the authority to establish it.

Within the IRB, there were separate electoral and administrative channels. The administrative side corresponded in a rudimentary way to what we expect of a civil service both in arrangement and in function. Of the thirty-four clauses of the 1873 Constitution, only four and the preamble deal with the IRB's governmental claim,[55] and virtually every other clause is concerned with administration and the security of the organisation in an Ireland governed, not by the IRB, but by a British government. Of the four clauses concerned with the claim that the Supreme Council was the sole government of the Irish Republic, only one defined governmental rights and duties;[56] the other three merely stated the claim. However, the whole justification for the IRB was expressed in the very first words of the constitution: 'Whereas the Irish People have never ceased to struggle for the recovery of their independence since the date of its destruction ...'[57]

1873–1917 Constitution

Ireland's history of intermittent rebellion, though unsuccessful, was the basis of the IRB's self-belief.

While the IRB claimed to respect its own civil authority, its operation was authoritarian. Indeed, although a provisional civilian government was appointed (not elected) by the IRB in 1916, it took no action apart from presiding over the Rising. Diarmuid Lynch, Munster representative on the Supreme Council from 1911 to 1918, described the 'democracy' within the organisation:

> The constitutional method of electing a Divisional Centre[58] was that a provincial Convention[59] comprising County and District Centres elected by ballot a special committee of five and the latter in turn elected by ballot a Centre for the Division. Thus, these five were the only members in the Province to whom the Divisional Centre was known as such … It was not a constitutional function of the Divisional Centre to enrol members; his duty was to keep in contact with the County Centres and thus keep posted on the state of the Organisation in his Division.[60]

All officers of the IRB held office for two-year terms and were 'subject to removal at any time by a two-thirds vote of the electoral body'.[61] In practice, the same men were usually re-elected.

The electoral body was never the total membership but was in stages – first, the Circles individually and then the Centres at County and then Divisional levels. At no stage was the entire membership formally involved in an election or in policy or in Supreme Council decisions.

The IRB was well aware of the general antagonism that the Irish diaspora felt towards England, especially in the United States, and was also confident of its ability to exploit emigrant feeling for its own interests. There was some action in Australia where an IRB training camp was set up to train men to fight in Ireland. Seven IRB members were arrested in June 1918 and the camp shut down.[62] Clan na Gael in the United States had the general support of the 4.75 million Irish people who had emigrated to the United States between 1841 and 1895.[63] As Alan Ward has said, 'though American citizens, they could still feel that they had political rights in Ireland'.[64] The Clan was the principal ally, financier and partner of the IRB (and its successors) ever since its foundation in New York in 1868 in succession to the Fenian Brotherhood.

Irish nationalism is irrevocably international.[65]

CHAPTER 5

Members

About 1908 or 1909 the Dublin Circles were re-organised; the Circles were reconstituted on the basis of the trades or employment in which the men were engaged. The organisation was strong amongst the drapers, grocers and vintners' assistants, and in the Civil Service. Each of these had their own Circles.[1]

Thomas Barry, 22 February 1947

Looking back at the pre-1916 IRB, Michael Hayes, a Dublin member, observed, 'There were no rich men in any part of the movement, very odd that. Teachers, civil servants, craftsmen, shop assistants. In all the Irish Ireland movements there were what you call – it's a horrible word – lower middle-class people. And that's why it wasn't a socialist movement to any extent.'[2] The composition of the Bartholomew Teeling Circle, although perhaps less typical than other Dublin Circles in that several members were middle rather than lower-middle class, generally supported Hayes' view. The Circle provided some of the core leadership of the independence struggle after 1916, and a great deal of that of the Rising too. Seán T. O'Kelly[3] joined the Teeling Circle through his Gaelic League activities around 1900.[4] At that time Arthur Griffith was a member of the Circle, although not a very active one,[5] and the Centre was a chemist, Tom Nally.[6] Richard Hayes, then a medical student who fought in 1916, was also a member of the Teeling Circle when O'Kelly joined.[7] Three other medical students were members at that time: John Ellwood, Donal Sheehan and Stephen Barry-Walsh. By 1907, when Piaras Béaslaí joined, Michael Cowley, a bank clerk, had become the Centre of the Circle.[8] Other members in 1907 were Tom Kelly,[9] Patrick McCartan (also a medical student),[10] Cathal Brugha,

Members 55

Bulmer Hobson (who succeeded Cowley as Centre in 1911), Frank Fahy (later Captain of 'C' Company, First Battalion, Dublin Brigade, Irish Volunteers[11] and later still Cathaoirleach (Chairman) of the Senate), Seán McGarry[12] (an electrician who in 1917 succeeded Thomas Ashe[13] as President of the Supreme Council),[14] Batt O'Connor[15] (a builder), George Nicholls (Chairman of the West Galway and Galway City Centres; later TD for Galway),[16] Diarmuid Lynch (a manager with an agricultural supply company) and Séamus Deakin (a chemist, Treasurer of the Circle and President of the Supreme Council, 1913–14).[17] Later on, members included Éamonn Ceannt[18] (a clerk with Dublin Corporation), Richard Mulcahy[19] (a post office engineer), Éamonn Duggan[20] (a solicitor), Con Collins[21] (a post office sorter), Páidín O'Keeffe[22] (then a clerk in the post office) and, according to Batt O'Connor, Michael (The) O'Rahilly[23] (manager of the Gaelic League's *An Claidheamh Soluis*).

In 1907 the Circle was divided into three – two new Circles and a smaller Teeling Circle – because it had become so large: around 120 members. But the new, smaller Teeling Circle grew so quickly that it was divided again.[24]

Circle meetings were opened by the Centre in the name of the Republic and then a roll-call was conducted when, in the Teeling Circle at least, members answered with Irish pseudonyms. The Teeling Circle met as the 'Bartholomew Teeling Literary and Debating Society'. The induction procedure required both the time and the patience of all concerned.

Ernest Blythe related his experience of joining this Circle.[25] He was first approached by Seán O'Casey, who asked him if he remembered the Fenians and what he thought about their aims and activities. Then, having received a favourable response from Blythe, O'Casey told him that the Fenians continued to exist and that Blythe was regarded as a possible member. In this, O'Casey did not follow the official procedure (which in general was probably more honoured in the breach than the observance), since he should only have asked Blythe's opinion at this stage, and not informed him of the continuing existence of the organisation.[26] Some months then elapsed while Blythe was scrutinised by other members of the IRB, and then he was formally approached, again by O'Casey, who, securing Blythe's agreement to join, brought him to a meeting of the Circle where he was sworn in by the Centre on a landing outside the meeting room. Blythe then entered and sat down with the rest of the Circle. The roll-call was taken by the Centre, and the false minutes of the Bartholomew Teeling Literary and Debating Society were spread in front of the Centre, who read them out to the meeting so that the members would know what to say about their meeting if questioned by the police.[27] After this, Blythe and any other new recruits were named, and each stood up so that other members could recognise them by sight, and each was greeted with clapping. Patrick Pearse was proposed twice for membership of the IRB at Teeling meetings but was rejected by Circle members, so his name did not go forward.[28]

Blythe thought recruiting was the most interesting and important business of Circles up to the outbreak of the First World War. A great deal of time was spent at Circle meetings discussing the suitability of potential recruits. Very often a man was known only by a few and his suitability for membership could not be discussed until more members had met him.[29]

The business of recruiting completed, the monthly subscriptions and contributions for *Irish Freedom* and for the Arms Fund were collected.[30] Members were divided into groups of eight to ten under 'Group Leaders' for this purpose.[31] Each group member had the names and addresses of the other members in his group so that the group alone could be assembled if necessary. In many Circles not enough was collected to buy every member a weapon and a raffle system was introduced to allocate whatever was obtained.[32] Finally, the 'Visitor' – usually a Divisional Board Centre – addressed the Circle on matters of policy.[33]

The strictness with which entry requirements were applied had a deleterious effect on membership, as did the opposition of the Church, the deep popularity of the IPP after it converted the Liberal Party to support Home Rule, and the fact that some IRB members found fulfilment in local political success instead of rebellious conspiracy. In Macroom, Co. Cork, for example, 'most of the members were suspended, one by one, for taking part in politics'.[34] In 1907 the funeral of John O'Leary, a founding member of the IRB, attracted a few hundred mourners, indicating the IRB's dwindling numbers and attraction over the previous decade. As F.S.L. Lyons pointed out, the Irish people had expressed no wish to inaugurate a war against England since 1798, so in the early twentieth century 'the Supreme Council of the IRB had been able with a clear conscience to devote itself mainly to the fascinating trivia of Dublin municipal politics'.[35]

The efforts of Bulmer Hobson, Tom Clarke and Seán MacDermott in the 1908–12 period started to rejuvenate the organisation and increase membership. Denis McCullough, one of the younger generation who would re-engage the Brotherhood with its revolutionary ethos, recalled his induction in a Belfast pub: 'I was duly sworn in by a large, obese man, a tailor by trade

Members 57

'... I was disappointed and shocked by the whole surrounds of this, to me, very important event and by the type of men I found controlling the Organisation; they were mostly effete and many of them addicted to drink.'[36]

McCullough's reaction to this experience was to try to bring the Brotherhood back to its founding principles by attracting like-minded men to join and replace the 'effete' alcoholics. With Clarke, Hobson and MacDermott in particular, new energy did percolate through the organisation. In Cork Thomas Barry dated this as beginning in 1911:

> I had a visit from Tom Clarke. The Cork Young Ireland Society, which organised the annual Manchester Martyrs demonstration, was being held together by the remnants of the older I.R.B. Group in the City. P.N. Fitzgerald was the old Centre and the activities of this group had dwindled to the holding of the Manchester Martyrs procession each year. Seán O'Hegarty[37] had a Circle of active younger men. On the instructions of Tom Clarke [we] went into the Young Ireland Society and I was elected President. This was the normal method by which the IRB influenced the policy and controlled the activities of all National organisations.[38]

The older group on the Supreme Council, while content to talk about rebellion rather than prepare one, were not inattentive to their administrative responsibilities. In Dublin, as Thomas Barry recounted, they reorganised Circles according to occupations.

In 1905 there were about ten Circles in Dublin city and county;[39] by 1916 there were at least twenty Circles in the city and county composed of about fifty members each.[40] Dublin city and county seem to have attracted the majority of organising efforts in Leinster with the exception of Co. Wexford, which was organised by local men;[41] no Circles were organised in Kildare.[42] Bulmer Hobson estimated that as the Leinster Division member of the Supreme Council in 1914, he represented about 75 per cent of the IRB's membership.[43] In 1913, on instructions from the Supreme Council, Diarmuid Lynch conducted a census of the IRB in the whole United Kingdom and found that it had increased from 1,500 in 1912[44] to 2,000 when he reported in 1914.[45] By 1916 the membership of the IRB in Ireland alone was at least 2,000.[46]

Outside Dublin, Circles averaged about ten members. Taking Hobson's estimate that about 1,500 members were in Leinster (including Dublin city), that left about 500 in the rest of the country and Britain, suggesting about fifty Circles plus assorted groups and unattached members. Outside Leinster, the majority were in Munster and Connacht, with very few in Ulster: Belfast had two Circles, Derry city one, and Tyrone five. In Munster in 1913, Cork city had five Circles, one based on members in the post office.[47] When the Irish Volunteers were created in 1914, four Circles formed the nucleus of the four Irish Volunteer companies in the city. In Co. Cork, there were seven active Circles and thirteen small groups, all of which were directly connected to Volunteer companies. In Kerry, there were seventeen active Circles and four groups all of which were again connected directly to Irish Volunteer companies. In the rest of Munster there were twelve Circles and twelve groups.[48] This tally might have represented about 550 members on the basis of about ten members in a Circle and five in a group, but Circle numbers were generally fewer and a more accurate figure was probably about 350. In Connacht, Co. Galway had sixteen Circles, Mayo five, and the rest of the Division four,[49] indicating a membership of up to 250, but again, probably fewer. In Leinster, Co. Dublin (excluding Dublin city) had seven Circles and Co. Wexford eight.[50]

In the South of England Division there were Circles in London, and in the North of England Division in Manchester, Liverpool, Newcastle-on-Tyne and Birmingham.[51] In Scotland Glasgow held the principal membership with ten Circles.[52] There may have been no Circles in Wales.

In Ireland, Circle distribution reveals no correlation when compared to population density. This indicates that – as was claimed – IRB members were chosen carefully at least up to 1916, and that at its base – Circle level – the IRB was concerned with individuals' qualities. Thus, when Diarmuid Lynch travelled to Connacht in 1915 to establish an IRB presence in the province, 'one of the few contacts I had in County Sligo was the name and address of a schoolmaster who was deemed eligible for membership'.[53] This schoolmaster was probably Alec McCabe.[54]

Recruitment was a careful affair, not only to filter out men who might not be resolute in pursuit of the IRB's objectives (and even then, exceptions inevitably occurred), but also to avoid men who were partial to alcohol. 'In the early twentieth century it was widely agreed that the country was drinking excessively,' Diarmaid Ferriter records. 'Over £15 million a year was being spent on drink in Ireland at the time of the First World War and there were over 15,000 licensed premises'[55] translating to a ratio of about 1 for every 287 of the population. Lloyd George, writing in 1933, observed about Britain: 'It is

Members 59

difficult for us today to realise how seriously excessive drinking contributed to diminish the output ... The sight of a drunken man or woman reeling down the street has grown a rare spectacle.'[56] In England and Wales the ratio of licensed premises was about 1 for every 415 of the population, suggesting that Irish drinking was even more serious.

In the Bartholomew Teeling Circle in Dublin, younger members were particularly anxious that possible recruits did not drink, since they were convinced that alcohol had ruined Ireland's efforts to free herself in the past and pressed for a rule of total abstinence. Real attention was paid to this requirement. Denis McCullough stressed: '[W]hen the I.R.B. was being actively organised, especially in the latter year [1915] when P.S. [O'Hegarty], Tom Clarke, Sean McDermott and myself got into a strong position in control, we insisted that only men of known sobriety and character be admitted.'[57]

Michael Collins was often criticised because he drank and bought drinks for others.[58] Garry Holohan reported Collins' drinking to his Circle: 'Barney Mellows[59] was employed in the National Aid office, and he reported to me that Collins was making a habit of going and drinking in the Deer's Head several times during the day. As this was a very grievous offence in my opinion I mentioned it at my Circle meeting of the I.R.B. This caused ructions.'[60]

Notably, the 1917 Constitution (principally drafted by Collins) and those that superseded it dropped any reference to 'sobriety' as a membership requirement.

The care with which members were recruited was instrumental in ensuring the security of the organisation. 'Nobody was allowed into the IRB who wasn't genuinely and committedly a republican,' said Patrick Mullaney. 'He had to be that.'[61] Michael Brennan, who joined the IRB in Limerick in 'about 1912' found that potential members were 'sounded out for about a year' before being asked to join.[62] In 1909 in Kerry, Dan Dennehy became a member and Centre of the Rathmore Circle. 'We recruited members slowly,' he recalled, 'accepting no one but teetotallers and men without any RIC connections.'[63] In Glasgow, the care taken when recruiting members was typical: '[A]ny person, whom we hoped to be eligible for admission to the I.R.B. organisation, was first asked to join the Wolfe Tone Memorial Club which had been earlier organised by the I.R.B. and, after being under observation there, if he proved himself to be the right type, he was then asked to join the I.R.B.'[64]

There were variations in recruitment procedures around the country. In Clare heredity was the key element, as Joseph Barrett explained: 'At the time I joined [1908], it was the practice in our part of Clare to invite the eldest sons of all the old Fenians to become members of the Brotherhood, and my father was an old Fenian ... There were fifteen of us, mostly the eldest sons of old Fenians, sworn in on the same night.'[65]

The spirit of the Brotherhood, however, was similar throughout its membership. Garry Byrne joined the IRB Mangan Circle in Dublin in 1911: 'The whole idea at that time was that there would be a "Rising", and we were left without any doubt about it.'[66] Moss Twomey, who joined in 1919, thought he was going to be with the real independence fighters. 'I thought, "By God! We'll have to buckle into it! If we're in the I.R.B. we'll have to bloody well fight whether we like it or not!"'[67] A Cork man who joined in 1917 testified to the IRB's commitment to force: 'It was a close-knit, practical, hard-headed body, and it evoked an extraordinary spirit of loyalty and brotherhood amongst its members. It was not propagandist; it sought rather to find and bind together men of good character who had reached the conclusion that there was no solution to the problem of achieving national freedom except through the use of physical force.'[68]

Richard Walsh, a senior figure in the IRB and on the Volunteer/IRA Executive, regarded the IRB with a cold eye, observing that members pledged that they were prepared to die for the IRB's objective: 'The I.R.B. did not press for a narrow point of view. Their attitude was to get the young manhood of Ireland to pledge their lives and service to Ireland and its people in the broad sense and, if the necessity arose, the great majority of the decent young men of the country would interpret their pledge in the unselfish and broad way.'[69]

Where IRB membership was sparse or non-existent, roving recruiters swore in members. Before 1916 Liam Mellows had an IRB commission to organise Circles,[70] as did Seán MacDermott, Ernest Blythe and Cathal Brugha, who, as a representative of his firm, travelled extensively.[71] Diarmuid Lynch, when he represented Munster on the Supreme Council, on occasion took men into the organisation in places where no Circle existed. In Lynch's case, as a member of the Supreme Council, he did so 'in the capacity of an "organiser" and not as Divisional Centre'.[72] In 1915 Lynch visited the Connacht Division (which Seán MacDermott then represented on the Supreme Council as an appointee) and swore in at least one new member, probably Alec McCabe, in County Sligo.[73] He also encouraged new members to recruit. Andrew Keaveney in Roscommon met Lynch and joined the Brotherhood in 1915:

In the summer of that year I met Dermot [*sic*] Lynch at a football match in Carrick-on-Shannon and he authorised me to tour North Roscommon and take selected men into the Brotherhood. He impressed on me the objects of the organisation and the type of men who were to be taken in. In those days and of necessity the organisation, which was very secret, had to be ultra selective in the type of men it took into its ranks.[74]

In Kerry and Clare, Ernest Blythe from early 1915 'was officially being employed by the Volunteer organisation [but really] by the headquarters of the I.R.B. He was to organise Volunteers certainly, but behind that he was to recruit for the I.R.B'.[75] Blythe advised his IRB recruiters, 'Only the very select few you want in the I.R.B. Take very, very few into it, only silent men.'[76] In Belfast, said Blythe:

We were suffering. If a fellow got great with a girl, her [relations] were sure to be [members of the Ancient Order of] Hibernians, and the next thing you'd hear was that this fellow wasn't attending meetings and then had resigned ... Hibernianism and all that was so strong in Belfast so that we had an undue proportion of Protestants in the Circle ... I think at one time out of our dozen we had perhaps four or five Protestants.[77]

Larry de Lacey in Wexford was an IRB Centre and recruiter:

Of course, there was an occasional blunder: a man that looked all right as a good fellow, but he got religion or something like that and he changed his mind and wanted to get out. Then he had to be sworn out. Sometimes you'd get a feeling of unrest and old Father Sheehy would go around and we'd call special meetings of the Circles for him – Father Sheehy or someone else, Father Sheehy mostly – to explain that the Fenian oath was not running against the religion.[78]

The Dublin membership of the IRB in 1916 was not diverse. 'The vast majority of the I.R.B. in Dublin,' said Diarmuid Lynch, 'comprised "workers" who were not associated with Liberty Hall:[79] clerks, grocers' assistants, workers in the Post Office and other Government Departments, mechanics, etc., etc.'[80] Recruitment in Dublin was more complicated than required by the constitution, involving all the Circles despite the authorised procedure:

When a member became acquainted with someone who was likely to prove a good member, he was not at liberty to approach him until he had obtained permission. He proposed the name at his Circle meeting. The names proposed were taken by the Secretary of the Circle to a meeting at which all the Secretaries of other Circles attended. The Secretaries exchanged the names and came back and read the list of men proposed in all the other Circles at their next Circle meeting.[81]

In this way every name proposed was open to comment in every Circle in the city, and any opposition that was not frivolous was sufficient to prevent a person being inducted. Only after a prospective candidate's name had survived this scrutiny was permission given to the proposer to invite him to join. This made recruiting slow but recruiting security tight.[82]

In 1922 the 'Police Intelligence Report' summed up British Intelligence's appreciation of the IRB:

The secret society known as the Irish Republican Brotherhood has been an organisation concerning which it has been exceedingly difficult to obtain information, and informers, members of the I.R.B. have been almost impossible to obtain. The only member of the I.R.B. who turned informer and whose information has been of the utmost value, was obtained through the agency of a Crimes Special Sergeant.[83]

This was remarkable.

CHAPTER 6

Supreme Council

Shortly after [Tom Clarke's] return he was co-opted to the S[upreme] C[ouncil] of the I.R.B., but he was dissatisfied with what he found there. The members were not alive. He felt that the organisation was still in the rut out of which it could not see in 1900 and turned his attention to the younger men in whom he could see a spirit of restlessness and impatience and a growing sense of impotence imposed from the top.[1]

Seán McGarry, 13 April 1950

There had been some hope within the IRB that the centenary of 1798 would see a revival of the organisation, but this did not happen. Commemorative meetings were not well attended. The IPP's campaign for Home Rule, with the Liberal Party's support, met general nationalist aspirations. This was Charles Stewart Parnell's legacy, undercutting the appeal of the IRB. Increasing acceptance of Catholics in British public life also helped to argue against insurrection.[2] As the twentieth century opened, a demoralised IRB found little support for 'overthrowing English power in Ireland'.

The RIC, embedded in the population, was the cornerstone of British authority. In 1908 Seán McGarry, then a young member of the IRB, presented a strategy for guerrilla activity to the Supreme Council that was later employed effectively by the IRA. Bulmer Hobson also advocated guerrilla action. They both maintained that a necessary preliminary to any forceful attempt to secure independence must be the ejection of the RIC from the countryside by attacking and burning its barracks and posts and making it impossible for it to find accommodation or to operate outside the larger towns. The Council approved the plan but made no attempt to implement it (and therefore launch another

64 The Irish Republican Brotherhood, 1914–1924

rising).[3] Tom Clarke's frustration with IRB inaction was easy to understand. Richard Connolly, on the Council with Clarke and MacDermott from 1913 as the South of England representative, gave a picture of Supreme Council meetings that substantiated this frustration:

> The time given to our meetings of the Supreme Council was short. Only on one occasion did the meeting run into two days – that was in September 1915. It usually started between 9 and 10 a.m. and ended about 7 p.m. A good deal of it was routine such as the taking of reports. Until 1915, when the military committee was formed, there were very few military discussions.[4]

Meetings of the Supreme Council at this time, according to Diarmuid Lynch, 'were largely devoted to reports on the state of the organisation in the several divisions, on finance, on publications; on such events as the Wolfe Tone and Emmet commemorations; on possibilities for the advancement of the Irish republican doctrine and ... to defeat denationalising schemes'.[5] Rebellion was given lip service, but nothing more. IRB members traded on past glories. Circle meetings took place perhaps two to four times a year and discussed principles and theories.[6]

In 1906 Patrick (known as 'P.T.') Daly, the most energetic of the society's leaders, threw what was left of the Brotherhood – then about 1,000 members – behind Arthur Griffith's Sinn Féin party, and used the money that Clan na Gael sent (Daly was the conduit for these funds) to support Sinn Féin Dublin Corporation election campaigns.[7] Two members of the IRB – Daly and Seán T. O'Kelly, a leading member of Sinn Féin – were elected to the Corporation. Fred Allan, periodically Secretary of the IRB, was employed by the Corporation. But while municipal politics may have provided an excuse for not actively fomenting rebellion, it was never a replacement. Daly, O'Kelly, Allan and their colleagues no doubt justified their participation as infiltrating the Corporation to persuade it to endorse more radical nationalist initiatives, as the IRB constitution directed.

Co-opted members of the Supreme Council offered the best hope of extending the range of IRB influence, and of energising the Council. Seán MacEoin explained the importance of co-opted members who

> couldn't go down the country to get elected as a Parish Centre and then to get elected as a County Centre and then to get elected as a Provincial

Supreme Council 65

Centre because that is what's known as coming up the road – the way I came up. I'd be no bloody good at a Supreme Council as a Secretary or a Treasurer or anything like that. You had to have a man that you could trust, in whom you had absolute confidence. And to appoint him to whatever position you wanted including sending him to America as an ambassador or the Argentine or wherever the hell you were sending him to.[8]

The need to appoint and to co-opt to pre-1913 Councils made it obvious that the IRB was weak outside Dublin: in the United States Devoy had been shocked to discover that the 'home' organisation in effect existed only on paper and, through Clarke, whom he knew and trusted, urged re-dedication to its revolutionary ethos. Bulmer Hobson considered that the Supreme Council before 1913 had 'almost stifled all activities'.[9] (Membership of Supreme Councils 1907–22 is set out in Appendix XI).

An embezzlement accelerated change. P.T. Daly, as was rumoured, had kept £300 of Clan money for himself.[10] When in 1910 this was discovered, the Supreme Council ejected him, but – despite clear regulations – without internal publicity and not from membership of the IRB. They were anxious to avoid scandal and risk the Clan's continued funding. Neil John O'Boyle, the president, and John Geraghty, the treasurer, also resigned – not that they were complicit with Daly, but probably because they felt they had a responsibility for not supervising Daly properly. This opened the Council to new blood. Seán MacDermott was co-opted to replace Daly.[11] In 1911 Tom Clarke joined as a co-opted member and was elected Treasurer,[12] essentially because he was known and trusted by John Devoy and the Clan and would ensure that Clan money kept flowing despite the scandal with Daly.[13]

Towards the end of 1910, Hobson, then on the Leinster Board and soon to join the Supreme Council, proposed that the Brotherhood should publish a new newspaper.[14] Two nationalist newspapers, *Sinn Féin* (Griffith's successor to the *United Irishman*) and *Irish Nation and Peasant*, had failed, leaving a gap that Hobson wanted the IRB to fill. On the Supreme Council, O'Hanlon and 'other conservative leaders'[15] opposed the proposal, and only gave way when Hobson threatened to start such a paper himself. Thus *Irish Freedom* was born. But the Supreme Council, nervous of a forthright separatist editorial stance, would not permit Hobson, who was widely known to be an IRB man, to be the editor and sought to make production difficult. They were

66   The Irish Republican Brotherhood, 1914–1924

content with the IRB as a political pressure group and did not want actual revolutionary activity that would displace their gains and standing in local politics. This was a recurring generational conflict between an older established group, conscious of the struggle they had endured, wishing to move slowly and carefully and not risk their positions, and a younger generation, full of enthusiasm for the national cause, eager to get things done. Patrick McCartan, then fully engaged in his final year as a medical student, was appointed editor but was clearly not really available to do the job if he wished to complete his studies. It was a move to dampen the project. However, McCartan and Hobson circumvented the Supreme Council by agreeing between themselves that McCartan would be editor in name while Hobson did the work.[16] The paper was supposedly financed by a special subscription of one shilling a month collected from members of the IRB, but Clan money actually kept it afloat.[17] Seán MacDermott was manager of the paper and administered its finance until he contracted polio in 1911.[18] The energetic Hobson, with the support of McCartan, Clarke and MacDermott on the paper's executive committee, kept the paper going until it was suppressed by the authorities in December 1914. Perhaps surprisingly, the content of *Irish Freedom* was somewhat subdued nationalism and not gung-ho revolution, but it was still strong enough for wartime suppression (and, as it happened, too much for the Supreme Council).

The struggle between the longer-serving and the newer members of the Council came to a head towards the end of 1911, ostensibly about the editorial direction of *Irish Freedom*.[19] In September, at a Robert Emmet commemoration, McCartan had proposed, with Tom Clarke seconding, a resolution against a loyal address to the king. Allan and the Supreme Council had vetoed such a resolution on the grounds that it was 'politics' and had so instructed McCartan. But McCartan went ahead:

> Tom jumped up after me and seconded it, and the thing went with a whoop. The resolution was passed with enthusiasm. Then there was consternation among the I.R.B. Supreme Council. We were charged with lack of discipline afterwards. There was a meeting of our Circle and something about me, my lack of discipline, or something was mentioned at the Circle meeting. I said, 'It's very funny that I am being denounced for taking a stand against loyal addresses to the King of England, when a man who is high in the organisation has mis-spent money belonging

to the organisation and there is no word about that.' It was to P. T. Daly I referred.[20]

As a consequence, Allan took on the editorship of *Irish Freedom* in November 1911, dismissing McCartan. McCartan asked Tom Clarke for financial help to publish a rival edition of the paper, which put Clarke, as IRB Treasurer, in a difficult position. Clarke gave McCartan the money he needed from his personal account, enabling McCartan and Hobson to publish an alternative issue of *Irish Freedom*. The result was two December 1911 issues of the paper, one by Allan and one by McCartan and Hobson. McCartan also appealed to his friend Joseph McGarrity, then the Clan's treasurer, who sent him funds to continue with the paper. Seán O'Hegarty, P.S. O'Hegarty's younger brother and Cork City Centre, described the conflict:

> There was a row in November 1911 between Allan [Secretary of the Supreme Council], O'Hanlon [who represented Leinster on the Supreme Council] and Crowe [co-opted member of the Supreme Council] on one hand, and McCartan and Hobson on the other. McCullough thinks it was something arising out of *Freedom* and Hobson thinks it was just an attempt by Allan to slow up proceedings generally by slowing up *Freedom*. My own very clear impression is that Pat (Dr McCartan) refused to accept a direction given him by the proper authorities of what nature I cannot remember ... and they tried to remove him from the editorship of *Freedom*. He refused to go with the result there were two issues of *Freedom* for December 1911 ... I know that a special meeting of the Supreme Council was summoned to deal with it.[21]

The outburst by McCartan about P.T. Daly and his disobeying the order from the Supreme Council not to propose the resolution at the Emmet gathering were the grounds for disciplinary action against him. Daly's dismissal from the Supreme Council was held to be a grave secret: he had friends and admirers throughout Dublin in Sinn Féin, the trade unions and the IRB. Having a public dispute would only damage all concerned. McCartan's edition of *Irish Freedom* was in direct conflict with the Council. But trouble with Daly propelled his scandal into view, as P.S. O'Hegarty recorded:

> Allan and O'Hanlon reported that Daly was not behaving himself, that

he was spreading stories that he had been badly treated and was the victim of a plot, and that he was causing a lot of mischief. It was then decided that he should be formally expelled and blacklisted, and that the whole story should be read to the Circles, and this was done.[22]

Proceedings against McCartan for his edition of *Irish Freedom* went ahead. Allan and John Mulholland, the president, called an emergency Executive meeting where they dismissed McCartan as editor, suspended Hobson from the paper and threatened Clarke with an IRB trial if he did not resign from the Supreme Council because of his support of McCartan and because he was suspected of telling McCartan about Daly. P.S. O'Hegarty found that Clarke and McCartan 'had made up their minds to resign from the Organisation altogether as they had decided it was quite useless so long as O'Hanlon and Allan ruled it'.[23] Together with Hobson, he persuaded them to fight back, and they did. Clarke was 'court-martialled' in Liverpool, away from Dublin and his supporters. Joseph Gleeson was the city's Centre:

> Some time in 1912 just after the publication of the two 'Irish Freedoms', Tom Clarke, who was then a ticket-of-leave man,[24] was brought over to England to stand trial by courtmartial on a charge of mutiny. The charge was the result of a difference of opinion between the younger men and the older men of the I.R.B. Clarke was associated with a group that was in favour of action which the older men were decidedly against. I was instructed to meet him at Birkenhead, which I did and conveyed him to the Morning Star Public-house in Scotland Place. This was where the courtmartial was held. The court comprised Mulholland, Jim Murphy, Jack O'Hanlon and Fred J. Allan. The result of the trial was an acquittal, and this result caused a split in the ranks of the I.R.B. in England and Ireland.[25]

The IRB split that Gleeson referred to was over the Clan's financial support for McCartan, Clarke and Hobson, enabling them – notably with *Irish Freedom* – to ignore the Supreme Council. Several IRB members considered this was interference in IRB affairs by the Clan, and the whole affair was discouraging. Patrick Kearney, an IRB member since 1900 or 1901, was in the ranks: 'The stories of the alleged misuse of I.R.B. Funds by P.T. Daly destroyed the great trust and confidence the members had in the leaders and led to the resignation of many more of the members. I left at this time.'[26]

Supreme Council

In January 1912 the Council (not simply the Executive) also met to judge McCartan.[27] The meat of the case was how did McCartan know about the Daly affair? If McCartan had said that Tom Clarke had told him the secret, then Clarke would have been dismissed and blacklisted:

> [T]hey were under the impression that it was Tom Clarke had given me the information. I was put on oath for this questioning. The first question I was asked was whether I had made this statement at the Circle meeting. I admitted that I had. Then I was asked where did I get this information and I replied that I had learned this from Joe McGarrity. When they heard this, the whole inquiry collapsed. They had no more to say to me because that was all.[28]

The trial was over. Allan completed proceedings saying that the whole affair was a 'misunderstanding' and, twice defeated, chose to resign from the Supreme Council (or was expelled) as did O'Hanlon, Cowley and Crowe.[29] At the next Council meeting, Clarke was jubilant. 'By God,' he said, exulting in the resignations, 'if we don't get something done it'll be our own fault.'[30]

The 'misunderstanding' had shock effects. Val Jackson found himself in the middle of them. He went to his Circle meeting and noticed a stranger there:

> The stranger, who by now I had learned was Bulmer Hobson, then announced that he was there by order of the Supreme Council and that his instructions were to suspend Cooke as Centre ... Hobson then made a statement that Cooke had with others entered into a conspiracy to disrupt the I.R.B. by seizing the paper, *Irish Freedom*, or to interfere with its publication. He made other charges that I cannot now remember ... Hobson ordered [Cooke] to leave the room, which he did. Hobson then said that the next duty of the Circle was to elect a new Centre and that he would temporarily take the chair while this was being done. I was proposed and seconded and unanimously elected ... He also ordered me to expel Allan and Ó hUadhaigh[31] from the I.R.B. and he gave me a slip on which was typed the form of oath that they should take ... I must say that the intervention of Hobson at the Circle meeting came to me as a bombshell, I had not the slightest inkling that trouble was brewing.[32]

70   The Irish Republican Brotherhood, 1914–1924

In March 1912, as word of the conflict spread, several ordinary members resigned too in protest at what was seen as interference by the Clan.[33] The resignations triggered more Divisional Board elections. In Munster Diarmuid Lynch was elected to the Supreme Council.[34]

Bulmer Hobson was startled to find himself also elected. Cowley had been the Centre of the Bartholomew Teeling Circle, and his departure in January 1912 created a highway into the Council for Hobson:

> When Michael Cowley resigned, I was surprised to find myself elected Centre without there being anyone else proposed. I thus became a member of the Dublin Centres Board and after a short time was elected Chairman of that body in succession to Séamus O'Connor. As Dublin Centre I became a member of the Leinster Executive,[35] also Leinster representative on the Supreme Council.[36]

This sequence indicated that, despite the IRB's poor state in 1910, two years later revivification efforts had some success: co-option and appointment were not necessary except in Connacht, where continuing membership weakness was reflected by the appointment of Seán MacDermott to represent the Division, although he was a co-opted member of the Council[37] and at no time an elected member.

In January 1913 the IRB in Dublin had begun instructing members in military drill.[38] The formation of the Irish Volunteers followed in November, planned by Bulmer Hobson, Tom Clarke and Seán MacDermott to be a front for an IRB army. Publicly, they were presented as a counterbalance to the UVF, which had been formed in 1912 to prevent the introduction of Home Rule in Ulster: the Irish Volunteers were to 'defend' Home Rule, their motto being 'Defence not Defiance'.

On 8 or 9 September 1914, shortly after the outbreak of the First World War, the Supreme Council met in Dublin. This meeting was the first since 1867 to concern itself with rebellion, as P.S. O'Hegarty, now a co-opted member of the Council, recorded:

> Its purpose was twofold, in the first place to revive the national spirit, and in the second place to bring Ireland's cause to the front internationally, with an eye on the eventual peace conference. It set up a small Military Committee, and determined to use the Irish Volunteers' organisation,

Supreme Council

equipment, and training, without the knowledge of the Executive of that body. For this purpose it was essential to have I.R.B. men, or men convinced of the necessity for an insurrection, in key positions in the organisation, and there was little difficulty in that. Many of them were already there and others were gradually manoeuvred into position so that, when the time came, full use could be made of the Volunteers. The sponsors of the insurrection decision on the Supreme Council were Tom Clarke and Seán McDermott.[39]

Tom Clarke and Seán MacDermott, Treasurer and Secretary respectively and thus a majority of the Executive, now effectively controlled the IRB. Hobson, a key Council member until he resigned from it in 1914, summed up their position:

> In the IRB the Supreme Council could not meet very frequently and when it was not in session the President, Secretary and Treasurer constituted a sort of standing Executive committee to act in any emergency. In 1914 the President was Denis McCullough, the Secretary Seán McDermott, and the Treasurer Tom Clarke. As McCullough was living in Belfast, this left McDermott and Clarke in charge in Dublin.[40]

McCullough acknowledged this: 'It will be remembered that P.S. O'Hegarty resided in London and I resided in Belfast. We were not always as close to passing events, at the centre of things, in those critical and stirring years, as were those of our colleagues who lived in Dublin.'[41]

In charge in Dublin meant in charge in Ireland and, in Dublin, said P.S. O'Hegarty, 'For the first time we had the men who meant business in complete control.'[42]

The next Council meeting was in January 1915. On MacDermott's motion all the members apart from Patrick McCartan, who had been co-opted in 1914,[43] agreed to a rising, setting September 1915 as the date for it.[44] McCartan urged caution and argued that another rebellion was not supported by public opinion, which was a requirement of the IRB constitution before committing the nation to war. Bulmer Hobson was later to make the same point. Denis McCullough chaired the meeting:

> I was in the chair when Dr Patrick McCartan pointed out that we were taking a great responsibility in committing the country to war, without

having, at least, a considerable section of the population behind us. I had to quieten the protests of at least two of those present and enthusiastically in favour of a fight, by pointing out that McCartan's contention was a very just and reasonable one and in accordance with the I.R.B. Constitution and must be considered calmly. Against that I stated that we had been organising and planning for years for the purpose of a protest in arms, when an opportunity occurred and if ever such an opportunity was to arrive, I didn't think any better time would present itself in our day. The whole matter was then discussed calmly and seriously and the unanimous decision arrived at was that preparations for a rising were to be pushed forward and a date arranged in any of the three following contingencies, viz. (1) Any attempt at a general arrest of Volunteers, especially the leaders. (2) Any attempt to enforce conscription on our people and (3) If an early termination of the war appeared likely.[45]

This argument – that the purpose of the IRB was to launch rebellions – had won the day.[46] 'The only thing at that meeting that I remember,' said Richard Connolly, 'was that Clarke was insistent that the Volunteers should be used for war and he got very excited at that meeting.'[47]

A noticeable number of senior IRB men left the society when they realised that rising plans were serious.[48] John Mulholland, the president, resigned from the Council and from the IRB after this meeting (suggesting that the decision to launch a rising was not, in fact, unanimous).[49] Séamus Deakin briefly succeeded him, but also resigned, and then Denis McCullough, since 1909 a co-opted member of the Council, was elected president.[50]

The 1915 IRB elections restored the elected composition of the Council. Recruiting and organising efforts by MacDermott and others had produced Circles in hitherto weak areas. Alec McCabe was the first elected member for Connacht since 1910 or 1911.[51] McCullough was re-elected president.

This Council was a break with its predecessor. Seven of the eleven members were new, and members of the previous Council who had disagreed with a rising had resigned or were not re-elected. With the exception of the cautious McCartan, who was not explicitly against a rising, Clarke and MacDermott finally had a Council that would bend to their will and that fully endorsed their determination to stage a rising and bring the IRB to a bloody climax.

A vital element enabling them to proceed was the support they received from John Devoy and Clan na Gael in the United States. Bulmer Hobson explained: 'The Clan-na-Gael organisation, the American prototype of the I.R.B., was an entirely separate and independent body, although there was a close connection between the two – the Clan being a source of funds for the I.R.B.'[52] Hobson might have said, more accurately, that the Clan was the principal source of funds for the IRB.

The connection with Clan na Gael was not catered for in IRB constitutions. This omission is all the more curious since the IRB was well aware of its financial dependence upon the Clan, as Seán Ó Murthuile, Secretary of the IRB from 1917 and its official historian,[53] testified: 'For more than 50 years the Clan na Gael gave the Home organisation the moral and financial support which enabled it to maintain its existence and propagate the republican principle.'[54] P.S. O'Hegarty provided a detailed explanation of all of the IRB's funding, most of which came from the Clan:

> I had better explain about the Council's finances. These came from the Divisions, and from the Clan na Gael. Of the 1/– a quarter paid by members ... I do not think the income from this source ever much exceeded £150 per annum [about £22,000 in 2024]. The Clan na Gael sent £300 per annum as its affiliation fee to the Organisation normally – the relations between the two [illegible] were simple. Each was supreme in its own place, but all decisions on policy [illegible] were the I.R.B.'s, and each sent an accredited delegate to the other, to see what was really being done was being done and what the prospects were. Now the Clan had for some years been sending a special extra £300 per year for the purposes of reorganisation, i.e., £600 per annum in all ... From the year 1910 the normal affiliation fee of the Clan of £300 was reverted to. John Devoy in his recollections states that the normal amount sent by the Clan was £1000 per annum, but this is an error of memory. The amount was £300. What confused him was that after the start of the Volunteers, two or three special sums of £1000 were sent over to be used for purchases of arms and [illegible] for purposes connected with the Volunteers.[55]

The IRB's close association with the Clan, said Hobson, 'was indicated by the fact that a delegate from the Supreme Council of the IRB attended the annual conventions of the Clan na Gael in America, but the latter body made it clear that the policy in Ireland was a matter for the men in Ireland.'[56]

74 The Irish Republican Brotherhood, 1914–1924

When Tom Clarke returned to Ireland from the United States in November 1907 with the single purpose of fomenting another rebellion, he simply transferred from the Clan to the IRB without any official instructions or position.[57] This transfer took the form of a letter from John Devoy, head of the Clan, to the then Secretary of the Supreme Council, P.T. Daly.[58]

Joseph O'Rourke, from 1912 Secretary of the Dublin Clarence Mangan Circle, dealt with smuggled American pistols, in all probability sent by the Clan, and pistols obtained directly through IRB connections:

> I was directly concerned in handling the lots of sometimes 50 to 60 mainly American automatic pistols, H & R Savage and Colt. These arrived in on the B&I boats, but later we got German automatics from Swedish timber ships bringing timber to T&C Martin Ltd. And occasionally at this time a rifle would be bought from a soldier out of one of the barracks.[59]

Once in Ireland, smuggled weapons remained under IRB control. After the Irish Volunteers were established, O'Rourke – as with most IRB members – joined one of the Volunteer battalions, but even then 'The munitions that we continued to import were always under the control of the IRB.'[60] Neil Kerr,[61] the Supreme Council member for the North of England, was a key person in the smuggling operation. His Council colleague Alec McCabe remembered: 'All the arms and messages and everything from America passed though Kerr in Liverpool. He was a terribly important man.'[62]

In 1914 Diarmuid Lynch was the envoy of the IRB to the biennial convention of the Clan, and in this capacity he consulted the Clan's Revolutionary Directory, conferred with the Clan's Committee on Foreign Relations and reported on the IRB generally to the Clan's leadership.[63] It was not until about Christmas 1919 that the Supreme Council, upon Michael Collins' suggestion, issued a statement to Clan na Gael on the relationship between the two organisations, 'and it was reiterated that the Insurrection of 1916 was the outcome of the work of the IRB and Clan na Gael'.[64] This was undoubtedly true.

Patrick Pearse, who was to be the military chief in the 1916 Rising, while arranging financial support for the Irish Volunteers, tried to ensure that IRB members controlled the Volunteers' finances. They could be trusted to use it for weapons, he wrote to one of the Clan leaders: 'I would suggest that in sending the money you do not entrust the expenditure of the whole of it to [any other men]. Not that I doubt their honesty but simply that they are not in or of our counsel and they are not formally pledged to strike, if the chance comes, for the complete thing.'[65]

IRB members regarded themselves as pledged to fight for independence. Diarmuid Lynch was clear about this: 'The sole purpose for which the IRB existed was the establishment of Ireland's national independence,' he wrote, simultaneously acknowledging that for decades the Supreme Council had talked and not acted because 'while its aims were revolutionary its leaders were circumspect'.[66]

By 1916 its leaders were no longer circumspect.

CHAPTER 7

Infiltration

The I.R.B. worked through Sinn Féin, the Gaelic League, the G.A.A. and eventually through the Irish Volunteers having key-men in each of them, to influence their policy in the direction required.[1]

Denis McCullough, 11 December 1953

The IRB recruited from, infiltrated and sought to control other nationalist political and cultural organisations. 'We were told to encourage national bodies: that was the big task at that time,' said Frank Daly of the pre-1916 period. 'Get into them and get likely men and recruit the men there.'[2] 'Fenianism,' argues Tom Garvin, saluting the IRB's efforts, 'persisted as the alternative to constitutional politics because of its influence in sporting and cultural associations.'[3]

The IPP's Ancient Order of Hibernians, especially strong in Ulster, was recognised as not being susceptible to IRB control, but individual members were brought into the IRB, and Hibernian activity was known to the Brotherhood. In Tyrone:

> a number of the members of the I.R.B. circles still retained membership of the A.O.H. after they had joined the organisation. This fact turned out a good policy as when the time came to organise the Volunteers the I.R.B. were able by their influence in the A.O.H. to get the divisions of the Hibernians to help to form the Volunteer Companies.[4]

The GAA, founded in 1884, was in large part an IRB initiative.[5] Two IRB men, Michael Cusack and Patrick Nally, sparked the Association's creation. From the outset it was Catholic, nationalistic and xenophobic. Archbishop Croke of

Infiltration 77

Cashel endorsed and protected it, directed priests to provide it with practical support and firmly opposed all IRB efforts to politicise it. Croke Park, the GAA's Dublin sportsground headquarters, is named after him.

Cusack wrote the GAA's founding manifesto as a cry against anglicisation, appealing to the deep nationalist undercurrent that reforms and lethargy had not yet eradicated:

> No movement having for its object the social and political advancement of a nation from the tyranny of imported and enforced customs and manners can be regarded as perfect if it has not made adequate provision for the preservation and cultivation of the national pastimes of the people; voluntary neglect of such pastimes is a sure sign of national decay and of approaching disillusion.[6]

Partly in response to the United Kingdom Amateur Athletic Association's wish to govern it, the GAA banned from membership sportsmen who played games under any other organisation's auspices. The government believed that the GAA was an arm of the IRB, and the RIC Special Branch regularly reported on its members and its activities. 'All this time we had been hearing rumours that the I.R.B. (Irish Republican Brotherhood) or Fenian organisation, was still in existence,' said Robert Brennan, a journalist and later Secretary of the IRB Wexford Board and a Sinn Féin publicist, 'and we got a thrill when it was whispered that some of the heads of the Gaelic Athletic Association were in it and that they were followed about by detectives.'[7]

In 1897 the GAA banned members of the RIC from membership. RIC attention was justified, but not to the extent suspected: it was not a hotbed of revolution. Robert Kelly in Newry recounted: 'In G.A.A. circles I found some very good lads whom I knew would make good soldiers of Ireland – and they did give their best in the fight later – but very few of them would join the I.R.B.'[8]

However, GAA events were used by IRB men to stay in touch with each other. 'The G.A.A. was a great blind and an organisation which had a good deal to do with the I.R.B. as under cover of a football match men could travel without suspicion and come together', confirmed P.J. Ruttledge, IRB Centre for North Mayo.[9] Dan McCarthy, in the IRB from 1902, explained:

> The G.A.A. was extensively used by the I.R.B. A man would be elected to represent, say, Wexford on the G.A.A. We worked in these counties

to get an I.R.B. man elected as a G.A.A. delegate. I was on the first Leinster Council of the G.A.A. We used this organisation extensively for I.R.B. purposes. For instance, a meeting of the G.A.A. Council would be held after a match so that if any of the executive I.R.B. in Dublin wanted to get in touch with any Leinster executives, he had a very good opportunity.[10]

When Michael Collins went to London in 1906 to start his job with the Post Office Savings Bank, one of his first actions was to join the GAA Notting Hill Geraldines Football Club, expecting only to enjoy sport. This brought him to the attention of the IRB, which he joined in 1909, sworn in by the then South of England Supreme Council member, P.S. O'Hegarty.[11] Sam Maguire, the London Centre, was a frequent captain of the Geraldines team and formed a lifelong bond with Collins. He was the person who, after several years of observation, recommended Collins as a member to O'Hegarty, illustrating not only the IRB's carefulness, but also that there was no assumption that GAA membership automatically qualified a man for the IRB. Most GAA members were sportsmen who were not politically engaged, spending most of their time on playing fields, not in secret sessions. Not many GAA members took part in the 1916 Rising who were not also members of another organisation or in the Volunteers/IRA.[12]

The major cultural nationalist organisation was the Gaelic League, founded in 1893 by Douglas Hyde, an academic linguist and the son of a Church of Ireland minister, Eoin MacNeill, then a civil servant, Fr Eugene O'Growney[13] and other Gaelic revivalists. Hyde was the League's first president. He attracted unionists (including at the League's foundation, most surprisingly, the Grand Master of the Orange Lodge[14]) and several Anglo-Irish aristocrats, making it an entrée to levels of society usually closed to the IRB. Hyde wanted it simply to be a cultural organisation. However, the size and connections of the League were attractive to the IRB not only as a recruiting ground but also as a subtle way of spreading separatism. It was a natural IRB target. Like the GAA, the League also provided regular cover for IRB meetings, since its more cerebral purposes explained regular indoor gatherings. Hugh Pollard, an intelligence officer in Dublin Castle in 1919–21, saw the League as 'a cult of hysterical nationalism'.[15]

Joseph Lawless, the son of an IRB Centre and himself an IRB member, described the IRB's effort to influence the League: 'The object aimed at by

Infiltration

the IRB was that all these national organisations should be under its control and guidance, so that while each was allowed or encouraged to pursue its own immediate aim, the aim of all would converge upon the ultimate Rising in arms, necessary as a further effort to shake off the yoke of foreign domination.'[16]

By 1915 the League had hundreds of branches in every county. Its teachers travelled around the country, which provided them with a perfect reason for being in any particular place. The membership of the IRB Keating Circle in Dublin, for example, drew heavily from the Keating Branch of the Gaelic League and used ostensible Branch meetings for its own purposes.[17] Batt O'Connor noted:

> The Gaelic League and the Gaelic Athletic Association were the two chief sources from which the Irish Republican Brotherhood recruited its members ... If a man belonged to either of these organisations you might be fairly sure that he was possessed of certain qualities – perseverance, sincerity, honesty of purpose, and moral courage – all of them invaluable in an I.R.B. man. When I joined the Brotherhood it gave me great delight to find these qualities in the men who became my comrades.[18]

A core IRB League group of Seán MacDermott, Piaras Béaslaí,[19] George Nicholls[20] and Padraic Ó Maille[21] met in Galway just before the June 1913 Gaelic League annual convention being held there.[22] Douglas Hyde was trying to exclude people he considered extreme nationalists from positions in the League. They needed to decide whether to oppose him or not. At the convention, Hyde attacked Thomas Ashe and other like-minded members of the Coiste Gnótha – the thirty-strong governing body of the League – accusing them of politicising the League and not adhering to the simple purpose of proselytising for the Irish language.[23] Hyde resigned, stood for re-election as a test of his support, and won.

Notwithstanding Hyde's views, MacDermott and his colleagues had decided to support him. They did not have the votes to secure control of the League, and they did not wish Hyde to resign at this stage and possibly establish another League excluding them, so they did not press for politically inspired motions that might have made him do so.[24] While Ó Maille maintained opposition to Hyde during the convention, presumably to keep the IRB's hand hidden since

80   The Irish Republican Brotherhood, 1914–1924

a sudden retreat from criticising Hyde would have been seen as suspicious, Éamonn Ceannt proposed and Michael O'Rahilly seconded Hyde's re-election. The value of a high-profile moderate nationalist at the head of the League made IRB influence not especially obvious.

The following year, 1914, the League's convention was held in July at Killarney and the Coiste Gnótha was increased from 30 to 45 members. In the elections to the enlarged body, two more IRB members were elected.[25]

Hyde and a majority of the Coiste Gnótha supported a speech made by John Redmond, leader of the IPP, at Woodenbridge, Co. Wicklow, on 20 September calling for the Volunteers to enlist in the British forces. This had already resulted in a split in the Irish Volunteers, with the Irish National Volunteers – 90 per cent of Volunteer members – following Redmond and the remainder under MacNeill breaking away. This split divided the whole nationalist community.[26]

In July 1915 a new struggle for control took place at the League's convention at Dundalk. Early in 1915, Seán MacDermott asked Seán T. O'Kelly, as a senior member of the League, to see that his branch proposed that the League's constitution be changed at the forthcoming convention to incorporate a statement that one of the League's aims was to obtain Irish freedom. O'Kelly refused. Then, on 20 June, Tom Clarke called a meeting of IRB members of the League to plan a takeover, by proposing an innocent-sounding motion reiterating the non-political and non-sectarian stand of the League that they correctly calculated Hyde would oppose as being 'political'. At the convention such a motion was proposed and passed despite Hyde's objection.[27] This was followed by eighteen separatists (including Tom Clarke, who spoke no Irish, and MacDermott, who was absent as he was in prison, having been arrested in May for giving an anti-conscription speech) winning election to the Coiste Gnótha. Hyde and the League's General Secretary, Padraigh Ó Dálaigh, resigned. Two years later Douglas Hyde gave a dry account of this takeover, confusing Sinn Féin with the IRB, as did most people after 1916:

> I was told by several people that Seán Ó Murthuile had got 50 proxies which instead of distributing to various Irish speakers as he was meant to do, he handed them over in one bunch to the Sinn Féin Secretary in Dundalk, who handed them over to fifty Sinn Féiners, who did not speak Irish, did not care for the language, had never even joined a branch of the Gaelic League, but who now got their orders to walk in as delegates

Infiltration 81

with passes in their hands and vote on a pre-arranged ticket for all the Sinn Féiners and politicians and followers of Arthur Griffith who were candidates for membership of the Coiste Gnótha.[28]

The convention, now effectively controlled by the IRB, went on to change the Gaelic League's constitution to include as one of its aims making Ireland 'free of foreign domination'. Eoin MacNeill was elected president and Seán T. O'Kelly as General Secretary in place of Hyde and Ó Dálaigh.

The Supreme Council now assumed that the League was under their control.[29] As usual, they depended upon top-down hierarchies, thinking that having majorities on committees would ensure that IRB decisions would be implemented. From 1914 to 1916 in the IRB itself, this was a reasonably safe assumption, but not elsewhere. And even in the IRB, as Seán T. O'Kelly had shown, blind obedience was not always given.

In 1909 Cathal Brugha had succeeded Fr Dinneen as President of the Gaelic League Keating Branch that was predominantly composed of IRB members. Dinneen had been president since its foundation in 1900. The Branch had been formed by Munstermen in Dublin, and it had great impact in the Gaelic League generally, introducing the first all-Irish language magazine, *Banba*, and pioneering the production of Irish-language plays. Its theatrical group included Piaras Béaslaí,[30] Gearóid O'Sullivan,[31] Fionan Lynch[32] – all members of the IRB – and Muiris Ó Catháin,[33] an Irish-language writer, actor and playwright. This Gaelic emphasis followed various internal disputes about playing the English game of soccer, and about supporting Fr Michael O'Hickey, Professor of Irish at Maynooth, in his campaign to have Irish made compulsory at the National University of Ireland. Seán MacDermott, initially a member of the Fintan Lalor Circle in Dublin, was a frequent visitor to the IRB Keating Circle that was within the Gaelic League Keating Branch and seems to have transferred to it in 1915. A group formed around him there, later providing senior Sinn Féin and Volunteer/IRA officers: Con Collins (who shared rooms with MacDermott in Russell Place); Piaras Béaslaí (transferred from the Teeling Circle);[34] Colm Ó Murchadha;[35] Fionan Lynch; Diarmuid O'Hegarty;[36] Gearóid O'Sullivan and Cathal Brugha.[37]

MacDermott introduced Michael Collins to membership of the Keating Branch and to the IRB Keating Circle in January 1916, no doubt because of Collins' affection for 'his' county (Cork) and province.[38] Collins remained an active member of the Gaelic League until 1919.[39]

82   The Irish Republican Brotherhood, 1914–1924

While Gaelic League and GAA politics engaged the IRB, the national organisation that was of paramount importance to the Brotherhood was the Irish Volunteers. The rooms of the Gaelic League Keating Branch at 46 Rutland Square (renamed Parnell Square in 1933) were used for IRB and Volunteer meetings and on Easter Sunday, 1916, were the headquarters of the First Battalion of the Volunteer Dublin Brigade.[40] The building had been purchased by the IRB through the agency of the Wolfe Tone Memorial Committee.[41]

The Irish Volunteers represented creation: a step beyond infiltration. Ironically, the creation of the UVF in September 1912 to prevent Home Rule applying to Ulster injected new life into Irish nationalism and, ominously, saw the formation of public private armies.

In January 1913 the Supreme Council, less restrained than the 1911 Council, had agreed to establish a public volunteer force in response to the UVF, including building a hall at the back of 41 Rutland Square, an IRB hotbed, for drilling its members in preparation for the formation of such a force, and as a headquarters.[42] Séamus Deasy, a Dublin IRB member for nine or ten years, was thrilled when news of the decision to create the Irish Volunteers was revealed:

> One day, early 1913, I was coming down D'Olier Street when I met Bulmer Hobson whom I had known for a number of years in various organisations in the city. He appeared to be excited and had just come from a Conference. He told me that an open organisation was about to be started in opposition to the Ulster Volunteers and was going to be known as 'The Irish National Volunteers'. He said they had got the support of Eoin McNeill [sic], who was a prominent Gaelic Leaguer, and also Andy Kettle who was a supporter of Redmond. He told me to spread the news quietly among the lads and that we should give it our full support as in this way we were bound to get rifles. At the next meeting of our IRB Circle Sean McDermott announced that every member would have to do a certain amount of drill, and arrangements were then made to make drill compulsory for all the younger members … Then came the big meeting in the Rotunda in November 1913, when the Irish National Volunteers were officially formed. Our Circle were all instructed to attend this meeting and hand in our names. We did this and we were all enrolled as members of the Volunteers.[43]

George Irvine, Centre of the Clarence Mangan Circle, Secretary of the Dublin

Centres Board and on the Leinster Board, credited an IRB colleague with the conception of the Irish Volunteers:

> The man who was responsible for the starting of the Volunteers was Cathal Kickham. He mentioned it several times at the Dublin Centres' Board of the I.R.B. but the rest of us did not take him seriously, thinking it was some kind of a police force he wanted. At last one night, in reply to a remark someone made about not wanting a police force, he said 'I don't mean a police force, I mean an army.' That made us think and we began to discuss the matter. I don't remember whether we made the arrangements at that meeting, but we finally arranged that the Chairman, Bulmer Hobson, and Séamus O'Connor [another Dublin Centre] should get in touch with some harmless nationalists like Eoin MacNeill and D.P. Moran[44] on the matter and see if it would be possible to form a committee to set things going. They (Bulmer Hobson and Séamus O'Connor) were not to mention the IRB or use the word republican at all, which at that time was worse than 'communist' at the present day, 1949. Simply to get an armed force to back up Home Rule, as the Unionists of the North had formed a force to oppose it.[45]

Hobson, perhaps because of Kickham, had been working to achieve the creation of the Volunteers since the formation of the UVF. He thought that if the IRB did not organise a counterpart to the UVF, the IPP probably would[46] – in the AOH the Party already had an organisation that could be militarised – and he realised that his and the IRB's roles needed to remain unobtrusive so that conventional nationalists would be willing to take part and not be frightened off by the IRB's physical-force reputation.[47] This awareness guided the Volunteers' formation and subsequent existence. Seán Fitzgibbon, a founding member of the Provisional Committee of the Volunteers, but never a member of the IRB, was clear about the care involved: 'The object of the Volunteers was, while securing that there should be a preponderance of men of separatist tendencies, at the same time the organisation should be sufficiently broad to include supporters of the IPP, otherwise it would lose its national appeal and become a sectional organisation.'[48]

In the autumn of 1913, Circles were told to support what was to be the Volunteers. Joseph O'Rourke remembered: 'At every meeting of the Circle there was supposed to be a visiting Centre to see we were doing our stuff.

84   The Irish Republican Brotherhood, 1914–1924

About August or September, 1913, the visitors were suggesting the idea of an open military organisation and requesting us to support the idea when it was officially launched.'[49]

In October 1913 the Midland Volunteer Force began in Athlone independently of the IRB, parading an estimated 5,000 men as a local counter to the UVF.[50] In November the Irish Volunteers and the ICA were formed – the Volunteers as an IRB initiative ostensibly to match the UVF but providing a marvellous opportunity to prepare a nationalist army that could be revolutionary;[51] the ICA by James Connolly as a workers' force to defend strikers against police violence.[52]

Having as leader of the Volunteers a moderate nationalist public figure who was not an IPP leader was an essential element to disguise their hand – as it had been with Douglas Hyde and then Eoin MacNeill in the Gaelic League. The IRB Executive spent time assessing who to approach, as Seán McGarry noted:

> The feeling that Volunteers should be started here was universal and there was some impatience shown in the Circles in Dublin but the S[upreme] C[ouncil] had the matter well in hand. A decision had been made [that] it was not intended that Volunteers should be started under the sole aegis of the I.R.B. Tom Clarke, McDermott and Pearse had been for some time working quietly and patiently interviewing people representing different aspects of National life including the labour movement; the object being to be ready to propose a provisional Executive that would be a cross section of the people.[53]

The general acceptability of Gaelic League figures was recognised. Eoin Mac-Neill, now Professor of Early and Medieval History at the National University, was well known and respected in Irish nationalist and cultural circles as a founder of the Gaelic League and the first editor of *An Claidheamh Soluis*. Hobson's intention was for MacNeill to emerge as the obvious leader behind whom varied nationalists might unite. To achieve this, he asked Michael O'Rahilly, assistant editor of *An Claidheamh Soluis* and not identified with the IRB, to approach MacNeill to write an article for the paper. MacNeill agreed.

In 'The North Began', published in *An Claidheamh Soluis* on 1 November 1913, MacNeill emphasised that the creation of the UVF meant that there was 'nothing to prevent the other twenty-eight counties[54] from calling into

Infiltration

85

existence citizen forces to hold Ireland "for the Empire". It was precisely with this object that the Volunteers of 1782 were enrolled, and they became the instrument of establishing Irish self-government.'

Immediately after the article was published, the IRB Executive (effectively Clarke and MacDermott) asked Hobson to sound out MacNeill about leading the proposed Irish Volunteers. Seán MacDermott secured Michael O'Rahilly's agreement that he would work with the IRB Executive.[55] O'Rahilly proposed that a meeting should be arranged to announce the formation of the Irish Volunteers under MacNeill's leadership.[56] MacNeill agreed: 'I had no doubt in my mind that [O'Rahilly and Hobson] came to me from the old physical-force party, whose organisation was the I.R.B., and I also had little doubt of the part I was expected to play.' But he was clear that he would not accept IRB control.[57] On 11 November, at Wynn's Hotel in Dublin, the establishing meeting took place with MacNeill presiding. Hobson did not attend, absenting himself on the grounds that as a well-known extreme nationalist, his presence would alienate moderates.[58] Nevertheless, of the ten men present, six were IRB members.[59]

Several more meetings of this group took place at Wynn's with Hobson present. He was not as unpalatable as was first assumed. He noted that his access to IRB funding may have played a part: 'The rent of the room for these early meetings was paid for by subscriptions from those present, but it was not realised that a sum of £1 which was provided by both Séamus O'Connor and myself came from the funds of the I.R.B.'[60]

On 14 November a self-appointed Provisional Committee took on the business of organising Volunteers nationwide with Eoin MacNeill and Laurence Kettle of the IPP as joint honorary secretaries. A majority were IRB members.[61] Hobson became the Executive's Secretary.[62] It was a first step, according to Seán McGarry, of Hobson breaking with Clarke and MacDermott: 'It had been already decided that no prominent member of the I.R.B. should accept office but Hobson allowed himself to be appointed [Secretary]. This had to be accepted as a *fait accompli* though with bad grace and everything went well for a while.'[63]

The stated object of the Volunteers in their 'Manifesto', drafted by MacNeill, was 'to secure and maintain the rights and liberties common to the whole people of Ireland'.[64] Privately MacNeill wrote that he was a supporter of John Redmond, and 'I pledge myself against any use of the Volunteer movement to weaken his Party (which is also my Party).'[65] The Volunteers were officially launched on 25 November 1913 as 'a corps of Irish Volunteers'[66] at

86 The Irish Republican Brotherhood, 1914–1924

a rally at Dublin's Rotunda Rink organised principally by Hobson.[67] About 7,000 people attended, filling the 4,000 places in the Rotunda, the rest milling around outside. A declaration of historical rebellious continuity, the constant refrain of Irish nationalists, was made: 'From time immemorial it has been held by every race of mankind to be the right and duty of a freeman to defend his freedom with all his resources and with his life itself. The exercise of that right distinguishes the freeman from the serf, the discharge of that duty distinguishes him from the coward.'[68] Hobson took this a step further, seeing the Volunteers as an opportunity to prepare for 'a defensive struggle using guerrilla tactics'.[69] Nevertheless, MacNeill's 'Manifesto', despite challenge from the IRB (and to an extent, Hobson), remained the Volunteers' official purpose.

'All the I.R.B. were instructed to be present at the meeting and to sign the enrolment forms,' Thomas Slater, who was present, recalled.[70] Members of the IRB in Dublin had an advantage when they joined the Volunteers because they had been drilling at 41 Rutland Square for about a year under the supervision of ex-British Army sergeants. 'Of course, these fellows who had done a little drill were the outstanding recruits,' Ernest Blythe pointed out, 'and a lot of them, purely democratically, were able to get elected to office.'[71] In Hobson's Teeling Circle, he and Éamonn Ceannt urged members to join the Volunteers.[72] 'On the formation of the Irish Volunteers we were instructed by the IRB to join and to do everything possible to get hold of the key positions in the Volunteers,' said Circle member Gerry Byrne. 'It was now perceived by the members of the IRB that this was a chance to do openly what we had previously to do in secret.'[73] In Clare Joseph Barrett, a founding member of the Volunteers in the county, confirmed IRB influence:

> The members of the I.R.B. started the Volunteers on their own, without assistance or instructions from any outside body or person, that is to say, we had no instructions from the Supreme Council, on the one hand, or the newly formed Volunteer Executive, on the other ... Limerick City was the Divisional Centre for Munster. Meetings of this Divisional Centre were held about every six months in Limerick City ... The general trend of the discussions at these meetings, however, was that the Council wanted to ensure that the I.R.B. was in control of the Irish Volunteer organisation because, through such control, it would be in a position to handle any situation that might arise. This objective, to a great extent, was successfully accomplished.[74]

Infiltration 87

Similarly, in Wexford, John O'Reilly joined the IRB in June 1914 and was impressed by the IRB's reach and energy:

> I did not realise how widespread it was until a special meeting in Enniscorthy ... I do know that practically all the officers of the Volunteers with very few exceptions were I.R.B. members and there was much activity by I.R.B. members that Volunteers were not aware of for security reasons. When an appointment or promotion in Volunteers or later I.R.A. was made it was mostly decided by I.R.B. beforehand.[75]

The farther away from Dublin, the looser the grasp of the IRB – a consistent element throughout the 1914–21 period.

In some cases, the IRB paid the costs of establishing Volunteer companies. 'From early in 1914 I was working full time on IRB work and Irish Volunteer organisation over the same area,' said James Tomney, Tyrone County Centre. 'My expenses for this work were paid by Denis McCullough.'[76] Diarmuid Lynch had travelled to New York in the summer of 1914 as an IRB envoy to the Clan na Gael's annual convention and returned in November with £2,000 for the Volunteers.[77]

In Clonmel the Centre of the local Circles Board, Frank Drohan, was ordered to form a Volunteer company by the IRB Executive. He received a separate request to do so from Eoin MacNeill. The three Circles in the town proceeded to form a company, and Drohan was elected captain.[78] 'Nearly every officer in the [Wexford] Volunteers,' said John J. O'Reilly, 'was an IRB man. That was one thing we tried to do although they were elected by popular vote.'[79] Mick Fleming in Tralee 'knew two men who went forward a few times as officers, but they were not returned as they were not I.R.B.'[80] Frank Daly in Dublin recognised that 'the IRB members were mostly the officers. They were the officers all round. I wasn't long in and I was promoted a lieutenant for a start; then I was made Captain of Engineers.'[81] Fionan Lynch, also in Dublin, found 'that nearly all the officers of the Volunteers were already members of the I.R.B. before they were elected officers'.[82] A similar procedure took place wherever there were IRB Circles, although this was not always co-ordinated.[83] For some IRB members – James Daly was one – the Volunteers began to rival the Brotherhood. It was a forewarning: 'During all this time, 1914 and 1915, I attended the usual monthly meetings of my I.R.B. Circle, but we did not give this part of our activities the same attention as before, as a lot of us felt the Volunteers were more important.'[84]

The creation of Volunteer companies did not depend only upon the IRB: many were formed where there was no IRB activity, in turn providing recruiting opportunities for the Brotherhood.[85] Volunteer officers in particular were targeted for membership. The end result was that while the IRB had influence in and knowledge of the Volunteers, neither it nor its members – although often in key Volunteer positions – fully controlled the new organisation. It rapidly became too large for that.[86] The IRB was not able to change the defensive profile established at the start of the Volunteers by Eoin MacNeill. Even after the Rising it took years for the Volunteers/IRA to be defiant. However, in 1913, for the first time in over a century, nationalist aspiration was given public organised militaristic presence.

In most cases, the Volunteer officers elected after September 1914 were members of the IRB principally because they were diligent Volunteers, and the IRB membership of a company would campaign and vote for IRB men.[87] As a result, nearly all the company captains, battalion officers and brigade officers were members of the IRB. Those officers who were not members, for the most part, joined willingly just before the Rising.[88]

The creation of the Volunteers inevitably drew the attention of the RIC which naturally suspected the IRB's hand. James McCullough joined the Armagh Circle in 1914 and immediately was made aware of RIC interest in the Circle: 'From 1914 onwards the R.I.C. got active in investigating the movements of the known members of the I.R.B. Instructions were issued by the Supreme Council that officer personnel were to be changed regularly and that substitutes were to be appointed to replace any officer of the organisation immediately an arrest was made.'[89]

The IRB's consistent emphasis on force, and the influence the society exerted in the Volunteers, was a deep worry to Arthur Griffith, who had become the leading public figure advocating national independence. He argued for a peaceful settlement and for a dual monarchy. He judged that this would provide Britain with an acceptable constitutional solution to Irish independence, and he never gave up his hope for it.

The principal impediment to Griffith's ambition was the IRB's commitment to force and to the establishment of a republic.

CHAPTER 8

Principals: Hobson, Clarke, MacDermott

It should be noted that the constitution specifically forbade an insurrection such as had taken place in 1867 when there was no public support, no adequate organisation and no chance of success. In swearing in men into the I.R.B. I was often asked if there was any assurance that their oath of obedience would not land them into a futile insurrection, and I frequently had to assure men that the constitution specifically forbade such a development.[1]

Bulmer Hobson, 17 October 1947

'That's ridiculous!' said Alec McCabe, making the point that the objective of the IRB was insurrection, and that a majority of people were most unlikely to vote for one first.[2] Hobson, however, was correct: clause 3 of the 1873 Constitution required popular support as a condition for a rising.

Hobson had highlighted the contradiction in the IRB constitution between constitutionalism and force, since this clause clearly held that before force was employed, a majority of the Irish people had to approve: how this was to be gauged was never addressed.[3] Denis McCullough acknowledged that 'We had not the country behind us; it was the active men who were overriding the general feeling and opinion of the Irish people who were behind Redmond and his party at the time.'[4] On the other hand clause 1 of the constitution held that Supreme Council decisions 'shall be the laws of the Irish Republic',[5] and in September 1914, and again in January 1916, the Council had determined on a rising.[6] Furthermore, clause 8 declared that 'the authority of the Supreme

Council shall be unquestioned'.[7] In other words, the Supreme Council had the authority to do what it liked. Hobson, in disagreeing, was held to be acting unconstitutionally and disregarding his oath to obey his superior officers. Hobson did not see this, thinking that he was dealing with an unconstitutional group within the society – the Military Committee – and not with a Supreme Council decision of which he seems to have been unaware.[8] The Committee had in fact been established within IRB rules, but Hobson did not know that – he had been kept out of Council plans ever since June 1914.

Hobson was born in Belfast into a Quaker family. His mother was English. She was politically active in support of suffragism and was a founder of an early Irishwomen's Association[9] – its book club met in the Hobson family home. As a teenager, Hobson joined the Gaelic League and the GAA. In 1904 he was sworn into the IRB by Denis McCullough. Hobson was recognised as an impressive IRB spokesman and in 1906 was chosen by the Supreme Council to represent the IRB to Clan na Gael.[10]

Hobson was energetic. Because he did not take part in the 1916 Rising, his importance has been underestimated. In January 1912, when he was elected to the Supreme Council for Leinster, he represented perhaps two-thirds of the IRB's total membership – itself largely his achievement – conferring on him far greater influence than any other member of the Council. He had been instrumental in maintaining and energising the IRB during the early years of the century.[11] He was a founder and a leader of the Volunteers and was their principal organiser. He was articulate, intelligent and self-confident. Denis McCullough described him as 'a very headstrong and somewhat egotistical person', but said that he 'was entirely unselfish'.[12]

From November 1913 Hobson concentrated on the Volunteers, taking a large part in their development, and it is from this point that he steadily grew away from Clarke and MacDermott.[13] Social differences played a part. Hobson was educated. He read books and quoted classical authors. He had a grand manner, yet never had any money. Hobson's transfer of his energies to the Volunteers may have been encouraged by these differences. No formal Volunteer Executive was appointed at first, but Eoin MacNeill, Hobson and Seán Fitzgibbon seem to have acted as such, joined from time to time by Sir Roger Casement, Michael O'Rahilly and Colonel Maurice Moore, who had been appointed Inspector General of the Volunteers.[14] In the manuscript of his *History of the Irish Volunteers*, written in 1917, Hobson, who knew better than most that the Irish Volunteers were an IRB initiative, put his view plainly if

Principals: Hobson, Clarke, MacDermott

speciously: 'The Irish Volunteer movement was the spontaneous creation of the Irish people.'[15] It was, therefore, in his opinion more deserving of support than the IRB. He thought the Volunteers offered the best prospect of securing real change for Ireland, if not independence, through guerrilla action. He was ahead of nearly everyone else. Guerrilla tactics, not the conventional approach of the Military Committee, were indeed the future of Irish rebellion.

In June 1914 Tom Clarke and Seán MacDermott broke with Hobson because of his support for the admission of Redmond's IPP nominees to the Provisional Committee of the Volunteers, which gave the Party a majority on the Committee. Hobson saw the Party's 'takeover' as inevitable: the Party could not allow the Volunteers to operate outside its control and become a rival military-type grouping. He reckoned it better to bend than to break on the issue and not risk fragmenting the Volunteers.[16]

Clarke and MacDermott had looked to Hobson to keep them informed about Volunteer activity and policy, but he let them down. During spring 1914, MacNeill and Casement had been talking to Redmond and senior IPP members about taking the Volunteers under the Party's umbrella.[17] The contact was not secret, but Hobson did not tell Clarke and MacDermott what he knew and did not follow their instructions to oppose an agreement with Redmond and the Party.[18] 'Bulmer Hobson was the most single-minded nationalist I knew in my time,' said Denis McCullough. 'He found it hard, however, to work under orders, as he had the supremest confidence (and still has) in his own judgement. A person of this temperament was bound to get at loggerheads, sooner or later, with those who were controlling the activities of the I.R.B. by methods which he did not understand & did not approve.'[19]

Patrick McCartan, in contrast, followed IRB instructions and argued with MacNeill and Casement against accepting IPP dominance.[20] On the evening of 15 June 1914, the Provisional Committee voted eighteen to nine to accept Redmond's twenty-five nominees, thus giving formal control of the Volunteers to the IPP. Six IRB members of the committee, doubtless influenced by Hobson, voted for them too.[21] Éamon Martin, in the IRB, Fianna Director of Organisation and Commandant of its Dublin Brigade 1915–16, and on the Volunteer Executive where he had opposed Hobson, remembered the debate: 'Hobson argued that Redmond wanted us to reject his demand, that he would be a very disappointed man if we accepted it and thereby kept the Volunteers intact. But his acceptance, and his persuading of the majority to accept earned for him very bitter criticism from Tom Clarke and McDermott and many others.'[22]

92   The Irish Republican Brotherhood, 1914–1924

Clarke and MacDermott had no wish to protect or to advance the Home Rule that was being legislated at Westminster: they saw it as the enemy of full independence and wanted a rebellion regardless of any consideration so as to keep the flame of independence alive and undermine the IPP, which they regarded as a British handmaiden. Seán McGarry was with Clarke when he heard the news of Hobson's support for Redmond's nominees:

> I was with Tom when the news came and to say he was astounded is understating it. I never saw him so moved. He regarded it from the beginning as cold-blooded and contemplated treachery likely to bring about the destruction of the only movement in a century which brought promise of the fulfilment of all his hopes. During his life he had had many very many grievous disappointments, but this was the worst and the bitterness of it was increased by the fact that it was brought about by a trusted friend. Had these proposals of Redmond been rejected [Redmond] would have to smash the organisation from the outside and his efforts might have caused a revulsion of feeling amongst his followers who were Volunteers, but now he was inside and in control. A way out had to be found but it was a deplorable one. It threw the onus of splitting the Volunteers on to the I.R.B.[23]

Hobson later described succeeding events, evincing surprise at the storm his action caused:

> I was completely taken by surprise when I was met [by Clarke and MacDermott] with a storm of hysterical abuse and accusations of having betrayed the movement … When they demanded to know how much I had been paid by Redmond for selling the Volunteers, I realised that I could not discuss policy on that level or work with people who thought like that. I was shocked to find that men so sincere and devoted had such paltry minds. Not wishing to prolong so unpleasant a scene, I resigned the editorship of *Irish Freedom*, which I had held since the paper was started, and announced my intention of resigning from the Supreme Council … I was quite well aware that my action would leave the direction of the I.R.B. in their hands [i.e., Clarke's and MacDermott's] and I was also aware that my resignation was exactly what Clarke and McDermott wanted. But if I could not work with them any more the

Principals: Hobson, Clarke, MacDermott 93

possible alternatives were to resign or to start a struggle for power within the I.R.B. which would have split the organisation from top to bottom … I chose to resign rather than render the I.R.B. impotent.[24]

Despite what Hobson said, this was obviously a power play. Hobson knew the strength of his position in the IRB and in the Volunteers, leaving Clarke and MacDermott with an uphill struggle to exercise control. 'We thought the I.R.B. was Hobson,' said Liam Gogan,[25] who was Assistant Secretary of the Irish Volunteers. Richard Connolly recalled the Supreme Council meeting when Hobson's opposition was discussed, seeing it as a struggle between Hobson and Clarke:

> The hottest meeting of the whole lot [of Supreme Council meetings] was in the end of September 1914, when Hobson was 'on the carpet' over the Volunteers, and Clarke … put forward his view that something should be done before the war ended. Clarke said definitely that, Volunteers or no Volunteers, he was going to let out some force during the occasion, that if they did not strike during the war, they were damned for posterity … That meeting finished up by agreeing with Clarke that before the war finished, the Council should take war action. I was quite certain Hobson was at that meeting. At the September 1914 meeting he tendered his resignation, and he was allowed out. At that meeting there was no provision made for a successor. It was a fight between Hobson and Clarke.[26]

Hobson's basic offence, as far as Clarke and MacDermott were concerned, was that as a senior member of the IRB he of all people should have accepted the Supreme Council's and Executive's decisions and not fought against them. Clarke immediately wrote to John Devoy saying that the Executive intended to expel Hobson from the IRB.[27] Hobson lost his job as Irish correspondent of the *Gaelic American*. This he no doubt correctly ascribed to Tom Clarke's influence with Devoy.[28] MacDermott probably advised Hobson's IRB colleagues in the Volunteers to distance themselves from him. Hobson later wrote of Pearse: 'Six months after I swore him into the I.R.B. he was writing to people in America, to whom I had introduced him, telling them that I was not sufficiently reliable, from a Revolutionary point of view, to be entrusted with funds or given support.'[29]

The Irish Republican Brotherhood, 1914–1924

That he maintained his membership of the IRB (he was not expelled), expected support from the Clan, and remained an officer on the Leinster Board meant that Hobson was aware of his strength and could campaign in the Dublin and Leinster Circles (where the great majority of IRB members were located) for his view that only a rising with a realistic hope of success should be attempted. He sought to widen the discussion within the IRB about the Redmondite takeover of the Volunteers, no doubt hoping that Circle opinion might generate opposition to Clarke and MacDermott:

> At the next meeting of the Teeling Circle of the I.R.B. I threw the question of the admission of Redmond's nominees open for debate, and I intended to resign if there was any of the hostility I had experienced with Clarke and MacDermott. There was, of course, difference of opinion, but the discussion was frank and friendly, and I continued to represent them on the Dublin Centres Board. I did the same thing at the Dublin Centres Board with the same result, and I continued to represent Dublin on the Leinster Board. At the next meeting of the Leinster Board I told them I could no longer represent them on the Supreme Council ... They were unanimous in pressing me not to resign, but I insisted that I could take no other course. At the subsequent biennial election [in 1915] I was re-elected Centre of the Teeling Circle and Chairman of the Dublin Centres Board without any opposition.[30]

The Leinster Board's 'unanimous pressing of Hobson not to resign' signalled the danger he could be to Clarke and MacDermott. That Hobson then stood for re-election was a declaration that he was combatting their willingness to split the Volunteers in order to obtain, as they must have seen it, a smaller more dedicated group that they would control. By remaining a member of the Leinster Board, he was in a position to thwart Clarke and MacDermott. Hobson was fighting for the integrity of the Volunteers, not the IRB.

Other IRB members in the Volunteers agreed with Hobson. Peadar Macken, an IRB member of the Provisional Committee, had voted for the acceptance of Redmond's nominees and had been instructed to do so by Seoirse Ó Ciatháin, the Centre of Macken's Circle. Ó Ciatháin so instructed Macken because he had received no directions from his IRB superiors on the matter, and personally thought it too early for a split to take place in the Volunteers.[31] This was, perhaps, Ó Ciatháin being wise after the event. Hobson was his immediate superior through whom Supreme Council and Executive instructions would have been passed, so it is possible that Hobson simply did not inform Ó Ciatháin or had suborned him.

Hobson's stand was reinforced by reality: the IRB simply did not have sufficient members throughout the country to achieve control of the Volunteers. If Redmond's demands were not met, the IPP could and would, as Redmond threatened, start a rival Volunteers, relegating an IRB-controlled Volunteers to a small rump grouping.[32] From the perspective of Clarke and MacDermott, that prospect was not a deterrent: all that mattered to them was that there should be even a small grouping for a rising that, however hopeless, would keep the insurrection tradition alive in a new generation.

Only in the summer of 1914, as it became clear that there would be war, did planning for a rising begin. This helps to explain Clarke and MacDermott's fury with Hobson for refusing to lend his weight to what they saw as the best chance for a strike for independence when England was distracted, extended and engaged elsewhere, in the core Fenian tradition that, as an IRB man, he could be expected to support. Hobson was not against a rising: he wanted a rising to have a prospect of success.[33] He was against Clarke and MacDermott's intended rising, which he saw as a hopeless demonstration of national spirit. He thought that occupying buildings and digging trenches was a recipe for disaster.[34]

Hobson was carefully isolated within the IRB by Clarke and MacDermott. In September 1914 they followed up the Supreme Council decision to launch a rising with a meeting at Gaelic League headquarters to which they invited senior Volunteers and nationalists. Their purpose was to float the idea of a rebellion during the war. Hobson, one of the five most senior Volunteers, was notably not invited. The Military Committee, active from May 1915, also by-passed Hobson (and the other members of the Supreme Council).[35] P.S. O'Hegarty recorded their effort:

> [Hobson] was still a member of the organisation and Chairman of the Dublin Centres Board. They knew he was opposed to an offensive, as distinct from a defensive, insurrection, and they knew his political intelligence and his single-minded independent integrity, so extraordinary precautions were taken to keep the decision a secret from him, everybody to whom it had to be disclosed being warned not to mention it to him or to discuss even the possibility of it with him.[36]

96 The Irish Republican Brotherhood, 1914–1924

After the Rising, Hobson was shunned and took no part in politics or the Volunteers/IRA. Early in 1917 he approached Val Jackson seeking an IRB hearing to clear his name. Jackson agreed to help and brought the question to the Dublin Centres Board:

> he was anxious to be given the opportunity of refuting the grave charges of cowardice and treachery that were in circulation concerning him. Collins, who, at the time, was standing near the window, spoke at once and said, somewhat sharply that surely I should know that Hobson could only be tried by his peers who were now all dead. I told him that I considered that he was already being judged and condemned without trial by many of his former colleagues and that surely there were still enough people left who could examine into and prove or disprove these charges. Collins now shifted his ground and said that was all very well, but that the organisation had much more important work in hand than the trial and not to be talking nonsense, or words to that effect. In face of this attitude, I could say no more.[37]

'Hobson,' said Larry de Lacey, 'was a first-class revolutionary and a first-class man, [who] failed in the end because he was so strict and solemn with himself and so careful that he isolated himself.'[38]

Tom Clarke

'I say with every confidence that Tom Clarke's person and Seán McDermott's energy and organising ability were the principal factors in creating a group and guiding events to make the Rising possible'[39] was Denis McCullough's forceful view. Clarke was a fanatic and, like Arthur Griffith, an anglophobe. 'To fight England was to him the most natural thing in the world,' said Seán McGarry,[40] who was 'a right-hand man of Tom Clarke'.[41] He was a man with a fixed idea, thought Larry de Lacey: 'Freedom and revenge. He'd been an English prisoner for years and suffered tortures, punishment and beatings and want of food and the black hole and all that sort of thing. A good, normal man otherwise – liked a joke. The secrecy of the organisation was supreme with him, and care for it. He lived for it.'[42] Imprisonment had nevertheless marked him. Piaras Béaslaí recorded calling on Clarke in his Dublin shop around 1912, finding: 'Tom sitting on a chair in the same position as, when a convict, he used to sit on a

Principals: Hobson, Clarke, MacDermott

stool in his cell, trunk erect, gazing into the distance, his eyelids hardly moving, his hands resting on his knees.'[43]

Clarke was born in 1857, probably in Tipperary. His father, James, was a Protestant from Co. Leitrim and a bombardier in the Royal Artillery. His mother, Mary, was a Catholic from Tipperary. He was brought up as a Catholic. The family travelled from Ireland when his father was posted to the Isle of Wight, then to South Africa and finally back to Ireland. Army life finished when his father was discharged as a sergeant in 1869. Dungannon, Co. Tyrone, became their home. In 1878 Clarke joined the IRB there, sworn in by John Daly (who was the uncle of Clarke's future wife, Kathleen Daly). When Billy Kelly joined the Dungannon Circle in 1880, Clarke was the Centre. They took part in an attack on some RIC men:

> On the night of the 16th August 1880, 11 of the R.I.C. were ambushed in Irish Street, Dungannon, by some members of the I.R.B. including Tom Clarke and myself – about 5 or 6 in all. We opened fire on the police and they escaped into a public house in Anne St. Reinforcements of police arrived on the scene and we had to retreat.[44]

Evading arrest prompted Clarke's travel to the United States. In contrast, his younger brother, Alfred, enlisted in the Royal Artillery. Billy Kelly went on to describe their experience in New York:

> In Sept. 1880, Clarke and I and a few others decided to emigrate to America. Previous to leaving for America we obtained a transfer from the Dungannon Circle of the I.R.B. to Camp No.1 Clan-na-Gael in New York (No. 4 Union St). We arrived in New York in October and called at Patrick O'Connor's, Chatham St, who was a member of the Clan-na-Gael ... Shortly after our admission to the Camp Tom Clarke was appointed recording Secretary of the Camp.[45]

In 1883 Clarke travelled to London under an alias (Henry Hammond Wilson) to take part in the 1881–85 bombing campaign organised by Clan na Gael. He was given away by an informer, was arrested in possession of dynamite and sentenced to life imprisonment. He was released in 1898 after fifteen years. He made a celebratory tour of Ireland, discovering that the IRB was a shadow of what it had been. He was dejected at the lack of commemorations of the 1798

98   The Irish Republican Brotherhood, 1914–1924

rebellion and infuriated by the complacency of the IRB leadership. 'There was no effort made to revive it until Tom Clarke was released from prison about 1898,' said Billy Kelly. 'After his return from prison he lived off and on in Dungannon. He organised some circles of the I.R.B. in the locality.'[46] He went back to the United States in 1899 where he married Kathleen Daly. He became an American citizen in 1905.

In New York, he worked for John Devoy, the secretary of Clan na Gael and its principal leader. Devoy constantly pressed the IRB to launch a rebellion, and regularly sent money to the Supreme Council. He was the IRB's principal contact in the Clan. With Tom Clarke he launched the *Gaelic American* newspaper in 1903 that was to become in America the leading voice of Irish nationalism and of IRB objectives.

Clarke returned to Ireland in November 1907 and opened a tobacconist shop in Dublin. His secret mission, funded by the Clan, was to organise another rising, if necessary, with a 'new' IRB committed to rebellion rather than to propaganda and municipal politics. Seán McGarry became close to Clarke and greatly admired him:

> He spoke of fighting for Ireland as casually as he did about any item of the day's news … He had wonderful energy, a great power of concentration and a tremendous capacity for mastering details and a quick judgement … He had no hankering after the limelight and any prominence was distasteful. He was always content to do the work and get it done; the credit could go anywhere.[47]

In Ireland, Clarke's natural initial connection was with Bulmer Hobson as a result of meeting him in 1907 in America when Hobson had represented the IRB to the Clan. Clarke soon surrounded himself with a group of IRB friends closely tied to Hobson, including Seán MacDermott, Denis McCullough, Patrick McCartan and P.S. O'Hegarty and his brother, Seán. In 1908 Hobson and Clarke persuaded MacDermott to devote himself to the IRB. This was the start of MacDermott's close association with Clarke, all due to Hobson.

Clarke's connection to Devoy made him the natural conduit for Clan funds sent to the IRB after the P.T. Daly scandal in 1910. He was determined to revive the IRB, which, as Diarmuid Lynch had noted and Clarke himself had witnessed immediately after his release from prison on parole in 1898, was moribund.[48] 'Outside the IRB there were few republicans,' said Patrick

Principals: Hobson, Clarke, MacDermott

McCartan about the years before 1916. 'We were mere propagandists and we realised it.'[49] Clan funds and Clarke himself were instrumental in achieving the IRB's revival. Had he not succeeded he intended to start a new organisation that would launch a rebellion.[50] It seems, however, that at the start of the First World War for a brief period he thought a rising would be unnecessary. Joseph Murray, a member of the O'Leary Circle in Dublin, proposed relieving the RIC of their weapons. The proposal reached Clarke:

> Before the outbreak of the war in 1914, I ascertained that there were 1,700 RIC barracks in Ireland and that each had five rifles and five revolvers and ammunition. I suggested to Pearse that the Volunteers should on some fixed date organise route marches in the vicinity of each of these barracks and seize the barracks and make off with the arms. Tom Clarke later told me that when this suggestion was brought before the Supreme Council of the I.R.B. a resolution in favour of doing so was defeated by his casting vote as Chairman. He explained to me that he did so because England was bound to be beaten in the war as she had never been up against a first-class Power before, and that we would get our freedom without any fight.[51]

Clarke quickly left his assumption behind, becoming with MacDermott the driving force behind the 1916 Rising. 'The only thing that was stated time and again [at Supreme Council meetings],' recalled Richard Connolly, 'was Tom Clarke's expressed intention and his determination to have a tryout before the war ended.'[52] He single-mindedly pursued rebellion[53] and bent the IRB to his will, using the IRB Executive to develop plans for a rising and with Supreme Council authorisation creating the Military Committee to implement them. Clarke's driving force was recognised by his Supreme Council colleagues, who, in the main, did not try to rein him in. Consequently the Executive and the Military Committee were effectively unsupervised.[54] Clarke concentrated on the IRB in Dublin, depending heavily on Bulmer Hobson and then Seán MacDermott, both of whom did the heavy lifting of organising, speaking, infiltrating other organisations, forming Circles and, finally, creating the Irish Volunteers – providing a greater force than the IRB itself could muster.

Those who control the money in organisations also tend to be the most powerful. Tom Clarke was IRB Treasurer in 1916[55] and Michael Collins formally occupied that position from 1917 to 1919[56] (and effectively until his death).

100   The Irish Republican Brotherhood, 1914–1924

IRB meetings started to take place in Clarke's rooms above his tobacconist shop.[57] From 1912 he was, in the opinion of Patrick McCartan, 'the real leader of the Republican movement'.[58] Batt O'Connor, who joined the IRB in 1909, said of him: 'Tom Clarke was the connecting link between Fenianism and what came to be called Sinn Féin. In his person was kept alive the tradition of the I.R.B.'[59] Denis McCullough gave him the credit for the 'new' IRB:

> It was only after the advent of Tom Clarke into the movement that it really shaped like taking serious action. His reputation enabled the younger men on the Supreme Council like Sean McDermott, P.S. O'Hegarty, Diarmuid Lynch and Bulmer Hobson etc., to move forward with his backing in organising, preaching and teaching the value and necessity of a physical-force movement. It protected them from the usual charges of youthful over-enthusiasm and of insincerity.[60]

Together with MacDermott, he strove not simply to infiltrate other organisations, but to see that qualified IRB members were elected or appointed to important positions, as Gregory Murphy, Secretary of the Leinster Board, remembered: 'Tom Clarke and Sean McDermott were very insistent that members of the I.R.B. should not seek executive positions in other organisations unless well qualified to hold such positions and have the confidence of the members of such organisations.'[61] This edict was particularly important in the Volunteers. George Irvine testified that: 'in Summer 1914 it was announced that officers would be elected in the companies, the men of the I.R.B. were ordered not to propose or vote for any other I.R.B. man unless he had the makings of a good officer and was competent to take command'.[62] The IRB system of electing Centres transferred to the Volunteers, whose officers were elected by their units, reflecting the IRB's founding influence.

Seán MacDermott

Seán MacDermott did not seek elected positions. He was known to many ordinary IRB members and Centres because of his countrywide organising. He was born in Co. Leitrim in 1883, one of ten children. His father was a tenant farmer and a carpenter, was in the IRB, and was a friend of John Daly, who provided a close link with Tom Clarke: both men looked up to Daly and often stayed with his family in Limerick.

Principals: Hobson, Clarke, MacDermott 101

MacDermott joined every nationalist organisation that he could. In 1903 he went to Scotland and worked as a gardener, moving in 1905 to Belfast where he worked as a tram conductor for about nine months.[63] In 1906 he met his contemporaries Bulmer Hobson and Denis McCullough, who probably swore him into the IRB.[64]

Very quickly, MacDermott adapted to the republican world, working closely with Hobson in the Dungannon Club, founded in 1905 by Hobson and McCullough. It was the first openly Irish republican club in the twentieth century, campaigning inter alia for the restoration of an Irish parliament.[65] Thomas Wilson, a young member, described its work:

> The I.R.B. was responsible for the formation of the Club. The idea behind its formation was to start an open organisation on the lines of the organisation subsequently known as Sinn Féin. Lectures and debates were held in the Club, and an effort was always made to instil the doctrine of physical force as a means to freedom and to shatter the confidence of people who had belief in the constitutional methods of the Irish Party. The overwhelming majority of the Nationalists in Belfast were good supporters of Joe Devlin [the Ulster IPP leader]. It was also hoped that the formation of the Dungannon Club would secure contact with young men who could be taken into the I.R.B. organisation.[66]

Belfast's 'No. 1 Dungannon Club' was chaired by Hobson and provided a nucleus of future republican leaders.[67] Seán MacDermott's reputation as an organiser and propagandist within extreme nationalist circles began in the Dungannon Club with Hobson's patronage.[68]

Later, a Freedom Club was also formed on the same lines as the Dungannon Club, with Denis McCullough as president.[69] It was aimed at younger men and members of the early Fianna Éireann, which had been formed in 1902 by Hobson in Belfast as a boys' sporting and cultural organisation, and provided members for the IRB and later the Volunteers/IRA.[70] According to Seán McGarry the Fianna was always 'under the guidance of the I.R.B.'.[71]

On 5 June 1906 MacDermott made his first public speech on a Dungannon platform. A month later he lost his job with the Belfast Street Tramway Company for smoking on a tram. He became a full-time paid recruiter, organiser and speechmaker for the Club, starting a career as a professional revolutionary. A whip-round was held within the Club that provided MacDermott with

102   The Irish Republican Brotherhood, 1914–1924

£1-10-0 (about £220 in 2024) a week, which was about twice the amount he earned as a tram conductor. They also bought him a bicycle.[72]

In 1907 he moved to Dublin, began to use the Gaelic form of his name, Seán Mac Diarmada, and worked as a recruiter and organiser for Sinn Féin. In 1910 he took on the same role with the IRB while also becoming manager of *Irish Freedom*. MacDermott visited England, Scotland and nearly every county in Ireland over the next six years recruiting for the IRB. Denis McCullough noted MacDermott's attractive personality[73] and recruiting skill: 'Sean McDermott was very skilful at this work and being a man of magnetic personality, the large measure of success achieved in it, may be attributed to him.'[74] The number of people who gave statements to the BMH about being present when MacDermott made a speech or were recruited by MacDermott testifies to his energy, determination and ability. Seán Fitzgibbon described MacDermott's recruiting argument:

> The main argument he mentioned was that in our day the national movement was kept alive by memory of the sacrifices of the Manchester Martyrs, and that the national sentiment voted [sic] by that act should be reinforced by action in our day. The idea that the national movement in my time should be merely one to provide further martyrs instead of being directed to a successful termination of our struggle for independence did not appeal to me. Another argument which, of course, was of a more practical nature, was that when men were wanted to take part in the gun-running for the Volunteers, it was only necessary to apply to the IRB.[75]

Thomas Furlong in Kilkenny, already a member of the IRB, experienced MacDermott's organising method:

> About 1912 Seán McDermott came to me with a letter of introduction from Ned Foley, IRB Centre in Wexford. McDermott discussed with me the possibility of restarting the Kilkenny Circle. He asked me to get those I knew to come together and restart the Circle. I knew that Peter de Loughrey was an old I.R.B. man and I sent McDermott to him. Subsequently de Loughrey called a meeting … Meetings which were [from then on] held frequently were concerned chiefly with the spreading of the organisation.[76]

In 1907 the first electoral test of combined IRB and Sinn Féin organisation occurred when Charles Dolan, MP, resigned his North Leitrim parliamentary seat in June in order to fight for it again as a Sinn Féin candidate. Leitrim was MacDermott's home county. The various nationalist political groups, including the Dungannon Clubs, banded together as Sinn Féin to fight the election. MacDermott threw himself into Dolan's campaign, using IRB resources.[77] With Hobson, he produced a local newspaper, the *Leitrim Guardian*, in support of Dolan. Hobson left soon after the start of the campaign: he was attacked mercilessly by local priests as a Protestant and agitator, and he considered that his presence in Leitrim would do more harm than good for Dolan. This left MacDermott as the principal campaign manager, bringing him to national notice. Voters in Leitrim were most interested in the land reform that the IPP was obtaining; talk of abstentionism and republicanism went over their heads. After six months campaigning, Dolan and MacDermott knew that they would not win. When the votes were counted, Francis Meehan, the IPP candidate, won with 3,103 votes to Dolan's 1,157. Nevertheless, it was considered a good result for Sinn Féin, and MacDermott was given the credit.

After the election, MacDermott shared lodgings with Bulmer Hobson and Patrick McCartan in Dublin. All three put their energies principally into the IRB, recognising that Irish voters did not support separatism and that infiltration of nationalist organisations was the best hope of gradually securing greater support. They hoped that Sinn Féin might become an IRB front, but Arthur Griffith policed his party and prevented any takeover.

MacDermott toured the country over the next two years, also visiting Scotland, trying to establish Sinn Féin branches and IRB Circles; with the support of Clarke and Hobson he was swearing in members without following official IRB recruitment procedures. In 1908 Denis McCullough, recognising that MacDermott was not formally approved as a recruiter, arranged for him to be appointed as national organiser by the Supreme Council.[78] In May 1909 he was given the same job by Sinn Féin, providing him with a proper reason to be anywhere. Hobson introduced MacDermott to Tom Clarke early in 1908 – probably soon after the Leitrim election – and by all accounts the two became inseparable, with MacDermott gradually displacing Hobson in Clarke's trust.

The connection to John Daly that the Clarkes and MacDermott shared must also have had a strong effect on all of them. This personal connection and Clarke's control of IRB funds ensured a close working relationship that, in

104   The Irish Republican Brotherhood, 1914–1924

turn, made the secrecy around the rising plans easier to achieve. MacDermott continued to travel around the country recruiting and giving speeches to IRB Circles, thereby also becoming known to the RIC. Clarke, who risked being re-arrested at any time, naturally preferred to stay in the background and depended upon MacDermott. Patrick Pearse was introduced to Clarke by MacDermott, who also proposed him as the speaker at the Robert Emmet commemoration in March 1911, bringing Pearse to the attention of IRB Circles. After the IRB elections that year, MacDermott was co-opted on to the Supreme Council where he soon was elected Secretary. He caught polio in September 1911 and from then on needed to walk with a cane.

MacDermott took the lead in making rising plans and policing their secrecy. Denis McCullough, hearing rumours of a rising just before Easter 1916, went to Dublin to see Tom Clarke and demanded to be told what was going on. As President of the IRB and thus one of the three members of the IRB Executive, he considered that he had every right to know. He found a wall of secrecy and a conflict going on between Hobson and Clarke and MacDermott, with Hobson 'advocating a policy of waiting, "that this was not Ireland's opportunity and that a more favourable time would come later",' while Clarke and MacDermott were determined on an immediate rising.[79]

Clarke was content to advise and support MacDermott, whose energy, dedication, willingness to defer to Clarke, and the trust Clarke placed in him gave him the authority to take the lead.[80] The need to maintain the IRB's record of rebellion was of supreme emotional importance to both men. Seán MacDermott put it simply: 'If this thing [the war] passed off without us making a fight, I don't want to live. And Tom feels the same.'[81] MacDermott (and probably Tom Clarke) kept plans away from McCullough not just to preserve secrecy, but probably because they also thought McCullough might be too friendly with his old colleague, Bulmer Hobson.

The Proclamation of the 1916 Republic was the culmination of the IRB's efforts. It was 'first and foremost, an IRB document, and the great separatist objective of the Fenians has central place,' John A. Murphy has stressed. 'Sovereignty and freedom are emphasised throughout; all else is secondary.'[82] The Supreme Council considered that the IRB had announced its purpose with the Proclamation. It was propaganda, aimed in part at future generations, and was not a constitution or a programme of government. In the event of victory only cursory thought was given to government. Patrick Pearse was considered for the position of president in the event that the Rising was successful, but Clarke, who was President of the 1916 Republic (which was provisional), thought him unsuitable as 'too Christ-like' and instead favoured John Devoy.[83]

CHAPTER 9

Guns and Plans

We used to be forbidden as members of the I.R.B. to fraternise with soldiers of the British garrison. This order was now reversed. We were encouraged to make contacts discreetly with the object of getting information or buying arms or ammunition.[1]

Séamus Daly, 2 March 1950

The fight with Hobson took place during mounting tensions over the probability of war in 1914 and over the Home Rule Bill, which was inexorably proceeding through Parliament to become law that year and was driving infuriated unionists to more extreme activity. In April 1914 the UVF had brought 24,000 rifles purchased in Germany to Larne on the Antrim coast. Eoin MacNeill then led a campaign to get weapons for the Irish Volunteers,[2] establishing on 23 June a secret Volunteer Arms Sub-Committee that reported only to him and not to the Provisional Committee.[3] O'Rahilly and Hobson were on this committee and took the lead in organising a gunrunning in July of (many fewer) German rifles and ammunition to Howth in Dublin and Kilcoole in Wicklow. The IRB had no part in buying these weapons, possibly because Hobson was trying to work only through the Volunteers and wanted to demonstrate that IRB connections were not needed. Patrick Pearse, who had been sworn into the IRB by this point,[4] interestingly wrote to Joseph McGarrity on 19 June that he hoped the IPP might help the Volunteers arm, and if they did then the surrender to Redmond would be worthwhile.[5] Pearse was speaking for himself but showed that Hobson had a point.

With the addition of the new IPP members, the Volunteers' Provisional Committee membership stood at fifty-four. Everyone recognised that this was

Guns and Plans 107

unwieldy. A Standing Committee of fourteen, chaired by MacNeill, was created to act in the full Committee's stead.[6] At its start, Hobson was the only IRB member, but he could no longer be regarded as an IRB representative.[7] Later, Seán MacDermott joined, thus securing IRB access to the inner councils of the Volunteers.[8] In June 1914 MacNeill created a Military Inspection Committee that soon took over Volunteer training. Hobson was the only IRB member of this committee too.[9] It can be inferred that Hobson and MacNeill sought to limit the influence of Clarke and MacDermott within the Volunteers.

While the IPP members of the Provisional Committee did little to change Volunteer administration and appointments, the northern leader of the Party, Joseph Devlin, was on the Standing Committee and was aware of the IRB's efforts to control the organisation. Together with the other IPP members, he welcomed MacNeill's call for arming the Volunteers, but tried to ensure that any weapons that were obtained stayed in the hands of IPP Volunteers.[10] In July 1914 MacDermott, Pearse, Ceannt and Seán Fitzgibbon[11] started working secretly to obtain arms for the 'sound men'.[12] Hobson was excluded. Meanwhile, unknown to the IRB and the Volunteers, Sir Roger Casement in London was successfully canvassing his friends to support the Volunteers with money that bought rifles and ammunition in Germany. He was incensed by the UVF's gunrunning and wanted to help the Irish Volunteers to match it.[13]

Hobson may have been the first in the IRB to learn of Casement's enterprise, and then only because Casement told MacNeill and O'Rahilly.[14] Hobson, with Thomas MacDonagh,[15] surveyed landing sites for Casement's rifles and ammunition. On 23 June Hobson met Casement and Erskine Childers at Buswell's Hotel in central Dublin and proposed Howth harbour as a good site, and this was agreed.[16] Childers, a friend of Casement, whose family home was in Wicklow, had offered to ship the munitions in his yacht. He and Hobson left together to inspect the harbour. Hobson's next step, benefiting from Dublin IRB Circles being organised according to trades, was to have about 200 oak batons made that Volunteers collecting the arms could use if they were attacked by police.[17] Despite his break with Clarke and MacDermott, Hobson's IRB connections were still excellent.

Clarke and MacDermott saw to it that the IRB controlled the arms landings and kept most of the weapons afterwards. Hobson did not object: he saw himself in a struggle with personalities, not with the IRB, and as yet a rising had not been agreed. Cathal Brugha was entrusted with command of the men who would receive the guns at Howth on 26 July.[18] With about twenty

IRB men, he went there early that morning. They placed themselves about the harbour, hired boats and generally tried to look as much like holidaymakers as possible. They were to protect the offloading of weapons from Childers' yacht, the *Asgard*, to about 800 Volunteers and Fianna members who had assembled at the harbour during the morning. The whole operation was completed within 40 minutes;[19] 900 rifles and 25,000 rounds of ammunition were landed. It was later discovered that the ammunition consisted of explosive bullets and the Irish Volunteers' Standing Committee decided that they should not be used because they contravened the rules of war.[20]

On 1 August, six days after the Howth landings, at Kilcoole, about 17 miles south of Dublin, 600 rifles and 20,000 rounds of ammunition arrived in another yacht, *Chotah*, owned and sailed by Sir Thomas Miles, a friend of Childers. The Kilcoole landing was not organised by Hobson, but by Seán Fitzgibbon who, through MacDermott, asked for and was given IRB men to collect the weapons and take them into Dublin. In contrast to Howth, Kilcoole was conducted in secret entirely by members of the IRB directed by Seán MacDermott, whom Fitzgibbon had asked to help.[21] As Thomas Wilson, a Belfast IRB man and member of the Belfast Irish Volunteer Executive Committee, noted: 'The I.R.B. influence in the Volunteers took particular care all along that the arms got into proper and reliable hands.'[22]

In August, with the outbreak of world war, Pearse and some of the IRB members on the Volunteers' Provisional Committee planned a coup d'état for November in Dublin where the IRB was strongest.[23] Tom Clarke, it seems, stopped this plan because he did not think it practical. In the United States, also in August, a Clan committee met the German Ambassador, Graf von Bernstorff, stating that Ireland would rebel and set up an independent government during the war and asking for German help with arms and officers.[24]

On 9 September 1914, probably following the Supreme Council meeting that established the Military Committee, a non-IRB meeting (without Hobson) was held in the Gaelic League library at 25 Rutland Square. Patrick Pearse, Thomas MacDonagh, Éamonn Ceannt and Joseph Plunkett (all of whom were later to be on the IRB Military Committee), Seán T. O'Kelly, John MacBride, Arthur Griffith, Seán McGarry and the trade unionists James Connolly and William O'Brien[25] were present. They discussed the prospect of a rising before the end of the war.[26] Seán T. O'Kelly, who used the library as his office, recalled that Clarke and MacDermott had arranged the meeting and that Clarke presided:

> [I]t was decided that a rising should take place in Ireland, if the German army invaded Ireland; secondly if England attempted to enforce conscription on Ireland; and thirdly if the war were coming to an end and the Rising had not already taken place, we should rise in revolt, declare war on England and when the conference was held to settle the terms of peace, we should claim to be represented as a belligerent nation.[27]

On 10 September the last meeting of the Volunteers' complete Provisional Committee of Redmondite and original members was held. The *Irish Volunteer* journal, which although not officially owned or controlled by the Provisional Committee was used to publish Volunteer appointments and orders, was now deemed editorially too extreme by the IPP members of the Committee and was disassociated.[28]

After John Redmond's Woodenbridge call to support Britain, Clarke and MacDermott had a firm reason to split the Volunteers, revealing who might follow the separatist path even if not in the IRB.[29] The next day, twenty members of the original Volunteer Committee met at 25 Rutland Square and resolved to renounce Redmond; to seize the Volunteer headquarters at 41 Kildare Street on 24 September, and on the same day to issue a counter-enlistment manifesto to weaken the impact of a recruiting meeting due to be held on 25 September in the Mansion House. That meeting was to be addressed by Prime Minster Herbert Asquith and by John Redmond. Simultaneously, Seán MacDermott, Tom Clarke and James Connolly were planning a joint IRB/ICA operation to seize the Mansion House and prevent the meeting. The plan included the use of weapons, if necessary, but at the last moment the operation was called off because soldiers turned out to guard the Mansion House.[30] This failure seems to have motivated Connolly to plan more thoroughly. He began training the ICA for rebellion and argued that since international socialism had failed to prevent the world war, Irish working people's cause was Ireland's cause.[31]

The Volunteers also formally split on 25 September 1914. Eoin MacNeill, on behalf of the original Volunteer Committee (and almost certainly aware of IRB pressure), sent out a press release separating the Volunteers from Redmond:

> Mr Redmond, addressing a body of Irish Volunteers last Sunday, has now announced for the Irish Volunteers a policy and programme

fundamentally at variance with their own published and accepted aims and pledges ... He has declared it to be the duty of the Irish Volunteers to take foreign service under a government which is not Irish. He has made his announcement without consulting the Provisional Committee, the Volunteers themselves or the people of Ireland, to whose service alone they are devoted.[32]

The split crystallised local IRB and Volunteer thinking. Robert Kelly in Newry found that some Volunteers and IRB members were already aware of potential differences between the two organisations, and that IRB Centres in Ulster understood that a rising might be on the cards. Behind this was the knowledge that the IRB and the Volunteers had to be cautious in Ulster:

> However, when Redmond made his Woodenbridge speech we could do nothing except leave the National Volunteers. We had not got much more recruits into the I.R.B. but a number of the men in the Volunteers were thinking that the Irish Volunteers were right ... In August or September 1914 a meeting of the Ulster Council of the I.R.B. was held in Belfast. I was a delegate at the meeting. It was decided that unless Germany could supply at least 100,000 men and 300,000 rifles we would not attempt a rising.[33]

Nevertheless, Clarke and MacDermott immediately began planning to move the Volunteers towards rebellion by strengthening IRB influence. 'Before the split in the Volunteers the I.R.B. did not interfere much in directing the policy of the Volunteers,' said Frank Booth, a Belfast Centre, 'but after the split the I.R.B. more or less took control, as all officers in the Volunteers were approached to join the I.R.B. and most of them did join the organisation.'[34] In October in Dungarvan, Co. Waterford, Patrick O'Mahony was asked to revive the local Irish Volunteer company that had dissolved after the split with the Redmondites: 'In my I.R.B. capacity I was able to make contacts and I acted on the request for revival, with the accepted I.R.B. policy, not so much of controlling but of being a power behind the movement.'[35]

Also in October, Patrick Pearse wrote excitedly to McGarrity that, if provoked, the 'MacNeill Volunteers' were prepared to rebel.[36] A Neutrality League was formed to campaign publicly against recruitment and the war, with Connolly as president and Seán T. as secretary.[37] It was suppressed by the

Guns and Plans

government two months later. In November Piaras Béaslaí and Joseph Plunkett began making Volunteer plans for insurrection in Dublin city and county.[38] Plunkett had joined the IRB probably in September 1914. He had an interest in military strategy and had been in the cadet corps at Stonyhurst,[39] where he gained a rudimentary knowledge of drill and tactics.

On his return to Ireland from New York in November 1914, with money from the Clan, Diarmuid Lynch was brought up to date by Clarke on Hobson, the Volunteers and rising plans.[40] Lynch replaced Seán MacDermott on the IRB Executive from May to September 1915 while MacDermott was in jail for incendiary speechmaking. Lynch suggested that a secret committee be established to work with the IRB Executive to make plans for an insurrection.[41] His proposal became the Military Committee:

> The 'Military Committee' originally comprised Padraic Pearse, Joseph Plunkett and Éamonn Ceannt. They were so appointed in the summer of 1915 on my motion at a meeting of the IRB Executive (Denis McCullough, Tom Clarke and myself). I was then acting Secretary of the 'Executive', as substitute for Sean McDermott who was then in prison. The three appointees (or perhaps only two of them) were present on that occasion, though neither of them was a member of the Supreme Council IRB.[42]

Lynch's date – 'the summer of 1915' – is probably wrong, and it may be that he confused its start with his experience on joining the Executive. The idea of a Military Committee was discussed at the September 1914 Supreme Council meeting, and the next Council meeting in January 1915 established it formally.[43] Béaslaí's and Plunkett's Volunteer plans now became the basis of the IRB's rising plans without the knowledge of MacNeill and Hobson. Richard Connolly met the Military Committee members at a joint meeting with the Supreme Council in January 1915:[44]

> [T]he military committee were sitting apart from us. The arrangement was that they were sitting in the next room which was separated from our room by folding doors, but these doors were pushed back. I was rather surprised when I saw Pearse there. It was the first time I knew he was in the I.R.B. He was sitting in the corner and I heard one of the other two who were with him was Ceannt. Before the discussion started

112 The Irish Republican Brotherhood, 1914–1924

> I was told this was the military committee … The Supreme Council had
> sanctioned the military committee.[45]

The Committee operated separately from the Supreme Council. Alec
McCabe was in prison when the Committee was formed, so Connacht was
not represented. After he was released on 9 November 1915, he asked Seán
MacDermott if he could help in some way:

> They didn't divulge their plans because they couldn't afford to. They were
> bound to be spoken of carelessly or there'd be some other corner where
> they'd get out. But they were to that extent a secret society within a
> society. They had control of the situation … Sean McDermott said to
> me, 'There's no need for you now, because everything is handed over to
> the Military Council.'[46]

By February 1915 Dublin Volunteer Brigades had been allotted positions for
a rising.[47] Also in February rising plans were revealed to IRB Dublin battalion
commandants.[48] Eoin MacNeill was told that the plans were for defensive
mobilisation if the government tried to suppress the Volunteers. He constantly
insisted on the defensive purpose of the Volunteers, and the information that
the Volunteer leadership was given conformed to his demand.[49]

Through Pearse, as Director of Organisation after the October 1914
Volunteer convention, IRB members were placed in senior Volunteer positions
where possible.[50] Since Volunteers elected their officers, a lot depended upon the
local standing of IRB members: Pearse's authority was simply confirmatory for
all but the most senior appointments.[51] An unelected Volunteer Headquarters'
Staff was created on 5 December 1914 by the Executive Committee (successor
to the Provisional Committee after the split with Redmond), giving Pearse the
opportunity to appoint IRB members.

By the end of March 1915, the Headquarters Staff was complete. Pearse
had confirmed the elections of Edward Daly (Clarke's brother-in-law), Éamon
de Valera and Éamonn Ceannt as commandants of Dublin battalions, and of
himself, Thomas MacDonagh (as Director of Training also on Headquarters
Staff), Hobson (Secretary of the Volunteer Executive and Quartermaster
General), Michael O'Rahilly (Director of Arms), and Joseph Plunkett (Director
of Military Operations) as commandants on the Headquarters Staff.[52] Except
for MacNeill (Chief of Staff), and possibly de Valera and O'Rahilly, all were

Guns and Plans

members of the IRB or were about to be. Hobson had a good idea of their general plan. Around this time MacDonagh persuaded de Valera to join the IRB.[53] Michael O'Rahilly, if not already a member, seems to have joined at some point between March 1915 and the Rising.

Also in March 1915 Clarke and MacDermott began to push for a rising in September that year. Lectures on tactics, signalling, scouting and musketry were given to Volunteer companies at the Volunteers' Kildare Street Dublin headquarters[54] and elsewhere in the country.[55] Seán T. O'Kelly was sent to the United States to inform the Clan of progress but did not have a specific date for the Rising. With security in mind, Patrick McCartan may have also been sent separately with the date at the same time as O'Kelly.

Sir Roger Casement travelled to the United States and then Germany representing only himself and not the IRB or Volunteers, seeking German aid for an Irish rebellion and trying to raise an Irish brigade from Irish prisoners of war. Seán McGarry recorded Tom Clarke's concern about Casement:

> Then it became known here that Casement had gone to Germany. Tom proposed that Plunkett should attempt to get there. Plunkett agreed to go, became very ill in Spain and it was a long time before word came from America that he had arrived [communication with Germany went through Clarke and John Devoy to and from the German Embassy in Washington DC]. He found that Casement's idea given to the German Government was that there could be no rising here unless the Germans landed an Army. Plunkett was able to tell them that the possibility of a German invasion was not even considered and that there would certainly be a rising. He asked for arms, was told at first that none could be spared but eventually [they] agreed to forward a cargo of Russian rifles with ammunition.[56]

Geraldine Plunkett reported her brother's experience:

> Joe's first really important task for the I.R.B. was the trip to Germany. He told me that the letters from Casement had been unsatisfactory and that the fears of the Supreme Council about him seemed to be justified ... He saw [the German Chancellor] von Bethmann Hollweg once only. Apparently Joe completely satisfied him, that [in dealing with Joe] he was dealing with a correct representative of Ireland. The Germans had had doubts of Casement's credentials and distrusted his temperament.[57]

114 The Irish Republican Brotherhood, 1914–1924

Plunkett returned to Ireland in June 1915, reporting to Clarke that Casement was pessimistic about his chances of securing a German expeditionary force to help them and had warned against a rising that might depend upon German support.[58] Germany's ally, the Austro-Hungarian Empire, contained several minority nations that would naturally be influenced by a successful Irish rebellion, and this no doubt acted to moderate German support. A failed Irish rebellion would be a propaganda coup for the Central Powers while also sending a message to their own minorities that rebellion would not succeed.

Pearse, in August 1915, was still expecting a September rising, but Plunkett's message and confirmation that the Germans would send weapons in spring 1916 caused it to be postponed, but until when was not settled.[59] Rising plans were kept tightly within the Military Committee. Neither the Supreme Council nor the Executive were informed of plans, as Denis McCullough remembered: 'The fixing of the date and time was left to the Military Council. I presume that this should have been referred to the Supreme Council or at least to its Executive, viz, the Chairman (myself), Secretary (Sean McDermott) and Treasurer (Tom Clarke). It never was so referred.'[60] Also in August 1915, Robert Monteith, a retired bombardier who had efficiently organised Volunteers in Limerick after the split with Redmond, was sent by the Military Committee to Germany to help with Casement's Irish Brigade. In September Diarmuid Lynch went to Kerry to scout with local IRB men a suitable landing site for a German arms shipment. He reported back to Pearse, Clarke and MacDermott that the Kerrymen favoured Fenit pier in Tralee Bay. Also in September, Joseph Plunkett went to the United States to inform the Clan of the changed plans.[61] Plunkett may have been on the Military Committee before he went to Germany, but more likely he joined upon his return in June.[62] The other members of the Committee – MacDermott, Pearse, Plunkett and Ceannt – were also on the Volunteer Executive and assumed that they controlled the Volunteers.[63]

There was no doubt that by Easter 1915, whether IRB or not, Irish Volunteer officers were being prepared for rebellion even if they did not know it. Most officers not already in the IRB, like de Valera, were sworn into it over Easter 1915.[64] The Supreme Council was readying for a rising. Early in May MacDermott travelled to Westport in Wales to inform P.S. O'Hegarty of the plans:

> I saw McDermott in May 1915 in Westport, he told me that the Council ... had decided to launch a rising before the war ended and

had established a Military Committee to plan and organise it. He told me who they were, told me the plan, with the various buildings to be held, and said that the plan was Plunkett's, that when they put him on the Military Committee they found that he had such a plan prepared for some time, and it was adopted without alteration. He said that he had been working on such a plan 'for years' as a hobby. It was to be a Dublin Rising only, a blood sacrifice – in his own words 'We'll hold for a week but it will save Ireland'.[65]

O'Hegarty told MacDermott that he was opposed to the Rising unless conscription was enforced in Ireland, and that nothing should be done to disturb the Volunteers – there should not be another split.[66] To MacDermott and Clarke this must have sounded as if Hobson had gained another follower. Then O'Hegarty reported: 'Some time in the summer of 1915 the regular election of all officers took place, and I was not co-opted. Naturally, they co-opted only people who were in favour of the Rising, and I had definitely asked to be recorded as against it.'[67]

Upon MacDermott's release from prison on 18 September 1915, he and Clarke became ex officio members of the Military Committee.[68] In January 1916, Connolly joined. In April, just before the Rising, Thomas MacDonagh became the seventh and final member of the Committee.[69]

CHAPTER 10

Disorganisation

[I]t is my recollection – that the actual date of the Rising was not definitely fixed. I remember Pearse saying in a vague sort of way, 'Around Easter would be a good time of the year to start a revolution.' Pearse spoke more like as if he was thinking aloud when he said this, rather than making any definite proposal.[1]

Patrick McCartan, 15 December 1952

By the end of January 1916, the Military Committee controlled the Volunteer Executive, the IRB and – through James Connolly – the ICA. 'The only curb on the Military Committee was the Executive,' said Richard Connolly. 'The Supreme Council did not count so much at all in 1914 and 1915. It was the Executive that counted.'[2] When the Supreme Council met on 23 January 1916, Easter Sunday was probably set as the new date for the Rising, using Volunteer 'manoeuvres' directed by Patrick Pearse as a cover. On the Supreme Council, Patrick McCartan remembered:

We must have discussed a revolution in some way at this meeting because I remember saying, in the course of the discussion, 'We don't want any more glorious failures.' ... The probabilities of German success in the war, whether or not they would send us aid and how much were all discussed at this meeting. I know that my attitude at the time was one of caution. I did not want our people to rush out into a revolution unprepared and without practical hope of success.[3]

This was the last meeting of the Supreme Council before the Rising. A 'new'

Disorganisation

IRB and Council would follow.

The major problem the Military Committee faced was keeping its plans secret from the British administration in Ireland, from the RIC and DMP, from all but a handful of IRB members, from Bulmer Hobson, Eoin MacNeill and the Volunteers, from the IPP, from James Connolly and the ICA, from Sir Roger Casement operating alone in Germany, while simultaneously trying to ensure as much support as possible when the rebellion was launched.

From January, as Volunteers were put on notice for manoeuvres at Easter and as IRB members were told that there would be a rising, the Military Committee inevitably found it difficult to maintain secrecy and their plans began to go wrong. Part of the trouble was undoubtedly their assumption that IRB members in the provinces would somehow understand what to do without being given explicit instructions. In Clonmel, for example, Dominic Mackey, the IRB Fianna Éireann leader, received orders to rise in 1916 which gave no details as to what was expected of him.[4] Seán Murphy, a Dublin Centre, was slightly better informed:

> I knew definitely in the month of January 1916, that a rising was to take place … There were four tentative dates arranged for the actual Rising. The first was St Patrick's Day, 1916, on which day a full armed parade of the Dublin Brigade was first held in Dublin. He told me that the arrangements would be in the event of the arms landing from Germany, the Rising would take place on St Patrick's Day, failing which it was to be postponed until Easter Sunday, again failing which it was to be postponed to Whit Sunday. If we had been again disappointed, final and definite arrangements were in hand for the insurrection to take place without fail, with or without German arms, on the August Sunday.[5]

Alec McCabe had been arrested at Sligo railway station on 6 November 1915 with a Gladstone bag containing forty-one gelignite cartridges, twenty detonators and six coils of fuse. His house, searched later that day, gave up one gelignite cartridge, two revolvers and a double-barrelled shotgun. He was charged with possession of explosives. MacDermott sent Éamonn Dore and Liam Tobin[6] to McCabe's home to rescue anything the authorities had not discovered. With more success he sent Dore and a Dublin IRB member, Paddy Daly (later head of Collins' Squad), to McCabe's parish priest to prevent him giving evidence against McCabe, and they also intimidated the Dublin jury,

118 The Irish Republican Brotherhood, 1914–1924

with the result that in February 1916 McCabe was acquitted.[7] IRB effectiveness had grown substantially since 1912.

Hobson was aware that a rising was being organised and undoubtedly warned MacNeill. In February 1916 MacNeill drew up a detailed memorandum arguing the case against a rising[8] and, in spite of assurance from Thomas MacDonagh and Patrick Pearse that no rising was imminent, MacNeill remained suspicious.[9] MacDermott and Clarke were almost certainly aware of Hobson's activity and of MacNeill's suspicions.[10] Probably in order to ensure IRB loyalty when the Rising occurred by cutting out men who might follow Hobson, shortly beforehand MacDermott advised Centres that members who had doubts should resign. Gregory Murphy gave an account of this:

> I was sent by Sean McDermott to Dundalk, Wexford, and Athlone during the month prior to Easter to inform members of the I.R.B. that the position was becoming acute and that any attempt to disarm the Volunteers should be resisted, and to inform them that if any of them wished to leave the Organisation (I.R.B.) it was then the time to resign. Very few as far as I am aware, resigned.[11]

Hobson insisted that MacNeill demand a clear and binding statement of commitment to the Volunteers' defensive policy from the Executive and the Headquarters Staff. On 5 April MacNeill called a meeting of the Staff and ordered that apart from routine orders, none were to be issued without his countersignature. This immediately made it clear to the Military Committee that although all the members of Headquarters Staff with the exception of MacNeill (and in effect Hobson) were members of the IRB, their control of the Volunteers was not as firm as they assumed. Hobson, of course, was a particular problem for them. That same week MacDonagh was made a member of the Military Committee.[12]

The Committee used Cumann na mBan and IRB members in the Volunteers to transmit their decisions to IRB Volunteer officers. James Connolly and Constance Markievicz also had networks of their own that were used.[13] As a result, IRB members in the country suspected (and some like Seán Murphy knew) earlier than others that a rising was in the offing. The experience of Joseph Lawless in Swords, Co. Dublin, and of Michael Brennan in Limerick is indicative. In March 1916 Lawless 'felt the hour was near at hand' when, at an IRB meeting, the appointment of Thomas Ashe to command the Fifth Dublin

Disorganisation 119

Battalion was announced as 'arranged' by the IRB as one of a series of moves preparing for imminent fighting.[14] Michael Brennan was told by his Circle Centre a week beforehand that a rising was planned for Easter Sunday, 'and that the Limerick Commandant, Colivet, had agreed to join the I.R.B. and had just been sworn in and he would give me detailed instructions'.[15]

Certainly, by March, there was widespread awareness that a rebellion was planned. Writing from Chicago to John Redmond on 6 March, Bernard MacGillian, an IPP supporter, warned that:

> a dastardly plot to drench Ireland in blood is being hatched in this country … The intention is to foment a 'rising' in Ireland next summer, which, of course, would be drowned out in blood. Then the conspirators would point to this crushing of the spirit of Irish liberty and say 'we told you not to trust Redmond. He and his Party have betrayed you. Behold the proofs.'

MacGillian's information came from someone who had attended the Irish Race Convention held in New York on 4–5 March, that, he wrote, was designed 'to give this scheme a big boost'.[16]

On Friday 14 April, Philomena Plunkett, Joseph's sister, arrived in John Devoy's office in New York with a request from the Military Committee that munitions the German government had promised should be landed at Fenit pier on Sunday night, 23 April. This proved impossible to arrange because the German arms ship, masquerading as a neutral Norwegian vessel with the name *Aud* (so as to avoid being stopped by the Royal Navy), had sailed without a wireless. The Military Committee assumed that these new instructions had been passed successfully to the *Aud* and that their plans would run exactly according to the precise timetable arranged around the landing date.[17]

However, Hobson's and MacNeill's opposition to a rising remained a serious obstacle. Hobson took advantage of the absence of a speaker at a Cumann na mBan meeting on Palm Sunday, 16 April, to step in and speak out publicly against a rising:

> I made a speech in very guarded language, so as not to excite the suspicions of the authorities, and yet sufficiently definite to be intelligible to the many Volunteers who were in the Hall. I warned them of the extreme danger of being drawn into precipitate action, which could only

120   The Irish Republican Brotherhood, 1914–1924

have the effect of bringing the movement to an end, and I said that no man had a right to risk the fortunes of the country in order to create for himself a niche in history.[18]

Liam Ó Briain was there: 'Hobson took advantage of the thing and made a speech: "Quiet! Quiet! Quiet! If you go to fight now you will last a week. It will be over. You should wait! Wait!" This was before I knew anything. I didn't know what he was talking about. I wished I'd paid more attention to what he was saying.'[19]

The publication of the 'Castle Document' on Wednesday 19 April must be seen in part as a ploy to weaken Hobson's and MacNeill's opposition. The document contained plans for British military occupation of Dublin, for the arrest of prominent nationalists and for the disarming of the Volunteers and the ICA. Its authenticity is still debated. Grace Plunkett, widow of Joseph Plunkett, explained its provenance:

> It did come out from the Castle. That is quite certain. I know who brought it. Donagh McDonagh was married to a girl, named Smith. It was her father who brought it out. Mr Smith was in the Castle ... He got out the information piece by piece. It was not a straight document. He got the bits around, pasted all together, and gave it to Joe.[20]

And while the Irish administration denied its authenticity, if they had not in fact arranged such precautionary measures, they were woefully incompetent.

The document was discussed at meetings of the Volunteer Headquarters Staff and, following the frequently stated policy that they would defend their arms, MacNeill finally issued orders to prepare to resist any attempt to disarm the Volunteers.[21] On Thursday evening, 20 April, Hobson discovered that Pearse had issued orders to the Volunteers for manoeuvres on Easter Sunday. With J.J. O'Connell[22] and Eimar O'Duffy,[23] Hobson went to see MacNeill and told him this news. MacNeill, Hobson and O'Connell immediately went to see Pearse at St Enda's and challenged Pearse's mobilisation authority.[24] The argument with Pearse ended, unresolved, at about 4 a.m. on Good Friday, 21 April.

Also on Good Friday, Seán Tobin, since 1915 the Leinster representative on the Supreme Council, asked Hobson to meet the Leinster Board. When Hobson arrived, four or five men produced guns and told him he was under arrest.[25] Éamonn Ceannt explained to another IRB man who wondered about

Disorganisation

Hobson's situation: 'Hobson has been an obstacle in our path. He is opposed to an insurrection. He is perfectly honest, he is not a traitor, but it would be better if he were as then we could shoot him.'[26] He was kept under guard in north Dublin at the home of Martin Conlon, a Centre, and released on Easter Monday evening when the Rising was underway.[27] He did not take part.

On Holy Thursday and Good Friday, trusted couriers (many of them women) carried messages to IRB Centres throughout the country that a rising was planned for Easter Sunday.[28] Women played an unsung but vital part in the 1914–21 period. They were an integral part of the independence movement, as the Irish Military Service Pensions Collection demonstrates. MacDermott (and later Collins) often employed women as informers, spies, couriers and smugglers, involving them with IRB operations, especially when it came to gunrunning and sending messages. Máire Comerford had no hesitation in stating in her memoirs that, '[E]ven the I.R.B. depended on Cumann na mBan extensively for their safety, night and day, their communications and sometimes for the holding and transport of their arms.'[29] The experience of Margaret Browne, sent by MacDermott to Galway on Holy Thursday with letters for two IRB leaders there, gives some idea of the tenuous nature of informing people of Rising plans, let alone having to change them within 48 hours:

> Sean McDermott came and gave me two despatches, one for Laurence Lardner[30] of Athenry and one for George Nicholls[31] of Galway. When I got to Athenry it was getting dark. I went to the hotel and left my case. I found Lardner's – a public house – at the corner of a street. It was full of people drinking. I walked through into a room at the back of the shop. Laurence was not there, but his brother and mother were. They told me he was in Dublin … The following morning Mrs Tina Power came and she brought me to George Nicholls in his office. When I handed him the message he seemed very disturbed and excited. He asked did I know what was in it. I said no, and he said no more about it.[32]

Denis McCullough on Good Friday was faced with objections to a rising from two nationalist priests at Patrick McCartan's home in Carrickmore, Co. Tyrone.[33] Some priests might be sympathetic to the IRB, but most followed the Church's condemnation of violence and secret societies.[34] To McCullough they maintained that the planned rising was a socialist plot:

They expressed the opinion – particularly the priests and also Burke [a Volunteer organiser] – that the whole thing was engineered and inspired by Connolly; that it was not a Volunteer, but a Socialist Rising; that it had no sanction etc., from McNeill [*sic*] ... I stated specifically that my allegiance was to the I.R.B. first and last; that I was satisfied that the proposed Rising was inspired and would be directed by the I.R.B. through its leaders in the Volunteers, with Connolly and the Irish Citizen Army, an integral part of any fighting force that would turn out; that I was taking my orders from the I.R.B.[35]

Afterwards, a question hung over McCartan: why were priests being consulted? Their involvement suggested that McCartan's IRB loyalty was not absolute and that he feared being complicit in a rising. Denis McCullough, too, was similarly suspected.[36]

Meanwhile, on Good Friday morning, Seán MacDermott, unaware that the *Aud* had no wireless reception, sent five IRB men to Caherciveen to seize the wireless station at Valentia Island to contact the *Aud*, and also to transmit a false story that a German attack on Scotland was underway, thus hopefully distracting naval attention from Kerry and the *Aud*. The idea for this had come from Michael Collins, who had come to Dublin in December 1915 and was working closely with MacDermott in the months before the Rising.[37]

As the IRB men were driven to Valentia in two cars that evening, one car lost its way and the other drove off the end of Ballykissane pier, leaving one survivor. The mission was over.[38] On Saturday afternoon MacDermott heard the news of the tragedy and of the arrest of Sir Roger Casement, who had landed from a German submarine at Banna Strand near Fenit. This was followed later by the news that the *Aud* had been intercepted by Royal Navy destroyers in Tralee Bay; that its captain had scuttled the ship with its cargo at the entrance to Cork Harbour, and that the IRB leader of the Tralee Volunteers, Austin Stack, had also been arrested. Everything that could go wrong had gone wrong. Casement had come to warn the Rising leaders that there would be no German support apart from the *Aud* arms shipment. By the time he landed in Kerry, that shipment was at the bottom of the sea.

Until Saturday morning MacNeill had considered allowing the planned Volunteer mobilisation.[39] However, conferring with Seán Fitzgibbon and Michael O'Rahilly, he concluded that the Castle Document was, in fact, a forgery designed to delude him and that there was no immediate government

Disorganisation 123

intention to suppress the Volunteers. News of the loss of the *Aud* seems finally to have convinced MacNeill on Saturday evening to send orders cancelling the manoeuvres that were to take place the following day and he arranged for these orders to be taken to Volunteers throughout the country and to be published in the next day's *Sunday Independent*. This ensured that any plan for a nationwide rising was ruined.[40]

The experience of Seán Murphy in Dublin was typical of the confusion amongst IRB and Volunteer members as a result of the conflicting orders they had received from Pearse for mobilisation on Sunday and from MacNeill cancelling Pearse's instruction. 'The unfortunate publication of the Proclamation over the signature of Eoin MacNeill who was undoubtedly inspired by Hobson,' Murphy considered, 'called off and upset all the arrangements for the Sunday morning mobilisation.'[41]

The Military Committee met on Sunday morning and decided to continue with a rising, but to postpone it by one day to Easter Monday, 24 April 1916.

CHAPTER 11

Rising

We were mobilised for a parade, and we were walked into a rebellion.[1]

Sam Irwin, 31 October 1972

Until Good Friday, the Military Committee believed the Rising would go ahead on Easter Sunday as planned. An anonymous memoir in Richard Mulcahy's papers gives a convincing account of the Military Committee's appreciation of events. According to its author, MacDermott learned of the loss of the *Aud* and the arrest of Casement at about 11 a.m. on Saturday morning and decided that the planned Rising was no longer possible on Easter Sunday. Pearse and MacDonagh, however, still hoped to change MacNeill's mind about cancelling the manoeuvres planned for Easter Sunday. They argued that the government was bound to move against the Volunteers, triggering Volunteer resistance.

However, even Pearse doubted the practicality of a Sunday rising at this stage. Postponement became the issue. Two days, MacDermott calculated, would elapse before the government took action. He was not worried about the rank and file, but about MacNeill's vacillation. If MacNeill joined in then he reckoned there would be 3,000 Volunteers in the Rising in Dublin alone, and powerful support in the country. With this hope in mind, MacDermott called upon MacNeill at about 2 p.m. on Saturday, only to find he was out. MacNeill had decided to issue his order cancelling the next day's manoeuvres. Apparently, Griffith had already told him of the Kerry failures. MacDermott stated that the problem they faced was that they had concentrated on trying to bring MacNeill and the bulk of the Volunteers into the Rising while now their problem was to prevent Connolly bringing out the ICA if they wavered. Pearse then decided to call a meeting of the Military Committee for 11 p.m.

Rising   125

that evening at MacDermott's lodgings in Hardwick Street, and meanwhile MacDermott would try to convince Connolly not to move alone on Easter Sunday. He managed to persuade Connolly to come to the 11 p.m. meeting. Pearse, MacDermott, Clarke, Ceannt and Connolly were present. MacDonagh arrived later, having tried but failed to find MacNeill, but left again on hearing that MacNeill was at Dr Seán Kelly's house at 53 Rathgar Road.

MacDonagh saw MacNeill at Rathgar Road and insisted that he had been told everything on Holy Thursday and had agreed to the Rising. MacNeill denied this, saying that he had agreed only to manoeuvres to distract attention from the landing of guns in Kerry and that he had not been told a rising was planned for Easter Sunday. MacDonagh said that a rising would take place regardless of MacNeill's views, and MacNeill replied that he would do all in his power short of informing the government to stop it. On this note MacDonagh departed, returning to the Military Committee meeting at Hardwick Street. A printer for the *Sunday Independent* was the next arrival. He came with a copy of MacNeill's order, which MacDermott read out to the Military Committee. Pearse replied, summing up their feelings and their decision: 'We will save the soul of the nation; Eoin MacNeill will preserve the body. The body will later respond when the soul is revived. We are both right. Eoin MacNeill is right and we are right.'[2] The decisions were taken by Pearse, MacDonagh and MacDermott with Connolly, Ceannt and Clarke assenting.

The Military Committee must have realised that there was no longer hope of a co-ordinated countrywide affair, and that the government must be preparing to act against the Volunteers. A serious flaw in the Rising plans must now have been apparent: no allowance had been made for a rising without MacNeill's support. Additionally, postponing a rising for any length of time could very well see James Connolly going it alone with the ICA, perhaps resulting in glorious failure, but unquestionably outflanking the IRB.

Even if everything had gone according to plan, the Rising was bound to fail. There were more RIC men than Volunteers. British Army units were dotted around the country. Unionist feeling in Ulster would have inspired counteraction there. And, as the events of Easter Week showed, the government proved an able suppressor.

Plans are imagination; good plans are great imagination; bad plans imagine certainties. The Rising plans were bad, making fundamental mistakes, especially the assumption of perfect compliance with orders and dispositions. They depended on faith, blind obedience and MacNeill. James Connolly believed,

'The British will never use gunfire in the city of Dublin. Capitalists will not destroy capitalist property.'[3] When fighting starts, General Chance commands. The Military Committee took no account of this. And during Easter Week, rebels took buildings and positions and then waited to be surrounded, cut off and attacked and shelled.[4] To be fair, as P.S. O'Hegarty pointed out, they did not expect to succeed.[5] Their purpose was simply to rebel, to spill blood and to depend upon the British reaction to mobilise national feeling. They did not succeed in this. While the Rising did start a national reappraisal, it was the threat of conscription in 1917 and 1918, not the Rising, that mobilised nationalist Ireland.

The Military Committee did not try to isolate MacNeill and had assumed that they had his support until Saturday evening when they heard that he had sent out his order cancelling the Sunday mobilisation.[6] Seán McGarry later insisted that Clarke believed that MacNeill had agreed to the Rising and described the effect his volte face had on him, Clarke and Michael Collins:

> McDermott called to my office on Wednesday in jubilant mood. He told me that everything was going well, that McNeill [*sic*] had agreed to everything[7]... The worst blow of all was to come. It was *The Independent* of Easter Sunday ... I got the paper and read the order countermanding the mobilisation. I walked home in a daze to find Mick Collins who had been staying with Plunkett and who came after Mass to breakfast in my house. I showed him the paper. He became dumb ... I found Tom Clarke afterwards and for the first time since I knew him he seemed crushed ... He regarded McNeill's action was of the blackest and greatest treachery.[8]

The Military Committee, apart from postponing the Rising to Monday, decided to go along with MacNeill's order and to depend upon IRB control of the Volunteers to overcome the setback. Clarke disagreed with this decision, preferring to stick to the original plan despite MacNeill.[9] But plans had been disrupted; MacNeill had caused great confusion. On Sunday IRB couriers were sent with new orders for a Monday rising, but often these did not reach Volunteer units.[10] On Sunday and Monday many Volunteers did not know what was expected of them. Joseph Barrett, an IRB Centre and Volunteer captain in Clare, recorded his experience, which was shared by many others elsewhere:

Rising

127

> On Easter Saturday, 1916, I got verbal instructions to mobilise on Easter Sunday ... I was satisfied myself that we were mobilising for armed insurrection. We got all the equipment necessary to take the field, trench-coats, boots, ammunition and twenty-four hours' rations. Our orders were to remain at Darragh Cross and await further instructions from Brigade Headquarters. Altogether, about thirty Volunteers assembled at Darragh Cross. With the exception of three, they were all members of the I.R.B. We remained mobilised on Easter Sunday until four o'clock on the Monday morning. As no orders had been received by that time, the men were dismissed and told to go home.[11]

The Military Committee's success in maintaining secrecy had made the appointment of IRB members to senior Volunteer positions useless outside Dublin because, on Sunday, most of them did not receive any explanation of the contradictory orders or instructions of what to do. They had sworn blind obedience to their superiors in the Brotherhood. When they received no instructions, they did not think that they were expected to act on their own. The absence of orders was taken as meaning they should not take initiatives. In the event, they were in the same position as non-IRB men.[12] Peadar McCann in Newry put it plainly: '[We did not receive] any communication from the Supreme Council. We resolved to take no action till we had received instructions from an official source.'[13]

The evidence suggests that the Military Committee accepted that they were unlikely to achieve a countrywide rising and simply went ahead with plans for Dublin where they were most sure of control (but even there confusion reigned).[14] By Easter Sunday, the IRB (presumably the Executive and Military Committee combined) had selected the members of a provisional government of a republic of which Alderman Tom Kelly was to be chairman.[15] However, during the Rising, Éamonn Dore in the GPO noted on Easter Tuesday that the 'government' was chaired by Tom Clarke with MacDermott as Secretary and with Connolly, Joseph Plunkett and the Pearse brothers taking part.[16] Denis McCullough stated that Clarke 'was made President in Liberty Hall on the day of the Rising'.[17]

Whether Patrick Pearse or Tom Clarke was President of the 1916 Republic is, as Charles Townshend has said, a 'murky' question. Pearse was named as 'President of the Provisional Government' on Easter Tuesday in the single issue of *Irish War News* published by the rebels.[18] But President of the Republic and

128   The Irish Republican Brotherhood, 1914–1924

President of the Provisional Government are two distinct offices, confused by the use of president for both. It was a confusion that continued in the Dáil government after 1918. Clarke, as his wife later insisted, was President of the Republic. At home for dinner on Monday 17 April after a Military Committee meeting, she recorded:

> On reaching home we settled down to supper, and during it he told me the great news, that the Rising had been arranged for the following Sunday, that a Proclamation had been drawn up to which he was first signatory. I said, 'That means you will be first President.' 'Yes,' he said, 'that is what it means.' … Pearse was made Commander-in-Chief of Ireland and Connolly Commander of Dublin. No other positions were created: the other signatories were all members of the Provisional Government.[19]

At about midday on Easter Monday 1916, Tom Clarke – not Patrick Pearse (who never claimed the title of President of the Republic) – almost certainly read the Proclamation of an Irish Republic, as Vincent Comerford relates:

> [T]here is the direct evidence of an anonymous journalist published within three weeks of the event, but little noticed since, stating that the proclamation was read by 'a small man in plain clothes' who came from the GPO and stood at Nelson's Pillar. This could not have been Pearse or Connolly, both of whom were in military uniform. On this evidence the reader of the proclamation is more likely to have been Tom Clarke, whose name was first and set apart on the printed list of seven signatories to the document by unanimous insistence of his fellows. Before presenting the proclamation the reader harangued the small crowd of chance onlookers about 'Ireland's wrongs and England's oppression'.[20]

The Proclamation was the first public announcement of the existence of the IRB in the twentieth century. 'I read down till I came to the phrase "Irish Republican Brotherhood",' remembered William Brennan-Whitmore, who served with James Connolly during the Rising. 'I nearly passed out because it was the first I heard of it!'[21] The Volunteers and ICA (with about thirty members of the AOH and about forty members of Cumann na mBan who had elected to join in) now formed a new army: the Army of the Irish Republic, the IRA. James Connolly on Palm Sunday, eight days before the Rising, had told the ICA that they were now soldiers in the IRA.[22] As a result of the IRB's recruiting drive within the Volunteers, most officers in this army were members of the Brotherhood.[23]

Collins was with a group of London Irish Volunteers and IRB men. Many of these men (though not Collins) stayed in the grounds of Count Plunkett's Kimmage home, Larkfield Manor, resulting in the London Irish being called the Kimmage Garrison.[24] Joseph Gleeson made the preparations for their stay with the Plunketts on behalf of the IRB: 'I think in December [1915] I was across in Dublin and made arrangements for a number of Volunteers from England and Scotland to go to Kimmage. I saw Tom Clarke and Sean McDermott and we arranged to take over the Old Mills at Kimmage.'[25] The move from Britain to Dublin was orchestrated by the IRB 'at Christmas, 1915, in fact, when all members of the I.R.B. were advised through the circles to get out'.[26] These IRB London members took part as a separate unit in the Rising.

The Proclamation appealed to the Irish diaspora, especially in the United States, and implied that Germany and Austria-Hungary were the rebels' allies, guaranteeing subsequent charges of treason and treachery:

> Having organised and trained her manhood through her secret revolutionary organisation, the Irish Republican Brotherhood, and through her open military organisations, the Irish Volunteers and the Irish Citizen Army, having patiently perfected her discipline, having resolutely waited for the right moment to reveal itself, she now seizes that moment, and supported by her exiled children in America and by gallant allies in Europe, but relying in the first on her own strength, she strikes in full confidence of victory.

The IRB's rebellion contained many 'firsts', not least its direct and radical appeal to women. 'Revolutionary republicanism,' as Peter Hart observed, 'is probably the most female-dependent major movement in modern Irish history.'[27]

Women were an integral part of the independence movement, as the Irish Military Service Pensions Collection demonstrates. In 1916 Helena Molony with nine other women fought alongside ICA men at City Hall. Margaret Skinnider fought in the GPO as a sniper and was wounded. Dr Kathleen Lynn (a Protestant) acted as the GPO's medical officer. Nurse Elizabeth O'Farrell tended the wounded in the GPO and took Pearse's offer of surrender to the

130   The Irish Republican Brotherhood, 1914–1924

British authorities, standing beside him as he surrendered. About 180 women took part in the Rising on the rebel side in some way; 79 were arrested and imprisoned.[28] Women in the Voluntary Aid Detachment, sponsored by the Irish administration, nursed British military casualties. Constance Markievicz, Cumann na mBan's leader after 1916, was the first woman elected to the Westminster Parliament (December 1918) and the first in Europe to hold a Cabinet post (Minister for Labour in the 1919–21 Dáil government). Women held important executive positions in Sinn Féin: Áine Ceannt (widow of Éamonn, executed after the Rising) was the party's director of communications, and Hanna Sheehy Skeffington (widow of Francis, murdered by a British officer during the Rising) was director of organisation. Kathleen Lynn was a vice-president. In 1921, when the second Dáil Éireann was formed, five more women were elected to it.[29]

The Republic could have given way to another form of government: Pearse, Plunkett, MacDonagh and Tom Clarke were not doctrinaire republicans, but rather regarded republicanism as the simple way of stating their belief in the complete separation of Ireland from Britain.[30]

When Patrick Pearse surrendered on 29 April he did so as 'Commander-in-Chief of the Army of the Irish Republic'.[31] This republic had been created and proclaimed by the Military Committee of the IRB Supreme Council and had been furnished with a president, a government, an army and in the broadest sense constitutional powers of its own.

For the IRB the important matter was that their republic had at last been established physically in Ireland; their government had been appointed, and their army defended it, however unsuccessfully. After the Rising a reformed IRB set about mobilising to continue fighting for their 'established' Republic. This was to be a vital strand in the complexity of the War of Independence from 1918 onwards.

The Rising had by no means been inevitable. Eoin MacNeill, in his February 1916 memorandum arguing against a rising, emphasised that pre-revolutionary conditions did not exist.[32] The families of the 100,000 or so Catholic Irishmen who had enlisted by 1916 in the British Army and the Royal Navy benefited financially from allowances. RIC reports throughout Ireland indicated that peace and prosperity, not widespread discontent, were the order of the day.[33] Ireland was enjoying a period of prosperity, particularly in farming and industry; exports were increasing, and there was a reasonably wide diffusion of wealth. Chief Secretary for Ireland Augustine Birrell and Under Secretary

Sir Matthew Nathan had a relaxed attitude to the marching and posturing of Connolly's ICA and of the Volunteers in large part because Ireland was on course for Home Rule.[34]

The Irish administration did not see itself as suppressing Irish nationalism; rather its view was that its job was to enable Home Rule to be established after the war.

CHAPTER 12

Post Mortem

The great majority of the Volunteers who fought in Easter Week belonged to the IRB; between 600 and 700 of the 800 or so that were in it. 800 in the Rising in Dublin in 1916, 600 or 700 of these would be IRB men.[1]

Liam Ó Briain, 7 December 1971

The Rising had been unpopular in Ireland and had presented the government with a chance to discredit extreme nationalists. More civilians had been killed or wounded during the Rising than there were military or insurgent casualties.

On 11 May, in the House of Commons, John Dillon delivered his famous speech against General Sir John Maxwell's executions of the Rising's leaders, pointing out that the rebels were rejected by the vast majority of Irish people and pleading that Asquith should recognise that:

> in this rebellion, for the first time in the history of Ireland, at least nine out of every ten of the population were on the side of the Government. Is that nothing? It is the first rebellion that ever took place in Ireland where you had a majority on your side. It is the fruit of our life work.[2]

On 12 May Asquith visited Dublin for a week and tried to stop the executions. Maxwell, however, had complete power under martial law. Evelyn Wylie was the Crown prosecuting officer at the trials of the condemned men. In 1941 he gave his account of the confrontation between Asquith and Maxwell to David Gray, the United States Ambassador to Ireland, who recorded it:

> A number had been convicted and executed, when Sir John Maxwell

Post Mortem 133

showed me a telegram he had just received from Asquith the Prime Minister. This instructed him to stop the executions as they were having a very bad political effect in England and might turn the forthcoming elections against the government.

Maxwell asked: 'Who is next on the list?'

Wylie answered: 'Connolly.'

Maxwell replied: 'We can't let him off; who is next?'

Wylie told him: 'De Valera', stumbling over a name as he later recalled.

Maxwell inquired: 'Is he someone important?'

Wylie made the immortal reply: 'No. He is a school-master who was taken at Boland's Mill.'

To which Maxwell's answer was: 'All right, we will go ahead with Connolly and stop with this fellow.'[3]

Of the ninety-three men and one woman (Constance Markievicz) sentenced to death, seventy-eight were not executed: de Valera because he was deemed unimportant and Asquith had intervened.[4]

The Rising was immediately termed contemptuously 'The Sinn Féin Rebellion' by the press. Nothing was further from the truth. 'Sinn Féin had as much to do with the 1916 rebellion as you had,' Seán MacEoin said to me in 1972, 'and that's nothing!'[5]

Sinn Féin under Griffith was non-violent, pro-Home Rule, monarchist and opposed to rebellion. The party had been developed by Griffith as a movement to add weight to the IPP's demand for Home Rule, and not as a republican political party. Bulmer Hobson and his IRB colleagues P.S. O'Hegarty, Séamus Deakin and Seán T. O'Kelly had tried to push Sinn Féin to more extreme policies but had not succeeded.[6] After 1911, Sinn Féin was failing. In 1916 it still had its paper, *Nationality*, but only one branch, the central branch in Dublin, having declined from 128 branches seven years earlier.[7] Seán T. O'Kelly, the party's joint secretary, estimated that it had perhaps 100 members in Dublin.[8] Its post-1916 dominance was due to it being identified with the rebels. Kathleen Clarke saw the Party's connection to the Rising as an IPP plot:

I suspected that the Irish Parliamentary Party were responsible for calling the Rising a Sinn Féin Rising, since the name Sinn Féin was to some extent associated with the idea of failure in the minds of the people. They were out to try and prove to the people the foolishness and uselessness of

134 The Irish Republican Brotherhood, 1914–1924

the Rising, especially when Home Rule had been promised for the end of the First World War.[9]

Tom Clarke had not been entirely unrealistic about Rising expectations: he envisaged defeat to be followed by another 'new' IRB and Supreme Council. He ensured that his wife had the money and the contacts for this. Five months after the Rising and the executions of her husband and MacDermott, Kathleen Clarke was in hospital having suffered a stillbirth. She gave an account of a dream she had that indicated the bond between both the Clarkes and MacDermott:

> I saw Tom's face and then Sean MacDermott's. Sean said, 'She must go back, Tom, she must.' Tom said, 'God, Sean, we can't send her back, it is too cruel', and Sean said, 'You know, Tom, she must go back. She has to do the work we left her to do.' … I felt myself being slowly but surely pushed down through the clouds … But now I knew what I had to do.[10]

This was a telling experience. The work she had to do was the rebuilding of the IRB. The history of the IRB provided models for each generation. The Invincibles of the 1880s were a model for the 1918–21 assassination Squad; Kathleen Clarke's post-Rising role paralleled that of the 1865 Ladies' Committee but was also more significant.

She had been entrusted by her husband with a list of Centres and the funds of the IRB, amounting to about £1,000. She was in effect the senior member of the society.[11] The three members of the Supreme Council for Scotland and England North and South had been told by Clarke and MacDermott to get in touch with Kathleen in the event that they survived a rising, as Joseph Gleeson, the North of England member, recounted:

> At the January meeting of the Supreme Council in 1915, there was discussion about the insurrection, that it could happen without us being there. Tom Clarke and Sean McDermott called Dick Connolly, Charlie Carrigan and myself after the meeting and told us that if it did happen and we were not in it that we were to get in communication with Mrs Clarke to keep up the threads of the organisation.[12]

Tom Clarke and Seán MacDermott had informed John Devoy immediately before the Rising that Kathleen Clarke had their trust, money and knowledge,

Post Mortem   135

and that she would act as the contact for post-Rising activity. MacDermott had proposed and the Military Committee had agreed that she should be informed of their decisions in case they were killed or captured.[13]

When Clarke's wife visited him in his cell at Kilmainham Gaol awaiting execution in 1916, he told her to use the IRB money and the Cumann na mBan, of which she was president, to care for the families of those who had taken part in the Rising.[14] Clarke's view was simple, and he expressed it to others imprisoned with him. Gerald Doyle was one:

> 'This is not the end of our fight for Irish Freedom; it is only the beginning and I believe from this last week's fighting that men will come forward to carry on from where we left off. Some of you will live to see Ireland respond to the call.' It was only later that I realised that Tom Clarke, although he knew that he would be facing the firing squad within the next six hours, believed in his heart and soul, that he and his comrades had defeated the British Empire, and that Ireland would win her freedom.[15]

Clarke saw that one way to make a renewed campaign for independence possible was to maintain the loyalty of the families of the dead and imprisoned by taking care of them financially.

Practicality alone indicated this course, but the government of the republic proclaimed in 1916 was, through the Clarkes, meeting its moral responsibility to those who had fought for it. Devoy sent Kathleen Clarke £1,000 via a priest, Fr McGuinness, visiting from America, bringing her IRB funds to £2,000.[16]

Spontaneous reorganisation of the IRB began immediately, undertaken around the country usually by local Centres, concentrating on maintaining existing Circles rather than recruiting new members. Three weeks after the Rising, Liam Clarke, who had been wounded in the face by a grenade on Easter Monday and had escaped arrest while in hospital, travelled to Limerick to see Kathleen Clarke. He proposed to start reorganising the IRB and the Irish Volunteers with the message that there would be another rising.[17] She provided him with expenses of £1-10-0 (£1.50) per week from the funds left in her care. Seán Keogh in Meath independently began IRB and Volunteer reorganisation, benefiting from an energetic Circle unfazed by the Rising's defeat:

> From the moment I joined the IRB in July 1916, I set about organising a company of Volunteers in my own area. I confided in five men at first

and, by the end of the year, had 25 men enrolled in the company. We started off drilling in the fields by night, using shotguns and wooden rifles. By March of 1917, our strength had reached 40.[18]

Volunteer reorganisation was noted by General Maxwell, but IRB activity was undetected, probably because there was not much in the months after the Rising. 'As far as can be ascertained,' Maxell reported, 'no secret meetings are being held but there are some signs of revival.'[19]

Secret meetings were being held. Seán Ó Murthuile and Diarmuid O'Hegarty had set about reorganising the IRB and the Volunteers that summer. O'Hegarty had been released on 18 May, apparently mistaken for another 'Hegarty' who had not been involved in the Rising.[20] Ó Murthuile was also released early. Both were long standing IRB men and saw to it that the Brotherhood was the driving force in rebuilding the Volunteers. Their message was that of Tom Clarke: the Rising was merely the first strike; there would be another. They contacted the leading members of the IRB in Dublin who had escaped imprisonment and in August 1916, just over three months after the Rising, senior Centres led by Séamus O'Doherty[21] gave the IRB a new start in Dublin at the Minerva Hotel, Rutland Square, using the Gaelic League annual convention as a cover. Most of those present had escaped arrest after the Rising.[22] They formed an unelected provisional Supreme Council with twelve members allotting themselves Districts and offices and Séamus O'Doherty as President. This Council met regularly throughout the autumn.[23]

One of the first actions of the provisional Council was to ask John Devoy for funds. He sent money and a messenger with news that Germany was prepared to support another rising with weapons but would not send troops. Ó Murthuile and O'Hegarty did not trust the message or the messenger and rejected the offer. In any case, they said, without troops there was no point.[24] Fresh membership and organising campaigns were planned. Ó Murthuile was appointed Secretary and kept this position until 1924.[25] Most of the members of the provisional Council were also members of the provisional Volunteer Executive, which they also established that autumn and which met monthly in Dublin, seeking to maintain the continuity of both organisations.[26]

The provisional Council concentrated on rebuilding the IRB. Val Jackson, who had been hospitalised before and during the Rising, was approached:

Towards the end of 1916, I received a visit from Sean Murphy and another Centre whom I cannot now remember. They told me that it had been decided to get the Circles going again. I said I felt very diffident about doing anything about this on account of being invalided for so long and of having taken no part in the Rising, but they said I need not have any doubt on that account as my case had been investigated and I had been exonerated from any blame.[27]

Joseph O'Rourke had been released from internment in September. He met Cathal Kickham:

He recognised me immediately and asked me if I knew how my Circle had gone through the Rising, and if any one of them had been killed. I told him we had had very heavy casualties; quite a number of the killed were of our Circle and about five or six were doing sentences of life imprisonment. I asked him, 'What do we do now?' He said, 'See if you can get in touch with any of the lads who have come back and if you find any number of them, get in touch with me.' I looked around and picked up about twenty which Kickham said would do for a quorum … The first sign of life was a meeting of the Wolfe Tone Memorial Association.[28]

The vitality of the IRB was demonstrated by these mid-level members taking the initiative of reorganisation. Joe O'Doherty, released from Frongoch in August, while not rejoining the IRB was conscious at the time 'that they held that they had the continuity of the Republican Government and of the Provisional Government of 1916, and they were exercising whatever influence they had to secure the dominance of that group in the Volunteers, in Sinn Féin and in everything'.[29]

This 1916–17 Council was seen as illegitimate by Joseph Gleeson, who had been elected as North of England representative in 1915 and came back to Dublin in June 1917 as one of the last remaining prisoners released that month. He considered that the provisional Council had ignored the imprisoned members who had been properly elected and co-opted in 1915: 'At the first meeting of our new Supreme Council in 1917 after the Rising there was a crowd of usurpers present, amongst others, Séamus O'Doherty, Liam Clarke, Pat McCartan, Gregory Murphy, Tom Breen from Sligo. Alec McCabe was on the "run".'[30]

138   The Irish Republican Brotherhood, 1914–1924

In May 1917 the provisional Council, with the participation of Count Plunkett, entrusted Patrick McCartan with a message to the new Russian Republic requesting recognition as a sister state. McCartan travelled to London and signed an appeal to the Russian government on behalf of the 'Provisional Government of the Irish Republic' that he gave to a Russian agent for onward transmission. He then went to Liverpool in an unsuccessful effort to find passage on a ship going to Russia. In June he joined the remaining prisoners who had been released on a mail ship on their way back to Dublin, using the opportunity to gain their support for an appeal for Irish independence to President Wilson:

> I asked for Diarmuid Lynch and Tom Ashe, whom I knew best amongst them, and I told them about my proposals. They suggested consulting de Valera on this, as he had been the prisoners' Commandant. De Valera came into the cabin where we were on the ship, and after some discussion he brought in Eoin McNeill [sic]. They all agreed with the proposition. Prof. McNeill then and there sat down to write out the draft statement on the way to Dublin ... The draft of the document, as it was written by McNeill, was taken by me to Séamus O'Doherty [and we went to see de Valera]. I was going to tell him about the other document which I had signed on behalf of the Provisional Government of the Republic, but Séamus advised me against this. He said, 'You have authority from the Supreme Council to sign and there's no use raking up difficulties, so you had better say nothing.'[31]

IRB distrust of non-IRB initiatives remained. According to Ó Murthuile 'without reporting to the I.R.B.'[32] (this seems unlikely since Séamus O'Doherty was party to the project), McCartan took the appeal to New York, consulted John Devoy, and then delivered it to the White House.

When Diarmuid Lynch was released in June 1917 he joined the provisional Council briefly as Treasurer. Kathleen Clarke gave him all the money still in her care with full accounting, thus completing the first post-1916 IRB reorganisation.[33] Séamus O'Doherty stayed in touch with John Devoy in New York, as his wife attested: 'Immediately after the Rising my husband had started organising the I.R.B. and he became the acting head of the Supreme Council of the Provisional Government of the Republic which met at our house. All communications from John Devoy came to him.'[34] Diarmuid Lynch noted that

Post Mortem

O'Doherty's effort was a new beginning of the IRB: 'I was not then a member of the new Supreme Council which had been formed since Easter Week but Séamus O'Doherty was and, as he knew I had been a member of the Supreme Council, he discussed matters freely with me, asking my advice on occasion as to how things were done by the older Council.'[35]

It was clear that the 'old' IRB had culminated with the Rising. Lynch and others on the pre-1916 Supreme Council did not automatically continue as Council members. A new IRB followed, concentrating on its own organisation and that of the Volunteers. Liam Gaynor in Belfast found the IRB at the heart of Volunteer reorganisation: 'Those who had escaped the British internment camps met a few times to piece together again the fabric of the Volunteer organisation. This was quickly done through the medium of the small, compact inner organisation of the IRB which contained almost all of the Volunteer section leaders and officers who had not been arrested.'[36]

Manus O'Boyle, in the Belfast IRB, remembered: 'During this time, although the Volunteers were smashed, the I.R.B. carried on their organisation.'[37] Patrick Colgan, a Co. Kildare Centre, at a meeting of the Leinster Board in June reported that 'the question of organising the Volunteers was discussed'.[38] The IRB was central to the continuing existence of the Volunteers/IRA.

The continuing existence of the IRB was, however, contested. Cathal Brugha, who, like Liam Clarke, had escaped internment, was its principal opponent. Wounds to his legs were so severe that he was hospitalised beyond the term of the warrant for his arrest. He had twenty-five wounds in all but had refused help and prepared to die defending a barricade in 1916, singing the Fenian anthem 'God Save Ireland'. A legend was born. Brugha very quickly was seen as a hero and was looked up to as such. As the senior officer not interned after the Rising, he was also accorded commanding status. When he was released from hospital in August 1916,[39] he refused to rejoin the IRB because, he said, he had seen men fight bravely during the Rising who were not members of the IRB while there had been several members of the IRB who had not, in fact, taken part at all.[40] He was not alone in this view. Michael Staines, Dublin Brigade Quartermaster 1913–16, fully agreed: 'While in Frongoch I was not approached about joining in any re-organisation of the I.R.B., possibly because I had openly expressed my views about the failure of a number of prominent members of that organisation to take part in the Rising.'[41] Seán Tobin, Patrick McCartan, Denis McCullough – all three in Ireland and on the Supreme Council – had not taken part.

140 The Irish Republican Brotherhood, 1914–1924

Initially, Brugha was not strident, accepting IRB help in reorganising the Volunteers. However, by June 1917 his opposition had hardened. George Lyons observed that some months later: 'Cathal Brugha, however, was of [the] opinion that Michael Collins ruled the Supreme Council already. He refused to return to the I.R.B. as he stated that the I.R.B. had not fulfilled its purpose and its men had not turned out at Easter Week.'[42]

Also, it should be said that returning might well have placed him as junior to Collins in the IRB.

Séamus O'Doherty, the leading member of the reconstituted IRB, had been in charge of the arrest and seclusion of Hobson and does not seem to have been blamed for not taking part in the fighting, but McCartan – who worked closely with O'Doherty in 1917 – was blamed. He had mobilised Volunteers in the North but, he said, he had been unaware of the decision to postpone the Rising and had sent them home when nothing happened on Easter Sunday; MacNeill's cancelling order had added to the confusion. Lack of clear information on the following days was the reason he gave for taking no action during Easter Week.[43] Together with McCullough's, Hobson's and Tobin's absence during the Easter fighting, this made the IRB's surviving leaders seem hypocritical and cowardly to Brugha and many others.

Brugha was not swayed by evidence that IRB members had comprised the great majority of the 1916 rebels.[44] He wanted the Volunteers/IRA to be the only separatist organisation. 'Divided counsels had caused the failure of the Rising,' he maintained, 'therefore there would be no more divided counsels.'[45] Batt O'Connor spoke to Brugha about the IRB: 'Cathal ... gave me his opinion that the IRB was "a spent force". I already knew him well enough not to argue with him. Once he made up his mind he never changed it. He was unbending and, once he decided that he was right, he would listen to no one who held an opposite view to his own.'[46] A more robust conversation in late 1916 was reported by John Matthews: 'I have a clear recollection of his telling me that he had left the I.R.B. for good and all, as he could see no use for it. When I asked him his reasons, he replied: "All that the I.R.B. in Dublin wanted was to pull their caps over their eyes, put up the collars of their coats and be shadowed by detectives".'[47]

Kathleen Clarke met Brugha in autumn 1916 and told him of her efforts. Brugha, who had organised for the IRB before the Rising, who had been trusted by the Rising leaders, was regarded as the natural leader of the separatists. But Brugha's opposition to the IRB and his failure to convince IRB men to allow the

Post Mortem

organisation to fade out and instead to concentrate all resources on building a unified movement based on the Volunteers meant that the issue of dual control within the Volunteers/IRA continued. Kathleen Clarke argued that Brugha's opposition to the IRB would only help create the very duality he feared:

> I told him that when the I.R.B. had started to plan for the Rising, it was decided that members should join every Nationalist organisation, such as the Gaelic League, and secure leading positions in them with the object of spreading the revolutionary idea and directing the people's minds towards the fight for freedom. As a result of this deliberate policy, decisions of the Supreme Council of the I.R.B. were carried into effect in other organisations, so that there were no divided counsels or conflicts. I said he would be undoing much that the Rising had done to bring the various groups together, and to break down any unfriendly spirit that might have existed. If he wanted the I.R.B. to die, let it die a natural death ... I failed to make an impression on him. About 9pm, he got up and banged the table, saying, 'I have decided, the I.R.B. must go!'[48]

Was Brugha correct that the IRB at large had not taken its proper part in the Rising? While it is difficult to draw detailed conclusions about the IRB background of the 1916 rebels,[49] nevertheless some indication of the social positions of those involved is available which can be tallied with the composition of the IRB (see Appendix XIII).

Generally, if we accept that the 1,333 men and women arrested after the Rising, whose occupations are known, are a fair representation of all those who actually took part, then some broad observations can be advanced. In the first place, tradesmen, who figured prominently in the membership of the IRB in Dublin, played a large part in the Rising. Secondly, farmers and tradesmen in the countryside, who also figured largely in the IRB's membership, also played a prominent part. Together with the distribution of occupations classified by the 1911 census, these observations indicate that the same sort of people who were IRB members took a major part in the Rising. 'It was mostly IRB men who held the Rising,' Mick Fleming, an IRB Volunteer in Kerry, observed.[50]

Brugha was wrong.

The 1917 reorganisers understood that if the IRB were again to recruit successfully, let alone command respect, the reasons for members not taking part in the Rising had to be investigated. The Volunteers had not come out countrywide, and especially not in Cork and Kerry where the IRB had been strong. In January 1917 Diarmuid Lynch was sent by the provisional Supreme Council to Cork to investigate the failure of the IRB Volunteers there to join the Rising. Lynch had been happy to remain in the IRB.[51] Tom Hales had pressed for an investigation:

> Early in 1917 there was some kind of enquiry into the action of the Brigade Officers at Easter, 1916. It was held in the Grinán in Queen Street, Cork, and there was a Gaelic League Dance going on while it was being held. I do not remember who conducted the enquiry, but Tom Hales made charges against the Brigade Officers, amounting to an imputation that they refused to fight. There were Officers from various parts of the County present, but, as far as I remember, Tom got no support.[52]

Hales amplified his accusation:

> My accusation against the Brigade officers at the time was that we had been left in a fog, that arms had been lost unnecessarily and that the loss of arms all over the South was due to the action of Cork ... Tomás MacCurtain said to me later, 'If I live I will redeem 1916.' The enquiry was carried out by Diarmuid Lynch and Dick Mulcahy.[53]

MacNeill's order cancelling the Easter Sunday 1916 manoeuvres, word of Casement's landing and capture, the *Aud* fiasco, Church opposition, and the failure of the Military Committee to inform most IRB members outside Dublin of changed plans were established as the cause of Cork's non-participation in the Rising, exonerating the Cork members. Circles were informed of Lynch's findings.[54]

There is no record of an investigation finding any IRB members at fault in 1916, and it certainly served the post-1916 IRB not to rake up the past as it prepared for renewed rebellion. In Cork's case, however, even Brugha considered that 'No blame attaches to the Brigade officers.'[55]

CHAPTER 13

Reorganisation

When we had all the places in which Volunteer Companies and I.R.B. Circles existed before 1916 reorganised, we tackled areas in which there was no previous organisation.[1]

Jack Shields, 9 March 1954

In September 1916, four months after the Rising, as the Volunteers/IRA began to reassemble, Liam Clarke, Seán Ó Murthuile, Diarmuid O'Hegarty and Séamus O'Doherty told Brugha of their IRB efforts, offering to help reorganise the Volunteers. Brugha welcomed their help, probably assuming that the Volunteers/IRA would consume their energies at the expense of their IRB efforts: his opposition to the Brotherhood only became strident during 1917 when IRB and Collins' influence in the Volunteers/IRA and Sinn Féin became obvious.[2]

In November 1916 Brugha presided at a Volunteer/IRA convention in Dublin at Flemings Hotel, Gardiner Row, organised by Ó Murthuile and O'Hegarty.[3] Brugha was on crutches. About fifty delegates attended. Until this point Eoin MacNeill had been Chief of Staff and Bulmer Hobson the secretary. MacNeill was in prison and Hobson had withdrawn from involvement. The convention was not representative, consisting mainly of the IRB men who had been working as Volunteers/IRA since the summer. Brugha was elected Chief of Staff to replace MacNeill, and a new Executive was also elected.[4] The reconstituted Volunteers/IRA now began to take formal shape with the IRB playing a crucial part.[5]

The principal activity of the IRB in 1917–18 was to form, officer and drill Volunteer/IRA units, often using GAA clubs as cover.[6] Dublin Volunteer/IRA

144   The Irish Republican Brotherhood, 1914–1924

officers who were members of the IRB began to co-ordinate their activities and plans and kept officers in the country who did not come to Dublin up to date – usually about organising Volunteer/IRA marches and parades.[7]

Outside Dublin, Volunteer/IRA reorganisation was based upon IRB members and whatever Circles were functioning. In August 1916, for example, most of the Tipperary IRB leaders were released from internment. They returned home and promptly began organising the IRB and the Volunteers/IRA in the county. Frank Drohan, the Clonmel Circle Centre, became O/C of the local battalion; in Tipperary town, also in August 1916, Seán Treacy[8] started an IRB-based revival of the Volunteers/IRA which enabled him to stage the first public post-Rising Volunteer/IRA parade there in August 1917 – to mark a visit by Éamon de Valera.[9] At a Circle meeting he appointed three IRB colleagues to carry on with Volunteer/IRA organisation should he be arrested.[10]

In Ulster, typically of the 1917 reorganisation, emphasis was placed on controlling the Volunteers/IRA. Jack Shields, the Tyrone County Centre from 1917, noted this: 'Another matter that received very close attention at meetings of the Ulster Council of the IRB was the question of controlling the Volunteer organisation. In those early days the IRB believed that members of their organisation should occupy all the important positions as officers in the Volunteer organisation.'[11] John McAnerney in Armagh was himself evidence of IRB influence in the reorganisation: 'At the time I joined the I.R.B. [in 1917] I would not be taken into the Irish Volunteers as I was considered both too young and of rather small stature. Shortly after I joined the I.R.B. I was admitted into the Irish Volunteers without further question.'[12] In Tyrone the IRB took over Volunteer/IRA organisation as Jack Shields recounted: 'it was decided that the I.R.B. be instructed to take over the organising of Volunteer Companies in all their local circle areas'.[13]

In Belfast Séamus Dobbyn, an energetic IRB Volunteer/IRA member, found a very depressing situation:

> In the month of May 1917, I was sent to Dublin to meet three members of the Supreme Council of the I.R.B., Diarmuid Lynch, Mick Collins and Sean McGarry. I was asked by them to go on a six months tour of inspection of the nine Ulster Counties, to find out the exact position of the I.R.B. in those Counties ... The position generally throughout Ulster was that they were doing nothing. A number of them thought themselves superior to the I.R.A. and were not even supporting the

Reorganisation

I.R.A. Some of the Centres had not met for years, and those who had met simply met to discuss current affairs. It was due to this state of affairs that I recommended the scrapping of the organisation. I was sent for about a month later, and informed that I had been co-opted a member of the Supreme Council and was given the duty of re-organising the I.R.B. in Ulster. That would be about the end of 1917 ... I carried on that organisation for about a year before being instructed to act as Inspector of the I.R.A.[14]

Dobbyn's efforts apparently transformed the reorganisation effort. Jack Shields recalled that IRB efforts were so successful that they resulted in a request to stop recruitment:

About the year 1918 I remember getting instructions through I.R.B. circles from Dublin not to form any more Companies of the Volunteers. The reason given was that Headquarters at this time were getting so many applications for the formation of new Companies that it would be impossible for them to give any attention to the personnel or the control of those new Companies.[15]

However, there was an undoubted falling off in the IRB. Diarmuid Lynch noted the departure of Brugha and de Valera from the IRB and that even members who had taken part in the Rising and remained in the IRB did not have the same respect for it: 'Others who had participated in the Insurrection felt that while remaining in the IRB they should no longer be subject to the old discipline.'[16] It must have occurred to many IRB members that the 'old discipline' – waiting for orders and not taking local initiative – had prevented a more general rebellion and that more devolved decision-making would result in more action. After the Rising, many IRB members acted locally without instructions from the Supreme Council or from the Volunteers. When William Redmond, John Redmond's son, won his father's seat for the IPP in the 1918 Waterford by-election, Seán MacEoin regarded himself as an officer in the IRB Republic's army. He took it on himself to mobilise the Volunteers and, relying on IRB and not Volunteer authority, banned IPP celebrations of Redmond's victory:

At this time the sole government of the Republic was the Supreme Council of the I.R.B., and the President of the Supreme Council

146   The Irish Republican Brotherhood, 1914–1924

was the President of the Republic ... From 1918 to 1919 there was the enforcement of law under the guidance and instructions of the Supreme Council of the I.R.B. ... The success of Captain Redmond in the Waterford by-election brought things to a head in Ballinalee. The Irish Parliamentary Party's supporters decided to organise a victory celebration. Acting under the authority vested in me I proclaimed the celebrations and enforced the decision with the aid of the Volunteers.[17]

Like MacEoin, Tom Hales in West Cork acted in 1918 without reference to the Volunteer/IRA chain of command. Additionally, he expanded his Ballinadee Circle by swearing in Volunteers/IRA men he judged suitable, creating a power base in the process that saw him become Third Cork Brigade O/C and, eventually, Supreme Council representative for south Munster.[18] This aspect of IRB membership – building voting blocs – naturally generated additional suspicion and animosity. Séamus McKenna in Belfast was convinced (correctly) that Volunteer/IRA promotions were based upon IRB membership and not ability,[19] although determined republicans did not need to be members of the IRB to be promoted or to command. Nevertheless, IRB favouritism was an underlying tension between the IRB and the Volunteers/IRA (despite the effective merging of the IRB with the Volunteers/IRA in 1919–21), between the IRB and Sinn Féin and between the IRB and the Dáil.

Many nationalists agreed with Brugha and de Valera that the IRB was unnecessary after the Rising.[20] Frank Gallagher in Dublin thought it 'plainly had plans of its own that were not those of an elected government ... What was to prove a tragedy later for the Volunteers, and for Ireland, was that a section of the I.R.B. continued its secret existence, and its struggle for control both of the Dáil and of the army.'[21] Many activists wanted public nationalist formations to operate without secret controls or agendas.[22] Denis McCullough agreed: 'I expressed the opinion which I still think is the right one that it had served its purpose in bringing about the Rising; that there was a government to be formed and that the I.R.B. had no further right to control things.'[23] In 1917 George Lyons thought that Brugha really objected to Michael Collins rather than the IRB, and that he in turn convinced de Valera: 'It was generally believed that Cathal Brugha mooted to de Valera that he should leave the I.R.B. as he might have to take orders from Michael Collins instead of being able to give orders.'[24]

Traditional IRB distrust of politicians continued after the Rising. John Madden, an IRB member in Galway, recalled an IRB organiser in 1917 or

Reorganisation   147

early 1918 who 'made a personal attack on de Valera ... He said that the IRB had no confidence in him',[25] indicating an early division between the physical-force devotees and the political wing of the national movement. Conversely, distrust of the IRB after 1916 caused rifts between the IRB and the Volunteers/IRA in Clare, Limerick and elsewhere.[26] Such episodes were straws in the wind presaging later conflict.

Throughout 1917 the IRB/Volunteer reorganisers faced the question, asked by de Valera, Brugha and erstwhile IRB members: what was the point, let alone the necessity, of the secret society? Did not open, political campaigning offer a greater opportunity for success than reverting to insurrection that had, so far, always failed? As Séamus O'Doherty's wife, Katherine ('Kitty'), put it: 'They considered that it had no further reason for existence as the Republic to establish which the organisation was founded had been solemnly proclaimed in Easter Week when the I.R.A. had taken the field openly, not as an oathbound society, but as an army of Irish citizens of all classes.'[27] Éamon O'Dwyer, a pre-1916 IRB Volunteer, in 1918 discussed the question of continuing the IRB with other prisoners in Belfast Gaol:

> [I]t was our opinion that the need for the I.R.B. had practically ceased to exist owing to the fact that the Irish Volunteers were now doing the I.R.B. work and that when an Irish Parliament was set up the Irish Volunteers would come under its control. They, the Volunteers, would then be titled the army of Ireland and continuation of the I.R.B. would not, therefore, be necessary.[28]

A different view was taken by Frank Henderson in the Dublin Brigade. He had not been a member before 1919 and tortuously explained his reasoning for joining:

> In late 1918, or early 1919, after I had become Commandant of the Second Battalion, it seemed to me that I could give better service to the Republic if I became a member of the I.R.B. A struggle that promised to be protracted and exacting had begun, membership would bind those in the organisation in the event of defections or attempts to compromise on the part of post-Rising recruits to the Volunteers or the political organisations who might not have such sound national foundations as those who had been trained in the old movement ... I was admitted to

membership ... It was considered desirable that Volunteer officers should belong to the I.R.B. so that a firm stand could be taken if a national stampede should threaten or the temptation should be presented of settled conditions or political power through a lowering of the national objective.[29]

In 1961 Florrie O'Donoghue in Cork wrote a considered memoir of his experience and his opinions about the personalities and events of 1916–22. He had been the principal intelligence officer in the Cork Volunteers/IRA. He succinctly agreed with Henderson: 'Knowing the compositions of the Volunteer mentality at the time, knowing the absence of official policy, and believing that whatever was attempted would emanate from the driving force of the hard core of the IRB men within its ranks, I had become convinced of the necessity of maintaining the organisation.'[30]

Liam Ó Briain, who joined the IRB in 1915, supported the continuation of the Brotherhood after 1916 because, he thought, it played a significant part in keeping men active in the Volunteers/IRA:

> Some very important people said after Easter Week – Cathal Brugha, de Valera – that there was no necessity to have the I.R.B. I think they're wrong there, completely, because it helped the lads. It strengthened their feeling of being soldiers under orders that they had sworn an oath to fight and therefore that when they got a call from the local Captain or other – think of 1917, '18, '19, '20, '21 – men might have sloped off. I believe the oath kept them together and kept them in it and kept them ready to go out and fight and die.[31]

Garry Holohan, commandant of the Fianna Éireann Dublin Brigade, saw the changes after 1916 as ushering in a new opportunistic calculation wherein the Volunteers/IRA became the ladder of opportunity for those who looked forward to benefiting economically and professionally from membership, elbowing aside the IRB's republican dedication:

> [T]he only men who were considered reliable before 1916 were the members of the I.R.B. We were in the centre of every action and held the key positions in every movement. This was completely altered after 1916. Every man who took part in the Rising was considered tried and

Reorganisation 149

true, as well as the other members of his family, so the new organisation grew to enormous dimensions and the ranks were swelled with the usual crafty place-hunters and seekers.[32]

Holohan, a worker in a Dublin pumping station, also felt that Sinn Féin and the Volunteers changed during 1917 as new men took over, displacing the IRB:

> The movement changed from a small party of idealists, who were ready to do and die in face of all adversity, to a huge political movement embracing all classes and types. The fighting men of limited education, like myself, devoted most of our energy to the re-organisation of military organisations, while the men of education took over control of the political machinery. In other words, men of my type were to accept the position of citizen soldiers.[33]

This was a natural change. Men who had not been prominent before 1916 inevitably formed the new leadership of both the Volunteers/IRA and Sinn Féin. The point that Holohan perceived was that traditional IRB recruits – as in the social groups that had taken part in the 1916 Rising – at least in Dublin post-1916 were no longer in many leadership positions.

Joseph O'Rourke was cautious about the thrust of IRB activity after 1917 and was committed to IRB secrecy. He had been acting Centre of the Dublin Clarence Mangan Circle while the previous Centre, George Irvine, was in prison. When Irvine was released in 1918 he resumed as Centre and, according to O'Rourke, focused Circle activity on the Volunteers/IRA:

> He was inclined to accept the precedence of the I.R.A. over the I.R.B. My argument was that the I.R.B. activities were not confined to military activities, but took place in economic, social, cultural etc., fronts with which the military did not concern themselves. George's argument was that the prestige of the I.R.B. as pioneers and ex 1916 would enable us to make propaganda effectively among the rank and file of the I.R.A. and convert them to our way of thinking. In a word, to raise their standards.[34]

In contrast Séumas Robinson, who had joined the IRB in February 1916, was in the Kimmage Garrison, took part in the Rising, and was interned and then released in December 1916, echoed Cathal Brugha's anger:

Shortly after the releases from internment young chaps mixed among us broadcasting the news that every member of the 'Organisation' was requested to attend a meeting in Parnell Square – No. 44 I think. At that meeting I saw young fellows with notebooks rushing round and about the ground floor (there were about 150 present) button-holing individuals with anxious whispers.– 'We must make sure that no one will be elected an officer of the Volunteers who is not a member of the "Organisation"' – as if that were something new or something that we would be allowed to forget, and without adverting to the fact that that sort of thing would undermine the authority and efficiency of the whole Volunteer movement. Without waiting for the meeting to start officially I walked out in disgust thinking of Tammany Hall. I never again bothered about the I.R.B.[35]

Michael Brennan in Clare 'looked on [the IRB], and most of the rest of us looked on [the IRB] as having done their job, and from then on it was a question of organising the Volunteers. We forgot all about the I.R.B. until the Treaty when we were told we could work whatever way we liked.'[36] Similarly, Eoin McArdle in the Dublin Brigade after 1918 'was all into the I.R.A.'.[37] James McCullough in Armagh saw the Volunteers/IRA simply replace the IRB:

The great achievement of the I.R.B. organisation was that they were mainly responsible for early re-organisation of the Volunteers after 1916. The strict selection of the I.R.B. confined its members to a small, handpicked band. The organisation of the Volunteers was on a more liberal basis where all young Irishmen of good national background were made welcome. In Blackwaterstown area, for instance, the I.R.B. Circle contained only 14 members while the Blackwaterstown Company of Volunteers numbered 80 to 90 men. It was only natural born that the Volunteers would break away from the control of the small band of I.R.B. who desired to control them.[38]

What was missed was that the Volunteers were doing what the IRB wanted, and that the Volunteer Executive was almost entirely composed of IRB men, as was the GHQ staff. As events would show, the IRB was not frightened of fighting. Michael Collins' domination of the IRB meant that criticism of the organisation was often a veiled criticism of Collins, and attitudes to Collins in the light of the 1922–23 Civil War doubtless coloured memories recorded later.

Reorganisation

On 22 December 1916 the remaining internees at Frongoch (about 600) had been released and over the next two days returned to Ireland. There remained about 150 prisoners scattered throughout prisons in England, and amongst them were the most senior survivors of the Rising as well as Arthur Griffith and Eoin MacNeill. Among the Frongoch releases, however, were many IRB men who immediately joined the Liam Clarke, O'Doherty, O'Hegarty, Ó Murthuile reorganisation.[39] Michael Collins was one of them.

Gearóid O'Sullivan (from Skibbereen, West Cork) introduced Collins to Seán Ó Murthuile (from Leap, West Cork) and through him to Séamus O'Doherty's provisional Supreme Council.[40] Collins, O'Hegarty and Gearóid O'Sullivan formed an unofficial triumvirate that met Volunteer/IRA and IRB men from the country when they came to Dublin, hearing their reports and requirements and working to provide them with as much support as possible, favouring requests from Co. Cork. 'We had a feeling that Collins was using his influence in favour of his own county,' said Michael Brennan.[41]

Diarmuid O'Hegarty (like O'Sullivan, from Skibbereen) was a vital connection for Collins. After 1916 he was as involved as Collins in reorganising the IRB and Volunteers before becoming the Dáil Cabinet Secretary in 1919. Joe O'Doherty, responsible for Volunteer communications with O'Hegarty, shared an office with Collins from 1917 at 32 Bachelor's Walk: 'I was well aware, first of all, that Diarmuid O'Hegarty was the brains. I don't know if anyone else has ever said this, but in my opinion he was the brains behind Collins. He was the real intriguer of the whole lot of them. Again, I couldn't prove that. But I always felt that.'[42]

CHAPTER 14

Collins Emerges

Michael Collins had a bellyful of fire and a head that was ice cold.[1]

David Lloyd George, c. 1921

Frongoch camp in Wales held most of the actual insurgents. The camp was divided into two sections, a north camp and a south camp. In the south camp, two IRB meetings had been held by September 1916. IRB members ran the camp and Michael Collins emerged as their spokesman and worked happily with Michael Staines,[2] the prisoners' official leader.[3] Many of the men who went on to revive Sinn Féin and to command the Volunteers/IRA came to know each other in Frongoch. Michael Collins, Jim Ryan,[4] Éamonn Dore, Gearóid O'Sullivan, Éamon Bulfin,[5] Frank Shouldice,[6] John Kilgallon[7] and Denis ('Dinny') Daly[8] formed a distinct IRB group that exercised together.[9] '[T]he I.R.B. – they were a power there,' remembered Thomas Malone. 'Collins, Richard Mulcahy and five or six more were the top men in it.'[10] 'Michael Collins seemed to be the principal man there,' said John O'Reilly, a fellow internee. 'After the Rising the IRB was already reorganised in Frongoch and Collins was the most forceful member.'[11] Collins did not attract the attention of the guards, conducting himself carefully.[12] He was also closely involved with the London Irish who had taken part in the Rising[13] and were threatened in Frongoch with conscription under the 1916 Military Service Act.[14]

Denis McCullough also worked to re-form the IRB while in Frongoch, involving Daniel Kelly:

> One day Dinny McCullough came to me and said: 'We are reorganising the I.R.B. and you will be representing Donegal. Could you nominate

a man to represent Derry?' ... We held a meeting of the I.R.B. in the YMCA Hall within the camp. [Men from every county in Ireland were present.] We had a very successful gathering and we raised the nucleus of the organisation for re-forming when we got out.[15]

Seán Murphy, Centre of the Dublin Thomas Clarke Luby Circle,[16] attended the meeting:

Mulcahy was Chairman. With him at the head of the table was Michael Collins who acted as Secretary, also Michael Staines, Gearóid O'Sullivan, Stephen Jordan[17] (Athenry) ... The object of calling them together was set out by Michael Collins; and that was to obtain their names and addresses so that they could be used as lines of communication in further activities if and when we were released.[18]

Collins was already preparing for future action: 1916 was the start that he was to build upon. He did not care for rules or for the IRB hierarchy, setting himself up as the overall organiser in the camp. There were inevitable reactions from other IRB members who did care for the IRB's formalities and saw Collins as an upstart. Éamonn Dore was one of these:

During our period of internment at Frongoch in 1916 there were several I.R.B. meetings held there. Mick Collins, who at the time was not very well known to us, called the first one and, acting entirely on his own initiative, swore in Bill Reilly as a member. Now, Collins had been a member in London for some time, but he had only come into our Circle a short time before the Rising and we, therefore, looked upon him as a newcomer. I discussed this matter of Bill Reilly's introduction as a member with Martin Murphy and some others at the time, as, in our opinion, Reilly was not a suitable type of man to bring in as a member of the I.R.B., nor should Collins have taken such action without the agreement of the other members there ... Collins was taken to task. Mick apologised for his action.[19]

This did not deter Collins, who became ever more involved in IRB discussions in Frongoch, including a decision setting aside the IRB's traditional reluctance to be formally engaged in political activity. Éamonn Dore again recalled:

154   The Irish Republican Brotherhood, 1914–1924

I was not invited to attend another meeting in Frongoch at which Collins, Dick Mulcahy and Frank Shouldice were present amongst others. Shouldice told me about this meeting afterwards, and that one of the things proposed and agreed to at this meeting, was that a policy of political action should be adopted by us on our release ... [I] gave my opinion against such a decision which, I felt, must only result in swamping the I.R.B. which was the only clear and genuine national organisation existing, in a sea of political intrigue and self-seeking.[20]

Nevertheless, political engagement was to become post-1916 IRB policy.

While interned, Collins gathered the nucleus of his personal countrywide IRB connections.[21] Joe Sweeney was also in Frongoch:

Collins got really busy there. He had quite a number of his own people from west Cork. We used to call them 'The Mafia'. They ran the whole camp. He saw everybody in charge of the camp was an I.R.B. man and people in pivotal positions were I.R.B. ... He organised classes of all kinds, both educational and military, and he saw to it that more attention was paid to guerrilla fighting. And we had fellows in there from all parts of Ireland in Frongoch, and he built up a great system of contacts that way, and it was then too that he began to get information about friendly police, you know, fellows who had done good acts for the lads after 1916 in various parts of the country, and he followed all those up and invariably he recruited those men.[22]

IRB influence in Frongoch secured general acceptance amongst internees that the Rising was the beginning of a new struggle for independence and not simply another demonstration of Fenian spirit. Richard Mulcahy reportedly expressed IRB intransigence:

'Freedom will never come', said he, 'without revolution, and I greatly fear that the Irish are too soft for the purpose of revolution. To bring a revolution to a satisfactory conclusion we need blood-thirsty, ferocious men who care nothing for death or slaughter or bloodletting. Revolution is not child's work. Nor is it the business of saint or scholar. In matters of revolution, any man, woman or child who is not for you is against you. Shoot them and be damned to them!'[23]

Collins Emerges

Subsequently Mulcahy denied saying any of this. Unfortunately, his later career suggests that he did.[24]

In Wandsworth, Knutsford, Stafford, Reading, Glasgow, Lincoln, Perth, Parkhurst, Woking, Lewes, Wakefield and Gloucester prisons, similar Frongoch-type contacts and friendships were made. As a result, by the time the last prisoners were released in June 1917, the participants in the Rising and those arrested because of it knew each other very well and were resolved to continue to struggle for independence.[25]

Dependants' Fund

On Saturday, 6 May 1916, three days after her husband was executed, Kathleen Clarke started the IRPDF with the money that her husband and John Devoy had given to her, and with the active support of Margaret Pearse, mother of Patrick and Willie (who had also been executed in 1916) and the wives of MacDonagh, Ceannt and Gavan Duffy.[26] John Reynolds, a friend of the Clarkes, was secretary of the Fund. Shortly afterwards, the IPP started the National Aid Fund (NAF) and Clarke was asked to amalgamate the IRPDF with it. She refused. She was asked a second time by Archdeacon John Murphy of Buffalo, New York, who was in Ireland as an emissary from the Clan and as a representative of the Irish Relief Fund of America. She then consented on condition that the Redmondites on the NAF's committee resign. They agreed to go. The two funds joined to form the INAVDF.[27]

Fred Allan had joined the NAF committee and had introduced a young IRB man, Joe McGrath, as secretary, who continued in that post in the amalgamated body, leaving after the release of Collins and the other internees from Frongoch in December 1916. Several men applied to replace McGrath. Collins campaigned for the job:

> Michael Collins and another ex-political prisoner applied for the position of secretary, and Collins called to ask me to support him. He was only just back from prison camp in England. After talking to him for a while, I decided he was just the man I was hoping for. He was I.R.B. and Irish Volunteer, and also reminded me in many ways of Sean McDermott.[28]

Clarke (who controlled the INAVDF) chose Collins. She was impressed by his energy and his republicanism and felt that of all the applicants he would best

156   The Irish Republican Brotherhood, 1914–1924

be able to take advantage of opportunities to reorganise the IRB that travelling throughout the country on aid work would facilitate. He would naturally become familiar with the men and the families of the Rising:

> He also agreed with my idea that the fight for freedom must be continued, the Rising to count as the first blow. As Secretary to the NAVDF, he would be free to move about the country without molestation. Everyone would be free to go into the office of the Fund without arousing suspicion as so many people were seeking help, and there contacts of every kind could be made. With the information I had been able to give him, he was not long in getting into a leading position. With his forceful personality, his wonderful magnetism and his organising ability, he had little trouble in becoming a leader.[29]

He had also worked closely with MacDermott and Joseph Plunkett in the weeks before the Rising. Kathleen Clarke knew and may have met him then. MacDermott seems to have made a point of endorsing Collins to her.[30] The close working relationship of Collins and MacDermott implied that in 1917 Collins was probably more knowledgeable than most about the IRB. Kathleen Clarke gave Collins all she knew of IRB affairs, including the names of members and its organisation, adding to the list that Collins had compiled in Frongoch. 'Mrs Clarke gave him the names of the three principal representatives of the IRB in each of the various counties,'[31] Richard Mulcahy confirmed. Collins' job with the INAVDF gave him the power of the purse as he determined the worthiness of applicants and visited and distributed funds to individuals and families.[32]

More than any Frongoch contacts and activities, Kathleen Clarke's choice of Collins as secretary in 1917 made his emergence as a leader in the IRB and in the national movement almost certain.[33] All that was required was energy, efficiency and dedication from Collins, and this he had. 'I saw Collins dictating to 3 typists at one time,' recalled one Volunteer/IRA officer.[34] Batt O'Connor, a builder at whose home Collins frequently stayed, was also struck by Collins' energy:

> Michael Collins was all the time attending to the recruiting side. He was getting together, so far as possible, an Active Service Unit for every area. He was forming his Intelligence staff, recruited from what was to

Collins Emerges 157

become the famous Dublin Brigade ... He was full of enthusiasm and hope. He said the fight had only begun, and that the real struggle lay ahead.[35]

He was also expanding the IRB's political activity. Tom Hales, an IRB officer in Bandon, met Collins early in 1917 shortly after his release from Frongoch:

> A Ceilidhe was organised in the [Cork] City Hall for all the released prisoners, which I attended. It was here that I first met Mick Collins. We discussed the future, and the lines on which the organisation was to move. The I.R.B. was to be the main activity and was to throw its weight behind Sinn Féin to ensure that it comprised men of grit and energy until such time as the Irish Volunteers came into the open again.[36]

Collins' entry to the Dublin IRB ruffled feathers. The two Circles he had organised amongst the Frongoch internees were outside IRB rules, and news of this had spread. Some members of the Dublin Centres Board were concerned that the traditional care taken with recruiting had not been observed and that the security of the organisation might be jeopardised if the new Circles were admitted. Joseph O'Rourke was on the Board and witnessed the opposition Collins faced:

> In May 1917, or June, there was a Centres Board meeting ... The Chairman got up and made a speech, the sense of which was 'As you may or may not know among your comrades in arms in Frongoch certain active individuals organised a branch of the I.R.B. in order that the fight should be carried on, and these men were tried in the furnace of action and we now propose that these two Circles should be admitted *en bloc* and attached to this Centres Board.' Two or three people got up and spoke in favour and as it appeared that nobody was going to object to it, I got up [and said] that I for one could not assent to their admission *en bloc* ... The Chairman stood up and said he was ashamed at us doubting the bonafides of these proved men, and a vote was taken (secret ballot) and the Chairman's motion was passed by nine to eight votes against. The Chairman then said that by a 'strange coincidence' the men 'to whom I refer are actually in the building, and if it is the will of the meeting I will introduce them' ... Then Collins came in ... We then got a 'pep talk' from Collins to 'get on with it'.[37]

The opposition to the two new Circles was likely to have had more to do with opposition to Collins than to the new members, since most of the men in Frongoch had probably been in the IRB in 1916. 'The Dublin members of the I.R.B.,' said Joseph Gleeson, 'did not like Collins.'[38]

Supreme Council

A 'legitimate' Council was formally re-established in June or July 1917.[39] From January 1917, internees released from Frongoch, especially Michael Collins, energised reorganisation not only of the IRB, but also of the Volunteers, initially funded by IRB money in the possession of Kathleen Clarke.[40] 'I got in touch with Dermot [sic] Lynch after his release from imprisonment,' said Patrick McCormack. 'This must have been at the earliest mid-1917. Shortly after Lynch's release a move was made to reform the Supreme Council of the I.R.B. Elections were held in each of the four Provinces and in England and Scotland.'[41] 'I met Mick Collins and Gearóid O'Sullivan,'[42] recalled Alec McCabe, 'and they told me to come to a meeting. And the meeting resolved itself into the I.R.B. I was the continuity member. And they summoned me there to create a continuity.'[43]

From 1917 onwards, because of absences (mostly in the United States) and arrests, the membership of the Supreme Council was constantly changing. Sometimes a new member was elected; more often co-opted. In Alec McCabe's view, from 1917 Collins 'dominated it and it was all his associates that were in the thing, and that was the beginning of Michael Collins' domination of the scene'.[44] Collins invited Gerry Boland, Harry Boland's older brother, to join the Supreme Council at this time (presumably as a co-opted member). He had met Gerry in Frongoch, but Boland refused on the grounds that he considered that the IRB was no longer needed.[45] The key 1917–19 members – Michael Collins (Treasurer), Diarmuid O'Hegarty (also Treasurer for a period), Seán Ó Murthuile (Secretary), Gearóid O'Sullivan, Seán McGarry (President) – were re-elected as members or co-opted in 1919.[46]

The Supreme Council was determined to continue the fight started in 1916. So was Cathal Brugha. But politics were inevitably involved. Collins and de Valera, more than any others, saw the opportunities of leadership in the post-1916 vacuum. Collins saw the IRB as his vehicle; de Valera saw Sinn Féin as his. Arthur Griffith had a clear opportunity to rival de Valera in Sinn Féin, but he did not have that ambition, seeing himself as a philosopher and not an

Collins Emerges 159

executive of nationalism. Brugha was too blunt for political success, but he could see Collins' growing power and influence with the Volunteers/IRA that he considered were his to lead, and he resented this deeply.

Part of Brugha's resentment must have been because Collins was not widely known in nationalist circles in 1916, unlike Brugha, and did not have a national reputation, again unlike Brugha. But Collins did not come from nowhere. He had been Treasurer of the IRB South of England Division and had been active in London Irish organisations. The 1913–16 Supreme Councils knew who he was. He seems to have been the Centre of an ad hoc London Irish Circle in Dublin in the months before the Rising.[47]

For Collins, generally regarded then and since as the single most important revolutionary, the IRB was to him, in the opinion of Richard Mulcahy, more important than anything else in 1918–19.[48] 'The secretive IRB is everywhere in [Collins'] diaries,' observed Anne Dolan and William Murphy in their study of the documents.[49] 'Collins received prominence because he was the principal Go Ahead man in [the] I.R.B. after Frongoch,'[50] was the view of John O'Reilly. Uniquely among nationalist leaders after 1916, through the IRB Collins possessed intimate knowledge of the personalities and undertakings of the other nationalist political, military and cultural organisations that the IRB had infiltrated, and of many British military, police and policy plans. Seán Ó Murthuile, the IRB's historian, emphasised the IRB's superior knowledge that Collins utilised:

> Of all the bodies contributing to the War I think the Supreme Council had perhaps the best knowledge of the actual strength or weakness of the forces operating under Dáil Éireann, because secrets that were not always available to other bodies were from time to time before the Supreme Council. In other words, a good deal of the 'bluff' that was essential in public was shed in the I.R.B. Council meetings, and realities were discussed. Collins and others who were high in the Volunteer councils were always present.[51]

Collins, through his command of the IRB after 1919, had more power than anyone else. He had connections through the IRB that the other leaders did not have. This gave him a direct and efficient way of securing his objectives and of knowing what his colleagues were planning and doing. 'The members of the I.R.B. were absorbed in the Intelligence Department that worked

160   The Irish Republican Brotherhood, 1914–1924

under Collins,' said Richard Mulcahy.[52] The IRB became Collins' intelligence organisation within the independence movement. 'I even had to send to Collins an account of the officers of the Volunteers,' said James Malone (Séamas Ó Maoileóin), an undercover agent in Cork. 'He required an accurate and precise knowledge of enemies and friends alike.'[53]

Born in West Cork in 1890, Collins had a fierce loyalty to his native county. In London as a young post office worker he socialised with other Cork men. He was Joseph Plunkett's aide de camp in the GPO during the Rising where he demonstrated his Cork romanticism:

> There was an instruction about prisoners that their boots should be removed. I had the boots of the two [RIC] Sergeants taken from them after they were brought into the GPO. Later the same day I had visited them and they complained of the cold. I reported the matter to Michael Collins. He went to see them, found they were two Cork men, had their boots restored to them and got them some tea.[54]

As he rose in the IRB and the Volunteers/IRA, he gave preference to colleagues from Cork and to weapons for the Cork Volunteers/IRA. 'In 1921 or something down in Cork they were running very short of guns and we had the guns, we had plenty of guns,' remembered Thomas Taylor.

> In any case, Mick Collins called a meeting in north county Dublin of our Battalion ... and he wanted those guns and our lads said he wouldn't get them. And one of our lads who was a TD afterwards said, 'Mr Collins, don't think you can come down here to walk on us.' 'Bejasus!' he said, 'I'll jump on you!' He was going to get the guns and he got them to go to Cork.[55]

There was a separate point that Collins did not make: pistols and revolvers are for urban killing; rifles and shotguns are for country killing and would best be with the men who were most active in fields and hills.

Personality

Collins had enormous self-confidence. On his last trip to Cork in August 1922 he angrily said he 'was not going to run from his own Corkmen' when he was

Collins Emerges

warned of the danger he would face.[56] Many colleagues perceived him as surrounded by a group of favourites, mostly from Cork, who promoted and defended him – and rose with him. It was not surprising that he was viewed by Cathal Brugha and Éamon de Valera as overly if not uncontrollably ambitious, especially since he had little time for formalities or colleagues' spheres of interest.[57]

'He had a mobile, expressive face, quick wit and a quick temper,' remembered Florrie O'Donoghue, a senior Cork IRB Volunteer/IRA man who knew Collins well. 'He was gay, boisterous, optimistic, bubbling with dynamic energy. That would not have made a man of him, of course, but behind the dashing exterior there was keen intelligence, great strength of character, steadiness, determination and vision.'[58] 'He was a remarkable man, was Collins,' said Robert Barton. 'He had quite a good mind but he hadn't got training. He'd only been to a National School. He had nothing more. And then he trained himself.'[59] Dinny Daly knew Collins as a twenty-year-old in London where he worked in the postal service. 'Through the GAA, I met Mick Collins, but he wasn't any good at either hurling or football and, when I was playing against him, I'd play for his toes and that would make him mad. It was always easy to vex Collins … Collins would be inclined to lose his temper at anything, talk or not.' But 'He had a big heart and would give you his last shilling.'[60] Tom Barry, the noted Volunteer/IRA guerrilla leader, described him as 'without a shadow of a doubt, the effective driving force'.[61] Charles Russell, a National Army major general in 1924, said unequivocally that Collins was 'the man. He was everything … Anybody knows that.'[62] Peter Carleton, a Fianna member in Belfast, said, 'Even up here, Collins had an aura that no one else had.'[63] Eoghan Plunkett's aunt, Geraldine, employed Collins in November 1915 to help manage Count Plunkett's estate and found him to be excellent. He was 'completely honest and direct', 'too trusting', 'a good actor', 'unsophisticated except financially', and 'really intelligent'. 'No one ever had a better clerk, he was far too good for the work I wanted done, quick and intelligent, a splendid organiser and took very little time to do much work.'[64] 'Collins was a man,' said Joe Sweeney, who became O/C First Northern Division in 1921. 'You'll never meet his like again. I think he was the most dynamic man I ever met in my life. I never met anybody like him. He could tear strips out of you and the next minute he'd have his arm round you chatting away about something else.'[65] 'Where were you in 1904 when I and others were founding the Sinn Féin movement?' asked a veteran whom Collins had addressed bluntly. 'I was playing marbles, damn you!'[66]

Conversely, Eoghan Plunkett, nephew of Joseph Plunkett, thought Collins

162   The Irish Republican Brotherhood, 1914–1924

boorish and unpleasant. 'My mother knew Mick Collins very well. He had an office in her flat and she despised him. He was a pup, a nasty piece of work. Whenever he came into their living room, the carpet on the living room floor was surrounded by a timber floor, but he walked on the timber part. Why? Because it made more noise. That's the sort of fellow that he was. She and he were both from west Cork; she recognised him for what he was.'[67] Garry Holohan, interned in 1916 with Collins at Frongoch, thought he was a bully: 'I must say I never liked him. I always considered him a rude, bouncing bully, but he was a very competent worker and very popular.'[68] 'Was he a bully?' asked Ernie O'Malley, an IRA general in an interview with Barney O'Driscoll, a 1916 Collins colleague. 'I don't know,' said O'Driscoll, 'but if you were ever in trouble he was a good man to have near you.'[69]

He liked to wrestle – literally – with colleagues and expressed his dislike of inaction by taking unusual action. In London, during the Treaty negotiations in October–December 1921, Kathleen McKenna, a secretary with the Irish delegation, reported to her brother:

> 'He came in at that unearthly hour that the Irish Mail used to arrive in London at 6 in the morning. He went down to Hans Place and he went in the door and you know what he did? He stole into all the bedrooms; he collected all their clothing ...'

> 'The girls' clothing?'

> '... and he went over to the men's clothing as well, and there were innumerable bathrooms and he threw them all into the bath and turned the taps on them, and then he went off on his own ... Every morning he'd come in, women's bedrooms, it didn't matter a damn who they were, and he'd put his hand under the blankets and he'd catch hold of their ankle and put them out to the middle of the floor, out of the bed! You really would have to barricade your door against him, and he'd say, "All the bloody time that's wasted in bed!" An hour was enough for him.'[70]

In Portobello Barracks in 1922, Willy McKenna remembered:

> [T]he officers had to barricade their doors: he couldn't stand the sight of a man in bed – he'd pull them out of it ... My sister told me many, many

Collins Emerges

times that he could dictate a letter and in between sentences he could shut his eyes for a fraction of a second and take a doze. Just doze off for a minute and be fully alert when he woke up.[71]

Turfing people out of bed might have had a part in his unpopularity. He rose to prominence 'by work, energy and ability', said Michael Hayes. 'I know why he became unpopular too, because I think efficiency is an unpopular thing, particularly if you've a nasty tongue.'[72] He was an excellent administrator and a guerrilla mastermind.

Views of Collins had a financial edge, flowing from his control of funds: secretary of the INAVDF; IRB Treasurer; Minister of Finance; Volunteer/IRA Executive Treasurer; in charge of the Dáil Loan to fund the Dáil government. IRB connections played an inevitable part in Collins' financial work. Tadhg Kennedy, a Volunteer/IRA intelligence officer in Tralee, recorded collecting subscriptions from 'Maurice Kelleher, one of the big millers and merchants and an I.R.B. man in his young days; John Griffin, merchant, another old I.R.B. man ... and other such monied people. We collected a large amount of money from these people.'[73] 'Michael Collins spent a lot of time thinking about money,' noted Ann Dolan and William Murphy: 'the money, the money the money possessed him for long stretches in 1920'[74] – and not just 1920. 'We can't forget that you hold the purse strings, and you're too close to them,' said Michael Kilroy, O/C Fourth Western Division, to him in 1922. 'Well,' said Collins, 'that's the meanest thing a man ever said to another.'[75]

After Frongoch

Within months of his release from Frongoch at Christmas 1916, Collins' drive and authority were established within the IRB, as he led the Brotherhood to be active in electoral politics. He was quickly sought out by those who had taken the lead in the post-Rising reorganisations and was emerging by mid-1917 as an IRB leader. His managerial ability and energy were promoting him to the top of the separatist hierarchy. In the opinion of Micky Joe Costello, later a National Army director of intelligence, Collins' rise was because of his personal qualities, not because of the IRB:

It was in his capacity as organiser and as a personality and not as an IRB man that he was influential, and the influence of the IRB was on Collins

164   The Irish Republican Brotherhood, 1914–1924

himself as an IRB man ... The IRA in England hardly existed as such apart from the IRB. And this is one of the reasons why Collins' influence was so dominant. These people [IRB members in Britain] were linked to Collins in two ways: because they were IRB men and because their main activities were Intelligence activities and so on. They were buying guns and sending them to Collins and from him they got the money for them.[76]

Richard Walsh had never met Collins but Collins found him, no doubt from one of the lists of IRB members that Kathleen Clarke had given to him:

> One day in 1917 in my own shop in Balla, a man walked in and presented me with a letter from Michael Collins, stating that the bearer would explain his business to me ... [H]is job in Co. Mayo was to organise the I.R.B. there. He asked me to give him a hand in pushing the organisation in the county. He told me that his proposition to me was Michael Collins' wishes and also that Collins looked on me as an I.R.B. member ... On the instructions of this man I undertook the organisation of the I.R.B. in Co. Mayo amongst active Volunteers. There was a system of extreme caution in selecting members for the organisation and, on account of this cautious attitude, the members of the I.R.B. were kept small.[77]

In June 1917 Collins joined the provisional Supreme Council together with Thomas Ashe, Seán McGarry and Diarmuid Lynch.[78] His work with the IRB since leaving Frongoch propelled him up the IRB ranks, as Lynch explained:

> When the 'Convict' prisoners were released from Pentonville in June, 1917, Dr MacCartan joined us – at Holyhead, I think – and informed me (I was the only member of the pre-Easter Week Supreme Council among them) that a temporary Council had functioned in our absence. The following Autumn the Supreme Council was regularly re-established – thanks to the preliminary work done by Michael Collins at Frongoch and during 1917 while Secretary of the National Aid Asscn.[79]

Darrell Figgis, a nationalist who preferred pacific action and disagreed with Collins' and the IRB's espousal of violence, left a memorable depiction of Collins in full flood at a Sinn Féin Executive meeting in June 1919. A Sinn Féin press announcement of a formal welcome in Dublin for 'President de Valera'

Collins Emerges

had appeared. Figgis, as a joint honorary secretary of the party, questioned on what authority this had been done:

> Characteristically, he swept aside all pretences, and said that the announcement had been written by him, and that the decision to make it had been made, not by Sinn Féin, though declared in its name, but by 'the proper body, the Irish Volunteers'. He spoke with much vehemence and emphasis, saying that ... Ireland was likely to get more out of a state of disorder than from a continuance of the situation as it then stood. The proper people to take decisions of that kind were ready to face the British military and were resolved to force the issue. And they were not to be deterred by weaklings and cowards. For himself he accepted full responsibility for the announcement, and he told the meeting with forceful candour that he held them in no opinion at all, that, in fact, they were only summoned to confirm what the proper people had decided.[80]

By this time the IRB had re-formed and then in effect merged into the Irish Volunteers: they were the 'proper people', as Richard Mulcahy confirmed:

> In the beginning of 1917 there was a group with, no doubt, Collins as the moving spirit, in a position and active, actively determined to speak as an I.R.B. authority, to communicate with and to link up the country for I.R.B. organisation purposes ... In relation to the subsequent development of organisation, as far as the Volunteers went it depended on persons, persons accepting responsibility in Dublin and assuming power to direct (and organise) ... It can be understood that in the inchoate initial circumstances ... that even after March 1918 and the setting up of the GHQ staff, that the development on the two lines would have to be in the hands of one man, as it was in the case of Collins.[81]

From December 1916 Mulcahy was in a position to know.

Centrality

Collins was the pivotal figure in IRB and Volunteer reorganisation, determined to continue the fight that he regarded as having started in 1916.[82] From then on his power and influence grew, as the positions he held attested:

166 The Irish Republican Brotherhood, 1914–1924

Secretary, INAVDF, 1917–18
Secretary, Liberty Party, 1917[83]
Treasurer, IRB, 1917–19
Executive, Volunteer/IRA, 1917–22
Executive, Sinn Féin, 1917–22
Treasurer, Volunteer/IRA Executive, 1917–22[84]
Director of Organisation, Volunteer/IRA Executive/GHQ Staff, 1917–20
Director of Purchases, GHQ Staff, 1917–21
Adjutant General, Volunteer/IRA Executive/GHQ Staff, 1917–20
Secretary, Volunteer/IRA Executive, 1918–22
Director of Intelligence, GHQ Staff, 1918–22[85]
President, IRB, 1919–22
Minister for Home Affairs, Dáil Éireann, 1919
Minister for Finance, Dáil Éireann, 1919–22
Acting President, Dáil Éireann, November–December 1920

Collins never held fewer than six important positions simultaneously. 'He was on everything,' said Emmet Dalton, who worked closely with him from 1919. 'Collins was an amazing man with an amazing capacity for work. He embraced everything. He was very intolerant of inefficiency so that if he had put somebody in a job and he didn't do it he put somebody else into it. This brought about a situation that was troublesome because he had as many as six jobs at one time.'[86] Páidín O'Keeffe, General Secretary of Sinn Féin (1917–23) and a TD, thought Collins' insensitivity generated antagonism, notably from de Valera: 'Collins was a right eejit because he took on so much that when Dev came back from America, the only person that people wanted to contact about affairs was Collins, thus apparently leaving Dev out in the cold.'[87]

Collins' energy, attention to detail and combination of roles also produced a completely new – and separate – power base, personal to him, as Robert Lynch has pointed out:

Thus in the midst of the War of Independence Collins was developing a new and multifaceted way of conducting a revolutionary insurrection reflected in his various roles as Minister for Finance, Director of Intelligence of the IRA and head of the IRB, which represented a formidable alternative power base to that of the political side of the movement.[88]

Collins Emerges

Cathal Brugha, while senior to Collins in the Volunteers/IRA, presided over rather than engaged in the daily grind.[89] De Valera, similarly to Brugha, had senior rank, but in America for eighteen months until December 1920 was even more removed from administration.[90] Collins was effectively untrammelled, free to bully and bark at his colleagues and co-workers, constantly chivvying them to greater effort, speed and efficiency, driving himself even harder, sleeping little, keeping accounts, administering the Dáil Loan, running the Dáil's Finance Ministry, plotting assassinations, conferring with agents, financing and arranging gun smuggling, meeting Volunteers/IRA men and requests from all over the country, regularly reporting to the Dáil, the Dáil Cabinet, Clan na Gael and the IRB Supreme Council.

As he energised IRB and Volunteer reorganisations, many saw him in 1917 and later as a political operator opportunistically developing the IRB for his own advantage.[91] Collins knew the whispers about his ambition, writing to Austin Stack in June 1919, 'All sorts of miserable little under-currents are working, and the effect is anything but good.'[92] Richard Walsh reflected much of the undercurrent: 'I totally disagree with his admirers and, I might say, worshippers, for attributing to him the gift of statesmanship and foresight. He had, in my opinion, none of those qualities, except to a very limited extent, if at all. His great weakness was his vanity and egoism.'[93]

In 1917–20, as Adjutant General of the Volunteers/IRA as they took shape, Collins built on his IRB connections, extending and solidifying his influence and being the person in GHQ that most Volunteer/IRA officers had met or knew about. He integrated the revived and reorganised IRB network with the Volunteers/IRA and used it for Volunteer/IRA expansion. He was so successful in this integration that by the end of 1917 most IRB Circles were the nucleus of a Volunteer/IRA Company (though not of every Volunteer/IRA Company).[94] By 1921 most Volunteer/IRA officers in Munster, down to company captains, were in the IRB, and a similar count could probably be made in each of the provinces.[95]

As Director of Intelligence on GHQ from 1918 to 1922, Collins used the IRB to support the Volunteers/IRA, especially with the purchase of arms and ammunition, again gaining admiration and loyalty from the Volunteers/IRA. Ernest Blythe saw him as inspirational:

> It was through his personal leadership and the fact that, as Griffith put it, Collins was 'The man who won the war' [that he was so respected]. It

168　　　　The Irish Republican Brotherhood, 1914–1924

was Collins' work as Chief of Intelligence, his collecting of money, his inspiring of people – everybody around him – even though he would be rough with some people and make enemies. 'No matter how black things look, boys, get on back to the job!' 'What the hell are you in Dublin for? Is there nobody to shoot in Tipperary?!' That sort of thing. So, Collins was more than any other person a figure of inspiration.[96]

He was also extraordinarily industrious, concerning himself with details. Máire Comerford recorded how in June 1921 a colleague received a note from Seán Ó Murthuile about laying a wreath on Wolfe Tone's grave: 'The Big Fellow says you are to lay a wreath at Bodenstown Sunday next. There will be a taxi at 41 Parnell Sq. at 10.30. There is seating accommodation for five people and you can bring who you wish.'[97]

President

Collins was elected President of the IRB in 1919, replacing Harry Boland. He was succeeded as Treasurer by Diarmuid O'Hegarty, who remained on the Council until 1923.[98] Eoin O'Duffy, one of the two Ulster representatives, joined the Council in 1919, succeeding O'Hegarty as Treasurer in 1921. Together with Seán Ó Murthuile and Gearóid O'Sullivan, both co-opted in 1917, this was the group that led the IRB up to 1923.

Collins' election as president confirmed his status.[99] His formation of the Squad and the Dublin Brigade 'Active Service Unit' to assassinate people and conduct special operations on his sole authority gave him the ability to command without first securing the agreement of Brugha or GHQ Staff.[100] Richard Mulcahy's quiet acceptance of Collins' pre-eminence played a vital part in this, with Mulcahy regularly informing Brugha about Volunteer/IRA affairs, including what Collins may have organised (and so covering for Collins), so that 'proper' procedures (never properly established) were seen to be observed. 'I opened and kept open for him all the doors and pathways he wanted to travel … I had no occasion to be questioning him. Over many matters we exercised a constructive and practical Cistercian silence.'[101] Tadhg Kennedy, one of Collins' intelligence officers, thought Collins stood apart from organisational structures: 'My idea of it was that surrounding Michael Collins was a gang of fellows, who rightly or wrongly regarded him as Chief of the Army and that nobody else counted under Collins, who was the "Big Fellow".'[102] Dan

Collins Emerges

McCarthy felt that this view of Collins and his standing with the Volunteers/ IRA was a major element in Brugha's hostility to him: 'There was great bitterness between Cathal Brugha and Michael Collins and I believe it all developed as a result of prominent I.R.A. Officers coming up from the country looking for Collins rather than Cathal Brugha who was Minister for Defence. Collins was always more popular with all these Officers. This was resented very much by Brugha.'[103]

Collins was careful with Brugha, unlike with Stack, and only hinted at his animosity. In early 1921 Pax Whelan, O/C Waterford Brigade, was in Dublin to argue the case for importing a shipload of weapons from Germany:

> Brugha called me over with some of these trifling complaints about how our fellows were behaving. Mellows was waiting at the door. 'Now,' said he, 'You see how difficult it is to persuade these people.' ... Then Mick cut in. 'I see Charlie and yourself were in a bit of an argument.' That startled me, because it was the first time I had heard his name, for which we all had an instinctive reverence, spoken that way. Mick seemed to say it in a derogatory way.[104]

Calling the determinedly nationalistic Brugha 'Charlie' indicated Collins' disrespect and must have annoyed Brugha.[105] It is no wonder that he was antagonistic and jealous of Collins, found it difficult to oppose him, and feared his secret influence and 'illicit' authority.[106] 'Collins, as you know, where he was he wanted to be boss,' said Liam O'Doherty, an IRB colleague.[107] Everything that Brugha had started in 1916 and 1917 had been taken over and accelerated by Collins. By attacking Collins, Brugha did himself a disservice while enhancing Collins' reputation.

Collins really was seen, with justice – as Griffith was to say in December 1921 – as 'the man who won the war'.[108]

CHAPTER 15

Elections

Sinn Féin to-day is allied with the physical-force Irish Republican Brotherhood of Ireland, which are a source of danger.[1]

Edward Shortt, Chief Secretary for Ireland,
in the House of Commons, 5 November 1918

As early as January 1917, Count Plunkett had been approached by a group of influential Roscommon men, led by Fr Michael O'Flanagan, to go forward as an anti-IPP candidate in the North Roscommon by-election caused by the death of the sitting MP. Séamus O'Doherty interviewed Plunkett, who agreed to stand as an abstentionist and on the 1916 Proclamation. O'Doherty undertook to be campaign manager and to put the IRB behind Plunkett, only to find that he had a problem with his provisional Supreme Council, as his wife remembered:

> My husband's activities in connection with the Roscommon election did not meet with the approval of his colleagues in the Supreme Council of the I.R.B. who did not seem to realise that the object for which that Body was founded and kept in existence up to the Rising had been realised and the Republic become a *fait accompli* by the Proclamation of Easter Week. Therefore, although they had ample funds in their treasury it was not made available for this 'constitutional' purpose.[2]

On 3 February 1917 Plunkett was elected with over 55 per cent of the vote, and in April he announced that he would form a new political party – the Liberty Clubs – and campaign for Irish representation at the peace conference that

Elections
171

would follow the end of the First World War. Sinn Féin had not yet emerged as the nationalist party of choice.

On 19 April 1917 Count Plunkett called a convention of his new party at the Mansion House, Dublin, with about 600 delegates from all over Ireland. Arthur Griffith and members of Patrick Little's Irish Nation League, both opposed to the IPP and to physical-force nationalism, were present.[3] Richard Walsh was a delegate:

> Each of the organisations had their own particular idea of what freedom meant. The Liberty Clubs – Count Plunkett's party – were out for the complete separation from England with physical force as their policy. Sinn Féin – Arthur Griffith's party – were out for economic and cultural advancement and an independent sovereign government, with a possible close association with England as independent entities. The third party – Paddy Little's party – were out for what was known as Colonial Home Rule, with a status similar to what Canada, Australia and New Zealand then enjoyed. Of the three elements, the most extreme and, as a consequence, the most influential as they had the support of the IRB organisations were the Liberty Clubs.[4]

Following on from the convention, Liberty Clubs were established seeking to replace the demoralised IPP and the newly popular Sinn Féin.[5] But Plunkett's convention had revealed nationalist differences that were not resolved. Dominion status – 'Colonial Home Rule' – effectively the IPP's position now in tune with Patrick Little – remained a strong nationalist view. The physical-force alternative of Plunkett and the IRB, while winning a majority at the convention, remained a minority choice nationally. Arthur Griffith opposed both Plunkett's Liberty Clubs and republicans (as separatists were now defining themselves), to everyone's surprise arguing against abstentionism – the policy he had pioneered – and expressing his resolve to maintain Sinn Féin's independence.[6] At this point in 1917 the political vehicle for separatism was not yet determined. Plunkett had national prestige as the father of Joseph. His handsome win in the Roscommon by-election on 3 February 1917 had made him a political force. His abstentionist stand appealed to the IRB.[7]

A 'Mansion House Committee' to co-ordinate nationalist political activity was formed immediately after the convention by Plunkett, Griffith, William O'Brien, Stephen O'Mara of the Irish National League, Cathal Brugha and Fr

172   The Irish Republican Brotherhood, 1914–1924

O'Flanagan. In 1918 the League and the Liberty Clubs agreed to merge with Sinn Féin under de Valera's leadership to fight the December 1918 general election on an abstentionist platform.

It was the popular, though inaccurate, connection of Sinn Féin with the Rising that would make Griffith's party the vehicle of choice. In return for the tremendous press publicity given to Sinn Féin in 1916, and the resulting growth of the party, in 1917 Griffith eventually accommodated his views to republicans and relinquished the leadership.

Griffith had been released from jail in December 1916. He brought out the first post-Rising issue of *Nationality* on 17 February 1917, devoting the whole paper to condemning Redmond and the IPP for their attitude towards the Rising.[8] He also echoed the hope of the Rising leaders that Ireland would have representation at the peace conference at the end of the war. His was a peaceful argument, placing him in opposition to the efforts of a revived IRB determined on fighting and not interested in arguing. The IPP was fading without any help from separatists. The continuing incarceration of those sentenced for their part in the Rising gave nationalists publicity as they campaigned for their release; their absence in prison enabled Collins to surge ahead in nationalist circles, rivalled only by Cathal Brugha.

The cult of dead leaders grew: frequent commemoration Masses in Dublin helped the growth of pro-Rising feeling; crowds – leaderless in 1916 – marched provocatively after these Masses. John Dillon, alone among the IPP leaders, recognised the dangers to the party of this change and as early as June 1916 had warned Redmond that they faced electoral difficulties.

Nationalist militancy was inflamed by Sir John Maxwell's presence in Dublin until he was replaced by Lieutenant General Sir Bryan Mahon in November 1916. Maxwell was personally, with justice, identified with executions. Mahon was Irish, a Roman Catholic, and was rightly seen as a conciliator. The continuation of martial law, also identified with Maxwell, was another grudge. A set of circumstances added to an increasing swing in popular opinion – the failure of the IPP's effort to secure Home Rule in 1916 (Unionists had proved intransigent, threatening the war coalition with disruption if Home Rule was implemented); the revelation that Redmond had agreed to partition presented the party as ineffective and in Britain's pocket; the hanging of Casement reawakened emotions; the publication of the report on the death of Francis Sheehy Skeffington, a Dublin cultural figure, that established that he had been killed unlawfully in 1916 by a British officer;[9]

Elections   173

and, above all, the threat in 1917 and 1918 of conscription in Ireland – all played into the hands of the IRB. William Brennan-Whitmore said to me in 1972:

> I was then and am now as convinced as I'm sitting on this settee that if the British had have kept us for, say, a fortnight in the various military barracks that we were confined in after the surrender and then opened the gates and given us a bloody good hard kick on the arse and told us to go home and be good boys, physical force would have been killed in Ireland for several generations anyhow. And the reason I'm so sure of that is this: the volume of opinion in Ireland was at that particular time solidly behind John Redmond and the Parliamentary Party and the whole bloomin' [Home Rule] Bill.[10]

William Oman was in the ICA and in the GPO during the Rising, and strongly agreed: 'My God! One British statesman in '14 would have saved it all because the country was looking for Home Rule. They were looking for Home Rule then, and they'd have voted it.'[11]

'The whole 1916 Rising would have died into ballad,' said Peadar O'Donnell, 'were it not for the issue of conscription immediately afterwards.'[12] The speed with which Clarke, O'Doherty, McGarry, Ó Murthuile and O'Hegarty acted in 1916 ensured that the IRB would significantly benefit from changing popular opinion.

Michael Collins had taken part in Plunkett's Roscommon election campaign on the last day as a poll watcher. He stayed on with Plunkett for two days, no doubt reconnecting with him as a Kimmage Volunteer and his son's aide de camp,[13] meeting O'Flanagan, O'Doherty and other activists. On 7 February, *The Freeman's Journal* reported Plunkett's return to Dublin 'accompanied by Miss [Geraldine] Plunkett, the Rev. Fr O'Flanagan, C.C., and Messrs Michael Collins, Séamus O'Doherty, John McCarthy and Joseph McGrath'. It was Collins' first mention in the national press.

In the United States Clan na Gael had formed the 'Friends of Irish Freedom' to publicise the cause of Irish independence and to support the families of the 1916 rebels – which, in effect, meant transferring funds to the IRB for the INAVDF. To the Clan, Ireland's fight meant the IRB's fight, and Clan money was always directed to IRB entities. Together, they lost no time in preparing to continue fighting.[14] They both calculated that after the

174   The Irish Republican Brotherhood, 1914–1924

Rising, to revert to parliamentary and traditional democratic methods would be to accept the platform of the IPP, which they were not prepared to do.

The entry of the United States into the First World War on 6 April 1917 transformed the Irish situation. President Wilson advocated the principle of national self-determination that was seen by Irish nationalists as offering the prospect of his strong support for Irish independence. Because of this, on 17 June 1917, following the release of the remaining 1916 prisoners the previous day, de Valera, Eoin MacNeill and twenty-four others had given Patrick McCartan their appeal to Wilson to endorse Irish sovereignty.[15] Wilson refrained: Ireland was part of the United Kingdom, America's ally in the war, and public support for Irish separation would have been unacceptable interference in United Kingdom affairs. Herbert Asquith had resigned as prime minister in December 1916 because of dissatisfaction with the conduct of the war and he was succeeded by Lloyd George. Wilson privately urged Lloyd George to address Irish nationalist feeling politically and not militarily.[16] Irish-American opinion was important; Wilson also had to be careful: Irish politics were American politics too.

Prompted by opposition to conscription, the release of the prisoners saw a spontaneous demonstration of the change in Irish popular opinion from anger against the 1916 rebels to support for them. Gerald Doyle was astonished by the reception his group of returning prisoners received: 'The climax came when Éamon de Valera, Thomas Ashe, Austin Stack, Harry Boland and Jack Shouldice appeared, and got on to the wagonettes. On seeing them, the crowd simply went mad. Rounds and rounds of cheers rent the sky.'[17]

Collins and the IRB activists concentrated on rebuilding and streamlining the Brotherhood to provide a solid base for a renewed Volunteer/IRA force, but they were also turning some of their attention to Sinn Féin.

On 9 May, Joseph McGuinness, a Rising prisoner in Lewes Prison, had won South Longford with a slender majority of thirty-seven. McGuinness had been an unwilling candidate, fearing along with de Valera that defeat would damage separatist political momentum.[18] But Michael Collins nevertheless put McGuinness' name forward and then campaigned vigorously for him. Collins had secretly conferred with Thomas Ashe in Lewes Prison about McGuinness and the wisdom of fighting the by-election.[19] Patrick McCartan, Diarmuid O'Hegarty, Seán Ó Murthuile and Séamus O'Doherty had also taken part in the campaign to elect McGuinness.[20] In contrast to Count Plunkett's election just three months earlier, McGuinness' election was an entirely IRB affair.

Elections 175

Irish politics was changing.

The lack of separatist unity and of political organisation gave local interests more influence. In East Clare there was a by-election on 10 July following the death during the Battle of Messines on 7 June of John Redmond's brother Major William Redmond, the MP for East Clare. Patrick Lynch, the IPP candidate, was well-respected and had deep Clare roots. Everyone understood that the by-election would be a crucial test of the IPP and of separatist strength. The Brennans, one of the influential and established political families in the county, favoured Eoin MacNeill as the separatist candidate. But there was strong resistance to MacNeill. Kathleen Clarke passed on to Michael Collins and other IRB organisers Tom Clarke's judgement that MacNeill had behaved treacherously in 1916.[21] MacNeill certainly did not regard the Rising as the first of more rebellions. Madge Daly, Kathleen Clarke's sister living in Limerick, approached the Brennans and suggested de Valera instead of MacNeill as the candidate. Neither sister knew de Valera or his political views but assumed that he would support the demand for independence. The Brennans came to agree and through their influence de Valera was nominated to fight the by-election.[22]

De Valera, recognising the sea change in Irish opinion, stood as an independent for East Clare in July in his uniform as a Volunteer commandant and accompanied by Eoin MacNeill, thus signifying a wish for a broad nationalist coalition.[23] This was a direct appeal to Volunteers in competition with the IRB. De Valera implied rejection of the IRB for yet again having carried out a failed rebellion, wearing his uniform and standing with MacNeill to balance his projection of a political rather than military future.[24] Éamonn Dore was at two meetings discussing the election:

> [M]ost of those present were I.R.B. members ... A discussion arose about Eoin MacNeill going down to Clare to assist in the election. Seán McGarry protested against this, but de Valera quashed all argument by saying that 'if MacNeill doesn't go – I won't go'. That appeared to overrule further argument on the matter ... [At a later meeting] Austin Stack asked why we were not all at our posts in Clare in accordance with de Valera's orders. And to this Seán McGarry replied, 'Who gave de Valera authority to order us about?' which query started a discussion on the desirability or otherwise of involving the I.R.B. in political activities. Finally the others all went off to Clare, but McGarry did not, he went back to Dublin. The point about this is that some of us strongly resented

176   The Irish Republican Brotherhood, 1914–1924

what we considered to be an unwarranted assumption of authority by those whom we looked upon as purely politicians. We, at the time, looked upon such things as election campaigns as frittering away the energies of the National Movement.[25]

On 10 July De Valera won massively with 71 per cent of the vote. His huge victory as a complete outsider in a constituency so closely associated with Redmond and against a strong and well-known local man was his launch as a national leader. Michael Noyk, a nationalist solicitor, noted: 'This was the "highlight" of the elections as, while up to this there may have been some doubts as to what Roscommon and Longford stood for, there was no doubt in this election as de Valera made it as clear as daylight that he and the party stood for a Republic.'[26]

On 10 August, William Cosgrave won the Kilkenny city election with 66 per cent of the vote. He was the first official Sinn Féin candidate in an election in ten years: Plunkett, McGuinness and de Valera had stood unaffiliated, but were identified with Sinn Féin. All four men refused to take their seats at Westminster, cementing abstention as the policy of the new politics.[27] The IRB had prompted the election successes identified with Sinn Féin, confirming the support of the new IRB leaders for political action, whereas before with Clarke and MacDermott the IRB had jealously persisted in its commitment to force alone.[28]

On 23 February 1917 Thomas Ashe, Seán Ó Murthuile, Séamus O'Doherty, Diarmuid O'Hegarty, Austin Stack and twenty-three others were arrested, charged with sedition and variously sentenced from one to two years' imprisonment. Collins visited them in Mountjoy prison before they departed for jails in England, gave them some money and a message of his own: he expected them all to escape as soon as possible.[29]

For ten weeks after these arrests Collins was effectively in charge of the IRB.[30] He arranged for some pistols to be bought in London and smuggled to Dublin: there was little doubt about his intentions. He was also thoroughly involved in INAVDF and Volunteer work. He followed up with plans for the escape of the prisoners, sending Fintan Murphy, an IRB colleague and drinking companion, on periodical visits to the prisoners to arrange the escapes.[31] In May, just before the Longford by-election, twelve of the twenty-eight men arrested in February broke out, including Ó Murthuile, O'Hegarty and O'Doherty. They found on their return that no changes had been made to the provisional Supreme Council since its formation in August 1916.

CHAPTER 16

1917–22 Constitution

The Fenians came and once and for all raised the banner of Ireland's freedom, with a definite military policy which, though unsuccessful at the time, had its full effect in bringing before men's minds the real road to Irish salvation.[1]

Michael Collins, The Path to Freedom

'When the bulk of the members returned to Dublin in 1917,' said George Lyons, an IRB member since 1898, 'it was found that the threads of the IRB were easily pulled together again and the whole position was regularised'.[2] The efforts of Liam Clarke, Collins, Ó Murthuile, O'Doherty and O'Hegarty had paid off. Diarmuid Lynch gave the principal credit to Michael Collins.[3]

IRB elections were held that summer and Lynch, Collins, Seán McGarry, Con Collins, Harry Boland and Thomas Ashe[4] became members of the new properly constituted Supreme Council formed in August. Ashe was elected president, shortly to be followed by Seán McGarry; Michael Collins secretary, and Diarmuid Lynch treasurer. A new constitution was drafted by Ashe, Con Collins and Lynch and then further revised by Lynch and Michael Collins.[5] Collins' growing influence is reflected in the attention to administrative procedures that were close to his heart – as the next years were to show – in the thirty-seven clauses of the constitution.[6]

Clause 1 came straight to the traditional point: 'The object of the Irish Republican Brotherhood (hereinafter sometime called the "Organisation") is to establish and maintain a free and independent Republican Government in Ireland.'

The most obvious difference from the 1873 Constitution was 1917's effort to deal with issues that had emerged in 1915 and 1916. The challenge of

178   The Irish Republican Brotherhood, 1914–1924

reorganising both the IRB and Volunteers was reflected in clause 2, introducing a new unequivocal element: 'The Irish Republican Brotherhood shall do its utmost to train and equip its members as a military body for the purpose of securing the independence of Ireland by force of arms.'

The consequences of this change – that the IRB was now conceived as an army – were that the Volunteers/IRA were intended to be that army; that the IRB would make every effort to control the Volunteers/IRA, and that any thoughts of non-violent efforts for independence were disregarded at the very start of the revived IRB campaign. A more encompassing phrase such as 'by all means possible' instead of 'by force of arms' would not have restricted the Brotherhood and, as events unfolded, would have more accurately reflected its activities. No doubt there was discussion on this point, but the final decision was a reavowal of complete dedication to force.

The 1873 provision that Hobson and McCartan had stressed for a majority decision by the Irish people as a prerequisite for war was dropped. A new death sentence for treason was introduced, emphasising the claimed reality of IRB government. A particular change was made to the Executive's powers. It was no longer allowed to declare war, or alter the constitution: the 1916 experience was not to be repeated.[7] Now, the Supreme Council would be in full control. Liam Mellows, who had been active in Galway during the Rising, voiced the concern that sparked this reform as he walked with Frank Robbins, a member of the ICA who had taken part in the Rising:

'If I had known as much in Easter Week as I know to-day I would never have fired a shot.' This immediately brought the response from me, 'Ah, ah, Liam, you have been listening to Dr. McCartan.' Liam was very angry at this remark … I suggested that if it was not a breach of confidence would he tell me what was troubling him. With that he told me that the Revolutionary Military Council had taken unto themselves powers to which they had no right; they had usurped the authority of the Supreme Council of the IRB which was the only authority with power to declare the Insurrection, and they had set themselves up as a military junta and ignored everyone else. These were the reasons for his astonishing statement, whereupon I asked him would he like to hear my point of view on the matter and replying he would be glad to hear it. I said, 'Liam, you have been going around this country telling the Irish people and the American people that the Insurrection of 1916 has

1917–22 Constitution   179

regenerated the soul of Ireland … in Christian charity you must give the benefit of the doubt to the men who made the supreme sacrifice, and made it so willingly, for what they believed in. That sacrifice, you and I must agree, is now bearing the fruits which we are looking forward to gather.' Liam turned to me and said, 'Thanks, Frank, I never looked at it that way. You have eased my mind considerably. I was very worried about the whole matter'.[8]

Membership procedures and the basic organisation remained the same. The IRB oath was unchanged. Men had to be Irish, of good character and obedient to 'superior officers'.[9] 'In cities, the District Board shall arrange for a special scrutiny of prospective candidates by submitting each name for the approval of the Circles in the District.'[10] Each District had a Board composed of the District Circle Centres who were to choose 'a Chairman, a Vice-Chairman, a Secretary and a Treasurer. The Chairman shall be entitled a "District Centre", and shall be responsible to the County Centre … Each City shall be considered a District.'[11] County Centres were to be elected by the Circle Centres in each County and were superior to the District Centres.[12]

There were to be at least two Districts in each Irish County. District Centres were to elect Divisional Boards of which there were to be eleven, two in each Irish province, two in England and one in Scotland. Each Divisional Board was to elect a Supreme Council representative. The elected members of the Council then co-opted four more members, 'thus laying the foundation for more intensive recruitment and incidentally enlarging the membership of the Supreme Council from 11 to 15'.[13]

Members were banned from belonging to any other oath-bound society 'without the express permission of the Supreme Council'.[14] This was another new element. Diarmuid Lynch explained: 'There was a particular reason for this in 1917 and the Supreme Council was determined that the I.R.B. should have but *one* object and that its members should not be dominated by any other secret organisation.'[15]

While no other nationalist secret society existed in 1917, Collins and his colleagues had leadership and control of the Volunteers/IRA in mind and thus wanted to ensure IRB primacy when it came to oaths of loyalty. They were also responding to incipient competition: from Brugha's growing opposition to the IRB combined with his seniority in the Volunteers; from Count Plunkett's independent initiatives that attracted a large body of Irish nationalist opinion;

from de Valera's opposition to McGuinness' election and to the IRB; from the popularity of the returning prisoners, led by de Valera, and the question of what – if anything – they as a group would do; from de Valera successfully taking the role of national leader and launching his own politico-military appeal entirely separate from the IRB and obviously competing for control of the Volunteers/IRA, and from the weakening but still significant IPP. The emergence of Sinn Féin as the holdall of the various more militant nationalist political groups had not yet occurred.

Subscriptions were another new element. The 1873 Constitution had simply stated that a member should 'contribute according to his means for the production of war materials and also towards the expense of keeping up communication in the different divisions of the IRB and for maintaining the efficiency of the Supreme Council'.[16] In contrast, the 1917 revision was detailed, showing Collins' hand:

> Each member of the Irish Republican Brotherhood shall pay a monthly fee of sixpence, one-third of which shall be retained by the Circle, one-third by the county treasurer, and one-third remitted to the Supreme Council through the Divisional Centre. Each member shall contribute according to his means for the purchase of war materials, and shall pay any special levies which the Supreme Council may impose as the necessity arises.[17]

Funding was, for the first time, made a regular and organised process. It was a signal of continuing rebellious determination, and of an awareness that dependence on Clan na Gael generosity[18] might have unwanted consequences, as Hobson, McCartan and Allan had experienced in 1911.

In the 1873 Constitution errant members could be fined (e.g. for losing weapons), expelled, or executed. The new constitution, probably because of the experience with Bulmer Hobson in 1916 who had not broken any rules (because he was circumvented, kept ignorant of plans, and not ordered to conform), introduced suspension as an intermediate step to expulsion.[19]

New provisions were made for several administrative initiatives. The energetic attention to detail and the obsession with records and procedures characteristic of Collins were apparent (although when it came to practicalities, he disregarded formalities). The transfer of members between Circles was set out, reflecting the experience of Collins and others who had come from Britain in 1915 and had

1917–22 Constitution

found no arrangements for their incorporation into local Circles.[20] Each County was to have 'two or more' District Centres responsible for County Circles and were required to send reports to their County Centres 'on the last day of each month ... relating to [their] numerical, financial and disciplinary standing' and to send on whatever funds were due. County Centres were to report onward to Divisional Centres 'on the 7th day of the month following'.[21]

Clauses about maintaining secrecy, election procedures, and the freedom of Divisional Centres 'to frame by-laws' subject to Supreme Council approval were introduced and a Military Council was established as a permanent sub-group firmly under the control of the Supreme Council with no policy authority.[22] The informal and untrammelled Executive of 1873 was being reined in. Again, retrospectively, Collins' hand can be seen imposing method on anything that was unclear or not included in the 1873 Constitution.

A key 1873 element was maintained: 'There shall be no State religion in the Irish Republic. Each citizen shall be free to worship God according to the dictates of his conscience.'[23]

Following on from the 1916 Proclamation of a Republic was a strong, new, social republican sensibility: 'There shall be no privileged persons or classes in the Irish Republic. All citizens shall enjoy equal rights therein.'[24]

The Supreme Council's claim to be 'the sole Government of the Irish Republic ... until ... a permanent Republican Government is established' was reaffirmed.[25] No compromise was allowed with devolution, Dominion status, Griffith's dual monarchy or any other form of government. The IRB's Ireland would be a republic. Partition, obviously a probability, was disregarded with a simple assumption of a united Ireland throughout, implying a traditional willingness to resort to force to achieve unity.

The functions of government were specified – another new feature: 'The Supreme Council of the Irish Republican Brotherhood shall have power to levy taxes, raise loans, make war and peace, negotiate and ratify treaties with foreign powers, and do all other acts necessary for the protection and government of the Irish Republic.'[26]

Despite the by-election victories during 1917, there was no mention of elections or political positioning. Altogether, the constitution reflected a determination to renew the fighting that had started in 1916 and – *pace* Éamonn Dore and others – not to be deflected from this purpose by electoral politics and compromises.

The IRB intended war.

CHAPTER 17

The Candidate

Collins declared his belief that de Valera would never hurt the IRB.[1]

George Lyons, 1947

In the summer of 1917 nationalists were not co-ordinated. Sinn Féin had yet to be galvanised nationally,[2] and the Irish Volunteers/IRA were only properly reorganised in Dublin. The IRB was still trying to re-establish its countrywide Circles that it used as the basis of Volunteer/IRA companies.[3] Count Plunkett, Arthur Griffith, de Valera and Eoin MacNeill competed in the public mind for separatist leadership. De Valera was known as the senior survivor of the Rising, but his connections were with the other prisoners released in June and not with the IRB Volunteer/IRA reorganisers and those who had campaigned in the two by-elections in February and May 1917. While in prison he had argued in favour of MacNeill's 1916 stand and against the continuation of the IRB. After the Rising he expressed serious doubts on religious grounds as to the validity of hopeless rebellion against an established government. Sam Irwin served with de Valera in Boland's Mill during the Rising and witnessed de Valera's declaration to this effect:

> Shortly after he was released in 1917 when the general amnesty took place, he assembled us all, if you don't mind, to explain the theology of the Rising and to point out the Church's doctrine on the thing. This is something not generally known; I've not seen it anywhere. I was present at the thing. That the Church's doctrine on this question of insurrection or rebelling of oppressed people is not justified. 'I will not get the blessing of the Church unless there is a chance of success'.[4]

The Candidate   183

De Valera gave notice of his wish to resign from the Brotherhood:

> At a meeting in August, 1917, a message came to the Centres Board that de Valera wished to be relieved of his oath and resign the organisation as he had conscientious scruples with regard to an oath and had never slept easily since he took the oath of the I.R.B. [so] de Valera did not leave as a mutineer, he resigned in the constitutional manner. Collins declared his belief that de Valera would never hurt the I.R.B.[5]

De Valera himself did not broadcast that he had religious scruples for resigning. He explained his resignation as being because a secret organisation was no longer necessary; because the Volunteers/IRA could work openly for independence; because the contradictory orders at Easter 1916 exemplified the problems arising between a public and a secret organisation; and because he disliked obeying an Executive of unidentified members.[6]

De Valera's departure was a marked change from the pre-Rising IRB. When members left the society or were expelled, there was a formal procedure. Fred Allan, for example, had to swear never to reveal anything about the organisation when he left. Now, in 1917 and later, with de Valera, Bulmer Hobson and presumably other members, no exit steps were taken. The post-Rising IRB was focused on reorganising itself and controlling first the Volunteer/IRA leadership and then the political leadership and was not so concerned about procedures for members leaving.

De Valera's political views were hard to pin down. He thought a republic unattainable and Dominion status a reasonable compromise. But in prison in 1916–17 he quickly realised that he was seen as a leader, and he knew he was competing with the IRB, so he had to maintain a republican stance. His East Clare election campaign was ambivalent. On the one hand it was an announcement that he would bid for both Volunteer/IRA and Sinn Féin leadership and wearing his commandant's uniform signalled that he supported continued militancy. On the other hand, he said that he was faithful to the 'spirit' of the Rising but did not explicitly endorse continued fighting. In 1921 he declared that during the period from mid-1917 to late 1919 'we were working under peace conditions then',[7] a statement at odds with the fact of growing violence during those years, and with the efforts of Brugha, Collins, the Volunteers/IRA and the IRB to continue fighting. It was a retrospective effort on de Valera's part to establish a fiction of constitutional action as

184   The Irish Republican Brotherhood, 1914–1924

the bedrock of the 1918–21 conflict, and to establish the pre-eminence of politicians: until late 1919, de Valera was asserting, the country had not actually been at war.

Razor-thin distinctions were to be de Valera's métier and ambiguity his defining element. He argued for an independent Ireland to have a seat at the peace conference that would end the war. The nature of this independent Ireland was left vague, enabling republicans to think he meant a republic, and Home Rulers to think that he did not. In August 1921, for example, he indicated that he was open to a Dominion status settlement.[8] He wanted to lead a broad nationalist alliance that he recognised was already forming. The IPP had been just such an alliance, having room both for IRB-minded men and for moderate constitutionalists. Just because the party had failed in the Irish mind did not mean that its constituents had become more narrow-minded. De Valera set about building on this awareness, and he was conscious of the mixed loyalties of most people. Significantly, there had been no mutiny in support of the Rising in the Irish units in the British Army or the Royal Navy. The Rising was put down by Irish soldiers in Irish regiments: 41 were killed and 106 were wounded. An English regiment, the Sherwood Foresters, which landed in Ireland on Easter Wednesday, suffered most with 220 killed and wounded. In addition, 17 RIC and DMP men were killed and 30 wounded.[9] Irishmen in British units fought without pause throughout the First World War.[10] De Valera understood that there was no popular mandate for killing constables and policemen and that careful politics was the best hope for independence. As Eunan O'Halpin has pointed out, 'the number of people killed as informers in County Cork between 1920 and 1923 – over 200 by one recent estimate – scarcely bespeaks either rock solid support for the IRA even in the rebel county, or IRA confidence that no one would betray them.'[11]

Irish voluntary enlistment in the British Army and Navy was substantial and merited de Valera's caution. During the war, about 210,000 men resident in Ireland served in the British forces. Of the estimated 680,000 United Kingdom fatalities, about 33,500 were Irish.[12] The journalist and author James Stephens, writing within weeks of the Rising, picked up on Irish enrolment from within the empire:

> The country was not with it, for be it remembered that a whole army of Irishmen, possibly three hundred thousand of our race are fighting with

The Candidate

England instead of against it. In Dublin alone there is scarcely a poor home in which a father, a brother, or a son is not serving in one of the many fronts England is defending.[13]

In Ireland, popular antagonism to the Volunteers/IRA was widespread both before and after the Rising.[14] There was never popular acceptance of the Volunteers/IRA by a majority of Irish people, and this meant a tricky political path for the IRB, the Dáil and Sinn Féin.

The task facing de Valera and the new nationalist political leadership was not to alienate the families of servicemen while also appealing to Plunkett's abstentionist Liberty Clubs, Arthur Griffith's reviving Sinn Féin, the Irish Nation League opposed to the IPP and to force, and the Volunteers/IRA and the IRB preparing for more fighting. The tensions between these groupings were never resolved.[15]

It is easy to depict de Valera as a very political operator, appealing to different groups without committing to any of them, constantly seeking pre-eminence. Yet he was sincere. He was a devout Catholic and a passionate nationalist. He did not like violence, although he benefited from it. His objections to the IRB were genuine. He had been set aside by his parents as a child, denied the experience of unquestioned love. He compensated by giving his deep love to an ideal of an independent Ireland that he sought to personify. He recognised in Cathal Brugha a similar commitment, and he recognised in Collins a pragmatist prepared to trade ideals for power – power to achieve a compromised independence, certainly, but not the pure ideal. De Valera was an idealogue masquerading as a politician.

De Valera's candidacy for nationalist leadership was supported by Thomas Ashe, President of the IRB. Ashe was a typical IRB leader, interested in action, in fighting the English enemy come what may. He had spent the eight weeks since his release in June 1917 delivering speeches in Kerry, East Clare, Longford and Dublin, urging defiance to British rule and to conscription. Early in August he was in Dublin to attend a meeting about reorganising the Volunteers/IRA. As many of the pre-Rising members of the Volunteer/IRA Executive as it was possible to gather attended, along with Brugha, de Valera and Collins.[16] Shortly afterwards, on 18 August, Ashe was again arrested and charged with sedition. He escaped but was recaptured and on 28 August he was tried, found guilty, and sentenced to two years' hard labour. In prison he went on hunger strike. On 25 September he died as a result of forced feeding.[17] The Right Rev. Michael

186   The Irish Republican Brotherhood, 1914–1924

Fogarty, Bishop of Killaloe, wrote in a public letter that the manner of his death was 'the triumph of English culture'.[18]

The Wolfe Tone Memorial Committee, an IRB front, took charge of his funeral, as they had two years previously for O'Donovan Rossa.[19] 'The funeral committee for the Ashe funeral in September 1917 was based on the O'Donovan Rossa funeral committee of August 1915,' noted Richard Mulcahy. 'It was activated by the IRB activists. It was no doubt due to this that Collins was selected to be the "speaker" at the graveside.'[20] The funeral committee's president was Seán McGarry, Ashe's successor as IRB president.[21]

De Valera was conspicuously absent. He was in Ennis where he delivered an assertive speech stating that Ashe's death showed popular determination to obtain freedom from Britain, and that Irish people 'were ready to perish, one after the other, rather than submit to be conquered'.[22] He did not admit that they had not been consulted nor the possibility that they might not wish to perish. His language made him out to be a diehard republican fighter.

Collins' emergence at the Ashe funeral marked the return of the IRB as a force in nationalist politics, as was to become obvious in the 1917 Sinn Féin and Volunteer/IRA conventions.[23] Its hidden hand was probably responsible for the successful marshalling of Volunteers/IRA from all over the country to attend the funeral in Dublin.[24]

Tadhg Kennedy was 'a kind of distant relative' of Thomas Ashe. He was a Kerry IRB man and was an intelligence officer for Austin Stack, who was both the IRB and Volunteer/IRA leader in Kerry. Kennedy was at the funeral: 'I recognised the fellow in charge of the Firing Party and he recognised me. It was Mick Collins … He asked me if I had any connection with the Irish Volunteers. "I have," I said, "but I have been appointed to a new job now, to Intelligence." "If that's so," said Collins, "I'm your boss."'[25]

The 1917 reorganisations of the IRB and the Volunteers/IRA had uneven results, as Kennedy's ignorance of Collins' position revealed. Over the following years, Collins' responsibilities became well known on all sides, but the lines of communication and authority became more and more frayed as they stretched, especially to the west and north from Dublin.

On Easter Sunday, 8 April 1917, a second Volunteer/IRA convention was held at the Plaza Hotel, Gardiner Row, Dublin. Brugha again presided, still on crutches. Many of those released from Frongoch took part. The night before the convention met, Collins held a meeting of IRB members of the Volunteers/IRA to secure acceptance by the convention of a scheme of organisation he

The Candidate

had drawn up. The week before he had been elected adjutant of the First Battalion, Dublin Brigade, giving him a more senior rank (in 1916 he had been a captain in the GPO). When the proposal for Collins' scheme came up, Liam Clarke joined Brugha in opposing it – successfully: Collins' overall dominance was not yet established (he had been released from Frongoch less than four months earlier), but nevertheless he advanced a modified 'General Scheme of Organisation' that was adopted. Its tone was moderate:

> All Irishmen also subscribe to the following objects:
>
> 1. To secure and maintain the rights and liberties common to all the people of Ireland;
> 2. To train, discipline and equip for this purpose an Irish Volunteer Force;
> 3. To unite, in the service of Ireland, all Irishmen of every creed and of every party and class are eligible for membership of the Irish Volunteers, having signed this declaration:
>
> 'I, the undersigned, desire to be enrolled for service in Ireland as a member of the Irish Volunteer Force. I subscribe to the constitution of the Irish Volunteers and pledge my willing obedience to my superior officers. I declare that in joining the Irish Volunteer Force I set before myself the stated objects of the Irish Volunteers and no others.'[26]

Collins took care to refer to 'Volunteers': the IRA from the Rising, let alone from the 1870s, was identified with the IRB, and Collins obviously wanted to keep the Brotherhood's hand hidden to avoid a rupture with de Valera and MacNeill. He also phrased his scheme so that the Volunteers/IRA would not be an oath-bound competitor to the IRB: this was probably his objective.

A new Volunteer/IRA Executive Committee was established together with a Resident Executive Subcommittee in Dublin for day-to-day affairs. The members of the Executive were elected at the convention. Brugha remained Chief of Staff and Chairman of the Resident Executive which included men from various parts of the country; it was not Dublin-centric. Five members of the National Executive were directors – of training, supplies, engineering, organisation and communications – and served on the Resident Executive. They had oversight responsibility. Later these positions overlapped with those on the

188   The Irish Republican Brotherhood, 1914–1924

GHQ Staff established in March 1918, but the Executive's overall authority remained – an element it never surrendered. Dublin had seven representatives on the National Executive, Munster and Ulster had four each, Leinster had two and Connacht three. Six more members were co-opted. Seán McGarry and Michael Staines acted as secretaries of the National and Resident Executives.[27] Staines was also Director of Supplies on the Executive.

Another convention to be held later in the year was agreed, aiming to integrate the growing Volunteer/IRA membership within the new structure.[28] As with the IRB, the GAA provided cover for Volunteer/IRA meetings, often at Croke Park.[29] In August 1917 Collins, Brugha, de Valera, Thomas Ashe and some others met to arrange this third post-Rising Volunteer/IRA convention.[30] It took place on 27 October at Croke Park. For the IRB, this convention was a key moment. De Valera was elected unopposed as President of the Volunteers/ IRA. Cathal Brugha continued as Chief of Staff and Chairman of the Resident Executive.[31] The IRB priority once again was to have firm control of the Volunteer/IRA leadership. Brugha may no longer have been a member of the IRB, but he was of an IRB mind and so did not represent a threat to their republican objective or their determination to continue fighting. De Valera and MacNeill presented the IRB with Hobson-like problems, but they could be circumvented. The point that was missed was that MacNeill and de Valera represented a majority Sinn Féin view, preferring to gain independence by replacing the British government with a Dáil government with a minimum of violence.[32]

On the Executive Committee that was elected, all but de Valera, Brugha and Joe O'Doherty were members of the IRB.[33] Seán McGarry became General Secretary and Collins became Director of Organisation. The IRB reorganisation of the Volunteers during 1917 had paid off but, as we have seen, had also reduced the importance of the Brotherhood to many of its members in favour of the Volunteers/IRA.

The next IRB priority was to gain control of Sinn Féin. On 25 October 1917, the tenth Sinn Féin convention was held at Dublin's Mansion House. The party had at last captured the public mind as *the* nationalist political grouping. Collins worked to have IRB men elected to the party's Executive Committee and to support de Valera for its presidency, providing a list of people that IRB members should vote for: 'I got an order from the I.R.B. to see Collins before the meeting,' said Robert Brennan, a Wexford delegate, 'in one of the houses on the west side of Parnell Square, I found a regular queue of men from all

The Candidate 189

parts of the country. Mick, sitting at a table, handed me a typed list. It was the ticket the Wexfordmen were to support for the National Executive.'[34] 'IRB men were instructed to have themselves elected delegates to that convention, if possible,' Séamus Dobbyn recalled, 'and to vote for the election of de Valera as President. I was ordered by the Supreme Council, and carried out the order, to give instructions to suitable IRB men to join the local Sinn Féin Club and if possible to have themselves elected as delegates to that Convention.'[35] Daniel Kelly was there, noting the delegates' awareness of the IRB:

> Mr de Valera was not a member of the Irish Republican Brotherhood, although he got their enthusiastic support for the Presidency of Sinn Féin. In the Mansion House, just before the meeting really got started – Arthur Griffith was in the chair – one of the O'Hanrahans got up and said that, before the meeting or any voting took place, he wished to make a strong protest as there was a big number of delegates present who belonged to an organisation and all of whom had pledged themselves to vote for a certain candidate. He was over-ruled by the chairman, Griffith.[36]

Darrell Figgis composed a rival list in favour of moderate nationalists that was not successful, triggering Collins' and the IRB's permanent hostility to him.[37] Joe O'Doherty, also at the convention, saw de Valera as stitching together a political alliance:

> There was a cloud over MacNeill, and it was he who brought MacNeill back again, do you see, and he was conscious of various types of mentality in the national movement: MacNeill signifying one section; the IRB another section; the Volunteers another section; Griffith another section. And it was the amalgamation of the whole lot he aimed at and eventually got that amalgamation at the Sinn Féin convention. And he was all the time trying to weld the various points of view together and succeeded – I take my hat off to him – up to a certain point.[38]

The shadow in the room was that there was no agreement about the form independence might take. Within Sinn Féin the whole range of nationalist opinion existed. Some wanted a republic, others wanted Dominion status while Griffith favoured a monarchy. The IRB wanted a republic and nothing

190   The Irish Republican Brotherhood, 1914–1924

else.[39] But the Volunteers/IRA had a life of its own and, while IRB influence was strong within the organisation, IRB republicanism was not fully accepted. And, as with Sinn Féin, the Volunteers/IRA contained different views about what it was willing to fight for.

The convention saw the consequences of these differences at work. There was a straightforward determination to have an executive of broad appeal. The rally to Sinn Féin had occurred only two or three months earlier, so the delegates had come together somewhat haphazardly. They were not the same people who formed the Volunteers/IRA and had not been as carefully targeted by the IRB. They were a mix of separatists and moderate nationalists, and this was reflected in the voting where relatives of 1916 leaders fared badly: a leavening of heroes was all that was wanted. Cathal Brugha (685) and Austin Stack (857) did well. Griffith received most votes (1,197) and was elected joint vice-president with Fr O'Flanagan (780). Stack was elected joint honorary secretary with Darrell Figgis (510). Eoin MacNeill (883) – after de Valera (elected unopposed) and Griffith – was the third most popular member of the Executive.[40] Joseph MacDonagh (421), Kathleen Clarke (402) and Geraldine Plunkett (345) received some of the lowest votes.[41] Collins came joint last in the poll (340 votes): other better-known members of the IRB received more votes than he did. If he was managing an effective IRB cadre, why then did he receive the lowest vote for a place? The suggestion is that in October 1917 he and the IRB had been flat-footed by the rapidity of Sinn Féin's growth: 1,700 delegates attended the convention.

Generally, moderate nationalists did better than separatists, and men and women from Dublin did better than those from elsewhere, which was probably a reflection of the composition of the convention. IRB men secured nearly half the places on the Executive, but Sinn Féin did not fall under IRB control. Liam Gaynor had to devote time and energy to keeping an eye on the party's activities in Belfast:

> [A] watching brief was held on the Belfast Sinn Féin organisation so as to prevent this body from getting into undesirable hands. Like most of my IRB and Volunteer colleagues I was always ... doubtful about the sincerity of most platform politicians. It was essential for me to take an active part in the Belfast Sinn Féin Executive meetings with some colleagues, so as to prevent a possible clash with the policy of our armed forces.[42]

The Candidate   191

In 1917 few outside the IRB thought of continued rebellion; most presumed that the struggle for independence would be political. By October the nationalist consensus was that the political effort would be conducted by Sinn Féin,[43] even though what the party stood for was not clear. Griffith wanted it to continue his campaign for an effectively independent Ireland, not bothering with the form it might take. But the Sinn Féin that emerged in October 1917 was quite different from the party Griffith had founded and led.

In September, a month before the convention, de Valera had published a compromise formula that he calculated would keep both Griffith and Brugha (representing diehard republicans) in Sinn Féin. He proposed it at the convention, and it was accepted by all. It formed the preamble to a new party constitution: 'Sinn Féin aims at securing the international recognition of Ireland as an independent Irish republic. Having achieved that status, the Irish people may by referendum freely choose their own form of government.'[44]

This was a form of words that would not stand application. Having secured a republic (if that were possible), why give it up? A referendum could opt for remaining within the United Kingdom or the Empire, negating the republican effort. And, if that was to happen, why not stick with Griffith's practical approach? Why insist on a status you were prepared to surrender? De Valera was postponing the confrontation between devolution and a republic while seeking to stifle debate until a republic was secured. Behind the words was a two-step power awareness: those who won a republic would be superseded by those elected to govern. De Valera led the political group waiting to govern. As all rebels discover, when the shooting stops politicians inevitably advance. Surprisingly, no reference was made to this 'republic first and then let's decide' clause during the Treaty debates of 1921–22 when a plausible argument could have been made that having achieved a republic, it was perfectly proper then to decide whether or not to stick to it. Perhaps the obviously theoretical nature of such a debate forestalled it.

The pressure for unity slowly penetrated the IRB. Its members on the Sinn Féin and Volunteer/IRA Executives gradually attached more importance to those organisations than to the Brotherhood. After all, Sinn Féin and the Volunteers/IRA were seen as working for an Irish republic, which was the IRB's objective too. But the call for unity suppressed deep differences of opinion, especially about 'force of arms'.

After 1917 there were no further Volunteer/IRA conventions or elections until 1922. That there could be divisive debate (as there was in Sinn Féin and the IRA in 1921–22) was recognised; avoiding debate and thus divisiveness by not convening was a way of maintaining focus, control and apparent unity, while putting off potential conflict. The Volunteer/IRA Resident Executive met fortnightly in Dublin during 1918, and infrequently after that.[45] As Executive members were arrested, new members were co-opted,[46] but IRB representation remained dominant. The effort to secure IRB members as officers after 1917 continued but was patchy. The election rather than appointment of officers pushed Circles to produce candidates who in many cases proved inadequate, especially when local loyalties were in play.[47] In Munster and Connacht, separatist feeling was sufficient to ensure separatist-minded Volunteer/IRA officers and companies, whether IRB or not. As Florence O'Donoghue explained, the election of officers worked 'because of the spirit in which men served'[48] rather than their competence. In Ulster, IRB activity was slight.[49] In Dublin, Leinster and Munster, however, there was a successful effort to elect IRB officers,[50] reflecting the preponderance and organisation of IRB members in the capital and the two provinces.

The 1917 effort to achieve public unity also obscured how an Irish republic would be obtained. For the Volunteers/IRA, directed by IRB members, there was no uncertainty about what to do: there was to be a campaign attacking the RIC and DMP. For de Valera and others, MacNeill's pre-1916 policy of 'defending arms if attacked' prevailed, and a political campaign through Sinn Féin was their choice. A confrontation between the two approaches was inevitable.

CHAPTER 18

GHQ

'We have got to organise movements in enemy-occupied territory comparable to the Sinn Fein movement in Ireland.'[1]

Hugh Dalton to Lord Halifax, 2 July 1940

The 27 October 1917 Volunteer/IRA convention elected the new twenty-six-member Volunteer/IRA Executive. Richard Mulcahy described it as 'the governing body of the Volunteer organisation, almost exercising ministerial control over the armed forces that were developing ... The organisation job was the principal thing that required to be done at that particular time and Collins was in a very strong and happy position to do it.' Nearly all those proposed for membership were in the IRB.[2]

It soon became clear that 'a body of a military kind' was needed to oversee the practical organisation and control of the Volunteers/IRA. In early March 1918 a GHQ at 'Dublin Headquarters' was formed by the Executive to direct the Volunteers.[3] The night before the Executive met, a group which included Collins, Mulcahy, Dick McKee, Gearóid O'Sullivan, Diarmuid O'Hegarty and Seán MacMahon – all members of the IRB – met to arrange who should hold the different positions on the staff.[4] Mulcahy was chosen as Chief of Staff.[5]

The night after the creation of the Staff, a meeting of the complete Executive confirmed Mulcahy's appointment and that of Austin Stack (IRB), upon Mulcahy's proposal, as Deputy Chief of Staff.[6] Collins continued as Director of Organisation on the Executive and on GHQ Staff and also as Adjutant General on the Staff. Joe O'Doherty (ex-IRB), Director of Communications on the Executive, was joined by Diarmuid O'Hegarty as Director of Communications on the Staff. Éamonn Duggan became Director of Intelligence.[7]

194   The Irish Republican Brotherhood, 1914–1924

Rory O'Connor (IRB),[8] who had been appointed Director of Engineering on the Executive in 1917, remained in the post on the Executive and as GHQ Director of Engineering; Piaras Béaslaí (IRB), editor of *An t-Óglách*,[9] completed the Staff.[10] They immediately faced administrative problems. Richard Walsh remembered:

> The question of wholetime work for the newly appointed Staff was subject to the availability of funds to pay the Staff … It was assumed that the only available cash was in the hands of the I.R.B. The Sinn Fein organisation had funds available, but we could not ask for their funds as Sinn Fein at that time contained men not favourable to physical force and they might not have been enthusiastically inclined to give any financial help to the Volunteers. When the question of approaching the I.R.B. for funds arose, Cathal Brugha approved of the proposition and pointed out that the IRB funds were intended for such use as the Volunteers would now put them to … Michael Collins stated that he knew the sources through which the I.R.B. organisation could be approached and influenced to advance the money.[11]

And so it was. The IRB underwrote the cost.

Séumas Robinson later asserted that the Staff self-interestedly controlled the Volunteers/IRA so that when the 1921 Treaty 'compromise' was presented, the opinions of lower ranks of the IRA were stifled:

> [T]his compromise has been lurking in the ante-camera of many a cerebrum for the past three years. It was conceived when the Volunteers were denied a general Convention three years ago [in 1919]; it passed through the embryo form when the Volunteers began to be controlled solely from Dublin Headquarters; it became a chrysalis when Dublin HQ became a wage-earning business, when District HQ were set up by General HQ and paid to control men who fought the war, aye, and won it, without any appreciable assistance from Dublin Headquarters.[12]

Dan Breen,[13] a Tipperary IRB man and Volunteer/IRA officer, echoed Robinson, noting that differences were suppressed for the sake of apparent unity: 'Our war policy was not popular. Our GHQ seemed to be lukewarm about it. The political wing certainly opposed it, and more than one TD privately

GHQ

denounced it. We succeeded in concealing our disagreements up to the time of the [July 1921] Truce.'[14]

Robinson and Breen spoke for a majority of the Volunteers/IRA and, as it turned out, the IRB too. They reflected the division of experience and outlook between Dublin activists and country activists. In Dublin the fight was about intelligence, protecting the nationalist political and military leadership, calculating political advantage, and assassination; in the country it was straightforwardly about ambushes and attacks on RIC barracks.

Two events occurred in 1918 immediately after the creation of the GHQ that delayed Volunteer/IRA development. The first was the conscription crisis of April–June; the second was the German Plot in May. Casualties in France during the war required replacing and Ireland, as the only nation of the United Kingdom not to have conscription, was the obvious place to extend it to. Lloyd George tied progress towards Home Rule to acceptance of conscription, but the Church, the IPP, Sinn Féin and all but Unionist associations and Unionist local government opposed it in a massive demonstration of national unity.

On 10 April, a day after Sir Horace Plunkett's Irish Convention ended in failure, Lloyd George introduced a Military Service Bill in the House of Commons that did not bring conscription to Ireland directly but, as A.J.P. Taylor put it, in 'another unconscious repudiation of the Union' made it possible through 'Orders in Council', again emphasising Ireland's separateness.[15]

John Dillon led the IPP's opposition to the Bill, convinced that the government was destroying the party. On 16 April the Bill passed in the House of Commons and the IPP withdrew from Westminster and made common cause with Sinn Féin, but it was too late: Sinn Féin was seen as the party willing to fight; the IPP as only willing to talk, not least because it had achieved its purpose – the enactment of Home Rule – and had not looked beyond that. De Valera drafted an oath of opposition to conscription that was administered at church doors throughout Ireland. The IPP retired a candidate in a by-election in favour of Sinn Féin. Defence committees were established in parishes and a National Defence Fund launched to oppose conscription. The Irish Trades Union Congress held a special meeting and called a twenty-four-hour general strike on 23 April to show workers' opposition too.[16] Enrolment in the Volunteers/IRA boomed, soon reaching 100,000.[17] 'During 1917 and '18,' said Eoin McArdle, 'there was a conscription scare here and everybody got into the IRA. But as soon as the scare went over, they fell out.'[18] Richard Mulcahy had a completely different impression: 'One of the last things Dick Mulcahy said to me,' said Joe O'Doherty, 'was that that period was one of the most important periods in the whole revolutionary struggle ... Because the cohesion, the cementing of the various forces took place at that time.'[19]

The crisis sparked an extreme reaction in the Volunteer/IRA Executive: it approved a proposal to assassinate the Cabinet in London.[20] Richard Walsh, on the Executive, gave an account of the decision:

> The actual decision of the Executive was that the most effective blow the Volunteers could strike in defence of their country to defeat conscription and the most destructive to the British was to make a personal attack on the lives of members of the British Cabinet, and to kill every one of them if possible ... The order containing the signatures of the members of the Executive was signed by every member of the Executive as far as I can remember. No member objected to signing it.[21]

Nothing came of this assassination proposal, although Brugha tried to implement it.

Then in May 1918 a German Plot for another rising was discovered. It had some basis in fact: one of Casement's Irish Brigade members, James Dowling, was arrested in Co. Clare having been put ashore by a U-boat with a cache of rifles and ammunition. He claimed that Germany was planning a military expedition to Ireland. This, and the interception by the Royal Navy of communications between John Devoy and Germany, convinced the government that there really was a plot for another rising and a German invasion.[22]

On 11 May Field Marshal Sir John French, now Lord French, replaced Lord Wimbourne as lord lieutenant of Ireland. On 15 May Lloyd George approved the arrests of Irish nationalist leaders. On 17 May about 150 men and women were arrested on the basis that there was a German Plot, including de Valera, Griffith, Kathleen Clarke, Constance Markievicz and more than half the Sinn Féin Executive.[23] On 3 July Sinn Féin, the Irish Volunteers, Cumann na mBan and the Gaelic League were declared 'dangerous' and effectively banned. Collins, who had several informers in Dublin Castle, had given advance notice of the impending arrests, but de Valera, Griffith and the Sinn Féin leadership decided to allow themselves to be arrested and gain popular sympathy,[24] calculating that this would increase support in a by-election scheduled for 20 June in East Cavan being fought by Arthur Griffith. Griffith won resoundingly. The ever-present threat of conscription had increased separatist support, demolished the

IPP, which was shown to be comprehensively ignored by the United Kingdom government, and further enhanced Collins' power as the only constant presence in the nationalist leadership. Darrell Figgis marked the German Plot arrests as the moment when Collins rose to dominance:

> The Brotherhood was, therefore, in a strong position now to capture the control [of Sinn Féin] it had sought so long; and it was to these men, indeed, that the [Sinn Féin] organisation naturally looked to take the places of those who had been removed. They did so at the very moment when the powerful revulsion of feeling all over the country, caused by the arrests, put Sinn Féin into undisputed leadership of the nation. And such was the curious chance by which the British Government made the IRB masters of the scene.[25]

Séamus O'Doherty was one of those arrested and deported to Leamington Spa. Liam Clarke sought out Séamus' brother, Joe, to go to England: 'Seamus had the code for communication with America and he wouldn't release it to these other fellows and would I go over and see him and see if I could get the code and let these fellows know ... It was I who brought it back to Diarmuid O'Hegarty.'[26]

Faced with the conscription and German Plot crises, Mulcahy as Chief of Staff worried that imprudent action anywhere by the Volunteers/IRA would prompt a clampdown. This was not appreciated by many Volunteer/IRA companies, and a feeling was prevalent that GHQ – frequently identified with the IRB – was dragging its feet. Robinson and many others looked upon this as cowardice: 'In those early days our young blood would boil at "caution" which we then regarded as "the better part of cowardice".'[27] GHQ's jurisdiction was patchy. It always had difficulty enforcing its authority outside Dublin, giving Mulcahy another set of headaches. Bridie O'Reilly, for example, working as a secretary for both Mulcahy and Brugha in 1918–21, thought 'West Cork mostly acted independently and simply sent their reports after the events'.[28] Pádraig Ó Fathaigh, the IRB Volunteer/IRA intelligence officer for South Galway and Mid-Clare, ascribed local action only to the IRB: 'During the Winter of 1919 the Kinvara IRB were active, and several ambushes were planned ... and some Beaghe IRB men came to assist.'[29]

With the creation of GHQ the actual control of the Volunteers/IRA rested with Collins and his colleagues. Collins emerged from this period as

198   The Irish Republican Brotherhood, 1914–1924

the dominant personality on the Executive and the Staff, where Mulcahy intelligently supported him as the de facto chief.[30] Batt O'Connor, an admirer of Collins, echoing Darrell Figgis, wrote accurately:

> Michael Collins now came to the forefront of the whole revolutionary movement. The control of all the important departments came into his hands, and he was not only, by his genius, perfectly well able to perceive and execute what had to be done, but the movement as a whole was enormously strengthened by the various branches being co-ordinated and directed by a single powerful mind.[31]

GHQ through which Collins operated was small, dedicated and made up nearly entirely of members of the IRB (see Appendix XII).[32]

Harry Boland, Collins' close friend on the Supreme Council and from 1918 Secretary of Sinn Féin, rivalled Collins in energy and ability and successfully managed an explosion of the party's membership, enabling Collins to concentrate on IRB and Volunteer/IRA activity.[33]

Mulcahy and Collins had very different relationships with the IRB. Both were loyal IRB members, in Mulcahy's case always as a simple member while Collins in 1917 had reached the top of the IRB, the Volunteers/IRA and Sinn Féin. His IRB connections – as Mulcahy noted – gave him great force. But as a member of the IRB Supreme Council he was committed to a separate line of command that did not recognise the Volunteers/IRA, the Volunteer Executive, GHQ, or Sinn Féin as anything but bodies to infiltrate and manipulate.

Richard Mulcahy had been told in 1913 to 'join the Volunteers and take your orders from your superior officers – that is the Volunteer officers' by his Bartholomew Teeling Circle Centre, Bulmer Hobson.[34] Before the Rising he had attended the monthly Circle meetings; after the Rising and his release from Frongoch in December 1916 he attended some meetings up to the time of Thomas Ashe's funeral, September 1917, when the Dublin Brigade was re-established. From 1919 to the Treaty in 1921, he had little contact with the IRB, years later recalling attending only one meeting in those three years, although he remained a member throughout.[35]

For Mulcahy, a loyal colleague and admirer of Collins, the principal importance of the IRB was that it provided Collins with an effective intelligence apparatus. It was always central to his purposes. The IRB organisation was also useful to the Volunteers/IRA and Sinn Féin, enabling de Valera and others

GHQ

to travel to and from the United States avoiding arrest, smuggling funds, purchasing and smuggling weapons, and keeping the Fenian spirit alive amongst Volunteer/IRA officers and the Active Service Units of 1920 and 1921.[36] Post-Rising, Mulcahy felt the suggestion that the IRB operated separately from the Volunteers/IRA – a suggestion he rejected – arose from Brugha's and later Stack's antagonism towards it and Collins:[37]

> There was never any conscious feeling even among ourselves in the work of the Volunteers of the time that there was any such thing as the I.R.B. in operation; still less was the I.R.B. in the public mind at all, and I doubt if it would have been given any prominence of any kind but for the attitude of Cathal Brugha and Stack.[38]

On the Volunteer Executive, Joe O'Doherty had a more nuanced view:

> The problem that beset us was that of duplication of control because many members of the Executive were also government Ministers and IRB men. McGarry was an IRB man but not a member of the government; Collins was a member of the IRB and of the government; de Valera and Brugha were no longer members of the IRB but were of the government. A great deal of this was surmounted by the very close bonds that existed between us, but the IRB tradition that the IRB Supreme Council was the Government of the Republic, and the fact that the IRB tended to look upon the Dáil as politicians, was a source of unease.[39]

Given that many members of the Volunteer Executive and GHQ Staff and many Volunteer officers were in the IRB, it is not surprising that no differences were felt by most of the people involved.[40] In their minds the IRB and the Volunteers/IRA were one, and Brugha and Stack were seeking difference when there was none. In Britain, IRB/Volunteer/IRA synonymity was natural, as Mulcahy observed: 'Any development of Volunteer units as such from new materials or in new areas was developed as such "from the clubs", namely from the most energetic members of the I.R.B. Centres in Britain.'[41] The value of the IRB in Britain was that it maintained a disciplined core of activists that smuggled guns and people, organised prison escapes and could murder and terrorise.

In Ireland the IRB and Volunteers/IRA worked in harmony. Joe O'Doherty, like Mulcahy, maintained that there was no problem with the IRB vis-à-vis the

200   The Irish Republican Brotherhood, 1914–1924

Volunteers/IRA: 'There was no split as such, do you see, because those who were Volunteers and not members of the IRB, they looked upon the members of the IRB as tried and true … It never occurred to me that there was anything sinister about the IRB insofar as its relations with the Volunteers were concerned.'[42] An example of the coincidence of IRB and non-IRB interests was in the first issue of *An t-Óglách* on 31 August 1918: an article entitled 'Ruthless Warfare' by Ernest Blythe argued that conscription would be an act of war that should be met by war (exactly the view of the IRB and the Volunteer/IRA leadership).

South Tipperary demonstrated the IRB focus on the Volunteers/IRA. Séumas Robinson was sent there from Dublin in 1917 as a Volunteer/IRA organiser to support the efforts of Seán Treacy, who was leading IRB and Volunteer/IRA activity in the county.[43] Robinson no longer considered himself a member of the IRB, but Collins and GHQ Staff were not concerned: they were happy with men they could count on to fight. In any case, IRB men led the local Volunteer/IRA companies. Treacy and Robinson organised these into battalions. In April 1918 both men were in prison. Treacy was elected *in absentia* as O/C but refused and Dan Breen was elected in his stead as first O/C Third Tipperary Brigade with 4,000 men in 57 companies in 8 battalions. Treacy was released in June, still refusing to be O/C. Robinson was released in October when he was unanimously elected brigade O/C with Treacy becoming vice-O/C and Breen becoming the brigade quartermaster.[44] The companies were based upon IRB Circles, and the officers elected were IRB members or, like Robinson, trusted men. All of this was the result of IRB action, strong in 1917, but thereafter gradually subsumed into the Volunteers/IRA.

By the end of 1917, IRB reorganisation was complete. About 350 IRB Circles were functioning throughout Ireland, representing a membership of 3–4,000. Furthermore, most Circles formed the nucleus of a Volunteer/IRA company.[45] This did not mean that every Volunteer/IRA company was based upon a Circle, but it did mean that most companies had an IRB contingent. The Supreme Council put little energy into IRB formalities, so much so that when Harry Boland became Secretary of Sinn Féin following the 1918 German Plot arrests, his move was not directed or even considered by the Council. Pre-1916, Clarke and MacDermott would have been closely involved in every aspect of such an appointment. Post-1916, the IRB focus was on building the Volunteers/IRA in order to resume fighting, not on managing Sinn Féin.

When Seán Treacy was arrested on 28 February 1918 by Sergeant Hamilton of the RIC, his colleagues proposed through the IRB hierarchy that Hamilton

GHQ

be kidnapped as a hostage for Treacy's release. Seán Ó Murthuile replied with a refusal and censured them: the IRB, he said, stood for something higher than the kidnapping of 'a bloody old policeman'. Ó Murthuile and GHQ did nothing to dispel the assumption that GHQ and IRB were one and the same, and this disadvantaged both. A result was that few – if any – IRB meetings were held in Tipperary in 1919–21 as many of the local IRB men left in protest and disappointment.[46] They simply wanted to proceed with the IRB objective of 'securing the independence of Ireland by force of arms'. For another reason, namely that Volunteer/IRA activity supplanted IRB activity, very few IRB meetings of any kind took place anywhere between 1919 and spring 1921.[47]

At Soloheadbeg, Tipperary, on 21 January 1919 two RIC constables guarding gelignite for quarrying were ambushed and killed.[48] Some days later near Macroom, Co. Cork, a group of Volunteers/IRA attempted to disarm some soldiers, injuring one. At Knocklong on 13 May 1919, an RIC sergeant died in an attack.[49] The Volunteers/IRA involved took tactical and organisational decisions in the spirit of the IRB, not referring to GHQ. Dan Breen, one of the Soloheadbeg ambushers, wrote later, capturing their view: 'The Volunteers were in great danger of becoming merely a political adjunct to the Sinn Féin organisation. Treacy remarked to me that we had had enough of being pushed around and getting our men imprisoned while we remained inactive. It was high time that we did a bit of the pushing.'[50]

Breen, Treacy and their colleagues spearheaded Volunteer/IRA activity in Tipperary, and this spread to other areas to the dismay of GHQ, and of the Dáil. 'After the conscription scare died things were a bit lackadaisical,' said Eoin McArdle. 'But they pulled them up, and Dan Breen and Treacy – God rest them – they started in the south … Quite a lot of the TDs didn't approve of that.'[51] Collins did approve and brought Breen and Treacy to Dublin later in 1919 to be under his personal direction.[52] For Collins, it is clear, the commitment to fight, the IRB spirit, was more important than membership of the IRB: membership was testament to commitment; commitment did not require membership. Only later would membership matter as the politics of independence were thrashed out. 'Mick didn't give a hoot about rules and regulations, so long as things were happening,' said one of his intelligence officers.[53]

The sense that the Volunteers/IRA were the continuation of the IRB spirit – as Mulcahy noted – was also possessed by many IRB members, once again raising the question of continuing with the IRB. Eoin McArdle put it well: 'Brugha and de Valera got an idea into their heads which was probably right: that the IRB

202   The Irish Republican Brotherhood, 1914–1924

was an underground movement while the IRA was an overground movement and they seemed to think there was no longer any necessity for underground movements. That was the difference between de Valera and Brugha and the IRB – nothing else.'[54] As early as mid-1918, IRB Volunteer/IRA prisoners in Belfast had debated the merits of the IRB versus the Volunteers/IRA. Éamon O'Dwyer, the IRB Tipperary County Centre, was one of them: 'Amongst discussions we had in Belfast Prison after that were some on the position of the I.R.B. and I.R.A., and the opinion was in favour of dropping the I.R.B., seeing that we had an Irish army which would be regularised in the course of time, and that there was scarcely any need to have a secret organisation as well.'[55] In January 1919 Austin Stack, who had been in prison with O'Dwyer, resigned from the IRB, accepting the Dáil as the Republic's government.[56] Debates about the IRB remained muted during 1917–21: clearly there was a general determination to maintain apparent unity.

CHAPTER 19

1918 Election

I gave a hand in the elections. But joining? Not at all! It was a sissy thing
to do.

Seán MacBride, 21 February 1973[1]

In the general election on 14 December 1918 Sinn Féin won seventy-three
constituencies, the IPP won six and Unionists twenty-two. It was a first-past-
the-post election. In twenty-five constituencies Sinn Féin was unopposed;
in the forty-eight contested constituencies which Sinn Féin won, a majority
of votes – 53 per cent – were cast for non-Sinn Féin candidates. Thirty-one
percent of the electorate did not vote. The election did not endorse Sinn Féin's
commitment to a republic, although that is what Sinn Féin and the Volunteers/
IRA claimed. Later, this led Republicans to overestimate their popular support:
a mistake that Michael Collins notably did not make. Sinn Féin fought on a
programme of:

1. Abstention from Westminster
2. The creation of an Irish parliament
3. Making England's power in Ireland impotent 'by military force or
   otherwise'
4. Securing recognition of Irish independence at the Versailles Peace
   Conference
5. Establishing the 1916 Republic[2]

The implication was that the IRB's Republic had not been established and that
force might be required to achieve this. Collins, always realistic, retrospectively

considered that the election had been 'fought on the principle of self-determination' and not for a republic.[3]

A corrective to Republican claims was delivered in the 1920 local and municipal elections when Sinn Féin, despite winning control of a majority of councils and corporations, won less than one-third (550) of the 1,806 seats. Donal Ó Drisceoil has noted:

> The turnout in the municipal elections was a very respectable 70 per cent. Sinn Féin emerged as the largest party overall, but less emphatically than in 1918 … The big surprise was the showing of the Labour Party, which had sat out the 1918 general election. It emerged as the second largest party, winning 394 seats. The Unionists came third with 368 seats, 302 of which were in Ulster. There was a surprisingly strong showing by the presumed-dead Nationalist Party (the former Home Rule/Irish Parliamentary Party), which secured 238 seats and outpolled Sinn Féin in first preferences in Ulster.[4]

Harry Boland, Diarmuid O'Hegarty and Collins personally selected candidates for the election,[5] resulting in the ensuing separatist parliament – the Dáil elected in 1918 – being fundamentally unrepresentative. Richard Mulcahy and Páidín O'Keeffe considered that resentment of Collins' IRB manipulations was a source of future antipathy towards him, the Volunteers/ IRA and the IRB.[6]

On 19 December 1918, four days after the general election, the Standing Committee of Sinn Féin decided 'to convoke Dáil Éireann' as an Irish parliament. The IRB had managed the creation of the Dáil. Most of the 'moderates' in the national movement had been arrested in 1917 and were still in prison, leaving Collins and the IRB a clear field. Richard Mulcahy knew the men who had been elected (he didn't think of including Constance Markievicz):

> As far as I know, all the candidates were I.R.B. men with the possible exception of Count Plunkett and Dr White … The I.R.B. activities and interference in the selection of candidates was caused by the fear, at that time, that men would be selected who would be weak on what they considered the national issue and would submit or agree to weak compromises. They attempted to influence the selection of candidates generally and succeeded in the majority of cases.[7]

1918 Election

Given the relationship between the Dáil and the Volunteers/IRA over the following two years, the candidates that Boland, O'Hegarty and Collins picked, and whom Mulcahy thought were almost all in the IRB, must have had a tenuous relationship with the Brotherhood. The Dáil and Sinn Féin were to prove more devoted to constitutional procedures than to guerrilla warfare. Time and again the Dáil, given the opportunity of endorsing the Volunteers/IRA, refused to do so.

There was also a great deal of personation.[8] John J. O'Reilly in Ferns, Wexford, spoke from his own experience of vote rigging:

> I know the vote was rigged. I'll tell you how it was rigged. During the troubles that were going on that time, the Register was done every three years, the Voters' Register. Well, it hadn't been done for five years, and nearly one-third of those on it were dead! … And every one of the dead men voted! Every one of them nearly. I had a first cousin who voted seven times! If there'd been an honest vote that time, Sinn Féin would hardly have got in at all.[9]

Joseph O'Rourke witnessed personation in Dublin: 'In the Patrick Street area during the 1918 elections various navvies turned up to Sinn Féin HQ unaccompanied by their wives (who had no intention of voting). Máire Ni Siubhlaigh and Sara Allgood of the Abbey Theatre, suitably costumed in shawls etc., doubled for quite a large number of these wives and accompanied the navvies to the polling booths.'[10]

Nevertheless, there was no denying Sinn Féin's success. Had the IPP stood in the constituencies where Sinn Féin was unopposed, the likelihood is that while it may have had another 90–100,000 votes, Sinn Féin would have increased its vote too. However, this was not the case. Forty-seven per cent of the vote gave Sinn Féin 70 per cent of the seats. Unionists were also successful, increasing their representation by one-third.

With this background, it is hard to maintain that Irish people wanted a republic in 1918. Led by the IRB, the election was the start of an extreme nationalist takeover of erstwhile popular and moderate nationalist leadership. De Valera, like Collins, retrospectively considered that the election had been 'fought on the principle of self-determination'[11] and 'for Irish freedom and Irish independence'[12] and not specifically for a republic.

The results reflected anger about conscription.[13] The arrest of the Sinn Féin leadership and suppression of the GAA and Gaelic League in the summer of

206 The Irish Republican Brotherhood, 1914–1924

1918 added to Sinn Féin's popularity.[14] Michael Hayes considered that the issue of conscription in 1917 and again in 1918 made Sinn Féin and the Volunteers/IRA the dominant forces: 'The Rising made the Volunteers the great barrier against conscription ... and that more than the IRB or anything else brought the country behind them in the 1918 election. It was conscription that convinced them, and by the way, silenced the bishops as well.'[15]

Vincent Comerford noted that it was the Catholic Church's opposition to conscription that gave Sinn Féin its support, and not a national surge in favour of revolution:

> The mobilisation against conscription was promoted by bishops and priests and was based, once again, on the Catholic parish. It enhanced the credibility of Sinn Féin enormously. The majority of Irish nationalists voted in December 1918 not for any revolutionary programme but (as so often before and after) for the party that seemed best equipped to look after their interests, including their country's place in the world. The fact that the Sinn Féin leadership identified with the rebels of Easter Week is no evidence that Sinn Féin voters in general (or even Sinn Féin leaders in general) were eager for any kind of reprise.[16]

Michael Collins, working to secure a strong Sinn Féin vote in the 1918 election, despite conscription no longer being an issue, understood that it had been Sinn Féin's identifier and that it would be a powerful reminder that the party would fight for Irish causes. The new nationalist leadership's determination that independence rather than Home Rule was now the objective was later stated by de Valera: 'we took advantage of that election [1918] to make it clear that the people wanted independence'.[17] Dan Breen reflected more extreme nationalist opinion: 'At first the general public did not want the war. They seemed to forget that their vote at the [1918] general election led to the formal establishment of the Republic. Many of them were of the opinion that freedom could be won without any effort on their part.'[18]

The defeat of the IPP in the election accelerated both Sinn Féin's dominance and the reborn Volunteers/IRA. And, despite what Dan Breen and many members of the Volunteers/IRA may have thought, only the IRB was fully committed to a republic.

The background strength of the IPP was reflected in the 210,000 or so Irish men who enlisted in the British armed forces during the war, joining at an

1918 Election 207

average of about 1,500 every month from the end of 1915 to November 1916 (the Rising made no difference to enlistment), and at an only slightly lower rate from then to the end of the war.[19] These men, predominantly Catholic (about three of every five who enlisted), were in addition to the approximately 60,000 who had enlisted before the war.[20]

This support for the British war effort was a constant if muted challenge to Sinn Féin, the IRB, and to republican political dominance. In 1915 more Catholics than Protestants had enlisted in Belfast and in 1914–17 more Ulster Catholics enlisted in proportion to the Catholic population than Catholics from elsewhere. Some of the richest counties had the highest enlistment rates, while the poorest had the lowest,[21] suggesting that poverty was not an incentive to enlist. A strong argument for the continuation of the IRB after 1916 was that it would stiffen the independence movement in the face of this popular support for the British war effort and a general and natural desire for peace.

Sinn Féin's agenda was clear: withdrawal from Westminster; establishment of an Irish parliament; making Westminster/Dublin Castle rule impossible (by pacifist methods) and appealing for Irish representation at the Paris Peace Conference. All this was presented as a glamorous and 'new' demand for an Irish republic which otherwise differed little from the IPP's election platform of Dominion status. And, having won the 1918 election decisively, Sinn Féin was perfectly justified to proceed on this basis.[22]

On 1 January 1919 a joint meeting of some of the elected Sinn Féin MPs and the Sinn Féin Executive Committee, summoned by Michael Collins and Piaras Béaslaí, agreed that there should be a secret session of the new Irish MPs to form an Irish parliament.[23] On 2 January Harry Boland, Sinn Féin Secretary, and Alderman Tom Kelly, Sinn Féin's leading politician still at liberty, sent a joint letter inviting the MPs to form what would be Dáil Éireann.[24] On 3 January Patrick McCartan declared to the United States government and the Washington diplomatic corps on IRB authority that the 'Republic of Ireland' existed in fact.[25] On 7 January the Sinn Féin Executive again met and set 21 January as the date for the first Dáil meeting[26] and appointed a select committee to draft standing orders and a constitution for the Dáil.[27] This was done over the next two weeks. At one of these meetings it was agreed that Cathal Brugha – a distinctly Fenian personality – would be proposed as the first president of the Dáil on the understanding that de Valera would take the position once he was out of jail.[28]

208   The Irish Republican Brotherhood, 1914–1924

The twenty-two Unionist and six IPP MPs elected in 1918 never attended the Dáil but did take their seats at Westminster. As a result it was a one-party, Sinn Féin, parliament in Dublin.

The republican principle was welcomed unreservedly by the twenty-seven MPs present at the first meeting of the Dáil.[29] The imprisoned leaders, however, were not so sure, feeling that a proclaimed republic had less chance of being accepted at a peace conference than would a purely nationalist appeal.[30] IRB influence in the Dáil kept the 1916 Republic as the Dáil's stated allegiance, but the Paris Peace Conference did not recognise it, and in any case almost certainly would not have recognised anything coming from Ireland that was not endorsed by the United Kingdom government.

The members of the Dáil present on 21 January, shorn of their imprisoned leaders, elected Brugha as Comhairle (speaker) and on 22 January as 'President of the Ministry pro. tem.', and approved his choice of ministers: Eoin MacNeill, Minister for Finance; Michael Collins, Minister for Home Affairs; Count Plunkett, Minister for Foreign Affairs, and Richard Mulcahy, Minister for Defence.[31] With Mulcahy and Collins as ministers, IRB and Volunteer/IRA interests would be protected. Collins was now a central figure in the IRB, Sinn Féin, the Dáil, the Cabinet and the Volunteers/IRA.

For IRB members the relationship with the Dáil and with the prime minister was determined by the claim of the Supreme Council to be the government of the Republic. The Council addressed this later in the year by withdrawing this claim. Seán MacEoin, a dedicated IRB member, explained the IRB view of the new situation:

> The fact that the head of that government was described as Príomh-Aire or Prime Minister should have been a clear indication to all reasonable and intelligent people that he was Prime Minister to a President ... From the date of the proclamation of the Republic in 1916 until the assembly of the First Dáil in January 1919, the government of the Republic was in the hands of the Supreme Council of the I.R.B. ... An entirely new situation arose with the assembly of the First Dáil ... There was then in existence an established government appointed by the legally elected representatives of the people, and to that government the Supreme Council of the I.R.B. at once voluntarily ceded all its powers except one. The President of the I.R.B. continued to be regarded by the Brotherhood as the President of the Republic until 1921.[32]

1918 Election 209

A Sinn Féin convention was held in April 1919, and this time Collins and Harry Boland spared no effort to pack the Executive with their candidates. Darrell Figgis, a steady opponent of Collins, was removed. He described his experience and the IRB machinations that, he noted, were applied not just to him or Sinn Féin:

> The method adopted in this case was to work through those members of the Volunteers who were sworn members of the I.R.B. and held important commands in their areas ... Beyond doubt, great organisation and tireless energy were required to produce this result. It was the negation of all freedom, of course, and utterly corrupt, but it was completely successful ... As I left the great hall, the Convention over, I was suddenly stopped by a strange sight. Behind one of the statues with which it is surrounded stood Michael Collins and Harry Boland. Their arms were about one another, their heads bowed on one another's shoulders, and they were shaking with laughter. They did not see me. Their thoughts were with their triumph.[33]

Packing Sinn Féin and the Dáil reflected deep distrust of politicians and democracy. Maintaining the IRB's claim to the presidency of the Republic was a statement of separateness, although not a public one. The Supreme Council was resisting the thrust of the Dáil presidency becoming the Republic's presidency – a title de Valera was to assume when in the United States from June 1919. And it was a caution that while the Sinn Féin Executive might have an IRB majority, the party was not fully controlled by the IRB and could – and did – have its own more peaceful agenda. Indeed, when Harry Boland went to America in May 1919 and resigned as Sinn Féin Secretary, Hanna Sheehy Skeffington, the widow of Francis, a pacifist, was appointed in his stead despite the IRB presence on the Executive.[34] Darrell Figgis may have been bounced out, but he was a representative Sinn Féiner and whenever there was a straightforward popular vote what he stood for had majority support.

De Valera was very aware of the importance of these competing presidencies and in August 1921 sought to establish his claimed presidency of the Republic unequivocally, accurately stating, 'The point about "President of the Republic" was very important. Though the office had been accepted it had never been constitutionally created. As a matter of fact the President was President not of the Republic but of the Ministry of Dáil Éireann.'[35] The Dáil accepted

210 The Irish Republican Brotherhood, 1914–1924

de Valera's argument that he was, in practice, President of the Republic and formally advanced him from the de facto to de jure status.

The separateness of the Dáil and IRB presidencies reflected the IRB's suspicion of the Dáil and politicians, and was so perceived by Brugha, de Valera, Stack and GHQ Staff. Seán MacEoin became the East Connacht representative on the Supreme Council in 1921. He regarded this position as making him responsible for encouraging IRB interest in every branch of the Dáil government's administration, and for ensuring that members of the IRB were active in every element of the national movement.[36] His was a hidden hand of manipulation, exactly as the IRB's opponents maintained.

The IRB's post-1916 penetration of Sinn Féin and recreation of the Volunteers/IRA had secured firmly separatist constitutions for both organisations. There had been a great deal of threatening of Sinn Féin opponents during the election – the unopposed Sinn Féin victories reflected this – which, together with the election victory, hid the moderation that always exists in any national electorate. The irony for Sinn Féin was that within thirty-seven months, the IPP's basic platform was adopted by a majority of Sinn Féin TDs who would win a Dáil majority followed five months later by an electoral majority. Hugh Pollard, on the British side, also maintained that most people stood aside from the Volunteers/IRA, and that even most 'Sinn Féin' prisoners were unclear about being republican:

> The Irish demand for an independent Irish Republic is, so far as the mass of the people is concerned, a purely hysterical manifestation. It is not a matter that touches them personally at all, and in my own experience less than five per cent of Sinn Féin prisoners, interrogated by a friendly guardian, could give any coherent idea of why they were Republican. They have been told that it is patriotic to be Republican, and the Republican slogan has been identified with the concept of anti-British manifestations ever dear to the Irish.[37]

Art O'Connor, Minister for Agriculture in the Dáil government, agreed, stating in 1921: 'The struggle of the Volunteers was a struggle with the Irish people more than a struggle with the invader.'[38] Colm Ó Gaora in Galway confirmed this view: 'Let nobody be under the illusion that we ever had a huge rush of recruits to the cause, however. There was always a large number of people who were happy to live from day to day and cared little whether Ireland was free or not. Indeed, we even had to "conscript" a few extra young men locally to increase the numbers in our training camp.'[39]

The IRB's success in influencing – if not subverting – the 1918 election hid its and the notional Republic's distance from the electorate but guaranteed a reckoning with representative democracy at some future point.

CHAPTER 20

Killing

The I.R.B. had secured their point: they had made sure that if the bulk of the people did not support them, at least they would not dare to inform and would shield the criminals.

H.B.C. Pollard, The Secret Societies of Ireland

IRB military efforts, apart from organising Circles and Volunteer/IRA companies, were concentrated in 1917 and 1918 on obtaining weapons, ammunition and explosives.[1] In 1918 IRB members in the Volunteers/IRA began raiding barracks and (Protestant) homes for weapons and confiscating land in the west and south against the direct orders of the Volunteer/IRA Executive.[2] Dan Breen recalled the tension involved:

> Our policy had been hitherto 'unofficial'. Dáil Éireann and General Headquarters of the IRA had neither sanctioned it nor accepted the responsibility. Mick Collins promised to push our war policy in the 'proper quarters', and it must be remembered that he was not only on the GHQ staff but was also the Finance Minister. Our war policy was not popular. Our GHQ seemed to be lukewarm about it. The political wing certainly opposed it, and more than one TD privately denounced it.[3]

Seán MacLoughlin had been on James Connolly's staff in 1916, and – as with Séumas Robinson – was sent to Tipperary as a Volunteer/IRA organiser in 1918. In April he proposed an attack on the army barracks in Tipperary town. His proposal was rejected by GHQ, and another organiser was sent to replace

Killing   213

him.[4] This followed on the heels of the Treacy/Hamilton affair and added to the alienation from GHQ felt in Tipperary. Dan Breen expressed their feeling:

> We had heard the gospel of freedom preached; we believed in it, we wanted to be free, and we were prepared to give our lives as proof of the faith that was in us. But those who preached the gospel were not prepared to practise it. Even from the Irish Volunteers, who were now known as the Irish Republican Army, we got no support.[5]

And not just in Tipperary. In Co. Cork, also in 1918, when Tom Hales (the IRB Supreme Council member for South Munster from 1919) led his Circle in a skirmish with the RIC at Innishannon River, killing a constable, Brugha and Mulcahy immediately attempted to discipline Hales, with Brugha pressing for Hales to answer to the Volunteer/IRA Executive.[6]

In Dublin and London the increasing activity of the Volunteers/IRA and of the IRB was noted by the Cabinet with concern. Edward Shortt, appointed Chief Secretary for Ireland in May 1918, told the House of Commons on 5 November:

> There is the question, again, of the Irish Volunteers, who are dominated today by the Irish Republican Brotherhood, and the question of their activities has once more arisen … but, small though their number may be, they are extremely dangerous, and they, unfortunately, do to a certain extent control the proceedings of the Sinn Féin Party … For a long time the physical-force party have been under, but they are now trying to come to the front again. I hope and believe we shall be able to avert anything like an armed Rising, or armed disturbance, but there is the means of it there unless we do keep a very firm hold. [7]

British Intelligence had an accurate knowledge of the IRB's influence and efforts.

The IRB's fanaticism, no matter the 1918 election, was not shared by the large majority of Irish people. That the Volunteers/IRA and Sinn Féin had no popular mandate for violence was immediately apparent to Dan Breen: 'The people had voted for a republic; now they seemed to have abandoned those who tried to bring that Republic nearer, for we had taken them at their word. Our former friends shunned us. They preferred the drawing-room as a battleground; the political resolution rather than the gun as their offensive weapon.'[8]

214 The Irish Republican Brotherhood, 1914–1924

Breen's was a common complaint, echoed by most Volunteer/IRA formations. Michael Collins explained why the Volunteer/IRA leadership was wary of military confrontation: in 1921, he said, there were only 1,617 IRA men with one weapon each and few bullets.[9] Apart from approving specific actions and distributing very limited guns, there was not very much support that GHQ could provide. Conserving weapons by preventing action was part of the political tightrope GHQ walked as it tried to satisfy both the Dáil and Volunteer/IRA units. Collins pretended to walk the tightrope, but actually supported action, gaining a reputation as the 'go-to' man amongst Volunteer/IRA activists. The concern that was prevalent in the Dáil and GHQ, Richard Mulcahy explained, was deniability:

> It is very simple to understand that it was very desirable that in circumstances where violent action was being taken ... members of the Government as such or of the Dáil as such should not have a rope put around their necks or be otherwise penalised unnecessarily by any formal or any apparent participation in any kind of responsibility for such acts.[10]

Since Collins, Mulcahy, Diarmuid O'Hegarty and Gearóid O'Sullivan – all IRB – were the leadership group within the Staff,[11] GHQ's identification with the IRB in the minds of Volunteers/IRA was not surprising. Probably to counter the view that they were in thrall to the politicians, they made a decision in early 1919 – after the Soloheadbeg incident – to attack the RIC.[12]

The strategy proposed by Bulmer Hobson and Seán McGarry – guerrilla warfare against the RIC – that Collins espoused while in Frongoch now became official policy. The Volunteer/IRA Executive and the Dáil Cabinet both approved the decision to undertake guerrilla warfare. The Cabinet's agreement, fearful of popular opinion and government reprisal, was not published.[13] Increasing violence and killings, with juries refusing to convict men charged with shooting soldiers and RIC men, and the launch of the Dáil Loan in August 1919 demonstrated the Dáil's determination to operate a parallel administration competing with the Dublin Castle administration. It resulted in the suppression of the Dáil on 13 September 1919 (and in November of the Gaelic League, Cumann na mBan and Sinn Féin). This promoted Volunteer/IRA aggression.

No matter what Treacy, Robinson, Breen and Hales thought of the IRB and GHQ, Collins was as determined as they were to take the fight to the RIC

Killing 215

and DMP, as became clear. He used the IRB to enable de Valera to escape from jail in February 1919 and then to travel to the United States in June.[14] On 30 March, Robert Barton, a Sinn Féin member of the Dáil, escaped from Mountjoy with nineteen other Sinn Féin prisoners, organised by Collins, Rory O'Connor and Harry Boland.[15] In Dublin in March 1919 Collins asked Dick McKee, O/C Dublin Brigade, to form his Squad – sometimes referred to as the 'Twelve Apostles' – which was under his personal direction. It was made up of IRB members. Collins' attachment to Cork was again expressed. Batt Murphy, in the Kerry Volunteers, observed: 'Take the Twelve Apostles and Collins: every one of them, bar one, was from the First Southern Division. They were all southerners, every one of them, bar one.'[16] Their purpose was to terrify the DMP detective corps – 'G' Division – and initially to kill two particular detectives – Smith and Hoey – who had identified 1916 leaders for trial resulting in execution.[17] Smith was killed on 30 July 1919 and Hoey on 12 September. Between March 1919 and July 1921, sixty men were targeted for assassination by Collins, and thirty-nine were killed by the Squad and the Dublin Brigade Active Service Unit, eight if not more in error.[18] Those targeted by Collins were detectives in the G Division, British informers, agents and undercover officers, and RIC men who diligently pursued Volunteers.

The climax of this 'intelligence war' came on 21 November 1920 – Bloody Sunday – when several British officers and secret service agents were assassinated by Collins' Squad working in conjunction with the Active Service Unit, and a player and spectators at a Croke Park Gaelic football match were shot by the RIC.[19] Overall, thirty people were killed or fatally wounded. It had a dramatic effect on British undercover agents. David Neligan knew the men who were killed: 'I said to Collins, "It's only a waste of money to be shooting these fellows. They're doing nothing at all only drinking and playing cards and playing billiards. Don't bother your backside shooting one of them because they're absolutely harmless." They had been thoroughly frightened by the Bloody Sunday bit.'[20]

The organisation of these killings was undertaken by Collins and two IRB colleagues, Dick McKee and Peadar Clancy, the Vice O/C of the Dublin Brigade.[21] Those who took part were all carefully selected for the purpose. Indeed, IRB Circles in Dublin were given to understand that assassinations were being rotated among Circle members, although ostensibly being conducted by the Dublin Brigade.[22]

Outside Dublin, attacks on the RIC were the purpose of the Volunteers/

IRA and did not need IRB sponsorship. In May 1919 in Tipperary, Éamon O'Dwyer and his colleagues took their identification with the Volunteers/IRA to the extreme of undermining the IRB:

> The IRB held its usual meetings all the time but there was very little that it could do that was not being done by the Volunteers. The Brigade Council at its meetings in Kilshenane and other places decided that it was about time to drop the I.R.B. They asked me would I cease to be County Centre and give all my time to the Brigade. As a way out, they suggested that we should appoint some other County Centre who would really be a wrecker and let the I.R.B. quietly die. I agreed and I resigned as County Centre, and the Supreme Council sent a red-haired man to call on me ... He said that the Supreme Council wanted me to remain on. I told him that I had too much work to do and it was better to have another man on the job.[23]

In 1919–21 the 3–4,000 members of the IRB compared directly with the number of active Volunteer/IRA men,[24] so the coincidence of IRB members and active Volunteer/IRA members, and the lack of separate IRB activity in 1919–21, is not surprising. James McCullough, an IRB Centre, considered that an element in the reduction of separate IRB activity flowed from an instruction:

> An order came from the I.R.B. Headquarters in Dublin about 1919 that all the elderly men in the I.R.B. organisation should be asked to resign ... This order created deep dissatisfaction amongst all the members of the organisation. The old fellows would not agree to be dispensed with. They paid their subscriptions and remained on, but they lost an influence in the control of the organisation. After 1919 the urge to spread the I.R.B. organisation seemed to fizzle out. We lost many of our active members through emigration, and the youngsters had a much keener interest in the Volunteers than in the I.R.B.[25]

Collins, because of his position in the IRB, in the Dáil government, and in the Volunteers/IRA could take initiatives without reference to Brugha or anyone except, in IRB theory, the Supreme Council, Executive and/or Military Committee, all of which Collins – because of his energy, contacts and successes – dominated. Through the Squad and the Dublin Active Service Unit, Collins

Killing

had a murder force of his own that took orders directly from him.[26] The Supreme Council, GHQ, Volunteer/IRA Executive, Brugha and the Dáil did not figure in these murderous operations: they were Collins' alone.

The Innishannon River incident in 1918 and the Soloheadbeg ambush in 1919 highlighted the tension between the military and political wings of the national movement. Both had taken place without any authority from the Volunteer/IRA Executive or GHQ, or from Collins and the IRB, and demonstrated that outside Dublin after 1916 chains of command were difficult to enforce when faced by local enthusiasms. Richard Walsh took part in the discussion in the Volunteer/IRA Executive that Soloheadbeg caused:

> The feeling at the Executive at the time was that the men involved in these operations had, without proper authority, taken what was then considered a very serious action, the consequences of which might be difficult to control, and that the country as a whole would not be willing to meet. The Executive also felt that disciplinary action in matters of armed operations was essential, and it was a matter of grave doubt if the country was prepared for such a policy.[27]

The Soloheadbeg ambush gained wide publicity because it coincided with the first meeting of Dáil Éireann.[28] It was immediately condemned by the Most Rev. Dr Harty, Archbishop of Cashel, and many local priests.[29] Reaction in the Dáil to the ambush was also hostile, but not public.[30] The imposition of martial law which followed in Tipperary prompted the South Tipperary Brigade to another act of defiance: a declaration of 'war' which was published even after GHQ had refused to sanction it.[31] In part, reluctance to encourage Volunteer actions in 1919 reflected the hope of securing recognition of Ireland's rights as a free nation from the Paris Peace Conference. The Dáil considered that a policy of peaceful resistance in Ireland would be more likely to lead to the recognition they desired.[32]

GHQ Staff inevitably had difficulty attempting to curtail Volunteer/IRA attacks in line with Dáil wishes without drowning Volunteer/IRA enthusiasm. De Valera in April 1919 gained the Dáil's support for a policy of ostracising the RIC that helped keep the Volunteers/IRA broadly in step with the Dáil. It was a passive and political step, but nevertheless it could be interpreted as tacit support for action.

Opposition to Volunteer/IRA actions came not only from the political

218   The Irish Republican Brotherhood, 1914–1924

wing fearful of alienating people, but also from Brugha, who wanted the Volunteers/IRA to train during 1919 and did not want confrontation with the RIC and the military until the Volunteers/IRA were ready. The Executive agreed with Brugha (and it was an easy way to avoid confrontation with him and with the Dáil). Richard Walsh confirmed the Executive's view: 'It was felt that armed operations would require considerable preliminary planning, and there was doubt about our ability to carry out successfully such a policy. The limited supply of arms available to the Volunteers was an ever-present problem which, to people who know the position, would not prompt any sane hope for success.'[33]

Mulcahy thought that Collins, and Béaslaí as editor of *An t-Óglách*, were in different ways responsible for many of the unauthorised Volunteer/IRA actions during 1919: Collins for bestowing unofficial encouragement and Béaslaí for his outspoken editorials. On 31 January 1919, for example, ten days after Soloheadbeg, *An t-Óglách* took an IRB position against the view of the Dáil and opined that the Volunteers/IRA were entitled to wage war against the RIC.

GHQ had some success restraining country units. On 10 January 1919 Seán Treacy ordered South Tipperary Battalion commanders to prepare plans to attack RIC and military barracks, and to submit these to him by 19 January. Michael Brennan, O/C Clare Brigade, similarly planned to attack RIC barracks over his whole Brigade area. He was ordered to Dublin by Richard Mulcahy, who had heard of his plan:

> Two days before the date of the attack, I was summoned to Dublin and handled very roughly by Dick Mulcahy who was Chief of Staff. His point was of course that the people had to be educated and led gently into open war, and what I proposed doing might scare them off. I disagreed, and anyway I knew that the R.I.C. rifles would no longer be available for the taking when the open war came. However, I obeyed orders and called off the operation.[34]

Treacy's plans in Tipperary were also not fulfilled, perhaps because he received the same message.

In January 1919, some days after the first meeting of the Dáil, the Volunteer/IRA Executive met. The meeting was attended by Mulcahy. The relationship of the Dáil government with the Volunteers/IRA was thrashed out. It would be unofficial, but the Volunteers/IRA would be regarded privately as the national army, and accordingly duty-bound to resist the 'invading' British.[35] No doubt, Soloheadbeg had forced this arrangement. It was, in effect, an agreement that Volunteer/IRA units could attack British forces, bowing to the inevitable, acknowledging both GHQ's and the Dáil's limited ability – even secretly – to control the Volunteers/IRA. Attacks on RIC barracks and ambushing members of the RIC had been frequent throughout 1917 and 1918, particularly in the south and west.[36] At some point in 1918 Seán Treacy was reported to have complained about the Volunteer/IRA leadership's reluctance to commit to action: 'If this is the state of affairs we'll have to kill someone and make the bloody enemy organise us,' he said.[37] At Soloheadbeg he did.

Other events pressed towards more Dáil acceptance of Volunteer/IRA action. On 3 February 1919, Michael Collins and Harry Boland, using Manchester IRB men in England, organised the escape of de Valera, Seán McGarry and Seán Milroy (a member of the Sinn Féin Executive) from Lincoln Prison.[38] 'The rescue at Lincoln Gaol was not for Mr de Valera,' said Seán MacEoin, 'but the rescue of [Seán McGarry,] the President of the Republic.'[39]

Instead of increasing repression after these escapes, the government relaxed. No new arrests were made, and on 6 March 1919 because of the 1918–20 influenza pandemic that killed millions worldwide, the remaining political prisoners were released.

CHAPTER 21

Relationships

We want an Irish republic because if Ireland had her freedom, it is, I
believe, the most likely form of government. But if the Irish wanted to
have another form of government, so long as it was an Irish government,
I would not put in a word against it.[1]

Éamon de Valera, East Clare by-election, July 1917

Dealing with the Volunteers/IRA was one of several pressures facing the Dáil. It
was responsive to public opinion that it judged – correctly – as hostile to attacks
on the RIC and to violence generally.[2] It tried to replace British government
with its own administration and was supported by the IRB and the Volunteers/
IRA in this effort, which was not cosmetic: in June 1919, for example, Robert
Barton secured Dáil support for a decree making provision for land for landless
men.[3]

Volunteer/IRA men guarded the Dáil when in session and provided a
rudimentary police force to enforce Dáil laws and courts' judgements in those
parts of the country where the Volunteers/IRA were strong.[4] The Dáil agitated
for representation at the Paris Peace Conference and for American money and
diplomatic support. It also authorised a National Loan to fund its enactments,
which Michael Collins as finance minister raised. This work and the publicity
surrounding it (a film of Collins issuing loan bonds was shown in cinemas)[5]
made Collins a national figure and demonstrated his administrative skill and
driving determination to a wide audience.

IRB membership, perhaps more than anything else, bound the Volunteers/
IRA and GHQ together in a common purpose – attacking the RIC and DMP
– separate from the Dáil. As Richard Walsh later observed, 'the difference

Relationships

221

between the I.R.B. and those not closely associated with the I.R.B., which subsequently became apparent, was not noticeable'.[6] This was a point that Richard Mulcahy, Volunteer/IRA Chief of Staff, later emphasised.[7] Collins went a step further in April 1920, writing to John Brennan, O/C Sligo Brigade, who had queried IRB activity: 'there is no difference between the aims and methods of the Irish Volunteer Organisation and the other one', referring to the IRB.[8] The exchange showed that, despite 'no difference', there was difference. The IRB may have been submerged in the Volunteers/IRA, but it was alive. Collins saw to that.

The first Volunteer/IRA attack sanctioned by GHQ Staff was also organised by GHQ: an attempted assassination of Lord French on 19 December 1919. But even then, caution was the watchword. Mulcahy called a meeting of Dublin Brigade officers and told them that the Dáil Cabinet reserved the right to repudiate the Volunteers/IRA and was anxious that no Volunteer/IRA action should be traced to it or to GHQ.[9]

The politicians kept their distance from the IRB and from Volunteer/IRA activity well into 1921, despite many TDs being IRB members. On 1 April 1919 the Dáil met for the second time. Fifty-two TDs were present, including for the first time the top leadership. Cathal Brugha resigned as Priomh Áire (prime minister/president of the Dáil) and as Ceann Comhairle, and de Valera replaced him as Priomh Áire. Seán T. O'Kelly was elected Ceann Comhairle and four clerks of the Dáil were appointed: Diarmuid O'Hegarty, Seán Ó Murthuile, Seán Nunan and Padraig Ó Síocháin. With the possible exception of Ó Síocháin, all were members of the IRB.[10] Brugha's ministers also resigned and on 2 April were replaced by de Valera's nominees – officially known as 'secretaries' – forming the Cabinet of the Dáil government. Arthur Griffith became Minister for Home Affairs and Cathal Brugha became Minister for Defence, replacing Mulcahy, who became his deputy while remaining Chief of Staff. Count Plunkett remained Minister for Foreign Affairs, Constance Markievicz, Minister for Labour, Eoin MacNeill, Minister for Industries, William Cosgrave, Minister for Local Government and Michael Collins, Minister for Finance.[11] Collins was the only active IRB man in the new Dáil Cabinet, which he certainly did not control (Plunkett was an IRB member but did not take part in the IRB after 1916).

IRB efforts to control nationalist organisations included the Irish trade unions. Martin Conlon, a co-opted member of the Supreme Council, was tasked by the Council with forming an Irish engineering union with nationalist

222 The Irish Republican Brotherhood, 1914–1924

principles to displace the British Amalgamated Society of Engineers (ASE) for factory workers and mechanics. Conlon chaired the IRB's Labour Board with a colleague on the Supreme Council, Luke Kennedy, as his deputy and another IRB man, Patrick McGuirk, as secretary. Collins took a direct interest in the Board, placing it within his intelligence operation. Thomas Maguire, one of the Board's organisers, summed up their mission:

> Our duty was to use our influence in our various trade unions, and in the Labour movement generally, on behalf of the Republic; to get hold of men in important key positions, such as power stations, railways and transport dockworkers, etc.; and most important of all, to undermine the amalgamated and cross-channel unions, and where possible to organise a breakaway from these unions, and establish purely Irish unions instead, manned and controlled by men with republican and national tendencies; in other words we were republican agents within the trade union movement ... We were in direct communication with Michael Collins, both as minister for finance and chief intelligence officer of the Army.[12]

Conlon worked to create a new union with the support of Constance Markievicz as Minister for Labour and Diarmuid O'Hegarty, who acted as Cabinet Secretary. The Irish Engineering Union was formed using men in the IRB, Sinn Féin and the IRA to recruit members. Its inaugural meeting was held on 9 May 1920 at the Abbey Theatre and by 1921 it had over 4,500 members, leaving the ASE with fewer than 1,800.[13]

De Valera, jailed in May 1918 for anti-conscription campaigning, had made it clear since his escape from Lincoln Prison in February 1919 that he felt his place was now in the United States where he could raise money and support for Irish independence. He remained in Ireland for four months in order to set up his government and was then spirited by the IRB to America in June.[14] Arthur Griffith, while remaining Minister for Home Affairs, was chosen to be Acting President of the Dáil in de Valera's absence.[15]

From about May 1919 the Dáil, subject to increasing harassment by the authorities, was driven underground, which limited its functioning as a government. On 27 October Griffith took the precaution of asking important Dáil members not to attend its proceedings because of the danger of arrest.[16] In November the Dáil Secretariat officers were arrested and the

Relationships 223

Dáil records seized. In all, between January 1919 and the July 1921 Truce there were only twenty-one meetings of the Dáil. As a result of this fugitive existence, there was little legislation, little debate, little direction and little opposition.

Ministerial successes reflected the quality of the individual ministers rather than the quality of the Dáil government. Collins was conspicuously successful as Minister for Finance, raising in Ireland a National Loan of £372,000 (about £24 million in 2024 values).[17] Munster, which Collins represented on the Volunteer/IRA Executive and where his constituency was (Cork South), contributed twice as much (£172,500) as Leinster (£87,400) and far more than Connacht (£58,000) and Ulster (£41,300).[18] This must have given Collins particular pleasure.

On 1 April 1919 the Volunteer/IRA Executive met to debate its relationship with the Dáil government and if it should relinquish its authority to Cathal Brugha as Dáil Minister for Defence. The debate continued for months. Richard Walsh took part:

> There was a very strong element in the Executive against handing over control of the army to the government, and the discussion revealed the existence within the Executive of two groups – one which may be described as the I.R.B., and the other the anti-I.R.B. wings … one associated with Michael Collins' views and the other with the views of Cathal Brugha.[19]

Opposition to accepting the Dáil government stemmed from the IRB's distrust of politicians that the emphasis on apparent unity suppressed. On the Executive Diarmuid O'Hegarty fronted the IRB's position. Collins was, no doubt, hanging back, unwilling to risk more resistance than he already faced. Richard Walsh described the IRB argument:

> The members opposed to this were led by Dermot [sic] O'Hegarty and held the opinion that Dail Eireann was composed of politicians who might if they – Dail Eireann – considered it expedient, abandon the republican position and compromise the I.R.A. by doing so.[20]

Cathal Brugha came up with wording that he said was taken from the oath that legislators, the military and civil servants swore in the United States. It was

224 The Irish Republican Brotherhood, 1914–1924

accepted by the O'Hegarty group. On 20 August 1919 the Dáil approved the oath:

> I, A.B., do solemnly swear (or affirm) that I do not, and shall not, yield a voluntary support to any pretended Government, Authority, or Power within Ireland, hostile or inimical thereto; and I do further swear (or affirm) that to the best of my knowledge and ability I will support and defend the Irish Republic, and the Government of the Irish Republic, which is Dail Eireann, against all enemies, foreign and domestic; that I will bear true faith and allegiance to the same, and that I take this obligation freely without any mental reservation or purpose of evasion, so help me God.

The oath was taken by all TDs in August 1919 and was accepted for the Volunteers/IRA by their Executive in July 1920, no doubt as a result of pressure from Brugha, but with reservations:[21] that the oath would only be binding as long as the Dáil remained the government of the Republic, and that the Executive would continue to be the governing authority of the Volunteers/IRA (thus also acting as a watchdog of the Dáil).[22] All but five members of the Executive were in the IRB.[23]

The formulation of the oath was unfortunate. It was still conditional. If the Dáil ceased to be the government of the Republic, or if the Dáil decided on a non-republican form of government, this oath could then be held to have been abrogated. It enabled Republicans in the 1922–23 Civil War to claim that since the Dáil had abandoned the Republic it forfeited IRA allegiance.

In September 1919 Ernie O'Malley gave the oath to some units of the South Tipperary Brigade: 'The oath was read out to the men – there was no compulsion on them to repeat the words aloud – some did so, others maintained a discreet silence or muttered under their breath – but all would have right hands raised, palms outward, at shoulder level.' Collins 'upbraided' O'Malley for doing this: the Volunteer Executive had not yet agreed to adopt the oath.[24] Tipperary discomfort and Collins' anger reflected general Volunteer/IRA and IRB wariness of politicians. Some other Volunteer/IRA units took the oath in 1919,[25] but a general administering waited for a year.

For their part the politicians were always careful of being identified with the IRA.[26] Not all TDs were simply politicians but being in the Dáil was a branding in the eyes of the IRA and IRB. The Dáil acted almost as if there were

Relationships 225

no British presence or government in Ireland and made little reference to the fighting. Not until 11 March 1921 did it acknowledge that there was a war going on and admit the existence of the IRA by name.[27]

In July 1920, fifteen months after the oath of allegiance to the Dáil was first discussed, a Volunteer/IRA constitution was drafted, requiring 'every member of the Irish Republican Army' to take the oath.[28] The objectives of the Volunteers/IRA in the new 1920 constitution were clear and firmly republican:

1. To secure and maintain the Irish Republic, and the rights and liberties common to the people of Ireland.
2. To train and equip for this purpose an Irish Volunteer Force, which shall be the Army of the Irish Republic.[29]

Direction of the Volunteers/IRA was now formally vested in the Dáil minister for defence but, once again, conditionally: 'The Minister of National Defence shall be approved by the Executive Council.'[30] In other words, the Executive's acceptance of the minister's authority could be withdrawn. The Executive also reinforced its position by continuing to ratify promotions and appointments in the Volunteers/IRA, and to determine military policy which GHQ Staff were to implement.[31] Despite these steps, the importance of the Executive had diminished with the creation of GHQ Staff, whose members effectively replaced the Executive's directors and came themselves to make 'Executive' decisions.

The Dáil did not exercise or formally acknowledge its relationship with the IRA until August 1921 after fighting was over.[32] Members of the Executive were aware that there was a conflict of authority between the Dáil and themselves. But the IRB's predominance in the Executive meant that there was no automatic willingness to accept the Dáil's and consequently Brugha's authority.[33] Despite being on the Executive himself and Chairman of the Resident Executive, Brugha's only effective source of authority was as Acting President of the Dáil and Minister for Defence – and that was conditional on the Volunteer/IRA Executive's assent.

In step with the Dáil's and Volunteer/IRA adoption of Brugha's oath, the Supreme Council amended the IRB constitution in September 1919 to accept this new allegiance, stressing that the people's will had been and would be expressed through the Dáil. IRB members in the Volunteers/IRA could now take the oath to the Dáil without contravening their IRB oath. In a circular to

226   The Irish Republican Brotherhood, 1914–1924

IRB County Centres the Supreme Council claimed that the Dáil was the IRB's creation and explained:

> In view of the fact that the policy of the I.R.B. has succeeded in establishing a duly elected public authority competent to declare the will and give expression to the desire of the Irish people to secure the international recognition of the Irish Republic; and whereas this public authority has decreed that all servants and soldiers of the Irish Republic shall take the ... oath. It is declared that members of the I.R.B. may, in accordance with the terms and spirit of their inception oath, loyally accept and obey this authority.[34]

The decision to accept the oath and the Dáil government's authority was left to each Volunteer/IRA brigade.[35] The overwhelming majority voted to accept without much – if any – IRB or Volunteer/IRA opposition to it. An immediate result was that the abbreviation 'IRA' became more frequently used from late 1919 onwards. 'After the first Dáil met and took over the Volunteers as the army of the Republic,' said Andrew Keaveney, 'all our members were required to subscribe to an oath of allegiance to the Republic and the Dáil as the elected government of such. All our 25 or 26 members took this oath without fail and we were then the I.R.A.'[36]

Florence O'Donoghue, an important chronicler of this period, recalled: 'The Dail decreed the oath of allegiance on 20 August 1919. The deputies did not take it until 27 October. Clearly, and I have some recollections about it, the delay was to enable the I.R.B. to make the necessary changes so that its members could take the oath.'[37]

Richard Walsh, although a Mayo Centre, was sympathetic to Brugha and suspicious of Collins. In his experience, after the oath was agreed, he was glad to say that the IRB did not interfere with the IRA's decision-making: 'I would like to state that as a body the I.R.B. organisation were not asked for any decisions on the question of the oath for the army. I was Co. Secretary for Mayo I.R.B. Co. Board and I got no orders to obtain a decision on the oath question.'[38] Richard Mulcahy was adamant that 'the I.R.B. never interfered in [Volunteer/IRA] policy in any way'.[39] This was not so: the Innishannon incident in Cork in 1918 was a local IRB affair, as was the 1919 Soloheadbeg ambush. Both were conducted without GHQ knowledge or approval.

Alec McCabe asked Collins about the IRB–Dáil relationship in 1919:

Relationships   227

I said to Collins as far as I am concerned we owe allegiance to the Dáil: the I.R.B. should not be in conflict with the newly-elected government, that we should all make ourselves servants of that government. So Michael Collins assured me – at this point I think it is right to confirm what Florrie O'Donoghue has said – that Collins said 'You can be absolutely sure if there is any conflict in allegiance you are absolved from allegiance with the I.R.B. You can take that for granted. There will be no conflict between the I.R.B. and the elected government of the country'.[40]

The Supreme Council had agreed the oath and what it entailed, namely that it dropped its claims to be the government of the Republic. Given O'Donoghue's account, the transition had been carefully choreographed. Additionally, since IRB meetings of all descriptions had tailed off from 1919 in favour of Volunteer/IRA activity, and since the Volunteers/IRA were officered mostly by IRB or IRB-minded men, it was probably assumed by the Supreme Council that the Volunteers/IRA could be depended upon to protect the 'republican position' that the IRB stood for.

With more reflection, this might have been seen to be doubtful. The Volunteers/IRA were too big for a small secret society fully to control, especially when that society and its methods and membership were known by its nationalist opponents, and when the unquestioned wish for peace in the population at large – and in the Church, always a strong influencer – was inevitably reflected in Volunteers/IRA ranks too.

With the oath to the Dáil, Brugha forced its members unequivocally to accept the Republic and forced the IRB to accept the Dáil.[41] A year later in August 1921, following de Valera's successful proposal that he should be formally recognised by the Dáil as President of the Republic, the Supreme Council also surrendered its claims to the presidency, altering the 1917 Constitution from 'The President of the Irish Republican Brotherhood is, in fact as well as by right, President of the Irish Republic' to 'The President of the I.R.B. shall direct the working of the Irish Republican Brotherhood, subject to the control of the Supreme Council or the Executive thereof.'[42] The two changes – recognising the Dáil and the Dáil presidency – were circulated in 1921 as a booklet within the IRB entitled *Constitution as Revised to Date, 1920*.[43]

For the IRB, retaining the presidential claim made little difference to the reality that it could no longer expect the undivided loyalty of its members because of its recognition of the Dáil as the government of the Republic, and

228   The Irish Republican Brotherhood, 1914–1924

because its members had been willingly subsumed in the Volunteers/IRA. There was no point in remaining separate from the structures of the Volunteers/IRA and the Dáil. The Volunteers/IRA had implemented the IRB's physical-force policy and the Dáil had adopted its ideology.

Michael Collins from the outset looked beyond the arguments about allegiance to the Dáil. In January 1920 he set out a plan for the IRB:

> I am anxious that an appreciation of say £500,000 be made as a permanent republican Trust Fund. The Principal to be untouched and untouchable. The interest annually say £30,000 to be available for republican Political purposes up to date of Recognition and Evacuation. Even then the Principal should not be realised and the interest should be added each year for perhaps 100 years or so. The Republic may not come in our lives and this Fund should be securely tied up against the possibility of Colonial or any other Home Rule landslide in the country for 15 or 20 years.[44]

Another part of his plan was that the Brotherhood would be part of 'a world-wide Irish Federation, each separate part working through the Government, and in accordance with the laws of the country where it had its being.'[45] The purpose of this federation, presumably, was to mobilise expatriate Irish people in the interest of an independent Irish republic.

Collins was revealing several vital appreciations: that a republic might not be achieved immediately; that the Irish electorate might well reject independence in favour of an IPP platform; and that the current fight was to secure British recognition of a republic and the 'evacuation' of British forces and officials. For him, the IRB was the guardian of the Republic that should be maintained and strengthened for generations into the future if necessary.

On 26 November 1920 Arthur Griffith was arrested and, after Brugha and Austin Stack declined the post, Collins was elected by the Dáil as Acting President, holding the position until de Valera returned at the end of December. It was testimony to the respect Collins enjoyed, and to his energy. Dorothy Macardle, generally regarded as de Valera's amanuensis, presented Collins' succession as significant from an IRB standpoint too:

> President de Valera was then at the climax of his labours in the United States. Michael Collins became acting President. Arthur Griffith might

Relationships 229

have been expected to nominate, as his successor in office, Cathal Brugha, but Michael Collins was head of the I.R.B. According to the Fenian tradition, the head of the Brotherhood was the real head of the whole movement and of the Revolutionary government; thus Collins was merely succeeding officially to the position which was already accorded him secretly by the I.R.B.[46]

This statement was published thirteen years after the event. It illustrated the view which de Valera, Brugha and Stack advanced that the IRB (and inferentially Collins) was subversive to civil authority. It did not accord with the facts, of which de Valera was well aware and of which Macardle should have been. The presidency was of the Dáil and not the Republic (as we have seen, that came in August 1921); it was not the secret IRB position; the Dáil presidency was not a permanent one; the appointment was made by the TDs, not Griffith, and both Brugha and Stack had been asked by Griffith to take over from him but both refused, citing pressure of work.[47] Collins used his position to give the Dáil staff a Christmas bonus of a week's pay.[48]

In December 1920, the Archbishop of Perth, the Most Rev. Patrick Clune,[49] on behalf of Lloyd George, joined Alfred Cope in negotiations for a truce with Collins. This may well have prompted de Valera to return to Ireland to re-establish his position as leader. On 25 January 1921 in the Dáil he called for less violence.[50] He was understandably anxious to present a narrative of statesmanship, of unity and determination, and to counteract the IRB and Collins' influence. Then, in a press interview in April, he claimed on behalf of the Dáil government that one of its first acts had been to establish the IRA: 'From the Irish Volunteers we fashioned the Irish Republican Army to be the military arm of government.'[51]

This was not correct. The IRB had done that job while the Dáil carefully stayed away, many TDs privately expressing disapproval of Volunteer/IRA violence as de Valera himself had done in January 1921. Over the following two months, de Valera must have seen that the Volunteers/IRA had the real power in the national movement and that he needed to come alongside in order to secure his leadership. The Dáil did not agree or disagree with de Valera, leaving his statement hanging. He also recognised that simply fighting would not secure independence: political compromise would inevitably be necessary. Signalling this on 16 August 1921, he said in a public session of the second Dáil (elected in May 1921):

230   The Irish Republican Brotherhood, 1914–1924

> Two and a half years ago, as you know, the old Dáil was elected as an expression of the will of the Irish nation in a general election which was, in effect, a plebiscite. The question was put to the Irish people, what form of Government they wanted, how they wished to live, so that they might have an opportunity of working out for themselves their own national life in their own way, and the answer that the Irish people gave was unmistakeable. I do not say that that answer was for a form of government so much, because we are not republican doctrinaires, but it was for Irish freedom and Irish independence, and it was obvious to everyone who considered the question that Irish independence could not be realised at the present time in any other way so suitably as through a republic.[52]

The Dáil then finally proceeded formally to embrace the IRA and accept responsibility for its activities.

De Valera was careful not to say that the 1918 election had been a vote for a republic and risk being repudiated in the press and by a section of TDs. His problem was the IRB/IRA. As events were to show, a majority of IRA men were doctrinaire republicans in the tradition of the IRB. Controlling the IRA was essential if there were to be peace and a settlement with Britain.

The Irish community in the United States was de Valera's chosen target group not only to raise money and support for Irish independence, but also to help him wrest authority from the IRB in Ireland. In this enterprise he had the unexpected help of Harry Boland, who joined him in the United States in May 1919. De Valera had appointed him as a 'special envoy of the Elected Government of the Irish Republic to the United States of America'.[53] The Supreme Council, at Collins' suggestion, simultaneously sent him as their representative to Clan na Gael.[54] Apart from his work in Sinn Féin, he had spoken on international affairs in the Dáil, so had some claim to diplomacy. His objective, as far as de Valera was concerned, was to persuade Devoy and his colleagues that the Clan should support de Valera and his policy statements.[55] He was also charged with obtaining weapons and ammunition by the Supreme Council.[56] Collins had arranged with Boland for these shipments to be handled by the IRB in Liverpool, writing to him on 23 November 1919: 'The scheme will be on the basis of sending a parcel perfectly open as ordinary merchandise, having secured entry through the Customs in Liverpool beforehand.'[57] He had real success in this IRB task, and the first shipments of weapons began

Relationships 231

arriving in early 1920. A year later Boland sent over the very first Thompson sub-machine guns (obtained by Larry de Lacey).[58]

The success of this operation was a tribute to the IRB's range, organisation and infiltration of Liverpool customs. Without this, supplying the Volunteers/IRA would have been far more difficult.

The Clan, in its previous form as the Fenian Brotherhood, had been the begetter of the IRB, encouraging, supporting and funding James Stephens and his successors. Its money had enabled the IRB to launch the 1916 Rising, and it had played a unique role in connecting the IRB and Germany before and after the Rising. Its funding enabled the IRB to be the principal (almost the sole) arms supplier of the Volunteers/IRA. John Devoy and the Clan leaders naturally looked upon the IRB as a supplicant partner and resisted being told what to do by Boland and de Valera. One of Boland's first actions was to make clear that he would be the conduit between the Clan and the Supreme Council.[59]

Soon after his arrival in the United States, Boland, supporting de Valera, conflicted with the Clan. The two principal leaders of the Clan, John Devoy, the secretary, and Judge Daniel Cohalan, active in American politics, wanted Boland and de Valera to follow their instructions about how to campaign. They did not want them to interfere in American politics that they regarded as their bailiwick. Nor did they welcome de Valera as the principal Irish spokesman in the United States: that was their claim to Irish-American pre-eminence.

Additionally, the Clan could not be seen putting Irish interests before American interests. In 1917 when America entered the First World War, Devoy and his colleagues – all born or naturalised American citizens – had been described as traitors because of their German connections. They needed to be careful. American interest after 1917 was to get along with its wartime ally, the United Kingdom – exactly what de Valera and Boland did not want.

The conflict must have reaffirmed de Valera's mistrust of the IRB while also worrying Collins about the differences between him and de Valera, and between Sinn Féin and the Volunteers/IRA. In December 1920 Collins had tried to heal the rift by sending Devoy a statement of the relationship between Clan na Gael and the IRB. He thanked the Clan for their support, asserting that the 1916 Rising was the culmination of co-operation between the Clan and the IRB, and giving an interesting statement of IRB policy: 'It has ever been the policy of the I.R.B. to secure easy and successful transmission of its aims and desires to the Irish people, and to make its will the will of the Irish people.'[60]

232   The Irish Republican Brotherhood, 1914–1924

The IRB may have wished this but never achieved it. It was always an extreme party unprepared for compromise. Collins' formulation implied that the political wing (de Valera) and the IRB and Clan had a unity of purpose that the IRB's 'will' would secure; that Devoy should not worry so much about de Valera who, ultimately, would be controlled.

Devoy accepted what was, in effect, Collins' guarantee that the IRB would manage the politicians and agreed to temper his criticism of de Valera and Boland. Perhaps with Hobson and McCartan's by-passing of Fred Allan and the Supreme Council in mind when they had used their connection to the Clan to win control of *Irish Freedom* in 1911, Boland, using his position as the Supreme Council's representative, asked the Clan if it regarded itself as subsidiary to or independent of the IRB, if it was prepared to supply more weapons and ammunition, and if it would give the IRB more money. It was an aggressive set of questions. No reply was received and the rift in America widened again.[61]

An interview with de Valera published in the *New York Globe* and the *Westminster Gazette* in February 1920 was the immediate cause of open disagreement. In it he indicated that he would accept less than full independence for Ireland. Comparing Ireland's relationship to Britain with Cuba's to the United States, he said:

> The United States safeguarded itself from the possible use of the island of Cuba as a base for attack by a foreign Power by stipulating [that Cuba would never take action endangering United States security]. Why doesn't Britain make a stipulation like this to safeguard herself? Why doesn't Britain declare a Monroe Doctrine for the two neighbouring islands? The people of Ireland so far from objecting would co-operate with their whole soul.[62]

This was immediately seen – correctly – as de Valera opening the door to compromise over a republic and surrendering the right of Ireland to conduct its own foreign policy. Cohalan and Devoy chose to have a public fight with de Valera about this interview, highlighting in the process the divisions beneath the surface unity in Ireland. The apparent divide was that de Valera and Sinn Féin were open to negotiated settlement while the Volunteers/IRA/IRB were not.[63] Matters came to a head in the summer of 1920 when de Valera, ignoring the Clan's advice, insisted on presenting the case for

Irish independence to the presidential election conventions of both major American political parties.[64] In August the *Gaelic American* published a report, 'Michael Collins speaks for Ireland', implying that Collins, not de Valera, was the real leader of Irish nationalism. Collins quickly told Devoy that when de Valera 'speaks to America, he speaks for us all'.[65] Implicit in this exchange was an assumption by Devoy that the IRB was *primus inter pares* and that Collins, as President, was in fact the real leader. Saying something to this effect publicly was designed to force de Valera to back down. Boland returned briefly to Ireland in September 1920 and explained the position to the Supreme Council, stressing the opposition both he and de Valera were facing from Devoy and Cohalan in the Clan and urging the Supreme Council to call them to order. Almost immediately after returning to the United States, Boland sent a cable to Collins which stated that on 18 October 1920 he had taken the step of severing the Clan from the IRB and had published this in the American press.[66] Shocked, Ó Murthuile and Collins called a meeting of the Supreme Council which decided not to recall Boland or withdraw his authority and to take no action until they received a full report from him.[67] Boland's next reports described de Valera's and his efforts to form a new American organisation which they called the 'Reorganised Clan na Gael'. Joseph McGarrity, President of Clan na Gael, and Luke Dillon, another leading Clan member appointed as Secretary by McGarrity, headed the new body and soon sent weapons and money to the IRB. Recognition, however, was not accorded to this new organisation by the Supreme Council.[68] Boland and de Valera with McGarrity and Dillon also formed the American Association for the Recognition of the Irish Republic as a new Irish-American political lobbying group.

The clash with the Clan signalled de Valera's firm resolve to be the head of the independence struggle and his expectation that the IRB, Volunteers/IRA, Sinn Féin, the Dáil and the Clan would all fall into line behind him in whatever settlement he might agree with the British government. In the United States he styled himself 'President of the Irish Republic' – something that Devoy must have resisted knowing the IRB's claims. And de Valera's Cuban analogy was an unmistakable signal that he would accept less than full independence.

Boland wrote suggesting that Collins join him in the United States to promote the second National Loan approved by the Dáil on 26 August 1920. A majority of the Cabinet thought Collins should go. Brugha and Stack in

234   The Irish Republican Brotherhood, 1914–1924

particular argued that he was the obvious choice to launch the new loan. No doubt they saw an opportunity to get Collins out of their way for a while. Other Cabinet members who did not approve of shooting constabulary and wrecking RIC barracks also seem to have pressured him to go, thinking that Collins' presence in the United States would reduce the number of such incidents.[69] Collins refused to go.[70] Secret talks to reach a truce had been underway for months and Collins did not want these to be taken over by someone else.

CHAPTER 22

Brugha

Because of his sincerity I would forgive him anything. At worst he was a fanatic – though in what has been a noble cause. At best I number him among the very few who have given their all that this country – now torn by Civil War – should have its freedom. When many of us are forgotten, Cathal Brugha will be remembered.[1]

Michael Collins, 7 July 1922

Darrell Figgis gave a brief sketch of Brugha: 'Stubborn, unbreakable, intractable … His life in the dream of the Republic – a Republic of name, without definition or constitution – was his reality. The public declaration of that name was all that to him was required to complete the reality that existed indivisibly in his mind.'[2] Emmet Dalton elaborated:

Brugha – you've got to understand the man. He was a likeable dedicated fanatic. His suggestions for the pursuit of the war of independence were such fantastic things … He had as much brains as a rabbit. Another of his ideas was to throw bombs into the assembled House of Commons. How do you deal with people like this? You just ignore them. And when he was ignored he was annoyed and he was Minister for Defence but nobody paid the slightest attention to him.[3]

'He wasn't a very intelligent man,' said Ernest Blythe. 'He was really, you might say, a natural fanatic. But not entirely oblivious to reason.'[4] Both Blythe and Dalton opposed Brugha in the Civil War, but they voiced a general opinion. Collins set reasonable objectives; Brugha was willing to cause mayhem.

236   The Irish Republican Brotherhood, 1914–1924

Born in 1874, Brugha was older than all the post-1916 leaders apart from Arthur Griffith (b. 1871) and Count Plunkett (b. 1851). De Valera was eight years younger, and Collins was sixteen years younger. Brugha was a stalwart member of the IRB Keating Circle from 1908, joining Seán MacDermott on IRB recruiting visits around the country. At about the same time he joined Lalor Ltd, chandlers supplying churches with beeswax candles, basing himself in its Dublin office for the next fourteen years and using travels on company business as cover for IRB organising. In 1912 he married and over the next four years had four children. He joined the Irish Volunteers at their inception in November 1913 and was elected Lieutenant of C Company of the Dublin Fourth Battalion. Within six months he had advanced to Battalion Adjutant. During the Howth gunrunning in July 1914 he led a group of IRB men to 'look as much like tourists as possible'.[5] They proceeded to unload the rifles and ammunition when the *Asgard* arrived, thus helping to ensure that they remained in IRB Volunteer hands. A week later he was similarly occupied when more rifles and ammunition were landed at Kilcoole in what was an entirely IRB exercise.[6] In early April 1916 he went to Kilkenny to ready local IRB Volunteers for the Rising.[7] On Easter Monday his battalion, commanded by Éamonn Ceannt, occupied the South Dublin Union. Very few Fourth Battalion members turned out: forty-four were counted at their surrender.[8] Brugha had been severely injured, suffering twenty-five separate wounds.[9]

The failure of the Rising and the low turnout grated with him. 'Cathal Brugha was fairly disgusted with the IRB,' said Michael Brennan. 'He thought that they were a pack of shilly-shalliers, a load of hot air. That's why he broke with them.'[10] For years he had put great energy into the IRB, and it had only delivered confusion. In Kilkenny, this resulted in parades and meetings but no insurrectionary action.[11] Brugha said to Seán Mathews, a Waterford IRB man, that '[T]he only two men who could keep that organisation free from graft and corruption were Tom Clarke and Sean McDermott, and they were dead.'[12] This feels like Brugha making a case rather than having evidence: because of the scandal of P.T. Daly's embezzlement in 1910–11, graft and corruption were associated with the pre-1912 Supreme Council, not with its successors. Éamonn Dore encountered Brugha in full anti-IRB flow in mid-1917 and reacted in the same vein as Kathleen Clarke did as Brugha, once again, banged a table:

When however, the name (I.R.B.) was mentioned, he got very excited and said that he was out to destroy it. He went on to say that if that organisation had ever been necessary, which he doubted, it was now unnecessary and even dangerous if it got into the hands of the wrong people. I remarked, 'Are you sure that what you are doing is the best way to end it? Knowing the Irish mind, will not your aggressive action make members more determined to stick to it? If you leave well alone, it may never become active again.' He made some answer to this which included reference to personalities, to which I replied, 'Will not your action push the organisation into the hands of those whom you do not wish to get control?' He got even more excited at this remark and striking the table with his fist, he said; 'I don't care. If it is the last act of my life I will lead a crusade to destroy it'.[13]

In public speeches and at Sinn Féin and Volunteer/IRA conventions, Brugha adopted a moderate tone, presenting himself as reasonable and within the non-violent consensus of 1917. But he was fixated on Collins and the IRB.

Figgis dated the start of Brugha's animosity towards Collins to the October 1917 Sinn Féin convention, when Brugha reacted against Collins' efforts to manipulate elections to the party's Executive in favour of IRB members: 'Cathal Brugha ... told me that he had seen what had been passing, but that he had been powerless to change events. It was at this meeting I saw for the first time the personal hostility between him and Michael Collins.'[14]

During 1919, Brugha became more and more hostile to Collins whom he correctly identified as flouting the chain of command and encouraging Volunteer/IRA activity that Brugha as Minister for Defence had not approved. In private Brugha also advocated violence, making the point that he did not disagree with Volunteer/IRA attacks but did disagree with unauthorised actions.

The control that Collins exercised through the IRB over the purchase and importing of arms and ammunition for the Volunteers/IRA contributed vastly to Brugha's growing antagonism. In Brugha's mind this came to revolve around the question of Collins' influence and the prestige accorded to Collins by the Volunteer/IRA rank and file as the man who could – and did – get arms and ammunition for them. The IRB was central to arms and ammunition supply. Eugene Loughran was a key Centre in Liverpool smuggling weapons to Ireland independently of the Volunteers/IRA and thus outside Brugha's chain of command: 'As far as I then knew the work of transporting arms and the traffic in arms in Liverpool generally was carried out by the IRB. The local Company of Volunteers in Liverpool knew nothing of our activities.'[15]

238 The Irish Republican Brotherhood, 1914–1924

Brugha resented this.[16] The IRB that Collins operated, and not the Volunteers/IRA of which Brugha had formal charge, possessed the contacts, the skill and the credit. Whereas Brugha had been instrumental in 1916 and early 1917 in the revitalisation of the Volunteers/IRA, Collins overtook him as the physical-force leader largely because of his countrywide contacts, facilitated by the IRB, and his administrative energy. At one point in 1920, Brugha attempted to organise a rival arms-purchasing operation in Britain but was frozen out by IRB men loyal to Collins.[17] Brugha's misjudgement was to assume that Collins' status and influence derived from the IRB when, in fact, it was Collins' ability and energy that secured his reputation. Michael Hayes was certain of this: 'Every conspiracy against the British here failed except the last one, because of lack of attention to detail. Now, Collins attended to details. That was one of the great differences – that's why, not because he was in the IRB at all.'[18]

Collins' brusque manner did nothing to soften offended colleagues, notably Brugha, who was no slouch in brusqueness either.[19] But while Brugha took offence, Collins never seemed to, and responded positively when people stood up to him.

An alliance between Brugha and Austin Stack against Collins developed. 'Collins used to pass remarks in fun about Stack's department to me,' said Tadhg Kennedy, 'and the other fellows to whom, perhaps, similar remarks were made would carry them back to Stack's men or to Stack.'[20] Collins was not alone in his view of Stack; Ernest Blythe thought Stack 'was as thick as you make them'.[21] Interestingly, both Stack and Brugha agreed in effect with Collins' criticisms, as Tadhg Kennedy recalled: 'During the Truce, Stack told me how unfitted he was for the job of Minister for Home Affairs. He hadn't either the education or the ability, he felt. He was a very humble man and he had no illusions about his own abilities. Cathal Brugha also spoke of his being unfitted for the job he'd held.'[22] The problem for the Volunteers/IRA was that they were the independence movement's only effective component and was constantly expected to perform civil functions.[23]

Towards the end of 1920 Brugha, supported by Stack, began to question sums of money sent by Collins to Glasgow for arms purchases and accused Collins of mishandling the money. There were gaps in accounting for the money Collins spent, not least because he commingled IRA and IRB funds. Brugha's own probity was unassailable. From 1919 he did not take his £350 per annum salary as Minister for Defence but gave it to Mulcahy.

In pursuit of Collins, Brugha went to the length at the end of 1920 of summoning the whole of GHQ and some others to a meeting at the home of Michael O'Rahilly's widow, Nancy, in Herbert Park, to discuss the accounts of arms purchases in Scotland. Mulcahy complained to de Valera about Brugha's action, declaring he would not continue as Chief of Staff if it went on. De Valera thought that Brugha was jealous of Collins. 'You know,' he said to Mulcahy, 'I think Cathal is jealous of Mick. Isn't it a terrible thing to think that a man with the qualities that Cathal undoubtedly has would fall a victim to a dirty little vice like jealousy.'[24] Matters were temporarily resolved by Mulcahy sending Brugha a series of forms for tabulating future accounts. But during 1921 Brugha pursued his allegations that Collins was using IRA funds for IRB purposes and for gifts to IRB people, especially in England and Scotland.[25] Brugha's grievance, although he did not say so, was that Volunteer/ IRA money was passing through IRB hands, and that in consequence the IRB and Collins were given the complete credit for arms supply. He attempted to dismiss Collins from GHQ, but Mulcahy and de Valera opposed him and Collins remained.[26]

Until August 1921 the conflict seethed, but then Brugha called a meeting of the IRA Executive at the Mansion House in order to discipline Collins (thus no doubt hoping to counteract the influence of the IRB within the IRA).[27] He sought to assert his authority over the Executive and to diminish Collins' status and power to the greatest degree he could. De Valera chaired the meeting. Brugha, supported by Stack, again demanded an investigation of Collins' arms purchases in Glasgow. The matter was put into the hands of a sub-committee that never reported back.

The Dáil Cabinet on 15 September 1921, prompted by Brugha and de Valera, had agreed to a 'new' army unequivocally responsible to the Dáil government.[28] This prepared the ground for new conflict between Brugha (with de Valera and Stack in muted support) and Collins. On 25 November the Dáil Cabinet met GHQ staff and attempted to restructure the Staff and create a new army, clearly designed to reduce Collins' and the IRB's influence.[29] The meeting endured an argument that had begun in September over the position of deputy chief of staff. Stack had been the deputy since the creation of GHQ but had never fulfilled the role. Mulcahy wanted Eoin O'Duffy – an active IRB member – to replace him. Brugha and de Valera wanted to keep Stack. Tempers were hot. Mulcahy's objections were taken by de Valera as mutinous, and he ended the meeting declaring, 'You may mutiny if you like, but Ireland will give me another army',[30] and stormed out. Brugha compromised and accepted Eoin O'Duffy as co-deputy chief of staff with Austin Stack.

GHQ Staff accepted the creation of a new army. Brugha immediately issued new commissions, for the most part confirming existing positions, that stated that the new army was solely responsible to the Dáil and no longer to the IRA Executive.[31] However, a change of the IRA to a new status required the approval of an IRA convention, and not just its Executive. The Executive could summon a convention, but there was no Executive meeting after October until 1922, and so no convention took place to endorse a new army. Liam Lynch, newly appointed O/C First Southern Division, refused to accept a new commission and resigned on 6 December in protest. To him, and many other IRB Volunteers/IRA officers and rank and file, the new army was a move to replace republican control of the IRA with compromise-minded political control that might well sacrifice the Republic.[32] From this point on, Lynch was acting as an independent commander of one-quarter of the IRA. He maintained relations with GHQ, but no longer accepted its authority. Mulcahy attempted to heal the rift by sending a message to the IRA commandants on 30 November saying that it was 'not really so' that a new army was being formed.[33]

The inevitable split in nationalist ranks between realists and idealists was taking place.

CHAPTER 23

Truce

I do believe that the more people that are killed, the more difficult will be the final solution, unless while killing is going on a body of opinion is growing up imbued with a strong idea that the Government have made a generous and definite offer to Ireland.[1]

General Nevil Macready, 20 June 1921

On 23 December 1920 the Government of Ireland Act came into force. It partitioned Ireland, with six of the nine counties of Ulster forming Northern Ireland within the United Kingdom, to be governed from Belfast, and the remaining twenty-six counties forming Southern Ireland to be governed from Dublin. A divided Ireland was now a fact. On 24 May 1921 two separate elections were held. In Northern Ireland, Unionists won forty seats and Sinn Féin and the Nationalists (the IPP in the North) each won six. In Southern Ireland there was no poll: Sinn Féin was unopposed in 124 seats. Similarly, Unionists were unopposed in the four seats for TCD. There was a general expectation among nationalists, and possibly with Lloyd George, that Northern Ireland would not be viable and would be re-integrated in a united Ireland. But by adopting these elections as its own the Dáil compromised a united Ireland, notwithstanding its refusal to recognise the validity of the Northern Irish government and parliament.

King George V, opening the Parliament of Northern Ireland on 22 June, appealed for reconciliation and successfully opened a door for new peace negotiations: 'I appeal to all Irishmen to pause, to stretch out the hand of forbearance and conciliation, to forgive and to forget, and to join in making for the land which they love a new era of peace, contentment, and goodwill.'[2]

242   The Irish Republican Brotherhood, 1914–1924

Three weeks later the IRA and the British Army agreed a truce.

At some point – probably in 1919 – the IRB had ordered its members to co-ordinate their military activities with those of the Volunteers/IRA. This co-ordination had been so successful that in March 1921 the Supreme Council was able to state baldly, 'The military functions of both bodies are similar to each other, the success or failing of one, is the success or failure of both.'[3] But the extent to which IRB men had identified with the Volunteers/IRA and integrated completely within the Volunteer/IRA structure now worried the Council because of growing differences between the Dáil government, the IRB and the Volunteers/IRA. Accordingly, the Council decided that the separate identity of the IRB should be stimulated. A strong IRB might be able to exert pressure on both the Dáil government and the army to present a united front.

Collins had kept the Council informed of peace discussions taking place secretly with Lloyd George's emissaries since spring 1920. Shortly before the July 1921 Truce, Lloyd George had agreed to a peace conference and the Council 'unanimously agreed that the ends of the Organisation would be advanced by representatives of Ireland entering into the proposed conference and that the influence of the Organisation should be directed towards that end'.[4] Simultaneously, revitalisation of Circles and recruitment of Volunteer/IRA officers into the IRB was implemented in order to improve IRB influence. Liam Gaynor in 1917 had been able to order an IRB man to accept a commission that he did not want: 'As an oath-bound member of the IRB he obeyed my command.'[5] Such obedience was no longer given in 1921. With a conference with Britain in mind that he knew would certainly not produce a republic, Collins must have looked to the IRB to support him in whatever position he took and so he needed to re-establish its discipline and his authority. In March a Supreme Council circular to all County Centres was prepared – no doubt prompted by Collins – re-asserting IRB claims to be the leader of the independence campaign, triggering a new effort to revitalise the organisation. IRB activity, separate from the IRA, now began again. The Council had not paid attention to the Brotherhood's organisation for the past two years, content to assume that its purposes were being met by the Volunteers/IRA. Now it had to scramble for its members' loyalty.

Collins presided at a South Munster Divisional Board at Easter (27 March 1921 was Easter Sunday) where it was agreed that Volunteer/IRA men who had proven themselves should be brought into the IRB.[6] At the end of April, Liam Deasy with the senior Cork officers came up to Dublin for discussions

Truce

with GHQ and for another IRB meeting with Collins again in the chair. The IRB meeting came first.[7] Deasy did not hear anything of Volunteer/IRA difficulties. Conversation focused on the IRB: 'For four hours down to a serious discussion on the IRB part in forcing activities in the area [West Cork]. One main decision, I recall, the IRB County and Centres were instructed to extend membership to all proven Volunteers, and this decision was carried out fully in the following months in the South.'[8]

Collins and his IRB colleagues decided to form Volunteer/IRA columns from active areas (which meant Munster) and send them to inactive areas to extend the range of conflict. This may have been the only 'military' meeting in 1918–21 under IRB and not Volunteer/IRA direction.[9] The pay-off for Collins' commitment to Cork and Munster may have been a factor in this meeting: these were 'his' people and at this point they followed his lead. The meeting also suggests that Collins understood the inevitability of the Volunteers/IRA becoming an instrument of the Dáil. Thus he wanted to re-establish the IRB as *the* fighting men that he could deploy separately as he – and the Supreme Council – thought best.

Tom Hales, O/C Third Cork Brigade, had been captured in July 1920. The South Munster Divisional Board elected Liam Lynch, the Cork County Centre, to replace him on the Supreme Council. Lynch nominated Florence O'Donoghue to replace him as County Centre and Seán O'Hegarty to replace the City Centre Donal O'Callaghan, Lord Mayor of Cork.[10] Seán Ó Murthuile wrote to O'Donoghue on 14 March 1921 informing him of his appointment. The eight months' time lag between Tom Hales' arrest and the March meeting in Dublin gives an indication of IRB disorganisation. Both Lynch and O'Donoghue were confirmed in these posts when the biennial elections were held in the summer of 1921.[11]

The previous IRB elections had been held in 1919 when there had been a discussion within the Supreme Council as to whether the IRB should continue to exist. This was generated in particular by de Valera's and Brugha's opposition to the society after 1916. The Council had decided that the organisation should continue, and now in March 1921 rejoiced in that decision, circulating to all County Centres:

> In the matter of co-ordinating the military work of the Organisation with that of the Irish Volunteers we have been very successful. In response to the orders issued Organisation men everywhere have shown tact and

244 The Irish Republican Brotherhood, 1914–1924

> wisdom in the matter, and to this may be attributed a good deal of the efficiency that has resulted in great military successes in the areas where the fighting has been most intense. This is only as it should be, and in strict accordance with the desires of the S.C.[12]

This was an interesting claim since the 'IRA' was then in official use. The Council was making a distinction here that there was a separate unspecified IRB military force – it would be assumed that this was the IRA, distinct from the Volunteers – but inferentially it was claiming that the IRB itself was the IRA.

In April and again in July 1921, Collins made this distinction clear within the IRB, stating that IRB members were expected to infiltrate and influence other nationalist organisations – including the Volunteers/IRA – rather than belong to them in preference to the IRB.[13] This was a defining statement. It showed that Collins saw the IRB as the harbinger of Irish resistance to Britain, as superior in the nationalist array to any other organisation, and that only the IRB could be depended upon to achieve independence. It also showed that the IRB was, in effect, Collins' party and that he was aware that his authority needed to be re-established: implicit in the March circular was the understanding that the Volunteers/IRA had effectively replaced the IRB and had become aligned with Sinn Féin.

The Dáil recognition of the IRA as its army in August 1921 completed its takeover by the politicians. It also revealed that de Valera and his supporters were not interested in collaborating with Collins to bring the IRB along with them in any peace settlement. They thought that they controlled the IRA. They were reassured by Richard Mulcahy that this was the case, and it was confirmed by the 25 May 1921 attack on the Customs House (ordered by de Valera as a test of IRA obedience to his authority).[14] They thought that IRB influence was no longer that great and had been overcome. The March 1921 circular was a political response on Collins' part to rebuild both the IRB and his authority in the face of de Valera's cloaked and Brugha's open opposition. It addressed the hidden fault line between politicians and the men of violence within the nationalist grouping.

The circular went on to claim that the IRB had been responsible for the 'regeneration' of Ireland, making it overwhelmingly republican, and had successfully maintained the Republic in arms. The areas in which there was most activity since 1916, it said (accurately), were also those where the IRB was strongest. The Supreme Council considered that the IRB had fulfilled its most important function: inculcating the 'fighting idea' throughout the independence movement. The clear inference was that violence, not debate, bred success. It saw the IRB as a 'national rallying centre' from which the 'Republican idea' had successfully spread through the Volunteers/IRA, Sinn Féin, the Gaelic League, the GAA, local government – indeed, the whole national movement – and now the IRB had to be maintained until Ireland was free of British forces. It also quietly set a new objective – 'the complete withdrawal of the enemy forces from Ireland' – that if achieved could be used to justify a peace settlement that did not produce a republic. Collins, who was certainly responsible for the circular, had been dealing secretly with Lloyd George for over a year. He was preparing the ground for a compromise.

Altogether, the circular smacked of chivvying propaganda: 'Organisation men who are unable or unwilling to act up to the spirit contained in their inception oath should be outside and not inside the Organisation.'[15] The Supreme Council and Collins were defensively self-justifying, making claims that could not be confirmed, anxious to secure loyalty but careful not to command and thus risk a direct challenge to their authority. They knew that they had a problem with their members.

Political moves also prompted this IRB initiative. From early 1920 and up to the Truce in July 1921, there were several peace feelers from both sides. Alfred Cope arrived in Dublin on 4 May 1920, sent by Lloyd George. He sought Sinn Féin contacts and opened a secret channel to Collins and Griffith. He worked tirelessly to bring about a truce and peace. The Bishop of Killaloe, the Right Rev. Michael Fogarty, met Cope and recalled, 'Alone among the die-hards in Dublin Castle, he kept Lloyd George's interest in the Truce alive. He was undoubtedly Lloyd George's man in Dublin, sent there to watch events ... [H]e expressed the view that were a Truce arranged, and had hostilities ceased on both sides, a splendid opportunity would present itself for a final settlement.'[16]

Lloyd George's strategy was to give Ireland devolution up to a maximum of semi-Dominion status. Cope's task was to persuade the republican leadership that a republic would not be allowed, but short of that they could have most of what they wanted; that the position of Northern Ireland would be negotiated; that if it was accepted that a republic was not achievable, then the fighting in Ireland was pointless. From December 1920, and probably earlier from spring 1920, Collins and Griffith understood this from the contacts that they had but could not acknowledge it to their colleagues and risk being accused of betraying

246 The Irish Republican Brotherhood, 1914–1924

the Republic. Moss Twomey was very conscious of the tightrope being walked: 'I remember 1918–19 I was always afraid that if the British came out that time and had offered full Dominion Home Rule, they might have split Sinn Féin from top to bottom, even at that time. And people would nearly give you a punch on the nose for saying it.'[17]

Carl Ackerman, the London correspondent of Philadelphia's *Public Ledger* newspaper, developed a strong relationship with Sir Basil Thomson, Director of Intelligence at the Home Office (effectively head of police intelligence), described as a key source on Irish affairs 'because everything of a confidential nature relating to Ireland and from Ireland passed through his hands before it reached the Prime Minister'.[18] In May 1920 Thomson gave Ackerman an IRB constitution and documents captured from Mulcahy and Collins in an effort, according to Ackerman, 'to prepare the ground for negotiation with the IRA leaders, weakening the movement's appeal as the expressed will of the Irish people by disclosing its secret and sinister puppeteers ... Thomson believed it "necessary for all parties to realize ... that the real leaders of Sinn Féin were not the men then in the public eye".'[19]

Lloyd George signalled that he wanted a settlement but had to keep this secret in order to maintain his coalition with Unionists and Conservatives and also so as not to undermine British forces and the RIC in Ireland. Home Rule was to be implemented separately in Northern and Southern Ireland, as the progress of a fourth Home Rule Bill through parliament ordained. His message to Collins was that partition was negotiable. For a settlement to be achieved, however, there needed to be at the least an apparently pacified country that could take administrative and government responsibilities, allowing an orderly British withdrawal.

The army naturally saw Irish matters in military terms, not appreciating Lloyd George's difficulties and subtleties. Cope himself in December 1920 observed British officers returning to London from Dublin to complain to Lloyd George about peace initiatives and commented: 'I do not like to see these fellows crossing in such strong numbers. They have convinced themselves that they have the boys in the hills beaten, and they want no talk of a Truce to interfere with them now. But the Prime Minister may not listen to them. Who knows? I still have hopes of that Truce.'[20]

It was a battle for Lloyd George's ear in London between Cope and the military, who were convinced that the IRA was being beaten. Lloyd George was in a delicate position as the leader of a coalition government wherein

Truce 247

the majority partner was the Conservative and Unionist Party that was committed to protecting Ulster unionists, that did not yet accept a Dominion-type settlement and that did not wish to be seen appeasing Sinn Féin and the Volunteers/IRA. He seized on the military appraisal of Volunteer/IRA weakness and the widespread reaction against Collins' killing of British officers, intelligence and otherwise, on Bloody Sunday to reassure his coalition partners that he could be trusted to deal harshly with Irish republicans, breaking off Archbishop Clune's peace initiative.

Several events sustained Lloyd George's view. Following the killings, Roger Sweetman, TD for North Wexford, wrote a letter to the press criticising the Volunteers/IRA, condemning Bloody Sunday and calling for peace. On 3 December six members (not a quorum) of Galway County Council publicly appealed for peace,[21] and on 6 December Fr O'Flanagan, Acting President of Sinn Féin (Griffith had been arrested on 26 November and de Valera was still in the United States), sent a telegram to Lloyd George asking for peace terms. Lloyd George waved O'Flanagan's telegram and the Galway resolution in front of Clune, declaring, 'Dr Clune, this is the white feather, and we are going to make those fellows surrender!'[22] Michael Brennan in Clare noted that O'Flanagan's and Galway's 'foolish action gave the impression that we were being beaten and couldn't hold out much longer. Many well-meaning people in England and elsewhere joined in and by January an atmosphere of defeatism was becoming evident.'[23]

Collins was depressed by this turn of events, recognising that republican weakness – a popular desire for an end to killings indicating limited support for the Volunteers/IRA – had been made apparent by Galway County Council and Fr O'Flanagan. He confided in an IRB colleague, Seumas O'Meara:

> Collins now informed me that they had almost reached terms with the British Government through the intervention of Archbishop Clune, but that Galway Co. Council had, by their famous resolution also a few other centres spiked it for the time being. The British Government had assumed we were weakening in our fight and withdrew their offers. He appealed to us to keep up the pressure and the British Government would be forced to seek peace in a short time.[24]

He urged Volunteer/IRA commanders to increase their activity. He needed to demonstrate that the 'white feathers' of Sweetman, Fr O'Flanagan and

248   The Irish Republican Brotherhood, 1914–1924

Galway County Council did not speak for him or the Volunteers/IRA. Collins doubtless calculated that in negotiations he could use the Volunteers/IRA to press for maximum devolution with Lloyd George and, ultimately, that the IRB and Volunteers/IRA would accept what he agreed to. He was one of the two or three most important Irish players in any peace agreement – and he knew it.

But there was an awareness that Collins did not voice: he knew that Britain would not accept a republic. The terms he claimed he had almost reached with Clune must have recognised this, yet it seems he never explained this to his colleagues in government or in the Volunteers/IRA. He may have kept the IRB Executive informed: a year later he went to great lengths to do so during the Treaty negotiations. But there is no evidence either way. Nor was he pressed by colleagues as to what terms were discussed with Clune. Altogether, this suggests that there was an unspoken general understanding, at least in the nationalist leadership, by the autumn of 1920 that a republic was not on the cards.

Cope and Collins had stayed in contact with each other despite the December 1920 setback and six months later between them arranged a truce as a prelude to negotiations for peace. When the Truce came into effect between the IRA and the British military, RIC and DMP, it gave a new opportunity for the IRA and the IRB to recruit and organise without harassment. On GHQ Staff, in addition to its preponderance of IRB members, Gearóid O'Sullivan, Adjutant General, and Seán MacMahon, Quartermaster General, were members of the Supreme Council or became members of it in October.[25] However, lower down IRB organisation was threadbare – another consequence of IRA pre-eminence of which the Supreme Council had begun to take account in March, when it ordered a new IRB recruitment drive.[26]

To many, the fact that the IRA had been recognised by the British Army (IRA officers wore uniforms in public; liaison officers were appointed by both sides) meant that they had won a position from which an advantageous peace could be achieved. Liam Hogan, in the Dublin IRB and IRA, felt the Truce was a godsend:

> If the British government had known the position we were in there'd never have been a Truce! We were in a terrible bad way … At the time I knew perfectly well, and everybody else knew we'd never see [a republic]. That was impossible. I knew all through. The only thing I believed we could have got was either a firing squad or a hangman's rope. That was the only thing. There was nothing else. The Truce was a miracle.[27]

Truce

249

Hogan's view was the reality that many IRA and IRB men refused to accept. When he heard that there was to be a truce, Patrick Mulcahy was commanding a flying column in north Tipperary. He was Richard Mulcahy's brother but had served with the Royal Engineers in France during the War. He spoke as an experienced soldier:

> The Brigadier came up and said 'Paddy, there's to be no more shooting after 11 o'clock on Monday.'
> 'Why?' I said.
> He said, 'The war is over. There's a Truce. We've won!'
> I said, 'Who won what? Where? Because we've won fuck all!'[28]

To counteract euphoric feelings, GHQ Staff emphasised that fighting might break out again at any moment. Training camps were established in all IRA commands and the command structure itself was formalised. Divisions were created, and officers began to be appointed by GHQ and no longer elected by companies and brigades.[29]

Circle meetings began to be held regularly once more during the Truce as a result of the Supreme Council's March circular (sent again in April), and many new members were sworn in – usually those with Volunteer/IRA experience.[30] Efforts were also made to win back members who had left because they did not see the value of the IRB after 1916. In May 1921 James Malone had a particularly difficult encounter with Seán Ó Murthuile and Collins because of this:

> Michael said that Seán [Ó Murthuile] had a word to say to me, and he asked me to oblige him. I knew what Seán had to say … What he wanted was that I should go back into the Republican Brotherhood. When Dáil Éireann had been founded, and when the Volunteers had been recognised publicly as the Army of the Dáil, Cathal Brugha and many others thought that there was no place anymore for a secret army. I agreed with them and left the Brotherhood … I refused to do what Seán wanted, although I was loath to refuse Collins. Seán did his level best to entice me. When he failed he threatened me with this and that. He said that Cathal Brugha and myself and our likes should be executed as deserters and it looked like that it might yet be done. I got very angry … Collins came between us and told Seán to get out …

250   The Irish Republican Brotherhood, 1914–1924

'I am sorry to lose you, Séamus,' said he, 'if you change your mind you will be welcome, at any time, but I doubt if you will. I told Seán last night that it was useless trying you on. Would you mind taking a verbal message to Donagh and Michael Sheehan in Tipperary for me?'

'Not at all,' said I.

'Tell them to give an opportunity to any Volunteer officer, who isn't in the Brotherhood already, to take an oath if he wants to.'[31]

At the Dublin meeting of south Munster IRB Centres two months earlier, Collins had given a similar instruction. 'After that we put any man of importance in West Cork into the IRB,' said Liam Deasy.[32]

The personal involvement of Supreme Council members[33] in the 1921 recruitment drive suggests that the chain from the Divisions down to the Circles was broken, and that the authority of Council members was needed when trying to connect to lower levels of the IRB that had been generally ignored since 1919, hoping that when politics inevitably supplanted guerrilla activity a strong IRB could influence negotiations and the Dáil government.[34]

Having set about re-establishing an IRB identity,[35] the Council next concerned itself with the IRB's biennial elections. Circle Centre elections were to be completed by 15 June 1921, County Centres by 15 August, and Divisional Centres by 15 October. As a result of these elections, a new Council was formed by the time of the Treaty in December 1921. Changes within the Council because of arrests since 1919 had been effected without regard to constitutional niceties, but the 1921 elections now properly confirmed its membership.

The Council in its March circular was confident that a final ending of the fight was coming – not surprising in the light of the various peace feelers from both sides since spring 1920: the IRB objective was now the withdrawal of enemy forces from Ireland, leaving in the air the matter of establishing a republic.[36] Although by 1921 the IRB had accepted that the government of the Republic was the Dáil government, no effort was made to make this clear in the circular. Collins was aware from Cope and others that a republic was not on the cards and probably kept his Supreme Council colleagues informed. To other colleagues, however, he presented a determinedly republican front while denying that the Truce was a first step to compromise about the Republic. Seán MacBride, a captain on Gearóid O'Sullivan's staff, had been involved in smuggling weapons:

Truce   251

I saw Collins, and for the first time I was angry. I said the Truce was a terrible mistake. I had thought de Valera responsible. 'Oh, ho,' said Collins, laughing, 'we can use it to reorganise and get more arms in; I want you to start working on that immediately.' … He told me that there was no *necessity* [*sic*] for the Truce, but that de Valera and the others were keen on it. He may have meant Mulcahy, whom at the time he did not like. I still felt that it was a mistake. I must say that Collins did not argue against that except to say that it would be a help in reorganisation and putting ourselves on a sounder footing.[37]

Dissembling, one cannot help feeling, was one of Collins' many attributes. To others, he had bemoaned the failure of Archbishop Clune's December 1920 peace efforts,[38] and had warned at the time of the Truce that the IRA's arms and ammunition were sufficient for only a few weeks of continued fighting.[39] Statements to this effect served to support compromise with Britain about a republic. Later opinions about IRA weaponry differed according to sides taken over the Treaty. Pro-Treaty IRA men said that there was a critical shortage of weapons and ammunition; anti-Treaty men said that while more supply was always welcome, the IRA had enough to continue fighting.[40]

Seán McGarry went to England to organise the IRA and the IRB there in late 1920 or early 1921 and was already warning that the IRA might not be able to continue fighting, telling John McGallogly in Manchester that 'they were nearly at the end of their resources in Ireland and might be compelled to abandon the struggle until the next generation'.[41] In the Glasgow/Motherwell area in Scotland where there were an estimated 600 IRB members, the IRA battalion (we can assume formed principally by IRB members) offered to come to Ireland to join the fighting. Collins said 'No', as James Byrne, an IRB member since 1905 and quartermaster of the Second Scottish Brigade responsible for munitions procurement, recounted. His opinion was perhaps more dispassionate than those of his colleagues in Ireland. Collins, he said, held that 'we could do better work by remaining in Scotland and get going on supplies; that ammunition was very short in Ireland and that it was a matter of urgency to get across all we could of it'. James Cunningham was clear that the IRB's 'main object was to get arms and send them home. To do so we had to contribute money ourselves, make money collections among our friends and run dances, lotteries, etc. to raise funds'.[42]

While the IRB internal elections proceeded during the summer and

252 The Irish Republican Brotherhood, 1914–1924

autumn of 1921, the Supreme Council commissioned a survey of the organisation.[43] Circles in every County were visited during July and August 1921 and the number of Circles, their geographical situation, their officers and their membership were listed. Most Circles had met last in September and October 1920. Seán Murphy conducted the survey of Westmeath, Longford and Louth in the Leinster Division.[44] Murphy was Centre of the Thomas Clark Luby Circle in Dublin from 1903 to 1922.[45] In Westmeath he reported that there were 106 members of the IRB with thirty more in prison. The two IRA brigades in Westmeath were commanded by the Centre and the sub-Centre of the County. In Longford, Murphy swore in two new members – both IRA battalion commandants. Longford had 102 members, sixteen of whom were in jail. Demonstrating the merging of the IRA and IRB since 1919, the Longford IRB County Board held a court of enquiry into a member's IRA performance and reported back to the Leinster Board.[46] George Irvine visited Louth where there were sixty-six members, of whom sixteen were in jail. The County Centre, who was also the IRA battalion O/C, was concerned that the Cooley Centre, who was captain of the Cooley IRA company, was unsuitable because he was a 'constitutionalist' and questioned military orders instead of simply obeying them. On 3 September 1921 Seán Boylan, the Westmeath County Centre (and brigade O/C) and Diarmuid O'Hegarty reported on Kildare where a complete reorganisation had been necessary. There were forty-nine members in the County arranged in seven Circles. A County Board had been elected, but O'Hegarty pointed out that as all the Circles had only just been formed, the members were 'very green' and would require constant attention for a considerable time. The southern part of the county was included with the IRA Carlow Brigade, and so northern County Kildare IRB members found themselves ignorant of membership and activity in the whole county: another example of the way the IRB had been subsumed into the IRA. O'Hegarty recommended that the Supreme Council ask the (south) Leinster No. 2 Divisional Centre to investigate, 'since he would be in touch with this area from the Volunteer angle'. The survey of Wicklow reported that the county was 'hopeless'.[47]

By 27 August 1921 the Leinster No. 1 Division had been reorganised. Its Board met at the end of September to elect a representative to the Supreme Council as instructed in the March circular. Two of the topics for discussion when they met were 'co-ordination of Division with I[rish] V[olunteer] Divisions' and the alteration of the IRB constitution. The Council met again on 21 October when the Divisional survey was presented.[48] The four Divisional County Centres were automatically members of the Divisional Board.[49] There were 89 Circles with 1,646 members in the Division. About half the members (911) and 25 of the Circles were in Dublin city and north Co. Dublin, apparently monitored by Diarmuid O'Hegarty. By October 1921 the Dublin membership had fallen to about 817, mostly as a result of transfers of Dublin members to country Circles. For example, on 3 November 1921 Ernie O'Malley, O/C Second Southern Division, was transferred from the Dublin Mitchell Circle to the Donohill Circle in Tipperary.[50] Expulsions also played a part. On 6 October 1921 Jack Reilly, a silkweaver of 30 Cork Street, Dublin, was expelled as unfit to be a member, and William McGinley, a tailor of FitzGibbon Street, was expelled for not attending IRA meetings. On 6 April 1922, at the last meetings of Dublin Circles recorded by O'Hegarty, the Dublin City IRB membership stood at 747.

Surveys were conducted in the other Divisions with new members, generally IRA officers, being sworn in. They also showed that many Circles had last met in September 1920, and had then lapsed until the Truce. Connacht was late: its survey was not delivered until 21 January 1922.

The Supreme Council also launched a major investigation in Cork. Donal O'Callaghan, Terence MacSwiney's successor as lord mayor of Cork, and IRB sub-County Centre, was accused of negligence and desertion and was tried on 11 December 1921 by an IRB 'court' appointed by the IRB Supreme Council and chaired by Martin Conlon.[51]

The events leading to the charge against O'Callaghan show the extent to which, in Cork at least, IRB members had permeated the entire national movement without necessarily controlling it. Instead they often devoted themselves to the organisations that they had joined. In January 1921, the County Board members were Liam Lynch County Centre, Donal O'Callaghan sub-Centre, Seán O'Hegarty Treasurer, and Michael Lynch Secretary. In the 1921 Divisional elections that spring, Liam Lynch was confirmed as Tom Hales' replacement on the Supreme Council.

O'Callaghan was also Cork City Centre, but under his leadership the seven city Circles met infrequently and irregularly. In order to impose some order and to find a replacement for Hales, a meeting of Centres in Cork City Hall on 12 August 1920 at 7.30 p.m. was arranged. Liam Deasy, Adjutant of the Third Cork Brigade, notified the Clonakilty and Bantry Centres of this meeting, and did so in a purely IRA capacity (again demonstrating the IRB's

254 The Irish Republican Brotherhood, 1914–1924

merging with the IRA), although those concerned knew that the meeting was an IRB affair:

> H.Q. 3rd Cork Brigade.
> 6 August 1920.
> TO: O.C. 2nd Battn.
> You are to attend at City Hall, Cork, on Thursday 12th August at 7 p.m.
> Brig. Adj.[52]

Five days later Deasy discovered that this message had been intercepted. He informed the Centres in his area and went to Cork to warn his city colleagues. He first sought Seán O'Hegarty but he was out to lunch, so he next went to see O'Callaghan, who was chairing a county council meeting and refused to see Deasy until 4.15 p.m. when the meeting ended. But by 7 p.m. O'Callaghan had not warned the City Centres. City Hall was surrounded by British military and Terence MacSwiney, then Lord Mayor and O/C First Cork Brigade, was arrested, having gone there for the IRB meeting.[53]

MacSwiney died on hunger strike in Brixton prison on 25 October. In November, O'Callaghan was elected to succeed him. He then left for the United States without informing his colleagues. Seán O'Hegarty discovered his absence quite casually. O'Callaghan was considered to have some responsibility for MacSwiney's arrest. Charges against him were framed by the South Munster Divisional Board and forwarded to the Supreme Council. An enquiry was ordered and Seán Ó Murthuile made the arrangements. O'Callaghan was notified of the charges against him. He acknowledged them on 17 October 1921 saying that he would defend himself and accept the findings of the court. On 22 November Ó Murthuile wrote to O'Callaghan:

> The following officers of the organisation have been selected by the S.C. to conduct the enquiry and you have the option of objecting to any two of them excluding No. 1 who is selected to act as chairman:

> 1. Martin Conlon   Dublin
> 2. Frank Crummy   Belfast
> 3. Éamonn Price   Dublin
> 4. P. Whelan   Dungarvan
> 5. Humphrey Murphy   Kerry[54]

The result is not recorded but was probably a decision to expel O'Callaghan.

Another enquiry was conducted into the financial irregularities of one Michael O'Flanagan in 1919 and 1920 when he was in charge of Dublin IRB finances that showed a deficit of £975–16–5 (£975.83).

Carelessness and irresponsibility were judged the cause. But, again, no record of judgement survives.

The 1921 IRB reaffirmation of its separateness from all other nationalist organisations was given force by these enquiries, and by its internal elections, together resulting in revived lines of acknowledged authority.

CHAPTER 24

Talking

A sovereign, independent Republic was our claim and our fighting ground, and I think we will all admit that men who decided to fight would be fools to fight for less than the fullness of their rights. But the fact that we were willing to negotiate implied that we had something to give away.[1]

Kevin O'Higgins, 19 December 1921

In July 1921, immediately after the Truce came into effect, de Valera thrashed out the basis for peace negotiations directly with Lloyd George in London. 'He came to see me in Downing Street,' recalled Lloyd George to his private secretary, Albert Sylvester.

'We sat and talked for three hours. It was all history and in those three hours we only got as far as Cromwell. de Valera [*sic*] is like riding on a hobby-horse at a fair,' he said. 'You gallop round and round at terrific speed but you never catch up with the other fellow in front of you.' ... That de Valera was a thoroughly sincere man, but quite impossible, was the general summing-up of his character by L.G.[2]

Tom Jones, a Cabinet Secretary and an intimate adviser to Lloyd George, provided an account of British understanding of de Valera and the Irish position:

The PM's account is that De V. is not a big man but he is a sincere man, a white man, and 'an agreeable personality'. He has a limited vocabulary, talks chiefly of ideals, and constantly recurs to the same

Talking 257

few dominating notions. He agreed to drop 'the Republic', the PM telling him there was no Irish or Welsh word for it, and therefore it was alien to the spirit of the Celt! He was willing to be within the Empire, to recognise the King, to go without a Navy. What he chiefly seemed to want was Irish unity – that we should not impose partition, that there should be an All-Ireland Parliament with real financial and other powers, while leaving to Ulster the autonomy she now enjoys so long as she wishes to retain it.[3]

Word of this obviously came back to Ireland, spurring worry. Tom O'Connor for example, sworn into the IRB in Kerry in September 1921, understood that 'Things were going wrong in England.'[4] Lloyd George secured his Cabinet's approval of formal proposals to Sinn Féin.[5] Tom Jones described the uncertainty that followed:

De V., while not accepting our proposals, agreed to make counter-proposals after consulting his colleagues. I think this means he is not unfavourable to the proposals in substance but must try and bring his left wing along with him. Michael Collins is all right but some of the gunmen will be irreconcilable. Meanwhile the Hierarchy, the Press, and all moderate opinion in Ireland is yearning for peace, and when De V. reaches Dublin he will come under this influence, it is hoped … Briefly [our proposals give] 'Dominion Status' with all sorts of important powers, but no Navy, no hostile tariffs, and no coercion of Ulster.[6]

Jones' understanding of Collins' position most probably came from Alfred Cope,[7] and possibly also from de Valera. Certainly, it reflected what Collins was saying privately.

Conflict about the terms of negotiation was first heralded in the IRA Executive. In August 1921, at an Executive meeting, Collins and Brugha had their stand-up row with Brugha insisting that Collins had mishandled arms purchase funds. It was also when Brugha first insisted on overruling Mulcahy's appointment of Eoin O'Duffy as Deputy Chief of Staff in favour of Austin Stack. On 26 August, quite possibly mindful of Brugha's suspicions of IRB and Collins' influence in the IRA, upon specific instructions from the Supreme Council (which meant Collins), Seán MacEoin in the Dáil proposed de Valera's

258 The Irish Republican Brotherhood, 1914–1924

election as President of the Republic: 'Then in August '21 the Supreme Council directed that the Presidency should be transferred from the Supreme Council to the elected Parliament and I was directed to propose Mr de Valera as President at the Dáil after he came back from London.'[8] It can be seen as an emollient gesture to calm fears about Collins and the IRB.

Years later – in 1961 – de Valera accosted MacEoin at the re-interment of John Moore, president of Wolfe Tone's 1798 Republic. MacEoin had been interviewed on television and had insisted that the president of the IRB was the president of the Republic until the IRB withdrew its claim and tasked him with nominating de Valera as president in the Dáil:

> He said, 'You know well that there was no President of the Republic until you proposed me in August of 1921.'
>
> 'Oh,' I said, 'was there not? Don't tell me that Old John Moore that you're after bringing back from Waterford to the West to re-bury him, don't tell me he wasn't President of the Republic. Don't tell me it was Humbert and his merry men that when they landed at Killala that appointed him to be President.'
>
> 'Oh, but you see,' he said, 'they weren't recognised.'
>
> 'Oh, no,' and I said that Tom Clarke was actually President of the Republic in 1916 … 'They got the same recognition and even more than you got even when I proposed you in '21 because Clarke had at least the German government in 1916 as a foreign ally and got recognition by a great country, and Moore got the French recognition of his government in 1798.' And I said, 'Before that, the Confederation of Kilkenny, King James got recognition as head or the monarch at that time.'
>
> The corpse came out after that and it ended.[9]

In America de Valera had caused the split with Devoy and Cohalan when he advocated a 'Cuban' relationship with Britain. Accepting his nomination as President of the Republic, he showed that he had learnt from that conflict and that he now firmly rejected such a compromise, adopting a hard-line republican position as he habitually did when faced with allegations of being soft on the question of a republic.[10]

While de Valera became more republican, Collins became less.[11] He knew that a failure to come to an agreement really would result in a massive increase in British 'sheer militarism' that the IRA could not withstand.

Talking

259

In the summer of 1921, Collins travelled around Ireland meeting IRB and IRA groups to encourage recruiting and training, and to talk about the reasons for and the possible outcome of the Truce. He was, no doubt, preparing for compromise while building as influential and as numerous an IRB as he could.

Loyalty to the Republic, not Irish unity, was at the heart of disagreements over a settlement with Britain. Lloyd George had stated explicitly to de Valera that insistence on a republic as a precondition for negotiations was to give 'a recognition which no British Government can accord. On this point they must guard themselves against any possible doubt.'[12] De Valera and the Dáil had quietly accepted this, and Treaty negotiations then began. Inevitably, word of compromise during the negotiations reached Ireland. Patrick McDonnell, a Clare IRA and IRB man, sought out Ernest Blythe, Minister for Trade and Commerce in the Dáil government, who was well known in Clare for his IRB activity before the Rising:

> I tried to find out Blythe for I felt certain he would know what was going on in Dublin ... 'How are these gentlemen going on?' I asked, referring to the London negotiations. 'I think Paddy it will be alright,' he said; 'if we get half this way, and then afterwards we can get the other half.' This he told me before the Treaty was signed, and then I knew that the whole thing was bungled.[13]

Later, Collins – as did Kevin O'Higgins – accurately noted why 'things were going wrong', pointing out: 'If we all stood on the recognition of the Irish Republic as a prelude to any conference we could have very easily have said so, and there would have been no conference ... It was the acceptance of the invitation that formed the compromise.'[14]

Collins did not want to be a member of the negotiating team that de Valera was arranging, but the Dáil insisted that he should go, as Ernest Blythe remembered:

> De Valera argued, however, that in order to get the best results it was essential that Collins should go. He intimated that as Collins was looked upon by the British as the leader of the fighting men, no delegation of which he was not a member would get the highest possible British offer, that if he were absent the British would feel that they had still to deal with him and still to conciliate him, said that they would hold back something

260 The Irish Republican Brotherhood, 1914–1924

from the other plenipotentiaries. This line of argument convinced the Dáil, and practically all present intimated either by speech or by applause that they wanted Collins to go. In the last resort he consented.[15]

In early October, as Collins prepared to go to London as a plenipotentiary to start negotiations with Lloyd George, he met Liam Lynch and other Munster IRB leaders in Cork and warned that obtaining a republic would probably be impossible.[16] 'You'd better not tell them about that when you go inside,' said Lynch, as they went to another, bigger IRB meeting.[17] 'When we came away from the IRB meeting in Cork,' said John Joe Rice, 'we had the idea that the Treaty, or something equivalent to it, was definitely accepted by these people, Collins, Ó Murthuile, etc.'[18]

Albert Sylvester was impressed by Collins at the very start of the Treaty negotiations:

And the first meeting with the Prime Minister and with them took place at No. 10 on October 11th at 11 o'clock. I was most interested to see, in the flesh, these representatives about whom I knew so much personally and officially, but had never seen. So I watched them enter No. 10, walk up the corridor to the hall, and to the door of the Cabinet Room. There L.G. stood to welcome them. The first was Arthur Griffiths [sic]. He was a very quiet man … The next one was Michael Collins. He shook hands with the Prime Minister, and his quick eye saw a row of old guns on the wall. Like a flash out of a gun, he went there, took off one of these old guns, the sort of type that would be operated by powder shot and wad, and he fooled about with this like a little schoolboy, but with the expertise of a gentleman who knew how to handle a gun. I was immensely impressed with him because it gave to me a knowledge of the man's whole temperament – gallant, brave, vivacious. I had a great opinion of Michael Collins – he was a very brave man, very brave man, and his exploits – they're fantastic. No wonder he was head of the Intelligence Service – the Director of the Intelligence Service – oh my goodness. So it was marvellous.[19]

Sylvester may not have grasped what he witnessed, but Lloyd George assuredly did: Collins had seized the first opportunity to assert equality with and indifference to Lloyd George and British power.

Talking

261

Collins depended upon his domination of the Supreme Council and of the Brotherhood generally to secure their acceptance of whatever position he took. Through the IRB in the IRA, and his personal status in the IRA, he expected the IRA to follow. 'What was good enough for me should be good enough for you,' he actually said about the Treaty to a group of IRA men in December 1921.[20] His commitment to the Brotherhood defined him as a hard-line republican to Lloyd George and to his political colleagues in Sinn Féin and the Dáil. This made him the man they had to court. Collins' agreement to a settlement was seen as essential for success. Identifying with and supporting the hard men of the IRA was a political tactic that both de Valera and Collins employed. They thought that by doing so they would have the support of the IRA for their political arrangements, and that the IRA would follow their leads.

While no Treaty would deliver a republic, it would be a first long step to one and Collins sought to project that he was the person most likely to achieve a republic down the line. He thought this would carry the IRB and IRA with him. He underestimated the sincerity and the simplicity of those who swore loyalty to the Republic, and he overestimated his IRB and IRA influence. The IRB recruitment drive within the IRA during the summer and autumn of 1921 strengthened support for a republic in the IRB and IRA and not, as it turned out, support for Collins. Since 1917 he had concentrated on dominating the Supreme Council and winning IRB majorities on the IRA Executive, GHQ Staff and influencing the Sinn Féin Executive, taking for granted that junior echelons would thus be marshalled behind whatever orders and policies emanated from their governing bodies. IRA pre-eminence seems to have been formally established at some point during the Truce when, as James Hogan, Intelligence Officer, First Western Division, noted, 'It was decided that an IRA order over-ruled an IRB order. When the IRB ceased to be in a position to act, it was ceasing to exist, and I would say that on the eve of the Truce the IRB was semi-moribund beneath, and alive only on top or in its upper levels.'[21]

Thomas Malone, Vice-O/C East Limerick Brigade, although a member of the IRB saw the IRB's recruitment drive during the Truce as an effort to gain votes: 'One thing that happened after the Truce was that the IRB started organising. They were all over the place ... so that ... the IRB would have a majority if it ever came to a question of the Treaty's acceptance or rejection.'[22]

The proposed formation of a new army demonstrated the jockeying for political power in Dublin. The Cabinet must have been aware of IRB

262 The Irish Republican Brotherhood, 1914–1924

reorganisation and recruiting during the Truce, and the proposal to create a new army was undoubtedly a move to counteract that. It was presented as a means of clarifying the relationship between the Dáil and the IRA.[23] In fact that relationship was clear: the IRA was loyal to the Dáil government as the government of the Republic. A new army under Dáil authority alone might not be so trammelled. The Dáil Cabinet must also have been aware that a republic would not be agreed by Britain and creating a new army loyal simply to the Dáil and not specifically to the Republic could be seen as a move to head off conflict.

From mid-November 1921 onwards, Collins knew he faced increasing domestic political difficulties.[24] 'Whilst the Treaty was being discussed,' said Emmet Dalton, the IRA chief liaison officer:

> We were being stabbed in the back by Brugha, Stack and Mr de Valera [who did this by] promoting the idea that there was no possible outcome of the Treaty other than a continuation of the war and their tendency was to promote a feeling of antipathy to the people who were the plenipotentiaries. Whatever efforts were being made towards a solution these particular people were satisfied with only one solution: that was to continue the war with Britain. Not de Valera because he was trying to sit on both sides of the hedge as always.[25]

The proposal of a new army, let alone the fuelling of divisions this generated when the prospect of a return to fighting was very real, emphasised the predominance of politics in the minds of de Valera and Brugha. It also suggests that de Valera, at least, was determined to reduce Collins and the IRB in order himself to control Sinn Féin and the IRA. It could not have been by chance that the effort to create a new army in November 1921 took place while Collins was fully engaged in London.

IRB elections had been held that summer and autumn, forming a new Supreme Council and Executive with Collins continuing as IRB President.[26] He kept the Council Executive abreast of the Treaty negotiations, at times asking for suggestions.[27] He was securing his base, flattering the Supreme Council while simultaneously engaging it in the slide away from the Republic that was the essence of the Treaty negotiation. He returned to Dublin more frequently for discussions with the Dáil Cabinet, and in particular with two of his IRB Executive colleagues, Seán Ó Murthuile, the secretary, and Eoin

Talking 263

O'Duffy, the treasurer.[28] On one of his visits back to Dublin, Seán MacBride met him:

> I felt that there was compromise. I felt that from one small incident particularly fairly early on. Collins came back one day describing how Lloyd George was a marvellous actor. He described in detail how clever Lloyd George was and what a good actor he was and how he had put his arms around him and said, 'Come on Michael, look at this map of the world with the British Empire printed in red on it. So why don't you come in and help us run this Empire? After all, much of this Empire consists of Irish people who can help us to run it.' And Collins gave this as an instance of Lloyd George's persuasive powers of acting, and that he wasn't taken in by it at all. But I knew that it had had an effect on him. I sensed – you sometimes have a sense that something has made an impact or made a lodgement – and I felt that this had made a lodgement.[29]

On 3 December 1921 Collins was unable to join a Supreme Council meeting that had been called at his request to discuss the outstanding issues facing the Irish delegation in London: the Holyhead to Dublin passenger boat had been in a collision that morning and so arrived late.[30] Collins had given the Council an outline of the progress of the negotiations in London and the text of the oath that had been presented by Lloyd George to the plenipotentiaries that read: 'I, A.B., solemnly swear to bear true faith and allegiance to the constitution of the Irish Free State; to the community of nations known as the British Empire; and to the King as Head of State and of the Empire.'[31]

The Council decided that there were three principal obstacles remaining: first, the oath of allegiance to the king; secondly, British control of Ireland's naval defences; and thirdly, partition: allowing the Northern Irish government to opt out of a united Ireland. The Council suggested a substitute oath of allegiance to 'Saor Stat Eireann' referring to the king in a secondary paragraph only, and rejected partition and British control of naval defences.

The Dáil Cabinet also rejected the oath and proposed an alternative: 'I do swear to bear true faith and allegiance to the constitution of Ireland and to the Treaty of association of Ireland with the British Commonwealth of nations, and to recognise the King of Great Britain as Head of the Associated States.' This was judged by the Supreme Council as compatible with its own position.

Ó Murthuile met Collins at Dún Laoghaire[32] harbour on the evening of 3 December as Collins returned to London. He informed him of the Supreme Council's endorsement of the Dáil Cabinet's proposed oath and their rejection of partition and British control of coastal defences.

The oath that was included in the Treaty read:

'I, A.B., do solemnly swear true faith and allegiance to the constitution of the Irish Free State as by law established and that I will be faithful to H.M. King George V, his heirs and successors by law, in virtue of the common citizenship of Ireland with Great Britain and her adherence to and membership of the group of nations forming the British Commonwealth of nations.'

It was considered that the new oath reflected the Dáil's and Supreme Council's concerns by not naming the king as head of state.

The 'Articles of Agreement for a Treaty' were signed in London on 6 December. Partition and British control of several naval facilities were incorporated in the Treaty. Albert Sylvester recorded Lloyd George's account of the night when the Treaty was signed:

L.G. often talked about the Irish Treaty and those fellows knew that if they signed the Treaty, they were signing their death warrant. He recalled what happened on the night of the Treaty. Oh I remember it so very well. It was very late in the evening. They had been expecting to be received somewhere early on, but it was now approaching midnight. And the first delegate to enter the Cabinet room was Arthur Griffiths [*sic*]. And L.G. said to him 'Well Mr. Griffiths, what have you to say?' And he said, 'I will sign'. And L.G. said to him, 'Does that mean that you are signing for yourself and your delegation?' And he said 'No, I'm signing for myself'. Then he turned to Michael Collins and he said to Michael Collins, 'Now it's your turn. What have you to say?' And he said 'If I go back and say that I've signed this Treaty, they will call me a coward.' 'Well' said L.G., 'Are you willing to take the responsibility? It is a very serious business. We put thousands of men against the German army. We do not want to do that in Ireland, and it would be a terrible thing. What have you to say?' And he said, putting his head in his hands, he said, 'I will sign'.[33]

Collins claimed that Lloyd George's 'threat of "immediate and terrible war" did not matter overmuch to me'.[34] But Lloyd George was prepared and was readying to flood Ireland with troops if the Treaty was rejected: he was not bluffing.[35]

The Treaty was signed without referring to the Supreme Council, de Valera or the Dáil Cabinet beforehand. A great deal was made of this and has been made of it ever since. De Valera had issued 'Instructions to Plenipotentiaries from Cabinet' in October stating that 'it is also understood that the complete text of the draft treaty' would be submitted to the Dáil Cabinet for approval before being signed.[36] It seems that the instructions may have been given to Griffith, who kept the understanding to himself: none of his colleagues referred to it then or subsequently. As plenipotentiaries, whatever the instructions, they were invested with the full power of independent action on behalf of the Dáil government.

From the outset, they had been left in no doubt that a republic would not be granted by Britain. It was politically impossible for a British government to accept that a constituent nation of the United Kingdom would become a republic overnight. No British government could hope for parliamentary or public approval of such a step. Refusing to accept this reality was placing ideology above all else. The best hope that republicans had was that the United States would take their side, but that was unlikely. Despite the efforts of Patrick McCartan, Joseph McGarrity, John Devoy, Judge Cohalan, Harry Boland, de Valera and their associated Irish-American organisations, President Wilson and then President Harding had made it clear that the United States would not cut across Britain on Ireland. The 1916 Republic that the Dáil represented was written in blood on water.

The Treaty gave Ireland practically everything except unity (but agreed that was to be negotiated) and a republic. The plenipotentiaries considered that it was the best they could achieve, even if they did not like it.[37] They argued that they had simply recommended the agreement to the Dáil and it was up to the Dáil to accept or to reject it. Collins seems to have been satisfied that the Treaty gave Ireland freedom, that a united Ireland was going to come, and that any need to fight had passed. 'The day after the signing of the Treaty,' related Liam McMahon, Centre of the Manchester Circle, 'I happened to be in Michael Collins' room in Hans Place, London ... I asked Michael Collins if we could keep the Republican movement intact in Britain, and his answer was: "No, it would be a hindrance".'[38] The republican movement in Britain was the IRB.

266 The Irish Republican Brotherhood, 1914–1924

McMahon took the anti-Treaty side and may have thought, in telling of this encounter with Collins, that it showed that Collins had sold out to British interests. But it also showed the opposite, that Collins believed that a boundary commission would produce an economically unviable Northern Ireland and so would work to produce Irish unity,[39] and that he recognised the point that Dominion status really was practical independence and a step to complete independence. Continued IRA/IRB action in Britain *would* be a hindrance.

On 8 December the Irish delegation returned to Dublin and went straight to a Cabinet meeting to discuss the Treaty. De Valera had been in Limerick where he had been taken aback by the news that a treaty had been signed. He felt betrayed. He had not been consulted. The Cabinet had not been consulted. Arthur Griffith had broken a promise that he would consult de Valera before signing anything. The plenipotentiaries had been bluffed. But de Valera's arguments did not succeed. By four votes to three the Cabinet backed the Treaty.[40] Collins held a meeting at the Gresham Hotel that evening or the next day with Richard Mulcahy and several other IRA leaders and said that he believed the proposed boundary commission would deal with partition and that he really did see the Treaty as a satisfactory settlement.[41]

On 10 December de Valera met GHQ Staff to establish what their attitude would be if the Dáil rejected the Treaty. Mulcahy answered first saying that the IRA would continue as the army of the Republic although he, personally, would probably make himself unacceptable as Chief of Staff to anti-Treaty IRA leaders: he was signalling that he would support Collins and the Treaty but that the IRA might not. His was an informed and realistic position. Collins next answered that if the Treaty were rejected and hostilities resumed, he would serve as an ordinary soldier with no other responsibilities. The rest of the Staff, however, agreed that they would continue in their posts. De Valera once again declared he would not stand for mutiny, thus showing his constant worry that the IRA might follow Collins and not him.[42] Doubtless, he hoped that his re-asserted republican credentials would gain the IRA's support, countering Collins' expectations.

Petie Joe McDonnell, O/C West Connemara Brigade and Deputy O/C of the Second Western Division, together with two other senior officers met Collins in Dublin shortly after 6 December:

> [H]e told me why we should accept the Treaty for we were out of ammunition and the only choice we had was to accept the Treaty for six

Talking

months, get in arms, and then we could tell the British to go to blazes. We couldn't carry on the fight for we had no hope of carrying it on successfully ... We told Collins that we didn't agree with what he said, and he didn't say much.[43]

In Cork, Liam Deasy understood that 'England had won the war',[44] and Tom Barry, an IRB Centre, despite maintaining that the IRA was stronger in 1921 than before, confirmed that they were losing:

> Here we were, coming to a darker night of a brighter summer, far more favourable to the enemy's huge round-ups; with the British Prime Minister publicly threatening to send in, if necessary, a quarter of a million troops and Black and Tans; with the British army staffs planning the 'blockhouse system' of cutting off area by area, with massive internment – and our chronic shortage of ammunition.[45]

In Ulster, Denis McCullough was sought out as a wise elder by the Third Northern Division (Belfast) leaders:

> Joe McKelvey, who had been attached to the staff of the Director of Organisation GHQ early in 1921 and who had some knowledge of the IRA strength etc., in other Divisional areas, gave it as his firm opinion that 'we could not stand up against open and unrestricted war for even two months though he thought that the 3rd Northern was one of the best armed Divisions in Ireland'. Séamus Woods pointed out ... from what he had seen in other Divisional areas that six months of Truce had seriously impaired the morale of the IRA and he feared that a return to war conditions would find the men much below pre-Truce standard.[46]

Séamus Woods confirmed McCullough's account.[47]

Within six months, surprisingly, given his view in December 1921, Joe McKelvey was commanding the anti-Treaty Republicans in Dublin's Four Courts. Conversely, some of Collins' closest confederates – notably Liam Tobin and Frank Thornton in his intelligence group, and J.J. O'Connell and Seán MacMahon on the GHQ Staff – were initially against or sceptical of the Treaty. 'When the Treaty was signed before the Civil War ever came along, Tobin and Thornton were against the Treaty,' Richard Mulcahy remembered. 'They held a meeting at the Gresham Hotel and Ginger O'Connell and Seán MacMahon and quite a number of others were there.'[48]

They may not have changed their minds, but they followed Collins. The 'fighting men' did not. On 10 December the First Southern Division followed Liam Lynch and declared itself against the Treaty.[49] On 12 December the Cork City Circles followed suit, calling for 'the rejection of the Treaty proposals being submitted to An Dail Eireann as being utterly at variance with the principles of the I.R.B., and treason to the Republic established in 1916'.[50] Theirs was a succinct summary of Republican thinking.

CHAPTER 25

Three Days in December

Our lust to kill had not been satisfied.[1]

Frank Aiken, Memoir

Liam Lynch as O/C First Southern Division (created in April 1921) became a key player in the run-up to the Civil War. The First Southern, largely based in Co. Cork, was one of the most active, largest (about 25 per cent of the total IRA strength) and best armed of the new Divisions, so Lynch carried more weight than most other IRA officers.[2] He regarded himself and the IRA as fighters for an established republic and was not willing to compromise on this.

Lynch was born in 1892 in Anglesboro, Limerick, near the border with Cork, the fifth of eight children – six boys and two girls. Two brothers, James and Jeremiah, died young. Another, Tom, became a priest, serving in New South Wales. A fourth, Martin, became a Christian Brother (a Catholic teaching order), and the fifth, John, took over the family farm. His sisters married locally. He did not join the Irish Volunteers or take part in Rising efforts. Instead in 1917 he joined the AOH, an avowedly Catholic fraternal organisation that was opposed to the secularism of the IRB and acted as the IPP's enforcers. He also joined the Gaelic League which drew him to the reorganised Volunteers in Fermoy where he was elected first lieutenant of the local company. The following year, because of the conscription threat, he became a full-time Volunteer and joined the IRB. In January 1919 he was elected O/C Second Cork Brigade, and from then on he advanced up the ranks of both the IRB and Volunteers/IRA as colleagues were arrested and imprisoned.

On 10 December 1921 the Supreme Council met to discuss the Treaty.[3] Only ten members were present.[4] Nine thought that it had been redrafted to

270 The Irish Republican Brotherhood, 1914–1924

Ireland's advantage, particularly noting that the oath had been changed as they had suggested and did not explicitly require allegiance to the king. However, there was no change in the clauses relating to the partition of Ireland and Ireland's naval defences that the Council had objected to. Strong opposition to the Treaty came from Liam Lynch. Writing to Florrie O'Donoghue he said:

> The situation is that I stood alone at the <u>meeting</u> [the Supreme Council meeting] I attended, and our Division seemingly stands alone in the army. GHQ staff and several others who have done actual army work are for the Treaty ... The position I have taken up I mean to stand by, even if the whole Division turn it down. On the other hand I do not recommend immediate war as our front is broken – which our leaders are responsible for.[5]

By a majority vote that should have been binding on all members, the Council had decided in favour of the Treaty but, no doubt anxious to give Lynch room to change his stance, decided that the IRB would not take action for or against it.[6] The deeper point was that the Council did not fully support Collins. On 12 December Ó Murthuile circulated two reports stemming from the Council meeting. One was to members of the IRB who were also TDs: 'The Supreme Council, having due regard to the Constitution of the Organisation, has decided that the present Peace Treaty between Ireland and Great Britain should be ratified. Members of the Organisation, however, who have to take public action as representatives are given freedom of action in the matter.'[7]

This was misleading: the Council had not decided that the Treaty should be ratified but had in fact remained undecided. It veered away from direct interference in the Dáil. It was a critical failure of leadership. Because of this statement, many IRB members were told by their Centres that the Treaty should be accepted. Paddy Mullaney in Kildare stated that he was instructed to ask any TDs he knew to support the Treaty: 'Every County Centre got instructions from the Supreme Council of the IRB that if there was any member of the Dáil that you had any influence with in your county that you were to ask them to vote for the Treaty.'[8]

Seán O'Keefe, an IRB and IRA commandant and county councillor in Clare, had a similar story. He had seconded a resolution by the county council supporting the Treaty. He did so, he wrote to de Valera on 22 December 1921, because the Divisional O/C (Michael Brennan) had told him that the Supreme

Three Days in December

Council and GHQ had ordered support for the Treaty, but 'It is contrary to my principle. I am a Republican.'[9] Tom Maguire remembered how when TDs arrived in Dublin for the Treaty debate, they were pressured by IRB men at railway stations to vote for the settlement.[10]

Ernie O'Malley attended an IRB meeting in Limerick in 1922 when members were ordered to support the Treaty.[11] Tom Maguire was told that the Council approved of the Treaty:

> I resented the fact that a man came along to me as an elected member of the Dáil – Thornton – to suggest to me though not to order that I should support him. It was supposed to get me thinking ... The Supreme Council honestly never decided and it was the Executive which met more frequently split 2:2 on the issue in December 1921 – January 1922 with Collins in the chair both times. He refused to cast a deciding vote arguing that if they were so divided that the thing to do was to aim to preserve the organisation. But people like Thornton and Conlon did go around implying strongly that the Supreme Council had decided in favour of the Treaty.[12]

Maguire and most IRB members rested on their oaths, and this pushed them to oppose the Treaty. For Collins, however, the Council's delaying statement dictated the objectives that he from now on strove to achieve: IRB and IRA unity; as republican a constitution as possible, and no civil war.

A second – accurate – report, 'The Organisation and the New Political Situation in Ireland', was sent to all IRB Centres. It appealed for patience, equivocating about a republic, urging that what mattered would be the constitution of the new State:

> The Supreme Council decided that no action for or against the present Treaty be taken by the Organisation as such ... Until the present issues are clearly defined, which cannot be until the draft Irish constitution can be considered by the Supreme Council, and the Council may be in a position to judge what use can be made of the new situation in the matter of gaining our ultimate aim, the sole policy of the Organisation shall be to maintain in the Organisation itself, in the army, and in the nation as a whole, that unity which is so essential to ultimate success, so that these forces may be available to support the Republic when the

272   The Irish Republican Brotherhood, 1914–1924

> proper opportunity arises ... The Dáil shall continue to be recognised as the government of the Irish Republic.[13]

Inevitably, there was confusion.[14] Both notes ignored the great opposition to the Treaty which had already been heard within the IRB and IRA. This became more coherent as the Treaty debates in the Dáil progressed. The heart of difference was that it was impossible to reconcile any oath mentioning the king with the oath to the Republic: the Republic and the Treaty simply could not exist together. As Florence O'Donoghue put it from the standpoint of the IRB: 'Members of the Organisation believed with passionate intensity in the *de facto* existence of the Republic, and they hotly resented that any group of men, even chosen leaders, should destroy what they had sworn to uphold.'[15] 'But there was an oath of allegiance in [the Treaty] too, do you see,' echoed Frank Ryan, 'and we already had an oath of allegiance so we couldn't really conscientiously take an oath of allegiance to the King of England and also one against him.'[16]

Collins' personal standing had swung a majority of the Supreme Council behind the Treaty, but lower down IRB members were not so persuadable. 'It is virtually certain that, were it not for his influence, the IRB – which really decided the issue – would have rejected it,' wrote Eoin Neeson in his history of the Civil War.[17] Instead, the Supreme Council sought to hold the organisation together, not by its traditional diktat, but by remaining indecisive in the hope that practical pro-Treaty arguments would win over members. This was counter-productive, effectively nullifying the 1921 recruitment drive which had been intended to provide a disciplined IRB cadre in the IRA that Collins could depend upon to follow his lead. But the experience of local Volunteer/IRA decision-making after 1919 infected the IRB, most of whose members had identified with the Volunteers/IRA. By 1921 members thought and were prepared to act independently. One Dublin Circle sent a message to the Supreme Council saying 'cease to consider us as Kindergarten Kids'.[18]

Responding to this feeling in the Circles, the Council meeting on 10 December extended to an extraordinary meeting with Dublin City and County Centres to consider the Treaty's ratification with them too. There was no provision in the IRB constitution for such a meeting, but the Executive considered that the political turmoil surrounding the Treaty warranted this gathering. At some point Collins chaired his Circle meeting to explain why the Treaty had come about. He said that he thought his first duty was to the

Three Days in December

IRB and that he cared for no other opinion, as P.S. O'Hegarty, who was in his Circle, recorded:

> On the Saturday week [17 December 1921] after the Treaty was signed, Michael Collins summoned a meeting of the IRB Circle of which he was Centre and I was a member. He said that he had summoned this meeting for the sole purpose of explaining how the Treaty position had arisen and added that he regarded his first duty as due to the IRB and cared nothing for any other opinion. He said that in June 1921 the total number of men in Active Service Units[19] all over Ireland, and counting everybody, was 1,617, that they had but one weapon per man for them, including rifles, automatics, sporting guns, blunderbusses, and weapons of all sorts; that they had not one cartridge per gun; that their ammunition supply routes had just been discovered by the British, and that they had not been able to organise another, and that he had had a message from Liam Lynch to say that new [British] tactics – consisting of the permanent occupation of key points after a 'sweep' instead of a return to Barracks until the next 'sweep' – had been adopted which were gradually constraining the area within which his Division could operate, and that they could not hope to operate much longer. To that situation the Truce came as a godsend. He went on to speak of the negotiations, and what he said of their inception and their course I do not recollect. But, dealing with his own appointment as plenipotentiary, he said:
>
> 'I did not want to go over. I told de Valera that I was not the person to go, that he would get a better settlement if he left me at home as a sort of dark horse. The British did not know me, and he would be able to say at a crisis "We cannot accept that! Collins and the IRB would not accept it." I wanted him to leave me at home and play up the IRB for all it was worth as a last card. But they were bent on sending me. They knew that it would embarrass me. They knew what had to be done. They had not the moral courage to do it, and they fixed on me. Well, I knew I was being made a scapegoat, and I went. And we got the utmost that could be got.'
>
> 'The men who are talking now about fighting the English are the men who did damn little fighting when the fighting was being done and gave us very little help in it. They denounced the fighting policy in the Cabinet when I was standing alone in the Cabinet in defence of it, when

I took the whole responsibility for it, and they only came over to it when they found that it was succeeding. If the Treaty is rejected and the war restarts, I will let them do the fighting this time. I will serve in the ranks but will accept no office and take no responsibility of any sort.'

'They are going about saying things about me. I don't mind that. But they are collecting arms, and they can only be collecting arms to strike at us.'

... The meeting asked a few questions and then unanimously passed a vote of confidence and approval of what had been done.[20]

Collins' closest henchmen would later state:

> [W]e all had one outlook and common aim, viz., 'The setting up and maintaining of a republican form of Government in this country'. In this ideal we followed [Collins] and accepted the Treaty in exactly the same spirit as he did. We firmly believed with him that the Treaty was only a stepping-stone to a republic ... [Collins] told us that he had taken an oath of allegiance to the Republic and that oath he would keep Treaty or no Treaty.[21]

The majority of Centres were opposed to the Treaty, and no compromise among them was reached.[22] This was when the IRB split. Sinn Féin had already divided. In late January 1922, as the Provisional Government of the Free State, formed to implement the Treaty with Collins as its head, started creating its National Army, Frank Daly, on the Dublin Centres Board, looked for direction from the Supreme Council:

> At every meeting of the Centre's Board a man from the Leinster Council came down. [Joe] McGrath came down from the Leinster Council, and I pressed for a direction of what we were to do. It was hot on the start of the Free State army. What were our directions? Were we to join it or not? ... I said that if we didn't get a direction within a week – and I was very well supported on it – if we didn't get a direction within a week what course we were to take from the Leinster Council, we'd have nothing more to do with them, we'd go our own way. And we got no instruction from them. That meeting broke up in a bit of disorder: we were insisting that we get a direction. We'd always had a direction on national policy,

Three Days in December

and we trusted the Supreme Council to give – the Leinster Council to give us and so on down the line – our instructions.[23]

The great difference in the IRB since 1916 was that Liam Lynch and other IRB members also commanded tens of thousands of the IRA (although they were nearly all unarmed) and no longer accepted the Supreme Council's directives. Now Collins was forced to recognise that the IRA and IRB would not follow his, GHQ's or the Supreme Council's orders.

At this stage, the consequence of these events seems to have escaped those involved. For the IRB, disintegration was the result. The Supreme Council had asserted its self-appointed role as watchdog of the Republic when it met on 3 December 1921 and considered in detail the outstanding issues in the Treaty negotiations. Yet within ten days it had met again and decided not to intervene in the debate about the Treaty but to wait until the constitution of the Irish Free State agreed by the Treaty was available, when a decision could be made as to whether it was sufficiently 'republican'. By procrastinating, the Council once again failed in its duty to lead.

Liam Lynch led the opposition to the Treaty within the IRB[24] and now led the opposition in the IRA too. Of all the members of the Council, apart from Collins, Lynch was the most important. His Division was dominated by IRB members under his supervision, and the men under his command in 1922 had carried out more actions against the British than any other Divisional area since 1918.[25]

On 10 December 1921 Lynch sent Mulcahy a resolution from all the senior officers of the First Southern Division (all of them also members of the IRB) that they would not accept the Treaty:

> At a meeting of Divisional Staff officers and all Brigade Commandants of the First Southern Division held in Cork on Saturday 10 December, the following resolution was unanimously adopted to be forwarded to the Chief of Staff with a request that it be transmitted to the Cabinet: 'The Treaty as it is drafted is not acceptable to us as representing the army in the First Divisional area, and we urge its rejection by the government.'[26]

The speed with which Lynch and his Division responded to the Treaty must have had its origins in the Supreme Council's discussions in November and early December, strongly suggesting that Collins' warnings that a republic was

276   The Irish Republican Brotherhood, 1914–1924

not then achievable had been given early on in the Treaty negotiations, perhaps even earlier, and that Lynch had sounded out his subordinates on the question of a republic before the Treaty was signed. At the end of January 1922 Lynch personally refused to obey IRB instructions and refused to distribute IRB directives throughout the South Munster Division of which he was Centre.[27]

The 12 December Supreme Council circular to IRB members in the Dáil increased differences and suspicions when its message reached other IRB men.[28] 'We didn't know what to do,' said Martin Dunbar, a Wexford IRB member and adjutant of the Third Battalion North Wexford Brigade. 'We thought they'd [IRB TDs] be voting against the Treaty, naturally, and it was left to ourselves whether we'd accept or reject the Treaty. So that, of course, was a very bad thing … It was a very bad idea leaving it to ourselves: it should have been unanimous one way or the other.'[29]

The statement that the Council was in favour of the Treaty can only have convinced Treaty opponents in the IRB that they would have to operate through the IRA and the Dáil. After the Treaty was accepted by the Dáil, officers of Lynch's First Southern Division spearheaded the Republican effort to gain control of the IRA.[30]

The split with Clan na Gael was another burning issue for the Supreme Council. During the Truce Harry Boland tried to persuade Seán MacEoin, who had been released from jail as part of the Truce agreement, to go to America as an IRB emissary to settle the disagreement with Devoy. MacEoin refused to go because he felt it might seem he was running away and because he was busy preparing for the outbreak of hostilities again.[31] In Dublin, Collins and Ó Murthuile met John McHugh, an envoy from John Devoy, who was also seeking rapprochement between the Clan and the IRB. They proposed that the Clan and McGarrity's Reorganised Clan should both send delegations to Ireland to meet the Supreme Council and thrash out their differences. Devoy rejected this, asking instead for a resumption of the pre-split relationship where the Clan and the IRB were each independent but co-operating fully. Collins did not want to alienate McGarrity who, like Devoy, had provided funding and weapons for the IRA, who was de Valera's supporter and who had split with Devoy over de Valera. Realigning with Devoy would be to take sides against de Valera, something that Collins in the summer of 1921 was not prepared to do. So the matter remained unresolved with Devoy. McGarrity, in contrast, came to Dublin himself and secured the Supreme Council's recognition of the Reorganised Clan.[32]

Both John Devoy and Joseph McGarrity supported the Treaty, persuaded by Collins' stepping-stone argument. During the Treaty debates in the Dáil in December, Devoy put himself and the Clan behind Collins in support of the Treaty. 'The only comfort I can take out of it,' he declared, 'is that it marks the disappearance of De Valera [*sic*] as the leader of the Irish people.'[33] McGarrity then changed his mind and threw the Reorganised Clan behind de Valera and the Republicans.

In March 1922 Denis McCullough, although no longer in the IRB, was entrusted by the Supreme Council with a mission to Devoy and McGarrity to bring them together in support of the Free State. He failed, principally because Devoy remained intransigent: he simply could not stomach reconciliation with McGarrity as a supporter of de Valera, whom he detested.[34]

By then, however, despite repeated reconciliation attempts, nationalist differences that were largely buried up to 1921 had become ever more confrontational.

CHAPTER 26

Divides

We have declared for an Irish Republic and we will live by no other law.[1]

Liam Lynch, 1919

The Dáil debated the Treaty over three weeks from 14 December. The evening before the first session, Collins met Liam Lynch and Liam Deasy at Vaughan's Hotel in Rutland Square, Dublin. 'He said,' remembered Deasy, 'that the "implication of the Treaty would mean a constitution which would be republican".'[2] To Kathleen Clarke, Collins expressed his hope that disagreement about the Treaty could be kept peaceful:

> 'Surely, Mick,' I said, 'you do not think people like me could vote for such an agreement?' 'No,' he replied. 'Nor would I like to see people like you vote for it. What I would like people like you to do would be to stand behind us and through your strength ensure that everything promised in the Treaty is got, and then we will work through it to complete freedom'.[3]

Seán Hales, a Cork TD and IRA officer, was convinced by Collins to vote for the Treaty as he explained to Éamonn de Barra, an IRA colleague: 'He had had a talk with Mick and … Mick had said that Britain had broken the Treaty of Limerick[4] and when the time was ripe they would break this one.'[5]

On 7 January 1922 the Dáil ratified the Treaty and its oath by a narrow margin – 64 to 57 – and progression to the Irish Free State was underway. The six women TDs all opposed the Treaty (and later a majority of Cumann na mBan did too). Of the pro-Treaty TDs, twenty-five (39 per cent) were members

Divides 279

of the IRB; of the anti-Treaty TDs, nineteen (33 per cent) were members of the IRB.[6] IRB TDs certainly swung the vote. Non-IRB TDs split evenly. De Valera blamed Collins and the IRB: 'M.C. had got the IRB machine working. The Dail members of the IRB were told that acceptance of the Treaty would be the quickest way to the Republic ... Tho' the rank and file of the army is right, the Headquarters Staff clean gone wrong – a part of the machine. Curse secret societies!'[7] 'The IRB was placing men for jobs then, just before the Treaty was signed and later,' remembered Denis Quille, an IRB IRA organiser in Kerry and Limerick.[8] Eoin O'Duffy was seen as buying support for compromise on the Republic even before the Treaty negotiations started, by offering jobs and positions in a new army at good rates of pay.[9] After the Treaty, Michael Collins did the same: 'He sent for a few of us,' remembered Stephen O'Neill in the Third Cork Brigade flying column, 'and he offered us anything we could want – positions or money if we would go his way.'[10] 'The money was there to be paid out,' said Frank Ryan. 'I was told I'd get a cheque for my Colonel's pension, and although I wasn't wealthy I wasn't willing to take it all the same. But when they recruited that army they gave them £4–10–0 [£4.50] a week which was a windfall for them all, to get them in. It was £10,000,000 given by the government to start up the army. The army was bought up.'[11]

As events were to show, Collins' influence with the IRB and the IRA may have nudged the Treaty over the winning line in the Dáil, but he and the IRB did not have the control they were accused of exercising. Micky Joe Costello discussed this with Diarmuid O'Hegarty, who disagreed with de Valera and thought that IRB influence one way or another did not make a difference to acceptance of the Treaty:

> O'Hegarty's opinion on this matter was most important because he was Secretary to the Cabinet and a man above everyone else, a leading IRB man and Collins' right-hand man in getting the Treaty through. But he believed that there were at least half a dozen people who voted against the Treaty only when they were certain it was going to be carried. They didn't want it to be rejected and they still wanted to maintain the banner of being sea-green incorruptibles and this was why there was so much uncertainty up to the very last moment as to what the majority would be. The position is that it would have been impossible for the IRB, even if they had as an organisation recommended their members to reject the Treaty, to secure its rejection.[12]

280   The Irish Republican Brotherhood, 1914–1924

IRB discipline that Collins assumed would continue did not withstand the IRA's claims. The IRA had fought for the Republic. The IRB now – because of Collins – was seen as surrendering the Republic – its historical objective. Days later, Tom Maguire was 'overwhelmed when the news came through that a Treaty such as this one had been signed. I was absolutely convinced that the Republic that the people had established had to be recognised.'[13] It was a clear sign that the IRA, not the IRB, now enjoyed first loyalty.

The distance between idealists and pragmatists over the Treaty was highlighted by Richard Mulcahy. Speaking in the Dáil on 22 December, he gave an appraisal of the political situation and admitted what Collins and GHQ Staff knew to be true: the IRA had not won; the Treaty was not victory: they had been defeated.

> We have not – those to whom the responsibility has been for doing such things – we have not been able to drive the enemy from anything but from a fairly good-sized police barracks. We have not that power … I see no solution of the Ulster difficulty or of the Six County difficulty at the present moment … We have suffered a defeat.[14]

This was realistic. 'We have suffered a defeat' left no room for equivocation. It accurately reflected Collins' opinion and his reluctant acceptance of the Treaty. Collins himself effectively conceded that the war had not been won, tellingly summing up that the Treaty was 'not the ultimate freedom which all nations hope for, but the freedom to achieve that end'.[15]

On 4 January 1922 nine TDs from both sides of the debate met and agreed that if the Treaty passed, de Valera was to remain president in order to maintain at least an appearance of unity so as to extract the maximum possible benefits from it.[16] On 7 January, the Dáil passed the Treaty and simultaneously in Cork the IRB County Centres formally notified the Supreme Council that they rejected it.[17] On 9 January, de Valera resigned as President of the Republic and of the Dáil. On 10 January he stood for re-election in the Dáil to both posts.[18]

He lost.

Arthur Griffith was elected to succeed him, although the Dáil chose to record his election as simply President of the Dáil.[19] Katheen Clarke then had an exchange with de Valera that highlighted at least her awareness that the Irish electorate was not necessarily wedded to the Republic:

Divides

The anti-Treaty members, as we were called, retired to another room ... De Valera was in the chair, and said that he wished to resign: he would go back to his teaching. He was prepared to be the leader of the Irish people but did not wish to be the leader of a party. I said that was all bunkum. He was never leader of the Irish people; he was leader of the Republican section of the Irish people.[20]

As was soon to be demonstrated, the 'Republican section of the Irish people' were – and probably always had been – a minority. But they were a passionate minority as Michael Hayes experienced in the Dáil. 'I was a hero in 1921 and when I accepted the Treaty I became a "Tool of the British". To say that I was a stupid ass is one thing; to say that I was a tool of the British was quite a different thing altogether.'[21]

From 7 January to the election on 16 June 1922, the Dáil and the Provisional Government ran in parallel with the same people occupying the same positions in both. After the election, the Provisional Government and then Free State government continued to refer to the Parliament of Southern Ireland, created by the 1920 Government of Ireland Act, as the Dáil and this nomenclature has continued to the present day. But when the Dáil ratified the Treaty, it meant that the Parliament of Southern Ireland supplanted the Dáil and the Treaty's Provisional Government replaced the Republic.[22] As William Cosgrave explained: 'The functions of the Second Dáil came to an end on June 30th [1922]. The meeting that was to have taken place on that date would have been purely formal for the purpose of bringing business to a conclusion. The Sovereign Assembly of Ireland is now the Parliament elected in June last whose authority the Irregulars have flouted.'[23]

In 1927 there was an interesting American footnote about the Republic, as related by Kitty O'Doherty, who was intimately involved in smuggling funds to Ireland from America:

A sum amounting to 5,123,640 dollars was subscribed by 257,988 people [for the Dáil Loan]; more than half of it was sent to the Minister for Finance of Dáil Éireann, thereby leaving about one million dollars in the New York banks. A second loan was launched just prior to the Treaty and a small amount only was subscribed to it. In August 1922, Mr Cosgrave [who upon Arthur Griffith's death on 12 August succeeded him as Chairman of the Provisional Government] sought an injunction

282 The Irish Republican Brotherhood, 1914–1924

from the Court to restrain the American Banks from paying the money to the two Trustees, Stephen O'Mara and Mr de Valera. At this time James O'Mara had resigned.[24] The third Trustee, Dr Fogarty, had supported Mr Cosgrave in his demand. Mr Cosgrave's claim was contested by the Republican Party thro' de Valera. Judge Peters, in May 1927, having heard all the evidence, decided that the Irish Free State Government was not legitimately entitled to the money which was subscribed for the Irish Republic.[25]

On GHQ Staff eleven of the thirteen officers were members of the IRB, four of whom were also on the Supreme Council.[26] Collins sought to deploy the IRB to maintain a unified IRA, but the relationship between the Supreme Council and Circles had been too weakened.[27] Billy Mullins, Quartermaster of the First Kerry Brigade, gave a direct account of the distance between the top and the lower levels of the IRB:

> There was a meeting of the IRB called in Tralee ... to discuss the Treaty in January 1922. There were about 25 there, a hell of a number of IRB. There was a discussion about our attitude to the Treaty. The meeting finished with a motion that further inquiries be made, but the result was that nothing happened, as it never seemed to come to anything. There were no outsiders there. The majority there present, I felt, were in favour of the Republic. We recognised that we could make no decision that would affect anything for we were low down in the line of the IRB.[28]

From February 1922 the IRB ceased to function as a national organisation. There were no meetings of the complete Supreme Council and only irregular meetings of Circles throughout the country. As barracks were vacated by British Army and constabulary units, Collins organised their occupation by Irish units, seeking to demonstrate his faith in the IRB and his trust in the goodwill of his IRB and IRA opponents. He personally selected Seán O'Hegarty, an opponent of the Treaty, to supervise such operations in Cork.[29] Nevertheless, effort after effort to maintain IRB and IRA unity failed.[30]

The Republican IRA considered that Mulcahy and the Dáil Cabinet, let alone the Provisional Government formed by the Treaty to oversee the creation of the Free State, did not have the authority to command the IRA. As long as the Dáil government was pursuing the establishment of a republic, the IRA

Executive, GHQ Staff and the IRA as a whole were prepared to take orders from the Dáil minister for defence and had eventually taken an oath to that effect. But since no IRA convention had been called to approve Dáil authority, once the Dáil no longer represented a republic, it and the minister could no longer claim the IRA's loyalty. Throughout, the Volunteer/IRA Executive had full authority over the IRA.[31]

The Executive called a convention for 26 March 1922. Both the Dáil and the Provisional Government banned the convention: they knew that the IRA would reject the Treaty by a large majority. Only four of the (theoretically) seventeen IRA Divisions obeyed the ban.[32] The convention was nonetheless held and the IRA split irretrievably.[33]

The paper strength of the IRA at the time was approximately 112,000, and 80 per cent of that strength was anti-Treaty and was represented at the convention.[34] Nine of the thirteen members of GHQ Staff were pro-Treaty. Of the seventeen Division commanders at the time, nearly every one was a member of the IRB. Eight took the pro-Treaty side, but most IRA members were Republican.[35] 'We still had three-quarters of the IRA, I mean the fighting IRA behind us,'[36] said Thomas Malone. The great majority of ordinary IRB members reflected the IRA split and were Republican too.

There was, however, a general desire to prevent civil war and to seek a new unity.

Joe McGarrity was in Dublin in early 1922 and secured the agreement of de Valera and Collins to meet. However, Collins changed his mind, feeling that it 'would be of no use. Nothing would come of it.' P.S. O'Hegarty admonished Collins:

> I forced him to go. I fell back on old authority. I'd been the recognised leader of the London nationalists for years, had sworn him into the IRB ... and had been the authoritative voice generally. I resumed that authority and told him he would have to go, that he was no longer representing himself but the people and would have to forget himself. I practically ordered him to go, as I would have done in other things ten years previously. And he went.[37]

As Collins foresaw, nothing came of the meeting.

Early in 1922, in a pre-emptive attempt to keep the IRB unified, the Supreme Council allocated £1,000 to fund a national weekly publication, *The Separatist*,

284 The Irish Republican Brotherhood, 1914–1924

edited by P.S. O'Hegarty. Its mission was publicly to reaffirm IRB ideology to IRB members in an effort to convince them that the Supreme Council's resolve had not changed and that the Free State was a stepping-stone towards a republic: 'We stand for the complete separation of Ireland from England … And in working for that we will use, as Separatists have always used, every movement which we can use, and take advantage of every situation which can bring us advantage.'[38] The weekly ran for six months until September. It had no discernible effect. The Treaty had demoralised IRB men. Christy O'Connell, an IRB IRA member in West Cork's Beara peninsula, attributed no importance to the IRB in 1922, seeing it as a disheartening influence:

> We came out into the open from about 1919 and then there was no need for swearing in or for secrecy. IRB men were proudly the moving spirits … Blythe came down here, an organiser for the IRB, in 1917 and he told the men that it would be the whole hog, the republic, or nothing. About two years or more after he took an oath of allegiance to the King of England. Men like that had a terrible effect on those who were proud to be members of the IRB and who remained faithful.[39]

In March a second extraordinary meeting of IRB Centres was held in the shadow of the ban of the proposed IRA convention and in the knowledge that the convention would be held despite the ban.

Those present were most concerned with the unity of the IRB. There was talk of electing a new Supreme Council, but nothing came of it:[40] IRB elections had been held in 1921 and the next elections were not due until 1923. Collins held that the IRB was 'supreme'.[41] It always had been and would be supreme for him. Liam Lynch and several others argued for a return to the 'old' constitution: presumably meaning that the IRB should reclaim the government and presidency of the Irish Republic.[42] The meeting ended without any resolution.

At the instigation of Liam Lynch and the Cork IRB IRA leaders, another extraordinary IRA convention was held on 19 April. As in January and again in March, the majority of those present opposed the Treaty. Discussion revolved around the possibilities presented by the Irish Free State constitution expected to be published around 10 May. Lynch impatiently dismissed speculations, saying that he could not wait three weeks for a constitution that might not alter the position in any way unless there was a guarantee that it would be

Divides 285

a republican constitution. Another IRB meeting was also held, probably just before the 19 April IRA convention. Patrick Mullaney was there:

The Cork division of the IRB sent a notice to the Supreme Council demanding an Extraordinary General Meeting. They could do that by a number of Country Centres getting together. The whole Southern Division of the IRA were members of the IRB and they made use of this and demanded a meeting. The purpose of the meeting – it was Liam Lynch that spoke first – was why did Collins sign the Treaty in England and was the Republic now finished with? Why was this if it were so? And it was an effort also to prevent a civil war coming on … Collins presided and the whole Supreme Council was there plus the Centres from every county in Ireland … They wanted to know what was the reason for this being signed. The general feeling that you got was that at the time it was signed the full Supreme Council weren't available in Dublin … Each one round the whole room was asked what would he do if he were in Collins' place. Would he sign or would he not? … As far as I can judge generally the number against Collins signing was far greater than the number that approved. The numbers would be, as I say, that if it went to a vote Collins would have been beaten, but he didn't put it to a vote. He said that there were two bodies framing a constitution and he said that that constitution would be a republican one. Liam Lynch interrupted him … 'I don't believe that', Lynch said … The result was that we appointed three on each side [to] examine the constitution and see if it was a republican one because Collins said: 'You'll examine that and come to an agreement.' The last words I ever heard out of his mouth were: 'And we'll be all together again, lads' … That was the last we ever heard of it and the last meeting of the IRB that I ever attended.[43]

The meeting proved to be the last chance for Lynch and Collins, now the principal spokesmen for the opposing sides in the IRA and the IRB, to come to some agreement. Unfortunately, the meeting only served to show once again that a majority of the Supreme Council was pro-Treaty, while a majority of the IRB was not.

The six men appointed to determine if the forthcoming Free State constitution would be republican instead occupied themselves with the immediate issue of the split in the IRB and the IRA. They decided during the next ten days that only senior IRA officers were competent to attempt once again to obtain IRA unity. Lynch declared that he had already waited too long and that unless he obtained a guarantee that the Free State constitution would be republican, he would continue the fight for the Republic.

On the morning of 16 June, the day of the general election called by the Dáil and the Provisional Government, the Free State constitution was published. It was not republican. Lloyd George's government, as entitled by the Treaty, had removed the republican elements, namely no oath, no mention of the Treaty, and a governor general's role that would be taken by 'the President of Ireland'.[44] Lloyd George had ruthlessly established that the settlement was Britain's, not Collins', Sinn Féin's, the Dáil's, the IRA's or the IRB's.

However, Lynch's wish to avoid civil war prevailed and he reached an agreement with Mulcahy to reunite the IRA.[45] On 18 June Lynch presented the plan to another IRA convention, but Rory O'Connor, GHQ Staff Director of Engineering, a Dublin Centre[46] and one of the leaders of Dublin Republicans, forestalled discussion by storming out with about half the delegates. He went to the Four Courts, which Republicans had occupied since 13 April as a prelude to renewed attacks against British forces still in Ireland, thinking that would force IRA reunification.[47] O'Connor 'hadn't the brains of a hen', said Peadar O'Donnell, who was with him on the IRA Executive. 'The First Southern Division were the only people who could have saved the situation if they had moved. They could have been the basis for a Republican constitution.'[48]

Within weeks the Civil War began when Collins ordered an attack on the Republican IRA in the Four Courts at the end of June 1922. And within weeks Collins 'called a number of us up to Dublin for a meeting,' Joe Sweeney recalled, 'the purpose of which was the reorganisation of the IRB in the [Free State] army.'[49] Tying the Volunteers/IRA/Free State Army to the IRB was clearly a principle for Collins, but the new IRB constitution that followed firmly established the IRB as separate from all other organisations.

CHAPTER 27

1922 Constitution

[T]he SC will appoint small Commissions or Committees to act as Vigilance Councils, to watch the progress of the various branches of Governmental, National, Economical, and Social Life of the Nation, in order to assure that they are kept in line with the Policy of the I.R.B.

Constitution of the Irish Republican
Brotherhood, 1922, clause 30

In July 1922 Collins drafted a new IRB constitution.[1] It was republican. It was part of his effort to convince Lynch and the other Republicans that despite the attack that he ordered on the Four Courts he could nevertheless be trusted to use the Free State to win a republic.[2] He incorporated more inclusive procedures so that Centres and not simply the Supreme Council could be involved in major decisions. The very first clause stated: 'The object of the Irish Republican Brotherhood (hereinafter sometimes called "The Organisation") shall be: To establish and maintain a free and independent Republican Government in Ireland.'

Mindful of the division over the Treaty, clause 2 incorporated political activity for the first time in the IRB's arsenal: 'The policy of the I.R.B. shall be to utilise every power and movement in the Nation: it shall influence them in their activities and co-ordinate these activities so as to secure that the maximum organised strength of the nation – armed, economic, political, social and otherwise shall be at all times available for the achievement of its objects.'

This was a recognition of the danger that the IRB now posed to the peaceful advancement of a republic. No previous constitution had allowed for political action, focusing solely on the use of force. IRB members had been expelled for

288 The Irish Republican Brotherhood, 1914–1924

taking part in the IPP, and distrust had marked the IRB's relations with Sinn Féin. Now, when force had failed to win a republic, Collins was arguing that penetrating and manipulating all elements of the new State was the best hope. Inferentially, it also endorsed Collins' actions and could be taken as supporting his positions as IRB President and Chairman of the Provisional Government.

A new oath dropped claims to be the government of the Republic and did not continue the 1919 constitutional amendment recognising 'the Government of the Irish Republic, which is Dáil Éireann':

> In the presence of God, I _____, do solemnly swear that I shall do my utmost to establish the National Independence of Ireland; that I will give true allegiance to the Irish Republic, and obedience to the Supreme Council of the Irish Republican Brotherhood, and preserve inviolable the secrets of the Organisation. So help me God.

On the face of it, this was a major change in the purpose of the IRB. But it is likely that this new oath was phrased so that if challenged a member could say that he had not sworn allegiance to an IRB government. Clause 27, however, maintained the IRB's governmental and presidential claims: 'While accepting the present Governmental position of An Saor Stait, the Supreme Council of the I.R.B. is declared the sole Government of the Irish Republic, until Ireland's complete independence is achieved, and a permanent Republican Government is established … its President shall be the President of the Irish Republic.'[3]

This, of course, was a rejection of the Dáil as the government of the Republic. It was back to the basic IRB position of being untrammelled by politicians, and it was more evidence of Collins' effort to convince republicans of the IRB's and his personal bona fides.

Dramatic changes in the organisation of the IRB were also made, focusing power with the Supreme Council Executive and president. 'Clubs' replaced Circles. A Club was to be between three and five members who would elect a Centre from amongst themselves. Each Club was to be based on a parish. This disrupted the traditional county/town/district basis of Circles, making Clubs particularly local and reducing the influence of Centres, and – as intended – it broke the direct connection with IRA units and made no connection with the new National Army being recruited by the Provisional Government. It was a move to make the IRB separate once again, showing an awareness that the IRA would not endorse the Free State and a hope that the IRB might provide a way

1922 Constitution

to unity. Centres and members of the Supreme Council had to be 'permanently resident in the area they represent'.[4] The Club Centres in sixteen Counties or Districts, each consisting of two or three actual counties or cities, were to elect a Centre. In annual elections, these County/Divisional Centres were to elect a nine-man County/Divisional Board that was to elect five of their number in turn to elect 'a member of the Irish Republican Brotherhood' to the Supreme Council.[5] The Council would co-opt four members who would only be known to Council members, producing a Supreme Council of twenty men. The Council's Executive was to be elected by the Council members and to consist of 'A President, a Secretary, a Treasurer and four other members':[6] there was no stipulation that the named officers should hold these positions on the Council itself. A 'General Election' could be held at any time if two-thirds of the Council or half the County/Divisional Centres requested one.[7]

There were no IRB elections in 1922, so this constitution probably remained inoperative. There is no evidence that it was promulgated or endorsed by the Supreme Council. It can be seen principally as a response to the turmoil of impending civil war with Collins, as president, drafting a text that he hoped would convince the IRB membership of the IRB's (and his) unflagging republicanism and that he, with their support, could win a republic through the Free State.

CHAPTER 28

Civil War

Irish republicanism was not a political theory but a secular religion.[1]

Tom Garvin, *1922: The Birth of Irish Democracy*[2]

On 14 January 1922 Collins became Chairman of the Provisional Government of the Irish Free State, answering to the Parliament of Southern Ireland.[3] Mulcahy replaced Brugha as Minister for Defence in both the Dáil government and the Provisional Government. Eoin O'Duffy became Chief of Staff of the Provisional Government's new National Army.

On 23 May 1922, a Sinn Féin Ard-Fheis that had been called in an attempt to agree a unified front in the forthcoming general election, despite the opposition of Arthur Griffith, ratified a pact between Collins and de Valera not to field opposing candidates and thus maintain the pro- and anti-Treaty balance in Parliament. Its purpose was to keep the argument about the Treaty and the Free State constitution within Sinn Féin, and hopefully, by keeping debate intra-party, avoid civil war. The pact did not last. Collins campaigned for pro-Treaty candidates.[4] The result on 16 June was ninety-two pro-Treaty TDs and thirty-six anti-Treaty.[5]

The assassination of Field Marshal Sir Henry Wilson on 22 June 1922 by two London IRB men, Reginald Dunne and Joseph O'Sullivan, was viewed by many as inspired if not directed by Collins. Whether Collins was responsible or not, it certainly supported his effort to prove his republican credentials, and he took advantage of it to this end. Wilson was an Ulster Unionist and ardent opponent of the IRA and Sinn Féin. In 1921–22 he was thought to be responsible for constabulary attacks on Catholics as well as what was publicised as an anti-Catholic pogrom in Northern Ireland.[6] P.S. O'Hegarty made a

Civil War 291

point of finding out what, exactly, had happened and asked Sam Maguire, the London Centre co-opted on the 1921–22 Supreme Council, who was in a position to know:

> I said to him, 'Do you know anything about the Wilson business?'
>
> He said, 'What do you want to know about it?'
>
> I said, 'Who did it?'
>
> He said, 'We did it.'
>
> That made me stiffen up in horrified incredulity. Sam and I worked in the closest association from 1903 to 1913, and we spoke the same language. When he said 'we', I took him to mean the IRB.
>
> I said, 'Surely to God, Mick never authorised that?'
>
> He was silent for a minute and then he said 'Collins knew about it.'
>
> I pressed him. I said 'Did he authorise it?'
>
> He would not say that, but he repeated, 'He knew about it.'
>
> And nothing else would he say.
>
> I had to leave it like that … Then I bethought me of Ben Kennedy. Ben was a member of the Organisation, a member of the Intelligence Section inside the PO which did such good work, in touch with Mick, and a great friend of Sam's. I knew that Sam used to stay with him whenever he was in Dublin … I asked him about the Wilson affair. I told him exactly what Sam had said to me and asked him whether he knew anything that would reconcile Sam's refusal to say that Mick 'authorised' it with his equally emphatic statement that Mick 'knew' about it.
>
> After some pressure, he said to me –
>
> 'I can tell you what happened, but only for your own private information. You must promise me neither to print it nor use it.'
>
> I gave the required promise, and he said –
>
> 'For a long time Sam was mad to shoot Wilson, because of the Belfast pogroms, and every time he came over he pressed Mick for authority and Mick invariably refused. But Sam persisted. The last time he saw him they had high words about it and Mick lost his temper and flared up and said, "God blast you! Get away to hell out of that and don't bother me, and do whatever you like!" Sam left him without a word and, although he was in Dublin several times afterwards, he never went near Mick again. When the thing happened, Mick was in an awful state' … Sam's own statement to me is proof of one thing, that it was he who carried it

out. Kennedy's further statement explains what puzzled me about Sam's statement, and makes the tragical sequence entirely credible. Anybody who saw Mick in the late Spring and early Summer of 1922, tired out, irritable, overburthened with work and responsibility, some new worry every day, and all the time brooding over the taunts that were freely thrown at him of being a traitor and so on (he was extremely sensitive on that point) can see the thing happening just as Kennedy described it. I believe that what I have recorded does constitute the truth about this wretched business. It does not, it cannot, remove from Mick the responsibility for it, but it does explain it ... I believe that Dunne and O'Sullivan acted under his instructions as members of the Organisation, and not as members of the Irish Volunteers.'[7]

Joe Sweeney, O/C First Northern Division and a National Army commandant, was told by Collins that he had, in fact, arranged Wilson's assassination. 'I said to him, "Was that an official job?" "Yes," he said.'[8]

Collins tried to save the assassins using IRB connections after the Civil War had started. The IRB in England was anti-Treaty, so Collins' effort was another way of reaffirming his republican credentials. He sent two members of the Squad, Joe Dolan and Vinnie Byrne, to Patrick O'Daly in Liverpool, with instructions to find and to shoot the hangman, John Ellis, and his assistant, William Willis.[9] O'Daly's opposition to the Treaty did not intrude and he worked to facilitate their mission, but Dolan and Byrne were unable to find Ellis and Willis. On 10 August Dunne and O'Sullivan were hanged.

In June Collins was behind swapping weapons between the IRA at the Four Courts and the National Army at Portobello Barracks in Dublin. The National Army weapons would replace the IRA's in Dublin[10] and the IRA weapons, which could not be traced to the Provisional Government, would be sent secretly to the IRA in Ulster by the National Army. There they would be used for attacks on the British Army and constabulary in Northern Ireland. A majority of the northern IRA had supported the Treaty; using them to attack the Royal Ulster Constabulary (the successor to the RIC in the North) and British military in Northern Ireland was yet another signal of Collins' republican intent.

By the end of June the IRA had split into three: the National Army, formed in February 1922, controlled by Collins and Mulcahy; the Republican IRA, principally in Dublin, Leinster and Munster controlled by Oscar Traynor (O/C

Civil War   293

IRA Dublin Brigade), and Liam Lynch (as IRA Chief of Staff), anxious to have unity and peace but not prepared to surrender the Republic; and the extreme republicans based at the Four Courts, under the command of Joe McKelvey, who wanted to smash the Treaty, the Provisional Government and the Free State and achieve unity by forcing the British to attack the Four Courts, expecting that then the National Army and Republican IRA would join them in a new fight with Britain.[11] Collins wanted to prevent civil war by securing general recognition of parliamentary authority, which meant that the pro-Treaty majority would still prevail within the Free State government but would face a parliamentary opposition.

De Valera, like Collins anxious to avoid civil war, wanted all sides to combine behind his Document No. 2 alternative to the Treaty. He had Brugha's support, but both had little influence in any section of the IRA and were essentially confined to political opposition.[12] Seán MacBride, who acted as de Valera's secretary for some years from 1922, thought that de Valera 'resented, I think, that the IRA – the militarists – would never accept, would never come under his orbit, would always maintain their independence. They were quite prepared to talk to him, to deal with him, to work with him, but always to maintain their independence and not be absolutely subservient to the political wing.'[13]

During June clashes had already occurred between the IRA in the Four Courts and National Army units at Beggars Bush Barracks.[14] When Sir Henry Wilson was murdered blame was immediately attached to the Four Courts.[15] Lloyd George demanded that the Provisional Government suppress McKelvey's group. Then Leo Henderson, a Four Courts officer, was arrested by the National Army on 26 June. When McKelvey in a tit-for-tat move kidnapped J.J. O'Connell, National Army Deputy Chief of Staff, Collins reluctantly agreed that action had to be taken. On 28 June the Four Courts was shelled. The Civil War had begun.[16] Seán MacBride, at that time in the Four Courts, remembered the surprise of the attack:

> We didn't expect an attack on the Four Courts at all … We had been negotiating with Collins during that period for the transfer of arms (which we were getting from the Free State army) to be transferred to the IRA for use in Donegal and in the north. And on the very day of the attack on the Four Courts we despatched a convoy of arms, I think four tenders of arms, right up to Donegal to help in the struggle in the north.[17]

294 The Irish Republican Brotherhood, 1914–1924

Two days later, McKelvey and his colleagues surrendered. Brugha fought around Sackville (from 1924 O'Connell) Street with a rearguard, enabling de Valera – who in early July after the attack on the Four Courts had re-enlisted as an ordinary Volunteer in the Third Dublin Battalion (his 1916 unit)[18] – to escape. A Cumann na mBan group was with Brugha, who insisted that they escape too, but three remained. Surrounded and without hope, on 5 July Brugha ordered everyone still with him to surrender but said that he would not. He then emerged and was shot, dying two days later.[19]

On 1 July John F. Homan of the St John's Ambulance Brigade, who had been at work in the Four Courts, took upon himself an effort to stop fighting expanding further, and went to see Collins, who said:

> Tell these men that neither I, nor any member of the government, nor any officer in the army (and I learned the feeling of every officer in Dublin on my rounds yesterday), not one of us wishes to hurt a single one of them in any way that can be avoided. They, and their leaders, are at liberty to march out and go to their homes unmolested if only they will – I do not use the word surrender – if only they will deposit their weapons in the National Armory, there to remain until and unless in the whirl of politics these men become a majority in the country in which case they will have control of them.[20]

This was a telling statement. Collins was now speaking as a democrat, not as an IRB republican. It suited him to do so: the June election had accepted the Treaty and his Provisional Government. He was also still trying to avoid civil war.[21] Dick Barrett, one of the IRA leaders in the Four Courts, 'once gave account of a talk between himself and Collins,' Peadar O'Donnell recalled, 'at which Collins had stated his plans in detail; he would use the Treaty to get strength but all the time he would operate a "dark hand" and according as undesirables pushed their way forward the "dark hand" would assassinate them.'[22]

There was no reason for Barrett to invent such a story. Collins was agreeing with Barrett's own view. The 'dark hand' was a bloodthirsty image, reminiscent of *Treasure Island*, so perhaps said for bombastic effect. And Collins had a dark fist in his Squad. But the stepping-stone that was Collins' plan for the Free State was perfectly serious. He depended upon IRB Executive colleagues to command the army (O'Duffy: IRB Treasurer) and the police (Ó Murthuile: IRB Secretary), securing their appointments days before he was killed, and he

Civil War 295

governed autocratically.[23] Collins was not a democrat before 1922. Nor were the anti-Treaty IRA. De Valera was not a democrat either: in November 1922 he recommended that the IRA 'act temporarily as a de facto military government'.[24] John Regan has pointed out that Collins was operating something close to a military dictatorship in July–August 1922: Parliament was prorogued; the National Army had no legal position with the Provisional Government, and Collins simply assumed executive powers. He consulted colleagues knowing that his will prevailed.[25]

Ernest Blythe, who was Minister for Local Government in the cabinets of both the Provisional and then the Free State governments, recounted how his colleagues worked with Collins:

> At first Collins agreed, and we were on the point of starting fighting ... But then Mulcahy said the Army wasn't ready for it and more time was needed for organising and training and so on, and then Collins agreed with him and it was off. And then from that time on it was only a point – it was only a matter of bringing Collins to the point of giving the word. All the Ministers were for fighting before then.[26]

All the skulduggery that he deployed in 1922 was directed at pushing the Free State towards a republic: the gun-swapping with the Four Courts to arm pro- and anti-Treaty IRA men in Northern Ireland fighting for a united Ireland against the Unionist government, and the effort to save Wilson's assassins by murdering the hangman and his assistant. In addition there was his IRB drumbeat of 'Trust me: I am an IRB diehard and I will work like blazes to secure a republic', and his authoritarian chairmanship of his Provisional Government.[27] And he might have succeeded. Liam Deasy was not alone on the Republican side in having 'great respect and trust in Michael Collins,' as Ernie O'Malley noted, 'possibly through [the] IRB'.[28]

The Provisional Government leading on to the Free State government (inaugurated on 6 December 1922) alone had a claim to popular endorsement.[29] Collins was the product of a closed and fanatical world that he was moving away from when he died. His idealism made him ambivalent about democracy, claiming democratic approval when it suited him but never shirking from rigging elections. He may well have become a democratic politician, as did de Valera, but his 1917 and 1922 IRB constitutions indicate that he was prepared to overturn democratic results. Unlike the 1873 Constitution, Collins' 1922

296   The Irish Republican Brotherhood, 1914–1924

Constitution had no references to 'the Irish nation', to religious freedom or to popular will: there was no provision for popular endorsement.[30]

Collins was attempting to meet IRB/IRA colleagues in Cork to force a peace when he was killed in an ambush at Béal na mBláth on 22 August 1922.[31] In the days before he had been trying to stop the Civil War using IRB contacts.[32] Thomas Malone, then a Republican prisoner, was visited by Collins:

> He asked me if I would attend a meeting of senior officers *to try to put an end to this damned thing*. He made arrangements with the Governor of the jail that I was to be released. As he went out, he slapped one fist into a palm in characteristic fashion: *That's fine, the three Toms will fix it*. The three Toms mentioned by him were Tom Barry, Tom Hales and myself. We were to meet in Cork with some of his officers and arrange for a cessation of hostilities. No political negotiations were entered into, nor were any political aspects alluded to by Collins, who appeared to be acting alone.[33]

Patrick Moylett, a Mayo businessman who acted as a go-between for Collins, Griffith and Lloyd George in 1920, met Collins just before he left Dublin on his fatal tour of Munster:

> Mick Collins told me that he was going to do a circuit of the country; that he intended to speak to the 'boys' – meaning his opponents – and to reason with them. He said he knew them all personally and he would explain to them the foolishness of their action. He said he would tell them that if they continued in their way of action he would use force and repressive measures to stop them. That was my last meeting with Michael Collins. He died a few days later.[34]

With Collins' death any realistic hope of using the IRB to end the Civil War passed, and the IRB's disintegration was underway. The Supreme Council continued for some days, but there is no evidence of continued Circle activity in the IRA or National Army or among neutral or civilian members. Micky Joe Costello thought Diarmuid O'Hegarty may have succeeded Collins as president of the IRB in a pre-emptive move to prevent the organisation falling into the hands of the IRA or of Collins loyalists:

Civil War 297

My impression was that O'Hegarty succeeded Collins and MacMahon succeeded O'Hegarty, but I can't give you any evidence as I wasn't a member of the IRB myself. There may well have been an interregnum and my supposition of that is that O'Hegarty's move in to be the head of the IRB was to prevent it falling into other hands and to attempt to wind it up. I think he was responsible for turning it into a kind of benevolent society. At that time he was Secretary of the Cabinet and this was his practice: he was always the power behind the throne rather than on the throne. It may well be that the threat from somebody else came from Martin Conlon who was likely to become President of it and revive it. O'Hegarty regarded this as a source of disaffection and possible mutiny and so on and moved in … Tobin and others would have been quite dangerous if they got hold of it as a going concern as an organisation with prestige and mystique attaching to its name, in particular the contacts with America. And I think O'Hegarty frustrated that.[35]

On the Republican side there was growing realisation that they would not win the war.[36] The executions of IRA prisoners by the Free State government, starting on 8 December 1922 with the leaders of the Four Courts IRA, Joe McKelvey, Liam Mellows, Rory O'Connor and Dick Barrett, all of whom were in the IRB (McKelvey on the Supreme Council), speeded the end of the war. Liam Lynch thought 'These executions may be intentional … to make the history … of the Organisation impossible.'[37] More official executions followed – eighty-one in all. 'A lot of people in Government Buildings were shaking in their boots that didn't have any confidence that it would be won by the government at this time,'[38] said Micky Joe Costello. 'It was the Army Council that [proposed the executions]: yes, Mulcahy and Gearóid O'Sullivan', said Michael Hayes, who was Minister for Education in the Provisional Government when the decision to execute IRA members was taken at the end of September 1922. 'It was obvious to everybody that you couldn't go on with this. We were all vulnerable. We couldn't guard however many members of the Dáil there were at that time – nearly 100 … But it had this great effect: it ended the Civil War, didn't it?'[39]

In November 1922, Lynch had proposed that the Republicans should restart the IRB, and that the pro-Treaty members of the 1921 Supreme Council should be taken to task by the County Centres for breaking their oath to a republic. On 7 November 1922 he wrote to his no. 2, Liam Deasy, now Adjutant of the First Southern Division and an IRB colleague:

298 The Irish Republican Brotherhood, 1914–1924

> Owing to (a) the importance of having a live I.R.B. organisation according to its constitution active at all times especially the present and (b) to save the honour of the splendid historic organisation through our generation, I consider it our duty as senior officers of same to exert ourselves at once … to have the [Supreme Council] now definitely account for its action in sanctioning treaty, account of each member in waging war on Republicans so that whole organisation can remain intact and get rid of all guilty members.[40]

Liam Deasy asked Florence O'Donoghue for advice. O'Donoghue had remained neutral during the Civil War. Neither man knew that on 31 August, nine days after Collins' death, Seán Ó Murthuile, while commandant of Kilmainham Gaol, called a meeting of Collins' pro-Treaty Supreme Council colleagues to secure his IRB papers and end the IRB.[41] Ó Murthuile may have considered that there was no longer any reason for the Brotherhood to continue, but more likely he recognised that a majority of members opposed the Treaty and the Provisional Government: ending the society would prevent that majority in the scheduled 1923 IRB elections that most probably would see anti-Treatyites overturning the existing Council and gaining control of whatever of the organisation remained.

O'Donoghue rejected the suggestion that the Centres should meet the Supreme Council, pointing out that the Council would reiterate that they had accepted the Treaty only as a stepping-stone to a republic. He proposed instead to play by the IRB's rules and ask the Council to call the biennial elections throughout the IRB due in 1923, including elections to the Council itself. If they ignored this demand, O'Donoghue argued, then IRB Republicans should proceed with the elections, producing a Republican Supreme Council.[42] Clause 29 of Collins' 1922 Constitution (although apparently not ratified) may have formed part of the process he had in mind:

> In the event of any crisis in the National Life of the Country that may call for any action by the Organisation, the S.C. will, in due course, prepare a plan of action concerning same, and in the event of the crisis being such that certain action on the part of the Organisation may endanger the integrity of the I.R.B., a Convention of Centres in each County shall be called to consider the matter.

Civil War 299

The clause was clearly introduced because of the then developing civil war and the split in the IRB. Such a convention would have firmly supported the Republican stance.

Lynch continued to toy with approaching the Supreme Council into 1923, noting that the IRB organisation in the south was intact and that there were moves in the National Army to re-form the IRB.[43] On 10 April Lynch was surprised by a National Army sweep around his headquarters in the Knockmealdown mountains on the Waterford–Tipperary border. He was shot while escaping and died later that day. With his death a Republican IRB reorganisation went no further.

Still, IRB ties remained strong and were seen by some Free State members as offering a means of honourable IRA surrender.[44] Tom Barry took a lead in the peace effort, apparently with the support of the Free State government. In March 1923 he approached Liam Lynch, proposing an end to the fighting. Patrick Ruttledge, a member of de Valera's Republican Cabinet, was with Lynch:

> Barry and Fr Duggan[45] came to see us. At first Barry did not press the point about surrender. It looked as if he had come up to satisfy some of the people in the south who wanted to surrender … Barry had a gun strapped on his leg. He was sneering at us for being afraid. He had helped to take three posts in Kilkenny. Later we found out that he had a free pass from the Staters. That is why he could stay in the Hibernian [hotel] and carry a gun.[46]

Barry persisted. At an IRA Executive meeting on 26 March he proposed that the IRA should unilaterally stop fighting. His motion was defeated by six votes to five. Lynch wrote to Barry telling him to stop trying to make peace.[47] After Lynch was killed on 10 April 1923, Ruttledge again encountered Barry at a meeting towards the end of April: 'I was amazed at Barry. He was advocating a "Cease Fire". They couldn't carry on the fight, and it was thrown back at Dev to arrange terms. The army was now "passing the buck" to the politicals.'[48]

On 30 April Frank Aiken, Lynch's successor as IRA Chief of Staff, announced a ceasefire and on 24 May followed this with an order to hide rather than surrender their weapons. De Valera simultaneously issued a statement acknowledging that the IRA had been defeated 'for the moment' and that fighting should stop.[49]

300 The Irish Republican Brotherhood, 1914–1924

On 25 May 1923, three and a half weeks after the Republican ceasefire, Seán Ó Murthuile as Secretary of the (now defunct) Supreme Council, and from January 1923 Quartermaster General of the National Army, received from Seán O'Hegarty an appeal from Barry for the IRB to use its influence to stop the National Army pursuing Republicans, so that the IRB at least might settle its differences and continue to work for a republic:

> T[om] B[arry] an officer in the Organisation in county Cork, appeals to the IRB to intervene with its influence to stop the now unnecessary and therefore vindictive pursuit of members of the Irish Republican Army (called the 'Irregulars') all over the country by Free State troops, these members having now for the most part dumped their arms and offering no resistance for the purpose of enabling him to create such feeling as will allow a fusion of the IRB elements which are now warring on both sides, so that the ideals of the Organisation may not be lost sight of, and for the purpose of counteracting the sinister reactionary elements which are rapidly gaining control of the life and government of the country.
>
> He appeals with confidence to the Supreme Council of the Organisation to take such effective action, without delay, as will save for future work for the Republic the members of the Organisation as a solid body, irrespective of their having taken one side or the other in the civil conflict.[50]

Ó Murthuile immediately passed this appeal to Mulcahy, Minister for Defence. Mulcahy rightly concluded that Liam Lynch had failed to create a Republican IRB, and that Barry's recognition of the Supreme Council was particularly important. It meant that the Free State could have in the Council a body to whose wishes about disbandment and arms surrender Republican leaders might acquiesce 'without feeling humiliated'. That both sides should look to the same Supreme Council showed that value was still placed on the integrity of the IRB. It was seen as providing a potential path to peace. At the same time Mulcahy was aware of the need to counteract any suspicion that he and the army were acting independently of the government.[51]

On 3 June Mulcahy told Eoin MacNeill, who had succeeded Michael Hayes as Minister for Education, about Barry's message. The next day Mulcahy discussed it with Ó Murthuile and Seán MacMahon, O'Duffy's successor as Chief of Staff. On 7 June he informed William Cosgrave, President of the

Civil War 301

Executive Council of the Free State, and Kevin O'Higgins, Minister for Home Affairs. Three days later they all met and agreed that they would rescind any steps taken to end the Brotherhood and conduct an IRB reorganisation within the Free State that might then provide the mechanism through which the IRA might surrender their weapons.[52] They were encouraged in this when Liam Deasy from prison suggested arranging an amnesty for the IRA in Cork through the IRB, indicating his ignorance of the August 1922 decision to end the organisation and his acceptance of the 1921–23 Supreme Council's authority that was still in place since no elections had been held.[53] To allay suspicion of the new IRB reorganisation, a new constitution was now drafted by Ó Murthuile and probably O'Hegarty and MacMahon, making the IRB's loyalty to the Free State explicit while seeking to enable IRA acceptance of its bona fides.

CHAPTER 29

1923 Constitution

[T]he IRA was a blind alley organisation now, and … those responsible for holding it together should get a chance of disbanding it. That the Second Organisation [IRB] was the only one that provided a pivotal point for arranging this. That the policy of the Second Organisation was fully controlled by us. That its policy could bear the light of day.[1]

Richard Mulcahy, 7 June 1923

A completely different vision of the Free State and of the IRB now replaced Collins' vision. At the end of 1922, reports had reached Ó Murthuile that Republicans were attempting to organise Circles in order to take over the IRB. IRB officers in the National Army had asked Ó Murthuile if there were any plans to counteract this danger.[2] Ó Murthuile consulted senior IRB members in the Army and in the Dáil. He obtained general agreement to try to counteract the anti-Treaty effort; that the traditions of the IRB should be handed on to a new generation; that any IRB reorganisation must be overseen by pro-Treaty members of the 1921 Supreme Council even if in the National Army, but that members in the Free State Cabinet should not be compromised by any direct involvement.[3] The Free State Minister for Home Affairs, Kevin O'Higgins, when told that Mulcahy (now Minister for Defence as well as Commander-in-Chief of the National Army) was involved in this initiative, objected on the grounds that the Free State should not have any association with the IRB.[4]

Ó Murthuile and his colleagues set aside objections and began work on their new IRB constitution. The April 1923 IRA ceasefire did not affect this. Tom Barry's letter may have energised the undertaking. The new constitution was completed in June. Ó Murthuile sent a draft of it to Mulcahy, who approved

1923 Constitution

each clause, making some minor wording changes, the most important of which was that a four-fifths majority of the Supreme Council would be required to change key clauses 'dealing with Policy, Objects, the Oath or Membership'.[5] It explicitly recognised the authority of the Free State. It reaffirmed once again the intention to establish a republican government in Ireland, and also arranged for the reorganisation of the part of the IRB within the National Army in the form of Clubs and Divisions corresponding exactly to the army's formations.[6] It did not continue the IRB's claims to the presidency and government of the Republic that had been restated by Collins in the 1922 Constitution. It stood on its 1919–21 watchdog role:

> [W]hereas National Sovereignty is inherent and inalienable and, while acknowledging that political authority is exercised through instruments legitimately established, the Irish Republican Brotherhood pledges itself the custodian of the Republican Ideal – the traditional expression of National Independence.
>
> The Policy of the I.R.B. shall be to utilise every power and movement in the Nation; it shall influence them in their activities so as to secure that the maximum organised strength of the Nation – armed, economic, political, social and otherwise shall be at all times available for the achievement of its objects.[7]

This was clearly calling for unity on all fronts to progress further to a republic, echoing Collins' 1922 Constitution. It was an implicit statement emphasising that the Free State had never been the final objective of the IRB but was a stepping-stone to a republic one day. This was wide open to a different interpretation: that the IRB's loyalty to the Free State was, as it had been with the Dáil government, conditional. The 1922 oath (retained in the 1923 Constitution), while dropping the IRB's claims to be the government, nevertheless left loyalty to the Free State up in the air. Ó Murthuile and his colleagues had tried to meet the difficulty of reconciling the IRB Republic to the Free State by not very skilfully equating 'National Independence' with 'Irish Republic'. But by not mentioning the Free State, Republicans might find it possible to accept the oath. It was an opening to them.

The basis of the Clubs was a complete reversal of Collins' 1922 Constitution that had aimed to break IRB correspondence to military units. The IRA might agree to use the IRB as an honourable vehicle for surrender, but there would be no question of the IRB's independence. The National Army would control the IRB: 'G.H.Q. shall constitute respectively a Division, and each Battalion, Corps and Army Service and Command Staff, shall respectively constitute a Club. (No soldier may be a member of a Civilian Club.)'[8]

This may have been a step to prevent IRA membership of the IRB, that is if IRA men were considered soldiers. However, the overall organisation was heavily skewed against IRA areas, making the question practically irrelevant. What it did ensure was that the National Army would be involved in any IRB contact with the IRA.[9] Civilian Clubs remained attached to parishes. Twenty-seven Divisions based on a combination of fifteen Counties, Britain and eight National Army formations elected members annually to the Supreme Council, which was to consist of twenty-eight members, including four co-opted, an increase of eight over the 1922 Constitution, and thirteen over the 1917 one.[10] The Executive remained seven strong as specified in 1922.[11] A 'General Election' could be held when nineteen or more members of the Supreme Council or fifty per cent of Divisional Centres voted for one.[12] Attention was paid to the geographical location of Divisional representatives on the Council: they 'must be permanently resident in the Division they represent'.[13] This requirement was aimed at focussing these members on their areas. The power and influence of Divisional members within the organisation was reduced by this requirement, and further by another stipulation that 'No Member will represent any Division for more than two consecutive years.'[14] The effect of these rearrangements was – as with the 1922 version – to make the organisation top-heavy, unwieldy, weak and ineffective, designed no doubt to reassure the government that the reorganisation was not a threat.

Two more openings to Republicans were included:

> In important public issues involving marked disagreement among members of the Organisation the Supreme Council before ordering a particular line of action, shall submit their proposals for consideration to each Divisional Board, and shall be guided in their decision by the advice of the majority of the Boards ... the S.C. will appoint small Vigilance Commissions or Committees to watch the progress of the various branches of Governmental, National, Economic, and Social Life of the Nation, in order to ensure that they are kept in line with the Policy of the I.R.B.[15]

1923 Constitution 305

The constitution was completed at the end of June 1923 and was given to Mulcahy for approval. He made some alterations. The pro-Treaty predilections of the majority of the members of the 1921 Supreme Council were recognised. Nearly every one of those involved in this reorganisation held a senior government post or position in the National Army.[16] Seán MacMahon, who had succeeded O'Duffy as Chief of Staff in 1922, now became President of the Supreme Council.[17]

The intimate involvement of several of the most senior National Army officers in the IRB could also be a threat to the very government they claimed to protect, and at the least could (and did) prove to be a source of suspicion within the National Army and the Cabinet. Ó Murthuile, MacMahon, Mulcahy and others involved did not seem to be aware of this and, having settled the new constitution, they waited to see if the IRA would make an approach about surrendering weapons through the IRB. But Barry's letter to the Supreme Council proved to be a solo effort. Aiken and the IRA did not approach the National Army, the Free State government, Ó Murthuile or the Supreme Council. The consequence was that the revived IRB was an entirely Free State affair and does not appear ever to have operated.

CHAPTER 30

Mutiny

As life runs on, the road grows strange
with faces new – and near the end
The milestones into headstones change,
'Neath every one a friend.[1]

James Russell Lowell, 'Sixty-eighth Birthday'

Simultaneously with Ó Murthuile's IRB reorganisation, unrest was growing among many of Collins' close associates in the National Army, particularly those who had been in the Squad. As early as the summer of 1922, Liam Tobin and Frank Thornton, both major generals, held a meeting of senior National Army officers to discuss their worries about the Free State. They had been particularly critical of Collins over the Treaty but had loyally followed his lead. After Collins' death they formed the 'IRA Organisation' in the National Army. This new society was composed almost entirely – if not entirely – of IRB members and was organised on the same lines. Its declared purpose was to ensure that the Free State was a stepping-stone to a republic. To this end they made contact with IRB members on the Republican side, some in Free State prisons.[2] They were upset about ex-British Army officers at senior levels in the National Army, and about the Free State government's contentment with the status quo. They claimed that the Free State IRB was counterfeit and had been set up to counteract and marginalise the IRA Organisation. Still, Tobin and his colleagues sought to be part of this IRB and only broke away because they were excluded.[3]

Tom Barry probably knew their concerns, hence his remark to Ó Murthuile about 'sinister reactionary elements'. On 15 May 1923 Michael Brennan, now a major general and O/C Limerick Command, sent a letter to Mulcahy stating

Mutiny 307

that he and others were worried by the prospect that the Free State was the end for which they had fought, not the means to that end.[4] This feeling was widespread amongst pro-Treaty IRA and IRB men in the National Army, as events were to show, and was exacerbated not only by the presence in the army of thousands of soldiers of all ranks without pre-1921 IRA experience, but also by personal and political divisions in the Free State Cabinet about the relationship of the army to the government.[5] On two occasions after the April 1923 Republican ceasefire that effectively ended the Civil War, Liam Tobin spoke to officers on a battalion commander's course at the Curragh, claiming that within a year ex-British Army officers would control the National Army and that all ex-IRA officers would be demobilised.[6]

On 25 June, Cosgrave and Mulcahy met with Tobin, Thornton and two colleagues. Tobin presented a statement that they had accepted the Treaty as a stepping-stone to a republic in the same spirit as Collins. They complained that GHQ Staff and Mulcahy were antipathetic to a republic and favoured men who did not have IRA experience:

[T]he present GHQ Staff since the Commander-in-Chief's death, their open and secret hostility to us, his officers, has convinced us that they have not the same outlook as he had. We require a definite 'yes or no' from the present Commander-in-Chief [meaning Mulcahy] if this be so.

Does the Commander-in-Chief understand the temper of the Old I.R.A. who are now in the National Army? He does not. Your Army is not a National Army. It is composed roughly of 40% of the Old I.R.A, 50% ex-Britishers and 10% ex-civilians. The majority of the civilians were and are, hostile to the National ideals. In the Army you have got men who were active British S[ecret] S[ervice] men previous to the Truce, and who never yet have ceased their activities.[7]

They also complained about the IRB reorganisation and threatened unspecified action:

[It is] a dishonest and corrupt effort to destroy any genuine effort to carry on a successful conclusion of Mick's ideals ... It is time this bluff ended. We intend to end it. Until satisfactory arrangements are come to, we will expose this treachery and take what steps we consider necessary to bring about an honest, cleaner, and genuine effort to secure the republic.[8]

308　　　　The Irish Republican Brotherhood, 1914–1924

This was mutinous, but Cosgrave did not react. 'One day there was a conference in Government Buildings about something involving Mulcahy, O'Higgins and myself,' said Ernest Blythe of this period. 'And when the business was over, this question of the IRB and the Army was mentioned, and we both said to Mulcahy that we'd stand for the dismissal from the Army of any officer whatsoever who was engaged in promoting the IRB. Mulcahy gave us no answer. We weren't sure that he was in it, we only thought that he was tolerating it.'[9]

From August 1923 to March 1924 meetings of the IRA organisation were held in Collins' old haunt, Vaughan's Hotel in Rutland Square. About two-thirds of the sixty-four battalion commanders in the army came at first but, as the government's and army leadership's opposition to the organisation and its activity became known, attendance declined.

With the end of the Civil War, the principal concern of the National Army's leaders was to develop an efficient, well-trained and disciplined force, responsive purely to the wishes of the government of the day. It had been obvious for some time that several senior officers with excellent IRA records were not suited to the discipline and manner of a conventional army, while several without any IRA experience were. The ensuing tensions were released when the Cabinet decided upon large reductions in the size of the army. The army was about 49,000 strong in June 1923 and with the end of fighting there was no longer a need for such size. In addition, the cost of this establishment was difficult to sustain. The reductions in numbers and in ranks were promulgated in February 1924 through GHQ Staff Memorandum No. 12, reducing the army to an overall strength of about 18,000. Nearly every member of the IRA was demoted or dismissed. The memorandum also showed that Mulcahy and MacMahon were not promoting IRB members in the army to the exclusion of others.[10]

The question of jobs sparked the IRA Organisation's abortive mutiny. On 6 March 1924 Tobin and Colonel Charles Dalton sent an ultimatum to the government on behalf of the IRA and the 'Old IRA', demanding the suspension of demobilisation and stating that the pro-Treaty IRA had only accepted the Free State as a step towards a republic.[11]

This ultimatum was rightly seen as mutinous. In fact, mutiny had already begun. In the previous week, deserters had absconded with weapons from several Army stations and there were several shooting incidents around the country. Kevin O'Higgins, Minister for Home Affairs and Acting President, insisted that the army must be made to accept the authority of the government and practically accused Richard Mulcahy of masterminding the formation of

Mutiny

309

the IRA Organisation. Mulcahy was sympathetic to the Old IRA men but was completely opposed to mutiny. Various steps were now taken. The Cabinet ordered the arrest of Tobin and Dalton on a charge of mutiny. Eoin O'Duffy, who had stood down as Chief of Staff to become Chief of Police, was appointed General Officer Commanding of the National Army. O'Duffy had taken no part in Ó Murthuile's bid to restart the Brotherhood.

On 18 March, Tobin and Dalton with about forty armed followers were surrounded by army units at Devlin's pub, Parnell Street, Dublin.[12] Gearóid O'Sullivan, having consulted Mulcahy, had ordered this action. Joseph McGrath, Minister for Industry and Commerce and sympathetic to the IRA organisation, successfully intervened to prevent shooting.[13] Tobin and Dalton managed to escape across rooftops and the mutiny was over. There was an IRA follow-up on 21 March when Cork IRA men wearing National Army uniforms attacked a party of British soldiers at Cobh Treaty port, killing one, wounding eighteen others and five civilians in what appears to have been an echo of McKelvey's 1922 Four Courts hope to prompt a British military response that might unify the Free State with Republicans and discredit it as a defender of national honour. The Free State government quickly apologised and paid compensation.[14]

McGrath resigned from the government in April 1924 in protest at the way Mulcahy had as he saw it precipitated the crisis by neglecting Old IRA men. He considered that if their grievances had been dealt with earlier there would never have been a mutiny.[15] O'Higgins and the Cabinet felt that IRB influence in the army had been, in part, responsible for the mutiny, and the government sacked MacMahon and Ó Murthuile.[16] Mulcahy resigned as Minister for Defence.

An inquiry by the Dáil into the mutiny drove home to those involved in the IRB reorganisation the overwhelming dangers of military secret societies within the State. Seán Ó Murthuile and seven other Supreme Council members met in July 1924 to wind up their reorganised Free State IRB.[17] 'You see,' said Seán MacEoin, who was one of them:

> in the new Army Act the government made it conditional of a commission that you would swear, not an oath of allegiance to the state, but that you were not a member of a secret society. Now we had to make up our minds what we were to do. We were going to do this or that. And we decided that we would wind it up. And therefore when the 1924 commissions were issued we could say then truly and swear faithfully that we were not then members of a secret society.[18]

310   The Irish Republican Brotherhood, 1914–1924

At a meeting in the Gate House at Phoenix Park, Eoin O'Duffy handed over the IRB funds to Martin Conlon with Seán MacEoin present.[19] On 5 August 1924 Conlon arranged for the funds, amounting to £3,809–14–0 (about £200,000 in 2024), to be put into trust with two other members of the Supreme Council, Eoin O'Duffy and Seán Ó Murthuile, as co-trustees. Of this, Ó Murthuile was given £2,059–14–0 (about £105,000) to pay outstanding debts and to write a history of the IRB. The remaining £1,750 (about £90,000) was placed in a deposit account at the Bank of Ireland.[20]

On the Republican side, attempts were also made to terminate the IRB. The IRA Executive decided on 27 and 28 January 1924 to instruct P.A. ('Pa') Murray, their Adjutant General, to summon all IRB County Centres who were still in the IRA to a meeting in Dublin and to order them to disband the IRB. Eleven Centres were contacted on 2 November 1924, but only six came. They were divided in their opinions, three favouring disbandment and three preferring reorganisation. However, they agreed unanimously to obey the IRA Executive and to instruct their local Centres accordingly. Pa Murray undertook to notify members in Scotland and England, and to inform the Clan in the United States. And he reported the conclusion to Frank Aiken.[21]

The ending of the Brotherhood in 1924 shows how firmly it had become part of the IRA, retaining this attachment in the IRA and also in the National Army even during the Civil War. It had lost any real separate identity. The death of Michael Collins ended any question of it becoming autonomous once again (not, it should be said, that Collins wanted it to be). The respect on all sides that Collins enjoyed personally had given the IRB status. It was a door to him. Without Collins it was fragmented, with its enthusiasts in search of a role. All reorganisation efforts after Collins' death were initiated and controlled by IRA and National Army leaders. On the Free State side this meant that it was directed in conformity with government objectives. On the Republican side, the IRA Executive supplanted the Supreme Council and controlled IRB organisation in Republican areas. Having created and organised the IRA and having been the republican watchdog of the IRA and the Dáil, by 1923 the IRB, to whatever extent it still existed, had become the servant and not the master of the military forces in the State.[22]

CHAPTER 31

'That's That'

No matter what issue it raises, the demand of the people is for Freedom, that is why I crossed out the paragraph in your letter where you say that if a majority of the people decided against us we would submit. I don't of course believe that they would so decide but our convictions are not conditional. They are absolute.[1]

Séamus O'Doherty to Patrick McCartan, 11 June 1917

IRB strategy was classic terrorist/guerrilla action, set out decades later by Frantz Fanon, the Martinican philosopher of class and political struggle:[2] to attack government forces and officers, prompting a reaction that would swing opinion in favour of rebellion, and then attacking again to generate a cycle of further reaction and greater popular support. The occupation of Dublin buildings in 1916, then sitting in them and waiting to be fired upon, followed by the government response of executing the Rising leaders, was a classic fulfilment (although unsuccessful) of this strategy. The attacks on the RIC in 1918–21 generated continuing (and at times excessive) government response. In 1922 the IRA occupation of the Four Courts was an attempted replay of the strategy.

What the IRB and the IRA were fighting for in 1918–21 is easy enough to understand: an independent republic of all thirty-two Irish counties. This descended to fighting against the British administration and further descended in 1922–23 to fighting against an Irish government created by Britain, armed and equipped by Britain, uniformed by Britain, manned in part by thousands of disbanded British Army soldiers who transferred to its National Army, with a constitution effectively drafted by Britain, and held by Republicans to be a government on behalf of Britain. Fronting for Britain was the Republican

312   The Irish Republican Brotherhood, 1914–1924

accusation against Michael Collins and, eighty-five years later, against Martin McGuinness.

Britain was fighting for several reasons: because its administration, constabulary and police were being physically attacked; because the new Northern Ireland created in December 1920 needed defending; because the British objective was Home Rule so that Irish governments could administer Ireland and themselves deal with Irish political unrest, freeing Britain of the cost and worry. Britain was also fighting against lawlessness. Once Northern Ireland and partition became a fact of life on 5 May 1921, the British were happy to stop fighting just over nine weeks later: Britain's political settlement had been imposed.

The 1918–21 conflict has been presented as Britain once again trying to suppress Ireland, and it was this view that motivated many of the men and women in Sinn Féin, the Dáil, the IRA and especially the IRB. But this was simply not the case. Britain wanted an orderly departure from Ireland, not a repressive power – as the British cross-party determination to impose Dominion Home Rule in 1921 demonstrated. A dawning realisation of this on the part of Michael Collins helps to explain his actions in 1920–22.

A republic was a political, not a military matter. Wars end with political settlements, and a republic outside the Empire was simply not negotiable. Realists understood this reasonably quickly and within eighteen months of Soloheadbeg (taken as the start of the War of Independence in 1919) Collins was secretly discussing with Alfred Cope and various go-betweens ways of ending the fighting and securing the maximum amount of independence that Britain would allow. He found he was pushing at an open door: somewhat circumscribed Dominion status was Britain's proposal, adopted by Lloyd George and his government coalition in 1921 and imposed in 1922.[3]

The 1921 Anglo-Irish Treaty was approved by the Conservative and Unionist Party, who formed the majority of the coalition government headed by Lloyd George, and by parliament.[4] Its acceptance by them was a definite statement of British disengagement from Ireland. But Sinn Féin did not present itself as coherent, and its Dáil representatives did not reflect the desire for peace found in the population at large.[5] In Peadar O'Donnell's view, shared by most Republicans:

> The way in which the [1920–21] war was conducted could only have led up to the Truce because it had been conducted not as a revolutionary

'That's That' 313

movement but as a movement that wouldn't upset any of the 'structures' that had been set up by the British ... But you can't fight as a revolutionary movement and hold on to all the structures. After all, Ireland's middle-class was a trading middle-class and all they really wanted was that all the power of patronage that had been in the Castle should be transferred to a government in Ireland. They never really were for anything more than Home Rule.[6]

The United Kingdom of Great Britain and Northern Ireland could not afford to have a lawless country on its borders from which criminality would inevitably spread, so Lloyd George's task was to find a path to Irish responsibility and then help to establish it. He was a psychologist of nations. He genuinely did not look through English eyes. He conceded that Scotland, Ireland and Wales were all distinct. He understood that Ireland was not the next parish but was the next country and that Catholic Ireland wanted to run its own affairs and was not concerned about much else. He made the Treaty as friendly to Ireland as far as was possible in British politics. He played on instruments of his own creation: thuggery, flattery, backchannels, partition, and an offer of substantial (though not complete) independence. He knew he had the resources to win a fight, and that the IRA did not. He saw himself as the principal Celt, addressing the Irish negotiators as 'We Celts', implying a common anti-English bond that he genuinely felt. He had been a leader of the Cymru Fydd ('Wales to Come'/'Wales to Be') Home Rule Party and, as he himself said about the Irish rebels, 'My sympathy with their cause was known,'[7] describing the conflict with Ireland as 'this unhappy feud that Britain has inherited from a foreign foe, who, having conquered England first, then proceeded to annex Ireland.'[8] His decision to negotiate a truce and then a settlement in 1921 caught nearly everyone by surprise, not least because it was believed that the IRA was almost finished. When his Cabinet colleagues made clear they would not shake hands with the Irish peace delegation in 1921, Lloyd George greeted each delegate at the door to the Cabinet Room at No. 10, shaking hands with each one.

Rebels only win when both sides can lose. In Ireland, only the IRA could lose, and Collins knew this. He accepted Lloyd George's overtures. Lloyd George advanced towards peace in 1920, pulling the rug away at the last minute, demonstrating that he would not have peace at any price and was prepared to keep the fight going. It was a classic negotiating tactic. It was also

314   The Irish Republican Brotherhood, 1914–1924

necessary to prove to his Conservative and Unionist Party coalition partners – and to the IRA – that he had the necessary determination to defeat the IRA. By July 1921 he had exhausted the IRA (and many of his own forces – but he had replacements), enabling him from a position of greater strength to enforce his terms for the British withdrawal that had been enacted government policy since 1914.

He realised that the only real hope of success was to persuade the hard men in the IRA and IRB, not Sinn Féin, that they could have nearly everything they wanted. Hard men in rebellions and revolutions are usually prepared to compromise; sentimentalists are not. Lloyd George sent Alfred Cope to Dublin to find and sound out Collins and other senior nationalist figures, effectively putting a *cordon sanitaire* around them protecting them from arrest: when de Valera was arrested in 1921, Lloyd George ordered his immediate release – the military wanted to charge de Valera with treason.[9] Cope on his own initiative released Arthur Griffith and Eoin MacNeill from prison while fighting was still going on, and Lloyd George backed him. Earlier than anyone else Collins grasped that every measure of practical independence except a republic was on offer. Lloyd George needed figureheads and *the* hard man, Collins, signed up to a settlement to achieve an orderly handover that would ensure the rule of law, thus protecting Northern Ireland and British imperial interests. He understood that a necessary prelude to successful negotiation was that the IRA should feel that they had forced a draw, that they had won something: 'I regarded the thing as finished and that we had won,' said Patrick Mullaney, 'and that we had beaten the British. That was the general opinion.'[10] Lloyd George allowed a formal truce between the IRA and his military, altogether de facto recognition of the IRA as an army; not attempting to disarm the IRA; and he treated de Valera with respect when they met in London in August 1921.

Lloyd George quickly realised that de Valera was a sentimentalist who could not be pinned down except, perhaps, on a cross, and that would have made any settlement one of long-term antagonism. De Valera embodied the great issues of Irish romantic history. He felt he was the holder of great memories that he should protect and couldn't think of anything else to do apart from making 'his' Ireland. Altogether, this made it too difficult to reach agreement with him, and there was no guarantee that 'his' Ireland was what Irish people wanted. It then became a process of elimination to identify an Irish leader who could and would make a settlement work. Griffith was not an obstacle to

'That's That'   315

agreement, was not interested in leadership, had no sway with the IRB or IRA, and therefore did not need to be 'won'. In any case he was overshadowed by de Valera and Collins. So Lloyd George concentrated on persuading Collins to accept the British settlement, and also to take power, correctly understanding that the qualities that made him such an effective opponent would make him an effective administrator of the new State.[11]

Public opinion in Britain might have been sickened by the fighting and sympathetic to Irish nationalism, but probably would have supported Lloyd George in refusing a republic, especially when Dominion status was the alternative, was reasonable and was seen as meaning effective independence, as Canada, Australia, New Zealand and South Africa were rapidly demonstrating.[12] Irish opinion was most anxious for peace and, as events demonstrated, was massively behind the Dominion settlement, and probably would have supported *any* settlement. Indeed, everyone except a majority of the IRB and IRA wanted the Dominion settlement as elections were to show. Fifty years later Ernest Blythe, who supported the settlement, observed that people 'didn't want any more fighting. That was the broad basis of it. And they would have felt we were a terrible lot of bunglers and idiots, do you see, [if we] had brought this war on again.'[13] Robert Barton went further, saying to me in 1973, 'I often wonder whether, seeing how the Empire's broken up, we weren't very wrong sacrificing all those lives.'[14]

A republic was the objective of the IRB and IRA and few others. It was a late-eighteenth-century possibility, but after the establishment of the British Empire, which was seaborne, Britain's own security, let alone the security of its Atlantic, African and Gibraltar sea lanes, could not allow Ireland to be fully independent: the 1921 Treaty kept British naval bases in Ireland. These bases were given up by Neville Chamberlain in 1938 to appease Irish feeling as expressed by de Valera in the hope of winning Irish goodwill. It was a miscalculation. In the Second World War a neutral Ireland – a demonstration of the reality of Dominion independence – was careful to prevent German exploitation but did not allow Britain to use its ports. The acceptance of a republic within the Commonwealth, brought on by Indian independence in 1947, made the declaration of the Republic of Ireland in 1949 irrelevant to Britain.[15]

To the present day, geography, that crucial underlying factor in history, inexorably connects Ireland and Britain. Irish and United Kingdom citizens can vote in each country; British common law remains the basis of Irish law; passports are not required for travel between the United Kingdom and Ireland; extra-territorial defence and maritime policing are conducted jointly; the United Kingdom and Irish governments share functions and interests in Northern Ireland; the two countries share a common border area outside the European Union's Schengen Area; somersaults are performed to prevent an obvious border between the United Kingdom and Ireland.

Revolutionaries rarely find that their high vision is achieved. They may come to do good but many stay to do well. If there is success it is followed by exhaustion, allowing the inevitable placemen to secure places, which was very much the accusation levelled at the Free State and its supporters, as Peadar O'Donnell suggested.

The 1922–23 Civil War, not the Rising, was the true birth of modern Ireland. Accounts of the 1916–23 period are coloured by Civil War battlelines. The victors and the losers were both anxious to claim democratic approval for their actions, on the one hand that the 1922 general election had provided massive popular support – about 3.5 to 1 – for the new twenty-six-county Free State,[16] on the other that the 1918 general election had endorsed a republic that the Dáil had no right to disestablish and that the Free State usurped. The democratic point that the electorate had changed its mind since 1918 and could change again did not carry weight: neither side was democratic in 1922–23 or earlier.

The Free State – it should be stressed only after Collins' death[17] – proceeded to execute captured and imprisoned Republicans in order to terrorise the terrorists, as they deemed Republicans to be. Similarly, the IRA targeted elected members of the Dáil who supported the Free State, murdering one and gravely wounding another. They were unapologetic, as was Ernest Blythe fifty years later:

> We decided that an act of terror, if you like, was necessary … What I thought we should do was to take six or eight of the leading Four Courts men, put them before a military committee the next day, and shoot them the day after. But when I went into the Cabinet meeting which was already in progress, I found that it was being proposed that four named persons should be shot the following morning.[18]

Unreconciled Republicans – those who continued in the IRA from 1922 – as with the 1916 rebels, did not claim or seek democratic approval. Theirs

'That's That' 317

was an ideological separation from most Irish people expressing an almost nihilist wish to undermine the operation of Ireland. Despite the idealism and bravery within the IRA, it had become a killing organisation; it did not have civil thinking: the IRB had more. The IRA sought to present voters, through violence and intimidation, with a *fait accompli* Republic that, once established, might employ democratic procedures only as long as it remained a republic in the eyes of the IRA. The difficulty that the IRB and the IRA faced was that democracies like peace and quiet.

The problem with ideology is that it allows for little, if any, deviation. A consequence is that ideologues easily break up with one another. The IRB, an ideological organisation, while grappling with reality, especially under Michael Collins' leadership from 1917 to 1922, could not accommodate ideological amendment. The proposal that the new 1922 State was a step towards a republic simply did not persuade ideological republicans. Collins in the last months of his life fought to make IRB members steer a rational course, only to find that without ideology the IRB fell apart. With Collins' death the IRB ended in failure, never achieving its sole objective: 'a free and independent Republican Government in Ireland'.

There were rumours of the IRB continuing within the Free State with Seán McGarry as president, together with Alec McCabe, Diarmuid O'Hegarty and Seán MacEoin on a Supreme Council.[19] John de Courcy Ireland, an Anglo-Irish Labour Party activist teaching in England, said that he was invited in about 1936 to join the Brotherhood, but refused.[20] In New York, Patrick O'Hanlon had been in a Dublin Circle before emigrating:

> In 1936 I was employed in a public garage here in New York where very often an American born man who was Chief Engineer for the New York City Dept of Highways dropped in. His salutation was always the same: 'UP THE REBELS'. On his way home one evening he stopped in to see me and said, 'Patrick, my boy, you are now relieved from your Oath of Allegiance to the Irish Republican Brotherhood, and the organization is now disbanded'. I asked him how he knew that, and he smiled and replied, 'Over here we know everything'. That was the last I ever heard about the IRB.[21]

Some Free State IRB members found an unofficial home (and effective pension) in the New Ireland Assurance Company (est. 1918). Similarly, some

318   The Irish Republican Brotherhood, 1914–1924

Republican members (including Army Mutiny members) came together in the
Irish Hospital Sweepstakes (est. 1930).

In 1960 Seán MacEoin, ever secretive, took part in the IRB's final act:

> When the last trustee [Martin Conlon] was very ill, the other two
> having died, and he was the sole owner of these monies [the remaining
> IRB funds banked in 1924], he got up off his sickbed and sent for me
> and we went into Michael Noyk's, solicitor, and a deed was drawn up
> transferring the money to a certain cause and signed by the two of us and
> got a receipt for it and that's that.[22]

APPENDIX I

Interviews

'I remember Liam Lynch said to me before he left here when he was killed, "I must write something about the I.R.B."'[1]

Moss Twomey, IRA Chief of Staff 1927–36, 11 December 1972

In the early 1970s I met a large number of outstanding men and women from all over the country. Most of the men had been members of the IRB. I met some more in 1979 and 1980 when I was associate producer of the BBC/RTÉ series, *Ireland: A Television History*, written and presented by Robert Kee and produced by Jeremy Isaacs. One person I regretted not meeting was Richard Mulcahy, who died on 16 December 1971. Mulcahy had spent years collecting documents, writing commentaries, essays and memoirs, and interviewing colleagues, all of which material was invaluable. His effort was, in part, a counter to Éamon de Valera's similar activity, a political opponent since 1922. A particularly interesting element in Mulcahy's collection was that he did not know much about the machinations of the IRB, although he was a member, and was always keen to find out more while presenting his own memory that there had been no effective difference between the Brotherhood and the IRA in the 1916–21 period.[2] He was anxious to show that the IRB had never been a threat to the Dáil or Free State governments. Mulcahy's collection is now in the Archives Department in UCD, where it sits beside de Valera's collection.

Joseph O'Doherty, from Derry, was on the post-1916 Volunteer Executive and the pre-1916 IRB and had sold copies in Ireland of *Bande Mataram*, a Bengali English-language anti-imperialist newspaper in the early years of the century: a reminder of the international background to Ireland's and the IRB's experience. Joe emphasised that the IRA Executive, of which he was a member,

320 The Irish Republican Brotherhood, 1914–1924

exercised real authority over the IRA in competition with the Dáil government. This is borne out by several witnesses. In 1922, during the debates about whether or not to accept the Treaty, Joe asked rhetorically, 'Who voted for the Rising?' as he opposed the Treaty and straightforwardly dismissed democratic arguments for accepting it.

I corresponded with Kathleen McKenna Napoli, who had been a secretary with the Irish delegation in London during the 1921 Treaty negotiations and remembered Michael Collins' boisterous relations with his colleagues (having pillow fights!), and Arthur Griffith's calmness. She gave me her (then unpublished) memoirs to read.

Liam Deasy, a brave and generous man, introduced me to men who had resisted interviews. Deasy was on the 1922 IRA Executive and succeeded Lynch as O/C First Southern Division. He had been captured during the Civil War by the Free State and sentenced to death. Once sentenced, expecting to be executed, he wrote an open letter urging Republicans to accept that they had lost and should end the fighting. His jailers reprieved him because of his letter. In 1924 the IRA court-martialled him and expelled him. Unhappily, for the rest of his life the most unjust whisper was that he had caved in to the Free State. At the end of his life he published his memoir, *Towards Ireland Free* (1973), and was then subjected to a nasty attack by Tom Barry (*Reality of the Anglo-Irish War, 1920–21, in West Cork: Refutations, Corrections and Comments on Liam Deasy's 'Towards Ireland Free'* (1974)), who wanted to show that his part in the war had not been recognised by Deasy.[3] In my judgement, Deasy's quality, modesty and honesty far outclassed Barry's ego. Dan Bryan had a career in military intelligence and was sent to interview Deasy when he was captured. He described him as 'a man of great moral strength'.[4]

Seán Fitzpatrick told me where the records of the Second Southern Division from the 1921 Truce to the run-up to the 1922 Civil War had been hidden (in a field gatepost in Tipperary) in 1923, which I recovered while a farmer (I presume: I could see his cap) dodged behind the hedge as I attacked gateposts with a pick. The records were in rolls one above another with a broken revolver pushed into the centre of the top roll. Their contents were mundane: correspondence between divisions, battalions and brigades; records of Second Southern Division strength and of training camps. Very useful if captured during the Civil War but shedding no new light on the 1922–24 period. There was no mention of the IRB. I gave the papers to the UCD Archives Department – and kept the revolver.

Interviews

I found IRB papers – membership rolls; constitutions; Supreme Council correspondence – aside from the IRA papers I found in Tipperary. I knew who had been members of the Supreme Council in 1921–22 and thought to see if any of them were still alive. I consulted a 1936 Irish telephone directory – one volume about an inch thick covered all twenty-six counties – and therein found the address of Martin Conlon in north Dublin. I went to the house and was met at the door by a lady who explained that Conlon had died in 1966 without a family and in his will had left the house to her: she had been his housekeeper. She had a tea chest full of his papers and gave them to me for £10 (which was a lot of money then – about £125 in 2024). They included IRB constitutions, membership and Circle lists, and correspondence. I also gave these papers to the UCD Archives Department.

Micky Joe Costello helped identify manuscripts in Mulcahy's papers. When I had access, they were stored in the upper floor of Earlsfort Terrace, and I brought Micky Joe up there (I very much doubt this would have been allowed if known). He recognised the handwriting of several otherwise anonymous documents, and at my request he wrote on them the names of those responsible. He was slightly taken aback to see transcripts of conversations between IRA prisoners that he had bugged during the Civil War. Aged nineteen in 1922, Micky Joe had been made a colonel in the National Army by Michael Collins after speaking to Patrick Mulcahy, commanding the Third Southern Division:

'What's wrong here,' [Collins] said, 'is that you have no Intelligence Officer.'

I agreed.

'I'll go round.'

He went around and I was told afterwards he said, 'Have I seen every officer now that you have?'

'Well, you have, except one. He's a Second Lieutenant in the Quartermaster's Stores. To tell you the truth he was a bloody nuisance, one of the Fianna boys. Two, three four o'clock in the morning if he had a bit of information he knocked you up to give it to you even though it might be time enough mid-day or later.'

He came back to me and said, 'You have an I.O. Michael Costello. I've appointed him now.'

I said 'Right', and Micky Joe was appointed like that by Michael Collins.[5]

322   The Irish Republican Brotherhood, 1914–1924

This anecdote said a lot about Collins' attention to detail and disregard for hierarchies. It also said a lot about Costello, who was recognised by his seniors as very able, being promoted aged twenty to be the National Army's Director of Intelligence in October 1923.

Larry de Lacey read Frantz Fanon in French sitting in his chair (all the chairs were covered in newspapers) on an earthen floor in his cottage in Wicklow, telling me about the IRB, Trotsky, gunrunning and nationalist publications before the Rising. He was a silent reminder that people of his generation and background should not have been and should not be underestimated.

Peadar O'Donnell was an old family friend (we spent some summers at his Donegal house), who was wistful about the Monaghan and Limerick Soviets that briefly existed in 1919 and was energised by discussion of the Civil War. 'The Four Courts,' he declared, 'should have been the anvil against which they would have smashed the Free State.'[6]

Todd Andrews, another old friend, was annoyed by my father (I think because he remained an unreconciled Republican while Todd had followed de Valera into the Free State). Todd was writing his memoirs at the time so a great deal of the period was once again fresh in his mind.

Emmet Dalton had joined the Royal Dublin Fusiliers in 1915 as he turned seventeen. Eighteen months later he won the MC as a lieutenant during the First Battle of the Somme, leaving the army in 1919 as a captain. He had been with Collins at his death. He took me through the engagement, drawing diagrams of where he had been during it, where Collins had been, and where other Free State soldiers had been during the brief firefight. Many people thought that Dalton had taken advantage of the affray to kill Collins on behalf of the British Secret Service; that Dalton all along had been a British agent. This was grossly wrong but, like Deasy, Dalton had to live with the whispers.

Robert Barton had been at Christ Church, Oxford (my college too), and told me about playing cricket as a boy with Charles Stewart Parnell and having tea with Gladstone in No. 10, and then being in No. 10 himself during the Treaty negotiations and first encountering Churchill. There was a screen around the door of the room where the negotiating teams met, and behind the screen a table with drinks. The first Barton heard of Churchill was the door opening and closing, a pause, and then a 'pop' as Churchill opened a bottle of champagne and then came around the screen with a glass in his hand. Barton tried to breach the walls of the Bureau of Military History on my behalf, but without success. He had not been in the IRB.

Interviews

323

Ernest Blythe, a pre-1916 IRB organiser and a Cabinet minister in the Free State government that determined on reprisal executions of captured Republicans during the Civil War, was unapologetic. His language was robust, giving a dramatic sense of the ruthlessness within the IRB and then the Free State administration. After the executions began in December 1922 a month later 'it was only a matter of hunting them down'.[7]

Emmet Clarke, son of Tom, a general practitioner in Blundellsands, Liverpool, where I visited him, gave me his mother's memoirs to read, subsequently published (with excisions) as *Kathleen Clarke: Revolutionary Woman* (1991). She was sometimes the sole witness of key moments pre- and post-1916, and was responsible for the promotion of Michael Collins, giving him her husband's list of IRB members and his contacts in the United States, which gave Collins a big part of his web of influence and intelligence. Kathleen kept her children away from the IRA and Irish politics but Emmet had clear memories of his mother's experiences that she told him. He was never in the IRB. Emmet's son and Kathleen's grandson, Thomas, went up to Sidney Sussex College, Cambridge in 1976.

Vinnie Byrne was twenty years old three days after Bloody Sunday. He was an original member of Collins' Squad and recalled its formation in 1919:

> Collins was there … It was explained to us what we were called for (there were eight of us there that night) and was there any objection – would our conscience allow us to shoot men. Some men would shoot in an ambush but it's different if a man walks up knowing deliberately he's going to take the life of another individual. But we said we had no objections; it was all in the cause … Barton was a well-known policeman and detective here in Dublin and he was the sweetest thing that ever walked on two feet, you know he'd take the birds off the trees, information off everybody … Collins sent word that Barton had to be got at all costs … 'There he is across the road!' We followed him up Grafton Street and every window he'd come to he'd look in the window where there'd be a mirror. Now we thought he was watching us. But that's a policeman's duty, walk four yards, stop, look in the mirror, turn round and look back … As he was stepping off the footpath … two or three shots flying out and he fell on his knee, he turned around and pulled his gun out of his pocket and he said, 'What did I do to deserve this?' Dead.[8]

324   The Irish Republican Brotherhood, 1914–1924

Murder always darkened nationalist romanticism.

Alec McCabe, on the Supreme Council of the IRB in 1915–16, was a Collins loyalist who went on to play a central part in the executions of Republicans during the 1922–23 Civil War. In 1932 the outgoing Cumann na nGaedheal government sensibly destroyed all records of Civil War executions. They were a scar on the start of modern Ireland.

Éamon de Valera, President of Ireland, in his nineties at Áras an Uachtaráin, the erstwhile Viceregal Lodge in Phoenix Park, recalled hearing news of the Treaty while he was in Limerick and then driving to Dublin on 'slushy roads' – 'a difficult, tiring drive' – to hear more. Charmingly, he said to me about his age, 'I never expected to be here.' He wore a Fáinne Airgid on his lapel, indicating a basic – not a fluent – ability in Irish. I had about half an hour with him, but my questions about the IRB clearly upset him and he kneed a button beneath his desk to summon a military aide who came in to say his next appointment was waiting. So I exited, pursued by relief.

List of interviewees

Frank Aiken, Dublin, 7 November 1972

C.S. ('Todd') Andrews, Dublin, 8, 23 March 1972; 3 November 1972

Leslie Mary Barry, 15 December 1972

Robert Barton, Annamoe, 26 November 1971; 3 September 1973

Florence ('Flor') Begley, Bandon, 2 March 1973

Ernest Blythe, Dublin, 4, 13 December 1971; 10 August 1973

Myles Breen, Ferns, 13 December 1972

Michael Brennan, Killiney, 18 December 1972

W.J. ('Whit') Brennan-Whitmore, Dublin, 2 November 1972

Charles Browne, Cork, 3 March 1973

Dan Bryan, Dublin, 12 December 1972; 1 March 1974; 15, 16 January 1975;
     31 May 1979

Ben Byrne, Dublin, 30 November 1971

Vinnie Byrne, Dublin, 19 April 1979

Seán Clancy, Dublin, 30 May 1979

Emmet Clarke, Liverpool, 30 January 1973

Joe Clarke, Dublin, 18 March 1973

Patrick Cloonan, Craughwell, 9 March 1974

Neilus Connolly, Skibbereen, 2 March 1973

Interviews

Madge Comer, Killarney, 23 September 1973

John A. Costello, Dublin, 25 September 1973

Michael J. ('Micky Joe') Costello, Dublin, 19 August 1973

Michael ('Micky') Crowley, Sligo, 26 February 1973

Emmet Dalton, Dublin, 7 March 1973

Frank Daly, Dublin, 14 December 1971

Patrick Daly, Dublin, 15 March 1973

Liam Deasy, Dublin, 12 August 1973

Eamonn de Barra, Dublin, 7 November 1972

Laurence ('Larry') de Lacy, Ballinapierce, 1 July 1972; 10 August 1972

Éamon de Valera, Dublin, 8 November 1972

Dan ('Sandow') Donovan, Mallow, 17 March 1972

Jim Donovan, Dalkey, 16 January 1973

Seán Dowling, Dublin, 31 October 1972

Thomas P. Doyle, Athenry, 9 March 1974

Martin Dunbar, Gorey, 19 December 1972

Seán Dunne, Dublin, 1 November 1972

Padraic Fahy, Laban, 8 March 1974

John Fanning, Fermoy, 28 February 1973

Michael Fitzpatrick, Tipperary, 23 November 1971

Seán Fitzpatrick, Dublin, 28 October 1971; 18 November 1971

Matt Flood, Fermoy, 28 February 1973

J.J. Garrett, Malahide, 12 December 1972

Peadar Glynn, Dublin, 18 February 1973

Liam Gogan, Dublin, 8 November 1972

Richard P. Gogan, Dublin, 7 November 1972

Michael Hayes, Dublin, 22 February 1973

Leo Henderson, Dublin, 28 October 1971

William 'Liam' Conor Hogan, Dublin, 10 November 1972

Sighle Humphreys, Dublin, 8 November 1972; 1 June 1979

Samuel Irwin, Dublin, 31 October 1972

Stephen Jordan, Athenry, 1 January 1973

Seán Kavanagh, Dublin, 10 May 1979

Henry Kelly, Dublin, 30 May 1979

Raphael P. Keyes, Bantry, 20 February 1973

Peter McArdle, Dublin, 6 November 1972

Seán MacBride, Dublin, 21 February 1973; 10 May 1979

326   The Irish Republican Brotherhood, 1914–1924

Alec McCabe, Dublin, 30 November 1971; 8 December 1971
James MacElligott, Blackrock, 3 September 1972
Tom McEllistrim, Ballymacelligott, 4 March 1973
Seán MacEntee, Dublin, 16 March 1973
Seán MacEoin, Dublin, 19 July 1972; 9 November 1972; 22 February 1973;
    8 March 1973
Patrick McGilligan, Dublin, 23 November 1973
W.J. McKenna, Athlone, 19 December 1972; 12, 14 February 1973
Thomas MacMahon, Dublin, 21 September 1975
Thomas Maguire, Cong, 27 February 1973
Thomas Malone (alias Seán Forde), Nenagh, 5 March 1973
Patrick Moylett, Dublin, 3 December 1971
Patrick Mulcahy, Dublin, 31 August 1973
Patrick Mullaney, Balla, 24 February 1973
Batt Murphy, Blackrock, 12 December 1972
Jim ('Spud') Murphy, Dundalk, 16 December 1972
David Neligan, Dublin, 20 February 1973
Harry Nicholls, Dublin, 8 December 1971
Seán Nunan, Dalkey, 18 March 1974; Dublin, 24 January 1980
Liam Ó Briain, Dublin, 7 December 1971
Leon Ó Broin, Dublin, 18 April 1973
Brendan O'Byrne, Dublin, 10 May 1979
Nora Connolly O'Brien, 12 November 1972
Patrick O'Brien, Liscarroll, 5 March 1973
Donal O'Cahill, Killarney, 4 March 1973
Christy O'Connell, Eyeries, 2 March 1973
Joseph O'Doherty, Dublin, 22, 25 March 1972; 18, 19 December 1972; 11,
    21 February 1973
Liam O'Doherty, Dublin, 7 March 1973
Peadar O'Donnell, Dublin, 31 October 1971
Liam O'Dwyer, Ardgroom, 2 March 1973
Michael O'Hara, Tobbercurry, 27 February 1973
Fergus F. O'Kelly, Dún Laoghaire, 30 October 1972
Phyllis O'Kelly, Donnybrook, 2 November 1972
William Oman, Dublin, 6 November 1972
John J. O'Reilly, Gorey, 13 December 1972
Tom O'Reilly, Dublin, 11 November 1972

Interviews

Patrick O'Sullivan, Aghada, 3 March 1973
Molly Reynolds, Dublin, 2 November 1972
Peter Reynolds, Watford, 26 January 1973
Harry Ridgeway, Dublin, 3 November 1972
Frank Robbins, Dublin, 28 October 1972
Patrick Ronan, Ferns, 14 December 1972
Jim Slattery, Sallins, 17 March 1973
Joseph Sweeney, Dublin, 10 December 1971; 2 September 1973; 1 June 1979; 24 January 1980
Albert Sylvester, Corsham, 11 July 1973
Thomas Taylor, Dublin, 5 November 1972
Maurice ('Moss') Twomey, Dublin, 11 December 1972
Richard Walsh, Dublin, 31 May 1979
Martin Walton, Castleknock, 17 December 1972
Patrick ('Pax') Whelan, Dungarvan, 18 January 1973
Seamus Woods, Dublin, 26 September 1973

APPENDIX II

IRB Constitution 1869–73[1]

Constitution of the Irish Republic

Preamble

Whereas it is necessary to the well being of the Irish Republic to enact and declare the constitution of the supreme and executive government thereof. It is hereby enacted and declared and promulgated by the aforesaid government, of the Irish Republic, in Council assembled, and by authority thereof, in the name of the people, that on this day, being the 18th day of August, anno domine [*sic*] 1869, and henceforth, the constitution of the Irish Republic, is and shall be as follows:

I That the government of the Irish Republic is and shall be composed of eleven members, to be designated the 'Supreme Council of the Irish Republic', and to be constituted as follows: seven of the said members to be duly elected by the seven electoral Divisions of the Irish Republic, and the remaining four shall be honorary members and shall be elected by the Irish provincial representatives, and the enactments of the government thus constituted shall be the laws of the Irish Republic, until the territory thereof shall have been recovered from the English enemy, and a permanent government established; and the manner of election of the Divisional representatives shall be as follows: the county or district centers shall be assembled in Convention, and shall elect a Committee of Five of their number, who under the superintendence of an officer deputed by the Executive, and under seal of an oath of secrecy shall elect the member of the Supreme Council for the Division whereunto they belong.

II That the Executive shall be composed of the President, the Secretary, and the Treasurer, the decision of any two of whom shall be binding on the executive of the Supreme Council, and that the President's duty shall be to direct the

IRB Constitution 1869–73

workings of the civil and military departments, subject to the ratification of the Supreme Council.

III That the authority of the Supreme Council shall be unquestioned by those who have sworn, or may hereafter swear allegiance to the Irish Republic, and the Supreme Council is hereby declared in fact, as well as in right, the sole government of the Irish Republic, and has authority to levy taxes, to negotiate loans, make war and peace, and do all other acts necessary to the protection of the Irish Republic, and that the Executive power shall never be entrusted to one man, but shall be vested in the President, Secretary, and Treasurer, of the Supreme Council, and that the members of the Supreme Council shall be bound to this constitution and to each other by an oath of fidelity and inviolable secrecy, and every act or attempted act to subvert the authority of the Supreme Council as aforesaid, shall be deemed treason, and punishable with death.

IV That the Supreme Council reserve to itself the right of treating with all friendly powers on all matters concerning the welfare of Ireland and the advancement of the Irish Republic, and that any interference, direct or indirect, with this provision shall be deemed treason.

V That every citizen or soldier of the Irish Republic and every member of the Supreme Council owes civil and military obedience to the executive of the Supreme Council, and the President thereof is in fact as well as by right, the President of the Irish Republic.

VI That each member of the Supreme Council is, and shall be finally elected, but may be removed by a two-thirds vote of the electoral body, and further, that any member of the Supreme Council may resign only with the consent of the Supreme Council, and the Supreme Council shall have the power to demand the resignation of any member, and should such member refuse to resign, the Supreme Council shall have authority by a two-thirds vote to remove him, and command a new election in his district; but that an honorary member can only be removed by a two-thirds vote of the Supreme Council.

VII That the military authority shall at all times be and remain subject to the civil government, and shall never be permitted to arrogate to itself the power of legislating, or restraining in any way the constitution, of the Irish Republic, as promulgated by the Supreme Council, and that all or any infraction of said constitution, shall be deemed treason.

VIII That the appointment, suspension and removal of all department officers shall be vested in the Executive, subject to the approval of the Supreme Council.

330   The Irish Republican Brotherhood, 1914–1924

IX That in the event of the Supreme Council being unavoidably reduced in number, the remaining member or members shall exercise the authority of the government until such time as the vacancies shall have been filled up, which shall be done as soon as possible.

X That in each of the seven electoral Divisions aforesaid, a Civil and Military Secretary shall be elected by the County District Centers thereof, and who shall act under the orders of the member of the Supreme Council of the Division. The duties of the Civil Secretary shall be to act in all respects as deputy of such member, and in the event of the removal of said member, by the act of the enemy: disability or death, said deputy shall assemble a Convention of the Division for the purpose of electing a new member, who shall be elected either permanently or temporarily, according to circumstances to be taken into account, and the said deputy shall exercise authority as member in the Division until after said election, but shall not be eligible on the Supreme Council, and further, it shall be his duty to attend to the civil correspondence of the Division.

XI That the duties of the Military Secretary shall be to execute all orders directed to him by the member of the Division in relation to procuring, distributing and safe keeping of arms and munitions, always under the supervision and subject to the Military Director of the Irish Republic.

XII That the citizens, soldiers, &c., of each county or district shall be ruled by a county or district center, who shall be elected by the centers of the county or district, and said county or district center shall be elected permanently, subject to removal by a two-thirds vote.

XIII That in England and Scotland the towns shall be grouped into Districts in the manner determined by the Divisional representative of the Supreme Council, and that a District Center be elected by each District, whose function, power and term of office shall be in all respects similar to those of a County Center, and the District Centers shall assemble in Convention and elect a Committee of Five as aforesaid, who shall proceed to elect a member of the supreme council for the Division. The voting in all cases to be by ballot, and the electors sworn to act according to their best judgment for the benefit of the Irish Republic, and to inviolable secrecy, regarding their proceedings in that behalf.

XIV That the County and District Centers shall on or before the last day in each month send in a report of the position and progress of affairs to the Civil Secretary of the Province or Division, who shall forthwith forward it to the

IRB Constitution 1869–73

Executive of the Supreme Council thro' the member of the Supreme Council for the Division.

XV That the oath of allegiance to the Irish Republic shall be tendered according to the orders of the Supreme Council by their agents or officers, and that no person shall be inducted into the army of the Irish Republic whose sobriety, truth, valour and obedience to authority cannot bear scrutiny, and that it shall be the duty of every soldier of the Irish Republic to state unreservedly his ability to obtain arms at once by purchase or otherwise, and that each soldier or citizen of the Irish Republic shall be bound to contribute according to his means for that special purpose, and also to the procuring of military material and instruction, as well as towards the expense of keeping up communications in each Province or Division to which he may belong, and for the purpose of maintaining the efficiency of the Irish Republic.

XVI That no member of the Supreme Council, or officer in the employment thereof shall be in receipt of salary from the funds of the Irish Republic.

XVII The Divisional officers shall have the power to make all bye-laws necessary for the local organisation, provided said bye-laws be not opposed to the spirit of the constitution of the Irish Republic.

XVIII That in each of the following large cities, to wit – Dublin, Cork, Limerick and Belfast, a Committee of Five be elected by the Centers, whose duty shall consist in directing local organisation, subject to the supervision and control of the County Center.

XIX That at each meeting of the Supreme Council the members thereof do hand in a summarised statement of receipts and expenditure of their respective Divisions.

XX That no citizen or soldier of the Irish Republic shall receive any information save what shall be necessary for the fulfilment of his duty.

XXI That there shall be no state religion, but that every citizen shall be equally free to worship God according to the dictates of his conscience, and perfect freedom of conscience and worship shall be guaranteed as a right, and not granted as a privilege.

XXII That whenever it is contemplated to make any alterations in the constitution of the Irish Republic, it shall be necessary to give one month's notice of the meeting of the Supreme Council at which such alteration is proposed to be effected, and it shall require a two-thirds vote of the Supreme Council to make the proposed change.

The Irish Republican Brotherhood, 1914–1924

Appendix

At recent sessions of the Council the following addenda was made to the constitution:

That the exercise of awarding capital punishment sought by certain local bodies is capable of being attended with danger to the peace and unity of the country, and is therefore reserved to the S.C.

That all losses which may result in the transmission of arms through negligence be traced to the department through the neglect of which the losses may have occurred, and that such department be responsible for the losses.

For the sake of uniformity and simplicity the following short form of oath is to be used by the organisation for the admission of members, viz – 'In the presence of God _____ do solemnly swear that I will do my utmost to establish the national independence of Ireland, and that I will bear true allegiance to the S.C. of the I.R., and the constitution thereof, and implicitly obey the orders of the officers of the S.C.I.R., so help me God'.

By order of the Supreme Council

APPENDIX III

1894 Rules and Regulations for the Government of the I.R.B.

Enlistment

1. No man to be admitted into the I.R.B. or recognised as a citizen or soldier of the I.R.B. until he has first taken the oath of allegiance to the Irish Republic. Previous to administering the oath of allegiance, the man's name must be proposed and seconded as a fit and proper person to become a member, at an ordinary meeting of the 'section' or 'circle', and if a majority of those present vote in favour of his admission, the oath can be administered.

2. No man known to be a member of the Ribbon, Hibernian or any other similar non-Republican or factional association, to be enlisted until he has first broken off his connection with such association.

3. No habitual drunkard, no man of bad character, dissipated habits, or dishonest occupation to be enlisted.

4. No man to be recognised a member of the I.R.B., unless enlisted by duly authorised officers of the I.R.B., said officers being the centre, B's, or C's of a circle or organisers commissioned by the Divisional executive.

Members' Duties

5. Every member of the I.R.B. in employment is required to pay a sum weekly towards the procuring of war material, and a further sum monthly to defray the expenses of the organisation; and also to contribute to the best of his ability to all extra levies or appeals which it may be necessary from time to time to make. Any member in employment

334　The Irish Republican Brotherhood, 1914–1924

who refuses or neglects his duty in this respect to be expelled the ranks of the I.R.B.

6. Every member is bound to obey the orders, instructions and commands of his superior officers in all matters relating to the I.R.B. Any member guilty of insubordination in refusing to obey the lawful commands of his superiors or speaking disrespectfully to or of them, to be expelled the ranks of the I.R.B.

7. Every member is bound to protect the secrets and guard the safety of the I.R.B. Any member speaking of his secrets to persons outside its ranks or neglecting to report a brother member so doing, to his knowledge, to be expelled the ranks of the I.R.B.

8. It is the duty of every member to defend the I.R.B. and the honour of it or its officers, whenever assailed by disunionists or factionists. Any member slandering or maligning a brother member, or allowing the same when possible to prevent it, or listening to slander or lies about the I.R.B. or any of its members, to be expelled.

9. It is the duty of every member to assist in preserving discipline in the ranks of the I.R.B. Any member creating any disturbance at any meeting of the I.R.B., any member attending such meeting under the influence of drink, or fighting with a member, is liable to expulsion from said meeting, and if the offence is repeated, to expulsion from the I.R.B.

10. Any member endeavouring to create distrust in the midst of brother members, to the detriment of the I.R.B., to be expelled.

Division of Circles, Election of Officers, etc.

11. Every Circle to be divided into Companies. A Company is to consist of not less than 30 or more than 80 men, and to be under the control of an officer, who shall be entitled to a B. A Circle is to consist of not less than 50 or more than 800 men, save and except in small country towns, where a section can be formed of any number over thirty men.

12. Every Company is to be divided into Sections. A Section is to consist of not more than ten men, including its officer, who shall be entitled to a C.

13. New Circles cannot be formed in any town where there are less than 400 men, save with the consent of the Civil Secretary for the Division.

14. Every Circle shall be governed by an Executive of three, namely Centre, Secretary and Treasurer. Any member is eligible for the post of Secretary or Treasurer if he possesses sufficient education. In circles numbering less

1894 Rules and Regulations 335

than fifty men the Executive to be elected by General Meeting; in Circles numbering over fifty and less than two hundred to be elected by the C's. In Circles numbering over two hundred only, the B's to be eligible for the position of Centre; in Circles less than two hundred, only the C's. In Circles numbering less than fifty men, any member to be eligible for the position of Centre if he possesses the necessary qualifications.

15. Each B is to be elected by the men of each Company, each C by the men of each section. The election of each B is to be superintended by the Centre, and the election of each C is to be superintended by the B of the Company to which the section belongs.

16. All elections to be by ballot and an absolute majority is necessary before an officer can be considered legally elected. In the event of there being more than two candidates and there not being a majority of the members present for anyone, the lowest candidate to be struck off and a fresh election to take place between the highest until an absolute majority be obtained for one of the remaining candidates. In the event of a tie between the two remaining candidates the chairman to have the casting vote.

Duties of Officers

17. The duties of a Centre are to receive all information and instructions for the Circle, to conduct all correspondence for the Circle, to settle all disputes between his B's and their men, to receive all reports from the Secretary and transmit them to the District Centre, to purchase and be responsible for the safe keeping of all war material for the Circle, to expel or otherwise punish all offenders in the Circle, to divide the Circle into Companies and superintend the election of a B for each Company, to issue orders for all general meetings of the members of the C's or B's of the circle, to appoint the Vigilance Committee for the Circle, to watch over the accounts of the Secretary and Treasurer, and to superintend the Circle generally.

18. The duties of the Secretary are to receive and keep an account of all the money from the B's and to hand it over to the Treasurer.

19. The duties of the Treasurer are to receive from the Secretary all moneys belonging to the Circle, and place the same in the hands of trustees duly elected to receive it by the officers of the Circle, if considered necessary, and to receive the same from the trustees whenever required by the Centre for the purchase of war material.

336 The Irish Republican Brotherhood, 1914–1924

20. The duties of the B are to receive and transmit all instructions from the Centre of his Company, to call all meetings of the C's or men of his Company, to receive and keep an account of all moneys from his C and hand said money to the Secretary of the Circle, to receive once a month from his C's report of their strength in men with one penny from each man reported, and hand the same to the Secretary; to divide the Company into Sections and superintend the elections of C's and to watch over and conduct his Company generally.

21. The duties of a C are to transmit all information from his B to the men of his section, to call all meetings of his Section, to collect weekly or fortnightly and hand over to his B the contributions of the men of his Circle for material, and keep an account of the same; to collect monthly the sum of one penny from each man in his Section which money he must hand over to his B.

Reports

22. On the last Saturday of each month each C is to give to his B a report of the number in his Section, with one penny for each man so reported. Each B must then transmit to the Secretary a full report of his Company, with one penny for each man. The Treasurer must report the amount of money in the funds of the Circle, and the Centre shall report the amount of material in the Circle. The Secretary shall then draw up a full report of the strength of the Circle in men, money and material and hand it to the Centre, who must transmit it to a District Centre on or before the first of the ensuing month. Any man refusing or neglecting to report and pay his monthly levy of one penny to be considered temporarily out of the I.R.B. Any C neglecting to report for his Section to be removed; any B neglecting to report for his Company to be removed; any Centre neglecting to report for his Circle to be removed. No communication, conversation or intercourse on matters connected with the organisation to be permitted with any member, Section or Company or Circle, put out of communication for neglecting to report, until the following month when, by payment of arrears, he or they shall be again admitted into communication. If three months elapse without he or they reporting, he or they shall be expelled the organisation finally.

War Material

23. The war material of each Circle is to be purchased by the Centre, who is held responsible by the Military Secretary for its safety and good

1894 Rules and Regulations

condition. He is empowered to make what arrangements he considers necessary for the safe keeping of the said material.

24. No member of the I.R.B, Centre, B, C or D, shall be allowed to carry material belonging to the Circle on his person, save and except on special occasion such as its removal to a place of greater safety, or when required to produce it for inspection, or when ordered to arm himself for a special purpose, such as the escort of material or protection of documents or officers of the organisation, or when exhibiting samples to new members or section of the I.R.B., or for practising or instruction. Any officer found guilty of having violated this rule to be reduced to the ranks.

25. The Centre shall be required, when called upon by the Military Secretary, to produce all material belonging to the Circle for inspection, and also to inspect himself all material belonging to the Circle at least once a month.

26. Any Centre, officer, or member, entrusted with the safe-keeping of material failing to produce it when called upon by the Military Secretary, Secretary or Centre to be expelled from the organisation and placed upon the black list afterwards.

27. The whereabouts of the material of a circle be known only to the Executive of the Circle, namely, Centre, Treasurer and Secretary.

28. Should the members of a circle be doubtful as to the amount of material reported by their centre, they shall have power to elect an Inspection Committee of Five, who, by giving the Centre a week's notice, shall be entitled to see said material, but not to know where it is stored, which knowledge must always be confined to the Executive.

Miscellaneous

29. Should want of employment or any other circumstance, save and except danger from the enemy on account of services performed to the I.R.B., cause any member of the I.R.B. to remove from one town to another, he shall be required to write back to his Centre through his B when settled, giving his address. His Centre will then communicate through his District Centre to the Centre of the town where he has taken up his abode, who will take steps to bring him into communication with the Circle of that place, always provided he be a good member of the I.R.B.; if he, on the contrary, be in arrears with the Circle he has left, he must not be recognised until he has first cleared off such arrears.

The Irish Republican Brotherhood, 1914–1924

30. Any Centre giving the address of any brother Centre, District Centre, or member of the Executive to any member except such member be a messenger or in danger of arrest on account of his connection with the I.R.B. shall be reduced to the ranks.

31. No stranger presenting himself to any Centre, unless properly accredited as a messenger or member in danger of arrest, to be received or recognised by such Centre. Any Centre receiving or holding communication with such non-accredited or unauthorised person to be removed from his position.

32. At all section meetings, the C shall conduct the business of the meeting, and the first duty shall be to inspect the men present, in order that no man outside his section shall take part in the proceedings. At all Company meetings the B shall conduct the business and the C's shall act as Inspection Committee and guards. At all general meetings of the C's or members, the Centre shall conduct the business, and the B's shall act as Inspection Committee and appoint guards.

33. No member or C can leave his section or Company to join another save with the consent of his B or Centre, and no member of any rank can leave one Circle to join another save with the consent of both Circles. Any member or members leaving one Circle to join another can claim none of the levy pay.

34. Any C, B, or Centre taking subscriptions from, giving information or instructions to, or in any other way interfering with the men of any other C, B or Centre to be reprimanded for the first, and reduced for the second offence.

35. In every Circle a Sub-Centre shall be elected from the B's, who shall act as Deputy during the Centre's absence, illness or temporary removal.

36. During the absence, illness or temporary removal of B or C, the Centre shall have the power of appointing an officer to act as his Deputy; said officer to be from the same Company or Section to which the B or C belongs.

37. No C, B or Centre shall be allowed to voluntarily resign save with the consent of the officer of his Company, Circle or District.

Vigilance Committee

38. Every Centre shall appoint a Vigilance Committee of not less than three or more than nine members who shall be known to no member or officer of the Circle save the Centre. Every Vigilance Committee shall act under

1894 Rules and Regulations 339

the control of a responsible officer appointed by the Centre who shall be appointed by the Vigilance C.

39. The duties of the members of the Vigilance Committee are to keep a watch upon all members of the Circle, to report to the Vigilance C all cases of drunkenness, violation of secrecy, etc., and to obey the orders of the Centre through the Vigilance C for the carrying out of any punishment or watching of any suspected traitor.

40. The members of the Vigilance Committee shall be unknown to each other. No member shall know any other member save the Vigilance C, unless two members are required to perform any duty beyond the power of one to accomplish, in which case the Vigilance C shall introduce the two members to each other.

41. The duties of the Vigilance C are to see each member of his Committee separately, at least once a fortnight, to receive from them any reports they may have to make, in Company with the Centre to privately investigate all cases reported and to choose the men for any special duty required and to keep a watch upon every individual member of the Vigilance Committee.

42. Any member of the Vigilance Committee speaking to another member of the I.R.B. on or about the secrets of the Vigilance Committee to be expelled the I.R.B. When such an event occurs, or when any member of the Vigilance Committee is removed from the Vigilance Committee, the said Committee shall be broken and a new one formed.

43. Should the Centre of a Circle discover that the Vigilance Committee or any member thereof are known to be members of the Vigilance Committee, he shall disband such Vigilance Committee and form a new one.

44. A black list of traitors, spies, swindlers and other criminals against the I.R.B. will be placed in the hands of each Centre, who shall read it to all the members of his Circle. Any member known to hold intercourse or correspondence with any man whose name appears on the black list to be immediately expelled and never to be readmitted into the I.R.B.

45. It shall be the duty of every member to forward to his own District Centre all cases of swindling, treachery, etc., in his Circle, with full description of the offender whenever such swindling or treachery occurs, and it shall be the duty of every Centre to preserve the black list given to him for reference whenever needed.

46. Any Centre or other member losing or mislaying any dangerous documents such as these rules, to be for ever expelled the ranks of the I.R.B.

APPENDIX IV

IRB Constitution 1873–1917

AMENDED CONSTITUTION OF THE IRISH
REPUBLICAN BROTHERHOOD

Whereas the Irish People have never ceased to struggle for the recovery of their independence since the date of its destruction and whereas it has on this 17th Day of March, the day of our Patron Saint, St. Patrick, 1873, been resolved by a Convention of Irish Patriots, held in Dublin and representing associations of Irishmen existing in various parts of Ireland, England and Scotland to amend the Constitution of the present Irish Revolutionary Organisation for the purpose of overthrowing English power in Ireland, and of establishing an independent Irish Republic.

Said organisation being known as The Irish Republican Brotherhood and governed by a Council entitled 'The Supreme Council of the Irish Republican Brotherhood and Government of the Irish Republic'. The following is declared to be and promulgated as the Amended Constitution of the Irish Republican Brotherhood and of the Supreme Council of the Irish Republican Brotherhood and Government of the Irish Republic.

CONSTITUTION OF THE IRISH REPUBLICAN BROTHERHOOD

1. The I.R.B. is and shall be composed of Irishmen, irrespective of class or creed resident in Ireland, England, Scotland, America, Australia, and in all other lands where Irishmen live, who are willing to labour for the establishment of a free and independent Republican Government in Ireland.

2. The I.R.B. whilst labouring to prepare Ireland for the task of recovering her independence by force of arms shall confine itself in time of peace to

IRB Constitution 1873–1917

341

the exercise of moral influences – the cultivation of union and brotherly love amongst Irishmen – the propagation of Republican Principles and a spreading of a knowledge of the national rights of Ireland.

3. The I.R.B. shall await the decision of the Irish Nation as expressed by a majority of the Irish people as to the fit hour of inaugurating a war against England and shall, pending such an emergency, lend its support to every movement calculated to advance the cause of Irish independence, consistently with the preservation of its own integrity.

4. The mode of initiating members into the I.R.B. shall be the rendering of the following Oath of Allegiance to its Government:

> 'In the presence of God, I ... do solemnly swear that I will do my utmost to establish the national independence of Ireland, and that I will bear true allegiance to the Supreme Council of the Irish Republican Brotherhood and Government of the Irish Republic and implicitly obey the Constitution of the Irish Republican Brotherhood and all my superior officers and that I will preserve inviolable the secrets of the organisation.'

5. No one shall be inducted into the I.R.B. whose character for sobriety, truth, valour and obedience to Authority cannot bear scrutiny.

6. Each member of the I.R.B. shall contribute according to his means for the production of war materials and also towards the expense of keeping up communication in the different Divisions of the I.R.B. and for maintaining the efficiency of the Supreme Council.

7. In every case where arms are lost through negligence the department through which the neglect of which the loss has occurred shall be responsible for the value of the arms.

8. The members of the I.R.B. resident in towns or parishes shall be directed and governed by an officer to be entitled a Centre and to be elected by the members of the I.R.B. each body of members electing the Centre for their own town or parish.

9. The members and centres of the I.R.B. shall be directed and governed by an officer to be entitled a County Centre and to be elected by the centres of the respective counties, and in England and Scotland the towns shall be grouped into Districts corresponding in population to the counties in Ireland and each District shall be directed and governed by a District Centre who shall be elected by the Centres of his District.

342 The Irish Republican Brotherhood, 1914–1924

10. The I.R.B. shall be divided into seven electoral Divisions – to wit – Leinster, Ulster, Munster, Connaught, North of England, South of England and Scotland and in each Division one Civil and one Military Secretary shall be elected by the County or District Centres and the duty of the Civil Secretary shall be to act in all respects as Deputy of the member of the Supreme Council of his Division and in the event of removal of said member by the act of the enemy, disability or death the Civil Secretary shall exercise authority in the Division until a new member of the Supreme Council shall have been elected in the manner provided for in the Constitution of the Supreme Council; and the duties of the Military Secretary shall be to execute all orders received by him in relation to the procuring, distribution and safe keeping of arms and ammunition

11. The term of office of all members of the I.R.B. shall be subject to removal at any time by a two-thirds vote of the electoral body.

12. The Divisional officers shall have power to make all bye-laws framed in accordance with the spirit of the Constitution – which they may deem necessary for the purpose of local organisation.

13. Each County or District Centre shall on or before the last day in each month send in a report of the position and progress of affairs to the Civil Secretary of his Division who shall forthwith send it to the member of the Supreme Council for the Division, by whom it shall be forwarded to the Secretary of the Supreme Council.

14. In each of the large cities, to wit – Dublin, Cork, Limerick, Belfast, London and Glasgow – a Committee of Five shall be elected by the Centres whose duty shall consist in directing local organisation subject to the supervision and control of the County or District Centres.

15. No member of the I.R.B. shall receive any information respecting the organisation, except what shall be necessary for the performance of his duty, and no member of the I.R.B. shall be at liberty to make use of any such information he may accidentally acquire.

AMENDED CONSTITUTION OF THE SUPREME COUNCIL OF THE I.R.B. AND GOVERNMENT OF THE IRISH REPUBLIC

1. The Supreme Council of the Irish Republican Brotherhood and Government of the Irish Republic is and shall be composed of eleven members; seven of said members shall be elected by the seven electoral

IRB Constitution 1873–1917 343

Divisions as marked out in the Constitution of the Irish Republican Brotherhood, and the remaining four shall be honorary members and shall be elected by the seven, to whom alone their names shall be known and enactments of the Government so constituted shall be the laws of the Irish Republic until the territory thereof shall have been recovered from the English Enemy and a permanent Government established.

2. The manner of the election of the before-mentioned seven members of the Supreme Council shall be as follows:

The County or District Centres shall be assembled in Convention and shall elect a Committee of Five of their number, who under seal of an oath of secrecy, shall elect the member of the Supreme Council for the Division whereunto they belong.

3. The term of office of the Supreme Council shall be two years but any member may be removed at any time by a two-thirds vote of his constituents or a two-thirds vote of the Supreme Council and any member of the S.C. wishing to resign will give one month's notice to his constituents and to the S.C.

4. There shall be an Executive of the Supreme Council, composed of the President, Secretary and Treasurer of that body, the decision of any two of whom shall be binding on all.

5. The duty of the President of the Supreme Council shall be to direct the working of the Irish Republican Brotherhood in all its departments, subject to the control of the Supreme Council.

6. The appointment, suspension and removal of all departmental officers shall be vested in the Executive subject to the approval of the Supreme Council.

7. No member of the Supreme Council or officers in the employment thereof shall be in receipt of any salary from the funds of the Supreme Council of the Irish Republican Brotherhood.

8. The authority of the Supreme Council shall be unquestioned by those who have become, or may hereafter become members of the I.R.B. and the Supreme Council is hereby declared in fact as well as by right the sole Government of the Irish Republic and has authority to levy taxes, negotiate loans, make war and peace and do all other acts necessary for the protection of the Irish Republic and members of the Supreme Council shall

344 The Irish Republican Brotherhood, 1914–1924

be bound to this Constitution and to one another by an oath of fidelity and inviolable secrecy and every act or attempted act of any member of the I.R.B. to subvert the authority of the Supreme Council shall in time of peace be a grave misdemeanour and punishable accordingly and in time of war every such act or attempted act shall be treason and punishable with death.

9. The Supreme Council reserves to itself the right of dealing with all friendly powers on all matters concerning the welfare of Ireland and the advancement of the cause of Irish independence.

10. Executive power shall never be vested in one man, but shall be vested in the President, Secretary and Treasurer of the Supreme Council.

11. Every member of the I.R.B. and every member of the Supreme Council owes Civil and Military obedience to the Executive of the Supreme Council and the President thereof is in fact as well as by right, President of the Irish Republic.

12. In the event of the Supreme Council being unavoidably reduced in number, the member or remaining members shall exercise the authority of the Supreme Council until such time as the vacancies shall have been filled up which shall be done as soon as possible and the same for the Executive.

13. The military authority shall at all times be and remain subject to the Civil Government and shall never be permitted to arrogate to itself the power of legislating or of restraining in any way the Constitution of the Irish Republic as promulgated by the Supreme Council.

14. At each meeting of the Supreme Council the members thereof shall hand in a summarised statement of the receipts and expenditure of the respective Divisions.

15. The Supreme Council shall have power to award Capital Punishment only in cases of treason and the crime of treason is hereby defined as any wilful act or word on the part of any member of the I.R.B. or of the Supreme Council calculated to betray the cause of Irish Independence and subserve the interest of the British or any other foreign Government in Ireland to the detriment of Irish Independence.

16. The Supreme Council shall appoint a secret court in each of the seven Divisions of the I.R.B. for the trial of all members charged with the commission of treason or grave misdemeanours.

17. The Supreme Council shall undertake the punishment of all minor offences committed by members of the I.R.B. once the offending members have

IRB Constitution 1873–1917

been removed from the Division whereunto they belong and in cases where members unlawfully appropriate moneys entrusted to them for national purposes, such members shall be expelled the I.R.B. and the Supreme Council shall draw up a list of the names of such members, and circulate it through all parts of the I.R.B. and forward copies of it to representative Irishmen in every part of the world in order that those who rob the treasury of their country may be held up to the execration of all honest men.

18. In the Irish Republic there shall be no State religion but every citizen shall be free to worship God according to his conscience, and perfect freedom of worship shall be guaranteed as a right and not granted as a privilege.

19. The Supreme Council shall have power to alter or revise the foregoing constitution of the Irish Republican Brotherhood and of the Supreme Council of the Irish Republican Brotherhood and Government of the Irish Republic but whenever it is contemplated to make any alterations it shall be necessary to give one month's notice of the meeting of the Supreme Council at which such alteration is proposed to be effected; and it shall require a two-thirds vote of the Supreme Council to make the proposed change.

By Order of
THE SUPREME COUNCIL

APPENDIX V

IRB Constitution 1917–22

<u>Objects</u>

1. The object of the Irish Republican Brotherhood (hereinafter sometime called the 'Organisation') is to establish and maintain a free and independent Republican Government in Ireland.

2. The Irish Republican Brotherhood shall do its utmost to train and equip its members as a military body for the purpose of securing the independence of Ireland by force of arms; it shall secure the co-operation of all Irish military bodies in the accomplishment of its object, and shall support every movement calculated to advance the cause of Irish National Independence – consistent with its own integrity.

<u>Membership</u>

3. Every Irishman, irrespective of class or creed, whose character for patriotism, truth, valour, sobriety and obedience to superior officers can bear scrutiny, and who accepts the constitution of the Irish Republican Brotherhood, is eligible for membership of the Irish Republican Brotherhood.

4. Names of prospective candidates for membership shall be proposed and seconded at a Circle meeting. If accepted by a Circle, the Centre shall direct a member to ascertain in an approved manner whether said prospect is willing to join the Organisation. When a prospect is approached for this purpose, only the investigator shall be present with him.

    On receipt of a satisfactory report the Centre shall proceed with the initiation of the candidate as early as possible.

    In cities, the District Board shall arrange for a special scrutiny of prospective candidates by submitting each name for the approval of the Circles in the District. Unless and until a satisfactory report is received from the District Board, no further steps shall be taken by the Circle.

IRB Constitution 1917–22

<u>Inception Oaths</u>

5. Each candidate who qualifies for admission into the Irish Republican Brotherhood shall affirm on oath that he does not belong to any other oath-bound society, and shall, as a requisite for acceptance, take the following oath:

> 'In the presence of God, I ... do solemnly swear that I will do my utmost to establish the National Independence of Ireland, that I will bear true allegiance to the Supreme Council of the Irish Republican Brotherhood and Government of the Irish Republic; that I will implicitly obey the Constitution of the Irish Republican Brotherhood, and all my superior officers, and preserve inviolable the secrets of the Organisation. So help me God!'

6. Should any man, while a member of the Irish Republican Brotherhood, be asked to join any other oath-bound society, he shall immediately inform his superior officer in the Irish Republican Brotherhood, who shall at once transmit the information to the Supreme Council in the appointed manner. Each officer of the Irish Republican Brotherhood shall be empowered to at any time demand that any member under his jurisdiction shall on oath affirm that he does not belong to any other oath-bound society.

    No man who is a member of any other such society shall be admitted to, or allowed to retain membership of, the Irish Republican Brotherhood without the express permission of the Supreme Council.

<u>Organisation</u>

7. (a) The unit of organisation shall be known as a 'Circle', the members of which shall elect an officer, entitled a 'Centre', to direct and govern same. Each Circle shall also elect a 'Sub-Centre', a Secretary and a Treasurer.

    (b) Each Circle shall be sub-divided into Sections of not more than ten men in each. Each Section shall be in charge of an officer, entitled a 'Section Leader'. He shall have an intimate knowledge of the men in his section, their names and addresses; he shall collect their subscriptions at the Circle meetings and hand same to the Treasurer; he shall submit a definite report regarding each man of his section absent.

348 The Irish Republican Brotherhood, 1914–1924

(c) Each Circle shall meet at least monthly.

8 Each county in Ireland shall, at the discretion of the Supreme Council, be divided into two or more 'Districts'. The Centres in each District shall form a Board for the purpose of directing the Organisation therein. Each District Board shall select a Chairman, a Vice-Chairman, a Secretary and a Treasurer. The Chairman shall be entitled a 'District Centre', and shall be responsible to the County Centre for the efficiency and discipline of the Irish Republican Brotherhood in his District. Each City shall be considered a District under this clause.

Where practicable, each District Centre shall arrange that each Circle in his District be visited at its monthly meeting by a representative from another Circle under his jurisdiction, who shall report thereon.

9. (a) In each County the local Centres of the Irish Republican Brotherhood therein shall hold a Convention at an appointed place and time for the purpose of electing a 'County Centre', a 'County Sub-Centre', a 'County Secretary' and a 'County Treasurer'. The County Centre shall be responsible for all matters pertaining to the Irish Republican Brotherhood in his County.

(b) A County Centre may, with the permission of the Divisional Centre, sub-divide any Circle under his jurisdiction into two or more Circles.

(c) In the event of the removal of the County Centre by the act of an enemy, disability or death, the County Sub-Centre shall exercise authority in the County until a new County Centre shall have been elected in the manner provided for.

<u>Supreme Council</u>

10. (a) The governing body of the Organisation shall be entitled 'The Supreme Council'. It shall consist of one member for each of eleven Divisions enumerated in this clause (10b). The eleven members so elected shall co-opt four additional members of the Supreme Council. The total membership of the council shall thus be fifteen.

<u>Divisions</u>

(b) The Irish Republican Brotherhood shall be divided into ELEVEN Electoral 'Divisions', to wit:

1. Part of Leinster, comprising the Counties of DUBLIN, WICKLOW, KILDARE, LOUTH, MEATH, WESTMEATH, and LONGFORD.

IRB Constitution 1917–22

2. Remaining portion of Leinster, comprising the Counties of WEXFORD, KILKENNY, CARLOW, QUEEN'S and KING'S COUNTIES.

3. Part of Munster, comprising the Counties of CORK, WATERFORD, KERRY.

4. Remaining portion of Munster, comprising the Counties of LIMERICK, CLARE, and TIPPERARY.

5. Part of Connaught, comprising the Counties of GALWAY and MAYO.

6. Remaining portion of Connaught, comprising the Counties of SLIGO, LEITRIM and ROSCOMMON.

7. Part of Ulster, comprising the Counties of DONEGAL, DERRY, TYRONE and FERMANAGH.

8. Remaining portion of Ulster, comprising the Counties of ANTRIM, DOWN, ARMAGH, MONAGHAN and CAVAN.

9. South of England.

10. North of England.

11. Scotland.

Election of Supreme Council

11. (a) The District Centres and County Centres in each Division shall, in Convention assembled, elect by ballot a Committee of FIVE of their number, who shall, under an oath of secrecy, elect by ballot a member of the Irish Republican Brotherhood as 'Divisional Centre', who shall represent the Division on the Supreme Council of the Organisation.

(b) The Convention shall, as a whole, also elect a 'Divisional Secretary'.

(c) In the event of the removal of the Divisional Centre by the act of an enemy, disability or death, the Divisional Secretary shall exercise authority in the Division until a new member shall have been elected in the manner provided for.

(d) While Dublin County remains one District as at present, the representation of the County at the Convention of Division No. 1 shall comprise six Centres elected by the Dublin District Board in addition to the County Centre. Should the County at a later date be divided into more than one District, the District Centres of same shall be among the aforesaid six representatives.

Subscriptions

12. Each member of the Irish Republican Brotherhood shall pay a monthly fee of sixpence, one-third of which shall be retained by the Circle, one-third by the County Treasurer, and one-third remitted to the Supreme Council through the Divisional Centre. Each member shall contribute according to his means for the purchase of war materials, and shall pay any special levies which the Supreme Council may impose as the necessity arises.

Suspension

13. Any member of the Irish Republican Brotherhood may be suspended by his Centre, or by a majority vote of the Circle, on any of the following grounds:– (a) Abstention from Circle meetings without valid excuse; (b) Failure to pay membership fees; (c) Failure to pay levies for purchase of arms; (d) Loss of arms entrusted to his care; (e) Speaking of the Irish Republican Brotherhood (I.R.B.) on any occasion other than at Circle meetings, unless with the express permission of his Centre or Circle; (f) Intemperance; (g) Being guilty of any act derogatory to the interests of the Irish Republican Brotherhood.

    Should any grave misdemeanour or serious breach of discipline warrant it, trial by court-martial may be ordered by a majority vote of the Circle, by the Centre or any other superior authority. If found guilty, said member shall be expelled from the Organisation and the expulsion reported to the Supreme Council through the proper channels. All charges against members shall be made in writing.

Transfers

14. When the change of residence on the part of any member necessitates a transfer to another Circle, said member shall so inform his Centre and furnish the latter with the new address at which he is to reside. The Centre shall immediately transmit this information to the County Centre through the County Board. The County Centre shall be responsible for the completion of all transfers within his County and inform the Divisional Centre of transfers required to any other County or Division.

    The Divisional Centre shall notify County Centres of inter-County transfers within his Division, and transfers from other Divisions as they affect each County Centre.

IRB Constitution 1917–22   351

Applications for transfers from one Division to another shall be reported to the Supreme Council.

All transfers shall be completed with the utmost despatch.

Reports

15. Each District Centre shall, on the last day of each month, furnish a report relating to the numerical, financial and disciplinary standing of the Organisation in his District to the County Centre; he shall also transmit to the latter all monies due from his District.

Each County Centre shall report and transmit in like manner to the Divisional Centre on or before the 7th day of the month following.

Secrecy

16. (a) No member of the Irish Republican Brotherhood shall receive any information respecting the work of the Organisation except what is necessary for the performance of his duty. Should any member inadvertently acquire such information he shall not be at liberty to divulge or make use of it, but shall report to his superior officer.

(b) At all meetings of the Organisation where any officer is elected the following oath shall be taken:–

'In the presence of God, I ... do solemnly swear that I shall not disclose to any person the business of this meeting or the names of those present thereat.'

Ordinary Elections

17. (a) General election for all officers of the Irish Republican Brotherhood shall be held every two years. They shall hold office until their successors shall have been elected, but an officer of a Circle, District, County or Division may at any time be dismissed from office by a two-thirds vote of his electoral body, by the Supreme Council or executive thereof.

(b) A special election for any Circle, District, County or Division may be ordered at any time at the discretion of the Supreme Council.

(c) All elections in the Irish Republican Brotherhood shall be by ballot.

352 The Irish Republican Brotherhood, 1914–1924

(d) The appointment, suspension and dismissal of all departmental officers, other than those mentioned in the foregoing clauses, shall be vested in the Supreme Council or Executive thereof.

By-laws

18. Each Divisional Centre, in conjunction with the County Centres of his Division, shall have power to frame by-laws in accordance with the spirit of the Constitution which may be deemed necessary for the purposes of local organisation. Such by-laws not to take effect unless and until ratified by the Supreme Council.

Religion and Social Standing

19. (a) There shall be no State religion in the Irish Republic. Each citizen shall be free to worship God according to the dictates of his conscience.

There shall be no privileged persons or classes in the Irish Republic. All citizens shall enjoy equal rights therein.

The Government

20. The Supreme Council of the Irish Republican Brotherhood is hereby declared in fact, as well as by right, the sole Government of the Irish Republic. Its enactments shall be the laws of the Irish Republic until Ireland secures absolute National Independence, and a permanent Republican Government is established.

The authority of the Supreme Council shall be unquestioned by members of the Irish Republican Brotherhood.

The Supreme Council of the Irish Republican Brotherhood shall have power to levy taxes, raise loans, make war and peace, negotiate and ratify treaties with foreign powers, and do all other acts necessary for the protection and government of the Irish Republic.

A Declaration of War shall be supported by at least TEN members of the Supreme Council, and a decision so arrived at shall be binding on all members of the Council.

Executive

21. (a) There shall be an 'Executive' of the Supreme Council composed of the President, Secretary and Treasurer of that body whose election

IRB Constitution 1917–22

shall, if possible, take place at the first meeting of a new Supreme Council to which all members shall have been summoned.

(b) This Executive shall be vested with all powers and prerogatives of the Supreme Council when the Supreme Council is not in Session, except those of declaring war and altering the Constitution.

A majority vote of the Executive shall be binding on all three of its members.

The President

22. The President of the Irish Republican Brotherhood is, in fact as well as by right, President of the Irish Republic. He shall direct the working of the Irish Republican Brotherhood, subject to the control of the Supreme Council or Executive thereof.

Vacancies

23. In the event of vacancies occurring in the Supreme Council or Executive thereof, the remaining member or members shall exercise the authority of the Supreme Council until such time as new members shall have been elected or co-opted in accordance with Clauses 11 and 12 of this Constitution. Vacancies shall, in all cases, be filled with the utmost despatch.

Meetings

24. (a) The Supreme Council shall meet at least once every three months. Special meetings shall be called by the Executive or at the written request of one member of the Executive and two other members of the Supreme Council.

(b) Nine members of the Supreme Council shall constitute a quorum.

(c) Members of the Supreme Council who absent themselves from two consecutive meetings of the Council without excuse which shall be considered valid by two-thirds of the members present on the occasion of his second abstention shall be dismissed from office.

(d) Notice of meetings at which a declaration of war or amendments to the Constitution are to be considered, shall be given by personal service to each member of the Supreme Council and a receipt obtained for such notification.

354 The Irish Republican Brotherhood, 1914–1924

Resignations, Dismissals, etc.

25. (a) Any member of the Supreme Council wishing to resign shall give one month's notice to a member of the Executive, and also (if an elected member) to the Secretary of his Division.

(b) Any member of the Supreme Council may be dismissed from office by a two-thirds vote of his electoral body, or of the Supreme Council.

26. At each meeting of the Supreme Council the elected members thereof shall furnish a report relating to the numerical, financial and disciplinary standing of the Organisation in their respective Divisions, and shall pay to the Treasurer of the Council all monies due.

The Treasurer of the Supreme Council shall furnish vouchers for all disbursements and submit a statement showing the financial standing of the whole Organisation.

27. The members of the Supreme Council shall give their services to the Organisation voluntarily. No member of the Council shall be entitled to remuneration as such.

28. The Supreme Council shall have power to appoint a secret court for the trial of any member or members charged with the commission of treason or grave misdemeanours.

Punishment

29. Any member of the Irish Republican Brotherhood who unlawfully appropriates money entrusted to him for National purposes shall be expelled from the Irish Republican Brotherhood. The Supreme Council shall circulate the name or names of such offenders throughout the Organisation, and to representative Irishmen living in foreign countries as may be deemed advisable.

30. The Supreme Council alone shall have power to inflict a sentence of Capital Punishment and give it effect; and this only in cases of treason. The crime of treason is hereby defined as any wilful act or word on the part of any member of the Irish Republican Brotherhood calculated to betray the cause of Irish Independence, or subserve the interests of the British or any other foreign government to the detriment of Irish Independence.

Military Council

31. There shall be a 'Military Council' of the Irish Republican Brotherhood which shall be attached to, and at all times subject to, the Supreme

IRB Constitution 1917–22

Council, and shall have no power to direct or interfere with the policy of the Government of the Irish Republic nor in any way to alter the Constitution of the Irish Republican Brotherhood.

<u>Amendment</u>

32. The Supreme Council of the Irish Republican Brotherhood shall have power to amend the foregoing Constitution of the Irish Republican Brotherhood, subject to the following restrictions:

33. Each member of the Council shall receive a month's notice of any amendment prior to the date of meeting at which such amendment is proposed to be effected.

34. Not less than a two-thirds vote of the Council shall be required to make any proposed change effective.

35. Clauses 1, 2, 3, 5, 21, 23, 24, 33, 35, 36, shall not be amended except with the consent and approval of a majority of the County Centres in Ireland of the Irish Republican Brotherhood.

36. Amendments to the Constitution or recommendations affecting the government and policy of the Irish Republican Government, emanating from any Circle, shall be submitted to the District Board. If accepted by the latter they shall be transmitted to the County Centre. This officer shall then transmit same, with his opinion noted thereon, to the Divisional Centre, who shall in due course submit said amendments or recommendations for the consideration of the Supreme Council.

37. This Constitution of the Irish Republican Brotherhood shall be read at the meetings of each Circle at least twice a year.

GENERAL ORDER OF BUSINESS AT CIRCLE MEETINGS

1. Post guard at door.
2. Centre opens meeting in the name of the Irish Republic, members standing to attention.
3. Roll-call by Secretary, and reports on absentees.
4. Introduction of new members.
5. Reports on candidates for membership proposed at previous meeting of Circle.
6. Nominations of prospective candidates.
7. Orders from District Board.
8. Collection of Subscriptions.

9. Announcement of next meeting date.
10. Other business.
11. Military training through lectures, discussions, etc., as arranged by District Board.
12. Centre declares meeting closed – members standing to attention.

APPENDIX VI

IRB Constitution Amendments 1919–21

SEPTEMBER 1919 CONSTITUTION AMENDMENT

Clause 20a. In view of the fact that the policy of the I.R.B. has succeeded in establishing a duly elected public authority competent to declare the will and give expression to the desire of the Irish people to secure the international recognition of the Irish Republic; and whereas this public authority has decreed that all servants and soldiers of the Irish Republic shall take the following oath:

> 'I, A.B., do solemnly swear (or affirm) that I do not, and shall not, yield a voluntary support to any pretended Government, Authority, or Power within Ireland, hostile or inimical thereto; and I do further swear (or affirm) that to the best of my knowledge and ability I will support and defend the Irish Republic, and the Government of the Irish Republic, which is Dáil Éireann, against all enemies, foreign and domestic; that I will bear true faith and allegiance to the same, and that I take this obligation freely without any mental reservation or purpose of evasion, so help me God.'

It is declared that members of the I.R.B. may, in accordance with the terms and spirit of their inception oath, loyally accept and obey this authority.[1]

AUGUST 1921 CONSTITUTION AMENDMENT

Clause 22, under the terms of 20a shall read:

> 'The President of the I.R.B. shall direct the working of the Irish Republican Brotherhood, subject to the control of the Supreme Council of the Executive thereof.'

APPENDIX VII

IRB Constitution 1922

(1) Objects:

The object of the Irish Republican Brotherhood (hereinafter sometimes called 'The Organisation') shall be:

To establish and maintain a free and independent Republican Government in Ireland.

(2) Policy:

The policy of the I.R.B. shall be to utilise every power and movement in the Nation; it shall influence them in their activities and co-ordinate these activities so as to secure that the maximum organised strength of the nation – armed, economic, political, social and otherwise shall be at all times available for the achievement of its objects.

(3) The Oath:

Each candidate who qualifies for admission to the I.R.B., shall take the following inception oath:

'In the presence of God I do solemnly swear that I shall do my utmost to establish the National Independence of Ireland; that I will give true allegiance to the Irish Republic, and obedience to the Supreme Council of the Irish Republican Brotherhood, and preserve inviolable the secrets of the Organisation. So help me God.'

(4) Membership:

Membership shall be open to Irishmen only. They shall be accepted without regard to religion or social distinction, provided their character and National standing is such as entitle them to membership. They must,

IRB Constitution 1922

of course, accept the Constitution of the I.R.B.

(5) Members of the I.R.B. may not join any other oath-bound society without the special sanction of the Supreme Council of the I.R.B.

(6) A man who is already a member of another oath-bound society may not be admitted to the I.R.B. without the special permission of the Supreme Council.

(7) Punishment:

Penalties in accordance with the nature of the offences, will be inflicted upon members for breaches of the Constitution, after trial by properly constituted Courts Martial, and after ratification by the Supreme Council.

(8) Sentence of death on a member of the Organisation by a Court Martial convened by the Supreme Council, can only be awarded with the express concurrence of the Supreme Council.

(9) All charges against members must be made in writing to the officer immediately superior to the member making the charge, and members must be immediately dealt with for any action or in-action, derogatory to the interests of the Irish Republican Brotherhood.

(10) Organisation:

The Unit of Organisation shall be known as 'A Club' the membership of which may not, without the permission of the County Board, be more than 3.

(11) The area to be served by each Club will be a parish, and for this purpose chapel areas are to be regarded as parishes.

(12) Where three is considered too small a membership, representation may be made to the County Board, and permission sought to have the number increased. The membership of a Club cannot be greater than 5 at any time, except with the assent of the Supreme Council.

(13) For the purposes of the Organisation, the following areas will be regarded as 'Counties':

   (a) County Antrim, including Belfast City.

   (b) The Counties of Armagh and Down.

   (c) The Counties of Tyrone, Fermanagh, and Derry, including Derry City.

   (d) The Counties of Cavan and Monaghan.

   (e) The Counties of Tirconnal and Sligo.

(f) The Counties of Galway and Mayo.

(g) The Counties of Leitrim, Roscommon and Longford.

(h) The Counties of Clare and Tipperary.

(i) The Counties of Kerry and Limerick.

(j) County Cork – including Cork City.

(k) The Counties of Waterford, Wexford and Kilkenny.

(1) The Counties of Carlow, Kildare, and Wicklow.

(m) Dublin City and County.

(n) The Counties of Leix and Offaly.

(o) The Counties of Louth, Meath and Westmeath.

(p) Great Britain.

(14) Each Club must meet frequently and at no time less frequently than once a fortnight. Its chief duties will be to see that the general activities in the Club area, and in accordance with the policy of the organisation, as set down in Clause 2.

(15) At its first full meeting each Club will elect one of its members to be its 'Centre'.

(16) When a Centre is thus elected his name is sent to the Supreme Council, and when Centres for all chapel areas are elected, a general meeting of all Centres in the County will be held. This meeting will be attended by a delegate nominated by the Supreme Council who will preside thereat.

(17) Where it is intended that further members should be admitted to any Club, the names of the candidates must be submitted at a County Meeting of Centres. No new Members may, however, be initiated except by a representative of the Supreme Council, who will be advised by the Members of the County Board of Centres.

(18) Each District, as described in Clause 13, will have a County Board consisting of:

> Chairman,
>
> Vice Chairman,
>
> Secretary and
>
> Treasurer, and
>
> 5 other members.

This Board will be selected at a Convention held annually. The Convention to be one of Club Centres in the area.

(19) The Chairman selected in accordance with Clause 18, shall be responsible to the S.C., for all matters pertaining to the Organisation in the area.

IRB Constitution 1922   361

(20) The County Board elected in pursuance of Clause 18 may, with the permission of the Supreme Council, sub-divide the area under its jurisdiction, into Districts suitable for organisation purposes.

(21) In the event of the removal, through any cause, of a County Chairman, the Vice County Chairman assumes control of the Office until a new Chairman has been elected by a Convention of County Centres in the manner provided for.

(22) <u>The Supreme Council:</u>

    (a) The Governing Body of the 'Organisation' shall be titled 'The Supreme Council'. It shall consist of one member for each of the 16 electoral areas enumerated under Clause 13, and in addition, 4 co-opted members. The 16 elected members shall co-opt the 4 members, whose names are to be known only to the members of the Supreme Council. The total membership of the Council shall thus be – 20.

    (b) <u>Election of Supreme Council</u>

    The Centre in each electoral area, as enumerated in Clause 13 will assemble in Convention annually and select by ballot a Committee of Five of their number, who shall, under an oath of secrecy elect by ballot a member of the Irish Republican Brotherhood to represent the area on the Supreme Council of the Organisation.

    (c) The Convention will also select by Ballot an area Sub-Centre, who will take control temporarily in the event of the removal of the area Head-Centre, while acting in the capacity of Centre, the Sub-Centre will exercise the full authority attaching to the Office. He will fill the office until a new head area Centre is elected in the prescribed manner.

    (d) At its first meeting after election and after the co-option of the four additional members mentioned in Clause 22a, the Supreme Council will elect from its members an Executive consisting of:

        A President,
        A Secretary,
        A Treasurer,
        and four other members.

    (e) A General Election may be declared at any time on the following conditions:

362   The Irish Republican Brotherhood, 1914–1924

(1)   When two-thirds of the Supreme Council consider it advisable.

(2)   When 50% of the County (area) Centres request an election.

(f)   A General Meeting of County (area) Centres can be called by the Supreme Council on a requisition signed by eight County Centres.

(g)   Members representing areas within Ireland on the Supreme Council must be permanently resident in the area they represent. A member spending the greater part of his time in any particular area shall be regarded as a permanent resident in the area.

(h)   When a member of the Supreme Council representing a County in Ireland finds it necessary to reside outside the area which he represents, he will resign membership of the S.C. An election will be held as soon as possible to appoint his successor, in the manner prescribed.[1]

(i)   No member will represent any Division for more than two consecutive years.

(23) Dismissals and Resignations:

(a)   A member of the S.C. may be dismissed from Office on a two-thirds vote of the S.C. Similarly, all Officers may be dismissed from their Commands by a two-thirds vote of their Units.

(b)   A member of the S.C. wishing to resign his membership of the S.C. will first have to give one month's notice to the President, and if he is not a co-opted member he will also give one month's notice to the Secretary to the County he represents.

(c)   Each member acting on the S.C., as the representative of a Division will submit, at each meeting of the Council, a report on the position of the Organisation in his County. Such report will also cover the financial position obtaining.

(d)   All members of the S.C. will give their services free as such.

(e)   The S.C. may appoint Secret Courts to try members for grave misdemeanour.

(f)   Any member of the Organisation may be suspended by his Centre, or by a majority vote of his Club or Unit, on any charge derogatory to the policy or Constitution of the I.R.B.

(g)   County Centres, in conjunction with their Boards of Centres may frame any necessary bye-laws to meet local circumstances. Such bye-laws must be in strict adherence to the Constitution, and have the sanction of the S.C., before becoming operative.

IRB Constitution 1922

(24) Subscriptions:

    (a)   Each member of the I.R.B., shall subscribe towards the expenditure necessary for the maintenance of the Organisation, in accordance with the manner prescribed by the S.C.

    (b)   The S.C., will, at the first meeting after election draw up the system of subscription, and arrange the method in which the membership fees are to be allotted.

(25) Transfers:

Transfers arising out of change of residence will be granted. Such transfers within a County will be arranged for by the Divisional Centre and reported to S.C. When a transfer from one Division to another is sought, it will be arranged for by the Executive of the S.C. All transfers must be speedily made.

(26) Secrecy:

    (a)   No member of the Irish Republican Brotherhood shall receive any information respecting the working of the Organisation except what is necessary for the performance of the duties attaching to his Office. Should any member happen to acquire inadvertently such information he shall not be in a position to divulge it, but shall communicate with his Superior Officer regarding it, at once.

    (b)   At all Meetings of the Organisation where Officers are elected, the following Oath of Secrecy shall be taken:

> In the presence of God I ＿＿＿＿＿＿＿
> solemnly swear that I shall not
> disclose to any person the business of
> this Meeting, or the names of those
> present thereat. So help me God.

(27) Government:

    (a)   While accepting the present Governmental position of An Saor Stait, the Supreme Council of the I.R.B. is declared the sole Government of the Irish Republic, until Ireland's complete independence is achieved, and a permanent Republican Government is established, and the authority of the Supreme Council shall be unquestioned by its members.

(b) There shall be an Executive of the S.C., in accordance with Clause 22d, and this Executive will be vested with all the powers of the S.C. when the S.C. is not in Session – except powers involving questions of policy.

(c) The S.C. being the sole Government of the Irish Republic its President shall be the President of the Irish Republic. He shall direct the working of the Organisation, subject to the control of the S.C.

(d) There shall be a meeting of the S.C. at least every three months, and of the Executive thereof, monthly, at least. A special Meeting of the S.C. may be called at any time by this Executive, or on the written request of any three members of the S.C.

(e) A quorum of the Council shall be constituted by 12 members and of the Executive by 5 members. Members absenting themselves from two consecutive meetings without permission shall automatically cease to be a member of the S.C.

(f) In the event of a vacancy occurring in the S.C. or Executive thereof, the existing members will exercise the full powers of the S.C. until vacancies are filled in accordance with procedure set down in Clause 21.

(28) Amendments

Amendments to this Constitution may be made from time to time by the S.C. in accordance with the following procedure:

(a) Each Club shall have submitted to it the substance of any causes for any amendment the S.C. propose making. Such proposed amendment must reach the Clubs one month in advance, and must be considered at once.

(b) Clubs or Centres desiring to have an amendment made may submit same for consideration of the S.C. Such recommendation shall be sent through the Club Centre and County Centre for transmission to S.C.

(c) Amendments to the Constitution may not be made except by a two-third vote of the full S.C.

(d) Clauses dealing with Policy, Objects, the Oath, or Membership, may not be amended, except with the consent of a four-fifth majority of the S.C.

Clauses shall be submitted.

IRB Constitution 1922

(e) The Constitution shall be read to all Members at least once a year.

(f) At its first meeting after election the S.C. will draw up and send out to all Clubs:

    (a) General Orders of Business at Club Meetings.

    (b) A general outline of the activities expected from all Clubs and members.

(29) In the event of any crisis in the National Life of the Country that may call for any action by the Organisation, the S.C. will, in due course, prepare a plan of action concerning same, and in the event of the crisis being such that certain action on the part of the Organisation may endanger the integrity of the I.R.B., a Convention of Centres in each County shall be called to consider the matter.

(30) In addition to the duties to be carried out by the Executive of the S.C., the S.C. will appoint small Commissions or Committees to act as Vigilance Councils, to watch the progress of the various branches of Governmental, National, Economical, and Social Life of the Nation, in order to assure that they are kept in line with the Policy of the I.R.B.

(31) Those Committees shall be selected from the members of the S.C., but permission will be given to co-opt certain other members of the Organisation. Such co-options shall have the sanction of the S.C.

APPENDIX VIII

IRB Constitution 1923

Objects

1.   The objects of the Irish Republican Brotherhood (hereinafter sometimes called 'The Organisation') shall be:
To establish and maintain a free and independent Republican Government in Ireland.

Policy

2.   (a)   Whereas National Sovereignty is inherent and inalienable and, while acknowledging that political authority is exercised through instruments legitimately established, the Irish Republican Brotherhood pledges itself the custodian of the Republican Ideal – the traditional expression of National Independence.

      (b)   The Policy of the I.R.B., shall be to utilise every power and movement in the Nation; it shall influence them in their activities so as to secure that the maximum organised strength of the Nation – armed, economic, political, social and otherwise shall be at all times available for the achievement of its objects.

The Oath

3.   Each Candidate who qualifies for admission to the I.R.B., shall take the following inception Oath:

> 'In the presence of God I _____ do solemnly swear that I shall do my utmost to establish the National Independence of Ireland; that I will give true allegiance to the Irish Republic, and obedience to the Supreme Council of the Irish Republican Brotherhood, and preserve inviolable the secrets of the Organisation, So help me God.'

Membership

4. Membership shall be open to Irishmen only. They shall be accepted without regard to religion or social distinction, provided their character and National standing are such as entitle them to Membership. They must accept the Constitution of the I.R.B.
5. Members of the I.R.B. may not join any other Oath-bound society without the special sanction of the Supreme Council of the I.R.B.
6. A man who is already a member of another Oath-bound society may not be admitted to the I.R.B., without the special permission of the Supreme Council.

Punishment

7. Penalties in accordance with the nature of the offences will be inflicted upon Members for breaches of the Constitution, after trial by properly constituted Courts Martial, and after ratification by the Supreme Council.
8. When a Member of the Organisation is to be tried on a Capital charge, the Court-Martial must be convened by the Supreme Council, and sentence of death may not be carried out unless confirmed by the S.C. Sentence of death shall only be inflicted in cases of Treason. Treason is hereby defined as any wilful betrayal by word or act on the part of any Member of the I.R.B., of matters vital to the objects of the Organisation.
9. All charges against Members must be made in writing to the Officer immediately superior to the member making the charge, and members must be immediately dealt with for any action, or in-action, derogatory to the interests of the Irish Republican Brotherhood.

Organisation

10. The Unit of Organisation shall be known as 'A Club' the Membership of which may not, without the permission of the Divisional Board, be more than three.
11. The area to be served by each Club will be a Chapel area, conditional on the provisions for Vocational representation in Clause 13.
12. Where three is considered too small a Membership, representation may be made to the Divisional Board, and permission sought to have the number increased. The Membership of a Club cannot be greater than five at any time, except with the assent of the Supreme Council. Clubs, except as

368   The Irish Republican Brotherhood, 1914–1924

is otherwise provided for by Vocational representation Clause 13, are to be designated in accordance with the names of the Chapel Areas they represent.

13. For the purposes of The Organisation, the following areas will be regarded as Divisions:

(a)   <u>Area Representation</u>

Division 1.   County Antrim, including Belfast City.

        2.   The Counties of Armagh & Down.

        3.   The Counties of Tyrone, Fermanagh and Derry, including Derry City.

        4.   The Counties of Cavan & Monaghan.

        5.   The Counties of Tirconnal and Sligo.

        6.   The Counties of Galway and Mayo.

        7.   The Counties of Leitrim, Roscommon and Longford.

        8.   The Counties of Clare and Tipperary.

        9.   The Counties of Kerry and Limerick.

       10.   County Cork – including Cork City.

       11.   The Counties of Waterford, Wexford and Kilkenny.

       12.   The Counties of Carlow, Kildare and Wicklow.

       13.   Dublin City and County.

       14.   The Counties of Leix and Offaly.

       15.   The Counties of Louth, Meath and Westmeath.

       16.   Great Britain.

(b)   <u>Vocational Representation</u>

(Military)

For the purpose of Vocational Representation each Command the aggregate Corps and Service, and G.H.Q. shall constitute respectively a Division, and each Battalion, Corps and Army Service and Command Staff, shall respectively constitute a Club.

(No soldier may be a member of a Civilian Club)

Division 1.   G.H.Q.

        2.   Dublin Command.

        3.   Curragh Command.

        4.   Donegal Command.

        5.   Claremorris Command.

        6.   Athlone Command.

        7.   Waterford Command.

IRB Constitution 1923

8. Limerick Command.

9. Cork Command.

10. Kerry Command.

11. Corps & Services.

Clubs at G.H.Q., shall not without the previous and special authority of the S.C., exceed 10 in number.

Club Centres will constitute the Divisional Board, and from its membership shall elect an Executive in accordance with the procedure prescribed in Clause 18. Such Division will elect from their Club Centres a Member to be known as the Divisional Centre. The Divisional Centres will elect from their number not more than eight representatives to the S.C. From the eight members three will be nominated to inform the Divisions not represented on the S.C., of all instructions etc., from the Meetings of latter.

14. Each Club must meet frequently and at no time less frequently than once a fortnight. Its chief duties will be to see that the general activities in the Club area are in accordance with the Policy of the Organisation, as set down in Clause 2.

15. At its first Meeting each Club will elect one of its members to be its 'Centre'.

16. When a Centre is thus elected, his name is sent to the S.C., and when Centres for all Chapel areas in a Division are duly elected the Divisional Board, or S.C., will divide the Division into areas suitable for organising purposes, and in each area so formed the Club Centres will meet, and from their Membership appoint a Centre to represent the areas at a Division Convention. The number of Clubs in an area to be not less than five, and not more than eight, such Unit to be called a Circle, and enumerated in order of their establishment. The area Centre above mentioned will act as the Centre, and be a Member of the Divisional Board.

17. Where it is intended that further Members should be admitted to any Club, the names of the Candidates must be submitted at a Divisional Board Meeting. No members may, however, be initiated except by a Delegate nominated by the Supreme Council, who will be advised by the Members of the Divisional Board.

18. The Membership of the Divisional Board shall consist of the Circle Centres, except as provided for in Clause 13 (b) and shall elect an Executive consisting of:

370   The Irish Republican Brotherhood, 1914–1924

Chairman,

Vice Chairman,

Secretary,

Treasurer, and

2 other Members.

This Executive will be elected annually. A Member will be elected to the Supreme Council by the Executive, except as provided for in Clause 13 (b) and the Election shall be by ballot vote. The Divisional Board shall meet every three months, and the Executive thereof, monthly.

19. The Chairman elected in accordance with Clause 18, shall be responsible to the S.C., for all matters pertaining to the Organisation in the Division.

20. (a) In the event of the removal, through any cause, of a Divisional Chairman, the Vice-Divisional Chairman assumes control of the Office until a new Chairman has been elected by a Convention in the manner provided for.

(b) Divisional Boards may frame any necessary bye-laws to meet local circumstances, such bye-laws must be in strict adherence to the Constitution and have the sanction of the S.C., before becoming operative.

<u>The Supreme Council</u>

21. (a) The Governing Body of 'The Organisation' shall be titled 'The Supreme Council'. It shall consist of one member for each of the 16 electoral areas enumerated under Clause 13 (a), the eight Members enumerated under Clause 13 (b), and in addition, four co-opted members. The twenty-four elected members shall, at their first Meeting co-opt the four members, whose names are to be known only to the Members of the Supreme Council. The total Membership of the Council shall thus be – twenty-eight.

(b) At its first Meeting after the co-option of the four additional Members mentioned in Clause 21 (a) the Supreme Council will elect from its Members an Executive consisting of:

A President,

A Secretary,

A Treasurer, and

Four other Members.

IRB Constitution 1923

(c) A General Election may be declared at any time on the following conditions:
1. When two-thirds of the Supreme Council consider it advisable.
2. When 50% of the Divisional Centres request an Election.

(d) A General Meeting of Divisional Centres can be called by the Supreme Council on a requisition signed by twelve Divisional Centres.

(e) Members representing Divisions within Ireland on the Supreme Council must be permanently resident in the Division they represent. A Member spending the greater part of his time in any particular County shall be regarded as a permanent resident in the Division.

(f) When a Member of the Supreme Council representing a Division in Ireland finds it necessary to reside outside the Division which he represents, he will resign membership of the S.C. An election will be held as soon as possible to appoint his Successor, in the manner prescribed.

(g) No Member will represent any Division for more than two consecutive years.

(h) The Executive of the S.C., in accordance with Clause 21 (b) will be vested with all the powers of the S.C., when the S.C. is not in Session – except powers involving questions of Policy.

(i) There shall be a Meeting of the S.C., at least every three months, and of the Executive thereof, monthly, at least. A special Meeting of the S.C. may be called at any time by this Executive, or on the written request of any seven members of the S.C.

(k) A quorum of the Council shall be constituted by seventeen Members, and of the Executive by five Members. A Member absenting himself from two consecutive meetings without permission shall automatically cease to be a Member of the S.C.

(1) In the event of a vacancy occurring in the S.C., or Executive thereof, the existing members will exercise the full powers of the S.C., until vacancies are filled in accordance with the Constitution.

22. In important public issues involving marked disagreement amongst members of the Organisation the Supreme Council before ordering a particular line of action, shall submit their proposals for consideration to each Divisional Board, and shall be guided in their decision by the advice of the majority of the Boards.

372 The Irish Republican Brotherhood, 1914–1924

23. (a) In addition to the duties to be carried out by the Executive of the S.C., the S.C. will appoint small Vigilance Commissions or Committees to watch the progress of the various branches of Governmental, National, Economic, and Social Life of the Nation, in order to ensure that they are kept in line with the Policy of the I.R.B.

(b) Those Commissions, or Committees, shall be selected from the Members of the S.C., but permission will be given to co-opt other members of the Organisation. Such co-options shall have the sanction of the I.R.B.

<u>Dismissals and Resignations</u>

24. (a) A Member of the S.C., may be dismissed from office on a two-thirds vote of the S.C. Similarly, any Officer may be dismissed from office by a two-thirds vote of his Unit.

(b) A Member of the S.C., wishing to resign his membership of the S.C., will first have to give one month's notice to the President, and if he is not a co-opted member he will also give one month's notice to the Secretary to the Division he represents.

(c) Each Member acting on the S.C., as the representative of a Division will submit at each Meeting of the Council a report on the position of the Organisation in his Division. Such report will also cover the financial position obtaining.

(d) All Members of the S.C. will give their services free as such.

(e) The S.C. may appoint Secret Courts to try members for grave misdemeanour.

(f) Any member of the Organisation may be suspended by his Centre or by a majority vote of his Unit on any charge derogatory to the Policy or Constitution of the I.R.B. All suspensions shall be immediately reported to the Executive of the Divisional Board, and the Executive of the Divisional Board will arrange for trials, and inflict the necessary penalties.

(g) Any Member of the Organisation, providing there is no charge pending against him, may at any time by notice to his immediate superior resign from the Organisation thereby relieving himself from the duties of allegiance and obedience, but not of secrecy. A Member so resigning may not be re-accepted as a Member.

Subscriptions

25. (a) Each Member of the I.R.B., shall subscribe towards the expenditure necessary for the maintenance of the Organisation, in accordance with the manner prescribed by the S.C.

 (b) The S.C. will at the first meeting after election draw up the system of subscription, and arrange the method in which the Membership fees are to be allotted.

Transfers

26. Transfers arising out of change of residence will be granted. Such transfers within a Division will be arranged for by the Divisional Centre and reported to the S.C. When a transfer from one Division to another is sought, it will be arranged for by the Executive of the S.C. All transfers must be speedily made.

Secrecy

27. (a) No Member of the Irish Republican Brotherhood shall receive any information respecting the working of the Organisation except what is necessary for the performance of the duties attaching to his Office. Should any member happen to acquire inadvertently such information he shall not be in a position to divulge it, but shall communicate with his superior officer regarding it at once.

 (b) At all Meetings of the Organisation, the following Oath of Secrecy shall be taken:

> 'In the presence of God, I _____ solemnly swear that I shall not disclose to any person the business of this Meeting, or the names of those present thereat. So help me God.'

Amendments

28. Amendments to the Constitution may be made from time to time by the S.C., in accordance with the following procedure:

 (a) Each Divisional Board shall have submitted to it the substance of any causes for any amendment the S.C. propose making. Such proposed amendment must reach the Divisional Board one month in advance, and must be considered at once.

 (b) Clubs or Circles desiring to have an amendment made may submit same for consideration of the S.C. Such recommendation shall be sent through the Circle Centre and Divisional Board for transmission to S.C.

(c) Amendments to the Constitution may not be made except by a two-third vote of the full S.C.

(d) Clauses dealing with Policy, Objects, the Oath, or Membership, may not be amended except with the consent of a four-fifth majority of the S.C.

(e) The Constitution shall be read to all Members at least once a year.

(f) At its first Meeting after election the S.C. will draw up and send out to all Clubs:

(a) General Orders of business at Club Meetings.

(b) A general outline of the activities expected from all Clubs and Members.

APPENDIX IX

IRB Supreme Council Circular March 1921

TO ALL COUNTY CENTRES.

You are to take charge of the foregoing general orders and have them conveyed to all Circles under your control with the least possible delay.

The matters contained therein call for your own personal attention, and you are hereby directed to see that the activities outlined are to be carried out in the manner directed under your own supervision.

BY ORDER,

S. C.

March, 1921

GENERAL ORDERS.

A. ORGANISATION

In reviewing the activities of the period that has elapsed since the elections were last held within the Organisation two years ago, the opinion then expressed regarding the importance of maintaining the I.R.B. in a virile and effective position throughout the country is now reiterated. The wisdom of the course adopted in the matter of preserving the Organisation should now be obvious. It was then said that the Organisation had been responsible for bringing about Ireland's strong and unconquerable position, had made all Ireland republican and had brought the country to the threshold of complete freedom.

An Ireland regenerated and overwhelmingly republican has during the past two years battled with the enemy to maintain the Republic, the part played in the struggle by the men of the Organisation has been of the most tremendous importance.

376 The Irish Republican Brotherhood, 1914–1924

That the Organisation made the fighting possible and contributed largely to the splendid stand made, and being still made by the fighting men of Ireland, is unquestionable. It is noted that areas in which most activity prevailed, and in which great successes have been achieved have been those in which the members of the Organisation have realised to the full the responsibilities attaching to their membership as set out in their inception Oath, and also in the Constitution of the Organisation, and have acted up to them, not necessarily by bringing great numbers into the Organisation, but rather by maintaining a state of efficiency among existing members. In these areas the Organisation fulfilled its most important function, that of inculcating the fighting idea not alone among the men of fighting age, but in addition through its other activities to band in support of the fighting men, and the fighting idea all through the national bodies.

In this regard the Organisation serves, as it is intended to serve, all the functions of a national rallying centre from which the Republican idea goes forth through the Volunteers, Sinn Féin, Public Boards, Gaelic League, G.A.A., and all parties helping in the cause of the Republic. In their own sphere these activities are essential until the enemy forces have finally been withdrawn from Ireland.

B. CO-ORDINATION

In the matter of co-ordinating the military work of the Organisation with that of the Irish Volunteers we have been very successful. In response to the orders issued Organisation men everywhere have shown tact and wisdom in the matter, and to this may be attributed a good deal of the efficiency that has resulted in great military successes in the areas where the fighting has been most intense. This is only as it should be, and in strict accordance with the desires of the S.C. The military functions of both bodies are similar to each other, the success or failing of one, is the success or failure of both.

C. MILITARY WORK

As stated above the fighting has been carried on more vigorously where the Organisation has been efficient. In the areas where the fight has been less vigorous, or not waged at all, the Organisation has been missing the importance of its most important function. The Supreme Council desires to see the fight waged everywhere. Untiring efforts in this regard will lessen the hardships of our men and the pressure of our forces.

D. ORGANISING WORK

It must be obvious that in order to maintain or create efficiency organising work must not be neglected. The present strenuous position of things is often given as an excuse for not holding regular meetings of Circles or Officers' Boards within the I.R.B.

Without such meetings at regular intervals the essential effectiveness cannot be achieved, and united efforts in accordance with the spirit of the Organisation may be missed.

Special stress is now laid on the importance of carrying on the work of the Organisation in the prescribed manner.

E. NEGLIGENCE

In view of the prevailing conditions, any form of negligence on the part of the officers or men of the I.R.B. is unpardonable and will henceforth be dealt with severely.

In some districts it has been noticeable, and dealing with it has been the cause of great waste of time and energy on the part of those charged with the responsibility of conducting the Organisation, and you are now directed to see to it that no such offences as negligence, or insubordination, are permitted in your areas, whether on the parts of the officers or men.

Organisation men who are unable or unwilling to act up to the spirit contained in their inception oath should be outside and not inside the Organisation.

What is needed is a good working Circle in each Circle District. Even though it be small it should be remembered that small bodies well organised and under proper control are always more effective than large numbers loosely held together.

F. THE ELECTIONS

The time has again come for the elections within the Organisation and an opportunity is thus offered for bringing all units together and reviewing their work and their conditions.

The dates for the completion of the elections are as follows:–
a.   Circle Elections–June 15th, 1921.
b.   County Elections–August 15th, 1921.
c.   Divisional Elections–October 15th,1921.

As there will be a lot of preliminary work to be done regarding those

378 The Irish Republican Brotherhood, 1914–1924

elections you are directed to take the matter up with the least possible delay, and arrange for the Circles under your control to meet at once.

You will be required to report frequently to your Divisional officer regarding the progress of the work generally in your county.

G. THE FUTURE.

It is now fully realised that Ireland can win out through physical force methods. In the past this was only seen by the minority who formed the I.R.B. Now it is a general and well justified belief, and the final ending in complete freedom of Ireland's struggle, is now rapidly approaching. Be the term long or short, the spirit underlying the Organisation will triumph in the complete withdrawal of the enemy forces from Ireland: but we must have courage, confidence, and physical force to the end. The length of the struggle will depend entirely on how these watchwords are inculcated among the people, and it is to the men of the Organisation that we must look not alone for their inculcation but for their maintenance however long the struggle and however great the stress.

Up to the present time the support given by the whole people to the fighting forces has been very great, and their attitude to the enemy has been in accordance with the wishes of the Government of the Republic. If this support and attitude are to be maintained the members of the Organisation must work whole-hearted and vigorously in accordance with the spirit of the Constitution.

At no time in the history of the Country have the enemies of Ireland been so violent in their attacks on the Organisation. Every attempt is being made to draw members from their allegiance to it. Every vile trick of the English and their apologists here is being used against it. No opportunity is lost to poison the minds of the people against it. In such a time the S.C. calls with confidence to all members to redouble their efforts in making the Organisation more and more potent against the foe, more and more vigorous in the service of Ireland.

By Order,
S.C.

March, 1921

APPENDIX X

Michael Collins' Note of the March 1922 IRB Meeting with County Centres and Supreme Council Members on 'The Post-Treaty Situation'[1]

Author's note: the Civil War division in the IRB is clear from this note. A number of entries are unexplained.

Saturday, 18 March 1922   SPECIAL SECY [Seán Ó Murthuile]

(1) Certain things brought into line   ) not an election.[2]
     Old Constitution – to get back to our old position[3]   )

(2) Miceal [Collins]. Org. supreme.

(3) Martin [Conlon]. Constitution not altered – election all round.

(4) Liam [Lynch]. Truce all right. Go back to old constitution.

(5). Diarmuid [O'Hegarty]. Treaty should be worked – keep org. intact – election desirable.

(6) Charlie D [Daly].[4] Should be kept the extreme Republican Party – outlook more military than political.

(7) Joe McK [McKelvey]. Withdraw add and revert to old constitution – favours election.

(8) Steve [?]. Poor chance, seeing England came out so well – duty to consolidate Brotherhood – agrees election.

(9) Joe V [Vize]. Agrees to use Treaty – Truce a Godsend.

(10) Harry [Boland]. Avoid question being put to Irish people. Bury Republic without contest.

380 The Irish Republican Brotherhood, 1914–1924

– stultify before people of the world. Disagrees with inter. of Con – endorsed an agreement – Force.

(11) Sean [MacMahon]. Was military now political – accept Free State for time being and work for the Republic.

(12) Dick [Barrett]. Ought to have election – alternative Policy – favours election.

TREATY. Right to secede – Republican administration.
Constitution of Free State – Policy for election.

ABSENT.

OFFALY.
CLARE. Dissociating the idea of a member of the Organisation as a member
TIPPERARY. From him [*sic*] in his capacity of public representative. [Unexplained]
LEITRIM.

(1) Awkward position.
Country members left in doubt definite one way or another.

(2) Shelving responsibility.
What authority would this organisation have.
Any man belonging to the Organisation should not have voted for the Treaty.

(3) Casey and proposal. [Unexplained]

(4) H.B. [Harry Boland] worse position to overthrow a Government.

Martin [Conlon]
Organisation never had the idea that the Irish Republic had been established.

Longford.	No.
Meath.	No.
Louth.	Sean G. [unidentified][5] not acted up.
Miceal O Droignean	– 1111111111111[6]
Sean Brennan	– 1111111

Co. centre (name unknown)   – 11111
Diarmuid O'H[egarty].   – 1111

Agree to the circular.
Question of the Constitution.

Monaghan   Joe McSweeney [Sweeney]   Dick himself [?][7]
George [?] – concur Before Dick [?]

APPENDIX XI

IRB Supreme Council Members 1907–22

Elections to the Supreme Council were held biennially usually in May. In 1907 the election returned the seven Provincial representatives who then co-opted four others to join the Supreme Council as specified in the 1873 Constitution that operated until 1917. The 1907–09 Council members were:[1]

Executive	Ulster and President	Neil John O'Boyle[2]
	Scotland and Treasurer	John Geraghty[3]
	Co-opted and Secretary	P.T. Daly[4]
Members	Leinster	John O'Hanlon
	Munster	Michael J. Crowe[5]
	Connacht	John MacBride[6]
	North of England	J. Murphy
	South of England	P.S. O'Hegarty[7]

Co-opted: Frederick (Fred) J. Allan,[8] John Mulholland, Seán Barrett.

1909–11 Supreme Council

In the next elections (1909) for the Council, P.T. Daly proposed Denis McCullough as a co-opted member to replace Seán Barrett, who resigned, and this was agreed;[9] otherwise, the composition remained the same.[10] McCullough was the first of a younger group, anxious to re-energise the Brotherhood, to join the Supreme Council.

Between 1909 and the next elections in 1911, 'at one period in between MacBride refused to be bothered anymore and in some way Michael Cowley was co-opted,' P.S. O'Hegarty recalled in 1936. 'I have a notion that either

IRB Supreme Council Members 1907–22

Allan or Daly was nominally assigned for Connaught and then Cowley was co-opted for the vacant co-option.'[11] Cowley probably joined in 1909 representing Munster. The proper course of action would have been for a special election to be held to replace MacBride, but the threadbare nature of the organisation outside Dublin and Belfast at the time meant that there were not Circles in many counties.

Fred Allan reluctantly agreed to rejoin the Council as secretary[12] and, because of his experience going back decades (he had first joined the Supreme Council in 1883), held a senior status. Michael Crowe was appointed to represent Munster. So the 1909–11 Council featured co-option rather than election as its norm, reflecting the Brotherhood's weakened state.

1911–13 Supreme Council

The 1911–13 Council elected in the summer had three energetic new members – Clarke, Hobson and MacDermott – determined to revive the society and displace the older members identified with letting the IRB slide away from rebellious activity.

Executive	Scotland and President	John Mulholland
	Co-opted and Treasurer	Tom Clarke
	Co-opted and Secretary	Fred Allan
Members	Ulster	Denis McCullough[13]
	Leinster	John ('Jack') O'Hanlon/Séamus O'Connor[14]/Séamus Deakin/ Bulmer Hobson[15]
	Munster	Diarmuid Lynch[16]
	Connacht	Michael Cowley
	North of England	James Murphy/Joseph Gleeson[17]
	South of England	P.S. O'Hegarty

Co-opted: Seán MacDermott, Michael J. Crowe.

Séamus O'Connor joined in 1912, replacing O'Hanlon as Leinster Divisional representative, but left a year later when Séamus Deakin joined.[18] James Murphy also left at some point in 1912 and was succeeded by Joseph Gleeson of Liverpool.[19]

384 The Irish Republican Brotherhood, 1914–1924

1913–15 Supreme Council

In September 1913, after a hectic two years of musical chairs, the 1913–15 Council was:

Executive	President	John Mulholland[20]/Séamus Deakin[21]
	Co-opted and Treasurer	Tom Clarke
	Connacht and Secretary	Seán MacDermott[22]
Members	Ulster	Denis McCullough[23]
	Leinster	Bulmer Hobson/Séamus Deakin[24]
	Munster	Diarmuid Lynch
	Scotland	John Mulholland/Charles Carrigan[25]
	North of England	Joseph Gleeson[26]
	South of England	Richard Connolly

Co-opted: Séamus Deakin, Dan Braniff,[27] P.S. O'Hegarty.[28]

Richard Connolly remembered that the first 1913–15 Council meeting concentrated on IRB organisation and administration, not on insurrection:

> At that meeting in September 1913, there was no talk of starting Volunteers at that time. There was some little trouble in the north-east of England and it was getting worse. Manchester and Liverpool were not pulling together very well and that occupied a lot of the business of the meeting. There was some trouble with Seamus Barrett, Manchester. He was a bit difficult, and representations were made to the Supreme Council, to the Secretary, and to Tom Clarke, to curb him. There were Dublin rows too. A lot of the business had to be left in the hands of the Executive. In fact, most of the business was left in the hands of the Executive as the duration of the meeting, that is, from 10.30 a.m. until 6.30 p.m., once a quarter, would not allow for much business being completed.[29]

Séamus Deakin and John Mulholland resigned at different times and had left the organisation by February 1915.[30] There may have been a short interlude before

IRB Supreme Council Members 1907–22 385

Denis McCullough was elected president in November 1915 (McCullough was in jail in September 1914).[31]

Early in 1915 – a Council election year – Seán T. O'Kelly, a trusted member of the Dublin Bartholomew Teeling Circle, was sent to Scotland to confirm Mulholland's resignation and to swear him to constant secrecy.[32] Seán T. probably conducted the Scottish biennial Divisional elections as well. Patrick McCormack[33] recalled:

> After Mulholland's resignation, some person from Dublin came to Scotland and held an election. I can't be sure now who the person who came was … At this election, Charles Carrigan, born in Stirlingshire, was elected. Carrigan was killed fighting at the GPO in 1916. Carrigan held office on the Supreme Council up to some time in 1915, when he had to leave Scotland to evade being conscripted for service in the British Army.[34]

1915–16 Supreme Council

In May 1915 MacDermott was arrested in Tuam, where he had gone to conduct the Connacht Divisional elections.[35] This task was taken over by Diarmuid Lynch, and Alec McCabe became the first elected member for Connacht since John MacBride's withdrawal in 1910 or 1911.[36] In September 1915 the new Council met in the Forrester's Hall in Rutland Square without MacDermott and McCullough, who was also in prison having been arrested in May for a bellicose speech. Four additional members were co-opted.[37] In November MacDermott and McCullough, having been released from prison, attended another Council meeting. McCullough was elected unanimously as president.[38]

The 1915–16 Council then was:

Executive	Ulster and President	Denis McCullough
	Co-opted and Treasurer	Tom Clarke
	Co-opted and Secretary	Seán McDermott[39]
Members	Leinster	Seán Tobin[40]
	Munster	Diarmuid Lynch
	Connacht	Alec McCabe
	North of England	Joseph Gleeson[41]

386   The Irish Republican Brotherhood, 1914–1924

South of England	Richard Connolly
Scotland	Charles Carrigan/Patrick McCormack[42]

Co-opted (in 1914):[43] Patrick Pearse,[44] Patrick McCartan.[45]

The Rising and what followed effectively brought the Council elected in 1915 to an end.

1916–17 Provisional Supreme Council

After the Rising, a provisional Supreme Council was put together by Séamus O'Doherty, Seán Ó Murthuile and Diarmuid O'Hegarty during 1916–17. Its members were:

Executive	Co-opted and President	Séamus O'Doherty[46]
	Co-opted and Secretary	Seán Ó Murthuile
	Co-opted and probably Treasurer	Diarmuid O'Hegarty[47]
Members	Leinster	Gregory Murphy[48]
	Ulster	Patrick McCartan/Liam Gaynor[49]
	Munster and Treasurer	Diarmuid Lynch[50]
	Connacht	Tom Breen/Alec McCabe[51]
	North of England	Patrick Lively/Neil Kerr/P.T. Daly
	Scotland	Patrick McCormack

Co-opted: Martin Conlon, Peadar Kearney, Luke Kennedy.

1917–19 Supreme Council

The 1917–19 Council's seven Divisional members were properly elected (a tribute to the work of the provisional Council) and the four co-opted, re-establishing its form and structure. There was a good deal of change because of arrests and the death of Thomas Ashe.

Executive	Co-opted and President	Thomas Ashe/Seán McGarry/ Harry Boland[52]
	Secretary	Seán Ó Murthuile/Michael Collins[53]

IRB Supreme Council Members 1907–22

	Treasurer	Diarmuid Lynch/Diarmuid O'Hegarty/Michael Collins/[54]
Members	Leinster	Luke Kennedy[55]
	Munster	Diarmuid Lynch
	Ulster	Liam Gaynor[56]
	Connacht	Alec McCabe/Andrew Lavin[57]
	Scotland	Patrick McCormack/Dan Braniff[58]
	England, north	Neil Kerr/Patrick O'Daly[59]
	England, south	Michael Collins

Co-opted: Séamus O'Doherty,[60] Gregory Murphy,[61] Gearóid O'Sullivan,[62] Diarmuid O'Hegarty,[63] Séamus Dobbyn,[64] Con Collins.[65]

1919–21 Supreme Council

The 1919–21 Council was more solid:

Executive	President and England, south	Michael Collins[66]
	Munster, north and Secretary	Seán Ó Murthuile
	Co-opted and Treasurer	Diarmuid O'Hegarty
Members	Connacht, east	Andrew Lavin
	Connacht, west (probably)	Michael Thornton
	Ulster, east	Liam Gaynor
	Ulster, west	Séamus Dobbyn/Eoin O'Duffy[67]
	Leinster, north	Luke Kennedy
	Leinster, south	Gearóid O'Sullivan
	England, north	Neil Kerr/Patrick O'Daly[68]
	Munster, south	Tom Hales
	Co-opted and Scotland	Daniel Branniff [69]

Co-opted: Seán McGarry, Harry Boland, Martin Conlon.[70]

1921–23 Supreme Council

When the Truce was signed in July 1921, the members of the Council[71] were:

Executive	England, south and President	Michael Collins
	Munster, north and Secretary	Seán Ó Murthuile

388   The Irish Republican Brotherhood, 1914–1924

	Ulster, west and Treasurer	Eoin O'Duffy
Members	Ulster, east	Joe McKelvey[72]
	Munster, south	Liam Lynch[73]
	England, north	Neil Kerr
	Scotland	Richard Connolly
	Leinster, north	Luke Kennedy[74]/Seán MacMahon
	Leinster, south	Gearóid O'Sullivan
	Connacht, west	Michael Thornton (probably)
	Connacht, east	Seán MacEoin

Co-opted: Diarmuid O'Hegarty, Harry Boland, Seán Boylan,[75] Sam Maguire.

This was the last complete Supreme Council.

APPENDIX XII

IRB Members in Senior Positions 1916–22

EASTER 1916: IRB MEMBERS OF THE DUBLIN BRIGADE STAFF

Commandant	Thomas MacDonagh[1]
Vice Commandant	John MacBride[2]
Adjutant	Éamon de Valera[3]
Assistant Adjutant	M.W. O'Reilly[4]
Quartermaster	Michael Staines[5]
Engineer	T. Sheehan[6]
Communications, Transport & Supply	Eimar O'Duffy[7]

EASTER 1916: IRB MEMBERS OF THE IRISH
VOLUNTEERS EXECUTIVE

General Secretary	Bulmer Hobson
Financial Secretary	Éamonn Ceannt
Press Secretary	Patrick Pearse
Publications Secretary	Pádraig Ó Riain
Co-Treasurer	Joseph Plunkett

EASTER 1916: IRB MEMBERS OF THE IRISH VOLUNTEERS
HEADQUARTERS STAFF

Director of Training	Thomas MacDonagh
Director of Military Operations	Joseph Plunkett
Quartermaster	Bulmer Hobson

390   The Irish Republican Brotherhood, 1914–1924

Director of Communications	Éamonn Ceannt
Director of Arms	Michael O'Rahilly
Director of Organisation	Patrick Pearse

1918–21 IRB MEMBERS, VOLUNTEERS/IRA GENERAL HEADQUARTERS STAFF[8]

Chief of Staff	Richard Mulcahy
Deputy Chief of Staff	Austin Stack;[9] Eoin O'Duffy
Assistant Chief of Staff	(J.J. O'Connell)[10]
Adjutant General	Michael Collins/Gearóid O'Sullivan
Quartermaster General	Fintan Murphy/Seán MacMahon
Director of Chemicals	(Séamus O'Donovan)[11]
Director of Engineering	Rory O'Connor
Director of Intelligence	Éamon Duggan/Michael Collins
Director of Munitions	Seán Russell
Director of Organisation	Éamon Price/Michael Collins/
Director of Communications	Diarmuid O'Hegarty
Director of Purchases	Joe Vize/Liam Mellows
Director of Training	Dick McKee
Editor of *An tÓglach*	Piaras Béaslaí

1921: IRB MEMBERS COMMANDING IRA DIVISIONS[12]

	Date Established	Commander	Treaty
1st Northern	29 May 1921	Joseph Sweeney[13]	Pro
2nd Northern	1 June 1921	Charlie Daly	Anti
3rd Northern	7 May 1921	Joe McKelvey	Anti
4th Northern	4 April 1921	Frank Aiken	Neutral/Anti
5th Northern	July 1921	(Dan Hogan)[14]	Pro
1st Western	2 September 1921	Michael Brennan	Pro
2nd Western	October 1921	Tom Maguire	Anti
3rd Western	October 1921	Liam Pilkington	Anti
4th Western	September 1921	Michael Kilroy	Anti
Midland	July 1921 (?)	Seán MacEoin	Pro
North Wexford Brigade	November 1920	Myles Breen[15]	Pro
Carlow Brigade	1917	(Liam Stack)[16]	Pro

IRB Members in Senior Positions 1916–22

1st Eastern	1 May 1921	Seán Boylan	Pro
2nd Eastern/ Dublin Brigade	1922	Oscar Traynor	Anti
3rd Eastern/South Dublin Brigade	July 1921 (?)	Patrick Fleming[17]	Anti
1st Southern	1 May 1921	Liam Lynch	Anti
2nd Southern	1 July 1921	Ernie O'Malley	Anti
3rd Southern	June 1921	Michael McCormick	Anti[18]

APPENDIX XIII

IRB Participation in the 1916 Rising

The official list of those tried for their part in the Rising together with the list of people arrested and their occupations published in the *Sinn Féin Rebellion Handbook*, compiled by *The Irish Times*, provides the best information.[1]

IRB members are not distinguished in these lists of those arrested, and only a minority of those listed actually took part in the Rising. Nevertheless, as Liam Ó Briain testified, 600–700 IRB members must have been included, and a rough picture of the social groups from which IRB members came can be inferred. Certainly, those arrested were suspected or known by the RIC and DMP to be involved in extreme nationalist politics and had been arrested because of this suspicion.

Of the 3,430 men and 79 women arrested in April and May 1916 following the Rising, the *Sinn Féin Rebellion Handbook* gives the occupations of 1,162, which can be broken down in the following way:

Arrested, April–May 1916

Socio-economic grouping	Dublin		Ireland	
	Number	**Percentage**	**Number**	**Percentage**
Professional and intermediate (merchants, teachers)	36	4.7	49(a)	12.5
Skilled, non-manual (printers, managers, compositors)	15	1.9	10(b)	2.5

IRB Participation in the 1916 Rising

Skilled, manual (tradesmen, farmers)	228(c)	29.6	177 (d)	45.3
Partly skilled, non-manual (salesmen, clerks)	120	15.6	37	9.5
Partly skilled, manual (apprentices)	68	8.8	27	6.9
Unskilled, manual and non-manual (shop assistants, labourers)	304(e)	39.4	91	23.3
Total	**771**	**100**	**391**	**100**

Notes:
(a) Includes one doctor and one barrister.
(b) Includes one 'priest's boy'.
(c) Includes thirty-two farmers and one market-gardener.
(d) Includes 110 farmers (28.1 per cent).
(e) Includes one Russian seaman.

From this breakdown, the large number of tradesmen arrested in Dublin stands out, particularly when set beside the correspondence of IRB Circles to trades in Dublin. If members of the IRB took part in large numbers in the Rising and/ or were arrested as a result, a significant number of tradesmen in Dublin would be expected, and this is confirmed.

In the countryside, farmers represented the bulk of those arrested. Again, this is to be expected because in the countryside the IRB naturally drew its members from those working on the land. It is also interesting to see that although a large number of labourers and shop assistants were arrested in Dublin and the rest of Ireland, many more tradesmen and farmers were arrested outside the cities, indicating that it was from these socio-economic groupings that the principal support for extreme Irish nationalist movements came.

A slightly different picture emerges from the breakdown of occupations of those men tried and found guilty for their parts in the Rising:[2]

Men court-martialled and found guilty, 1916

Socio-economic grouping	Number	Percentage
Professional and intermediate	35	20.5
Skilled, non-manual	13	7.5
Skilled, manual	58 (a)	34
Partly skilled, non-manual	24	14
Partly skilled, manual	3	1.8
Unskilled, manual and non-manual	38	22.2
Total	**171**	**100**

Note: (a) Includes twenty-seven farmers (15.8 per cent).

In this group, which includes the leaders of the Irish Volunteers, the ICA and the IRB, as might be expected, a very much higher proportion compared to the previous table is drawn from the 'professions and intermediate' group – teachers, doctors, shop-owners. A high proportion still came from the 'skilled, manual' group, particularly tradesmen and farmers, while a slightly lower proportion was composed of labourers and shop assistants, 'unskilled, manual and non-manual'. Compared to the distribution of occupations in Ireland classified in the 1911 census, the 1,333 arrested as a result of the Rising and whose occupations are known were employed in the following way:

Occupation comparison, 1911 census classification[3]

	Percentage arrested in 1916	Percentage in 1911 census
Professional and governmental	9.08	4.72
Domestic	0.68	1.17
Commercial	23.63	4.62
Agricultural	12.84	32.91
Different working class	50.81	19.87
Persons not producing	2.93	36.71
Total	**99.97**	**100**

Again, the strength of the representation of the 'commercial' class reflects the large number of tradesmen arrested in Dublin. While many 'agricultural' (169) were arrested, they seem markedly under-represented compared to the census percentage. However, we obtain a more realistic picture of the part agricultural people played if we look at the division between those people arrested in the countryside and those arrested in Dublin. Farmers comprised 28.1 per cent[4] of those arrested in the countryside. Labourers were heavily over-represented in Dublin and in the countryside, but what is interesting is that the unemployed (classed as 'persons not producing', together with retired people, old age pensioners and presumably housewives) were greatly under-represented. The lure of taking the king's shilling to fight for the rights of small nations during the First World War may have reduced the numbers of unemployed men in Ireland. But those arrested following the 1916 Rising were, for the most part, employed, and not merely standing around with nothing better to do.

ENDNOTES

GLOSSARY

1 D.M. Leeson, *The Black & Tans: British Police and Auxiliaries in the Irish War of Independence* (Oxford, 2011), p. 87; Jim Herlihy, *The Black & Tans 1920–1921: A Complete Alphabetical List, Short History and Genealogical Guide* (Dublin, 2021).

2 Petie Joe McDonnell, interview in Ernie O'Malley (ed. Cormac O'Malley), *The Men Will Talk to Me: Galway Interviews by Ernie O'Malley* (Cork, 2013), p. 43.

3 Cmdt Padraic Kennedy, 'Key appointments and the transition of the Irish Volunteers, the Irish Republican Army and the National Army (1913–23)', *Defence Forces Review 2016* (Dublin, 2016).

4 Seán Gibbons, Bureau of Military History Witness Statement (BMH WS) 927.

5 Michael Collins, *The Path to Freedom* (Cork, 2018), p. 119.

BIOGRAPHIES

1 Liam McMullen, BMH WS 762.

2 Albert Sylvester, transcript of an interview given to the author by Albert Sylvester, n.d.

3 Richard Ellmann, *Letters of James Joyce* (New York, 1966), vol. ii, p. 167.

4 Maud Gonne MacBride, BMH WS 317.

5 Patrick Kearney, BMH WS 868.

PREFACE

1 Keith Jeffrey (ed.), *The Sinn Féin Rebellion as They Saw It* (Dublin, 1999), p. 102. Arthur Norway (1859–1938) was appointed secretary of the Irish post office in 1912. He went on to say: 'and saved the British Government from a failure more disgraceful than can easily be found in its great history'.

2 J. Bowyer Bell, *The Secret Army: The IRA, 1916–70* (London, 2017), p. ix.

3 Thomas Bartlett (ed.), *The Cambridge History of Ireland*, vol. iv (Cambridge, 2018); Roy Foster (ed.), *The Oxford History of Ireland* (Oxford, 2001); Richard Bourke and Ian McBride (eds), *The Princeton History of Modern Ireland* (Oxford and Princeton, 2016); W.E. Vaughn (ed.), *A New History of Ireland. Volume VI: Ireland under the Union, 1870–1921* (Oxford, 1989); J.R. Hill (ed.), *A New History of Ireland. Volume VII: Ireland 1921–1984* (Oxford, 2003).

4 Maurice ('Moss') Twomey, interview, 11 December 1972.

5 Dermot Meleady, *John Redmond: The National Leader* (Dublin, 2018), p. 339.

6 Joseph E.A. Connell Jnr, *The Terror War: The Uncomfortable Realities of the War of Independence* (Dublin, 2021), p. 107.

7 Ben Byrne, interview, 20 November 1971. The 'Knocking Squad' was one of the names that it was called by its members. T. Ryle Dwyer, *The Squad and the Intelligence Operations of Michael Collins* (Cork, 2005), pp. 45–6.

Endnotes

8   Máire Comerford (ed. Hilary Dully), *On Dangerous Ground: A Memoir of the Irish Revolution* (Dublin, 2021), p. 90.

9   See Glossary under 'Republicans'.

10 Clann na Poblachta was formed in 1946 by several Old IRA men as a determined republican and reform party in contrast to de Valera's Fianna Fáil. 'Following Éamon de Valera's eventual entry into the Free State Dáil in 1927, a section of the Republican Army continued to oppose what they claimed to be his betrayal of true republicanism' (Noël Browne, *Against the Tide* (Dublin, 2007), pp. 96–7).

11 In 1960 Edna O'Brien's novel *The Country Girls* and in 1965 McGahern's novel *The Dark* were banned by the Censorship of Publications Board as a risk to public morality because they frankly addressed sexual matters.

12 Frank O'Connor, *The Big Fellow* (Dublin, 1965), p. 4 quotes Collins saying, 'If there is a God, I defy him.' Parish priests helped Collins' efforts to raise money: Collins was well aware of the power of the Church in Ireland and was careful to maintain good relations.

13 Patsy McGarry, 'An Irishman's Diary', *The Irish Times*, 12 May 1997. My father changed the spelling 'O'Byrne' to 'O'Beirne' on the grounds that Gaelic has no 'y' in its alphabet. He added 'Ranelagh' to designate our particular Byrne sept.

14 Joseph O'Doherty, interview, 22 March 1972.

15 Vinnie Byrne, interview, 19 April 1979.

16 Charles Townshend, *The Partition: Ireland Divided 1885–1925* (London, 2021), *passim*.

INTRODUCTION

1   Theobald Wolfe Tone (ed. Thomas Bartlett), *Life of Theobald Wolfe Tone* (Dublin, 1998), p. 178.

2   Michael Walters, 'Wolfe Tone: footnote or founding father to modern Ireland?', Drew University, Transatlantic Connections Conference, 28 October 2016, www.academia.edu/36423423/ Wolfe_Tone_Footnote_or_Founding_Father_to_Modern_Ireland?email_work_card=title: 'Given that Tone was not Catholic, the significant remembrances of him in Ireland, excluding northeast of partition, is testament not only to his force as a symbol, but the power of mythology surrounding him.' Gerry Adams, President of Sinn Féin (1983–2018), the party associated with the Provisional IRA, and TD for Louth, speaking at the Wolfe Tone Commemoration, 16 June 2014: 'What we are committed to is the radical republican politics of Theobald Wolfe Tone, brought to bear on the conditions of our time', www.youtube.com/watch?v=N_bYCkspk0A.

3   *Dáil Éireann Proceedings*, 19 December 1921: Michael Collins, 'The history of this nation has not been … a struggle for the ideal of freedom for 750 years symbolised in the name Republic. It has been a story of slow, steady, economic encroachment by England.'

4   *Irish Freedom*, September 1912.

5   The Irish government gave a grant of £15,000 towards the cost.

6   Philikí Etaireía ('Society of Friends') was the Greek society. The Greek war of independence (1821–30) against the Ottoman Empire was successful only when Russia, France and Britain actively supported the rebels. The Carbonari, a Franco–Italian–Spanish-connected group of secret societies, provided the impetus for Italian independence. The origin and meaning of Carbonari ('Charcoal Burners') is obscure.

7   They had a point. 'Perhaps the most pervasive legacy of British government in Ireland was the partnership that had developed between the Catholic Church and the British State, giving to the religious organisations the tasks of educating the young, running much of the health system and controlling much of the civic life of the society' (Tom Garvin, *Preventing the Future: Why was Ireland so Poor for so Long?* (Dublin, 2005), p. 3).

398 Endnotes

8 John Borgonovo (ed.), *Florence and Josephine O'Donoghue's War of Independence* (Dublin, 2006), p. 61.

9 Mícheál Ó Fathartaigh and Liam Weeks, *Birth of a State: The Anglo-Irish Treaty* (Dublin, 2021), pp. 92–4.

10 Mulcahy, 'Talk on Michael Collins', 11 December 1964 (UCD, Richard Mulcahy papers, P7/D/66.

11 Lawrence de Lacey (1885–1973), interview, 17 July 1972. A journalist, he also printed the Volunteer newsletter, *Irish Volunteer*.

12 Carol Coulter, *The Hidden Tradition: Feminism Women and Nationalism in Ireland* (Cork, 1993), p. 16: 'Mary Jane O'Donovan Rossa, Letitia Luby, and the sisters of John O'Leary, Ellen and Mary, were among its most prominent members ... and it continued its work for six years.' Rose Novak, '"Keepers of important secrets": The Ladies' Committee of the IRB', *History Ireland*, vol. 16, iss. 6 (November–December 2008).

13 Patrick McCartan, BMH WS 99; Robert Brennan, BMH WS 779: 'Seán T. O'Kelly happened to be in Wexford some time later and swore Úna in as a member of the organisation. About that time [*c*. 1909] somebody told me that there was only one other lady a member ... I think it was Maud Gonne.' See also Patrick McCartan, BMH WS 99; Maud Gonne MacBride, BMH WS 317; Geraldine Plunkett Dillon (ed. Honor Ó Brolcháin), *All in the Blood* (Dublin, 2006), p. 300.

14 David Neligan, interview, 20 February 1973. The parson's son was Thomas Clarke Luby (1822–1901), a journalist, author and revolutionary; the Catholic was James Stephens (1825–1901), a single-minded revolutionary. Neligan was referring to the renewed violence in the 1970s in Northern Ireland.

15 Eoin O'Duffy, who rose to become Chief of Staff and Commander-in-Chief of the Free State National Army in 1922–24, was a particularly successful example of someone who came to prominence because of his membership of the IRB and ensuing patronage from Michael Collins.

16 Joseph O'Doherty, interview, 25 March 1972.

17 Thomas Maguire, interview, 27 February 1973.

18 Thomas McEllistrim, interview in Ernie O'Malley (eds Cormac O'Malley and Tim Horgan), *The Men Will Talk to Me: Kerry Interviews* (Cork, 2012), p. 184. He related this to 1918. John Madden, interview in Ernie O'Malley (eds Cormac O'Malley and Cormac Ó Comhraí), *The Men Will Talk to Me: Galway Interviews* (Cork, 2013), p. 212. Madden, a Galway IRB Volunteer, was swayed by the appeal of an 'open' Volunteers and Sinn Féin in 1917: 'From that day none of us thought much about the IRB,' he said of the Galway Volunteers. Galway was not alone: there was a widespread assumption among IRB members from 1917 that the Volunteers were to be the nationalist focus, and this was ever more the case the further members were from Dublin.

19 Thomas Maguire, interview, 27 February 1973.

20 Patrick Mullaney, interview, 24 February 1973.

21 Richard English, *Irish Freedom: The History of Nationalism in Ireland* (Basingstoke and Oxford, 2007), p. 384; M.J. Kelly, *The Fenian Ideal and Irish Nationalism* (Woodbridge, 2009), *passim*.

22 Mulcahy, 'Conversation with Denis McCullough', 1961 (UCD, Richard Mulcahy papers, P7/D/15).

23 Dr Patrick O'Daly, BMH WS 814. Dr Daly, sometimes O'Daly, not to be confused with Patrick (Paddy) Daly, sometimes also O'Daly, of the Squad.

24 Risteárd Mulcahy, *My Father, The General: Richard Mulcahy and the Military History of the Revolution* (Dublin, 2009), pp. 63–4.

25 Collins, *The Path to Freedom*, pp. 101–2.

Endnotes

26 Robert Evans, letter to the author, 14 November 1972; Peter Hart, *The I.R.A. and Its Enemies: Violence and Community in Cork 1916–1923* (Oxford, 1999), p. 192.

27 Seán Fitzpatrick, 'The Third Tipperary Brigade', *The Nationalist*, 16 November 1957: 'The Volunteers … had become since Easter week, the Irish Republican Army.' Harry Nicholls, interview, 8 December 1971: 'In Frongoch a lot of fellows used to sign autograph books and you always signed yourself as "Captain, IRA". It was never "Irish Volunteers".' During the Rising, the Volunteers became the Army of the Irish Republic. Technically, since the post-Rising separatist effort was acknowledged as a continuation of the 1916 republic, the Volunteers were the IRA. But the new name did not have national currency, and calling themselves Volunteers was less confrontational, so the use of 'Volunteers' continued. In 1921 this changed and 'IRA' became the norm. Still, 'Volunteers' kept recurring in order to differ from 'IRA' which was seen – with justice – as the IRB's army. IRB witnesses in their statements to the BMH tended to refer to the IRA after 1916 and not the Volunteers.

28 Seán Ó Riain, *Provos: Patriots or Terrorists?* (Dublin, 1974), pp. 31–2.

29 First attributed (1856) to Daniel O'Connell, and popular in nationalist circles at the start of the First World War, *The Oxford Dictionary of Proverbs* (Oxford, 2008).

30 Eunan O'Halpin and Daithí Ó Corráin, *The Dead of the Irish Revolution* (Yale, 2020), p. 543 (covers 21 April 1916 to 31 December 1921).

31 Niamh Gallagher, *Ireland and the Great War: A Social and Political History* (London, 2020), pp. 146–8.

32 Francis McQuillan, BMH WS 338.

33 Dr Emmet Clarke, letter to the author, 6 May 1972.

34 President Biden provided an example of nationalist memory. In November 2020, having just won the presidential election, he was asked by a *BBC News* correspondent, Nick Bryant, for 'a quick word for the BBC' as he walked along a corridor. 'The BBC?' Biden responded without stopping, adding with a smile: 'I'm Irish' (*The National*, 8 November 2020). This gave rise to Biden being called 'Irish Joe'. Biden told an interviewer 'how much his mother hated the English. His parents were Irish and she had written several poems about her hatred of the English. He went off to find them and returned with hundreds of poems describing how God must smite the English and rain blood on our heads. He also told me that when his mother visited the United Kingdom she had stayed in a hotel where the Queen had once stayed. She was so appalled that she slept on the floor all night, rather than risk sleeping on a bed that the Queen had slept on.' Georgia Pritchett, *My Mess is a Bit of a Life* (London, 2021), p. 275.

35 The Anglo-Norman FitzGerald family which identified with Ireland and provided the leadership of several insurrections against British rule from the fourteenth to the eighteenth centuries.

36 Eamon Broy, BMH WS 1280.

37 Dr James McElligott, interview, 1 November 1972.

38 1862–1927. Born in England, his father was a staff surgeon in the British Army. The Chartres family, originally French Huguenots, had been established in Ireland since *c.* 1650. Chartres was educated at Wellington College, the University of London, and the King's Inns, Dublin. He was a legal adviser to the Irish team during the 1921 Treaty negotiations. James McGuire and James Quinn (eds), *Dictionary of Irish Biography* (Cambridge, 2018).

39 Brian P. Murphy, *John Chartres: Mystery Man of the Treaty* (Cambridge, 1995), p. 22. Chartres became one of Collins' intelligence agents in London and was involved with gunrunning for the IRA. De Valera described Collins' intelligence operation as his 'special department'.

40 *Dáil Éireann Proceedings*, 21 December 1921. She continued, 'and, as the things of the spirit have always prevailed, they prevail now'.

41 Christopher M. Byrne, BMH WS 1014.

400 Endnotes

42 Liam Ó Briain, BMH WS 6.

43 Liam Ó Briain, interview, 7 December 1971. In Clare, for example, 'the Irish Republican Brotherhood was always known as the Fenian Brotherhood, being, as it was, handed down directly from the Fenian organisation of 1867' (Joseph Barrett, BMH WS 1324).

44 Most famously called for by Patrick Pearse in his oration at the funeral of O'Donovan Rossa in 1915.

45 Patrick H. Pearse, *Political Writings and Speeches* (Dublin, 1924), p. 216. The bloodletting on the Western Front 1914–18 was the background to this bloody talk. It was not 'normal' times and consciousness was not 'normal' either.

46 Fergus O'Kelly, interview, 31 October 1972.

47 Diarmuid Ferriter, *A Nation and Not a Rabble: The Irish Revolution 1913–1923* (London, 2015), p. 34; Ernie O'Malley, *On Another Man's Wound* (Cork, 2013), p. 94.

48 Richard English, *Ernie O'Malley: IRA Intellectual* (Oxford, 1998), p. 101.

49 Desmond FitzGerald, *The Memoirs of Desmond FitzGerald* (London, 1968), p. 141. Prince Joachim (1890–1920) was the youngest son of Kaiser Wilhelm II.

50 Robert Brennan, BMH WS 779, section 2: at the 1917 Sinn Féin Ard-Fheis (political convention), 'Dev's formula declared the object of the organisation was the achievement of the Independence of Ireland as an Irish Republic and added that when that had been achieved, the people would decide on the form of government they wished to have. In his speech, Dev said that if they decided to have a king, he would not come from the House of Windsor.'

51 Dorothy Macardle, *The Irish Republic* (London, 1937), p. 242.

52 Charles Townshend, 'Force, law and the Irish revolution', in Senia Pašeta (ed.), *Uncertain Futures: Essays About the Irish Past for Roy Foster* (Oxford, 2016), p. 161; Roy Foster, *Modern Ireland 1600–1972* (London, 1989), p. 506.

1. POLITICS AND IDEALS

1 D.G. Boyce, 'How to settle the Irish Question: Lloyd George and Ireland, 1916–21' in A.J.P. Taylor (ed.), *Lloyd George: Twelve Essays* (London, 1971), p. 163.

2 Richard Mulcahy, 'Conversation with Denis McCullough', 18 October 1963 (UCD, Richard Mulcahy papers, P7/D/15). Inferentially, McCullough was denying that Protestant unionists were Irish.

3 The Government of Ireland Act received royal assent on 18 September 1914, but under the Suspensory Act that was simultaneously enacted, Home Rule was deferred for the duration of the First World War. In 1910 the IPP, campaigning for Home Rule, won 74 seats at Westminster. Another ten Irish MPs supported Home Rule. Herbert Asquith's Liberal Party won 272 seats; the Conservative and Unionist Party won 271 seats, and the Labour Party won 42 seats. So Asquith needed the support of the IPP to stay in government: the price was the enactment of Home Rule in 1914.

4 Major General Douglas Wimberley in William Sheehan, *British Voices, From the Irish War of Independence 1918–1921: The Words of British Servicemen Who Were There* (Cork, 2005), p. 227: 'At last the British Government in July 1921 decided to treat and compromise with the rebel leaders. To my mind this was the only sensible course left open to them, for though no doubt we, in the Army, given the powers of life and death, and official policy of ruthlessness, could easily have quelled the actual active Sinn Féin revolt, by means of really stern measures backed by the British Government, I feel certain the discontent would have merely smouldered underground. It would have burst into flames as soon as we withdrew.' Wimberley served with the Cameron Highlanders in Cobh as a brigade adjutant.

Endnotes 401

5   Daniel M. Jackson, *Popular Opposition to Irish Home Rule in Edwardian Britain* (Liverpool, 2009), *passim*; Jeremy Smith, *The Tories and Ireland 1910–1914: Conservative Party Politics and the Home Rule Crisis* (Dublin, 2001), *passim*.

6   Nicholas Mansergh, *The Irish Question, 1840–1921* (London, 1975), p. 5.

7   David Lloyd George, *War Memoirs of David Lloyd George*, vol. i (London, 1938), pp. 417–18.

8   Keith Jeffery (ed.), *The Sinn Féin Rebellion as They Saw It* (Dublin, 1999), p. 95.

9   Lloyd George, *War Memoirs*, vol. i, pp. 416–18. 'The failure of the [1919 Versailles Peace Conference] to deal with the Irish question, despite the discreet efforts of President Wilson and Colonel House, disappointed and alienated many Irish Americans and contributed significantly to the defeat of the Versailles Treaty and US membership in the League of Nations.' Francis M. Carroll, *America and the Making of an Independent Ireland: A History* (New York, 2021), pp. 199–200.

10   There were some demonstrations in support of Irish Home Rule too, but the most significant politically were those in support of Ulster unionists. Unionism was an Empire-wide movement. '[T]here were over 5,000 Orange lodges worldwide, including some 1,700 in Canada and Newfoundland, 1,600 in Ireland and 800 in the United States. The key figure, however, is not the number of lodges reported, but the dues paid – which reflects total membership. Here we find that Ireland and British North America account for at least 90 percent of the total … membership is dominated by Canada, Newfoundland and Northern Ireland in the twentieth century.' Eric Kaufmann, 'The Orange Order in Ontario, Newfoundland, Scotland and Northern Ireland: A macro-social analysis', in David. A. Wilson (ed.), *The Orange Order in Canada* (Dublin, 2007), pp. 42–3.

11   Donal Lowry, 'Ulster resistance and loyalist rebellion in the Empire', in Keith Jeffery (ed.), *An Irish Empire? Aspects of Ireland and the British Empire* (Manchester, 1996), p. 192.

12   Charles Townshend, 'The Irish Republican Army and the development of guerrilla warfare, 1916–1921', *The English Historical Review*, vol. 94, no. 371 (April, 1979), p. 341: 'De Valera's announcement, at the end of March, that the Dail accepted responsibility for the actions of the IRA, can be seen as something of an admission of defeat by the "politicians" who had not achieved any real control over the Republican military forces.'

13   Ferriter, *A Nation and Not a Rabble*, p. 197. About 418 men – 19 per cent – of a sample of 2,200 Tans from a total enlistment of 7,684 were Irish born; Diarmuid Ferriter, 'Black and Tans: "Half-drunk, whole-mad" and one-fifth Irish', *The Irish Times*, 4 January 2020. But Jim Herlihy, *The Black & Tans 1920–1921: A Complete Alphabetical List, Short History and Genealogical Guide* (Dublin, 2021), lists 882 Irish-born Tans in a total of 7,684 in what he calls the 'Royal Irish Constabulary Special Reserve' – in three categories: 381 recruited in Britain, 312 temporary constables, and 189 Veterans and Drivers Division. David Leeson, in an email to the author, 10 November 2021, said, '[What percentage of the Tans were Irish] is surprisingly difficult to answer. What makes it difficult, is the fact that the Black and Tans (unlike the Auxiliaries) were not a separate force or formation. They were simply constables in the Royal Irish Constabulary, and were counted as members of that Force. In his recent book, Jim Herlihy claims they were part of a "Royal Irish Constabulary Special Reserve", but no such formation ever existed. So I'm not sure where he got that idea. What is more, Britishness was a defining feature of the Black and Tans. That nickname was applied to new British recruits, who stood out from the rest of their Force in their militarized uniforms. So, I'm not sure it was even possible to be an "Irish Black and Tan". That's why I didn't talk about them in my book. Irishmen continued to join the RIC in Ireland by the usual procedure throughout the War of Independence. And they were trained separately, at Phoenix Park, instead of being trained (sort of) with the Black and Tans at Gormanstown. In October 1920, for example, 74 Irish recruits joined the RIC as constables, in

402 Endnotes

Ireland, compared to 1153 British recruits joining the force from Great Britain. But a number of Irishmen did join the RIC in Great Britain, alongside British recruits ... Those men were probably the closest thing there were to "Irish Black & Tans".'

14 Leeson, *The Black & Tans*, pp. 3, 4: '[T]he Irish police took part in reprisals as well ...The government primarily relied on the [RIC] to defeat what became known as the Irish Republican Army.' W.H. Kautt, *Ground Truths: British Army Operations in the Irish War of Independence* (Dublin, 2014), p. 185.

15 O'Halpin and Ó Corráin, *The Dead of the Irish Revolution*, p. 544; Herlihy, *The Black & Tans*, pp. 272–77, 419–20; Kautt, *Ground Truths*, p. 165. A total of 413 British military died in 1920–21. Of these, 152 died by suicide, accident or as a result of ill health.

16 Collins, *The Path to Freedom*, p. 119. Sinn Féin obtained about 47 per cent of the vote in 1918, but if the twenty-five constituencies where Sinn Féin was unopposed had been contested, Sinn Féin might have received 67 per cent or more of the recorded vote: www.ark.ac.uk/elections/h1918.htm.

17 David Fitzpatrick (ed.), *Terror in Ireland 1916–23* (Dublin, 2012), *passim*.

18 David Fitzpatrick, 'The geography of the War of Independence' in John Crowley, Donal Ó Drisceoil, Mike Murphy (eds) and John Borgonovo (ass. ed.), *Atlas of the Irish Revolution* (Cork, 2017), pp. 534–43; RTÉ, *The Irish War of Independence, 1919–21*, Document Pack Part 1, Map: 'Structure and organisation of the IRA, 1919–21'.

19 Erskine Childers, 'Rough minutes from Anglo-Irish Conference', 14 October 1921 (papers of Robert Erskine Childers and his wife Mary Alden Childers (née Osgood), TCD, 7799/7802).

20 *Dáil Éireann Proceedings*, 22 December 1921.

21 Marc Mulholland, 'How revolutionary was the 'Irish Revolution?', *Éire-Ireland*, vol. 56: 1 and 2 (Spring/Summer 2021), p. 148: 'Did the generation of 1913–23 actually believe that they had lived through a revolution? This is not at all clear. A search of the online British Library Newspaper Archive finds 858 uses of the term 'Irish revolution' for the period 1879–98, many of which referred to the period of the Land War. For the years after 1916, up to 1935, there are only 237 hits, most of these expatiating on various alleged plots rather than seeking to characterise the Irish independence and partition period as a whole. The equivalent figures for the online Irish Newspaper Archive, in contrast, are 102 hits for 'Irish revolution' in the 1879–98 period compared to 214 for the years 1916–35. For the 1916–35 period, however, the terms 'Irish Troubles' (458), 'Tan War' (833) and 'Anglo-Irish War' (2542) predominate. In the 1,773 witness statements and 334 sets of contemporary documents collected by the BMH to track the 'history of the movement for independence' from 1913 to 1921, the term 'revolution' brings up only 65 hits, disproportionately from veterans of the Irish Citizen Army. Even these labour-movement veterans usually talked about revolution in general rather than of an Irish revolution.'

22 Jim Maher, *Harry Boland: A Biography* (Cork, 2020), p. 65.

23 Derek Molyneux and Darren Kelly, *Someone Has to Die for This – Dublin: November 1920–July 1921* (Cork, 2021), p. 119.

24 Peter Hart, *Mick: The Real Michael Collins* (London, 2005), p. 230.

25 Peter Hart, *British Intelligence in Ireland 1920–21: The Final Reports* (Cork, 2002), p. 15; Charles Townshend, *The British Campaign in Ireland* (Oxford, 1975), p. 80: 'Working to secret instructions from Lloyd George, who often, in Cabinet, disowned his moves, Cope tirelessly struggled to establish common ground for negotiations.' Geoffrey Sloan, 'Hide seek and negotiate: Alfred Cope and counter intelligence', *Intelligence and National Security*, vol. 33, no. 2 (2018), pp. 176–95: 'It has not been possible to locate evidence of direct communication between Cope and Lloyd George' (p. 189).

26 The 1931 Statute of Westminster gave the Free State the freedom to make treaties.

Endnotes

27   The Commission reported privately in 1925 recommending some small changes, but the British, Northern Irish and Free State governments agreed to confirm the existing county borders unchanged.

28   Seán MacEoin, BMH WS 1228.

29   Townshend, *The Partition*, p. 205–9; Séamus Woods, note of a discussion with the author, 26 September 1975; Eoin Neeson, *The Civil War 1922–23*, (Dublin, 1989), p. 21: 'according to PS O'Hegarty and others, Churchill was one of those who had given the guarantee to Collins that he would see to it that the North would consist of only four counties which could not survive as an economic unit'.

30   Proportional representation was introduced in Ireland by the 1920 Government of Ireland Act. John M. Regan, *Myth and the Irish State* (Dublin, 2013), p. 117, points out that votes may have been for the pact between Collins and de Valera rather than straightforwardly for the Treaty settlement. It has also been pointed out that the prospect of peace was an argument for a pro-Treaty vote that risked but did not guarantee civil war, that an anti-Treaty vote would ensure renewed fighting with Britain, and that the June 1922 general election result was taken as endorsing the Treaty. Several Republican leaders, including Liam Lynch and Liam Deasy, opposed the Treaty but acknowledged that most people supported it. Like Collins, they were in favour of using the Treaty as a stepping stone to a republic, but their loyalty to the Republic determined their eventual choice. Florence O'Donoghue and Seán O'Hegarty withdrew from active IRA involvement and, as neutrals, spent the Civil War trying to halt fighting.

31   Peadar O'Donnell, interview, 22 March 1972.

32   Sir Alfred Cope to Elizabeth Foxe, 3 January 1951, BMH WS 469.

33   The parallels did not stop there: Stern (1907–42) was killed while being arrested by three policemen in his hideaway in Tel Aviv. At the time they claimed that Stern had tried to escape through a window; later two of them (one unambiguously, the other privately) alleged that their leader, Geoffrey Morton, had purposefully shot Stern, who was unarmed. Stern was similar to Patrick Pearse: he was a poet and thought in terms of a 'blood sacrifice'.

2. CONSPIRATORS

1   Alphonse de Lamartine, *Histoire de la Révolution de 1848* (Paris, 1849, trans. by the author), vol. i, p. 66.

2   Desmond Ryan, *The Fenian Chief: A Biography of James Stephens* (Dublin, 1967), p. 58. In 1856 Jeremiah O'Donovan Rossa formed the Phoenix National and Literary Society in Dublin with Young Irelanders as a physical force organisation. It merged with Stephens' IRB.

3   Peter Hart, 'The Fenians and the international revolutionary tradition', in Fearghal McGarry and James McConnel (eds), *The Black Hand of Republicanism: Fenianism in Modern Ireland* (Dublin, 2009), p. 193.

4   Security was not as tight as the Carbonari model suggested, largely because as clause 11 of the IRB's 1894 Rules stated: 'Every Circle to be divided into Companies. A Company is to consist of not less than 30 or more than 80 men … A Circle is to consist of not less than 50 or more than 800 men, save and except in small country towns, where a section can be formed of any number over thirty men.' This was tightened up after 1916.

5   Desmond Ryan, *The Fenian Chief*, pp. 87–91; Joseph Denieffe, *Recollections of the Irish Revolutionary Brotherhood* (New York, 1906), ch. 2, p. 14 *et seq.*

6   T.W. Moody and Leon Ó Broin, 'The I.R.B. Supreme Council, 1868-78', *Irish Historical Studies*, vol. 19, no. 75 (March 1975).

7   1869 Constitution, clause XV.

404   Endnotes

8   Kathleen Clarke (ed. Helen Litton), *Revolutionary Woman* (Dublin, 2008), p. 132, asserted that Cumann na mBan was started by the IRB. Aine O'Rahilly, BMH WS 333, credited various nationalist women with its creation. See Eve Morrison, 'The Bureau of Military History and female republican activism,1913–23' in Maryann Gialanella Valiulis (ed.), *Gender and Power in Irish History* (Dublin, 2008), ch. 5, for an account of Cumann na mBan's importance that was publicly acknowledged by Michael Collins and Cathal Brugha.

9   The IRB infiltrated the AOH, and these infiltrators may have been the thirty or so AOH members who took part.

10   *Dáil Éireann Proceedings*, 11 March 1921.

11   Bulmer Hobson, *Ireland Yesterday and Tomorrow* (Tralee, 1968), p. 36; Diarmuid Lynch, *The I.R.B. and the 1916 Insurrection* (Cork, 1957), p. 26. On the Supreme Council of the IRB in 1916, Denis McCullough, the President, was a shop assistant; Thomas Clarke, the treasurer, a tobacconist; Seán MacDermott, the secretary, an ex-bartender turned journalist and professional revolutionary; Patrick Pearse, a barrister and headmaster; Alasdair ('Alec') McCabe, a schoolmaster; Diarmuid Lynch, a commercial traveller; Dr Patrick McCartan, a general practitioner.

12   T. Desmond Williams (ed.), *Secret Societies in Ireland* (Dublin, 1973), *passim*; Marcus Bourke, *John O'Leary* (Dublin, 2009), *passim*; Tom Garvin, *Nationalist Revolutionaries in Ireland 1858– 1928* (Oxford, 1987), pp. 52–3.

13   Twenty-eight men were arrested. Five were tried of whom two were found not guilty. Edward O'Meagher Condon had cried 'God save Ireland' from the dock.

14   Geraldine Dillon, BMH WS 358. 'There's the man, says Joe.' (Joe Hynes in James Joyce's *Ulysses*.) 'There he is sitting there. The man that got away James Stephens.' (James Joyce, *Ulysses* (London, 2000), p. 552.)

15   1841–1914. Holland was a native Irish speaker, learning English only in his teens. He emigrated to the United States in 1873 and became a mathematics teacher in Paterson, New Jersey, for several years. Holland's brother, Michael, had emigrated to America earlier and joined Clan na Gael. Through Michael's contact with O'Donovan Rossa, Holland met John Devoy, the head of the Clan, and secured the Clan's backing to build a submarine (a term Holland apparently invented). The submarine was named *Fenian Ram* by the *New York Sun* newspaper. It submerged to 45 feet with a crew of three. A pneumatic gun fired six-foot-long dynamite-filled steel projectiles out of her bow like a modern torpedo. Holland went on to design submarines for the United States Navy and the Royal Navy, and his design was licensed by other navies, including the Austrian whose Holland design U-5 was commanded by Georg Ritter von Trapp of *The Sound of Music* fame, the most successful submariner of the First World War. The company created to build Holland submarines evolved into General Dynamics, the world's sixth largest defence contractor. The *Fenian Ram* is on display at the Paterson City Museum. Richard Knowles Morris, 'John P. Holland and the Fenians', *Journal of the Galway Archaeological and Historical Society*, vol. 31, no. 1/2 (1964/1965).

16   Jeffery (ed.), *The Sinn Féin Rebellion as They Saw It*, pp. 93–4.

17   Thomas Taylor, interview, 5 November 1972.

18   Military rigour was not confined to Irish rebels. Conscientious objectors in 1914 were sent by the military authorities to France, a war theatre, where they fell under military law, and could be tried by court martial and sentenced to death for refusing to fight. Only Prime Minister Asquith's intervention saved their lives.

19   Lloyd George did not want the job. He was scheduled to join Lord Kitchener, the War Minister, travelling to Russia on HMS *Hampshire* to see for themselves the Russian situation. *Hampshire* was sunk by a mine and Kitchener was one of the 737 on board who died. 'But my plans were

Endnotes 405

upset by Mr Asquith's proposal … it saved my life! … I should have been with [Kitchener] and shared his fate. This escape, at least, I owe to Ireland.' Lloyd George, *War Memoirs*, vol. i, p. 420.

20 Townshend, *The Partition*, pp. 100–12.

21 See, for example, James McCullough, BMH WS 529: 'The I.R.B. after 1916 played a very important part in the procuring of arms for the Volunteers. We had contacts with I.R.B. Circles in Belfast where quantities of arms were procured and transported to Armagh by our members … The I.R.B. were useful in obtaining information through police channels and through Unionist supporters.'

22 Michael O'Leary, BMH WS 797.

23 Arthur Greene, BMH WS 238. Greene joined the Dundalk Circle in 1912 and remained a member until 1916.

24 Robert Haskin, BMH WS 223.

25 Valentine Jackson, BMH WS 409.

26 James Slattery, interview, 17 March 1973.

27 Seán MacBride, interview, 21 February 1973.

28 Michael Hayes, interview, 22 March 1972.

29 Maurice ('Moss') Twomey, interview, 11 December 1972.

30 Liam O'Dwyer, interview, 2 March 1973.

31 Seán Gibbons, BMH WS 927: 'In our Brigade area, particularly from 1919, the Irish Republican Brotherhood was a great moulding and constructive force. Their members were active, individually and as a body, in the Sinn Féin Clubs, in the Irish Republican Army and in all the activities that streamed from those two bodies. I myself was Secretary to the Sinn Féin Club, Company Adjutant of Westport Company of Volunteers, Assistant Brigade Adjutant, Clerk of the Parish Court – all at one time.'

32 Some IRB members were in the AOH, but its IPP affiliation made secret IRB control of it impossible. See, for example, James McCullough, BMH WS 529.

33 Liam O'Doherty, interview, 7 March 1973.

34 Lieutenant General A.E. Percival in Sheehan, *British Voices*, p. 156.

35 Frank Crozier, *Ireland Forever* (London, 1932), p. 220.

36 Townshend, 'The Irish Republican Army and the development of guerrilla warfare, 1916–1921', p. 343.

37 Thomas Maguire, interview in Ernie O'Malley (eds Cormac O'Malley, Vincent Keogh), *The Men Will Talk to Me: Mayo Interviews by Ernie O'Malley* (Cork, 2014), p. 194.

38 For example, 'The IRB never developed much in Clare' (Patrick McDonnell, interview in Ernie O'Malley (ed. Pádraig Óg Ó Ruairc), *The Men Will Talk to Me: Clare Interviews by Ernie O'Malley* (Cork, 2016), p. 173); in Armagh the IRB 'lost control' (James McCullough, BMH WS 529). In South Tipperary, after 1918, members drifted away. 'There was only an odd IRB man here and there in East Mayo' (Johnny Grealy, interview in O'Malley, *Mayo Interviews*, p. 254). But the 'IRB had a hold on Galway, and it was also powerful around the county' (John Madden, interview in O'Malley, *Galway Interviews*, p. 219). 'The IRB was very strong in Kerry … I expect that all the officers in Kerry were IRB' (Dennis 'Dinny' Daly, interview in O'Malley, *Kerry Interviews*, p. 320).

39 Thomas Harris, BMH WS 320. It was probably thought that British military presence made IRB recruitment in the county less secure.

3. INFAMY

1 *The Freeman's Journal*, 18 February 1867. Sermon delivered at Killarney Cathedral.

2 T.W. Moody and F.X. Martin (eds), *The Course of Irish History* (Cork, 1967), p. 279.

Endnotes

3 John Henry Whyte, *Church and State in Modern Ireland 1923–70* (New York, 1971), p. 3; W.J. Lowe, 'The Lancashire Irish and the Catholic Church, 1846–71: The social dimension', *Irish Historical Studies*, vol. 20, no. 78 (September 1976), p. 130, noted that perhaps fewer than 40 per cent attended Mass regularly in the mid-nineteenth century.

4 Whyte, *Church and State*, p. 8.

5 Lowe, 'The Lancashire Irish', p. 154.

6 Rev. Fr Aloysius, OFMCap., BMH WS 207. The Third Order was secular, for married men and women who met in regular religious gatherings. The First Order was monks; the Second Order was nuns. William Cosgrave, who fought in 1916 and became President of the Executive Council of the Free State, refused to join the IRB and had an oratory built at his home where Mass could be celebrated. Kevin O'Higgins, who became Cosgrave's deputy in the Free State, had studied to be a priest. Éamon de Valera at all times was a devout Catholic.

7 Clarke, *Revolutionary Woman*, p. 136.

8 Patrick Joseph Ruttledge (1892–1952), interview in O'Malley, *Mayo Interviews*, p. 277. Mayo TD 1921–51. A pupil at St Enda's. A friend of Seán MacDermott's. IRB Centre, North Mayo. Intelligence Officer, North Mayo Brigade and later of Fourth Western Division. Vice-O/C Fourth Western from September 1922 and on IRA Army Council. Minister for Home Affairs in the Republican Cabinet (paralleling the Free State) from November 1922. Acting President of the Republic from August 1923. A founder-member of Fianna Fáil in 1926, and a minister 1932–41.

9 MacDermott made this list in New York in 1913 while conferring with Clan na Gael (Seán Cronin, *The McGarrity Papers* (Tralee, 1972), p. 330).

10 F.S.L. Lyons, *The Fall of Parnell 1890–1* (London, 1960), *passim*.

11 David W. Miller, *Church, State and Nation in Ireland* (Dublin, 1973), p. 459; Emmet Larkin, *The Roman Catholic Church and the Creation of the Modern Irish State, 1878–86* (Dublin, 1975), *passim*.

12 Edward R. Norman, *The Catholic Church and Ireland in the Age of Rebellion, 1859–73* (London, 1965), p. 94. The animosity of the Church lived on: F.X. Martin, 'The 1916 Rising: A "Coup d'État" or a "Bloody Protest"?', *Studia Hibernica*, no. 8 (1968), did not mention the IRB.

13 Norman, *The Catholic Church and Ireland*, p. 131.

14 Ryan, *The Fenian Chief*, pp. 217–61.

15 Giovanni Costigan, *A History of Modern Ireland* (New York, 1969), pp. 214–15.

16 'Editorial', *Irish People*, 21 May 1864. The paper was suppressed in 1865.

17 P.S. O'Hegarty, *A History of Ireland under the Union* (London, 1952), pp. 427–44.

18 Norman, *The Catholic Church and Ireland*, pp. 94–5.

19 *The Times*, 20 February 1867; Norman, *The Catholic Church and Ireland*, p. 118: Cullen, however, was angered by Moriarty's sermon for having caused 'great offence'.

20 Norman, *The Catholic Church and Ireland*, pp. 120–2.

21 Robert Kee, *The Green Flag* (London, 1972), p. 367; Donal McCartney, 'The Church and secret societies' in Williams (ed.), *Secret Societies in Ireland*, p. 73.

22 K.B. Nowlan, 'Thomas Clarke, MacDermott and the IRB' in F.X. Martin (ed.), *Leaders and Men of the Easter Uprising: Dublin 1916* (London, 1967), pp. 109–10.

23 Miller, *Church, State and Nation in Ireland*, p. 322; Patrick McCartan, BMH WS 766, gives the names of two priests who were members; John Devoy, *Recollections of an Irish Rebel* (New York, 1929), p. 119, recounts how IRB men could go to confession at the Jesuit church in Gardiner Street, Dublin, where the priest did not ask difficult questions.

24 Lynch, *The I.R.B. and the 1916 Insurrection*, pp. 22–3. At the start of the Rising on Easter Monday, 'One of the interesting things that Ceannt said was that we had the Papal Benediction,

Endnotes

that we had the Pope's Blessing' (Thomas J. Doyle, BMH WS 186); Éamonn Ceannt had felt it necessary to reassure his men.

25 'When Seán McDermott told us what we were to do, this man got very disturbed and said he would like to go to confession. Seán told him to go over there in the corner and make an act of contrition. The man knelt down in the corner of the room and prayed fervently. It is more than I did' (Kevin McCabe, BMH WS 926).

26 Daniel Kelly, BMH WS 1004.

27 Thomas Barry, BMH WS 1. Valentine Jackson, BMH WS 409, remembered another Clontarf meeting – not the same as Fr O'Sullivan's – at about the same time: 'Sometime about 1909 or 1910, the members of the Dublin Circles were instructed (or requested) to attend a general meeting which was held one summer Sunday evening at the old Town Hall, Clontarf, to hear a lecture from the Rev. Father Sheehy, brother of David Sheehy, MP. He was himself, I was told, a member of the IRB. The various Centres were gathered in the entrance hall to identify the rank and file. I had not the gumption to count the number who attended, but I would say there were between two and three hundred. The lecturer was enthusiastically received. I have now no idea of the subject matter of his lecture, but I know that it dealt only with the IRB.' Father Sheehy seems to have been used fairly often to reassure members (Lawrence de Lacey, interview, 17 July 1972).

28 Francis Daly, BMH WS 278.

29 Patrick McCartan, BMH WS 766.

30 Norman, *The Catholic Church and Ireland, passim*: British diplomacy in this respect certainly influenced the Pope.

31 Patrick McCartan, BMH WS 766.

32 Joseph Barrett, BMH WS 1324.

33 Lynch, *The I.R.B. and the 1916 Insurrection*, p. 23: Fr O'Sullivan was born in Valentia Island, Co. Kerry, but emigrated to the United States; Patrick Daly, BMH WS 220: 'Father O'Sullivan from America addressed the meeting explaining the Church's attitude to secret societies and proved to us that the I.R.B. was not banned by the Church.' Thomas Barry, BMH WS 1, thought the 1910/11 meeting 'was the only general meeting of the I.R.B. ever held during my period of membership'. Frank Ryan, interview, 14 December 1971: Ryan thought the 1913 meeting was 'The only occasion when the IRB all came together in Dublin.' Probably there were two meetings with different attendance.

34 Ernest Blythe, interview, 10 August 1973.

35 Henry O'Brien, BMH WS 1308.

36 Séamus Daly, BMH WS 360. Daly signed his statement as 'James Daly'.

37 James Lalor, BMH WS 1032.

38 Batt O'Connor, *With Michael Collins in the Fight for Irish Independence* (London, 1929), p. 90.

39 Miller, *Church, State and Nation in Ireland*, pp. 324, 329–484. Seven bishops denounced the Rising but twenty-two remained silent.

40 Patrick McCartan, BMH WS 766. St Saviour's Priory, Church Street, Dublin.

41 Michael Brennan, *The War in Clare, 1911–21: Personal Memoirs of the Irish War of Independence* (Dublin, 1980), p. 39.

42 Manus O'Boyle, BMH WS 289.

43 Donal McCartney, 'The Church and secret societies', p. 78.

44 Mulcahy, 'Talk on Michael Collins', 11 December 1964 (UCD, Richard Mulcahy papers, P7/D/66). This was a Squad operation. The officer was probably Paddy Daly.

45 Macardle, *The Irish Republic*, p. 241; Longford and O'Neill, *Eamon de Valera*, p. 66.

46 Frank O'Connor, *An Only Child* (London, 1968), pp. 130–1: 'The bishop, Daniel Cohalan – locally known as 'Danny Boy' – was a bitter enemy … and every Sunday we had to be ready for

408 Endnotes

a diatribe at Mass ... and some young man would rise from his seat and move into the nave, genuflect, and leave the church ... Sometimes this went on for minutes till a considerable group had left. They stood and talked earnestly in the chapel yard, all of them declared rebels.'

47 Brigade Chaplain to Brigade Adjutant, 15 December 1920 (National Library of Ireland (NLI), Florence O'Donoghue papers Ms 31,170).

48 Patrick J. Twohig (trans.), *Blood on the Flag: Autobiography of a Freedom Fighter* (Cork, 1996), p. 94 (Séamas Ó Maoileoin, *B'fhiú an Braon Fola* (Dublin, 1958)). In 1909 at a London Sinn Féin Club Collins said that the way to deal with the Irish hierarchy was 'to exterminate them'. During the Rising he mocked men in the GPO who sought confession. Then, in September 1921 he visited the Drogheda shrine of the Blessed Oliver Plunkett (beatified in 1920 and canonised in 1975, the first Irish saint since St Laurence O'Toole was canonised in 1225). From 12 October 1921 during the Treaty negotiations in London he went to the 8 a.m. Mass at Brompton Oratory every day, followed by Special Branch detectives (Mary Kenny, 'Michael Collins' religious faith', *Irish Historical Studies*, vol. 96, no. 334 (Winter 2007), pp. 424–6). The change in Collins' view seems sudden. Attending Mass and visiting the Plunkett shrine may have been political moves, with attending Mass in London also a cover for meeting people secretly. Kevin O'Higgins, a minister in the 1922 Provisional Government of the Free State, described Collins as 'a pasty-faced blasphemous fucker from Cork' suggesting that Collins' religious faith was political, not profound (Tom Garvin, *1922: The Birth of Irish Democracy* (Dublin, 1996), p. 101). Collins himself declared about his part in the GPO in 1916, 'I am the only man in the whole place who wasn't at Confession or Communion!' (O'Connor, *The Big Fellow*, p. 15).

49 Whyte, *Church and State*, pp. 89–90, 320–2, 372, 375.

50 David Moriarty, 'A Letter on the Disendowment of the Established Church' (1867), quoted in Norman, *The Catholic Church and Ireland*, p. 118.

4. 1873–1917 CONSTITUTION

1 Christopher Byrne, BMH WS 167.

2 1873 Constitution, preamble, and clause 2.

3 1873 Constitution, 'Supreme Council', clause 18.

4 1873 Constitution, clause 1.

5 1873 Constitution, 'Supreme Council', clause 18.

6 In 1922, Michael Collins drafted a new constitution that did not mention religion but was probably not presented for approval by the Supreme Council before his death.

7 F.S.L. Lyons, *Ireland Since the Famine* (London, 1971), p. 123.

8 Donal McCartney, 'The Church and the Fenians', *University Review*, vol. 4, no. 3, Special Fenian Issue (Winter, 1967). For more than fifty years after 1921, the separation of Church and State was more a formal than a practical distinction.

9 Ryan, *The Fenian Chief*, p. 91.

10 Ibid.

11 Ibid., p. 92.

12 1873 Constitution, clause 4.

13 Valentine Jackson, BMH WS 409. Not every member was so enthralled. A few members enlisted during the First World War, not as revolutionary agents but most likely in search of excitement and regular pay. They were probably expelled from the Brotherhood. One – Michael O'Toole, a lance-corporal in the Irish Guards – volunteered for Casement's Irish Brigade, recruited from prisoners of war to fight for Germany. Richard S. Grayson, *Dublin's Great Wars: The First World War, The Easter Rising and The Irish Revolution* (Cambridge, 2018), pp. 79, 411, 432.

Endnotes

409

14 Seán MacEoin, interview, 22 February 1973.

15 Seán MacEoin, interview, 9 November 1972; 19 July 1972.

16 Anne Dolan and William Murphy, *Days in the Life: Reading the Michael Collins Diaries 1918–1922* (Dublin, 2022), p. 47.

17 UCD, Michael Conlon papers, P97/9.

18 Valentine Jackson, BMH WS 409.

19 'Committee', 'Board' and 'Council' were used interchangeably by members, but 'Board' was the official name.

20 Lynch, *The I.R.B. and the 1916 Insurrection*, p. 22.

21 Ibid. Ordinary members could propose men for membership, but responsibility for ensuring that they met requirements was the Centre's.

22 Séamus Daly, BMH WS 360.

23 Gilbert Morrissey, BMH WS 1138.

24 Joseph Furlong, BMH WS 335.

25 Joseph Barrett, BMH WS 1324.

26 Valentine Jackson, BMH WS 409; Jack Stafford, BMH WS 818: in his Circle, 'as far as I could see, very little attempt was made to procure arms'.

27 'Laws, Rules and Regulations for the Government of the I.R.B.' (1894), clause 39. See Appendix III.

28 Patrick Mullaney, interview, 24 February 1973.

29 In 1917 the Divisions were divided in two resulting in fourteen Divisional representatives on the Supreme Council.

30 1873 'Constitution of the Supreme Council of the I.R.B. and Government of the Irish Republic', clause 10.

31 1873 Constitution, clause 14.

32 1873 Constitution 'Supreme Council,' clauses 1, 2, 4; T.W. Moody and Leon Ó Broin, 'The IRB Supreme Council, 1868–78', pp. 286–332.

33 1873 Constitution, clause 12.

34 1873 Constitution, clause 13.

35 1873 Constitution, clause 6.

36 1873 Constitution, 'Supreme Council', clause 14.

37 1873 Constitution, clause 7.

38 1873 Constitution, 'Supreme Council', clause 8.

39 1873 Constitution, 'Supreme Council', clause 11.

40 Lyons, *Ireland Since the Famine*, pp. 116–23, for the Church's antagonism to Fenianism at the time the 1873 Constitution was drafted.

41 Alec McCabe, interview, 6 December 1971; Seán MacEoin (listed as 'MacKeon' in the Bureau index), BMH WS 1716; Seán MacEoin, interview, 19 July 1972: MacEoin, a member of the 1921 Supreme Council, regarded the governmental and presidential claims of the IRB as real and binding.

42 1873 Constitution, 'Supreme Council', clause 1.

43 1873 Constitution, 'Supreme Council', clause 8.

44 1873 Constitution, 'Supreme Council', clause 9.

45 1873 Constitution, 'Supreme Council', clause 15.

46 1873 Constitution, 'Supreme Council', clause 16.

47 1873 Constitution, 'Supreme Council', clause 17.

48 1873 Constitution, 'Supreme Council', clause 17.

49 1873 Constitution, 'Supreme Council', clause 19.

410 Endnotes

50 1873 Constitution, clause 2.

51 1873 Constitution, clause 3.

52 1873 Constitution, 'Supreme Council', clause 5.

53 1873 Constitution, 'Supreme Council', clause 13.

54 1873 Constitution: 'Supreme Council', clause 11.

55 1873 Constitution clause 4, 'Supreme Council', clauses 1, 8 and 11.

56 1873 Constitution 'Supreme Council', clause 8.

57 1873 Constitution, preamble.

58 The title 'Divisional Centre' was not given in the Constitution.

59 1873 Constitution, 'Supreme Council', clause 2

60 Diarmuid Lynch, *The I.R.B. and the 1916 Insurrection*, p. 22.

61 1873 Constitution, clause 11.

62 J.R. Hill (ed.), *A New History of Ireland. Volume VII: Ireland 1921–1984* (Oxford, 2010), p. 672.

63 Alan J. Ward, *Ireland and Anglo-American Relations* (London, 1969), pp. 1–6; *Report of the Commission on Emigration and other Population Problems, 1948–54* (Dublin, 1954), chap. vii, p 254

64 Ward, *Ireland and Anglo-American Relations*, p. 9.

65 Lyons, *Ireland Since the Famine*, p. 128. But not internationally connected. Peter Hart, 'The Fenians and the international revolutionary tradition', in McGarry and McConnel (eds), *The Black Hand of Republicanism*, p. 197.

5. MEMBERS

1 Thomas Barry, BMH WS 1.

2 Michael Hayes, interview, 22 March 1972. Count Plunkett, Robert Barton and Erskine Childers could be classed as 'rich'.

3 1882–1966. Librarian, Irish language campaigner, a founder of Sinn Féin, politician. Later President of Ireland.

4 Seán T. Ó Ceallaigh (ed. Proinsias Ó Conluain; trans. Pádraig Ó Fiannachta), *Seán T.* (Dublin, 1972), p. 47.

5 Ibid., p. 47; Mrs Arthur Griffith, BMH WS 205: 'My husband was a member of the I.R.B. and of the Volunteers and had been present at the Howth gun-running with his Unit.'

6 Ó Ceallaigh, *Seán T.*, p. 47.

7 Ibid., p. 48. Richard Hayes (1882–1958). Doctor and author. O/C Fingal Battalion, Irish Volunteers. Medical Officer at Ashbourne (1916). TD for Limerick (1919–24). Film censor (1940–54). Author: *Irish Swordsmen of France* (1934) and *The Last Invasion of Ireland* (1937). Awarded the *Légion d'honneur*.

8 Piaras Béaslaí, 'A nation in revolt', *Irish Independent*, 5 February 1953; Ó Ceallaigh, *Seán T.*, p. 47; in 1901 Cowley swore in Seán T. as a member. In 1911 Cowley joined the Supreme Council representing Connacht (probably appointed rather than elected).

9 Alderman Thomas Kelly led the Sinn Féin group in Dublin Corporation.

10 *Sunday Independent*, 21 November 1965.

11 Béaslaí, 'A nation in revolt', *Irish Independent*, 5 February 1953.

12 1886–1958. Thomas Clarke's assistant in the GPO during the Rising. General Secretary, Irish Volunteers (1917–22). President of the IRB (1917–18). Escaped from Lincoln Prison with de Valera and Seán Milroy in 1917. TD for Dublin Mid (1921–24). Supported the Treaty. His son, Emmet, died from burns when republicans set fire to the family home in December 1922. Resigned from the Dáil in 1924 in sympathy with McGrath and army mutineers.

Endnotes 411

13 1885–1917. Teacher. Irish language activist. A founding member of the Irish Volunteers. On the governing body of the Gaelic League. Proved to be an effective commander at Ashbourne during the Rising.

14 NLI, Florence O'Donoghue papers, f.72.

15 1870–1935. Stonemason, builder. Joined the IRB in 1909. Built secret rooms for Collins and others (1919–21).

16 Béaslaí, 'A nation in revolt', *Irish Independent*, 5 February 1953; Thomas P. Doyle, interview, 9 March 1974; Jack Comer, interview in O'Malley, *Galway Interviews*, p. 232: 'George Nicolls was one of Collins' pet aversions. Ketterick left him drunk for they were on a skite in Kirwan's Public House for Collins to see. Nicolls was no bloody good.'

17 1874–1952. Anglican. Chemist and shopkeeper. Succeeded John Mulholland as President of the IRB. Resigned from Supreme Council and IRB in 1914. Succeeded as President by Denis McCullough.

18 1881–1916. Born Edward Kent. From Belfast. Accountant. Irish language activist. On the governing body of the Gaelic League. Sinn Féin organiser. Sworn into the IRB in 1912 by Seán MacDermott. Member of the IRB Military Committee that planned the Rising. Executed.

19 1886–1971. Second in command to Thomas Ashe (1916). Minister for Defence in Dáil Government and Chief of Staff, IRA (1919–22). Chief of Staff, National Army (1922–24).

20 1878–1936. Solicitor. IRA Director of Intelligence (1919–20). TD (1919–33).

21 1881–1937. Born Cornelius Collins. Arrested just before the Rising. TD (1919–23).

22 1881–1973. Born Patrick O'Keefe. General Secretary of Sinn Féin (1917–22); TD (1919–22). Later Assistant Clerk of the Senate. O'Connor, *With Michael Collins*, p. 23.

23 1875–1916. Adopted the honorific title 'The O'Rahilly', the head of a Clan. A founding member of the Irish Volunteers and Director of Arms. Directed the Howth gunrunning (1914). Killed during the Rising. O'Connor, *With Michael Collins*, p. 22. A friend, Sydney Czira, claimed: '[O'Rahilly] and Griffith, however, were deeply opposed to the I.R.B. ... [O'Rahilly] did not belong to the I.R.B.' (Sydney Czira, *The Years Flew By* (Dublin, 1974), pp. 61–2). It is more likely that he was an ordinary IRB member, sworn in at the same time as de Valera.

24 Earnan de Blaghd, *Trasna na Bóinne* (Dublin, 1957), pp. 110–13. Translated for the author by Síle Dudley Edwards.

25 Ibid., p. 108.

26 Ibid., p. 109.

27 Joseph O'Rourke, BMH WS 1244: 'Our Circle, No. 17, was known as the Clarence Mangan Literary and Debating Society.' Circles' cover as literary and debating societies was widespread.

28 Piaras Béaslaí, 'A nation in revolt', *Irish Independent*, 5 February 1953; Seán McGarry, BMH WS 368. Tom Clarke also initially resisted Pearse.

29 De Blaghd, *Trasna na Bóinne*, p. 110.

30 Ibid.; Ó Ceallaigh, *Seán T.*, p. 47; Joseph O'Rourke, interview with Fr F.X. Martin, OSA, declared that in 1911 members had to pay one shilling each month to the 'Guarantee Fund' of the Circle. In 1910 one shilling was worth approximately £4 today. The average income in 1910 was £70 per annum, so this level of contribution was extraordinarily high, especially since many IRB members were in less well-paid occupations. O'Rourke may have been well-off; it seems probable that he may have contributed this amount and others much less according to their means. Patrick McCartan BMH WS 100: 'I don't think the shilling subscription was from each member of the organisation but from selected members who volunteered that amount. The normal subscription for each member was one shilling a month.' Officially it was sixpence a month.

31 'My recollection of the method of financing the paper does not coincide with Hobson's. He

Endnotes

suggests that it was financed by a monthly contribution of 1/– per member. My recollection is that it was financed entirely by the Supreme Council and not by personal subscriptions.' Denis McCullough, BMH WS 111.

32   De Blaghd, *Trasna na Bóinne*, p. 177.

33   Ibid., pp. 110–12.

34   Dan Corkery, BMH WS 93.

35   Lyons, *Ireland Since the Famine*, p. 315.

36   Denis McCullough, BMH WS 914.

37   1881–1963. Younger brother of P.S. O'Hegarty. Post office clerk. Probably in 1901 he joined the GAA and captained the post office hurling team. In 1906 he joined the IRB and was Centre of the Cork City Circle. In 1907 he joined the Gaelic League. In December 1913 he was a founding member of the Irish Volunteers in Cork. In 1917 he became vice-O/C IRA First Cork Brigade, becoming O/C in 1920. He opposed the 1921 Treaty but remained neutral during the Civil War.

38   Thomas Barry, BMH WS 1.

39   Ibid.

40   Hobson, *Ireland Yesterday and Tomorrow*, p. 36.

41   Lawrence de Lacey, interview, 17 July 1972.

42   Thomas Harris, BMH WS 320; Michael O'Leary, BMH WS 797: 'the position in Kildare in the years 1910, 1911, 1912 and 1913 was hopeless; the same apathy applied to practically the whole of Ireland. The garrisoned towns of Kildare, Newbridge, Naas and the Curragh Camp – the chief training centre – had a demoralising effect on the people of those districts which left its mark, and to find an Irish-Ireland mind within this orbit would be a rare find, but after events proved that was wrong; the mind was there but latent then.'

43   Hobson, *Ireland Yesterday and Tomorrow*, p. 52.

44   Ibid., p. 36.

45   Lynch, *The I.R.B. and the 1916 Insurrection*, p. 24; NLI, Joseph McGarrity papers, Ms 17,505.

46   Lynch, *The I.R.B. and the 1916 Insurrection*, p. 35.

47   Seán O'Hegarty's Circle was based on the post office.

48   Matthew Connolly (BMH WS 1746); Alfred Cotton (BMH WS 184); Dan Dennehy (BMH WS 116); Patrick Harris (BMH WS 80); Tadhg Kennedy (BMH WS 135); Diarmuid Lynch (BMH WS 4); Jack McGaley (BMH WS 126); Matthew McMahon (BMH WS 115); Gilbert Morrissey (BMH WS 874); Liam Murphy (BMH WS 19); Michael Spillane and Michael J. O'Sullivan (BMH WS 132); J. Anthony Gaughan, *Austin Stack: Portrait of a Separatist* (Dublin, 1977) pp. 29–30: there were ten or more Circles in the Tralee area and 'invariably the IRB Centre in a District was either O/C or an important officer in the local Battalion or Company of the Irish Volunteers'.

49   Charles Desmond Greaves, *Liam Mellows and the Irish Revolution* (London, 1971), pp. 50–1, 73–84.

50   Lawrence de Lacey, interview, 17 July 1972; J.J. O'Reilly, letter to the author, 13 September 1972.

51   Greaves, *Liam Mellows*, p. 81.

52   Patrick McCormack, BMH WS 339.

53   Diarmuid Lynch, *The I.R.B. and the 1916 Insurrection*, p. 26.

54   Alec McCabe, interview, 30 November 1971; Alec McCabe, BMH WS 277; Lynch, *The I.R.B. and the 1916 Insurrection*, p. 26.

55   Diarmaid Ferriter, 'Drink and society in twentieth-century Ireland', *Proceedings of the Royal Irish Academy*, vol. 115C (2015): in 1927 'the government was particularly conscious of figures which

Endnotes

413

revealed that in England and Wales there were 86,722 licensed premises (a ratio of 1 for every 415 of the population), in Scotland 56,841 (1:695) and in Ireland 16,396 (1:263).' In Britain 'heavy drinking' had affected British war production during 1914, 1915 and 1916.

56 David Lloyd George, *War Memoirs*, p. 192

57 Denis McCullough, BMH WS 914.

58 Éamonn Dore, BMH WS 392: 'I knocked around a lot with Collins and others such as Fintan Murphy, Mick Staines and Dr Jim Ryan. I did not drink then or now but I went with the others into such places as Davy Byrnes' or Nearys' in Chatham Street in the evenings where they had a drink or two, and we would then go to the Gaiety Theatre or some such place for the night.' Hart, *Mick*, pp. 35, 144, 291–2.

59 1896–1942. Brother of Liam Mellows. Assistant clerk in the Inland Revenue. He joined Fianna Éireann in 1911, the IRB in 1912, and the Irish Volunteers at their inception in November 1913. He took part in both the Howth and Kilcoole gunrunnings in 1914 and fought in the GPO in 1916. He was interned at Frongoch in 1916 and was arrested and interned again in 1917 and 1918. He was a Fianna Éireann liaison officer with the IRA while also working with Michael Collins' Intelligence Department. He took the anti-Treaty side during the Civil War.

60 Garry Holohan, BMH WS 336.

61 Patrick Mullaney, interview, 24 February 1973.

62 Michael Brennan, interview, 18 December 1972.

63 Dan Dennehy, BMH WS 116.

64 Daniel Kelly, BMH WS 1004.

65 Joseph Barrett, BMH WS 1324.

66 Gerald Byrne, BMH WS 143.

67 Maurice ('Moss') Twomey, interview, 11 December 1972.

68 Charles Townshend, *The Republic: The Fight for Irish Independence* (London, 2013), p. xiv.

69 Richard Walsh, BMH WS 400.

70 Greaves, *Liam Mellows and the Irish Revolution*, pp. 71–7.

71 John McKenna, BMH WS 1025: 'It was in the year 1910 that a traveller for Lalor's of Dublin, named Cathal Brugha, on one of his visits to Listowel swore myself and Mick Griffin into the I.R.B. Mick Griffin, who became the Centre, subsequently took into the I.R.B. a number of local men.'

72 Lynch, *The I.R.B. and the 1916 Insurrection*, p. 22.

73 Ibid., pp. 25–6.

74 Andrew Keaveney, BMH WS 1178.

75 FitzGerald, *The Memoirs of Desmond FitzGerald*, pp. 63–4; Ernest Blythe, interview, 10 August 1973. 'Archie Heron was an organiser of the I.R.B. He was doing the North; Ernest Blythe was doing Kerry and the South, and Liam Mellows was doing the West' (Joseph Gleeson, BMH WS 367).

76 Patrick McDonnell, interview in O'Malley, *Clare Interviews*, p. 172.

77 Ernest Blythe, interview, 10 August 1973.

78 Lawrence de Lacey, interview, 17 July 1972.

79 Liberty Hall was the headquarters of the Irish Transport and General Workers' Union. The implication is that IRB members were not unionised workers.

80 Lynch, *The I.R.B. and the 1916 Insurrection*, p. 89; Williams (ed.), *Secret Societies in Ireland, passim*; Bourke, *John O'Leary, passim*; Garvin, *Nationalist Revolutionaries in Ireland 1858–1928*, pp. 52–3: 'Occupationally, the leaders were middle class, as is usual among revolutionary leaders everywhere ... Of 248 whose occupations at the time could be ascertained, eighty-eight were members of the professions, divided more or less equally between the higher professions

414   Endnotes

(medicine, law, academia, accountancy) and the lower professions (teaching, journalism). The retail trade, so conspicuous in Irish politics both before and after independence, was fairly well represented, at least thirty-nine being involved in it. Civil servants and "clerks" amounted to thirty-six. The proportion engaged in farming was probably no greater than one-fifth, in view of the fact that although eighty-six of 212 were born in rural places, most of these had non-farming occupations. It should be recalled that over 50 per cent of Irish Catholics earned their living in agriculture at that time ... The occupations of the parents of 157 leaders were ascertained; extraordinarily, half of these 157 leaders had parents of agrarian background, most of them "comfortable", if not large, farmers. A further quarter had parents in business of some kind, very often in connection with rural produce. It should be remembered, however, that unascertained occupations of parents are likely to have been humble.'

81   Hobson, *Ireland Yesterday and Tomorrow*, p. 36.
82   Ibid., pp. 36–7. In Frongoch internment camp after the Rising, Collins fell foul of several IRB members because he recruited – without authority – and did not observe these strict requirements.
83   Hart (ed), *British Intelligence in Ireland 1920–21*, pp. 71–2. This informer was probably in Armagh. The Irish Papers in the Public Record Office, London, CO 904/91, 904/97 quote an Armagh informer giving detailed information about IRB Circles, numbers of members, and weapons held in 1913 and 1914: Co. Tyrone IRB membership was 350, with 24 Circles, 23 Centres, and 5 or 6 District Centres. In November–December 1914 the number of arms in the possession of the Ulster Volunteer Force were estimated to be 55,166, the National Volunteers 8,947, and the Irish Volunteers 2,275 (CO 904/29; CO 904/95). Tadhg Kennedy, BMH WS 1413, relates that in 1916 in Tipperary 'I soon realised that the RIC kept a constant watch on the activities of all the national organisations and up to that time were able to keep a "representative" in the republican secret organisation, the I.R.B., and so were in a position to know what was going on fairly well. They were well supplied with items of information also from the Masonic Lodge whose members worked hand in hand with them.'

6. SUPREME COUNCIL

1   1886–1958. Seán McGarry, BMH WS 368.
2   There were several instances that were widely publicised in Ireland. Several IRB men had joined the IPP and been elected to Westminster. A Catholic was appointed for the first time as assistant commissioner of the DMP in 1894. A Mayo man was elected mayor of Manchester in 1910, the first ever Catholic. The most important event in the acceptance of Catholics in British public life was in 1864 when the Catholic University, established by Fr (later Cardinal) John Henry Newman in 1854, was recognised by the government as the National University of Ireland, enabling Catholic education from childhood to graduation. The Church used this to counter the IRB's influence by developing an 'Irish Ireland' nationalism, harking back to Gaelic times, with Catholicism and the Irish language as the defining elements of Irish nationhood. Most of the Irish leaders after 1916 came from this background and had this sense of nationality.
3   O'Hegarty, *A History of Ireland*, p. 738.
4   Richard Connolly, BMH WS 523.
5   Diarmuid Lynch, BMH WS 4.
6   For example, in Waterford (Liam Walsh, BMH WS 1005).
7   Denis McCullough to Patrick McCartan (UCD, Denis McCullough papers, P120/24(4)).
8   Seán MacEoin, interview, 22 February 1973.
9   Bulmer Hobson, BMH WS 30.

Endnotes

415

10   Ó Ceallaigh, *Seán T.*, p. 60; P.S. O'Hegarty, BMH WS 26.

11   P.S. O'Hegarty to Diarmuid Lynch, 3 November 1936 (NLI, Florence O'Donoghue papers, Ms 31,409/1); P.S. O'Hegarty, BMH WS 26: O'Hegarty remembered MacDermott becoming secretary immediately upon his co-option, but this is unlikely.

12   P.S. O'Hegarty to Diarmuid Lynch, 3 November 1936 (NLI, Florence O'Donoghue papers, Ms 31,409/1); P.S. O'Hegarty, BMH WS 26; Ó Ceallaigh, *Seán T.*, p. 60.

13   P.S. O'Hegarty, BMH WS 26; Thomas Slater, BMH WS 263: the Clan sent people to Ireland to check on the Supreme Council after the Daly affair. Dr Emmet Clarke, letter to the author, 24 February 1973: 'The reason why my father was Treasurer of the I.R.B. after he returned from America was that the Clan na Gael had been sending money over to Ireland but there was no proper accounting of what had happened as most of the people in the organisation at that time were living on past memories and not active.'

14   Hobson, *Ireland Yesterday and Tomorrow*, p. 38.

15   Ibid., p. 39.

16   Ibid., pp. 38–9.

17   John Devoy had made support for the IRB a principal purpose of Clan na Gael in the United States, sending about $3,000 (about £97,000 value in 2024) a year to the Supreme Council (Carroll, *America and the Making of an Independent Ireland*, p. 4).

18   Hobson, *Ireland Yesterday and Tomorrow*, p. 38; *The Capuchin Annual* (Dublin, 1966), p. 156, gives the date as 1912. He was weak on his left side and needed a cane to balance.

19   Hobson, *Ireland Yesterday and Tomorrow*, p. 39.

20   Patrick McCartan, BMH WS 766.

21   Seán O'Hegarty to Diarmuid Lynch, 3 November 1936 (NLI, Florence O'Donoghue papers, Ms 31,409/1).

22   P.S. O'Hegarty, BMH WS 26. Expelling Daly from the IRB was required by the IRB Constitution. 'Charges against Daly of being a spy were in the air from 1907 onwards. Sir Henry Campbell, Town Clerk of Dublin, who had the entry to Castle circles, made the statement freely and privately in the Corporation, and, I think, dropped broad hints in public also, but he was known to be a personal enemy of Daly's. Daly did, when this campaign of Campbell's was at its height, apply to the Council for permission to kill Campbell, which was refused ... I never saw Daly save at meetings of the Council, but the Dublin members (O'Hanlon, Allan and Crowe) were quite convinced of his integrity, and they knew him intimately ... [If he] had been giving information, he would never have needed to embezzle the £300 ...'

23   P.S. O'Hegarty, 'Recollections of the IRB', manuscript written 7–11 November 1917 (NLI, Sir Roger Casement additional papers, Ms 36,210).

24   A 'ticket-of-leave man' was a convict released from jail before his sentence was completed who could be rearrested and returned to prison at any time.

25   Joseph Gleeson, BMH WS 367.

26   Patrick Kearney, BMH WS 868.

27   P.S. O'Hegarty, BMH WS 26.

28   Patrick McCartan, BMH WS 766; Michael Cowley, BMH WS 553.

29   P.S. O'Hegarty, 'Recollections of the I.R.B.' (NLI, Sir Roger Casement additional papers, Ms 36,210); P.S. O'Hegarty, BMH WS 26; Valentine Jackson, BMH WS 409: Hobson 'ordered me to expel Allan' and Jackson proceeded to swear him out.

30   P.S. O'Hegarty, 'Recollections of the I.R.B.' (NLI, Sir Roger Casement additional papers, Ms 36,210).

31   1886–1959. Born John Woods. An Irish language enthusiast. Solicitor. Member of IRB. Joint Secretary with Tom Clarke of the Dublin Wolfe Tone Club. Defended Kevin Barry in 1920. He

416 Endnotes

took the anti-Treaty side in 1922 and was on the Sinn Féin Standing Committee and the Gaelic League's Coiste Gnótha.

32 Valentine Jackson, BMH WS 409.

33 Diarmuid Lynch, *The I.R.B. and the 1916 Insurrection*, p. 22. Cathal Brugha, the travelling organiser of the IRB, also resigned.

34 Ibid., p. 21.

35 Hobson, *Ireland Yesterday and Tomorrow*, p. 39. By 'Leinster Executive' Hobson clearly means the Leinster Divisional Board.

36 Ibid., p. 36; Owen McGee, *The IRB: The Irish Republican Brotherhood from the Land League to Sinn Féin* (Dublin, 2007), pp. 353–4.

37 Diarmuid Lynch, *The I.R.B. and the 1916 Insurrection*, pp. 25–6; P.S. O'Hegarty to Diarmuid Lynch, 3 November 1936 (NLI, Florence O'Donoghue papers, Ms 31,409/1).

38 David Fitzpatrick, *Harry Boland's Irish Revolution* (Cork, 2004), p. 34; McGee, *The IRB*, pp. 253–4.

39 O'Hegarty, *A History of Ireland*, p. 697. The Military Committee began to function in 1915.

40 Hobson, *Ireland Yesterday and Tomorrow*, p. 52.

41 Denis McCullough, BMH WS 914.

42 P.S. O'Hegarty, 'Recollections of the I.R.B.' (NLI, Sir Roger Casement additional papers, Ms 36,210).

43 Patrick McCartan, BMH WS 766, says that he was co-opted 'some time in late 1914'.

44 Maureen Wall, 'The plans and the countermand: The country and Dublin' in Kevin B. Nowlan (ed.), *The Making of 1916: Studies in the History of the Rising* (Dublin, 1969), p. 181; Denis McCullough interview with Richard Mulcahy, 1961 (UCD, Richard Mulcahy papers, P7/D/14).

45 Denis McCullough, BMH WS 915. McCullough was not sure if the meeting took place in December 1914 or January 1915.

46 Denis McCullough interview with Richard Mulcahy, 1961 (UCD, Richard Mulcahy papers, P7/D/14).

47 Richard Connolly, BMH WS 523.

48 Séamus Deakin, John Mulholland, P.S. O'Hegarty (who, opposed to a rising, did not stand for re-election in 1915), Séamus O'Connor, Thomas Craven (O/C Liverpool Volunteers) and Seán Barrett (none of whom were on the 1915 Council).

49 Patrick McCormack, BMH WS 339, recalled: '[A] discussion must have arisen at the Supreme Council about the possibility of a rising and, as a result of whatever happened at the Council meeting, John Mulholland resigned from the Supreme Council. He later called a meeting of his Division in Scotland and explained his action and tendered his resignation to the Division and also from the organisation.' Éamon Dore, BMH WS 392: '[A]bout nine months before the Rising, Séamus O'Connor announced one night at a Circle meeting that information had been got out of the Castle that action was in contemplation against the Volunteers or rather against individuals by the British Authorities, to seize arms and ordering us to safeguard our arms. This information was to the effect that the British contemplated raiding the houses of certain individuals for arms, and we were ordered to stand by and if necessary defend our arms rather than surrender them. O'Connor said something to the effect that "this is just the usual sort of thing" or, in other words, made light of the warning, but at the same time showed that he himself was somewhat alarmed by it. It was soon after this incident that he disappeared from the Circle and Sean McDermott took his place there.' Dore places this event in August 1915. Séamus O'Connor had been the Centre.

50 Lynch, *The I.R.B. and the 1916 Insurrection*, p. 25, refers to McCullough being a member of the

Endnotes 417

Executive in November 1914. Since Clarke and MacDermott filled the positions of treasurer and secretary, the only other position on the Executive was that of the president.

51 Alec McCabe, BMH WS 277.

52 Bulmer Hobson, BMH WS 30.

53 Seán Ó Murthuile, *History of the I.R.B.* (UCD, Richard Mulcahy papers, P7/C/I/52), p. 94. He was probably secretary until 1924. At some point between 1917 and 1922 he shared the role with Michael Collins.

54 Ó Murthuile, *History,* p. 93; Leon Ó Broin, *Revolutionary Underground: The Story of the Irish Republican Brotherhood, 1858–1924* (Dublin, 1976), p. 134.

55 P.S. O'Hegarty, BMH WS 26. If £150 annually was collected from the 6/– annual subscription (1/6 each quarter), then the membership of the IRB in good standing was about 500 (150x20/6). Less well-off members were allowed not to subscribe. If there were about 1,500 members in 1912, this suggests that then perhaps half of the IRB's membership was of low economic rank.

56 Bulmer Hobson, BMH WS 30.

57 Louis N. Le Roux, *Life of Thomas Clarke: Thomas Clarke and the Irish Freedom Movement* (Dublin, 1936), p. 81.

58 Clarke, *Revolutionary Woman,* p. 50.

59 Joseph O'Rourke, interview with Fr F.X. Martin, 2 June 1961.

60 Ibid. During the winter of 1915 several arms shipments were received. 'Thomas Clarke paid for this by writing an order to Mrs Clarke (on a paper snuff bag) which I duly presented to Mrs Clarke in Richmond Rd and received between £500 and £600.'

61 1867–1939(?). Born in Co. Armagh. Purser on the Cunard line. O/C Liverpool Irish Volunteers and IRB Centre. Masterminded Liverpool arms and passenger smuggling (1917–20). Arrested in November 1920 and found guilty of incendiary attacks on warehouses. Released from prison in December 1921. Took the pro-Treaty side in the 1922–23 Civil War.

62 Alec McCabe, interview, 8 December 1971.

63 Lynch, *The I.R.B. and the 1916 Insurrection,* p. 24.

64 Ó Murthuile, *History,* p. 94.

65 Pearse to McGarrity, 19 October 1914 (NLI, Bulmer Hobson papers, Ms 13,162).

66 Lynch, *The I.R.B. and the 1916 Insurrection,* p. 85.

7. INFILTRATION

1 Denis McCullough, BMH WS 914.

2 Frank Daly, interview, 14 December 1971.

3 Tom Garvin, *The Evolution of Irish Nationalist Politics* (Dublin, 2005), p. 76.

4 Arthur McElvogue, BMH WS 221; Patrick McKenna, BMH WS 911: 'Later these men were able to smash up the organisation of the local division of the A.O.H. in 1917.' Joost Augusteijn has argued that IRB members of the AOH helped to radicalise its nationalism, thus inciting the IPP's takeover of the Volunteers. Joost Augusteijn, *From Public Defiance to Guerilla Warfare: Experience of Ordinary Volunteers in the Irish War of Independence* (Dublin, 1996), pp. 32–6, 40–2.

5 W.F. Mandle, 'The IRB and the beginnings of the Gaelic Athletic Association', *Irish Historical Studies,* vol. 20, no. 80 (September 1977), pp. 418–38; Dr Feargus (Frank) de Burca, BMH WS 105: 'The first job I got for the I.R.B. was the organisation of the G.A.A. in London with the object of making as big a splash as possible and, by activities in [the] G.A.A. Organisation, to collect possible recruits for the I.R.B.'

6 Michael Cusack, 'A word about Irish athletics', *The Irishman,* 11 October 1884.

418   Endnotes

7   Robert Brennan, BMH WS 779.
8   Robert Kelly, BMH WS 181.
9   Patrick J. Ruttledge, interview in O'Malley, *Mayo Interviews*, p. 238.
10 Dan McCarthy, BMH WS 722.
11 P.S. O'Hegarty, 'Notes on certain things which had not been written down, and of which I imagine nobody but myself has now any cognisance', 15 December 1946 (NLI, Florence O'Donoghue papers, Ms 31,333(1)).
12 David Hassan and Andrew McGuire, 'The GAA and revolutionary Irish politics in late nineteenth- and early twentieth-century Ireland' in Richard McElligott (ed.), *A Social and Cultural History of Sport in Ireland* (London, 2018), p. 60. Seán McGarry, who had taken part in the Rising and in 1917 was IRB president and GAA general secretary, was unrepresentative.
13 1863–99. Irish-language scholar. Professor of Irish Language, Literature, and Antiquities at Maynooth (1891–6). His *Simple Lessons in Irish* (1894) was a bestselling book. He died of tuberculosis in Los Angeles.
14 A Protestant unionist order based in Northern Ireland with branches in Ireland, Britain, the British Empire and the United States.
15 H.B.C. Pollard, *The Secret Societies of Ireland* (London, 1922), p. 103.
16 Joseph V. Lawless, BMH WS 1043.
17 Béaslaí, 'A nation in revolt', *Irish Independent*, 7 June 1953. The McHale Branch of the Gaelic League in Dublin was similarly involved with the IRB.
18 O'Connor, *With Michael Collins*, pp. 19–20.
19 1881–1965. Member of IRB. Author, playwright, biographer and translator. Vice-O/C First Battalion, Dublin Volunteers (1916). Fought at the Four Courts during the Rising. GHQ Staff (1918–21). Editor of *An tOglach*. TD (1919–23). First biographer of Michael Collins.
20 1884–1942. Galway City Centre. Solicitor. Founding member of Sinn Féin. Gaelic League enthusiast. Chairman of Galway County Council (1920–25). TD (1922–27).
21 1878–1946. Farmer. A founder of Sinn Féin and of the Gaelic League in Galway. TD (1919–27).
22 Piaras Béaslaí, 'Memoirs', *Irish Independent*, 13 May 1957.
23 Béaslaí, 'Memoirs' *Irish Independent*, 14 May 1957. Elections to the thirty-strong Coiste Gnótha at the convention returned only a handful of separatists including Ashe, Ó Maille, Nicholls (Mac Niocaill), Ceannt, Diarmuid Lynch – all members of the IRB – and O'Rahilly (who may have also been a member of the IRB).
24 This was in contrast to Clarke's and MacDermott's fury with Hobson for taking a similar position vis-à-vis John Redmond and the Irish Volunteers in 1914.
25 Béaslaí, 'Memoirs', *Irish Independent*, 13 May 1957. The two new members were Béaslaí and Seán T. O'Kelly.
26 Béaslaí, 'Memoirs', *Irish Independent*, 15 May 1957: on 15 December 1914, Hyde expressed disappointment in the Volunteers' split with the Redmondites and hoped that the League might be the mechanism of renewed unity: both the Irish Volunteers and the National Volunteers had marched with Hyde through Cork that day. Hyde's constant theme, however, was that the League must look to moderates for support and remain outside politics.
27 Seán T. O'Kelly, 'Memoirs', *The Irish Press*, 11 July 1961.
28 Douglas Hyde, 'Memoir', UCD Folklore Archive.
29 Béaslaí, 'A nation in revolt', *Irish Independent*, 13 January 1953; Ruth Dudley Edwards, *Patrick Pearse: The Triumph of Failure* (London, 1977), pp. 27, 230–1; Foster, *Modern Ireland*, pp. 475–6.
30 1881–1965. Born Percy Beazley in Liverpool. Journalist, playwright, Irish language campaigner. Director of Publicity, Volunteers/IRA (1919–21).

Endnotes 419

31 1891–1948. Born Jeremiah O'Sullivan. Barrister, teacher, Gaelic scholar. Adjutant-General, IRA (1920–22).

32 1889–1966. Teacher, barrister, judge and politician. Assistant Director of Organisation, Volunteers/IRA (1920–22). Joint secretary for the Irish negotiators of the 1921 Treaty.

33 1890–1960. Teacher. A founder of the Irish language theatre company, An Comhar Drámaíochta.

34 Brugha brought Béaslaí from the Branch into the IRB and the Teeling Circle.

35 1889–1939. Born Clement Murphy. Irish language activist. Dáil Cabinet Assistant Secretary (1919–22). Deputy Clerk and then Clerk of the Dáil (1922–39).

36 1892–1958. Civil servant. Founding member of the Irish Volunteers and member of its Executive (1916–1921), Volunteer/IRA Director of Communications (1918–1920), Volunteer/IRA Director of Organisation (1920–1921). Secretary, Dáil Cabinet (1919–22). Clerk of the Dáil (1919–22). O'Hegarty was on the Supreme Council and a close colleague of Michael Collins from 1917. He was IRB treasurer and possibly acting president after Collins' death in 1922. He was Secretary to the Provisional Government and Free State cabinets.

37 Fionan Lynch, BMH WS 192.

38 Ibid.: 'it was also natural that Gearóid O'Sullivan and myself should choose the Keating Branch as this was the Branch that sponsored Munster Irish'.

39 Béaslaí, 'A nation in revolt', *Irish Independent*, 7 June 1953.

40 Ibid. After the Rising, the reconstituted Bartholomew Teeling IRB Circle met regularly in the Keating Branch rooms.

41 Thomas Barry, BMH WS 1: 'The Wolfe Tone Memorial Committee was the public body under cover of which the I.R.B. operated. The Circles had Wolfe Tone Clubs under various names such as the '98 Club, the William Orr Club, etc. The public proceedings of these Clubs were reported. From about 1908 on, Tom Clarke was President, Seamus Stritch Treasurer, and Sean Ó Húadhaidh Secretary … I was Chairman of the Wolfe Tone Club. A house was purchased in Parnell Square and sub-let to various National organisations.'

42 Fitzpatrick, *Harry Boland's Irish Revolution*, p. 34; Harry Nicholls, interview, 8 December 1971. No. 41 was also owned by the IRB (Comerford, *On Dangerous Ground*, p. 127).

43 Séamus Daly, BMH WS 360.

44 1869–1936. An arch-conservative cultural nationalist, journalist and author. Gaelic League activist, principal advocate of Gaelic Catholic Irish nationalism through his journal, *The Leader*.

45 George Irvine, BMH WS 265.

46 Bulmer Hobson, 'A short history of the Irish Volunteers', vol. iia (NLI, Bulmer Hobson papers, Ms 12,178), p. 54; Hobson, 'A short history of the Irish Volunteers', vol. i (NLI, Bulmer Hobson papers Ms 12,177), p. 27.

47 Fitzpatrick, *Harry Boland's Irish Revolution*, p. 34; McGee, *The IRB*, pp. 353–4.

48 Seán Fitzgibbon, BMH WS 130.

49 Joseph O'Rourke, BMH WS 1244.

50 *The Freeman's Journal*, 13 October 1913: 'It is estimated that 5,000 men took part in the day's events, and at its close drill books, with instructions for parading, trench digging, and rifle positions were freely distributed. The Athlone force represents the first military style opposition, in favour of Home Rule, to line up against Carson's Ulster Volunteers.'

51 O'Hegarty, *A History of Ireland*, pp. 669–70.

52 Formed on 23 November by the leaders of the Irish Transport and General Workers' Union – James Larkin and his deputy, James Connolly – during the August 1913 to January 1914 Dublin strike and lock-out.

53 Seán McGarry, BMH WS 368.

Endnotes

54 MacNeill was identifying Counties Londonderry, Antrim, Down and Armagh as Ulster Volunteer Force strongholds.

55 Le Roux, *Life of Thomas Clarke*, p. 126; Pádraig Ó Snodaigh (Oliver Snoddy), *Comhghuaillithe na Reabhloide, 1913–1916* (Dublin, 1966), p. 9 (translated by Oliver Snoddy for the author). The Supreme Council approved but did not direct the effort: this was its Executive Committee's work.

56 F.X. Martin, 'Eoin MacNeill on the 1916 Rising' *Irish Historical Studies*, vol. 12, iss. 47 (March 1961), p. 260. O'Rahilly's part in the Volunteers strongly suggests that he was in the IRB in 1913. In any case, he acted in collaboration with Hobson, MacDermott and the Executive Committee. O'Connor, *With Michael Collins*, p. 22, remembered O'Rahilly as a colleague in the Teeling Circle prior to 1916. FitzGerald, *Memoirs*, p. 26, states that in November 1913 'O'Rahilly did not belong to the I.R.B. at that stage.' Hobson, who as Circle Centre was in a position to know, says O'Rahilly was not a member (Hobson, *Ireland Yesterday and Tomorrow*, p. 43). However, the Teeling Circle grew so quickly and was accordingly separated into at least three Circles that in turn were divided into more Circles (Ernest Blythe, *The Irish Times*, 3 April 1969) that it is possible that O'Rahilly was a member of a Teeling spin-off Circle and that FitzGerald and Hobson did not know.

57 Bulmer Hobson, *A Short History of the Irish Volunteers* (Dublin, 1918), p. 19; Martin, 'Eoin MacNeill on the 1916 Rising', p. 260.

58 Bulmer Hobson, 'Foundation and growth of the Irish Volunteers, 1913–1914' in F.X. Martin (ed.), *The Irish Volunteers* (Dublin, 1963), p. 25; Seán Fitzgibbon, BMH WS 130: 'I became more determined that even on matters of detail I would just act on my own judgment and even went out of my way at times to adopt a different line from that followed by Bulmer Hobson, whom I regarded then inaccurately, as I subsequently found out, as an extreme delegate of the I.R.B.'

59 Seán Fitzgibbon, BMH WS 130: 'At the first meeting of the Provisional Committee of the Volunteers I saw that nearly all those present were members of the I.R.B. … It was then pointed out by some of the members that all those present were, broadly speaking of the one school of thought, i.e., Sinn Féin, Gaelic League, I.R.B., and it was agreed to by all that the basis of the Provisional Committee should be widened and suitable people, known as supporters of the Irish Parliamentary Party, should be asked to join the Committee.'
Non-IRB: Eoin MacNeill, William J. Ryan, Seán Fitzgibbon, Joseph Campbell.
IRB: Seán MacDermott, Éamonn Ceannt, Séamus Deakin, Piaras Béaslaí, Patrick Pearse and possibly Michael O'Rahilly. Deakin, Ryan and Campbell soon dropped out. Deakin gave as his reason that he had a business to run and found it difficult to attend meetings (Hobson, 'Foundation and growth of the Irish Volunteers', pp. 25–6). A year later, Deakin left the Supreme Council and the IRB, so he may have had cold feet about a rising.

60 Hobson, 'Foundation and growth of the Irish Volunteers', p. 26.

61 IRB: Piaras Béaslaí, Éamonn Ceannt, Bulmer Hobson, Michael Lonergan, Peadar Macken, Seán MacDermott, Liam Mellows, Séamus O'Connor, Colm O'Laughlin, Robert Page, Patrick Pearse, Michael O'Rahilly and three Fianna Éireann officers, Con Colbert, Éamonn Martin and Padraig Ó Riain.
Non-IRB: Eoin MacNeill, Laurence Kettle (IPP), John Gore (IPP), Sir Roger Casement (Gaelic League), Seán Fitzgibbon (Gaelic League; Sinn Féin), Liam Gogan (Gaelic League), Michael Judge (IPP), Thomas Kettle (IPP), James Lenehan (IPP), Thomas MacDonagh (Gaelic League), Maurice Moore (IPP), Peter O'Reilly (IPP), Joseph Plunkett (Gaelic League), John Walsh (IPP).

62 *The Freeman's Journal*, 17 November 1913.

Endnotes   421

63 Seán McGarry, BMH WS 368. McGarry inaccurately said that Hobson was appointed Honorary Secretary. Gregory Murphy, BMH WS 150: 'I was aware that it was a recognised policy in the I.R.B. that anyone who had taken an active part in hostility to the Parliamentary Party should not be openly associated with the initial stages of the formation.'

64 'Manifesto of Irish Volunteers'. Hobson, 'Foundation and growth of the Irish Volunteers', p. 26.

65 John J. Horgan, letter, *The Irish Times*, 9 December 1963: in December 1913 MacNeill addressed the Cork Volunteers and called for cheers for Edward Carson (who had created the UVF).

66 *The Freeman's Journal*, 21 November 1913.

67 Hobson, *Ireland Yesterday and Tomorrow*, p. 45; Hobson, *A Short History of the Irish Volunteers*, p. 19. Hobson sat on the platform at the Rotunda meeting.

68 'Manifesto of the Irish Volunteers'.

69 Bulmer Hobson, BMH WS 51.

70 Thomas Slater, BMH WS 263.

71 Ernest Blythe, interview, 10 August 1973; Harry Nicholls, interview, 8 December 1971: in 1916 Nicholls was a member of the IRB and a Captain in the Dublin Fourth Battalion. 'The IRB were looking after things before the Army began drilling and consequently you see, when the Volunteers were formed, the I.R.B. men were the most able to take up the jobs as officers.'

72 Béaslaí, 'Memoirs', *Irish Independent*, 24 April 1961. Ceannt joined the Teeling Circle in April/May 1913 (Béaslaí, 'Memoirs', *Irish Independent*, 14 May 1957).

73 Gerald Byrne, BMH WS 143; Charles Donnelly, BMH WS 824: 'When the Volunteers were formed in 1913, we were instructed by the I.R.B. to join the Volunteer companies in our own areas. This was to ensure that there would be I.R.B. members in almost all the companies formed.'

74 Joseph Barrett, BMH WS 1324.

75 John J. O'Reilly, letter to the author, 13 September 1972.

76 James Tomney, BMH WS 169. McCullough was the Ulster representative on the Supreme Council.

77 Diarmuid Lynch, BMH WS 004; Lynch, *The I.R.B. and the 1916 Insurrection*, p. 25. A 'Memorandum by Joseph McGarrity on 1916 Rising' states that the Clan gave Lynch £2,300 in or not long after March 1914 for the Volunteers (Seán Cronin, *Irish Nationalism: A History of its Roots and Ideology* (Dublin, 1980), p. 317): £2,000 in 1914 equates to about £200,000 in 2024.

78 Hobson, *A Short History of the Irish Volunteers*, p. 17; Frank Drohan, BMH WS 702.

79 John J. O'Reilly, interview, 13 December 1972.

80 Mick Fleming, interview in O'Malley, *Kerry Interviews*, p. 57: in 1914–16 in Kerry, 'The IRB was growing very quickly as Stack believed in it and he made use of it to develop the Irish Volunteers.' Austin Stack, a member of the IRB since 1908, was commandant of the Kerry Irish Volunteers.

81 Frank Daly, interview, 14 December 1971.

82 Fionan Lynch, BMH WS 192; Michael Spillane and Michael O'Sullivan, BMH WS 132: in Killarney there was no IRB Circle before 1914. When it was formed by the leading local Volunteers, 'This Circle did not make any active effort to control the Volunteer organisation and had no instructions to do so. Our policy was to let the Volunteer organisation develop naturally, knowing that it included men of different political opinions.'

83 FitzGerald, *Memoirs*, p. 71. In Tyrone: 'Generally there was a circle of the I.R.B. in each Irish Volunteer Company area and the I.R.B. held the controlling influence in each Volunteer Company. It was not considered essential that an Irish Volunteer Officer should be a member of the I.R.B. Most of the officers were, however, in the I.R.B. Only I was a member of the I.R.B. I would not have been selected as a representative at the Irish Volunteer Convention' (John

422 Endnotes

'Jack' Shields, BMH WS 224); in Maryborough: 'For all practical purposes the I.R.B. controlled the Volunteers in that area at the time, because practically all members of the local Volunteer Company were members of the I.R.B. organisation ... From the time I joined the I.R.B. [in 1915] I was given to understand that the Volunteers would take definite action to strike for freedom before the Great War ended. With this object in view, the local Company was always kept in trim' (Michael Gray, BMH WS 489). Brennan, *The War in Clare*, p. 8: 'At our meetings all our members [in the Fianna, the Wolfe Tone Club and the I.R.B.] were directed to press their friends and associates everywhere towards having a committee formed to organise a meeting which would launch the newly-formed Irish Volunteers in Limerick. As there was hostility to us amongst the Redmondites, we were not ourselves to take a public lead, but rather to induce supporters of Mr Redmond to appear as the moving force. This was managed and a Provisional Committee was formed ... many of our members got themselves selected to represent trades unions and such bodies. As a result I think we were a majority on this Committee from the beginning.'

84 Séamus Daly, BMH WS 360.
85 Frank Booth, BMH WS 229: 'All I.R.B. men were members of the Volunteers at the start of the Volunteer organisation. The members of my Circle were scattered over different Companies of the Volunteers. I would not say that the I.R.B. were mainly responsible for getting the Volunteer organisation going. All the Volunteer Officers in Belfast were not members of the I.R.B. There were a number of Volunteer Officers very active in building up the Volunteer organisation who were not members of the I.R.B.'
86 Dan McCarthy, in the IRB from 1902, emphasised about the creation of the Volunteers: 'The main thing I want to get at is that the I.R.B. was not a big body at all, but in the background' (Dan McCarthy, BMH WS 722).
87 Seán Ó Lúing, 'Bulmer Hobson', *The Irish Times*, 6 May 1971. Hobson stated that with about 500 trained members of the IRB in Dublin, 90 per cent of Irish Volunteer officers there were already IRB members, and this was because 'our men were the most efficient'.
88 Ó Ceallaigh, *Seán T.*, pp. 155–6. However, Wall, 'The plans and the countermand', pp. 165–7 argues that Clarke and MacDermott ignored the constitution and the traditions of the IRB when ordering this mass swearing-in of new members. But it must be remembered that these officers had proved themselves as worthy of membership by their continued Volunteer activity. No one thus approached seems to have refused to join. Volunteer/IRA ranks in ascending order were: volunteer; section commander; 2nd lieutenant; lieutenant; captain; brigadier; commandant; general (introduced with Divisions in 1921); director (on Executive and GHQ staff, ranked as general after the 1921 Truce); chief of staff, ranked as general after the Truce.
89 James McCullough, BMH WS 529.

8. PRINCIPALS: HOBSON, CLARKE, MACDERMOTT

1 Bulmer Hobson, BMH WS 30.
2 Alec McCabe, interview, 8 December 1971.
3 Hobson, *Ireland Yesterday and Tomorrow*, pp. 76, 78; Bulmer Hobson, 'A short history of the Irish Volunteers', vol. i (NLI, Bulmer Hobson papers, Ms 12,177), p. 206.
4 Denis McCullough in Mulcahy, 'Talk given to the members of the 1916–21 Club', 20 February 1964 (UCD, Richard Mulcahy papers, P7/D/66).
5 1873 Constitution, clause 1.
6 Lynch, *The I.R.B. and the 1916 Insurrection*, p. 31. The implication is that Clarke and MacDermott, together on the Executive since 1913, had developed plans during the course of

Endnotes

423

  1914 that were approved by the Supreme Council in September, the start of the First World War providing an opportunity to take advantage of potential German help and of a distracted Britain.

7 1873 Constitution, clause 8.

8 Hobson, *Ireland Yesterday and Tomorrow*, p. 78.

9 Not to be confused with the Irish Women's Association founded in London in 1915 'to aid Irish Regiments and Prisoners of War'.

10 Le Roux, *Life of Thomas Clarke*, pp. 79–80.

11 Ibid., p. 48, describes Hobson as a member of the 'Ulster Group' of Denis McCullough, Seán O'Hanlon, Patrick McCartan and Seán MacDermott. Except for O'Hanlon, who did not believe in public activity, all worked hard to establish Dungannon Clubs and to revivify the IRB.

12 Denis McCullough, BMH WS 111.

13 Hobson, *Ireland Yesterday and Tomorrow*, p. 46; Le Roux, *Life of Thomas Clarke*, p. 126, says that from the start Hobson disobeyed IRB instructions about the Volunteers.

14 Maurice Moore (1854–1939). Born in Ballyglass, Co. Mayo. He served with the Connaught Rangers in South Africa during the Zulu and Boer Wars. He was horrified by the treatment of Boer civilians in concentration camps. He retired from the army in 1906 and became a Gaelic League enthusiast. He joined the United Irish League that campaigned for land reform and became a member of the Provisional Committee of the Volunteers in 1913 as a representative of the League. Hobson, *Ireland Yesterday and Tomorrow*, p. 47; Lynch, *The I.R.B. and the 1916 Insurrection*, p. 96, confirms the Provisional Committee consisted of thirty members, sixteen members of the IRB, thirteen non-members, and Michael O'Rahilly.

15 Hobson, 'A short history of the Irish Volunteers' (NLI, Bulmer Hobson papers, Ms 12,177) p. 26: Hobson was making his argument that the Volunteers were a better vehicle than the IRB for resistance to British rule.

16 Bulmer Hobson to Joe McGarrity, 1934 (NLI, Bulmer Hobson papers, Ms 13,171/4).

17 NLI, Colonel Maurice Moore papers, Ms 10,561/3.

18 Le Roux, *Life of Thomas Clarke*, p. 134.

19 Denis McCullough, BMH WS 916.

20 Le Roux, *Life of Thomas Clarke*, p. 134.

21 If O'Rahilly was a member, then Hobson and seven IRB members voted for the Redmondites. Two IRB members were not present for the vote (NLI, Bulmer Hobson papers, Ms 13,174/10); Bulmer Hobson 'Foundation and growth of the Irish Volunteers', p. 49.

22 Éamonn Martin, BMH WS 591.

23 Seán McGarry, BMH WS 368.

24 Hobson, *Ireland Yesterday and Tomorrow*, pp. 52–3; Denis McCullough, BMH WS 916: 'Tom Clarke, who was a man of a very simple mind, loved & admired Hobson immensely. Consequently, when Hobson was guilty of what Tom considered a betrayal, the rift was very bitter & Tom would not forgive him or trust him again.'

25 Dr Liam Gogan, interview, 3 November 1972.

26 Richard Connolly, BMH WS 523. Hobson, *Ireland Yesterday and Tomorrow*, p. 76: Seán Tobin succeeded Hobson as chairman of the Leinster Council and on the Supreme Council.

27 Clarke to Devoy, 25 June 1914 (NLI, Patrick J. Madden papers, Ms 31,696), but since Hobson remained a senior member, the implication is that he had too much support to be quietly expelled.

28 Lynch, *The I.R.B. and the 1916 Insurrection*, p. 53.

29 NLI, Bulmer Hobson papers, Ms 13170/11.

30 Hobson, *Ireland Yesterday and Tomorrow*, pp. 53–4. The biennial election was throughout the IRB and included elections to the Supreme Council. As Chairman of the Dublin Centres Board,

424 Endnotes

Hobson also continued on the Leinster Divisional Council (which he referred to as the 'Leinster Board').

31 Seoirse Ó Ciatháin to Diarmuid Lynch, 2 September 1946 (NLI, Diarmuid Lynch papers, Ms 11,130).

32 Seán T. O'Kelly, 'Memoirs', *The Irish Press*, 7 July 1961, considered that the split in the Volunteers over Redmond's nominees mirrored a split in the IRB between Hobson and MacDermott, lending force to the view that Hobson may have been trying to wrest control of the IRB from Clarke and MacDermott. Ó Snodaigh, *Comhghuaillithe na Reabhloide*, p. 51.

33 Robert Brennan, BMH WS 125: 'Sometime previous to the outbreak of war (I think it was early in 1914) Bulmer Hobson addressed a meeting of members of I.R.B. in my house at Somerville, Wexford, and stated that war between Germany and England was practically certain and that when it occurred, we would certainly have a rising.'

34 Liam Ó Briain, interview, 7 December 1971: 'He worked out a business by which if it came to conscription – if they were going to conscript this country – then the whole people of Ireland would rally against it and then they would go in for guerrilla warfare.'

35 Lynch, *The I.R.B. and the 1916 Insurrection*, p. 25; NLI, Diarmuid Lynch papers, Ms 11130. MacDermott had been arrested on 15 May and Lynch replaced him as acting secretary on the Executive. Lynch claims the Military Committee was his proposal, but the Supreme Council had created it in September 1914. Lynch nominated Pearse, Ceannt and Plunkett as its founding members in May 1915 and that is when the Committee became active.

36 O'Hegarty, *A History of Ireland*, p. 698.

37 Valentine Jackson, BMH WS 409.

38 Lawrence de Lacey, interview, 17 July 1972.

39 Denis McCullough, BMH WS 914.

40 Seán McGarry, BMH WS 368.

41 Joseph Gleeson, BMH WS 367.

42 Lawrence de Lacey, interview, 17 July 1972.

43 Piaras Béaslaí, 'My friend Tom Clarke' (NLI, Piaras Béaslaí papers, Ms 33,935/2).

44 William Kelly, BMH WS 226.

45 Ibid.

46 Ibid: 'one in Dungannon, John McElvogue Centre, and another in Donoughmore where James McElvogue was Centre. Later on, another Circle was started in Coalisland – James Tomney was Centre. Another one was organised at Ardboe – James Devlin was Centre of it. A Benburb Centre [*sic*] was organised with John Shields as Centre.'

47 Seán McGarry, BMH WS 368.

48 Michael T. Foy, *Thomas Clarke: The True Leader of the Easter Rising* (Dublin, 2014), p. 61.

49 Patrick McCartan, BMH WS 99.

50 Le Roux, *Life of Thomas Clarke*, p. 81; Séamus G. O'Kelly, 'Thomas Clarke', *The Kerryman*, 8 April 1961.

51 Joseph Murray, BMH WS 254: 'I remember Pearse asking me at a later date if I had any other scheme. I said it was too late now as England was getting stronger & the element of surprise had gone.' Clarke was never 'chairman' or president of the IRB. He may have been acting president when Diarmuid McCullough was absent.

52 Richard Connolly, BMH WS 523.

53 Wall, 'The plans and the countermand', pp. 157–200.

54 Richard Connolly, BMH WS 523.

55 Lynch, *The I.R.B. and the 1916 Insurrection*, p. 28.

56 Ó Murthuile, *History*, p. 160.

Endnotes

57 Denis McCullough, BMH WS 915.

58 Patrick McCartan, 'Notes on Louis Le Roux, *Life of Thomas Clarke*' (NLI, Ms 44,683).

59 O'Connor, *With Michael Collins*, p. 23.

60 Denis McCullough, BMH WS 914.

61 Gregory Murphy, BMH WS 150.

62 George Irvine, BMH WS 265. But inevitably, nothing was absolute. Liam Murphy in Cork remembered: 'There was a case in which a vacancy for Brigade Adjutant occurred in 1915 when Daithi Barry, who occupied that post, lost his civil employment and had to leave the city. An examination was set and a man named Liam Rabette, Adjutant of 'D' Company, and Sean Nolan sat for it. It was stated at the time that although Rabette got the highest marks, Nolan was appointed because he was an I.R.B. man' (Liam Murphy, BMH WS 19).

63 Brian Feeney, *Seán MacDiarmada* (Dublin, 2014), pp. 25–38; Bulmer Hobson, BMH WS 82: Hobson recorded a different set of events. 'McDermott was a native of Glenfarne, in County Leitrim, and he began his career as a pupil teacher in the local National School. A quarrel with one of the clergy led him to emigrate to Glasgow, where he worked as a bartender. Shortly afterwards he came to Belfast, where he first worked as a bartender, and then as a conductor on one of the city trams.'

64 Feeney, *Seán MacDiarmada*, p. 62. MacDermott may have been sworn into the IRB by his father as a teenager (Rev. Charles J. Travers, *Seán Mac Diarmada 1883–1916* (Cavan, 1966), p. 6).

65 Hobson, *Ireland Yesterday and Tomorrow*, pp. 8, 21. P.S. O'Hegarty established a Club in London and Dan Braniff one in Newcastle-upon-Tyne. Le Roux, *Life of Thomas Clarke*, p. 78. In 1906 Seán MacDermott became the organiser of the Clubs.

66 Thomas Wilson, BMH WS 176. Joe Devlin ran the Ancient Order of Hibernians.

67 Liam Gaynor, BMH WS 183. Hobson was chairman of the Club. Seven Club members, including Hobson, were to be on the Supreme Council: Denis McCullough, Seán McGarry, Seán MacDermott, Dan Braniff, Neil John O'Boyle, P.S. O'Hegarty. Other Club members included: Séumas Robinson, later a senior IRA officer; Cathal O'Shannon, an influential trade unionist, editor of the Irish Trades and General Workers' Union's paper, *Voice of Labour*; Robert Lynd, writer, close associate of Hobson and friend of Sir Roger Casement.

68 Hobson, *Ireland Yesterday and Tomorrow*, pp. 8–9, 21, 26.

69 Thomas Wilson, BMH WS 176.

70 This Fianna withered away when Hobson moved to Dublin in 1907. In 1909, with Constance Markievicz, he founded a new Fianna as a boy scouts movement that was organised nationally and of which he was president.

71 From 1909 the IRB organised Fianna clubs. Mick Fleming in Tralee recalled, 'The Fianna was started by 2 or 3 of the IRB' (Mick Fleming, interview in O'Malley, *Kerry Interviews*, p. 57). Seán McGarry, BMH WS 368. Hobson claimed 'that the I.R.B. was not formally consulted and did not play an official part in the establishment of the Fianna' (Marnie Hay, 'The foundation and development of Na Fianna Éireann, 1909–16', *Irish Historical Studies*, vol. xxxvi, no. 141 (May 2008), p. 56). Bulmer Hobson, 'The I.R.B. and the Fianna' in F.X. Martin (ed.), *The Irish Volunteers 1913–1915: Recollections & Documents* (Dublin, 1963). Eamon Martin, Chief of Staff of the Fianna (1917–20), stated that by 1913 most senior Fianna officers were members of the IRB (Eamon Martin, BMH WS 591).

72 Feeney, *Seán MacDiarmada*, p. 66.

73 There were some people MacDermott disliked: 'Diarmuid Lynch … was undoubtedly trusted but Sean McDermott was usually very irritated by Diarmuid's rather pompous manner. He would get out of [Tom Clarke's] shop or house whenever he saw Diarmuid coming' (Dr Emmet Clarke, letter to the author, 24 February 1973).

426   Endnotes

74   Denis McCullough, BMH WS 914.
75   Seán Fitzgibbon, BMH WS 130.
76   Thomas Furlong, BMH WS 513.
77   Richard Walsh, BMH WS 400: '[Among] the main points of policy of the I.R.B., [were] opposition to the Ancient Order of Hibernians, support for the infant organisation of Sinn Féin, and the encouragement of all Irish-Ireland activities.'
78   Martin (ed.), *Leaders and Men of the Easter Uprising*, p. 101; Le Roux, *Life of Thomas Clarke*, p. 83.
79   Denis McCullough, BMH WS 915.
80   Foy, *Thomas Clarke*, pp. 206–7: only at the very end was Clarke let down by MacDermott who united the Military Committee in agreeing to delay the Rising by one day; Clarke urged that the Rising should start as planned on Easter Sunday.
81   P.S. O'Hegarty, 'Recollections of the I.R.B.' (NLI, Sir Roger Casement additional papers, 36,210), p. 20.
82   John A. Murphy, 'The Proclamation of the Irish Republic, 1916' in Crowley, Ó Drisceoil, Murphy (eds) and Borgonovo (assoc. ed.), *Atlas of the Irish Revolution*, p. 269.
83   Foy, *Thomas Clarke*, pp. 197–8.

9. GUNS AND PLANS

1   Séamus Daly, BMH WS 360.
2   Writing editorials in *Irish Volunteer* on 20 June and 4 July.
3   Hobson, *A Short History*, p. 52. Apparently, the sub-committee never met as a whole.
4   Hobson, 'A short history of the Irish Volunteers' (NLI, Bulmer Hobson papers, Ms 12,179), vol. iib, p. 19. Pearse seems to have been appointed Director of Organisation later at the first convention of the Volunteers on 25 October 1914 (NLI, Bulmer Hobson papers, Ms 13,170/11).
5   NLI, Bulmer Hobson papers, Ms 13,162/2.
6   Hobson, 'A short history of the Irish Volunteers' (NLI, Bulmer Hobson papers, Ms 12,177), vol. i, p. 198.
7   Ibid.
8   Ibid., p. 175.
9   Ibid., p. 172.
10   Patrick Pearse to Joe McGarrity, 17 July 1914 (NLI, Bulmer Hobson papers, Ms 13,162/2). Pearse wrote that he considered Hobson to be completely dependable. On 17 August 1914 he wrote to McGarrity, 'I think they have been too hard on Hobson on your side.'
11   Seán Fitzgibbon, BMH WS 130. Fitzgibbon was trusted by MacDermott.
12   Ibid. Christopher Byrne, BMH WS 167: 'the I.R.B. supplied us with rifles and ammunition. There was a rifles' fund in the I.R.B. and we paid one shilling per month for rifles and ammunition. They were British pattern long Lee-Enfield rifles. We did not get the short Lee-Enfield. Small arms and ammunition were also supplied by the I.R.B.'
13   Sir Roger Casement to Fitzharding Berkeley, 19 July 1914 (NLI, Fitzharding Berkeley papers, Ms 7,879): Casement claimed that Redmond would use the Volunteers for political bluff.
14   Hobson, *Ireland Yesterday and Tomorrow*, p. 59.
15   1878–1916. Born Thomas Stanislaus MacDonagh. Teacher. Deputy Headmaster, St Enda's school. Lecturer in English at UCD. Gaelic League enthusiast. On Irish Volunteers' Provisional Committee. Commandant of Volunteers' Dublin Brigade. Sworn into the IRB possibly as late as 1915. Executed after the 1916 Rising.
16   Hobson, *Ireland Yesterday and Tomorrow*, p. 60.

Endnotes

427

17 Ibid. On 25 July MacDermott and Seán Tobin supervised baton making at Tobin's house (O'Kelly, 'Memoirs', *The Irish Press*, 7 July 1961).

18 Hobson, 'A short history of the Irish Volunteers' (NLI, Bulmer Hobson papers, Ms 12,177), vol. i, p. 68; Macardle, *The Irish Republic*, p. 117.

19 Hobson, 'A short history of the Irish Volunteers' (NLI, Bulmer Hobson papers, Ms 12,177), vol. i, pp. 222–6.

20 NLI, Bulmer Hobson papers, Ms 13,162/2.

21 Hobson, 'A short history of the Irish Volunteers' (NLI, Bulmer Hobson papers, Ms 12,177), vol. i, p. 208. Casement had asked Hobson to take care of the Kilcoole landing but Hobson handed over to Seán Fitzgibbon. 'The Howth landing was deliberately organised in a spectacular way to win the utmost publicity for the Volunteers and to wake up the country. The Kilcoole cargo, which was as big as the first one, was deliberately organised as a secret operation' (Seán Fitzgibbon, BMH WS 130).

22 Thomas Wilson, BMH WS 176.

23 Pearse to McGarrity, 12 August 1914 (NLI, Bulmer Hobson papers, Ms 13,162/2).

24 Devoy, *Recollections of an Irish Rebel*, pp. 403–4; Seán T. O'Kelly, 'Memoirs', *The Irish Press*, 8 July 1961. O'Kelly stated that the Clan approached von Bernstorff at the request of the Supreme Council.

25 1881–1968. Labour leader. 'The dominant member of the transport union executive from 1918 until his retirement in 1946, he served as president of the Trades' Congress in 1913, 1918, 1925, and 1941. He also had an abbreviated career as a public representative, being elected an alderman to Dublin Corporation (1920) and serving brief terms as a member of Dáil Éireann (1922–3, June–September 1927, 1937–8)' (*Dictionary of Irish Biography*).

26 O'Hegarty, *A History of Ireland*, p. 697; Bulmer Hobson, *Ireland Yesterday and Tomorrow*, pp. 71–2.

27 'Typescript copy of the report in *An Phoblacht* of the speech Ó Ceallaigh made in New York on Easter Sunday, 1926, commemorating the 1916 Rising' (Seán T. O'Kelly papers, NLI, Ms 27,689).

28 Lawrence de Lacey, interview, 17 July 1972; Béaslaí, 'A nation in revolt', *Irish Independent*, 12 January 1953. The *Irish Volunteer* was edited by de Lacey, the Enniscorthy IRB Centre.

29 Pearse to McGarrity, 24 (26?) September 1914 (NLI, Bulmer Hobson papers, Ms 13,162/2).

30 Béaslaí, 'A nation in revolt', *Irish Independent*, 12 January 1953; Piaras Béaslaí, *Michael Collins, Soldier and Statesman* (Dublin, 1937), vol. i, pp. 46–7; Ó Ceallaigh, *Seán T.*, pp. 158–9; Ailbhe Ó Monachain, 'Seachtain na Caiga i nGaillimh', *An Aghaidh* (Eanain 1967), p. 7; Wall, 'The plans and the countermand', pp. 166–7; Joseph O'Doherty, interviews, 22 March 1972, 11 February 1973, stated that the seizure of the Mansion House was to be led by Connolly, that MacDermott had mobilised IRB men for the action, and that all the men involved that day were IRB men.

31 Wall, 'The plans and the countermand', pp. 167–8; Ó Snodaigh, *Comhghuaillithe na Reabhloide*, ch. 3; James Connolly (ed. Desmond Ryan), *Labour and Easter Week* (Dublin, 1949), p. 2.

32 Francis P. Jones, *History of the Sinn Féin Movement and the Irish Rebellion of 1916* (New York, 1917), pp. 211–12. Redmond's National Volunteers numbered about 175,000, while the Irish Volunteers were reduced to about 13,500.

33 Robert Kelly, BMH WS 181.

34 Frank Booth, BMH WS 229.

35 Patrick O'Mahony, BMH WS 118.

36 Pearse to McGarrity, October 1914 (NLI, Bulmer Hobson papers, Ms 13,162/2).

37 Seán T. O'Kelly, 'Memoirs', *The Irish Press*, 8 July 1961, lists those present at its inaugural

428 Endnotes

meeting: Thomas Clarke, Seán MacDermott, Patrick Pearse, John MacBride, Thomas MacDonagh, Éamonn Ceannt, Joseph Plunkett, William O'Brien, Seán Tobin, Seán McGarry, Seán T. O'Kelly – all members of the IRB – Arthur Griffith and James Connolly (both of whom may have been members but were inactive). Wall, 'The plans and the countermand', p. 166, argues that this group formed a nucleus of activists, of whom James Connolly was most active, from which sprang the impetus for the Rising. Padraig Ó Snodaigh, *Comhghuaillithe na Reabhloide*, examines the differences and suspicions between Connolly, the IRB and the Volunteers throughout 1914 and 1915 that were only resolved shortly before the Rising. Robert Brennan, BMH WS 125, 779: there may have been more than one such meeting. 'After the war started in 1914, I attended a Leinster Council meeting of the I.R.B. in the Foresters' Hall, Parnell Square. Tom Clarke presided and stated the Rising would occur at a suitable time before the War ended ... Tom said that if any of us had hitherto taken our duties lightly we were to do so no more because there was a war on now and that meant business. We would get our chance to rise before the war ended.'

38   Béaslaí, 'A nation in revolt', *Irish Independent*, 15 January 1953.

39   An English Jesuit boarding school in Lancashire.

40   MacDermott was in prison when Lynch returned. Clearly Clarke's and MacDermott's split with Hobson directed Clan help for the Volunteers via Lynch and not Hobson. Carroll, *America and the Making of an Independent Ireland*, pp. 8–9: 'The Clan sent money to the IRB: £2,000 in both September and November, and larger amounts later, totalling about $100,000.'

41   Lynch, *The I.R.B. and the 1916 Insurrection*, p. 25.

42   Diarmuid Lynch, BMH WS 4; Richard Connolly, BMH WS 523.

43   Richard Connolly, BMH WS 523: 'The Supreme Council had sanctioned the Military Committee before the May meeting of 1915 and the Committee had been formed.'

44   It seems that this meeting followed the Clontarf Town Hall meeting.

45   Richard Connolly, BMH WS 523. Plunkett probably was with Pearse and Ceannt. Diarmuid Lynch, *The I.R.B. and the 1916 Insurrection*, p. 25, states that he was acting secretary and therefore with Clarke on the Executive for some months in 1915 while MacDermott was in prison (16 May–18 September). Clarke emerges alone as the consistent presence at the top of the IRB in the year before the Rising. Lynch also states that upon his return to Ireland from the United States in November 1914, he reported to the two available members of the Executive, Thomas Clarke and Denis McCullough. Wall, 'The plans and the countermand', argues that the Military Committee was a semi-IRB body, and that Pearse, Ceannt, Clarke, and Plunkett were seeking to give a semblance of authority to their actions. Lynch, Wall suggests, was doubtless primed by Clarke, and that since the IRB constitution had no provision for the substitution of its officers, this whole operation was a sham. However, substitutions did occur (Lynch and others referred to colleagues as 'acting' in a position until regular procedures took place), and the principle at work seems to have been of absolute secrecy, where people knew only that which related to them. Denis McCullough, interview with Richard Mulcahy (UCD, Richard Mulcahy papers, P7/D/14), states that the Military Committee was appointed at the January 1916 meeting of the Council. If so, this suggests that the Military Committee was kept secret throughout 1915 even from the Supreme Council, and this is improbable, not least given Richard Connolly's statement. Rather it suggests that McCullough was not informed.

46   Alec McCabe, interview, 8 December 1971.

47   Mulcahy, 'Commentary upon Piaras Béaslaí, *Michael Collins and the making of a new Ireland*' (UCD, Richard Mulcahy papers, P7/D/67), vol. i, p. 8; Béaslaí, 'A nation in revolt', *Irish Independent*, 15 January 1953. Béaslaí had been making plans on instructions from Joseph Plunkett.

Endnotes

48 Béaslaí, 'A nation in revolt', *Irish Independent*, 15 January 1953. This meeting of Dublin battalion commandants was probably that referred to by Longford and O'Neill, *Eamon de Valera*, p. 24, as having met on 13 March (but more likely on 13 February according to Béaslaí who kept a diary at the time). It was chaired by Pearse, and the possibility of a September 1915 rising was discussed and the plans for the Dublin battalions were outlined.

49 Wall, 'The plans and the countermand', pp. 170–1, argues that at this time the IRB did not exert any real control over Volunteer policy. But they did not need to: the 'defensive' plan was accepted and after that waiting for an opportune moment to rebel and ensuring that Volunteer officers would do so was their focus. The Volunteer Executive, by doing their job of maintaining Volunteer morale and training, did not need any more IRB control.

50 Hobson, 'A short history of the Irish Volunteers', vol. i (NLI, Bulmer Hobson papers, Ms 12,179), p. 19; Ó Snodaigh, *Comhghuaillithe na Reabhloide*, pp. 94–125 details these appointments.

51 Martin (ed.), *The Irish Volunteers*, p. 175; Béaslaí, 'A nation in revolt', *Irish Independent*, 8, 15 January 1953, where he relates that not only captains were elected by companies, but that the captains elected battalion commandants.

52 Longford and O'Neill, *Eamon de Valera*, p. 40, gave the date of these appointments as 13 March 1915; Piaras Béaslaí, 'A nation in revolt', *Irish Independent*, 15 January 1953, gave the date as 13 February 1915; Béaslaí had noted these events in his diary at the time.

53 Wall, 'The plans and the countermand', pp. 172–3; Éamonn Dore, BMH WS 392; Joseph V. Lawless, BMH WS 1043; Longford and O'Neill, *Eamon de Valera*, p. 25; Seán Murphy, BMH WS 204: 'On that day [Holy Thursday, 1 April 1915] I had a mission to carry out at No. 2 Dawson Street, which was to introduce to Thomas MacDonagh, Commandant Eamon de Valera, I previously having been asked by Sean Tobin [Leinster representative of the Supreme Council 1915–16] if I had any idea if De Valera was a member of the I.R.B. I said as far as I knew he was not.' De Valera probably joined the IRB at this meeting with MacDonagh shortly after he was made commandant, Third Battalion, Dublin Brigade in March 1915.

54 Longford and O'Neill, *Eamon de Valera*, pp. 172–4. Connolly was also giving lectures to the ICA, declaring that the British would not destroy property in Dublin.

55 Seán MacEntee, *Episode at Easter* (Dublin, 1966), p. 60.

56 Seán McGarry, BMH WS 368. From about 2,200 Irish prisoners of war only 56 volunteered for the brigade: a telling indication of Irish contentment with Home Rule and rejection of the 1916 rebels.

57 Geraldine Dillon, BMH WS 358.

58 Seán McGarry, BMH WS 368: 'On his return Plunkett brought with him some films which I enlarged and which were photographs of the agreement between Casement and the German Government for the starting of the Irish Brigade. This was all Casement's efforts in Germany achieved.' Through Clarke, the Military Committee was in touch with John Devoy in the United States who, in addition to sending money to Clarke for the Rising, was also relaying messages from Germany.

59 Wall, 'The plans and the countermand', p. 174.

60 Denis McCullough, BMH WS 916.

61 Wall, 'The plans and the countermand', pp. 176–7.

62 Ibid., pp. 177–9, argues that IRB constitutional procedures meant little after Clarke and MacDermott were together on the IRB Executive, and that if the IRB had functioned according to its constitution during the years before 1916, the likelihood of a rising taking place would have been remote. But the IRB was an authoritarian organisation; the only opinions, deliberations and decisions of importance to it were those of its Supreme Council and Executive. Indeed, the appointment of Diarmuid Lynch as acting secretary while MacDermott was in prison, if

430   Endnotes

anything, shows Clarke's anxiety to maintain secrecy while conforming as far as possible to the practices of the IRB.

63   Bulmer Hobson, 'A short history of the Irish Volunteers' (NLI, Bulmer Hobson papers, Ms 12,179), vol. i, p. 157; Wall, 'The plans and the countermand', pp. 181–2. However, the plans of the Military Committee were based upon their assumption that they could control the Volunteers through the 2,000 members of the IRB – most of whom were also Volunteers – without making it clear to them when the time came that IRB orders were superior to Volunteer orders. Wall argues further that the Military Committee's expectations were misplaced because they did not realise that by changing the system of recruitment with co-options, and by undermining the practice of absolute obedience to immediate superiors, they had weakened the IRB power in the Irish Volunteers. I have found no evidence of a change in recruitment procedures (apart from the high level of co-options to the Supreme Council and MacDermott's recruiting efforts before 1913) or of undermining the practice of obedience to immediate superiors. Richard Mulcahy was told by his IRB Centre to join the Volunteers and to take orders from his Volunteer superiors; Denis McCullough maintained that the IRB controlled everything up to the 1916 Rising, and that the only authority he recognised, notwithstanding his appointment as a commandant in the Volunteers, was that of the Supreme Council (Denis McCullough interview with Richard Mulcahy, 1961 (UCD, Richard Mulcahy papers, P7/D/14)).

64   Joseph Lawless, BMH WS 1043. These new 1915 inductions (e.g. de Valera) imply a lowering of IRB recruiting standards in favour of gaining authority over Volunteer officers sufficient to order them into a rising not authorised by MacNeill and the Volunteer Committee.

65   P.S. O'Hegarty, BMH WS 27. This must have been in the first days of May since on 16 May MacDermott was arrested.

66   P.S. O'Hegarty, BMH WS 27; Thomas Young, BMH WS 531; P.S. O'Hegarty to Diarmuid Lynch, 27 September 1950 (NLI, Florence O'Donoghue papers, Ms 31,409/13). O'Hegarty's view was akin to Hobson's. Hobson and O'Hegarty were lifelong friends (*Dictionary of Irish Biography*).

67   P.S. O'Hegarty, BMH WS 841.

68   Rev. Charles J. Travers, 'Seán Mac Diarmada, 1883–1916', *Breifne*, vol. iii, No. 9 (1966); Lynch, *The I.R.B. and the 1916 Insurrection*, p. 102.

69   Donagh MacDonagh, 'Thomas MacDonagh', *The Irish Press*, 6 April 1956.

10. DISORGANISATION

1   Patrick McCartan, BMH WS 766

2   Richard Connolly, BMH WS 523.

3   Patrick McCartan, BMH WS 766.

4   Padraig Tobin, 'The Third Tipperary Brigade', *The Nationalist*, 9 November 1957.

5   Seán Murphy, BMH WS 204.

6   1895–1963. One of Michael Collins' chief lieutenants. Led the 1924 Army Mutiny.

7   B. Mac Giolla Choille (ed.), *Intelligence Notes, 1913–16* (Dublin, 1966), pp. 159–60; Alec McCabe, interview, 16 January 1972.

8   F.X. Martin, 'Eoin Mac Neill on the 1916 Rising', pp. 226–71. There is no evidence that the memorandum was circulated or read to anyone by MacNeill. Hobson, 'A short history of the Irish Volunteers' (NLI, Ms 12,177 and Ms 12,179), for example, makes no reference to this memorandum.

9   Wall, 'The background to the Rising', p. 184; Hobson, 'A short history of the Irish Volunteers'

Endnotes

431

(NLI, Bulmer Hobson papers, Ms 12,177), pp. 155–7. MacDonagh was not yet a member of the Military Committee.

10 Gregory Murphy, BMH WS 150. 'Early in Holy Week I was at a meeting of the Dublin Centres Board, I.R.B., at 41 Parnell Square. Among others I recollect the following being present – George Irvine, Tom Hunter, P.J. Farrell, Seán Murphy, Con Colbert, Seán Tobin, Bulmer Hobson and George Lyons. At that meeting P.J. Farrell of Loughlinstown asked if the instructions he had received to interfere with the Railway were all right. Bulmer Hobson told him that nothing should be done without instructions from Eoin MacNeill. I knew that Bulmer Hobson went to see Eoin MacNeill after the meeting.'

11 Gregory Murphy, BMH WS 150.

12 Wall, 'The background to the Rising', p. 184, points out that MacDonagh, as commandant of the Dublin Brigade and director of training of the Volunteers, was not of central importance to the Rising plans. While MacDonagh had committed himself to a rising in the summer of 1915, Clarke and MacDermott may have delayed recruiting him on to the Committee because he was close to MacNeill personally. As the remaining senior Volunteer who was not privy to the Rising plans (with the exceptions of MacNeill and Hobson), by putting him on the Committee (a) he would know the plans in full, and (b) his participation would present a united senior Volunteer front and would ensure his authority behind Dublin Brigade orders. They therefore left it to the last to bring him into their plot. The Dublin Rising plans had already been made when he joined the Committee.

13 Michael O'Halloran, 'Perilous days', *Sunday Press*, 17 January 1960.

14 Joseph V. Lawless, BMH WS 1043.

15 Brennan, *The War in Clare, 1911–21*, p. 13.

16 Bernard MacGillian to John Redmond, 6 March 1916, in Dermot Meleady (ed.), *John Redmond: Selected Letters and Memoranda, 1880–1918* (Dublin, 2018), pp. 227–8. These conventions are held intermittently as gatherings of Irish nationalists. The first was held in Chicago in 1881. Others have been held in Melbourne (1919), Buenos Aires (1921) and Paris (1922), but the majority have been in the United States, most recently in New York in 1994.

17 Wall, 'The background to the Rising', p. 183; Devoy, *Recollections*, pp. 458–9, stresses that the Rising was intended to take place before arms were landed.

18 Bulmer Hobson, BMH WS 81.

19 Liam Ó Briain, interview, 7 December 1971.

20 Grace Plunkett, BMH WS 257. Lorcan Collins, *1916: The Rising Handbook* (Dublin, 2016), pp. 15–16. The key is probably that 'He got out the information piece by piece', and from that Plunkett constructed a document. P.J. Little, 'Memoirs', *Sunday Press*, 7 May 1961, recounts that as editor of *New Ireland* in February 1916 he was approached by Rory O'Connor, an IRB member close to Joseph Plunkett, and asked to publish the document. O'Connor explained that Eugene Smith, a telegraphist in the GPO, had obtained the original ciphered document, smuggled it out piecemeal and given it to O'Connor, and that the main body of the document was substantially accurate and correct. Smith testified to the published document's authenticity. Little agreed to O'Connor's request and also joined a committee that was formed to publicise the document. Joseph E.A. Connell Jnr, 'The "Castle Document"', *History Ireland*, vol. 24, iss. 2 (March/April 2016): '[I]n Kilmainham Gaol, on the night before he was executed, Seán MacDermott swore to Msgr Patrick Browne that the document was genuine. Moreover, it had several "errors" that Joseph Plunkett was unlikely to have made.' Éamonn Dore, BMH WS 392: 'Concerning the Plunkett document; Joe Plunkett was at that period suffering from serious tubercular glands, so serious that despite the Rising and the preparations for it, he had to have an immediate operation by Surgeon Charlie McAuley. It is not reasonable to suppose that a

432 Endnotes

man in such a condition would concern himself in the details of forging such a document, even assuming that he wanted to do so.' Bulmer Hobson, BMH WS 81: 'As a result of subsequent investigations in 1917, I discovered that MacNeill had got this document from P.J. Little, who had got it from Rory O'Connor, who had got it from Joseph Plunkett, a member of our Committee [i.e. Volunteer Executive], who was actively associated with Pearse and who had taken, apparently, elaborate precautions to plant the document on MacNeill.'

21 Hobson, 'A short history of the Irish Volunteers' (NLI, Bulmer Hobson papers, Ms 12,179), p. 203.
22 1887–1944. Jeremiah Joseph ('Ginger') O'Connell. MA UCD. Emigrated to the United States and served in the 69th Infantry Regiment (New York). Returned to Ireland in 1914. Subsequently on IRA GHQ and a senior officer in the National Army.
23 1893–1935. Eimar Ultan O'Duffy. Writer.
24 Bulmer Hobson, 'A short history of the Irish Volunteers' (NLI, Bulmer Hobson papers, Ms 12,179), pp. 205–6; O'Kelly, 'Memoirs', *The Irish Press*, 12 July 1961, states MacNeill had been told of the expected German arms landing a few weeks before and that the Sunday mobilisation was to act as a cover for the landing, and that MacNeill had agreed to this.
25 Hobson, *Ireland Yesterday and Tomorrow*, p. 76; Charles Townshend, *Easter 1916: The Irish Rebellion* (London, 2005), p. 137, credits Clarke and MacDermott with the decision to arrest Hobson; Marnie Hay, 'Kidnapped: Bulmer Hobson, the IRB and the 1916 Insurrection', *The Canadian Journal of Irish Studies*, vol. 35, no. 1 (Spring 2009), pp. 53–60, gives a comprehensive account of the affair.
26 Quoted in Marnie Hay, 'Kidnapped'. Ceannt was speaking to Séamus O'Connor whose statement to the BMH is with the Eoin MacNeill papers (UCD, Eoin MacNeill papers, LAI/G/117) but is not in the Bureau's own collection.
27 Martin Conlon, BMH WS 798: 'I am confining myself to the episode of Mr Bulmer Hobson's "imprisonment" in my house in Phibsboro – 11 Altinure Terrace, Cabra Park, subsequently changed to 76, Cabra Park. I acted under orders, as it were, to give the prisoner and his escort accommodation in my premises. As an I.R.B. man it sufficed, to ensure my co-operation in the matter, to have learned through I.R.B. channels that higher authority had decided on Mr Hobson's arrest and to be asked through the same channels to participate on the lines indicated ... I also had occasion to calm down the Volunteers in charge of the prisoner. By Easter Monday when it was known that the Rising was taking place, they had begun to bemoan the fact that they were engaged on this job of prisoner-guarding and so would be out of things now that the fight was on. They felt so keenly on the point as seriously to contemplate drastic action to rid themselves of the prisoner. They were even suggesting he should be executed and dumped on the railway line which runs at the back of my place, but, possibly, they were not really in earnest about this. In any case, I made it clear to the Volunteer guards that I would not countenance any unauthorised action and that I had the means to oppose it – I had my revolver and indicated that it would be used if necessary. I succeeded in carrying my point that they would have to await orders as to what was to be done with the prisoner. Such orders did in fact arrive in the course of the afternoon of Easter Monday. They were brought by Mr. Seán T. O'Kelly ... [They] were in writing and came from Seán MacDiarmada ... They were to the effect that Mr Hobson could now be released. These instructions were given effect to by whoever was in charge when they reached my house.'
28 Wall, 'The plans and the countermand', pp. 201–51.
29 Comerford, *On Dangerous Ground*, p. 89.
30 Laurence ('Larry') Lardner, 1882–1936. An Athenry native. Publican and auctioneer. Secretary of the Galway GAA and of the Gaelic League. Centre for Athenry. O/C Galway Volunteers (1916). Arrested and imprisoned after the Rising. IRB Supreme Council representative for Connacht (1917–19).

Endnotes   433

31 George Nicholls (1884–1942). Solicitor, originally from Dublin. An early member of Sinn Féin. Galway County Centre and founder of the Galway Irish Volunteers. Arrested at the start of the Rising and was interned in Frongoch.

32 Margaret MacEntee (née Browne), BMH WS 322.

33 Probably Fr Eugene Coyle and Fr James O'Daly. Terence Dooley, *The Irish Revolution 1912–23: Monaghan* (Dublin, 2017), p. 67.

34 For example, Éamonn Dore, BMH WS 392: 'In discussion with Fr Augustine, he said he resented very much that despite his friendship with the people in the National movement he was never allowed to know that there was a secret society governing it of which we all appeared to be members. He said that membership of a secret society put us outside the Church and turning to me said, "Even your great Bishop Thos O'Dwyer of Limerick could not absolve you if he knew you were members."'

35 Denis McCullough, BMH WS 91.

36 Dr Feargus de Burca, BMH WS 105: 'When I took Pearse's orders to Denis McCullagh [*sic*] on the Wednesday prior to the Rising, he cried. McCullagh's activities during the Rising were not approved of by the IRB, and he was refused readmission to the I.R.B. after the Rising.' Denis McCullough, BMH WS 914, dated his severance later: 'on the formation of the First Dáil [19 January 1919], I could see no further use for the I.R.B. and severed my connection with it.'

37 Joseph Furlong, BMH WS 335: 'In 1911 there were large scale Labour troubles and lock-outs in Wexford, and Matt (my brother) and I went to London. We were transferred to the I.R.B. in London. Mick Collins was our centre there. Dan Sheehan, who was drowned at Ballykissane on Good Friday 1916 and Dan Murphy were members of this Centre [*sic*].'

38 Denis Daly, BMH WS 110.

39 O'Kelly, 'Memoirs', *The Irish Press*, 11, 12 July 1961, states that on 9 April MacDermott secured MacNeill's agreement to Easter manoeuvres, and in the same week Pearse informed MacNeill of their plans. MacNeill objected strongly at first but finally agreed to co-operate. However, MacDermott felt that MacNeill might change his mind and blamed this on the advice he was getting (from Hobson), and on Monday 17 April Clarke and MacDermott resolved to deal with Hobson. A week later, following the news of the sinking of the *Aud* and Casement's arrest, MacNeill insisted to Seán T. on Easter Saturday that he had never agreed to an insurrection and denied the claims of Clarke and MacDermott to the contrary, showing him copies of a countermanding order he had already sent out.

40 Hobson, O'Connell and O'Duffy all distributed MacNeill's order, ensuring that whatever – if anything – took place on Sunday would be a muddle.

41 Seán Murphy, BMH WS 204.

11. RISING

1 Samuel Irwin, interview, 31 October 1972.

2 Anonymous memoir (UCD, Richard Mulcahy papers, P7/D/24); Liam Ó Briain, BMH WS 3: MacNeill seems to have sought to join the Rising later in the week.

3 William J. Brennan-Whitmore, interview, 2 November 1972. Brennan-Whitmore was present when this was said. Gregory Murphy, BMH WS 150, gives a different account: 'I remember on one occasion when speaking to James Connolly, he left me under the impression that Pearse believed that the British would not shell Dublin owing to the damage they would cause to their own "garrison". James Connolly did not agree with that view.'

4 Gregory Murphy, BMH WS 150: 'Pearse gave a lecture generally about street fighting and house to house fighting. Mobilisers for the Unit were appointed. After the meeting I remained behind

434 Endnotes

with Pearse, McDermott, McBride and J.R. Reynolds, discussing the situation. McBride did not entirely agree with remaining in Dublin as he was of opinion that the British would surround the Volunteers and slaughter them. He thought that guerilla warfare should be adopted, attacking communications, etc. Pearse believed that something spectacular should be done, otherwise the rest of the country would not rise. It appeared to me that he was impressed by the Robert Emmet plan to seize Dublin Castle, the centre of British administration in Ireland.'

5 P.S. O'Hegarty, BMH WS 27.

6 Béaslaí, 'A nation in revolt', *Irish Independent*, 16 January 1953.

7 Liam Ó Briain, BMH WS 3: 'The other letter was a curious one from Mick Lennon, District Justice. Do you know him? He said he had tried to put McNeill's recollections together. He had interrogated him repeatedly as if he were a witness in the box before him, and he had found him a slippery witness dodging all sorts of questions especially about these matters concerning Easter Week ... McNeill, president of the Volunteers, had more and more frequently tended to absent himself from executive meetings, to slip back into the 10th century and The Book of the Dun Cow and to leave the chairmanship of the weekly meetings to Pearse; that therefore he had morally lost the right to be offended when he suddenly came back to modern times and found that things had been done unknown to him. The point would be worth verifying. The second was put some years ago by Desmond FitzGerald. It was that MacNeill had the support of the majority of the Volunteer Executive for his cancelling order: Michael O'Rahilly, Séamus O'Connor, Seán Fitzgibbon, and himself; four out of seven. (Were there really only seven?) If true it is a good point.'

8 Seán McGarry, BMH WS 368. Seán MacDermott agreed: 'He said what a pity that it had prevented the Rising being a respectable rising, that it would have been over a considerable part of the country, employing a lot of British troops, and that, as far as the Germans were concerned, it would have been a more valuable thing than the mere flash in the pan that it was' (Patrick Browne, BMH WS 729). MacDermott ignored the approximately 17,000 well-armed men in the RIC – about 30 per cent more than the Irish Volunteers (numbering about 12,000) – and the lack of weapons and ammunition available to the Volunteers. Frank Thornton, BMH WS 510: after the Rising, MacNeill was arrested. 'Eoin MacNeill arrived in a cab, a prisoner. He tried to shake hands with Sean McDermott, but Sean turned his back and walked away.'

9 Dr Emmet Clarke, note of a discussion with the author, 6 May 1972. This seems to be the only recorded time that Clarke and MacDermott disagreed.

10 O'Kelly, 'Memoirs', *The Irish Press*, 11, 12 July 1961.

11 Joseph Barrett, BMH WS 1324. In Kildare, Tom Harris met an IRB colleague, Michael O'Kelly, on Easter Sunday: 'He said he had got the Sunday paper where MacNeill had issued the countermanding order. He did not attach any importance to MacNeill's order because, he said, he was not a member of the I.R.B. ... O'Kelly was aware that McNeill was not trusted as he changed his mind so often' (Thomas Harris, BMH WS 320). Robert Kelly looked to the IRB for instruction and, as with Michael O'Kelly, would only accept IRB orders: 'Immediately before Easter Week I understood from the Ulster secretary of the I.R.B. Seán Southwell, that the Newry Volunteers were for Dungannon at the start of hostilities and that we would get our orders through the I.R.B. No such order came when the time for action arrived but we got an invitation from the Irish Volunteers in Louth to join up with them. This would have been a convenient arrangement as Dundalk was a much nearer mobilisation centre for us than Dungannon. There was, however, a crux in the matter, of the invitation as the man who invited us to Dundalk – Paddy Hughes – was not himself a member of the I.R.B. and refused to join the organisation' (Robert Kelly, BMH WS 181).

12 Wall, 'The plans and the countermand'; O'Kelly, 'Memoirs', *The Irish Press*, 11, 12 July 1961.

Endnotes 435

13   Peadar McCann, BMH WS 171.

14   The Military Committee met for the last time on Easter Sunday, very likely at 18 North Frederick Street (Mulcahy, 'Cathal Brugha', 28 April 1965 (UCD, Richard Mulcahy papers, P7/D/86)).

15   O'Kelly, 'Memoirs', *The Irish Press*, 14 July 1961; Sheila Carden, *The Alderman: Alderman Tom Kelly (1868–1942) and Dublin Corporation* (Dublin, 2007), p. 104. Clarke and his colleagues had given some thought to a government in the event of the Rising's success, selecting a wide range of interests. Apart from the members of the Military Committee, other members of the proposed government were Alderman Tom Kelly (IRB) who was named as chairman, with Arthur Griffith, William O'Brien, Johanna ('Hanna') Sheehy Skeffington (suffragette and labour activist), and Seán T. O'Kelly (IRB, Gaelic League, Sinn Féin). If Kelly refused, Seán T. was to be chairman. There is no evidence that these men and Sheehy Skeffington knew that this was planned for them (Dudley Edwards, *Patrick Pearse*, p. 276). John M. Heuston, *Headquarters Battalion* (Dublin, 1966), p. 62, lists the Provisional Government as Thomas Clarke, Patrick Pearse, Éamonn Ceannt, Joseph Plunkett, Thomas MacDonagh, James Connolly.

16   Éamonn Dore, BMH WS 392.

17   Mulcahy, 'Conversation with Denis McCullough' (UCD, Richard Mulcahy papers, P7/D/15).

18   Charles Townshend, *Easter 1916*, p. 161.

19   Clarke, *Revolutionary Woman*, pp. 99–100.

20   R.V. Comerford, 'Stephens, Devoy and Clarke', in Eugenio F. Biagini and Daniel Mulhall (eds), *The Shaping of Modern Ireland* (Dublin, 2016), p. 22.

21   William J. Brennan-Whitmore, interview, 2 November 1972.

22   William Oman, interview, 6 November 1972.

23   Seán Fitzpatrick, 'The Third Tipperary Brigade', *The Nationalist*, 16 November 1957, 'Most of the active officers [of the IRA in 1916] were members of the IRB.'

24   Collins did not stay at Larkfield but with Gearóid O'Sullivan at the home of his aunt, Mrs Julia O'Donovan, at 16 Airfield Road, Rathgar, Dublin; Julia O'Donovan, BMH WS 475.

25   Joseph Gleeson, BMH WS 367.

26   Denis Daly, Padraig Ó Conchubhair and Michael Breathnach, BMH WS 786.

27   Peter Hart, 'Definition: defining the Irish Revolution' in Joost Augusteijn (ed.), *The Irish Revolution 1913–23* (Basingstoke, 2002), p. 22.

28   Ruth Taillon, *The Women of 1916: When History Was Made* (Dublin, 2018), pp. 22–8.

29   They were Kathleen Clarke, Margaret Pearse (mother of Patrick and William), Mary MacSwiney (sister of Terence), Ada English and Kathleen O'Callaghan. All were members of Cumann na mBan. None took their seats at Westminster.

30   Mrs Richard Mulcahy, interview with Richard Mulcahy, 1965 (UCD, Richard Mulcahy papers, P7/D/49). Tom Clarke told Min Ryan (Mrs Richard Mulcahy) in the GPO during the Rising that a republic 'was the only way to emphasise to the world the separateness of Ireland and England and what Ireland's claim was'. The Rising's purpose, according to Clarke, was to secure Irish independence at the peace conference that would be held at the end of the war. Notwithstanding the IRB's dedication to a republic, Clarke was willing to accept a monarchy if it secured independence. Lyons, *Ireland Since the Famine*, pp. 270–1, 278–9, 330–8, 342–5.

31   Michael McInerney, 'Gerry Boland's story', *The Irish Times*, 9 October 1968.

32   Martin, 'Eoin MacNeill on the 1916 Rising', pp. 226–71.

33   B. Mac Giolla Choille (ed.), *Intelligence Notes*, pp. 135–54.

34   Lyons, *Ireland Since the Famine*, pp. 261–2.

436

Endnotes

12. POST MORTEM

1 Liam Ó Briain, interview, 7 December 1971.

2 Hansard, 11 May 1916.

3 Tim Pat Coogan, *Eamon de Valera: The Man Who Was Ireland* (New York, 1996), p. 78.

4 It is frequently asserted that in 1916 Britain was anxious not to have difficult relations with the United States government and that executing de Valera, an American citizen, might well cause difficulties and for that reason he was not executed. In fact, de Valera's citizenship was not an issue. Tom Clarke was also an American citizen: there was no protest from the United States at his execution.

5 Seán MacEoin, interview, 19 July 1972.

6 Davis, *Arthur Griffith and Non-Violent Sinn Féin*, pp. 67–8; Ó Murthuile, *History*, p. 45.

7 Garvin, *The Evolution of Irish Nationalist Politics*, pp. 116–17.

8 William O'Brien (ed. Edward MacLysaght), *Forth the Banners Go* (Dublin, 1969), p. 118.

9 Clarke, *Revolutionary Woman*, p. 168.

10 Ibid., pp. 161–2.

11 Ibid., p. 173; Ó Corráin and Hanley, *Cathal Brugha*, p. 70, state that she had £3,100 in IRB funds.

12 Joseph Gleeson, BMH WS 367.

13 Dr Emmet Clarke, note of a discussion with the author, 2 August 1973. Dr Emmet Clarke, letter to the author, 24 February 1973: 'My mother had no direct connection with the I.R.B. after the Rising but the following, some of which I think I have mentioned, maybe of use to you.

  "She was made confidant of the decisions and the reasons for the decisions of the S.C. of the I.R.B. before the Rising and given a list of names in each area to contact should there be any upset in the plans such as wholesale arrests before the Rising. She was given the names of the first, second and third in command in each area. But after the Rising nearly all the names she had been given were in jail or could not be contacted e.g. Pat MacCartan.

  "She was helped by Liam Clarke, a young man arriving out of the Richmond Hospital swathed in bandages who agreed to go around the country making contact saying that the Rising was but the first blow and to prepare to continue the fight for freedom. She instructed him not to let the young men know that she was acting but to say that the word had come from the Clan na Gael in America. Some time later she met Dick Mulcahy as he was on the run."'

14 Séamus G. O'Kelly, 'Memoirs', *The Kerryman*, 8 April 1961; Dr Emmet Clarke, letter to the author, 6 May 1972: 'On Easter Monday my father and mother walked down Richmond Avenue from our home which was at the very end. As he turned into Richmond Road, they did not say goodbye but he remarked that if they lasted as long as [Robert] Emmet's they would be doing well. When she saw him later in Kilmainham he was overjoyed at the length they had been able to hold out and said that Ireland would never lie down until full freedom was achieved. He believed that the British Empire would not last more than fifty years.'

15 Gerald Doyle, BMH WS 1511.

16 Clarke, *Revolutionary Woman*, pp. 173, 180–81; Rex Taylor, *Michael Collins* (Dublin, 1961), p. 62; Piaras Béaslaí, *Michael Collins and the Making of a New Ireland* (Dublin, 1926), vol. i, pp. 135–43; Séamus G. O'Kelly, 'Memoirs', *The Nationalist*, 24 March 1956.

17 Dr Emmet Clarke, note of a discussion with the author, 2 August 1973.

18 Seán Keogh, BMH WS 1615.

19 Sir John Maxwell to Sir Henry Duke, Chief Secretary, 5 September 1916 (Public Record Office, Crime Special Branch Papers 23).

20 James O'Driscoll, interview in Ernie O'Malley (ed. Andy Bielenberg, John Borgonovo, Pádraig Óg Ó Ruairc), *The Men Will Talk to Me: West Cork Interviews by Ernie O'Malley*, p. 39.

Endnotes
437

21 1882–1945. Gaelic League activist. Commercial traveller for M.H. Gill & Son Ltd, publishers. Sworn into the IRB by Patrick McCartan in 1910. Joined the Irish Volunteers in 1913. Was an armed custodian of Bulmer Hobson in 1916. At Tom Clarke's direction, he did not take part in the Rising. He was ambivalent about the post-1916 violence and left the IRB in 1919.

22 Ó Murthuile, *History*, p. 51.

23 Ibid., p. 50.

24 Lyons, *Ireland Since the Famine*, pp. 395–6; Ó Murthuile, *History*, pp. 50–3; Cronin, *The McGarrity Papers*, pp. 64–5.

25 Liam Gaynor, BMH WS 183; Ó Murthuile, *History*, pp. 50–1, 220–3: Ó Murthuile indicates that he was secretary from 1916 and remained secretary until 1922 when the Council and IRB were brought to a formal end after Collins' death (although he seems to have continued to act as secretary in the recreated 1923 Supreme Council up to 1924 when that, too, was brought to an end). Liam Archer, interview with Richard Mulcahy, 9 February 1967(UCD, Richard Mulcahy papers, P7/D/33).

26 Liam Gaynor, BMH WS 183.

27 Valentine Jackson, BMH WS 409.

28 Joseph O'Rourke, interview with Fr F.X. Martin, 2 June 1961.

29 Joseph O'Doherty, interview, 25 March 1972.

30 Joseph Gleeson, BMH WS 367. Gleeson does not say if he was properly re-elected in 1917 and does not remember that Patrick McCartan had been co-opted in 1915 and so was 'legitimate'.

31 Patrick McCartan, BMH WS 766.

32 Ó Murthuile, *History*, p. 59.

33 Ibid.; Liam Gaynor, BMH WS 183; P.S. O'Hegarty, *Sunday Independent*, 26 August 1945: 'Mrs Clarke, who had kept the threads and contacts of the I.R.B. in her capable hands while the men were in prison, handed them on, on their release, to Diarmuid Lynch, Harry Boland, and these two, with Collins, McGarry and others, took up the threads again and put them together.'

34 Kitty O'Doherty, BMH WS 355.

35 Diarmuid Lynch, BMH WS 4. But he was active in the IRB in 1917.

36 Liam Gaynor, BMH WS 183.

37 Manus O'Boyle, BMH WS 289.

38 Patrick Colgan, BMH WS 850. Present were Martin Conlon as chairman, Seán Murphy as secretary, Diarmuid Lynch, Diarmuid O'Hegarty, Christopher Byrne and Michael Collins.

39 September may have been his release date.

40 Lynch, *The I.R.B. and the 1916 Insurrection*, pp. 22, 32; Arthur McElvogue, BMH WS 221: '[McCartan] also told me a rising was taking place in Dublin and that the contemplated rising in the North would only lead to slaughter.' Kevin McCabe, BMH WS 926: 'After breakfast we went to Sean Tobin's house in Hardwicke St. Sean was not there but Jim was and he said Sean had gone away on some business and had told himself to remain at home till he came back. We met Sean McDermott later in the day at the GPO and we reported the result of our journey to him. He asked us where was Jim Tobin, that he knew where Sean was. I heard afterwards that Sean was sent with a dispatch – I presume to Dundalk – to Donal Hannigan who was in command of the Volunteers there, but Donal said he never delivered the dispatch to him, but stayed in the hotel during the whole of Easter Week. Both the Tobins dropped out of everything after 1916.' John McGallogly, BMH WS 244: 'Towards the end of 1917 I returned to Glasgow. A split had developed in the ranks of the I.R.B. there and, as a consequence, in the other organisations too. Joe Robinson was at the head of one party composed mostly of those who had been in the Rising. Seamus Reader was with, but not at that time at the head of those who had not taken part. Some of them were in the IRB beforehand and had been informed of its

438   Endnotes

coming. One of them was alleged to have been in Dublin during Easter Week without turning out, and to have given a false account afterwards in Glasgow.'

41   Michael Staines, BMH WS 944. He claimed that he was never a member of the IRB but considered that up to the Rising 'they trusted me'. In fact he had probably joined before the Rising – Dublin Brigade quartermaster was too important a position for the IRB to ignore – but like Brugha was disillusioned by the failure of some IRB leaders and Circles to take part in the Rising.

42   George Lyons, BMH WS 104; Clarke, *Revolutionary Woman*, p. 18; Ó Murthuile, *History*, pp. 51–2; Mulcahy, 'Commentary', vol. i, pp. 6–7, 21–4; Liam Archer, interview with Richard Mulcahy, 9 February 1967 (UCD, Richard Mulcahy papers, P7/D/33).

43   Patrick McCartan, BMH WS 766.

44   Clarke, *Revolutionary Woman*, p. 183.

45   Ibid., p. 182.

46   O'Connor, *With Michael Collins*, p. 100.

47   John Matthews, BMH WS 1022.

48   Clarke, *Revolutionary Woman*, pp. 182–3: 'I did hear that he went all out to smash the I.R.B. I also heard that he soon saw the error of his action and abandoned it. Judging by later events, the mischief that I feared had already been done.' Dr Emmet Clarke, letter to the author, 24 February 1973: 'Cathal Brugha who had come out of prison determined to get rid of the I.R.B. as he said there was to be no more divided counsels. [My mother] tried to prevent him making a direct onslaught on the organisation as she said that in loyalty to the men who had been executed the members would rally to its defence and it would tend to cause splits instead of unity. She said that if he wanted to let the organisation die [then let it die] but not to attack it.'

49   Jim Thomas, 'Theory, method and the Irish Revolution', *Social Studies*, vol. iii, no. 4 (September, 1974), pp. 381–402; Williams (ed.), *Secret Societies in Ireland, passim.*

50   Mick Fleming, interview in O'Malley, *Kerry Interviews*, p. 60.

51   Eileen McGough, *Diarmuid Lynch: A Forgotten Irish Patriot* (Cork, 2013), pp. 82–96. In February 1918 he was arrested and, as an American citizen, deported to the United States.

52   Patrick Twomey, BMH WS 46.

53   Thomas Hales, BMH WS 20; Kitty O'Doherty, BMH WS 355: 'According as batches of prisoners were released from time to time from British camps and jails a lot of unfair comment was reported from various places against the leaders of those Volunteer Brigades – such as Cork and Kerry – which had taken no part in the Rising. My husband, as head of the Supreme Council, attended an inquiry into the matter which resulted in a complete exoneration of the leaders in question.'

54   Ó Murthuile, *History*, p. 59; McGough, *Diarmuid Lynch: A Forgotten Irish Patriot*, p. 86.

55   Florence O'Donoghue, *Tomás MacCurtain* (Tralee, 1958), p. 205.

13. REORGANISATION

1   John Shields, BMH WS 928.

2   Mulcahy, 'Talk given to the members of the 1916–21 Club', 20 February 1964 (UCD, Richard Mulcahy papers, P7/D/66).

3   Liam Archer, interview with Richard Mulcahy, 9 February 1962 (UCD, Richard Mulcahy papers, P7/D/35); Mulcahy, 'Notes' (UCD, Richard Mulcahy papers, P7/D/5); Richard Walsh, BMH WS 400; Daithí Ó Corráin and Gerard Hanley, *Cathal Brugha, 'An Indomitable Spirit'*, p. 71.

4   Ó Murthuile, *History*, p. 52; Liam Archer, interview with Richard Mulcahy, 9 February 1967

Endnotes

439

(UCD, Richard Mulcahy papers, P7/D/33). Archer's memory was that the first post-Rising Volunteer convention was held late in 1916 at Flemings Hotel, Gardiner Row, Dublin, when most delegates were from the country with only a few from Dublin (Archer, Liam Clarke, Diarmuid O'Hegarty), and that Cathal Brugha was not present. He also remembered that a second convention was held in March or April 1917 at the Plaza Hotel, Gardiner Row, and at this Brugha presided on crutches. Liam Gaynor, BMH WS 183, placed the first 1916 Volunteer convention in December.

5   M.V. Sugrue, interview with Richard Mulcahy, 1964 (UCD, Richard Mulcahy papers, P7/D/94). Mulcahy, for example, became O/C First Battalion, Dublin Brigade in January 1917.

6   Ó Murthuile, *History*, pp. 52–5; Seán Boylan, BMH WS 1715.

7   Seán Boylan, BMH WS 1715.

8   1895–1920. Jailed in August 1917–November 1917. Jailed again in February 1918–June 1918. A leader of the Soloheadbeg ambush that started the 1919–21 fighting. Killed in October 1920 in a street shoot-out in Dublin.

9   Padraig Tobin, 'The Third Tipperary Brigade', *The Nationalist*, 9, 16 November 1957.

10 Mulcahy, 'Preliminary note on Dan Nolan's questions', 4 December 1963 (UCD, Richard Mulcahy papers, P7/D/46). Treacy made this arrangement in July 1918. Treacy was central to Volunteer reorganisation in Tipperary.

11 John Shields, BMH WS 928.

12 John McAnerney, BMH WS 528.

13 John Shields, BMH WS 928.

14 Séamus Dobbyn, BMH WS 279; Liam Gaynor, BMH WS 183: Gaynor proposed this Ulster survey to the Supreme Council and nominated Dobbyn to conduct it. John Shields, BMH WS 928: Seán Ó Murthuile came to see Dobbyn's progress. 'O Murthuile's visit to County Tyrone was for the purpose of inspecting the officers and getting information to make a report on the state of the organisation. During his time with me I supplied him with a full verbal report on all matters concerning both the Volunteers and the I.R.B.'

15 John Shields, BMH WS 928.

16 Diarmuid Lynch, BMH WS 4.

17 Seán MacEoin, BMH WS 1716 part 2. Redmond won convincingly with 62 per cent of the vote and kept the seat until his death in 1932 – a sign of latent IPP support. Indeed, Redmond in 1926 formed the National League Party in the Free State. It appealed to IPP and Unionist supporters and won eight Dáil seats in the 1928 election.

18 Peter Hart, *The IRA and its Enemies: Violence and Community in Cork 1916–1923* (Oxford, 1999), p. 193.

19 Séamus McKenna, BMH WS 1016.

20 Other IRB men left because, like de Valera, they saw no place for the society once public political action and the IRA emerged after 1916. Senior IRB men Seán T. O'Kelly, Ernest Blythe and Desmond FitzGerald all left the IRB after 1916. The confusion caused by MacNeill's cancellation order convinced both pro- and anti-IRB men to avoid a repeat of that confusion. Collins thought that by operating strong secret control confusion would be avoided; conversely, de Valera, like Brugha, thought that continuing the society would ensure confusion.

21 David Hogan (Frank Gallagher), *The Four Glorious Years* (Dublin, 1971), pp. 246–7.

22 Taylor, *Michael Collins*, p. 11 quotes Collins on the question of continuing the IRB: 'There are many things to be said in favour of Sinn Féin, many of whose ideals are but the re-weighed ideals of the I.R.B. But the things to be said in favour of Sinn Féin do not outweigh the uses of the I.R.B. which is respected and acknowledged by many who will think twice about the prospects of Sinn Féin.'

440 Endnotes

23 Denis McCullough in Mulcahy, 'Talk given to the members of the 1916–21 Club', 20 February 1964 (UCD, Richard Mulcahy papers, P7/D/66); Mulcahy, 'Conversation with Denis McCullough', 18 October 1963 (UCD, Richard Mulcahy papers, P7/D/15): 'When I came back from jail [in 1917] I found the I.R.B. in the hands of people like Sean Ó Murthuile and Seamus O'Doherty and a boy called Clarke from Dundrum and a few others in Dublin and in Belfast it fell into the hands of one called Liam Gaynor. I came up to a meeting here [in Dublin] and I was kept in the outer darkness while these people met inside until I got fed up and I opened the door and I said, "What authority have you to meet here or who the hell are you?! As far as I'm concerned you can meet as often as you like; I'm through, there's no more use for the I.R.B."' McCullough gave a different story to the BMH: 'on the formation of the First Dáil, I could see no further use for the I.R.B. and severed my connection with it' (Denis McCullough, BMH WS 914). McCullough and Patrick McCartan were both viewed suspiciously after 1916 because they and their Volunteer units did not take part in the Rising (Joseph O'Doherty, interview, 18 December 1972), so being kept out of the meeting might have been a signal of this to McCullough. 'When I took Pearse's orders to Denis McCullagh [sic] on the Wednesday prior to the Rising, he cried. McCullagh's activities during the Rising were not approved of by the I.R.B., and he was refused readmission to the I.R.B. after the Rising' (Dr Feargus de Burca, BMH WS 105). William Kelly, BMH WS 226: Kelly's son reported an incident during Easter Week. 'Nora Connolly wished to be taken to Carrickmore to see Dr McCartan and my son Tom volunteered to accompany her in a car to Carrickmore. They proceeded to Carrickmore and I understand Miss Connolly saw Dr McCartan and had angry words with him over the obeying of the countermanding orders'. McCartan never explained how or why two priests were at his home over the 1916 Easter weekend arguing against the Rising.

24 George Lyons, BMH WS 104.

25 John Madden, interview in O'Malley, *Galway Interviews*, p. 211.

26 Thomas Malone, interview, 10 March 1973: Donnchadh O'Hannigan and Liam Manahan, both members of the IRB, had quarrelled about conflicting orders, the role of the IRB, and their own actions in 1916. 'When Collins came out of gaol, he asked me to go down and see if I could do something about this row in east Limerick. And he told me to go first to Thomas MacCurtain in Cork who was an I.R.B. man … He gave me the names of I.R.B. men [in Limerick] … I got the two of them quiet … Some of them threatened that if their opponents came [on an attack on a Barracks] they'd shoot them! But once the fight started all that trouble was forgotten: they were united then' (Liam Manahan, BMH WS 456).

27 Kitty O'Doherty, BMH WS 355.

28 Éamonn O'Duibhir, BMH WS 1474. Austin Stack, Ernest Blythe and Joseph MacDonagh (Tipperary TD (1919–22); director of the Belfast Boycott (1920–21)) agreed.

29 Frank Henderson, BMH WS 821.

30 O'Donoghue met the problem of dual IRB/Volunteer control when an IRB member in his battalion shot an RIC man, causing public outcry. Several Volunteer officers denounced the shooting. It raised the question of who actually commanded the Volunteer Brigade, the official leadership or the IRB? Good personal relationships smoothed away this particular incident (Borgonovo (ed.), *Florence and Josephine O'Donoghue's War of Independence*, pp. 58–60).

31 Liam Ó Briain, interview, 7 December 1971.

32 Garry Holohan, BMH WS 336.

33 Ibid.

34 Joseph O'Rourke, interview with Fr F.X. Martin, 2 June 1961.

35 Séumas Robinson, BMH WS 1721: Robinson's anti-IRB feeling was probably generated by his anti-GHQ, anti-Collins, anti-Treaty opinions. Florence O'Donoghue papers, NLI, Ms 31,390.

Endnotes

441

36 Michael Brennan, interview, 18 December 1972.

37 Peter (Eoin) McArdle, interview, 6 November 1972.

38 James McCullough, BMH WS 529. Two other Armagh members gave the same judgement: 'as the Volunteers took control of the matters which the I.R.B. were organised to encourage and foster' (Patrick Beagan, BMH WS 612), and 'I remained in the I.R.B. up to 1918 when I joined the Irish Volunteers. When I joined the Volunteers I ceased being a member of the I.R.B.' (Eugene Loughran, BMH WS 1774). Seán Gibbons, Adjutant of the West Mayo Brigade, concurred: 'With the formation of the I.R.A. and the Oath of Allegiance in 1919, the Irish Republican Brotherhood drifted more or less into disuse, as the things for which it stood began to be well catered for' (Seán Gibbons, BMH WS 927). James Hogan, an IRB member who fought in the East Clare Brigade in 1920–21, and later became National Army Director of Intelligence, reflected: '[T]he Volunteer movement was growing strong and taking the whole burden of the national fight on its back, it was absorbing and assimilating the I.R.B. ... the secret organisation was losing itself in the open organisation' (Maj. Gen. James Hogan, 'Statement to the Committee of Inquiry into Army Mutiny, 12 April 1924' (UCD, Richard Mulcahy papers, P7/C/30)). In Tyrone, 'When the Volunteers got strong and properly established, the I.R.B. ceased to exist' (Patrick McKenna, BMH WS 911). Florence O'Donoghue, *No Other Law* (Dublin, 1954), pp. 188–9, regarded IRB activity in Southern Ireland as minimal, and that while there were approximately 31,000 men in the IRA in Kerry, Cork and Waterford, in the same area there were about 1,170 in the IRB.

39 Ó Murthuile, *History*, p. 53; Kitty O'Doherty, BMH WS 355: 'Mick Collins and Harry Boland with some others worked hard both in detention and after their release to form a powerful instrument of the organisation and they eventually dominated it.'

40 Ó Murthuile, *History*, p. 53. O'Sullivan and Diarmuid O'Hegarty were, with Collins, the IRB/ IRA decision-making group. Dinny Daly, interview in O'Malley, *Kerry Interviews*, p. 323: 'Gearóid and Diarmuid O'Hegarty and Mick Collins were the inner circle.'

41 Brennan, *The War in Clare*, pp. 38–9: 'Neither then [1919] nor later did I ever succeed in extracting even one rifle from GHQ. This was much resented as we knew that a certain number of rifles were going to Cork.' John Madden, interview in O'Malley, *Galway Interviews*, p. 217: 'Dick Walsh bought Lee-Enfield rifles from England before the Tan War, but like a bloody fool he reported to Collins who said to him, "God, you're a Godsend, you've just arrived at the right time, they're planning a big thing down in Cork and I'll guarantee to get the rifles back for you." Dick handed them over and we never got them back, nor did we get anything in exchange for them.'

42 Joseph O'Doherty, interview, 11 February 1973. Ernie O'Malley agreed: O'Hegarty's 'mind worked quickly, shrewdly and surely' (Arthur Mitchell, *Revolutionary Government in Ireland: Dáil Éireann 1919–22* (Dublin, 1995), p. 45).

14. COLLINS EMERGES

1 Albert Sylvester, interview transcript, n.d.

2 Michael Joseph Staines (1885–1955). Born in Newport, Co. Mayo, where his father served in the RIC. In 1904 the family moved to Dublin. Joined the Gaelic League and, in 1913, the Volunteers. Probably joined the IRB in 1915. In 1916 he became quartermaster of the Irish Volunteers. Fought in the GPO in the Rising. On GHQ Staff and Volunteer/IRA Executive. A TD in the First and Second Dáils. First commissioner of the Garda Síochána.

3 Mulcahy, 'Commentary', vol. i, p. 16; Béaslaí, *Michael Collins*, vol. i, pp. 110–20.

4 1891–1970. From Wexford. Doctor and politician. Sinn Féin TD. Later Fianna Fáil minister.

442   Endnotes

Part of a closely connected political family. Two of Ryan's sisters, first Mary Kate (who died early) and then Phyllis, married Seán T. O'Kelly, a future Cabinet colleague and a future President of Ireland. Another sister, Josephine ('Min') married Richard Mulcahy. A fourth sister, Agnes, married Denis McCullough.

5   1892–1968. Born in Argentina. Family from Offaly (King's County). A pupil at St Enda's. Raised the 'Irish Republic' flag over GPO in 1916. Interned at Frongoch. Deported to Argentina in 1917. He returned to Ireland in July 1922 and was active in Offaly politics. His sister, Catalina, was secretary to Austin Stack 1919–22 and married Seán MacBride.

6   1882–1974. From Mayo/Roscommon. Gaelic footballer. IRA officer. Intelligence, Oriel House, National Army 1922.

7   1887–1965. Born in New York. Pupil at St Enda's.

8   1886–1965. Civil servant in London. Sent to Valentia on Good Friday in an aborted attempt to capture the radio station there to contact the *Aud* and confuse the Royal Navy.

9   Mulcahy, 'Commentary', vol. i, p.16; Liz Gillis, *The Hales Brothers and the Irish Revolution* (Cork, 2016), p. 43; Seán O'Mahony, *Frongoch: University of Revolution* (Dublin, 1995), pp. 66–7, adds Seán Hales, Joe Sweeney and Seán Ó Murthuile to the IRB group around Collins in Frongoch. He also credits Henry Dixon (1859–1928) with IRB organising in the camp. Dixon was an old Fenian and friend of Arthur Griffith. He was transferred to Reading Prison not long after being interned. Ó Murthuile was released early. So both men, while becoming aware of Collins, did not have much contact with him before 1917.

10 Uinseann MacEoin, *Survivors* (Dublin, 1980), p. 82, quoting Tomás Ó Maoleóin (Thomas Malone), brother of James Malone (Séamus Ó Maoleóin); Pádraig Ó Caoimh, *Richard Mulcahy: From the Politics of War to the Politics of Peace, 1913–1924* (Dublin, 2019), p. 31: Gerald Boland, an IRB member who had fought in 1916 and been interned with Mulcahy and Collins, asserted that Mulcahy was part of the Collins IRB group in the camp. 'Dick Mulcahy was very friendly at the time with Collins' (Dinny Daly, interview in O'Malley, *Kerry Interviews*, p. 319). Mulcahy denied this. Opinion was divided about Collins among the internees at Frongoch, and Mulcahy may have wanted to present himself as uninvolved in Collins' group so as to add weight to his positive judgement of Collins.

11 John J. O'Reilly, letter to the author, 13 September 1972.

12 Hart, *Mick*, pp. 103–6.

13 Mulcahy, 'Commentary', vol. i, p. 16; Piaras Béaslaí, *Michael Collins*, vol. i, pp. 110–20.

14 The Act came into force on 2 March 1916. After the Rising, heeding political feeling, the government decided that it would not be applied to Ireland. If the Frongoch men had been conscripted they would have faced military courts and possible death sentences if they refused orders.

15 Daniel Kelly, BMH WS 1004.

16 Thomas Clarke Luby (1822–1901). A founder of the IRB.

17 Stephen Jordan (1887–1995). Born and lived in Athenry. Shoemaker. Played hurley for Galway in the GAA (1903–13), became secretary of the Galway County Board (1918–20). Joined the IRB in 1906. Organised the Irish Volunteers in Galway with Liam Mellows. Arrested after the Rising and interned at Frongoch. Organised the Galway Volunteers in 1917. Arrested and imprisoned in 1918–19 and again in 1920–21. Took the anti-Treaty side in the Civil War.

18 Seán Murphy, BMH WS 204.

19 Éamonn Dore, BMH WS 392.

20 Ibid.

21 Gerry Boland to Michael (Hayes), 9 April 1966 (UCD, Richard Mulcahy papers, P7/D/118). Gerry Boland, who had joined the IRB in 1904, objected to Collins' activities on the grounds

Endnotes

443

that 'we should give up sneaking in and out of 41 Parnell Square and come into the open as a republican party'.

22 Joseph Sweeney, interview, 24 January 1980.

23 Twohig, *Blood on the Flag*, p. 56. Mulcahy threatened to sue James Malone for libel for including this in his book, *B'fhiú an Braon Fola* (1958). Collins echoed this sentiment when discussing the Bishop of Cork with Malone (p. 94). James' brother Tomás Ó Maoileóin (Thomas Malone), interview in MacEoin, *Survivors*, pp. 82–3, quotes the same statement by Mulcahy. During the 1922–23 Civil War, Mulcahy certainly acted in the spirit of the quote: 'Mulcahy boasted that he had so many of the higher [IRA] officers that he would execute three of them' (Michael Kilroy, interview in O'Malley, *Mayo Interviews*, p. 69).

24 Florence O'Donoghue left a memoir that lends further credence to Mulcahy having uttered these sentiments. He met Mulcahy in 1918: 'I was shocked by Mulcahy's deliberate, cold-blooded blasphemy. I attributed it to a weakness of character, a desire to appear tough and ruthless' (Borgonovo (ed.), *Florence and Josephine O'Donoghue's War of Independence*, p. 56). Borgonovo observes that Mulcahy 'held no great love for O'Donoghue' (p. 73).

25 Béaslaí, *Michael Collins*, vol. i, pp. 110–20.

26 Muriel MacDonagh, Áine Ceannt and Margaret Gavan Duffy whose husband, George, was Casement's defence barrister in London.

27 Clarke, *Revolutionary Woman*, p. 176.

28 Ibid., p. 177.

29 Ibid. Batt O'Connor, 'Statement' (NLI, Piaras Béaslaí papers, Ms 33,914/7) gives an account where returning prisoners found that dependants of rebels were often not receiving funds, while less deserving people were, so they determined to get Collins appointed to the secretaryship of the INAVDF. 'Joe Gleeson came to me and said Michael Collins was the right man for the job but he was not known. He suggested that when names were proposed we should distribute ourselves throughout the room and call "Michael Collins". I got standing on a chair and Joe on another. People said some man was wanted who knew who was who. Joe shouted "Collins" and others followed and that carried the crowd. The committee of women, Mrs Thomas Clarke, etc, did not know Michael Collins but arranged the interview. The committee was impressed by his ability, but nettled by his apparent conceit. Nevertheless, Mrs Clarke's views were definitive.'

30 Kitty O'Doherty, BMH WS 355, recounts how Seán MacDermott introduced her to Collins four days before the Rising: '"Did you ever meet this man?" I said "No." Standing near was Mick Collins. That was the first time I saw Mick Collins.' Dr Emmet Clarke, letter to the author, 24 February 1973: 'When Mick Collins was released the position of Secretary to the National Aid was becoming vacant and my mother could arrange to have anybody she liked appointed to the position. She had heard of Collins from Sean McDermott before the Rising who had a very high opinion of Collins. Collins applied for the job and Mam had him out to our house in Richmond Avenue [and] she asked him what ideas he had and whether he felt that the Rising was but the first blow and that the country should be organised for the next. His views were in line with hers and she said it would give him an opportunity to organise the Volunteers and the I.R.B. under the cloak of travelling for the National Aid. She had him appointed.'

31 Mulcahy, 'Talk given to the members of the 1916–21 Club', 20 February 1964 (UCD, Richard Mulcahy papers, P7/D/66); Richard Mulcahy, 'Notes as a background to talk on Collins', 21 October 1963 (UCD, Richard Mulcahy papers, P7/D/66): Mulcahy received this information from Kathleen Clarke.

32 Brennan, *The War in Clare*, p. 21: 'Michael Collins visited us several times in his capacity as Secretary of the Irish National Aid Association.'

33 Collins met opposition within the IRB when he stood for election as the Centre of the Fintan

Endnotes

Lalor Circle because of his unauthorised recruiting in Frongoch (Hart, *Mick*, pp. 275–6). Kathleen Clarke was careful to give the IRB funds in her possession in 1917 to Diarmuid Lynch as treasurer of the reconstituted IRB.

34   Dinny Daly, interview in O'Malley, *Kerry Interviews*, p. 323. Daly was vice-O/C Third Kerry Brigade.

35   O'Connor, *With Michael Collins*, p. 100.

36   *The Southern Star*, 23 August 1953.

37   Joseph O'Rourke, interview with Fr F.X. Martin, 2 June 1961.

38   Joseph Gleeson, BMH WS 367.

39   Diarmuid Lynch, BMH WS 4.

40   Ó Murthuile, *History*, p. 59; Liam Gaynor, BMH WS 183.

41   Patrick McCormack, BMH WS 339.

42   1891–1948. From Cork. Irish language activist. Sinn Féin politician. Adjutant General in the IRA and National Army. Barrister. Raised the tricolour over GPO in 1916. Supreme Council 1921. Very close to Michael Collins.

43   Alec McCabe, interview, 6 December 1971.

44   Ibid.

45   McInerny, 'Gerry Boland's story'; Gerry Boland to Michael (Hayes), 9 April 1966 (UCD, Richard Mulcahy papers, P7/D/118). Gerry did not like or trust Collins (*Dictionary of Irish Biography*).

46   Ó Murthuile, *History*, p. 160. Liam Gaynor proposed this change in 'about 1918' (Liam Gaynor, BMH WS 183).

47   Joseph Furlong, BMH WS 335: 'I also transferred to the I.R.B. in Dublin. When I arrived there Mick Collins was again our Centre, and we had a lot of our old members from London here with us. We met at 48, Parnell Square.' Furlong did not give the name of this Circle.

48   Mulcahy, 'Commentary', vol. i, p. 45.

49   Dolan and Murphy, *Days in the Life*, p. 46.

50   John J. O'Reilly, letter to the author, 13 September 1972.

51   Ó Murthuile, *History*, p. 160.

52   Mulcahy, 'Talk given to the members of the 1916–21 Club, 30 February 1964' (UCD, Richard Mulcahy papers, P7/D/66).

53   Twohig, *Blood on the Flag*, p. 80.

54   Denis Daly, BMH WS 110. Later, when Rising prisoners were being identified, the two sergeants did not pick out Collins or Daly as being significant, so they were sent to Frongoch (Denis Daly, interview in O'Malley, *Kerry Interviews*, p. 322). William J. McKenna, interview, 19 December 1972: in August 1922 McKenna asked Collins if he could go to Cork with him. 'He said, "What use would you be in Cork?" "I can drive a car." "I've got plenty of drivers enough."… I just saw the scowl there, and I saw a little bit of indecision, and I said to him "I'd love to see Cork, sir." That was very cute, you see, Collins loved Cork and used to say, "You'll never know Ireland until you've seen Cork!" "You can come but be there on time."'

55   Thomas Taylor, interview, 5 November 1972.

56   Margery Forester, *Michael Collins* (London, 1971), pp. 332–3; Hart, *Mick*, p. 266.

57   T. Ryle Dwyer, *Michael Collins, 'The Man Who Won the War'* (Cork, 1990), pp. 130–1, 140.

58   NLI, Florence O'Donoghue papers, Ms 31,124/1–3; Kitty O'Doherty, BMH WS 355: Collins demonstrated his bluntness in a letter to the editor of the *Gaelic American*, 15 October 1920. 'I don't like writing to newspapers for many reasons, particularly because the Editor always has the last word.' The last word was what Collins himself always wanted.

59   Robert Barton, interview, 3 September 1973. Dolan and Murphy, *Days in the Life*, p. 14: Collins

Endnotes

445

as a young man in London kept a notebook 'in which he created a personal dictionary' of uncommon words. 'Espionage' he defined as 'Employment of spies'; 'Erotic' as 'An amorous poem'.

60   Dinny Daly, interview in O'Malley, *Kerry Interviews*, pp. 318, 323.

61   Tom Barry, *Guerilla Days in Ireland* (Dublin, 1949), p. 164. Thomas Bernadine Barry (1897–1980), O/C Third Cork Brigade Flying Column from mid-1920. He had a chequered career, first as a soldier in the Royal Artillery during the First World War; then as an IRA fighting man winning some notable engagements but gaining a reputation for ruthlessness and egocentricity.

62   Maj. Gen. Charles Russell, 'Statement to the Army Inquiry', 10 May 1924 (UCD, Richard Mulcahy papers, P7/C/29).

63   Peter Carleton, interview in MacEoin, *Survivors*, p. 306.

64   Geraldine Plunkett Dillon, 'Memoir' (NLI, Geraldine Plunkett Dillon papers, Ms 37,331/1); Geraldine Plunkett, BMH WS 358.

65   Joseph Sweeney, interview, 10 December 1971.

66   Liam Ó Briain in Mulcahy, 'Talk on Michael Collins', 29 October 1963 (UCD, Richard Mulcahy papers, P7/D/66).

67   www.irishcentral.com/roots/history/michael-collins-nasty-1916-relative-plunkett, 13 August 2020.

68   Garry Holohan (Gearóid Ua h-Uallachain), BMH WS 336. Holohan ascribed Collins' popularity to his position as secretary of the Dependants' Fund in 1917 because, 'Like everyone else who has the giving of money or jobs, he became very popular.' Hart, *Mick*, p. 145, quotes Leo Henderson saying, 'Collins was a bully'.

69   James O'Driscoll, interview in O'Malley, *West Cork Interviews*, p. 44.

70   William J. McKenna, interview, 14 February 1973: McKenna was reporting the experience of his sister, Kathleen McKenna.

71   Ibid.

72   Michael Hayes, interview, 22 March 1972.

73   Tadhg Kennedy, BMH WS 1413.

74   Dolan and Murphy, *Days in the Life*, p. 90.

75   Michael Kilroy, interview in O'Malley, *Mayo Interviews*, p. 46. Kilroy was trying to get money from Collins to pay IRA debts. Ronan Fanning, *The Department of Finance, 1922–1958* (Dublin, 1978), pp. 26–7: Collins provided detailed reports on the Department of Finance and appointed a professional auditor for the Department and secured the Dáil's agreement to an auditor for the Dáil accounts too.

76   Michael Joseph Costello, interview, 19 August 1973.

77   Richard Walsh, BMH WS 400. Walsh swore in Thomas Maguire, O/C South Mayo Brigade from 1920, and O/C Second Western Division from August 1921 (Thomas Maguire, interview in O'Malley, *Mayo Interviews*, p. 187).

78   They were all probably co-opted. Seán Ó Murthuile dates their joining the Council to June.

79   Diarmuid Lynch, BMH WS 4.

80   Darrell Figgis, *Recollections of the Irish War* (New York, 1927), p. 243.

81   Mulcahy, 'Commentary', vol. i, pp. 132A–B.

82   Desmond Ryan, *Remembering Zion* (London, 1934), p. 233.

83   Collins took the position of secretary of the Liberty Clubs founded after the Rising by Count Plunkett (who had joined the IRB in April 1916, sworn in by his son, Joseph (Dillon, *All in the Blood*, p. 211)). Geraldine Plunkett Dillon, 'The North Roscommon election', *Capuchin Annual* (Dublin, 1967), p. 339; Richard Walsh, BMH WS 400: As with the Dungannon and Freedom Clubs, the Liberty Clubs were an IRB front. 'This organisation was the public or outward expression of the IRB's policy. In other words, the Liberty Clubs were sponsored by

446   Endnotes

the IRB to give public expression and support to the IRB's policy of physical force as a means of gaining complete independence, meaning separation from English rule.'

84　Michael Staines was co-treasurer.

85　In an exercise of power, he simply took over from Éamonn Duggan (to Duggan's relief) as Director of Intelligence on GHQ Staff, being formally appointed to the post in 1919 (Richard Walsh, BMH WS 400). It was not surprising that Collins should have generated suspicions about his purposes and motivations.

86　Emmet Dalton, interview, 7 March 1973.

87　Risteárd Mulcahy, *Richard Mulcahy (1886–1971): A Family Memoir* (Dublin, 1999), p. 113.

88　Robert Lynch, *Revolutionary Ireland, 1912–25* (London, 2015), p. 72.

89　Brugha was chief of staff from 1917 until March 1918 when the Volunteer/IRA GHQ Staff was created and Mulcahy replaced him as chief of staff. Brugha resigned from the Sinn Féin Executive in April 1918 in protest at its collaboration with the IPP during the conscription crisis. President of the Dáil (January–April 1919). Minister for Defence (April 1919–22).

90　President of the Volunteer/IRA Executive (1917–22). President of the Dáil government (April 1919–1922). President of the Republic (1921–22).

91　Richard Walsh, BMI I WS 400· 'From the start of Collins' organising activities, there were people, differing from him in their ideas, who suggested that he was building himself up with a view to being able later on to direct the Volunteers and the national policy. This feeling of suspicion of Collins started, in my opinion, at least in Frongoch, and possibly in some cases, it started before 1916 in the Kimmage Garrison … On the release of Collins, O'Hegarty, Mulcahy, etc., in late 1916, this group got together again and were, to a great extent, responsible for the reorganisation of the military and political elements existing after 1916. This group did great work, which was undoubtedly due to careful planning by them whilst interned in Frongoch. Dermot [*sic*] O'Hegarty was the ablest man in the group, in my estimation. Collins was outstanding as a forceful personality who was able to get things done.'

92　Ryle Dwyer, *Michael Collins*, p. 61. Richard Walsh demonstrated the suspicions Collins faced. 'One night at an Executive meeting in Parnell Square, Collins surprised many of the members by resigning his position as A.G. and asking that he be appointed as Director of Intelligence. Certainly a lot of us were astounded that he should wish to relinquish the A.G-ship and take over the position of D.I. (Director of Intelligence) … Rory and myself … realised that the position of D.I. would give Collins an opportunity of establishing any contacts he liked and really placed him in the position that he could have intercourse with practically any individual he desired; that he could always use the excuse that he was seeing an individual or individuals for the purpose of getting information' (Richard Walsh, BMH WS 400). It seems that Collins remained Adjutant General until 1920, combining the post with Director of Intelligence.

93　Richard Walsh, BMH WS 400.

94　Seán Ó Murthuile, *History*, p. 64.

95　Maurice ('Moss') Twomey, interview, 11 December 1972.

96　Ernest Blythe, interview, 13 December 1971: 'He had personally devoted followers and people who may have been slammed by him like Michael Brennan. He was once up in town and he was glad to see Mick and he was expressing his pleasure to meet him – "What the hell are you doing in Dublin?" – was Mick's polite reply to him.'

97　Comerford, *On Dangerous Ground*, p. 207.

98　Seán MacEoin, interview, 22 February 1973, was adamant that O'Hegarty was secretary and Ó Murthuile treasurer. This may have been the case after Collins' death.

99　Seán MacEoin, interview, 8 March 1973. Harry Boland succeeded Seán McGarry as president in 1918 but resigned when he went to the United States in June 1919. Collins succeeded Boland. Richard Mulcahy, 'Notes on the Chief of Staff position' (UCD, Richard Mulcahy

Endnotes

447

papers, P7/D/96); Richard Mulcahy, 'Notes on 1916' (UCD, Richard Mulcahy papers, P7/D/I/30).

100 Mulcahy, 'Commentary', vol. i, p. 46; *The Nationalist*, 14 December 1957; Dan Breen, *My Fight for Irish Freedom* (Dublin, 1933), pp. 115–16; Desmond Ryan, *Seán Treacy and the Third Tipperary Brigade I.R.A.* (Tralee, 1945), pp. 108–9. Mick McDonnell was the first O/C of the Squad. Paddy Daly succeeded him. The other members were Vinnie Byrne, Ben Byrne, Jim Slattery, Frank Bolster, Eddie Byrne, Jim Conroy, Paddy Griffin, Mick Kennedy, Thomas Keogh, Joe Leonard, Bill Stapleton and Mick Reilley. Many of these men were later to be active in Liam Tobin's IRA Organisation in 1923–4.

101 Leon Ó Broin, *Michael Collins*, p. 49.

102 Tadhg Kennedy, interview in O'Malley, *Kerry Interviews*, p. 91.

103 Dan McCarthy, BMH WS 722.

104 Pax Whelan (Pax Ó Faolain), interview in MacEoin, *Survivors*, p. 139.

105 Collins' 'Charlie' was a jibe at Brugha's less than 100 per cent Irish background.

106 Ó Broin, *Revolutionary Underground*, pp. 201–2; O'Connor, *The Big Fellow*, p. 141: 'Mulcahy went to de Valera and informed him he must either control Brugha or accept his own resignation as Chief of Staff. De Valera agreed. "Cathal is jealous of Mick," he said. He did remonstrate with Brugha and Brugha broke down. "I could not do wrong," he said. After this Brugha went back to his old mania – assassinating the British cabinet.'

107 Liam O'Doherty, interview, 7 March 1973.

108 *Dáil Éireann Proceedings*, 19 December 1921.

15. ELECTIONS

1 House of Commons, 5 November 1918.

2 Kitty O'Doherty, BMH WS 355.

3 Patrick Little (1884–1963). The Irish Nation League supported abstentionism. Fiona Devoy, 'The Mansion House Conference: Ireland's "First National Cabinet"', *University of Limerick History Society Journal*, vol. 9 (2008).

4 Richard Walsh, BMH WS 400: 'One of the first moves made by Collins after his release was his managing to get himself appointed as Secretary to Count Plunkett and also Secretary to the Liberty Clubs which contained all the extreme elements of the survivors of 1916, men who still visualised another resort to physical force, numbering many key men in the local districts all over Ireland.'

5 Thomas Dillon, 'Birth of the new Sinn Féin and the Convention 1917', *Capuchin Annual* (1967), p. 395.

6 O'Brien, *Forth the Banners Go*, pp. 146–7.

7 William O'Brien, BMH WS 1776.

8 While the IRB had funded *Nationality* before 1916, its post-16 iteration was funded privately and not by the Brotherhood. Together with IRB criticism of de Valera in 1917–18, IRB antagonism towards the political wing of the movement, though not strident, was already present (John Madden, interview in O'Malley, *Galway Interviews*, p. 211).

9 Francis Sheehy Skeffington had tried to prevent looting during the Rising. He was arrested and shot without trial.

10 William J. Brennan-Whitmore, interview, 4 November 1972.

11 William Oman, interview, 6 November 1972.

12 Peadar O'Donnell, note of a discussion with the author, 31 October 1971.

13 Richard Walsh, BMH WS 400; Michael Staines, BMH WS 944: 'The first time I saw Michael

448 Endnotes

Collins during the election was in Frenchpark on the actual day of the election. He had charge of one of the booths there and I had charge of the other one – there were two in the town. Count Plunkett, if elected, was quite prepared to do anything we wanted him to do and he told us so.'

14 Ó Murthuile, *History*, p. 54.

15 Macardle, *The Irish Republic*, p. 231.

16 Lyons, *Ireland Since the Famine*, pp. 384–5.

17 Gerald Doyle, BMH WS 1511.

18 Lyons, *Ireland Since the Famine*, pp. 382–3; Longford and O'Neill, *Eamon de Valera*, pp. 56–8.

19 Richard Mulcahy, 'The Irish Volunteer Convention, 27 October, 1917', *Capuchin Annual* (1967), p. 403; Tim Pat Coogan, *Michael Collins: A Biography* (London, 1991), p. 67, gives an account of the returning officer who, threatened with a gun, 'found' uncounted ballots that gave the election to McGuinness.

20 Richard Mulcahy, 'Notes' (UCD, Richard Mulcahy papers, P7/D/102). They based themselves in Forester's Hall, Rutland Square.

21 Clarke, *Revolutionary Woman*, p. 137.

22 Kathleen Clarke, *Memoirs*, p. 122 (Ms from Dr Emmet Clarke, Blundellsands, Liverpool), provides this account. It was not included in her published book, *Revolutionary Woman*. Brennan, *The War in Clare*, pp. 24–5, does not mention Kathleen Clarke's or Madge Daly's involvement. 'A meeting of Volunteers and Sinn Féin supporters from all over the constituency was held in Ennis and they asked me to stand. I declined promptly and suggested de Valera as the penal servitude prisoners were being released and he was their recognized leader ... There was strong opposition as all the old people and nearly all the clergy wanted John MacNeill ... [But] the Volunteers wouldn't accept him because of his action in the Rising but would run de Valera as the Volunteer candidate. This settled the question and eventually de Valera was agreed to unanimously.'

23 Longford and O'Neill, *Eamon de Valera*, pp. 63–5.

24 David McCullagh, *De Valera: Rise 1882–1932* (Dublin, 2017), pp. 122–5.

25 Éamonn Dore, BMH WS 392.

26 Michael Noyk, BMH WS 707.

27 Arthur Griffith had first proposed abstention from Westminster in 1902. The Sinn Féin Party is dated as starting in 1905. It was a coalition of nationalist groups, including the IRB's Dungannon Clubs that would also meet as Sinn Féin clubs.

28 Michael Laffan, 'The unification of Sinn Féin in 1917'.

29 Ó Murthuile, *History*, p. 56.

30 Lyons, *Ireland Since the Famine*, pp. 393–4; Ó Murthuile, *History*, pp. 54–6; Forester, *Michael Collins*, pp. 84–6.

31 Ó Murthuile, *History*, pp. 57–9.

16. 1917–22 CONSTITUTION

1 Collins, *The Path to Freedom*, p. 97.

2 George Lyons, BMH WS 104.

3 Diarmuid Lynch, BMH WS 4.

4 Con Collins, Harry Boland and Thomas Ashe were released from prison in June.

5 Diarmuid Lynch, BMH WS 4.

6 Ibid. The 1873 Constitution had thirty-four clauses with approximately 2,160 words. The 1917 Constitution had thirty-seven clauses with approximately 3,600 words. See Appendices IV and V.

7 1917 Constitution, clause 21(b).

Endnotes   449

8   Frank Robbins, BMH WS 585. Robbins had been a sergeant in the ICA in 1916. It would seem that McCartan, as with McCullough, had sought to explain his non-participation in the Rising.
9   1917 Constitution, clause 3.
10 1917 Constitution, clause 4.
11 1917 Constitution, clause 8.
12 1917 Constitution, clause 9(a). '[A] "County Sub-Centre" a "County Secretary" and a "County Treasurer"' were also to be elected by the County Centres.
13 Diarmuid Lynch, BMH WS 4; Liam Gaynor, BMH WS 183, misdates the new composition: 'The Supreme Council agreed, about 1918, to my proposal to increase the Irish Provincial representation from one to two, thus increasing the Council from eleven to fifteen members.'
14 1917 Constitution, clause 6.
15 Diarmuid Lynch, BMH WS 4.
16 1917 Constitution, clause 6.
17 1917 Constitution, clause 12.
18 Terry Golway, *Irish Rebel: John Devoy and America's Fight for Ireland's Freedom* (New York, 1998), pp. 202, 209, 211, 220: between September and December 1914, for example, $18,500 (about £90,000 in 2024) was sent to the IRB by the Clan; in 1915 $8,000 (about £43,000) was sent to Casement in Germany for his Irish Brigade; in the months before the Rising, $100,000 (about £500,000) was sent to Clarke; a further $10,000 (about £50,000) was sent in March 1916.
19 1917 Constitution, clause 13. Hobson was never expelled. Nor did he resign. He was simply allowed to retire without any ceremony, theoretically 'suspended' under this new clause.
20 1917 Constitution, clause 14.
21 1917 Constitution, clause 15.
22 1917 Constitution, clauses 16, 17, 18, 31.
23 1917 Constitution, clause 19(a).
24 1917 Constitution, clause 19(b).
25 1917 Constitution, clause 20.
26 1917 Constitution, clause 20. Patrick McCartan's missions to Russia and the United States were probably conducted before the new constitution was introduced and no doubt prompted this clause.

17. THE CANDIDATE

1   George Lyons, BMH WS 104.
2   Michael Laffan, 'The unification of Sinn Féin in 1917': 166 Sinn Féin Clubs, about 11,000 members, 9 July 1917; 336 Clubs, about 21,000 members, August 1917; 1,200 Clubs, about 250,000 members, October 1917.
3   Ó Murthuile, *History*, p. 9; Liam Gaynor, BMH WS 183: members were told 'when organising a Circle to form also a Company of Volunteers'.
4   Samuel Irwin, interview, 31 October 1972. Eoin MacNeill's influence can, perhaps, be seen here. George Lyons, BMH WS 104, erroneously claimed that there was a constitutional provision for release on religious grounds: there was no such provision in either the 1873 or the 1917 constitutions.
5   George Lyons, BMH WS 104.
6   Longford and O'Neill, *Eamon de Valera*, p. 66.
7   *Dáil Éireann Proceedings*, 23 August 1921.
8   Ibid.; Béaslaí, *Michael Collins*, vol. i, p. 150; Tim Pat Coogan, *De Valera: Long Fellow, Long Shadow* (London, 1995), p. 94.

Endnotes

9 Neil Richardson, *According to their Lights: Stories of Irishmen in the British Army, Easter 1916* (Cork, 2015), p. 390 and *passim*: the 3rd Royal Irish Regiment, 3rd, 4th, 5th and 10th Royal Dublin Fusiliers, 3rd Royal Irish Rifles, 3rd Reserve Cavalry Brigade, 5th Leinster Regiment, Trinity College Officers Training Corps, the Volunteer Training Corps and the Ulster Composite Battalion.

10 James Cullen, BMH WS 1343: 'When the Rising started, a native of Enniscorthy who was in the English Army was home on leave. He threw off his uniform and joined the Volunteers. He rejoined his regiment when the Rising was over.'

11 Eunan O'Halpin, 'Collins and Intelligence 1919–23' in Gabriel Doherty and Dermot Keogh (eds), *Michael Collins and the Making of the Irish State* (Cork, 1998), p. 74.

12 David Fitzpatrick, 'Ireland and the Great War' in Thomas Bartlett (ed.), *The Cambridge History of Ireland*, vol. iv, pp. 494–8, suggests 'about 206,000' enlistments in Ireland and 32–35,000 fatalities. Niamh Gallagher, *Ireland and the Great War: A Social and Political History* (London, 2020), p. 18, gives 210,000 enlistments from all thirty-two Irish counties with about 63,000 from Ulster. Richardson, *According to their Lights*, p. 6, estimates about 150,000 Irish recruits during the war of whom 31,000 were UVF and 32,000 Redmondite National Volunteers. In a population of 4.4 million (1911) with about 890,000 Protestants, the non-Protestant population was about 3.51 million of whom about 25 per cent of men aged 18–41 voluntarily enlisted in 1914–18 or were already in the military. In 1918 enlistment age was increased from 41 to 51, but by then voluntary enlistments had tailed off. A consequence of so many Irishmen in the armed forces was that most families had a member in the military.

13 Stephens, *The Insurrection in Dublin*, p. 87.

14 Brennan, *The War in Clare*, pp. 11, 20–21: 'In the summer of 1915 a big parade of Volunteers was held in Limerick … When we got to the poorer quarters, crowds of women showed strong disapproval … These women were in the main wives of men serving in the British Army and were known to us as "Separation Allowance" women … [After the Rising we] had been "seen off" at Limerick station by a crowd of British soldiers' wives ("separation allowance ladies") who howled insults, pelted us with anything handy and several times had to be forced back physically by the military escort.'

15 Longford and O'Neill, *Eamon de Valera*, pp. 51–61; Lyons, *Ireland Since the Famine*, p. 383; Macardle, *The Irish Republic*, pp. 220–34; Ó Murthuile, *History*, pp. 60, 62–3.

16 Mulcahy, 'Notes' (UCD, Richard Mulcahy papers, P7/D/96). The meeting was held at the Gaelic League's Keating Branch rooms in Rutland Square.

17 Macardle, *The Irish Republic*, pp. 236–9; Mulcahy, 'Notes on Thomas Ashe' (UCD, Richard Mulcahy papers, P7/D/26).

18 *Weekly Freeman*, 6 October 1917.

19 Mulcahy, 'Notes on Thomas Ashe'.

20 Mulcahy, 'Notes as a background to talk on Collins'.

21 Ó Murthuile, *History*, p. 64; Macardle, *The Irish Republic*, p. 238. After Ashe's death, Seán McGarry was co-opted. Harry Boland was probably co-opted when Seán McGarry was arrested in May 1918 during the German Plot.

22 *Irish Independent*, 1 October 1917; Kee, *The Green Flag*, pp. 608–9.

23 Mulcahy, 'Notes' (UCD, Richard Mulcahy papers, P7/D/59).

24 Richard Walsh, BMH WS 400: 'The Volunteer Executive at the time was greatly surprised by the influx of men and organised plans to get officers from each part of the country to meet trains from their own districts and to take charge of the men coming into the city.'

25 Tadhg Kennedy, interview in O'Malley, *Kerry Interviews*, p. 82.

26 'Irish Volunteers General Scheme of Organisation, 1917' (UCD, Richard Mulcahy papers, P7/D/33).

Endnotes

27 Seán McGarry was secretary of the National Executive until 17 May 1918 when he was arrested. Mulcahy, 'Note on M.W. O'Reilly' (UCD, Richard Mulcahy papers, P7/D/96); Richard Walsh, BMH WS 400, lists the 1917 Resident Executive as Éamon de Valera, Chairman; Éamonn Duggan, Deputy Chairman; Rory O'Connor; Michael Staines; Cathal Brugha; M.W. O'Reilly; Diarmuid O'Hegarty; Michael Collins and Richard Mulcahy.

28 Liam Archer, interview with Richard Mulcahy, 9 February 1967 (UCD, Richard Mulcahy papers, P7/D/33). Archer thought that Brugha did not preside at the December 1916 convention but did at this one. He also thought that Brugha's enmity towards Collins developed with Collins' IRB election-fixing at this convention.

29 Patrick J. Ruttledge, interview in O'Malley, *Mayo Interviews*, p. 271: 'On Sunday, before matches at Croke Park, the IRB would meet in Dublin.'

30 Mulcahy, 'Commentary', vol. ii, p. 4. Also present were Richard Mulcahy, Austin Stack, Michael Staines and Diarmuid Lynch.

31 Richard Mulcahy was Director of Training until March 1918 when he became Chief of Staff. Dick McKee succeeded him, also as O/C Dublin Brigade. Michael Staines was Director of Supplies, Rory O'Connor, Director of Engineering. De Valera, Brugha, Mulcahy, Staines, O'Connor, M.W. O'Reilly and Dick McKee represented Dublin on the National Executive. Collins, Director of Organisation (later Director of Intelligence), represented Munster with Diarmuid Lynch, Austin Stack and Gearóid O'Sullivan. Seán MacEntee, Joseph O'Doherty (Director of Communications – Diarmuid O'Hegarty and Diarmuid Lynch also had communications roles), Paul Galligan and Eoin O'Duffy represented Ulster. Séamus Doyle and Peadar Bracken represented Leinster. Larry Lardner, Dick Walsh and James Keaveney represented Connacht. Six members were co-opted: Éamonn Duggan, Gearóid O'Sullivan, Fintan Murphy, Diarmuid O'Hegarty, Dick McKee (all from Dublin and members of the Resident Executive) and Paddy Ryan from Tipperary (Joseph O'Doherty, interview, 22 March 1972); Richard Mulcahy, 'Notes' (UCD, P7/D/39)). Diarmuid Lynch was arrested in February 1918 and when he was deported to the United States at the end of April Collins took over his communications responsibility (Mulcahy, 'Note on M.W. O'Reilly', UCD, Richard Mulcahy papers, P7/D/96). Richard Walsh, BMH WS 400: 'The Chairman of the Convention was Eamon de Valera. Behind him, lying on the pile of hay, were Michael Collins, Cathal Brugha, Austin Stack, Dermot Lynch, Eamonn Duggan, Dermot [*sic*] O'Hegarty, Michael Staines, Liam Lynch of Cork, Terence McSwiney of Cork, Ernest Blythe, Joe McKelvey, Dick Barrett and Frank Barrett of Clare, Mick Brennan and one of his brothers of Clare, Sean MacEntee of Belfast, James Keaveney, Sligo, Alec McCabe of Sligo, Rory O'Connor, Dick McKee, Oscar Traynor, William M. O'Reilly and some of the McQuills of Dundalk, Brian O'Higgins, Laurence O'Toole, etc. All the prominent men in the republican physical-force movement of that time were present.'

32 The search for peace conducted by Galway County Council, Fr O'Flanagan and Sinn Féin in 1920 and the substantial electoral support for the 1921 Treaty reflected popular dislike of violence.

33 Joseph O'Doherty, interview, 22 March 1972. O'Doherty had left the IRB after 1916 for reasons similar to Brugha although his brother, Séamus, became president after the Rising.

34 Robert Brennan, *Allegiance: An Account of the Author's Experiences in the Struggle for Irish Independence* (Dublin, 1950), p. 154.

35 Séamus Dobbyn, BMH WS 279; Brennan, *Allegiance*, p. 154.

36 Daniel Kelly, BMH WS 1004.

37 McInerney, 'Gerry Boland's Story'; Figgis, *Recollections of the Irish War*, pp. 217–18.

38 Joseph O'Doherty, interview, 25 March 1972.

39 For most people, 'republic' was shorthand for complete independence. Nationalists generally

452 Endnotes

were not doctrinaire republicans (Aidan J. Beatty, 'Royalism in Republicanism: The political vocabulary of Irish sovereignty, 1912–1924', www.aidanbeatty.com/essays. I am grateful to Mariana Bonnouvrier for identifying Beatty's site).

40 Hugh Hehir, BMH WS 683: 'One thing that I can recall very clearly concerned the opposition to Eoin MacNeill's election to the Executive. He had been nominated and De Valera and Arthur Griffith both spoke eloquently in his favour. He was strongly opposed by Countess Markievicz and Dermot [*sic*] Lynch. The chief reason for the opposition was because of his action regarding the mobilisation orders for Easter Week, 1916.'

41 Mulcahy, 'Notes' (UCD, Richard Mulcahy papers, P7/D/39). W.T. Cosgrave, Hon. Treasurer, 537; Laurence Ginnell, Hon. Treasurer, 491; Dr R.F. Hayes, 674; Seán Milroy, 667; Constance Markievicz, 617; Count Plunkett, 598; Piaras Béaslaí, 557; Joseph MacGuinness, 501; Fionan Lynch, 475; Harry Boland, 448; Dr Kathleen Lynn, 425; J.J. Walsh, 424; Fr M. Ryan, 416; Fr T. Wall, 408; Diarmuid Lynch, 390; David Kent, 386; Seán T. O'Kelly, 367, Dr Thomas Dillon, 364, Seán MacEntee, 342. Ernest Blythe came joint last with Collins, with 340 votes.

42 Liam Gaynor, BMH WS 183: Gaynor placed this in 1918.

43 *Irish Independent*, 26 October 1917.

44 *Irish Independent*, 24 September 1917; Macardle, *The Irish Republic*, p. 242. De Valera had first proposed this clause on 10 October.

45 Piaras Béaslaí to Dr Risteárd Mulcahy, 20 February 1962 (UCD, Richard Mulcahy papers, P7/D/96).

46 When the Resident Executive last met at the end of 1921, its members were de Valera, Brugha, Austin Stack, Con Collins, Seán MacEntee, Joseph O'Doherty, Séamus Doyle, Rory O'Connor, Michael Staines, Paul Galligan, Diarmuid O'Hegarty, Fintan Murphy, Éamonn Duggan, Seán McGarry, Richard Mulcahy, Michael Collins, Eoin O'Duffy and Gearóid O'Sullivan (Joseph O'Doherty, interview, 22 March 1972).

47 James McCullough, BMH WS 127.

48 O'Donoghue, *No Other Law*, p. 20.

49 Thomas Fitzpatrick and Bob McDonnell, BMH WS 395; Séamus McKenna, BMH WS 1016: in Belfast, 'I cannot recall any useful purpose served by our particular Circle.'

50 Joseph Martin, BMH WS 1723; Thomas Brady, BMH WS 1008.

18. GHQ

1 M.R.D. Foot, *SOE – The Special Operations Executive 1940–46* (London, 1984), p. 19. Dalton was proposing the Special Operations Executive.

2 Mulcahy, 'Talk on Michael Collins'.

3 Mulcahy, 'Commentary', vol. ii, p. 56; the meeting took place in the Typographical Society's rooms in Middle Gardiner Street. Brugha was Chairman of the Resident Executive but, according to Mulcahy, after the formation of GHQ Staff, Brugha took no part in Volunteer/IRA or Staff affairs.

4 They met at the Keating Branch of the Gaelic League, 46 Rutland Square.

5 Mulcahy, 'Commentary', vol. ii, p. 41. The choice was between Collins and Mulcahy, but Collins was opposed by Dick McKee and others because they felt his temperament was unsuited to being chief of staff (UCD, Richard Mulcahy papers, P7/D/96).

6 Mulcahy, 'Commentary', vol. i, p. 121; Mulcahy, 'Notes' (UCD, Richard Mulcahy papers, P7/D/96).

7 The *Dictionary of Irish Biography* asserts that Duggan was a member of the IRB. I have found no evidence of this after 1916 and consider it to be unlikely. He was a battalion adjutant in the

Endnotes

453

Dublin Irish Volunteers Brigade in 1915–16, and may have been a member then.

8   1883–1922. Civil engineer. A graduate of the National University, he worked as a railway engineer in Ireland, then in Canada for the Canadian Pacific Railway and Canadian Northern Railway. Joseph Plunkett asked him to come back to Dublin in 1915 where he was employed by Dublin Corporation. He joined the AOH and took part in the Rising as an intelligence officer in the GPO.

9   In July 1918 the Executive decided to publish the journal as *The Official Organ of the Irish Volunteers* for circulation among Volunteers. The first issue was published on 31 August 1918.

10   Mulcahy, 'Notes on the Chief of Staff position' and 'Notes on M.W. O'Reilly' (UCD, Richard Mulcahy papers, P7/D/96); Béaslaí, *Michael Collins*, vol. i, pp. 198–200; Joseph O'Doherty, interview, 22 March 1972.

11   Richard Walsh, BMH WS 400. At this stage, Brugha did not seem to be anti-IRB, no doubt suppressing his animus, seeing an opportunity to gain IRB funds.

12   *Dáil Éireann Proceedings*, 6 January 1922.

13   1894–1969. Son of a small farmer in Soloheadbeg. Plasterer. Linesman on Great Southern Railway. Sworn into the IRB by Seán Treacy in 1912.

14   Breen, *My Fight for Irish Freedom*, p. 102.

15   Taylor, *English History*, p. 56.

16   Lyons, *Ireland Since the Famine*, pp. 390–2; Macardle, *The Irish Republic*, pp. 249–52.

17   Padraig Tobin, *The Nationalist*, 23 November 1957.

18   Peter (Eoin) McArdle, interview, 6 November 1972.

19   Joseph O'Doherty, interview, 25 March 1972.

20   Ibid.; Richard Walsh, BMH WS 400; Longford and O'Neill, *Eamon de Valera*, p. 87; Mulcahy, 'Commentary', vol. ii, p. 56.

21   Richard Walsh, BMH WS 400, claimed that Collins and de Valera were enthusiastic supporters of the assassination project: 'I know that Collins gave it his enthusiastic support. Mr de Valera also supported it and made most useful contributions to the discussion; his ideas were incorporated in the final draft authorisation which the Executive members signed.'

22   Paul McMahon, *British Spies and Irish Rebels: British Intelligence and Ireland, 1916–1945* (Woodbridge, 2008), p. 24; O'Hegarty, *History*, pp. 721–2; Macardle, *The Irish Republic*, p. 253; Calton Younger, *Ireland's Civil War* (London, 1968), pp. 65–6; Lyons, *Ireland Since the Famine*, pp. 393–4; London, Public Record Office, Cabinet Paper 2392.

23   Between May and November 1918, there were over 1,000 arrests.

24   Longford and O'Neill, *Eamon de Valera*, p. 75; Taylor, *Michael Collins*, p. 71; Richard Mulcahy, 'Commentary', vol. ii, pp. 5, 8–9.

25   Figgis, *Recollections of the Irish War*, p. 218.

26   Joseph O'Doherty, interview, 25 March 1972; Thomas O'Connor, BMH WS 1070: Liam Clarke probably did not know about O'Connor who was the principal courier between John Devoy and the IRB from 1915 and kept a copy of the IRB code: 'it was built up of the figures 1,2,3,4 and 5 and excluded the figures 6,7,8,9 and 0 (zero). The latter figures when used, as undoubtedly they would be, were to be ignored, as they would only be included for the purpose of misleading those into whose hands a message might fall. The code was as follows:

A.	B.	C.	D.	E.
11	12	13	14	15
F.	G.	H.	I.	J.
21	22	23	24	25
K.	L.	M	N.	O.
31	32	33	34	35

P.	Q.	R.	S.	T.
41	42	43	44	45
U.	V.	W.	X.	Y.
51	52	53	54	55

The letter Z was left out.'

27 Séumas Robinson, BMH WS 1721.

28 Bridie O'Reilly, BMH WS 454.

29 Pádraig Ó Fathaigh (ed. Timothy G. McMahon), *Pádraig Ó Fathaigh's War of Independence: Recollections of a Galway Gaelic Leaguer* (Cork, 2000), p. 52.

30 Leon Ó Broin, *Michael Collins* (Dublin, 1991), p. 49; Emmet Dalton, interview, 7 March 1973: 'Personally, I didn't get on too well with Mulcahy ... Mulcahy as Chief of Staff was ornamental. I'm not an egotist; I'm speaking the truth as I see it. But he was a man who never made an utterance until a decision was really made and then came in on the winning side.'

31 O'Connor, *With Michael Collins*, pp. 109–10.

32 Kee, *The Green Flag*, pp. 618–20; Mulcahy, 'Note on Thomas Ashe' (UCD, Richard Mulcahy papers, P7/D/26).

33 Lyons, *Ireland Since the Famine*, p. 395; Béaslaí, *Michael Collins*, vol. i, ch. x; Taylor, *Michael Collins*, pp. 71–2; Edgar Holt, *Protest in Arms: The Irish Troubles, 1916–23* (Dublin, 1960), pp. 163–5.

34 Mulcahy, 'Note on Thomas Ashe' (UCD, Richard Mulcahy papers, P7/D/26).

35 Ibid.

36 Ibid.; Mulcahy, 'Commentary', vol. ii, pp. 45, 174.

37 Collins came to be openly dismissive of Stack and scornful of his management abilities, and this was the source of Stack's antagonism.

38 Mulcahy, 'Commentary', vol. ii, p. 46.

39 Joseph O'Doherty, interview, 22 March 1972.

40 But there were differences. In April 1919 in Cork, Harry Varien, an IRB member, shot and severely wounded an RIC constable. The RIC, in reply, raided Volunteer/IRA homes and arrested an innocent man. Within the Volunteers/IRA Varien claimed IRB authority for his action, thus challenging the authority of local Volunteer/IRA leaders versus the authority of local IRB leaders. The upshot was that Seán O'Hegarty, the IRB County Centre, resigned as vice-O/C Cork No. 1 Brigade, and Florence O'Donoghue, the brigade adjutant and IRB County secretary, offered his resignation which was not accepted by Tomás Mac Curtain, Brigade O/C. 'It was not a complete solution,' said O'Donoghue, 'but it was a gesture to the authority of Tomas' (Borgonovo (ed.), *Florence and Josephine O'Donoghue's War of Independence*, pp. 58–60).

41 Mulcahy, 'Commentary', vol. ii, p. 174.

42 Joseph O'Doherty, interview, 25 March 1972.

43 Thomas Ryan to Richard Mulcahy, interview, 1964 (UCD, Richard Mulcahy papers, P7/D/107a).

44 Mick Fleming, interview in O'Malley, *Kerry Interviews*, p. 57; Padraig Tobin, *The Nationalist*, 16 November 1957: on 6 April 1918 the Brigade was formed. Seán Fitzpatrick, letter to the author, 21 April 1975: 'All the senior Divisional and Brigade officer personnel in South Tipp. Bde. area were in the I.R.B.; the ratio in re Battn. and Coy. officers would be about 50% and an unknown number of the rank and file were also members. In relation to the overall numerical Bde. strength (over 3,000 officers and men at the "Truce" date 11 July 1921) the total number of I.R.B. men was comparatively small – approx. 60.'

45 Liam Gaynor, BMH WS 183; Ó Murthuile, *History*, p. 64; Seán Fitzpatrick, letter to the author, 21 April 1975: 'I.R.B. "Circles" in South Tipp. after 1916 did not form in I.V. (I.R.A.)

Endnotes

455

Companies, nor did they form in "units" as such, in townlands; members of the organisation simply joined their local IV (I.R.A.) Coys. as individuals, and they were not obliged to advertise the fact of their I.R.B. membership.'

46 Seán Fitzpatrick, interview, 1 March 1974.

47 Richard Mulcahy, 'Notes on Thomas Ashe' (UCD, Richard Mulcahy papers, P7/D/26).

48 Those who took part were Séumas Robinson, Seán Treacy, Dan Breen, Seán Hogan, Tadhg Crowe, Michael Ryan, Michael McCormick, Jack O'Meara and Patrick O'Dwyer. With the exception of Robinson (who had been a member), all were members of the IRB. Seán Fitzpatrick, 'The Third Tipperary Brigade', *The Nationalist*, 27 October 1951; Seán Fitzpatrick, note of a discussion with the author, 1 March 1974; Breen, *My Fight for Irish Freedom*, p. 77.

49 Those who took part were Séumas Robinson, Seán Treacy, Dan Breen, Éamon O'Dwyer and his brother John Joe, Seán Lynch, Jim Scanlon and Ned Foley. Seán Hogan had been arrested but was freed by his comrades in this incident. Padraig Tobin, *The Nationalist*, 7 December 1957; Breen, *My Fight for Irish Freedom*, p. 85.

50 Ibid., p. 72.

51 Peter (Eoin) McArdle, interview, 6 November 1972.

52 Breen, *My Fight for Irish Freedom*, pp. 115–17; Ryan, *Seán Treacy and the Third Tipperary Brigade*, pp. 108–92.

53 Twohig, *Blood on the Flag*, p. 81.

54 Eoin McArdle, interview, 6 November 1972.

55 Éamon O'Dwyer, BMH WS 1474: 'Austin Stack, Joe McDonagh, E. de Blaghd [Blythe], myself and others took part in the discussions and generally it was our opinion that the need for the I.R.B. had practically ceased to exist.'

56 Billy Mullins, interview in O'Malley, *Kerry Interviews*, p. 62. Cathal Brugha had sworn Stack in as an IRB member, so it is likely that Stack's resignation from the IRB was also in support of Brugha's stand.

19. 1918 ELECTION

1 Seán MacBride, interview, 21 February 1973.

2 Arthur Mitchell and Pádraig Ó Snodaigh (eds), 'General Election: Manifesto to the Irish People', in *Irish Political Documents, 1916–1949* (Dublin, 1985), p. 48.

3 Collins, *The Path to Freedom*, p. 119: Collins was no doubt seeking to justify his endorsement of the 1921 Treaty. But: 'General Election: Manifesto to the Irish People' (Sinn Féin, 1918): 'Sinn Féin gives Ireland the opportunity of vindicating her honour and pursuing with renewed confidence the path of national salvation by rallying to the flag of the Irish Republic.'

4 Donal Ó Drisceoil, 'The victory of Sinn Féin: The 1920 local elections', www.ucc.ie/en/theirishrevolution/collections/mapping-the-irish-revolution/the-victory-of-sinn-fein-the-1920-local-elections/.

5 Ó Broin, *Michael Collins*, p. 36; P.S. O'Hegarty, *Victory of Sinn Féin: How It Won It and How It Used It* (Dublin, 1924), p. 75; Richard Walsh, BMH WS 400; Mulcahy, 'Notes on the use and origin of the title Irish Republican Army' (UCD, Richard Mulcahy papers, P7/D/99); Mulcahy, 'Position of the Chief of Staff' (UCD, Richard Mulcahy papers, P7/D/96). Mulcahy was selected in this way.

6 Mulcahy, *Richard Mulcahy*, pp. 112–13.

7 Mulcahy, 'Notes on the use and origin of the title Irish Republican Army' (UCD, Richard Mulcahy papers, P7/D/99). Mulcahy records that the feeling at the time was that the struggle for independence was in the hands of the Sinn Féin and Volunteer leaderships.

Endnotes

8 John Bruton, 'The 1918 election in Ireland', Wynn's Hotel, Dublin, 15 December 2018: 'there are credible allegations that intimidation played a part in ensuring that Sinn Féin would not face a contest in these seats. IPP meetings were broken up in Cahir, Rathmines, Bohar in Louth, Jonesboro Co. Armagh, Moate Co. Westmeath, Clones, Gorey, and Castleblaney. Candidates who had agreed to stand for the Parliamentary Party backed out in face of this activity. The [Parish Priest] of Kiltimagh, Dr O'Hara, told John Dillon of "young roughs going around the roads at night saying they will burn down any house that will vote for Dillon and threatening to destroy cattle". On polling day, Republican "peace patrols" stood outside polling stations, and it is claimed they discouraged thousands of Irish Party supporters from going to vote … I myself knew a man, a 1916 veteran, who was reputed to have voted 40 times for Sinn Féin, in the names of different people.'

9 John J. O'Reilly, interview, 13 December 1972: 'I only voted once because they knew me too well … In Ballygarrett I had all the dead men voting before 9 o'clock, before the [IPP] fellow … [who] didn't come until 10 o'clock. And we crossed all the names that voted off the Register, and after looking at the names [he said], "By Jaysus! This man is dead!" "He might be dead, but he voted here this morning anyhow!"'

10 Joseph O'Rourke, interview with Fr F.X. Martin, 2 June 1961.

11 Collins, *The Path to Freedom*, p. 119: Collins was no doubt seeking to justify his endorsement of the 1921 Treaty.

12 *Dáil Éireann Proceedings*, 16 August 1921.

13 *Tipperary Star*, 19 June 1965.

14 Richard Mulcahy, discussion with Risteárd Mulcahy and Mrs Richard Mulcahy, 1965 (UCD, Richard Mulcahy papers, P7/D/99).

15 Michael Hayes, interview, 22 March 1972.

16 R.V. Comerford, 'Stephens, Devoy and Clarke' in Biagini and Mulhall (eds), *The Shaping of Modern Ireland*, p. 23.

17 Maurice Moynihan (ed.), *Speeches and Statements by Éamon de Valera, 1917–1973* (Dublin, 1980), p. 599.

18 Breen, *My Fight for Irish Freedom*, p. 103.

19 Timothy Bowman, William Butler and Michael Wheatley, *The Disparity of Sacrifice: Irish Recruitment to the British Armed Forces, 1914–1918* (Liverpool, 2020), p. 11; Michael Wheatley in www.westernfrontassociation.com/the-latest-wwi-podcast/ep-178-irish-recruitment-in-world-war-one-dr-tim-bowman-dr-michael-wheatley-dr-william-butler/; Gallagher, *Ireland and the Great War*, pp. 172–3: Irish responses to the war and the 1916 Rising showed rural recruitment lagging behind Britain, 'a trend that was not true of urban Ireland, at least until the introduction of conscription in Britain in 1916 – [but Ireland's] commitment to agricultural production for the war effort was high, particularly in 1917 and 1918 … Rural society took the defence of Ireland seriously: the low commitment rates do not reflect the attitudes of people whose primary relationship to the war effort was agricultural … there is no obvious trend to indicate a causal link between support for the war effort and political change within nationalism … A considerable degree of stability and continuity thus underlined Ireland's war effort to an extent that has gone unacknowledged.'

20 David Fitzpatrick, 'Ireland in the Great War', pp. 498, 500: 'About 58,000 Irish servicemen were mobilised at the outset, including 21,000 regular soldiers, 18,000 reservists (former regulars), 12,000 special reservists (incorporating former militiamen), 5,000 naval ratings, and perhaps 2,000 officers … Catholics accounted for 53 per cent of naval recruits, 68 per cent of army reservists, and 57 per cent of military recruits, the Catholic component in army recruiting being much higher in 1915 (61 per cent) and 1916 (63 per cent) than 1914 (46 per cent).'

Endnotes

21 David Fitzpatrick, 'Ireland in the Great War', pp. 501–2: 'Though not closely correlated with Ireland's economic geography, the county rankings indicate heavier enlistment in Ulster and the midlands, with lighter enlistment in most coastal counties, especially those marked by poverty and "congestion" along the Atlantic seaboard. Some of the richest counties had high enlistment rates, contradicting the superficially plausible assumption that military enlistment appealed most strongly to the poor and unemployed ... The provincial returns for 1914–1917 show that Catholics were consistently more likely than Protestants to enlist in both Leinster and Munster. In Ulster as a whole, the Protestant rate was higher, yet Ulster Catholics were markedly more likely to enlist than Catholics elsewhere. County returns by religion, available only for 1915, indicate that Catholics were actually more inclined than Protestants to join up in the Belfast region, belying the innuendo that Belfast Catholics "shirked" while their Orange and Unionist adversaries answered the empire's call ... No wonder that Redmond set such store in these enlistment returns, tirelessly requesting and manipulating the figures to refute Unionist slurs against nationalist Ireland.'

22 Collins, *The Path to Freedom*, p. 119.

23 *Sinn Féin Minute Book, 1919* (NLI, Ms 15,400); Brian Farrell, 'A note on the Dáil Constitution, 1919', *Irish Jurist*, vol. iv, new series, part 1 (Summer 1969), pp. 132–67.

24 Mulcahy, 'Correspondence concerning proposed articles' (UCD, Richard Mulcahy papers, P7/D/60).

25 Patrick McCartan, *With de Valera in America* (New York, 1932), pp. 3, 9–12, 64, 73; Padraig Tobin, *The Nationalist*, 30 November 1957.

26 Mulcahy, 'Correspondence concerning proposed articles' (UCD, Richard Mulcahy papers, P7/D/60). This was probably the meeting arranged by the new MPs and the Sinn Féin Executive on 1 January.

27 NLI, George Gavan Duffy papers, Ms 15400. The members of the committee were: George Gavan Duffy, James O'Mara, Seán T. O'Kelly, Éamonn J. Duggan, Piaras Béaslaí and Eoin MacNeill.

28 Mulcahy, 'Commentary', vol. ii, p. 160.

29 Mulcahy, 'Comments on Frank Gallagher, *The Anglo-Irish Treaty*' (UCD, Richard Mulcahy papers, P7/D/49). However, at the Dáil meeting of 20 August 1919 Thomas Kelly objected to the oath of allegiance to the Dáil as the government of the Republic on the grounds that a man who would not keep his word would not keep his oath, and that the IRA should be kept separate so as not to involve the Dáil in the IRA's guerrilla warfare. The oath was carried 30:5.

30 Figgis, *Recollections of the Irish War*, pp. 234–7.

31 *Dáil Éireann Proceedings*, 21 January 1919, p. 26.

32 Seán MacEoin, BMH WS 1716, part 2. The Supreme Council did not act 'at once', but in September 1919 ceded to the Dáil government its claims to be the government of the Republic. Richard Mulcahy and others thought that MacEoin always overstated the importance of the IRB (Richard Mulcahy, 'Talk between de Valera and McKeon [*sic*] on the occasion of the Requiem Mass for Pat McCrea', 10 February 1964 (UCD, Richard Mulcahy papers, P7/D/68)).

33 Figgis, *Recollections of the Irish War*, pp. 245–7; O'Connor, *The Big Fellow*, pp. 67–8, echoes Figgis' account of election rigging at a Sinn Féin convention that he dates as 8 May 1919.

34 Dwyer, *Michael Collins*, p. 60. Collins was angry at Sheehy Skeffington's appointment, which obviously reduced IRB influence, and complained about the Sinn Féin Executive as 'malcontents' and 'bargaining' people.

35 *Dáil Éireann Proceedings*, 23 August 1921.

36 Mulcahy, 'Commentary', vol. ii, p. 121.

37 Pollard, *The Secret Societies of Ireland*, p. 247.

458   Endnotes

38   Ferriter, *A Nation and Not a Rabble*, p. 186.
39   Colm Ó Gaora (trans. Mícheál Ó hAodha; eds Ruán O'Donnell, Mícheál Ó hAodha), *On The Run: The Story of an Irish Freedom Fighter* (Cork, 2011), p. 296.

20. KILLING

1   Mulcahy, 'Commentary', vol. ii, p. 174.
2   *Irish Independent*, 23, 26, 28, February 1918, 2, 4, 9, 15, 19 March 1918.
3   Breen, *My Fight for Irish Freedom*, pp. 273–4.
4   Seán Fitzpatrick, interview, 1 March 1974.
5   Breen, *My Fight for Irish Freedom*, p. 98.
6   Mulcahy, 'Notes on the Chief of Staff position' (UCD, Richard Mulcahy papers, P7/D/96). Brugha was also seeking to establish the authority of the Executive. Hales found himself in difficulty with GHQ on another occasion when the Rathcaren Company determined to attack the local RIC. Hales in his IRB capacity gave the local Circle permission to go ahead, making it another IRB affair (Liam Deasy, note of discussion with author, 20 November 1973).
7   Hansard, 5 November 1918. Shortt's speech was prescient. He raised the questions of coercing Ulster into a united Ireland; of RIC men being shot without witnesses willing to come forward, and of the demand for an Irish republic.
8   Breen, *My Fight for Irish Freedom*, pp. 97–8.
9   Ó Broin, *Revolutionary Underground*, pp. 196–7.
10   Mulcahy, 'Commentary', vol. i, p. 102.
11   James O'Donovan, interview, 20 September 1975.
12   Mulcahy, 'Commentary', vol. i, pp. 69, 89; Mulcahy, 'Notes on the Chief of Staff position' (UCD, Richard Mulcahy papers, P7/D/96): Brugha agreed to Joe McKelvey's request for a Volunteer/IRA action in Belfast and Mulcahy agreed to MacSwiney's appeal for one in Cork – both without reference to Brugha.
13   Richard Mulcahy to the Most Rev. Dr Fogarty, letter, 12 January 1925 (UCD, Richard Mulcahy papers, P7/D/98).
14   Mulcahy, 'Commentary', vol. ii, p. 173. Dick O'Neil, an IRB messenger, interrupted a Supreme Council meeting to say that the IRB was needed to smuggle de Valera to the United States.
15   Mulcahy, 'Note on the Chief of Staff position' (UCD, Richard Mulcahy papers, P7/D/96). O'Connor's involvement enhanced his status in GHQ and the Volunteers (Mulcahy, 'Commentary', vol. i, p.117).
16   Bartholomew ('Batt') Murphy, interview, 5 November 1972. Vinnie Byrne was the 'one': a Dubliner.
17   The first Squad assassination, and the first of a DMP officer, was of Detective Sergeant Patrick Smith on 30 July 1919. The other DMP officers who were killed were Detective Daniel Hoey on 12 September; Detective Michael Downing on 19 October; Detective Sergeant John Barton on 29 November; RIC District Inspector William Redmond on 21 January 1920; Detective Constable Harry Kells on 14 April 1920; Detective Laurence Dalton on 20 April 1920.
18   Michael ('Mick') McDonnell, BMH WS 228: 'Although the Active Service Unit known to us as the "Squad" was formed on May Day 1919, it did not become a fulltime unit until early 1920.' McDonnell was confusing the Unit with the Squad: they were separate.
19   David Leeson, 'Death in the afternoon: The Croke Park massacre, 21 November 1920', *Canadian Journal of History*, vol. 38, iss. 1 (Spring 2003), pp. 43–68. Two Courts of Inquiry were held *in camera* immediately afterwards. They determined that shooting started from the spectators' stalls, and that the deaths were caused by rifle or revolver fire by the RIC. They also

Endnotes

459

found that the RIC firing was unauthorised, and – most interestingly – that no firing came from the uniformed Auxiliaries or the military, except those soldiers in an armoured car at an exit who fired a burst of 50 bullets into the air to stop people from running out of the ground. Much of the evidence given to the courts differs from that of other eyewitnesses. But the contradictions and detail in the court statements indicate what probably happened, namely that the RIC, and not the Tans or Auxiliaries, fired into the crowd (Public Record Office, WO 35/88).

20   David Neligan, interview, 20 February 1973.

21   James Gleeson, *Bloody Sunday* (London, 1962), pp. 198–209; Charles Dalton, *With the Dublin Brigade* (London, 1929), pp. 101–7; Mulcahy, 'Commentary', vol. ii, pp. 48–50; Jane Leonard, '"English Dogs" or "Poor Devils"? The dead of Bloody Sunday morning' in Fitzpatrick (ed.), *Terror in Ireland 1916–1923*, pp. 127–71; J.B.E. Hittle, *Michael Collins and the Anglo-Irish War: Britain's Counterinsurgency Failure* (Washington DC, 2012), pp. 160–76: Hittle considers that fifteen of the twenty-five men targeted were intelligence officers, and suspects that others targeted were also intelligence operatives.

22   Dan Bryan, interview, 30 May 1975.

23   Éamon O'Dwyer, BMH WS 1474. There is an element of protesting too much in O'Dwyer's account of his view of the IRB, probably because it was blamed for the 1921 Treaty passing in the Dáil. O'Dwyer remained neutral during the Civil War and greatly admired Michael Collins.

24   Ó Murthuile, *History*, p. 64; Forester, *Michael Collins*, p. 156.

25   James McCullough, BMH WS 529.

26   Eoin Neeson, 'University College Cork Historical Society', 12 January 1967 (UCD, Richard Mulcahy papers, P7/D/65); Richard Mulcahy, discussion with Risteárd Mulcahy, 9 August 1963 (UCD Richard Mulcahy papers, P7/D/100).

27   Richard Walsh, BMH WS 400; Davis, *Arthur Griffith and Non-Violent Sinn Féin*, pp. 1–6.

28   Breen, *My Fight for Irish Freedom*, pp. 34–40.

29   *The Irish Times*, 24, 27, 28 January 1919; *Tipperary Star*, 25 January 1919; Padraig Tobin in *The Nationalist*, 30 November 1957.

30   *Dáil Éireann Proceedings*, 1919–21, p. 243. Roger Sweetman, TD, in particular, opposed IRA violence. Mulcahy, 'Commentary', vol. i, p. 55; vol. ii, p. 35. Séumas Robinson, BMH WS 1721. Collins approved of the ambush; Diarmuid O'Hegarty and Gearóid O'Sullivan did not.

31   Séumas Robinson, BMH WS 1721.

32   Mulcahy, 'Commentary', vol. i, p. 85.

33   Richard Walsh, BMH WS 400.

34   UCD, Richard Mulcahy papers, P7/D/54.

35   Padraig Tobin, *The Nationalist*, 23 November 1957.

36   Department of Defence, *Chronology, 1913–21*, vol. iii, part 1 (Dublin, 1952).

37   Ryan, *Seán Treacy and the Third Tipperary Brigade I.R.A.*, pp. 55–6.

38   Seán MacEoin, interview, 9 November 1972, stated that the escape was intended primarily to release McGarry. McInerney, 'Gerry Boland's story': de Valera was taken to Manchester by Harry Boland with the help of Neil Kerr, North of England representative on the Supreme Council and Manchester Centre. Richard Mulcahy, 'Commentary', vol. i, pp. 71, 117. Béaslaí, *Michael Collins*, vol. i, pp. 281, 363: the prestige Collins accrued for organising this escape helped to advance him in the estimation of the IRA and IRB. Liam McMahon, BMH WS 274.

39   Seán MacEoin, interview, 9 November 1972: MacEoin had a most formal appreciation of the IRB and regarded it as the government of the Republic established in 1916 with the Dáil government only having the authority and the governmental positions that the IRB ceded to it. 'The British suspected. They knew all about it prior to 1916, but by Heavens they never knew anything after that! They didn't know who was who.' In fact, the British knew a great deal about

460 Endnotes

the IRB as Edward Shortt had demonstrated in the House of Commons in November 1918 (cf. Pollard, *The Secret Societies of Ireland*, and Hart (ed.), *The Final Reports*).

21. RELATIONSHIPS

1   Ronan Fanning, *A Will to Power* (London, 2015), p. 57.

2   Kee, *The Green Flag*, ch. 4; Garvin, *1922: The Birth of Irish Democracy*, p. 73: most people, appalled at the violence, were carefully neutral, 'keeping their heads down and praying for peace'.

3   David Hogan, 'Books from my shelves', *Sunday Press*, 17 January 1960.

4   GHQ General Order No. 12, 1 November 1920; Mulcahy, 'Commentary', vol. i, pp. 112, 137.

5   Collins' reputation for being camera shy is challenged by this film. Notably, Collins stood up and shook hands only once for a subscriber, J.J. Walsh, TD Cork City. Walsh and Collins had shared a room in the GPO where Collins was guarding a roof entrance/exit and Walsh was operating the telephone switchboard. Collins' fealty to Cork was constant.

6   Richard Walsh, BMH WS 400.

7   Peadar MacMahon, interview with Richard Mulcahy (UCD, Richard Mulcahy papers P7/B/181).

8   Maryann Gialanella Valiulis, *Portrait of a Revolutionary: General Richard Mulcahy and the Founding of the Irish Free State* (Dublin, 1992), p. 48.

9   Séumas Robinson, *Evening Telegraph and Press*, 17 October 1932. Mulcahy was simply relaying the official position so that there would be no surprise if the Dáil condemned the attack which would inevitably be seen as a Volunteer/IRA affair: it was unrealistic to expect otherwise.

10   Ó Murthuile, *History*, p. 50; Seán Nunan, interview, 18 March 1974: Nunan was sworn into the IRB by Collins.

11   *Dáil Éireann Proceedings*, 1919–21, pp. 30–8. Alec McCabe, the sole TD present who had been on the 1916 Supreme Council, proposed Collins, and Harry Boland seconded.

12   Quoted in Padraig Yeates, 'Michael Collins' "Secret Service Unit" in the trade union movement', *History Ireland*, vol. 22, no. 3 (May–June 2014), p. 42.

13   Conlon's union was officially the 'Irish Engineering, Shipbuilding and Foundry Workers Trade Union' (Yeates, 'Michael Collins' "Secret Service Unit" in the trade union movement', pp. 42–3).

14   Longford and O'Neill, *Eamon de Valera*, p. 89; Mulcahy, 'Commentary', vol. i, p. 161. Brugha met de Valera in Liverpool immediately after his escape and added his voice to Collins', persuading him not to travel directly to the United States, but to come to Dublin and head the government.

15   De Valera was in the United States from 22 June 1919. He returned to Ireland on 24 December 1920.

16   *Dáil Éireann Proceedings*, 1919–21, p. 158; Mulcahy, 'Commentary', vol. i, pp. 43, 89; Padraig Tobin in *The Nationalist*, 14 December 1957.

17   Gary Evans, *The Raising of the First Internal Dáil Éireann Loan and the British Responses to it, 1919–21*, M. Litt. Thesis, National University of Ireland Maynooth (2012), p. 69. The loan was closed on 31 July 1920. It was oversubscribed by £121,849 with a total of £371,849.

18   Dolan and Murphy, *Days in the Life*, p. 93. Munster contributed about 46 per cent of the total Loan.

19   Richard Walsh, BMH WS 400. Walsh also stated that some IRB members on the Executive supported the Dáil's claim. Non-IRB members of the Executive were aware of the IRB presence and sense of separate identity (Joseph O'Doherty, interview, 22 March 1972).

20   Richard Walsh, BMH WS 400.

Endnotes   461

21 Mulcahy, 'Commentary', vol. ii, pp. 22, 93, thought that Brugha probably insisted on the oath in an attempt to weaken the IRB, since members were not allowed to belong to other oath-bound organisations.

22 Joseph O'Doherty, interview, 22 March 1972.

23 These were de Valera, Joseph O'Doherty, Cathal Brugha (all three being former IRB members), Seán MacEntee and possibly C. Deviney (about whom I have found no information).

24 Seán Fitzpatrick, letter to the author, 21 April 1975; notes of a discussion with Seán Fitzpatrick, 1 March 1974, dated this to September 1920.

25 Andrew Keaveney, BMH WS 1178.

26 UCD, Richard Mulcahy papers, P7/D/49: Thomas Kelly TD, for example, opposed the oath in the Dáil on the grounds that it would make no practical difference and that TDs should be excused fighting responsibilities.

27 *Dáil Éireann Proceedings*, 11 March 1921.

28 Constitution of the Irish Volunteers, 1920 (UCD, Richard Mulcahy papers, P7/D/33); Margery Forester, *Michael Collins*, p. 127.

29 Constitution of the Irish Volunteers, 1920 (UCD, Richard Mulcahy papers, P7/D/33).

30 Ibid. The 'Executive Council' was the Volunteer/IRA Executive.

31 Ibid.; Joseph O'Doherty, interview, 22 March 1972.

32 *Dáil Éireann Proceedings*, 1919–21, pp. 264, 278–9. At the end of March 1921, de Valera had assumed public responsibility for the IRA on behalf of the Dáil, but it was not until August that the Dáil officially accepted this.

33 Joseph O'Doherty, interview, 14 August 1973.

34 Appendix VI, 'IRB Constitution amendments 1919–21', clause 20(a) (NLI, Martin Conlon papers, P97/14; NLI, Florence O'Donoghue papers, 31,233; NLI, 27,628).

35 Seán Fitzpatrick, letter to the author, n.d.: The 'relationship between Vols. and Dáil E. showed that relationship between Vols. and Govt. was not yet officially established or satisfactorily defined. The Vols., by their Constitution, bound to obey their own Exec., and no other body.'

36 Andrew Keaveney, BMH WS 1178.

37 Florence O'Donoghue to Fr F.X. Martin, 28 March 1964 (NLI, Florence O'Donoghue papers, 31,300); Ernest Blythe, interview, 13 December 1971: 'I regarded it as a nonsense because I knew we weren't going to have a republic. I mean, that was my firm belief in view of the Northern situation, which a lot of people didn't consider at all ... I was a Northern Protestant ... and I'm sure that it was my views that excluded me from being on the inner Cabinet which de Valera formed when he started the negotiations [in 1921].'

38 Richard Walsh, BMH WS 400. He went on to say, 'I have no definite proof that individual I.R.B. men were asked to use their influence at Brigade conventions to influence them against giving allegiance to Dáil Éireann, but ... I have a hunch that some IRB were prominent in opposing the oath of allegiance, probably under advice ... I attended the convention of the Mayo Brigade at Balla at which 300 to 400 men attended. At this time Co. Mayo was all in one Brigade. The question of taking the oath was opposed by a small number of officers led by Joe McBride who was then county centre of the I.R.B. The overwhelming majority of the delegates were in favour of taking the oath, so it was not pushed to a vote as in all only about 6 officers were against it.'

39 Mulcahy, 'Talk given to the members of the 1916–21 Club', 20 February 1964 (UCD, Richard Mulcahy papers, P7/D/66): 'I ask anybody who was an army officer from March 1918 to say there was any occasion upon which he got instruction from an I.R.B. official.'

40 Alec McCabe in Mulcahy, 'Talk given to the members of the 1916–21 Club', 20 February 1964 (UCD, Richard Mulcahy papers, P7/D/66).

462　　　　　　　　　　　　　Endnotes

41　UCD, Richard Mulcahy papers, P7/D/96. Mulcahy later thought that the oath of loyalty to the Dáil 'arose principally from Cathal that there being a group of people in the country who were supposed to have taken an oath to the Irish republic: that is the members of the I.R.B., Cathal wanted that the Dáil and the Volunteers would at least be as good as they … he might have had at this time certain objection to Collins, but I don't think that is so. His objection in the matter would arise out of his shock and disappointment with some people belonging to the I.R.B. who did not turn out in the Rising.'

42　Éamon de Valera, 'Note, 7 February 1964' (UCD, Éamon de Valera papers, P150/3447); see Appendix VI, 'IRB Constitution Amendments 1919–21'.

43　'IRB Constitution as revised to date, 1920' (NLI, Florence O'Donoghue papers, Ms 31,233; NLI, Ms 27,628). It was not a new constitution; it was the 1917 Constitution with the September 1919 and August 1921 amendments incorporated. These were the only changes to the 1917 Constitution. The first page was headed, 'Addenda to Constitution, September 1919'. That it was dated 1920 was, perhaps, to suggest that the IRB had accepted the Dáil presidency earlier than was, in fact, the case so as to demonstrate that it was in complete harmony with the Dáil.

44　Hart, *Mick*, p. 194.

45　Michael Collins, letter to John Devoy, February 1922, quoted in Golway, *Irish Rebel*, p. 302.

46　Macardle, *The Irish Republic*, p. 421.

47　Mulcahy, 'Commentary', vol. ii, p. 60; Béaslaí, *Michael Collins*, vol. ii, p. 81. Collins was acting president from 26 November 1920 to 24 December 1920, the day de Valera returned from the United States. There are no records of Dáil meetings in this period. Arthur Griffith was not released from prison until 30 June 1921 (Department of Defence, *Chronology, 1913–21*, vol. iii, part 3, p. 487).

48　Hart, *Mick*, p. 25.

49　1864–1935. Born in Ennis, Co. Clare, and sent as a newly ordained priest to Australia. He was the uncle of Conor Clune, an IPP supporter arrested as a suspect in the Bloody Sunday killings of British officers on 21 November 1920, who was murdered in Dublin Castle that evening by enraged Auxiliaries.

50　*Dáil Éireann Proceedings*, 15 January 1921.

51　*Irish Bulletin*, 4 April 1921.

52　*Dáil Éireann Proceedings*, 16 August 1921.

53　Fitzpatrick, *Harry Boland's Irish Revolution*, p. 120.

54　Kitty O'Doherty, BMH WS 355: 'Harry Boland who was in America at that time having been sent over largely through the influence of Mick Collins who wanted to have a direct link with Clan na Gael … As he was on the Supreme Council of the I.R.B. he would have the entrée to the meetings of the councils of Clan na Gael and de Valera would not, because, after the Rising and when released from prison, he had refused – as did Cathal Brugha – to have anything more to do with the Brotherhood.'

55　Ó Murthuile, *History*, pp. 73–7.

56　Ibid., p. 92; Macardle, *The Irish Republic*, p. 312; Cronin, *The McGarrity Papers*, pp. 98–9.

57　Ó Murthuile, *History*, p. 93.

58　Ibid., p. 92; Lawrence de Lacey, interview, 17 July 1972; Cronin, *The McGarrity Papers*, pp. 98–9. Thomas Ryan, an investor and a senior member of Clan na Gael, contacted Michael Collins who agreed to finance the development of the Thompson guns with money channelled through Boland to Ryan. De Valera apparently knew nothing of this. Possibly only two of the guns reached Ireland (Liam Farrell, 'The Tommy Gun – The Irish connection', *History Ireland*, vol. 8, iss. 4 (Winter 2000)).

Endnotes
463

59   Fitzpatrick, *Harry Boland's Irish Revolution*, p. 154.

60   Ó Murthuile, *History*, p. 93.

61   Ibid., p. 94.

62   Moynihan (ed.), *Speeches and Statements by Éamon de Valera, 1917–1973*, p. 33.

63   Máire Comerford, interview in MacEoin, *Survivors*, p. 45, speaking about the arguments for and against the 1921 Treaty: 'De Valera had led them on with his Cuban speech to the brink of compromise … the Treaty side knew that de Valera wanted only a favourable opportunity in order to jettison the Republic.'

64   McCartan, *With de Valera in America*, pp. 134–200.

65   Coogan, *De Valera*, p. 190.

66   Ó Murthuile, *History*, p. 95; Cronin, *The McGarrity Papers*, pp. 83–4. Prior to this they used the pseudonyms 'William Field' (Collins) and 'William Woods' (Boland) in the normal post. Before Boland returned to the United States he and Collins arranged that future communications should be cabled by Boland to Éamonn Duggan at his office in Dame Street. Patrick McCartan tried to stop Boland publishing the severance on the grounds that it was not helpful to reveal a schism. Luke Dillon countered by explaining that Boland was denied access to the Clan's membership list and so his only way of informing them was through a public announcement (Cronin, *The McGarrity Papers*, p. 95; McCartan, *With de Valera in America*, p. 186).

67   Ó Murthuile, *History*, p. 96; Cronin, *The McGarrity Papers*, pp. 84–5; Macardle, *The Irish Republic*, p. 425, says that Boland was ordered by the IRB to sever the connection with the Clan. This is unlikely: the Clan's financial support, if nothing else, was a vital connection that the IRB would not wish to jeopardise. Ó Murthuile's account – that Boland acted alone – is far more likely to have been the case.

68   McGarrity fired John Devoy, the secretary of the Clan, and four other members of the Clan Executive; Devoy, in turn, expelled McGarrity, Dillon and the Clan treasurer, Hugh Montague, who had sided against Devoy.

69   Ó Murthuile, *History*, p. 92; Cronin, *The McGarrity Papers*, pp. 73–92; McCartan, *With de Valera in America*, pp. 133–241; Forester, *Michael Collins*, pp. 106–7. Roger Sweetman, TD Wexford North, resigned from the Dáil in January 1921 in protest at the support being given to what he considered the IRA's campaign of murder (*Dáil Éireann Proceedings*, 1919–21, pp. 243–4, and *Dáil Éireann Proceedings*, 25 January 1921).

70   Ó Murthuile, *History*, p. 92: writing to Boland on 13 September Collins said: 'You will readily see that there are other reasons, for instance communications, Volunteers, etc., why I should remain here. Then there is my own predilection against going.' By 'communications' Collins probably meant his IRB network of informants and arms smugglers.

22. BRUGHA

1   Coogan, *Michael Collins*, p. 387; Taylor, *Michael Collins*, p. 236, is the source for this letter to a mysterious friend, 'O'Kane', who has not been identified.

2   Figgis, *Recollections of the Irish War*, pp. 217, 220.

3   Emmet Dalton, interview, 7 March 1973. An element of the Civil War divide is present here, but Dalton's fundamental point – that Brugha was ignored – seems to be correct.

4   Ernest Blythe, interview, 13 December 1971.

5   Richard Walsh, BMH WS 400.

6   Francis Daly, BMH WS 278: 'The Manager of the Dolphin's Barn Brick Works was John Cassidy, who was in the IRB. The Kilcoole stuff came to Cassidy's place – the major portion of it – after it was collected.'

464 Endnotes

7 Thomas Treacy, BMH WS 590.

8 James Coughlan, BMH WS 304.

9 Joseph Doolan, BMH WS 199.

10 Michael Brennan, interview, 18 December 1972.

11 P.J. Hennessy and Jim Maher from notes left by Thomas Treacy, Jim DeLoughry, Jim Byrne V.E.C. and Peter DeLoughry, 'The Irish Volunteers in Kilkenny in 1916', https://kec1916project. files.wordpress.com/2015/01/the-irish-volunteers-in-kilkenny-in-1916.pdf.

12 Seán Mathews, BMH WS 1022.

13 Éamonn Dore, BMH WS 392. Brugha's reference to 'personalities' probably meant Collins.

14 Figgis, *Recollections of the Irish War*, pp. 239–40; Richard Walsh, BMH WS 400, dated the Brugha–Collins 'feud' seven months later to the time of the 1918 German Plot: 'Cathal Brugha asked Michael Collins did he know of any intercourse the Volunteers or any other political group had with German representatives here, or was he (Collins) aware of any German agent working in the country. This meeting was about the first time the first whispers of what was known as the German Plot got about. Michael Collins was emphatic in his denial of any knowledge of these matters. He was supported in his denial by Diarmuid O'Hegarty and both stated that the prominence given to the German Plot in the British Press was laughable. Cathal Brugha did not appear to be satisfied with the denials … His whole attitude towards Collins's and O'Hegarty's denials was sceptical, and his general attitude towards Collins after this was one of suspicion. This incident … was, in my opinion, the real start of the feud that subsequently existed between Michael Collins and Cathal Brugha.'

15 Eugene Loughran, BMH WS 526.

16 Margery Forester, *Michael Collins*, p. 212; Charles Townshend, *The Republic*, pp. 326–30.

17 Richard Mulcahy, 'Commentary', vol. ii, p. 174.

18 Michael Hayes, interview, 22 March 1972.

19 Joseph O'Rourke, interview with Fr F.X. Martin, 2 June 1961: 'I had been showing Joe Leonard some special munitions (a self-loading Luger) with a drum magazine which I had bought abroad, and I was trying to convince him of its merits. Shortly afterwards I was summoned to North Frederick Street and ordered to bring the weapon with me. I went, but without the weapon. Collins himself was there and ordered me to produce it. I told him it was my own personal property and that if it was required I could operate it. His reply was, "Produce the gun or else!"'

20 Tadhg Kennedy, interview in Ernie O'Malley, *Kerry Interviews*, p. 91; Richard Mulcahy, 'Notes' (UCD, Richard Mulcahy papers, P7/D/96): from his appointment in June 1920 as Minister for Home Affairs, Stack was unsuccessful. He was not a good manager. He wanted to use Volunteer/ IRA networks for his Ministry's purposes, and in 1920 and 1921 had several arguments with Gearóid O'Sullivan, Adjutant General, who did not want to overwork local units. On two occasions GHQ stretched the Volunteers'/IRA's limited resources to organise a police force for Stack, and each time it melted in his hands. The last occasion in May 1921 was marked by GHQ pressing Stack to organise civilian trials instead of courts martial, and for judicial functions to be conducted quite separately from the Volunteers/IRA by his ministry.

21 Ernest Blythe, interview, 13 December 1971.

22 Tadhg Kennedy, interview in O'Malley, *Kerry Interviews*, p. 93: 'There was no personal element in Stack's antagonism.' Ernest Blythe, interview, 13 December 1971: 'He never achieved anything, Stack you know. Like when the Kerry arms thing was to be on and Casement was arrested, he got himself arrested too by walking into the barracks to speak to Casement. Now there are people who would say that he did that for safety, to be safely under lock and key. I don't accept that. I just take it as part of his natural stupidity.'

Endnotes

23 .Sinn Féin's organisation had become threadbare under the pressure of guerrilla warfare and fears of retaliation: men identified with the party were frequently harassed and worse by the military and the Black and Tans and Auxiliaries.

24 Mulcahy, 'Commentary', vol. ii, p. 73.

25 Collins' interest in controlling funds in every organisation he joined gave rise to rumours, originating from his time in London, that he embezzled. There is no evidence that he did, but Brugha was referring to these rumours in his attacks. Hart, *Mick*, pp. 144, 263. Seán McGrath to Art O'Brien, letter, 20 September 1922 (NLI, Art Ó Briain papers, Ms 8,442/1).

26 Richard Mulcahy, 'Commentary', vol. ii, pp. 51, 57, 73, 82, 144, 164.

27 Mulcahy, 'Note on Cathal Brugha' (UCD, Richard Mulcahy papers, P7/D/96); Mulcahy, 'Commentary', vol. i, pp. 50–1.

28 Joseph O'Doherty, interview, 19 December 1972. The last meeting of the pre-Treaty Volunteer Executive took place in October 1921 to issue the commissions in the new army.

29 Mulcahy, 'Commentary', vol. i, pp. 6, 94–5.

30 Mulcahy, 'Commentary', vol. ii, p. 167; Richard Mulcahy, 'Notes' (UCD, Richard Mulcahy papers, P7/D/96).

31 Mulcahy, 'Notes on de Valera' (UCD, Richard Mulcahy papers, P7/D/79); 'Notes on the Chief of Staff position' (UCD, Richard Mulcahy papers, P7/D/96); 'Notes on the IRA' (UCD, Richard Mulcahy papers, P7/D/99).

32 Richard Mulcahy, discussion with Risteárd Mulcahy (UCD, Richard Mulcahy papers, P7/D/100); O'Donoghue, *No Other Law*, pp. 199–200; Maurice ('Moss') Twomey, interview, 11 December 1972, had an interesting IRB Circle meeting with Liam Lynch reporting on his time in Dublin. 'The last meeting of the Circle we had was the night, I remember, before the Treaty was signed – in fact the night the Treaty was signed. [Lynch] had come back from Dublin where he'd met Collins and those on their way back when they were over that weekend, and he told us that they were going to reject the offer that was made and that we were going to be at war.'

33 Townshend, *The Republic*, p. 330.

23. TRUCE

1 Parliamentary Archives (London), Lloyd George papers, LG/F/36/2/19. Letter to Frances Stevenson who was Lloyd George's mistress and secretary.

2 Pádraig Óg Ó Ruairc, *Truce: Murder, Myths and the Last Days of the Irish War of Independence* (Cork, 2016), pp. 57–8: Jan Smuts, the South African Prime Minister, at the king's request, advised on the speech. It was drafted by Lloyd George's government with the intention of opening formal peace negotiations.

3 See Appendix IX, 'March 1921 Supreme Council Circular to All County Centres' (NLI, Florence O'Donoghue papers, Ms 31,237/1–2; UCD, Martin Conlon papers, P97/14(32)).

4 Ó Murthuile, *History*, p. 160.

5 Liam Gaynor, BMH WS 183.

6 Denis Quille, interview in O'Malley, *Kerry Interviews*, pp. 30–1: 'About September 1920, there was a hint given that we should get in as many IRB as possible.' Quille also credits Austin Stack with this hint.

7 Liam Deasy (ed. John E. Chisholm), *Towards Ireland Free: The West Cork Brigade in the War of Independence 1917–1921* (Cork, 1973), pp. 258–9.

8 Liam Deasy in Richard Mulcahy, 'Note on Liam Deasy at Lissenfield', 18 October 1962 (UCD, Richard Mulcahy papers, P7/D/45). IRB organising had never stopped, however. In

466 Endnotes

Maryborough, for example, Laurence Brady was the County Centre: 'In May 1920, I was elected County Centre of the Irish Republican Brotherhood, and from that period, in addition to my Volunteer duties, I was busy extending the Irish Republican Brotherhood, organising and establishing about twelve Centres' (Laurence Brady, BMH WS 1427).

9 Liam Deasy, note of a discussion with the author, 10 August 1973. Carlow, Wicklow and Wexford were the three particular areas. Seán MacBride was sent to Wicklow and Wexford to organise an Active Service Unit – a flying column (Seán MacBride, interview, 10 May 1979).

10 O'Callaghan had left for the United States leaving his IRB position open.

11 Seán Ó Murthuile to Florence O'Donoghue, 14 March 1921 (NLI, Florence O'Donoghue papers, Ms 31,237/1–2).

12 See Appendix IX, 'March 1921 Supreme Council Circular'.

13 UCD, Richard Mulcahy papers, P7/A/5–6.

14 Padraig Ó Conchubhair, BMH WS 813; Richard Mulcahy, discussion with Risteárd Mulcahy, 8 August 1963 (UCD Richard Mulcahy papers, P7/D/100); Mulcahy, conversation with Paddy Daly, 28 November 1962 (UCD, Richard Mulcahy papers P7/B/178); Macardle, *The Irish Republic*, p. 479. De Valera, Mulcahy states, upon his return from the United States in December 1920, said that the Volunteers/IRA were 'going too fast' and that all that was needed was 'one good battle about once a month with about 500 men on each side'. Apparently, GHQ Staff were not consulted and were simply ordered to attack the Customs House (Mulcahy, 'Commentary', vol. ii, p. 10). Mulcahy, 'Notes' (UCD, Richard Mulcahy papers P7/D/96): 'The government ordered, as a unique intervention in army matters, the burning of the Customs House.' Collins and some others opposed the attack because of its suicidal nature. Collins ensured that the Squad was not involved but did not challenge de Valera's authority. As a result of the attack, the effective fighting sections of the Dublin Brigade were captured together with their weapons.

15 See Appendix IX, 'March 1921 Supreme Council Circular'.

16 Monsignor J.T. McMahon, BMH WS 362; Albert Sylvester, interview transcript: 'Very little was known of Sir Alfred Cope [knighted in 1922], even in those days; little or nothing is heard of him now, but I learned a great deal of Cope, and I admired him immensely. Suddenly, a prisoner was released in Ireland to the great concern of our members of the cabinet, because, and it was released by Cope without any official sanction from London … he was Arthur Griffiths [*sic*]. Cope was inspired with one idea, and that was to bring about a better relationship between Ireland and this country. That is why he released Griffiths. When the Cabinet meeting was held at Inverness, Winston Churchill said to L.G., when he observed Cope there, "Who is this poop?" Winston had yet to learn the true calibre of this remarkable man. Cope was a high Civil Servant. He was, as I said, a remarkable man. He'd got enormous determination and enterprise, and he was a very brave man too. He was ruthless to a degree. And also, he was unorthodox. He was totally unlike most Civil Servants. He was full of push and go. Indeed, he had more energy and determination and push and go than some of the whole Departments of State in Whitehall, as you will see. He felt that the only thing for him to do was to make personal acquaintance with some of the rebels, and this he did. And it's an amazing story – I'll tell you how it happened. He told me himself and I recorded it … This is what he said. "I used to go out in the dead of night from Dublin Castle, secretly, by secret means, and there I established contact with the rebels. And the one man I met was Michael Collins. And I met him in the remote countryside, in his hideout. And when I first met him, I said to him "Put your revolver on the table, I have nothing, I carry nothing." Michael Collins pulled his watch chain out of his pocket – his waistcoat, and at the end of it he took off a tiny imitation revolver, and he put it on the table and he said, "There, that's mine." And that, if you please was the beginning of a better understanding which led, in the end, to the Treaty.'

Endnotes

467

17 Maurice ('Moss') Twomey, interview, 11 December 1972.

18 Maurice Walsh, *The News from Ireland: Foreign Correspondents and the Irish Revolution* (London, 2008), p. 143.

19 Ibid., p. 147.

20 Monsignor J.T. McMahon, BMH WS 362.

21 Councillor James Haverty, a 1916 veteran, O/C Mountbellew Volunteer/IRA Brigade and a Dáil court judge proposed the appeal.

22 Coogan, *Michael Collins*, p. 197. The Conservatives and Unionists disagreed among themselves about the working of partition in a proposed federal system, with the Westminster parliament responsible for common concerns. Lloyd George needed time to persuade them to endorse a Dominion settlement that would not result in a federation and would clearly open the door to full independence.

23 Brennan, *The War in Clare*, p. 65.

24 Seumas O'Meara, BMH WS 1504.

25 Richard Mulcahy, 'Notes on GHQ Staff' (UCD, Richard Mulcahy papers, P7/D/102); Béaslaí, 'A nation in revolt', *Irish Independent*, 4 February 1953; Joseph O'Doherty, interview, 22 March 1972; Mulcahy, 'Commentary', vol. i, pp. 98–100. GHQ Staff in July 1921 had grown since 1918. The 1921 Staff was: Richard Mulcahy, Chief of Staff; Eoin O'Duffy, Deputy Chief of Staff; Austin Stack, theoretically co-Deputy Chief of Staff; J.J. O'Connell, Assistant Chief of Staff; Gearóid O'Sullivan, Adjutant General; Michael Collins, Director of Intelligence; Rory O'Connor, Director of Engineering; Éamonn Price, Director of Organisation; Emmet Dalton, Director of Training; Seán Russell, Director of Munitions; Seán MacMahon, Quartermaster General; Liam Mellows, Director of Purchases; Piaras Béaslaí, Director of Publicity; James O'Donovan, Director of Chemicals.

26 Ernie O'Malley, *The Singing Flame* (Cork, 2012), pp. 36–7. '"There was a reorganisation before the Truce," said Johnny O'Connor of the Second Kerry Brigade, "but we didn't take the matter seriously."' Conversely, Andy Cooney, O/C First Kerry Brigade, remembered, 'During the Truce there was a big reorganisation' (Johnny O'Connor and Andy Cooney in O'Malley, *Kerry Interviews*, pp. 178, 238). In November–December 1921 Seán Ó Murthuile was in Limerick encouraging IRB recruitment.

27 William Conor ('Liam') Hogan, interview, 10 November 1972. Statements about the Volunteers'/IRA's ability to continue guerrilla activity need to be conditioned by attitudes to the 1921 Treaty. Hogan supported the Treaty.

28 Patrick Mulcahy, interview, 31 August 1973.

29 Liam Robinson in the *Sunday Express*, 18 May 1969; Mulcahy, 'Commentary', vol. i, pp. 126–34; vol. ii, pp. 118, 126–7.

30 'Survey' (UCD, Michael Conlon papers, P97/9(16)).

31 Twohig, *Blood on the Flag*, pp. 155–6. Seán Ó Murthuile is referred to as 'Seán Hurley' in the text, 'Hurley' being the anglicised Ó Murthuile.

32 Deasy, *Towards Ireland Free*, pp. 258–9; O'Malley, *West Cork Interviews*, p. 28.

33 Thomas Maguire, interview in O'Malley, *Mayo Interviews*, p. 194: Martin Conlon led the drive in Mayo. Eoin O'Duffy was also organising IRA Divisions during the Truce (Michael Kilroy, interview in O'Malley, *Mayo Interviews*, pp. 45–6).

34 O'Malley, *On Another Man's Wound*, p. 376: shortly after the Truce, O'Malley briefed de Valera, Collins and Mulcahy about the IRA in the West. When it was over and de Valera had left, '"What did you think of the interview?" asked Collins. "He did not know much about the army in the south," I said. Both laughed as if amused. Collins mentioned some of the questions the President had asked; they laughed again. I felt uncomfortable. Dev was the President. After all, I

Endnotes

35 Bertie Scully, interview in O'Malley, *Kerry Interviews*, p. 162: 'There was some move on in the Truce to get the IRB distinct from the IRA.'

36 Twice in the circular the objective is so described, bound only to a general hope that IRB principles would permeate the nation.

37 Seán MacBride, interview in MacEoin, *Survivors*, p. 114; Brennan, *The War in Clare*, p. 105: 'Collins, Mulcahy, Gearóid O'Sullivan and others all emphasized that they didn't expect the Truce to last very long and that it must be used to improve our organisation and training. I left them quite convinced that we had only got a breathing space and that the resumption of the fighting was an absolute certainty.'

38 Julia O'Donovan, BMH WS 475: 'I have a distinct recollection of Mick Collins's excitement at the time Archbishop Clune was over in connection with the Peace negotiations. He did not usually talk about his business to us in fact he was close; but that time he was bubbling over with the excitement which he could not keep altogether to himself. He was making a lot of jokes about the matter such as, "I must be in the state of grace now that I am going to see His Grace", but at the same time I could see that he was very serious about it. He went to see him on a Sunday to a house in Merrion Square probably Dr Farnan's. He was very wroth with Father O'Flanagan for sending about that time the wire to Lloyd George. He said, "That ruins things for us", and he was not surprised when the negotiations broke down.' Collins, *The Path to Freedom*, p. 50: 'In my opinion the Truce of July 1921 could have been secured in December 1920 at the time his grace Archbishop Clune endeavoured to mediate, but the opportunity was lost through the too precipitate action of certain of our public men and public bodies.'

39 M.E. Collins, *Ireland, 1868–1966* (Dublin, 1993), p. 63: Richard Mulcahy supported Collins' view: 'There was not one of us who did not know that the Truce came just in the nick of time. I think that if the war had gone on much longer it might have ended in collapse.' While Collins' concerns coincided with the Truce, it should be kept in mind that Mulcahy's opinion, when uttered, was – at least in part – a justification of his support of the Treaty.

40 W.H. Kautt, *Arming the Irish Revolution: Gunrunning and Arms Smuggling 1911–1922* (Kansas, 2021), in a detailed analysis of IRA weapons and ammunition between December 1920 and December 1921, concludes that, 'The protreaty claim of insufficient ammunition does not stand up to scrutiny and would appear to have been a fabrication on at least the QMG's [quartermaster general's] part, if not Collins's and Mulcahy's. Thus, any claim that the truce was necessary due to lack of ammunition is demonstrably false' (pp. 194–5). Weapons were another matter. Around Easter 2021, the IRA had 559 rifles, 569 revolvers, 947 shotguns (p. 191). By January 1922, 'The arms stockpiles grew from 2,075 firearms to 16,156, while the ammunition supplies had grown from 33,393 in the spring of 1921, to 391,951.' However, ammunition did not match weapons, so the increase in supplies was not as effective as might appear (p. 193). Seán MacMahon, a member of the IRB Supreme Council from mid-1921, was quartermaster general from December 1920 to February 1922 (Military Service Pensions Collection, 24SP5162).

41 John McGallogly, BMH WS 244: McGarry wanted to make sure that the IRB remained strong 'in the younger element'.

42 James Cunningham, BMH WS 922.

43 'Survey' (UCD, Martin Conlon papers, P97/9(10)).

44 This would have been the Leinster No. 1 Council; the No. 2 Council represented the southern counties in the Division. Similar designations – 'No. 1' and 'No. 2' – applied to all the Irish

Endnotes

469

Divisions. George Irvine helped survey Louth. Irvine, a Protestant from Fermanagh, joined the IRB in 1907 and became Centre of the Clarence Mangan Circle in Dublin (George Irvine, BMH WS 265).

45 Seán Murphy, BMH WS 204.

46 'Board' and 'Council' were used interchangeably by IRB members.

47 'Survey' (UCD, Martin Conlon papers, P97/9(10)).

48 Michael Collins, Martin Conlon (Dublin Labour Board), Seán Farrelly (Meath Centre), Diarmuid O'Hegarty, George Irvine, Seán Murphy and Joseph Plunkett were on the Leinster No.1 Council.

49 Seán Murphy, Martin Conlon, Seán Farrelly and Seán Boylan; Seán MacEoin was the 'Visitor' to the Division Council from the Supreme Council.

50 O'Malley's transfer at this point in 1921 was another demonstration of the IRB not functioning properly during the period 1919–21: O'Malley had been sent to Tipperary in 1920 (UCD, Martin Conlon papers, P97/16).

51 UCD, Michael Conlon papers, P97/17.

52 NLI, Florence O'Donoghue papers, Ms 31,237/1.

53 MacSwiney, according to Florence O'Donoghue, had left the IRB after the Rising (Borgonovo (ed.), *Florence and Josephine O'Donoghue's War of Independence*, p. 60).

54 NLI, Florence O'Donoghue papers, Ms 31,237/1.

24. TALKING

1 *Dáil Éireann Proceedings*, 19 December 1921.

2 A.J. Sylvester, *The Real Lloyd George* (London, 1947), p. 64.

3 Thomas Jones (ed. Keith Middlemass), *Whitehall Diary: Ireland 1918–1925*, vol. iii (Oxford, 1971), p. 90.

4 Thomas O'Connor, interview in O'Malley, *Kerry Interviews*, p. 138.

5 Winston S. Churchill, *The World Crisis: The Aftermath*, vol. iv (London, 1923), p. 65: from the start of negotiations, Churchill had Dominion Home Rule in mind for Ireland.

6 Jones, *Whitehall Diary*, p. 91.

7 Cope 'through his contact with the rebels, particularly Michael Collins, he was able to understand their minds. And certainly to understand the romantic figure of Collins. And in so doing he was able to give truly remarkable information to the Prime Minister which helped him in dealing with their representatives. No wonder then, when L.G. signed the Treaty, he turned to Cope and he said "You have done great work"' (Albert Sylvester, interview transcript).

8 Seán MacEoin, interview, 19 July 1972; Seán MacEoin, BMH WS 1716, part 2: 'It was not declared that he was taking the place of the existing President [of the Republic: Michael Collins as president of the IRB]. He [de Valera] was then, like now, Prime Minister or Head of the government. The President wrote out, in Irish, the speech that I was to make, proposing it.'

9 Seán MacEoin, interview, 22 February 1973. John Moore was proclaimed president by General Humbert, commander of the French expeditionary force that landed at Killala, Co. Mayo on 23 August 1798 to support Tone's rising. On 13 August 1961, after a funeral mass in Castlebar, Moore's remains were reinterred at The Mall in Castlebar at a State funeral attended by President de Valera, the Taoiseach Seán Lemass, and the ambassadors of Spain and France.

10 *Dáil Éireann Proceedings*, 26 August 1921.

11 Collins was not a doctrinaire republican. In London before 1916 he had argued that a constitutional monarchy was just as good (Mary Kenny, 'Michael Collins' religious faith', p. 424).

470 Endnotes

12 David Lloyd George to Éamon de Valera, 29 September 1921, in Ronan Fanning and Michael Kennedy (eds), *Documents of Irish Foreign Policy, 1919–22* (Dublin, 1998), vol. i.

13 Patrick McDonnell, interview in O'Malley, *Clare Interviews*, pp. 170–1.

14 Benjamin Kline, 'Churchill and Collins 1919–22: Admirers or adversaries?', *History Ireland*, vol. i, no. 3 (Autumn 1993), p. 39: Robert Barton came to the same conclusion. 'The English refused to recognise us as acting on behalf of the Irish Republic and the fact that we agreed to negotiate at all on any other basis was possibly the primary cause of our downfall.'

15 Ernest Blythe, BMH WS 939.

16 O'Donoghue, *No Other Law*, p. 192.

17 Liam Deasy, interview in O'Malley, *West Cork Interviews*, p. 182.

18 John Joe Rice, interview in O'Malley, *Kerry Interviews*, p. 282. Rice placed this meeting as just after the Truce, but there was only one Cork IRB meeting with Collins and Ó Murthuile, and that was in early October before the Treaty negotiations started in London.

19 Albert Sylvester, interview transcript.

20 Stephen O'Neill, interview in O'Malley, *West Cork Interviews*, p. 50.

21 Maj. Gen. James Hogan, 'Statement to the Committee of Inquiry into Army Mutiny, 12 April 1924' (UCD, Richard Mulcahy papers, P7/C/I/30).

22 Thomas Malone, interview, 10 March 1973.

23 Mulcahy, 'Note on M.W. O'Reilly' (UCD, Richard Mulcahy papers, P7/D/96).

24 Seán Ó Murthuile, *History*, pp. 166–7; Mulcahy, 'Commentary', vol. ii, p. 230; Mulcahy, 'Notes on the IRA (UCD, Richard Mulcahy papers, P7/D/99); McInerney, 'Gerry Boland's story'. Collins realised that anything he obtained during the Treaty negotiations would be opposed by Brugha and Stack before he even left for London.

25 Emmet Dalton, interview, 7 March 1973.

26 Appendix IX, March 1921 Supreme Council Circular. The eleven Divisional representatives on the Supreme Council were elected on 15 October 1921. Collins was re-elected president by the Council.

27 Ó Murthuile, *History*, pp. 166–7.

28 Since August 1920 the Executive consisted of five members. In 1921 these were Collins, Ó Murthuile, O'Duffy, Boland and probably Gearóid O'Sullivan. Ó Murthuile, *History*, pp. 167–8, names only himself, O'Duffy and Collins meeting as the Executive in November 1921.

29 Seán MacBride, interview, 10 May 1979. Lloyd George's 'lodgement' smacked of Collins appreciating that he too could reach the heights of influence in the British Empire, as had Jan Smuts who had fought against Britain during the 1899–1902 Boer War. In 1922 Collins sent a message to Churchill that tends to support MacBride's view: 'Tell Winston that we could never have done anything without him' (Robert Rhodes James (ed.), *Winston S. Churchill: His Complete Speeches* (New York, 1974), vol. v, p. 348). An indication of the close relationship Collins had formed with Lloyd George and Churchill was when after his death in August 1922, Churchill sought out Collins' sister Hannie in London and personally reserved a compartment on the boat train for her and paid all her expenses to attend her brother's funeral (James Mackay, *Michael Collins: A Life* (Edinburgh, 1996), p. 292).

30 Ó Murthuile, *History*, pp. 168–9.

31 Macardle, *The Irish Republic*, pp. 983, 988, 990. The oath had been presented to the plenipotentiaries on 1 December together with a draft of the Treaty.

32 Built as a Dublin port between 1817 and 1859 and named Kingstown in 1821. Renamed Dún Laoghaire in 1920. It was the principal passenger port between Dublin and Britain.

33 Albert Sylvester, interview transcript.

34 Collins, *The Path to Freedom*, p. 52.

Endnotes   471

35 'At the end of May 1921 ... 18–20 battalions, 3 cavalry regiments with a proportion of armoured cars' were planned to deploy in Ireland. 'If conducted properly, there would be little the IRA could have done to counter such operations' (W.H. Kautt, *Ground Truths*, p. 164).

36 Moynihan (ed.), *Speeches and Statements by Éamon de Valera 1917–1973* (Dublin, 1980), p. 55; Longford and O'Neill, *De Valera*, p. 150.

37 Collins and Griffith argued with Robert Barton and George Gavan Duffy, the two plenipotentiaries who were reluctant to accept the Treaty terms, that not signing would result in more terrible war, as Lloyd George threatened. '[F]or three hours we had a most frightful battle in the delegation, among ourselves, at which the most terrific things were said to Gavan Duffy and to me by Collins and Griffith and Duggan. They called us murderers, stated that we would be hanged from lamp-posts, that we would destroy all they had fought for. The most terrible prospect was held out by Collins and Griffith to us' (Robert Barton, BMH WS 979).

38 Liam McMahon, BMH WS 274.

39 Collins, *The Path to Freedom*, p. 153: 'Shorn of [Counties Fermanagh and Tyrone, Ulster] would sink into insignificance ... Thus, union is certain. The only question for north-east Ulster is – *How soon?*'; Townshend, *The Partition*, pp. 139–41, 197–209, for the development of a boundary commission.

40 The Cabinet consisted of Éamon de Valera, President of the Republic; Arthur Griffith, Minister for Foreign Affairs; Austin Stack, Minister for Home Affairs; Cathal Brugha, Minister for Defence; Michael Collins, Minister for Finance; William Cosgrave, Minister for Local Government; Robert Barton, Minister for Economic Affairs. De Valera, Brugha and Stack voted against the Treaty.

41 Séamus Woods, note of a discussion with the author, 26 September 1975.

42 Mulcahy, 'Notes on the Chief of Staff position' (UCD, Richard Mulcahy papers, P7/D/96).

43 Petie Joe McDonnell, interview in O'Malley, *Galway Interviews*, p. 44.

44 Liam Deasy, note of a discussion with the author, *c.* September 1973.

45 Tom Barry, *The Reality of the Anglo-Irish War 1920–21 in West Cork: Refutations, Corrections and Comments on Liam Deasy's 'Towards Ireland Free'* (Tralee, 1974), p. 42. Barry's ambivalent role during the Civil War (he sought to make peace rather than maintain a hard-line Republican position) and his animus towards Liam Deasy perhaps influenced his view, although many contemporaries were alive in 1974 and they did not take issue with his statement. Molyneux and Kelly, *Someone Has to Die for This*, p. 307, note that roundups and area sweeps supported with spotter planes were beginning to harry the IRA successfully.

46 Denis McCullough, BMH WS 636.

47 Séamus Woods, in Denis McCullough, BMH WS 636.

48 Mulcahy, 'Conversation with Denis McCullough', 18 October 1963 (UCD, Richard Mulcahy papers, P7/D/15).

49 NLI, Florence O'Donoghue papers, Ms 31,239; Mulcahy, 'Commentary', vol. ii, pp. 233–5.

50 NLI, Florence O'Donoghue papers, Ms 31,237/1.

25. THREE DAYS IN DECEMBER

1 Frank Aiken, *Memoir* (1925) (UCD Frank Aiken papers P104/1308).

2 John Borgonovo, 'Atlas of the Irish revolution: The war in Cork and Kerry', *Irish Examiner*, 20 September 2017: 'The Military Service Pensions Collection shows an overall national strength of 115,476 Irish Republican Army (IRA) Volunteers; the IRA brigades in Cork accounted for 17,976 of that total, or 16 per cent. The national estimated strengths of all IRA flying columns and active service units in 1921 totalled 1,379 IRA full-time fighters, of which 466 (34 per

Endnotes

cent) served in County Cork … [T]he 1st Southern Division possessed 26 per cent of the IRA's rifles, 25 per cent of its pistols, and 58 per cent of its machine guns. The Cork IRA was responsible for roughly eighty-six of 403 Royal Irish Constabulary (RIC) dead (21 per cent), and forty-nine of 158 British military fatalities (31 per cent). The importance of Cork is further evident in the Crown forces dispositions. Five of the nineteen RIC Auxiliary Division companies operated in County Cork (26 per cent); eighteen of the British army's seventy-seven battalions or equivalent units (23 per cent) deployed in Ireland by July 1921 were based there.' Michael Collins estimated that there were 1,617 armed IRA men in July 1921 (Patrick O'Mahony, BMH WS 745). O'Donoghue, *No Other Law*, pp. 219, 334.

3 Ó Murthuile, *History*, p. 172; O'Donoghue, *No Other Law*, p. 190, states that this was the first Supreme Council meeting that Liam Lynch attended. Ó Murthuile, who as secretary and the historian of the IRB was in a position to know, presents Lynch as present and taking the lead at the earlier 3 December meeting.

4 Dr Patrick O'Daly, interview, 15 March 1973: Daly was the north of England representative, but because of some irregularity in his election did not attend the Supreme Council in December 1921 and was thus unable then to join Lynch in opposing the Treaty.

5 O'Donoghue, *No Other Law*, p. 192.

6 Ibid., p. 190; Seán Ó Murthuile, *History*, pp. 172–3; Lyons, *Ireland Since the Famine*, p. 438.

7 Ó Murthuile, *History*, p. 160; Tadhg Kennedy, interview in O'Malley, *Kerry Interviews*, p. 93: 'Stack showed me the IRB Supreme Council's recommendation of the Treaty, but it stated that members could take any side they wished.'

8 Patrick Mullaney, interview, 24 February 1973.

9 Mulcahy, 'Notes on the Falinge File Papers as a background to a talk on Collins', 24 October 1963 (UCD, Richard Mulcahy papers, P7/D/66).

10 Nollaig O'Gadhra, *Civil War in Connacht, 1922–23* (Cork, 1999), pp. 13–14.

11 O'Malley, *The Singing Flame*, pp. 36–7.

12 Thomas Maguire, interview, 27 February 1973. The IRB Executive in January 1922 was Collins, Diarmuid O'Hegarty, Eoin O'Duffy – pro-Treaty – and Harry Boland and Liam Lynch – anti-Treaty.

13 Ó Murthuile, *History*, pp. 173–5; O'Donoghue, *No Other Law*, pp. 231–3.

14 Séamus Hennessy, interview in Ernie O'Malley, *Clare Interviews*, p. 68.

15 O'Donoghue, *No Other Law*, p. 90.

16 Frank Ryan, interview, 14 December 1971.

17 Neeson, *The Civil War*, p. 68.

18 UCD, Martin Conlon papers, P97/16(1).

19 The Active Service Units were formed by men with weapons.

20 P.S. O'Hegarty, 'Notes on certain things which had not been written down, and of which I imagine nobody but myself has now any cognisance', 15 December 1946 (NLI, Florence O'Donoghue papers, Ms 31,333(1)). Patrick O'Mahony (listed as 'O'Mahoney' in the Bureau index), BMH WS 745: 'In 1918 the Conscription Act drove practically all the young men into the ranks of the IRA and there was very little difficulty in organising except that, the lack of armament proved a great obstacle to adequately equipping them and, while giving all of them a good military training, only the selected few could be retained in the actual fighting ranks while the remainder formed the Reserve.' This situation had not changed by 1921. About 10 per cent of the nominal members of the IRA were armed and formed the guerrilla bands by 1921.

21 Liam Tobin (foreword), *The Truth About the Army Crisis* (Dublin, 1924); John Madden had been taken to a meeting in the Gresham Hotel that Collins was using as his base where 'They

Endnotes — 473

talked about using the Treaty as a steppingstone' (John Madden, interview in O'Malley, *Galway Interviews*, p. 213).

22 O'Donoghue, *No Other Law*, pp. 231–3.

23 Frank Daly, interview, 14 December 1971.

24 O'Donoghue, *No Other Law*, pp. 190–1. Lynch, in two letters he wrote on 11 and 12 December 1921, said that he 'stood alone' opposing the Treaty at the 10 December Council meeting, and that the First Southern Division was 'alone in the army' in opposing the Treaty. Thomas Hales to Florence O'Donoghue, 30 April 1953 (NLI, Florence O'Donoghue papers, Ms 31,431/2): 'Liam told me that all except himself were for accepting the Articles of Agreement "when signed". His words were "at first" all were in favour except one – I am certain of this.' In the end there were four Council members opposed to the Treaty: Liam Lynch, Joe McKelvey, Harry Boland and Patrick O'Daly (Neil Kerr's replacement): 'Two of the Governing Body stood against the Treaty;' wrote Lynch on 21 December 1922, 'one of these was in America at the time [Harry Boland]; two others a short while afterwards also stood against it [McKelvey and O'Daly]. Of the four, two have been killed [Boland and McKelvey] and another is in jail [O'Daly, presumably]' (Liam Lynch to Seán McGarrity, 21 December 1922, NLI Seán McGarrity papers, Ms 17,455/1). Harry Boland to Seán McGarrity, 25 July 1922 (NLI, McGarrity papers): 'All the old Supreme Council save four or five are now in arms against the Republic.' Macardle, *The Irish Republic*, p. 653, incorrectly states 'Eight of the twelve members of the Supreme Council favoured acceptance.' There were fifteen members; only ten attended the 10 December meeting. Ó Murthuile, *History*, p. 224, says that Harry Boland was at first in favour of the Treaty (see *Dáil Éireann Proceedings*, 7 January 1922).

25 Department of Defence, *Chronology, 1913–21*: of thirteen (Volunteer/IRA) actions in 1918, five were in what became the First Southern Division's area; in 1919, 10 of 44; in 1920, 168 of 455; in 1921, 201 of 738.

26 NLI, Florence O'Donoghue papers, Ms 31,239; Mulcahy, 'Commentary', vol. ii, pp. 233–5.

27 Ó Murthuile, *History*, p. 175. Lynch attended the Supreme Council meeting on 12 January 1922 that approved the circular to County Centres informing them of the Council's neutral stance on the Treaty. On 30 January Lynch wrote to Ó Murthuile, 'I took it that it was an order to have this circular reach all Circles. The document will not reach them, but I take it that District Centres will explain the situation.'

28 'The Organisation and the new political situation in Ireland, 12 January 1922' (NLI, Florence O'Donoghue papers, Ms 31,244).

29 Martin Dunbar, interview, 19 December 1972.

30 O'Donoghue, *No Other Law*, provides an authoritative account of this contest; O'Malley, *The Singing Flame*, pp. 36–7.

31 Seán MacEoin interview with Richard Mulcahy, 15 June 1967 (UCD, Richard Mulcahy papers, P7/D/87).

32 Ó Murthuile, *History*, pp. 162–3.

33 *Gaelic American*, 24 December 1921.

34 Ó Murthuile, *History*, pp. 164–74; Golway, *Irish Rebel*, pp. 268–83.

26. DIVIDES

1 O'Donoghue, *No Other Law*, p. 231.

2 Liam Deasy, interview in O'Malley, *West Cork Interviews*, p. 183.

3 Clarke, *Revolutionary Woman*, p. 262.

4 1691. Ended the Jacobite war, creating the 'Wild Geese' (Jacobites who left Ireland by

474   Endnotes

agreement). The government reneged on the Treaty's guarantees of Catholic religious freedom and of property rights with the introduction, starting in 1695, of the anti-Catholic Penal Laws.

5   Éamonn de Barra, note of a discussion with the author, 7 November 1972; Séamus Woods, note of a discussion with the author, 26 September 1975: Woods, too, was swayed by Collins and ended accepting the Dáil's vote for the Treaty.

6   Ó Fathartaigh and Weeks, *Birth of a State*, p. 86.

7   Éamon de Valera to Joseph McGarrity, 27 December 1921 (NLI, Joseph McGarrity papers, Ms 17,440). De Valera had a history of dealing with 'the I.R.B. machine'. In 1911 he had stood for election to the Gaelic League Executive Committee and had lost but, while then unaware of the IRB, felt that the election had been rigged (Coogan, *De Valera*, p. 43). An anti-Treaty 'machine' also operated. P.S. O'Hegarty, 'Notes on certain things' (NLI, Florence O'Donoghue papers, Ms. 31,333(1)), related that 'Cathal Brugha asked my brother [Seán O'Hegarty], then Commandant of No. 1 Cork Brigade, to kidnap the Cork pro-Treaty deputies just before the Final Vote so that their votes could not be recorded.'

8   Denis Quille, interview in O'Malley, *Kerry Interviews*, p. 31.

9   Petie Joe McDonnell, interview in O'Malley, *Galway Interviews*, pp. 94–5; Fearghal McGarry, *Eoin O'Duffy: A Self-Made Hero* (Oxford, 2005), pp. 94–5.

10   Stephen O'Neil, interview in O'Malley, *West Cork Interviews*, p. 51.

11   Frank Ryan, interview, 14 December 1971. £4–10–0 was worth about £320 in 2024: not so much; in fact, the equivalent of a basic Irish State pension.

12   Michael Joseph Costello, interview, 19 August 1973.

13   Thomas Maguire, interview, 27 February 1973.

14   *Dáil Éireann Proceedings*, 22 December 1921. This admission had huge political consequences. It provided a cast iron reason for the Treaty ('If we don't accept it, we'll be pulverised because we don't have enough guns or bullets'), but simultaneously played to Unionist conviction that the Treaty was an unnecessary surrender by Lloyd George and Britain.

15   O'Malley, *The Singing Flame*, p. 44; Robert Barton, interview, 3 September 1973. Barton thought that there was another reason that Collins signed the Treaty in 1921, apart from his judgement that the war had been lost: 'He'd found out that he was no longer the mystery man of Ireland. His headquarters had been raided and his principal aide [Broy in the RIC] had been arrested. So had the other man, McNamara. He had no staff left. He was exploded as a mystery man who always knew all the information … If he'd gone back he'd have to recruit new staff and he had no means of getting any. Broy was the link between the British and the Irish authorities and every word he learned he brought to Collins. When he was caught all that was gone … He felt himself that he was finished and no longer could he be Intelligence chief because his staff was gone, his means of getting information were all gone … That, in my opinion was one of the principal reasons why Collins was prepared to make peace.'

16   UCD, Richard Mulcahy papers, P7/B/242: the pro-Treaty side was represented by Patrick Hogan, Joseph McGuinness, Michael Hayes and Eoin O'Duffy, the anti-Treaty by Seán T. O'Kelly, Liam Mellows, Patrick Ruttledge, Art O'Connor and Seán Moylan.

17   Cork County Centre to South Munster Divisional Secretary, 7 January 1922 (NLI, Florence O'Donoghue papers, Ms 31,237/2/3): 'The whole county organisation is against acceptance of the Treaty, and three District Boards have sent forward resolutions to this effect. Two of these, Cork city and Bantry, have already been sent forward through you to the S.C. and the other is attached herewith.' This third resolution was probably from Skibbereen District Board on 29 December 1921.

18   Clarke, *Revolutionary Woman*, p. 262: 'He said … he was sure he would be re-elected; the vote was not against him personally, and he felt sure they would still want him as President … What

Endnotes

475

I took exception to was that he had resigned his position as President of the Republic, and that even if he was elected as President, it would not be as President of the Republic.'

19   *Dáil Éireann Proceedings*, 10 January 1922. Griffith's election was confusing. He said that he would succeed to the position de Valera had left; de Valera said that was president of the Republic; the vote was recorded as president of the Dáil. 'MR DE VALERA: It is President of Dáil Éireann, which is written down as the Government of the Republic of Ireland. So I was President of the Republic of Ireland. MR GRIFFITH: I do not mind a single rap about words. I say whatever position – if you like to put it that way – that the President resigned from yesterday, I will, if I am elected, occupy the same position until the Irish people have an opportunity of deciding for themselves ... THE SPEAKER: The original motion – that Mr Griffith be appointed President of Dáil Éireann – was then put and carried unanimously by those remaining in the House.'

20   Clarke, *Revolutionary Woman*, p. 264.

21   Michael Hayes, interview, 22 March 1972.

22   Michael McDunphy, BMH WS 1396, summarised the complicated constitutional relationships of 1922: 'a Provisional Government was established in Ireland on 16th January 1922. It included many of the members of the Cabinet of Dáil Éireann, the independent Parliament of Ireland which had come into being as a result of the General Election of December, 1918, as the First Dáil Éireann, and which with its successor, the Second Dáil, had existed and operated in the face of opposition, military and otherwise, from the British authorities. With the coming into existence of the Provisional Government in January 1922, the Cabinet of Dáil Éireann did not come to an end. It continued to exist and operate side by side with the Provisional Government, with the result that for a time there were two national governments, to some extent identical in personnel, acting as a dual government. With the election of the Third Dáil Éireann in May, 1922, the Second Dáil, of which the then Dáil Cabinet was the Government, came to an end. The Dáil Cabinet, however, in theory at least, continued to exist pending the election by the Second Dáil of its successor, but with the election of a new Government by the Third Dáil at its first meeting in September, 1922, both the Dáil Cabinet and the Provisional Government which had been formed in January, 1922, ceased to exist, their place being taken by the new Government – again entitled a "Provisional Government – responsible to the Third Dáil Éireann".' McDunphy (1890–1971), Assistant Secretary to the Provisional Government (1922); Assistant Secretary to the Executive Council of the Irish Free State (1922–37); Secretary to the President of Ireland (1937–54); Clerk to the Council of State (1937–54); Director, BMH (1947–57). The 'Third Dáil Éireann' was the renamed Parliament of Southern Ireland and did not actually represent continuity from the Second Dáil.

23   *Irish Independent*, 7 August 1922.

24   Both O'Mara brothers were 'Fiscal Representatives' of the Dáil in the United States.

25   Kitty O'Doherty, BMH WS 355. Curtis A. Peters was a Justice of the New York Supreme Court. The case was *Irish Free State v. Guaranty Safe Deposit Company*, 1927. Carroll, *America and the Making of an Independent Ireland*, p. 79: Judge Peters concluded 'that the Dáil government never constituted a de facto government in Ireland, being unable to drive British forces out of any significant part of the country. The terms of the Anglo-Irish Treaty made no reference to the Dáil, but rather established the Provisional Government through the machinery of the Southern Irish Parliament, created by the Government of Ireland Act 1920 enacted by the British parliament. In Judge Peters' opinion, the Irish Free State had no claim to the money. The judge also denied the defendants' claim, concluding that the original terms of the sale of the bond certificates on behalf of the Irish Republic, to be exchanged for gold bonds upon international recognition of the Irish Republic, could no longer be fulfilled. Judge Peters, having rejected the arguments of both the plaintiffs and defendants ... ordered that the money be returned to the original purchasers.'

Endnotes

26   The two exceptions were J.J. O'Connell and James (Séamus) O'Donovan. O'Donovan had never been a member; O'Connell had been but left after the Rising. Collins, Diarmuid O'Hegarty, Eoin O'Duffy and Gearóid O'Sullivan – members of GHQ Staff – were elected or co-opted in 1921 to the Supreme Council.

27   O'Donoghue, *No Other Law*, pp. 231–46, 282–8.

28   Billy Mullins, interview in O'Malley, *Kerry Interviews*, p. 64.

29   Seán Ó Murthuile, *History*, pp. 177–8: Collins 'allowed certain barracks to be taken over by southern Volunteer officers in the name of the Provisional Government. Seán O'Hegarty was the officer he selected to take over the Cork barracks.' Relations between Collins and the anti-Treaty IRA were friendly and co-operative in the first months of 1922. Collins probably could have chosen a pro-Treaty officer to supervise these handovers without causing trouble: the IRA units that took over in Cork were inevitably anti-Treaty, so the officer making handover arrangements would not change the result.

30   Collins was prepared to go a long way to meet his IRA opponents. A new GHQ Staff representing both pro- and anti-Treaty officers was proposed. 'In these arrangements, the Free Staters would grant us any position except Chief of Staff' (P.J. Ruttledge, interview in O'Malley, *Mayo Interviews*, p. 239). 'After the Truce … There was a meeting in Dublin at which O'Duffy and Collins were present. Collins asked if we were prepared to give a guarantee that we wouldn't use our arms against the Irish people and all of us agreed that we would not [use arms]' (Thomas Maguire, interview in O'Malley, *Mayo Interviews*, p. 194).

31   Joseph O'Doherty, interview, 22 March 1972; Hogan, *The Four Glorious Years*, pp. 245–7; O'Donoghue, *No Other Law*, pp. 42–3.

32   O'Donoghue, *No Other Law*, pp. 219–21, 334–5; Macardle, *The Irish Republic*, pp. 1001–2. The Divisions that did not attend the convention were 2nd and 3rd Eastern, 4th Southern and 5th Northern. The 2nd Eastern never functioned. It was meant to consist of the Dublin and South Co. Dublin brigades. These two brigades and the Wexford brigades of the 3rd Eastern were officially represented at the convention.

33   Joseph O'Doherty, interview, 22 March 1972. There were three IRA conventions between March and July 1922. The first on 26 March revoked acceptance of Dáil control and placed it back with the IRA Executive. The second was on 9 April when a new anti-Treaty Executive was elected. The third was on 18 June when there was a split between those who wanted to attack British forces in Ireland and thus force a renewal of the independence fight, and those who were anxious to prevent civil war without renouncing the Republic.

34   O'Donoghue, *No Other Law*, pp. 219, 334. Tom Barry estimated that Republican IRA strength was no more than 8,000 men; other estimates of Republican strength were about 13,000 with about 6,800 rifles (Diarmuid Ferriter, *Between Two Hells: The Irish Civil War* (London, 2021), pp. 41–2).

35   Macardle, *The Irish Republic*, pp. 1001–2; O'Donoghue, *No Other Law*, p. 334. The theoretical strength of the pro-Treaty divisions was approximately 34,800 compared to Republican strength of approximately 77,850.

36   Thomas Malone, interview in MacEoin, *Survivors*, p. 99.

37   P.S. O'Hegarty, 'Notes on certain things' (NLI, Florence O'Donoghue papers, 31,333(1)). Collins was nevertheless thinking ahead about the future of republicanism. In early 1922 he is quoted as writing to John Devoy expanding on his thinking in 1920, when he had floated the idea of a £500,000 republican trust fund that would finance efforts to achieve a full republic, saying that he had had in mind a vital principle of 'a world-wide Irish federation, each separate part working through the Government, and in accordance with the laws of the country where it had its being' (Michael Collins, letter to John Devoy, February 1922, quoted in Golway, *Irish*

Endnotes

Rebel, p. 302, referring to the John Devoy papers, NLI 18,001. I have not found the letter in these papers). Exactly what form this federation would have taken, and how it would operate legally, remained unexplained.

38   *The Separatist*, 18 February 1922.

39   Christy O'Connell, interview, 1 March 1973.

40   Cronin, *McGarrity Papers*, pp. 113–14. McGarrity met Collins and members of the Supreme Council and gained the impression that a large majority of the IRB was pro-Treaty.

41   UCD, Richard Mulcahy papers, P7/A/62.

42   UCD, Richard Mulcahy papers, P7/D/13.

43   Patrick Mullaney, interview, 24 February 1973.

44   'Under such a constitution there was no way that those who supported the Treaty and those loyal to the isolated Republic could coexist in one government' (Bill Kissane, *The Politics of the Irish Civil War* (Oxford, 2005), p. 71).

45   O'Donoghue, *No Other Law*, pp. 232–46; Seán MacEoin, BMH WS 1716, part 2: 'Having voluntarily divested itself of its executive powers at the commencement of 1919, the Supreme Council of the Irish Republican Brotherhood, however, did not dissolve itself until five years later. As long as the struggle continued, there was danger that the elected government and Dáil might, at any moment, find themselves extinguished by enemy action and, should that happen, the Supreme Council held itself in readiness to carry on the fight as a "caretaker" government.' This was a fanciful retrospective justification that did not accord with reality.

46   Fergus O'Kelly, interview, 31 October 1972.

47   'Proposals', n.d. (NLI, Florence O'Donoghue papers, Ms 31,249); O'Donoghue, *No Other Law*, pp. 245–6. The Kildare Street Club, Kilmainham Gaol and a Freemasons' Hall were also occupied.

48   Peadar O'Donnell, interview, 22 March 1972.

49   Ernie O'Malley (eds Síobhra Aiken, Fearghal Mac Bhloscaidh, Liam Ó Duibhir, Diarmuid Ó Tuama), *The Men Will Talk to Me: Ernie O'Malley's Interviews with the Northern Divisions* (Dublin, 2018), p. 37.

27. 1922 CONSTITUTION

1   'Constitution of the Irish Republican Brotherhood', 1922 (UCD, Michael Conlon papers, P97/14).

2   Seán Ó Murthuile, 'Statement to the Committee of Inquiry into Army Mutiny, 29 April 1924' (UCD, Richard Mulcahy papers, P7/C/13).

3   1922 Constitution, clauses 27(a) and 27(c).

4   1922 Constitution, clause 22(g).

5   1922 Constitution, clause 22(b). The person elected therefore did not have to be a Centre, but since the member was subsequently referred to as 'area Head Centre' the probability is that members were to be Centres (clause 22(c)).

6   1922 Constitution, clause 22(d).

7   1922 Constitution, clause 22(e).

28. CIVIL WAR

1   Garvin, *1922: The Birth of Irish Democracy*, p. 144.

2   This and the following chapters draw upon John O'Beirne Ranelagh, 'The I.R.B. from the Treaty to 1924', *Irish Historical Studies*, vol. 20, no. 77 (March 1976).

478   Endnotes

3   Mulcahy, 'Notes on the IRA' (UCD, Richard Mulcahy papers, P7/D/99). Collins handed the
      day-to-day chairmanship to W.T. Cosgrave. The Provisional Government formed on 7 January
      1922, the day the Dáil accepted the Treaty (Townshend, *The Partition*, p. 223), was officially
      established on 16 January (Michael McDunphy, BMH WS 1396).

4   Macardle, *The Irish Republic*, p. 751; Mulcahy, 'Notes on the IRA' (UCD, Richard Mulcahy
      papers, P7/D/99). Collins gave an ambiguous speech in Cork on 14 June that was reported
      as a breach of the election pact with de Valera. Instead of asking voters to support agreed pact
      candidates, Collins had instead urged voters simply to support candidates they thought best.

5   Of the 128 members of the 1922 Dáil/Parliament, there were 92 pro-Treaty members in different
      parties: Sinn Féin 58, Labour Party 17, Farmers' Party 7, Independents 9, Business Party 1. Anti-
      Treaty were the 36 Republican Sinn Féin members. Seventeen pro-Treaty, 16 Republican and 4
      independent members were elected unopposed. In total 641,271 votes were cast – a turnout of
      about 63 per cent of the electorate.

6   Glennon, 'The dead of the Belfast pogrom': between 21 July 1920 and 5 October 1922, 498
      people were killed in Belfast. 'The population of Belfast in the 1911 Census was split 24%
      Catholic and 76% Protestant. But the 498 killings were split 56% nationalist and 44% unionist,
      so nationalists' share of the fatalities was more than double their share of the population. Of
      the 498 people killed, 74, or 15%, were female; of whom 54 (73%) were nationalists and 20
      (27%) unionists. This proportion of female fatalities is relatively high compared to the rest of
      Ireland and reflects the degree to which the violence in Belfast was directed at civilians … In the
      sixteen months up to October 1921, there were 165 killings – 81 nationalists and 84 unionists.
      In other words, an almost-even split. But … in November 1921, the Unionist government of
      Northern Ireland gained control of policing and security and re-mobilised the U[lster] S[pecial]
      C[onstabulary]. In the twelve months from then until the end of the conflict in October 1922,
      there were 333 killings, twice as many as in the first sixteen months. However, in this period, the
      tide turned decisively against nationalists – they were the victims in 199, or 60% of these killings
      … [M]embers of all combatant organisations, whether state or Republican, make up only 13%
      of the killings. The remaining 432 are split between 251 Catholic and 181 Protestant civilians.
      To describe all of these as "non-combatants" would be a misnomer, as many were killed during
      rioting.'

7   P.S. O'Hegarty, BMH WS 897. This account suggests that Maguire may have obtained Collins'
      permission months if not a year before Wilson was killed, and that Collins was exasperated rather
      than considered in what he said to Maguire. Joseph Sweeney, interview (UCD, Richard Mulcahy
      papers, P7/D/43): '[Collins] told me it was a couple of our lads that did it, that they had sanction
      for it.' Macardle, *The Irish Republic*, p. 737, thought Collins ordered the murder. Joe Dolan, *Sunday
      Press*, 27 September 1953, stated that Collins in March had ordered Sam Maguire to kill Wilson.
      Dolan had been in the Squad and was part of Collins' intelligence apparatus. In his statement to the
      BMH, Dolan was less certain: 'There is nothing more I can say from my personal knowledge on this
      incident except to express my firm belief that Collins did instruct Dunne to carry out the execution
      of Wilson' (Joseph Dolan, BMH WS 900). Connie Neenan, interview in MacEoin, *Survivors*, p.
      243: '[Sam Maguire] was with Frank Thornton, one of Collins' men, "the job on Wilson is on",
      said he. I was not to breathe a word. I could not. It was a profound secret. And I did not breathe it.'
      MacEoin, *Survivors*, p. 256: 'Rex Taylor in *Assassination* records that the order went from Collins
      on the 8th of June though, according to [Connie] Neenan it went in May. There is corroboration of
      this in a note to the author from a certain Mr J. of Dublin, whose mother, from Castlecomer, was
      a courier in the Collins entourage. She informed her son that she personally travelled to London
      with the order and was met at Euston by Liam Tobin and [Frank] Thornton, both reliable Collins
      men.' O'Malley, *Interviews with the Northern Divisions*, p. 48: Dr Pat McCartan met Tobin after

Endnotes

479

Wilson's death. Tobin, he said, 'was afraid to see or to meet [Richard] Mulcahy. When he met Collins, Collins said to him, "to Hell with Mulcahy. I'll make it alright [*sic*]".' Frank O'Connor, *The Big Fellow*, p. 203: 'Collins, half demented, was receiving Reggie Dunn [*sic*] and discussing the killing of Henry Wilson … No one can help wondering whether, as with American gangsters, killing hadn't become too easy to him.' Peter Hart, 'Michael Collins and the assassination of Sir Henry Wilson', *Irish Historical Studies*, vol. 28, no. 110 (November 1992), provides a forensic examination of Wilson's murder, concluding 'There is no solid evidence to support a conspiracy theory linking Michael Collins or anyone else to the murder. In the absence of such evidence, we must accept the assertion of the murderers that they acted alone in the (grossly mistaken) belief that Wilson was responsible for Catholic deaths in Belfast.' Hart did not have access to P.S. O'Hegarty's statement to the Bureau and may not have been able to decipher Ernie O'Malley's Notebooks. Liam Ó Briain, BMH WS 784, quotes Frank Martin, a London IRB and IRA member, as saying that the Four Courts IRA had ordered Wilson's murder: 'One day, the Captain, Reggie Dunne, came to me and asked me would I take part in a big job. The Four Courts people, he said, had decided to shoot Sir Henry Wilson. This would precipitate an attack on the Four Courts by the British military forces still in Dublin. The "Portobello people" (that is, the Army under Mulcahy and Dáil Éireann) could not stand by and see old comrades attacked by the British and would have to come to their assistance, and so the split would be healed up and we would be "all one again", fighting the British, and there would be no further question of the Treaty.' Michael Hopkinson, *Green Against Green: The Irish Civil War* (Dublin, 1988), p. 112: 'The testimony of many of those who were involved in the events surrounding the affair suggests strongly that Collins was directly implicated.' Ronan McGreevy, *Great Hatred: The Assassination of Field Marshal Sir Henry Wilson MP* (London, 2022), pp. 381–3, considers that Collins was complicit.

8   Kenneth Griffith and Timothy E. O'Grady, *Curious Journey: An Oral History of Ireland's Unfinished Revolution* (London, 1982), p. 281; Hopkinson, *Green Against Green*, p. 112; O'Malley, 'Notebook' (UCD, Ernie O'Malley papers, P17B/29, p. 97).

9   Dr Patrick O'Daly, interview, 15 March 1973; Mulcahy, 'Discussion papers' (UCD, Richard Mulcahy papers, P7/D/100); Joseph Dolan, BMH WS 900. 'Willets' is the name O'Daly and Dolan use, but there was no hangman or assistant hangman of that name. William Willis worked with John Ellis.

10   NLI, Florence O'Donoghue papers, Ms 31,258; Macardle, *The Irish Republic*, p. 761.

11   Mulcahy, 'Notes on Gerry Boland' (UCD, Richard Mulcahy papers, P7/D/118); O'Malley, *The Singing Flame*, p. 83, puts Joe McKelvey as IRA O/C in the Four Courts.

12   McInerney, 'Gerry Boland's Story'. De Valera was refused entry to the Four Courts on all but one occasion, and then only to consult Liam Mellows about the June election. Brugha's support of de Valera and of Document No. 2 surprised many people who knew him and thought that he was incapable of compromise.

13   Seán MacBride, interview, 21 February 1973.

14   Mulcahy, 'Commentary', vol. ii, p. 37; Macardle, *The Irish Republic*, pp. 740–4; McInerney, 'Gerry Boland's story'; Gerry Boland to Michael Hayes, 9 April 1966 (UCD, Richard Mulcahy papers, P7/D/118). Harry Boland was the go-between for Collins and de Valera negotiating their election pact.

15   De Valera and the Four Courts IRA thought Wilson's killing was an IRB affair (Maher, *Harry Boland*, p. 296).

16   Mulcahy, 'Notes on the Civil War' (UCD, Richard Mulcahy papers, P7/D/100). When the Four Courts was attacked, Mulcahy ordered the release of Liam Lynch and Liam Deasy who had been arrested on their way back to Cork after meeting Mulcahy in Dublin, because he thought they would work to stop civil war spreading.

Endnotes

17 Seán MacBride, interview, 10 May 1979; Griffith and O'Grady, *Curious Journey: An Oral History of Ireland's Unfinished Revolution*, p. 275: Joseph Sweeney in Donegal in this way received 200 British Army rifles that had to have their identification markings removed to hide their origin.

18 Longford and O'Neill, *Eamon de Valera*, p. 196; O'Donnell, *Not Yet Emmet*, pp. 27, 31: 'The I.R.A. Executive was little less estranged from de Valera than from Collins … The I.R.A. Executive was not only bankrupt of ideas itself but was scarcely within speaking distance of the politicians who also opposed the Treaty; they were not even within speaking distance of de Valera or Brugha.'

19 Linda McWhinney, BMH WS 404.

20 Peter Young, 'Michael Collins a military leader', in Doherty and Keogh (eds), *Michael Collins and the Making of the Irish State*, p. 88.

21 Ernest Blythe, interview, 4 December 1971: 'If it hadn't been for Collins' reluctance to fight old comrades, the Civil War would have been started months before then.'

22 Peadar O'Donnell, *The Gates Flew Open* (Cork, 1965), p. 16: Collins was not bloodthirsty. He approved specific, not general killings. On 29 July 1922 he wrote to W.T. Cosgrave, Chairman of the Provisional Government, that 'I am against shooting down unarmed men in any circumstances when it is known the men are unarmed' (Michael Collins to William Cosgrave, 29 July 1922, UCD, Richard Mulcahy papers P7/B/29).

23 Ó Murthuile, *History*, p. 192; Seán MacEoin, interview, 19 July 1972, refers to Ó Murthuile as IRB treasurer in this post-Collins period. This may be because he took responsibility for the IRB's funds in 1923–4.

24 'Notice from Éamon de Valera, 22 November 1922' (UCD, Dr James Ryan papers, P88/82). This can be seen as an effort by de Valera, with an eye on history, to put himself behind the reality that the IRA was not governed or directed by him so that he would not appear to have been set aside.

25 Regan, *Myth and the Irish State*, pp. 120–3.

26 Ernest Blythe, interview, 4 December 1971.

27 Regan, *Myth and the Irish State*, pp. 120–2: Collins simply announced that he was commander-in-chief of the National Army and that there would be a war council of himself, Mulcahy and O'Duffy.

28 O'Malley, *West Cork Interview*, pp. 190, 200.

29 The Free State was created by the Irish Free State Constitution Act, passed by Westminster and receiving royal assent on 5 December 1922. On 7 December the Parliament of Northern Ireland exercised its right, agreed in the Treaty, to opt out of the Free State. The 27 August 1923 general election saw Cumann na nGaedheal (in April 1923 the Free State government re-formed Cumann na nGaedheal as its party, distinguishing itself from Sinn Féin) win about 57 per cent of the vote.

30 Appendix IV, 1873 Constitution, clauses 2 and 3. J.J. Lee, 'The challenge of a Collins biography', in Doherty and Keogh (eds), *Michael Collins and the Making of the Irish State*, points out that we cannot know what Collins would have become had he lived; that he was 'still developing rapidly at the time of his death'. He might, for example, have broken from his conservative colleagues in Cumann na nGaedheal and formed a quasi-republican party (as de Valera was to do).

31 William J. McKenna, interview, 19 December 1972: McKenna kept the wireless messages between Dalton in Cork and Collins in Dublin. He had worked in one of Collins' offices in 1920–21, was in Collins' communications office at Beggar's Bush barracks and was with Collins on this trip. On 18 August 1922 Dalton forwarded 'terms by prominent Cork citizens' (one of whom though not from Cork was Frank Aiken) to Collins calling for a truce and peace negotiations

Endnotes

481

with 'Republican opposition to the government and Parliament to be on constitutional lines', no persecution of Republicans, Republicans wishing 'to join the National Army will be received therein with due recognition of rank and service', Republican arms and munitions to be handed over 'to a committee to be mutually agreed upon', and 'a general amnesty for all political prisoners'. Collins asked if the offer was agreed by the Republican military and political leaders, and Dalton confirmed that it was. Collins then agreed to a meeting on 22 August. Dalton was given details of mines and mined bridges, and Collins was 'assured a safe conduit [sic]', but as time would not enable all Republican units to be informed an armoured car escort went with him. Attempts were made to dissuade Collins from going, but 'Collins went, so anxious it is said, that if all else failed he would push out his bike, commenting "If I am not safe in Cork, then I am safe nowhere".' William J. McKenna, interview, 14 February 1973: 'Wasn't it strange: they'd come all the way down from Dublin and down into Cork, and drove around Cork for 48 hours, and this was the only attack that was made. The only attack that there was. I mean, they had come all the way down through Limerick and down into Mallow and into Fermoy and into Cork City without a shot being fired at them.' Frank Thornton to Seán T. O'Kelly, 25 February 1965, quoted in Ó Ceallaigh, Seán T., pp. 212–14: Collins 'traced out the means by which he hoped to end the civil war quickly. He told me that he had arrangements made to try to meet Liam Lynch, Liam Deasy [IRA deputy chief of staff], Dan Breen [IRA column leader], Dinny Lacey [O/C IRA Third Tipperary Brigade] and several others during a visit he proposed to pay to Cork at the weekend of 18th August ... As far as I know, all these arrangements were being made by Collins on his own; also the officers on the other side in the war did not know what day he would come or anything about his movements while he was in the south.' Liam Deasy, note of a discussion with the author, 19 February 1973: Deasy said he did not know about this peace initiative or that Collins was in the area. W.J. Brennan-Whitmore, Letters to the Editor, Evening Herald, 12 July 1968: Séumas Robinson (O/C IRA Second Southern Division) may have been another of those Collins hoped to meet.

32   Yellow was the colour associated with the IRB. As the Civil War began IRB Republicans were told that IRB members in the National Army would wear a yellow diamond behind their cap badge and should not be fired upon (Memorandum by James O'Beirne, n.d., in possession of the author). There is some evidence for this: the cap that Collins was wearing when he was killed had such a diamond. It can be seen at the National Museum of Ireland. The yellow diamond is obviously sewn on inexpertly: Collins may have made the modification himself. It may be that only Collins sported the yellow diamond to make his identity clear to the many new members of the IRA, the 'Trucileers', enrolled in 1921–22 who may not have recognised him. The Leyland Eight car that Collins was travelling in when he was killed was yellow – probably specially painted: it was a most unusual colour for a car at the time. Altogether suggestive of Collins advertising his IRB presence. The regular diamond on National Army caps was dark green. Different coloured diamonds – possibly yellow to identify a member of the IRB – seem to have been used for years afterwards. An tÓglach, 1 December 1928, p. 18: 'All officers are directed to note, by G.R.O. No. 55, that the wearing of a cloth "Diamond" of any kind whatever underneath the new official cap badge is forbidden and A.P.M.s [military police] are directed to consider the wearing of such "Diamonds" as "Irregular Dress".'

33   Thomas Malone, interview in MacEoin, Survivors, p. 99. All three Thomases were senior IRA officers and IRB men. Thomas Malone, interview, 10 March 1973: 'We had a little bit of an argument about the Treaty ... and he said we'll wait long enough and get the stuff and we'll finish it. And I believe, mind you, that he might have ... He said "I'm trying to put a stop to this damn thing. I'm trying to call a meeting of Southern officers of both sides" ... And Mick said, "Three Thomases, Bejasus!"' Michael Joseph Costello, interview, 19 August 1973: 'I was present

Endnotes

but I have no recollection [of Collins saying this to Malone]. There is no evidence that would support that and a lot of imagination was running away with him.' Costello also gave a different view of Collins' intentions: 'The people that wanted to make peace were primarily Fr Duggan and the one he persuaded to do something about it was Thomas Barry. And Collins didn't believe that Barry could deliver the goods, and at this stage Collins had the bit between his teeth and he wasn't prepared to make peace on terms.'

34 Patrick Moylett, BMH WS 767; Éamonn de Barra, note of a discussion with the author, 7 November 1972: 'Dan Breen stated that Collins had been in touch with him on his last trip south, and that Collins had told him he was trying to make peace.'

35 Michael Joseph Costello, interview, 19 August 1973.

36 Maurice Twomey, interview, 11 December 1972: 'I was in touch with Dev all the time he was in the South [in 1923]. I remember one day he kept me for hours in Fermoy Barracks. He wanted me to go in to Lynch. And I said, "Why don't you go in yourself then? Why should I do that? Can't you go in yourself and say what you're saying to me?" Dev was for quitting at that time, and he might have been right looking back at it now.'
'Lynch didn't want to see Dev because Dev was for quitting?'
'Oh yes, he avoided him.'
'And this isn't generally known that Dev was for quitting?'
'But all of us down there knew it at the time.'

37 Liam Lynch to Seán McGarrity, 21 December 1922 (NLI, Joseph McGarrity papers, Ms 17,455/1).

38 Michael Joseph Costello, interview, 19 August 1973.

39 Michael Hayes, interview, 22 March 1972; Ernest Blythe, interview, 4 December 1971: 'And then a statement already prepared by the [National] Army people was submitted to the cabinet as the announcement [of the execution policy].'

40 Liam Lynch to Liam Deasy, 7 November 1922 (NLI, Florence O'Donoghue papers, Ms 31,240/2).

41 Richard Mulcahy, 'Statement to the Committee of Inquiry into Army Mutiny, 29 April 1924' (UCD, Richard Mulcahy papers, P7/C/10); Seán Ó Murthuile, 'Statement to the Committee of Inquiry into Army Mutiny, 29 April 1924' (UCD, Richard Mulcahy papers, P7/C/I3); Seán MacEoin, interview, 8 March 1973. Ó Murthuile called the meeting 'to consider certain questions in connection with the Organisation and the death of the late Commander-in-Chief'. It was held on 3 September 1922. Attending were Ó Murthuile, Mulcahy, Peadar MacMahon (General Officer Commanding, Curragh training camp), Eoin O'Duffy (Police Commissioner since September 1922), Martin Conlon, Gearóid O'Sullivan, Diarmuid O'Hegarty, Michael Brennan (Western Command), Seán MacEoin and Daniel Hogan (Eastern Command). It was not a Supreme Council meeting. Mulcahy was kept fully informed of IRB activities in 1923 and 1924.

42 Liam Deasy to Florence O'Donoghue, 30 November 1922 (NLI, Florence O'Donoghue papers, Ms 31,240/4); Florence O'Donoghue to Liam Deasy, 2 December 1922 (NLI, Florence O'Donoghue papers, Ms 31,240/5); Florence O'Donoghue to Liam Deasy, 29 December 1922 (NLI, Florence O'Donoghue papers, Ms 31,240/7). O'Donoghue was also trying to start a new political party to be controlled by the IRB without 'the millstone of ambiguity of Document No. 2'.

43 Liam Lynch to Liam Deasy, 4 January 1923 (NLI, Florence O'Donoghue papers, Ms 31,240/12).

44 This did not mean that IRB members on either side in the Civil War fared better than non-members. John Joe Rice in Kerry 'had an idea that any important IRB who didn't go Free State were wiped out' (John Joe Rice, interview in O'Malley, *Kerry Interviews*, p. 281).

45 Fr Thomas Francis Duggan (1890–1961), a Cork nationalist priest and friend of Barry's, who

Endnotes 483

was a British Army chaplain in both world wars, in 1940 winning an MC for heroism at Dunkirk and in 1946 being awarded an OBE for his wartime service. In 1955 he was appointed archdeacon of Cork. In 1977 the Archdeacon Duggan Bridge over the Bandon River was named in his memory.

46 P.J. Ruttledge, interview in O'Malley, *Mayo Interviews*, p. 274. Barry was probably trying to emphasise his credentials, albeit in a vulgar way, in order to make the point that no disgrace was involved.

47 C.S. Andrews, interview, 15 January 1975: Andrews was sharing a bed with Lynch some days after Lynch had sent his letter when Barry stormed in, kicked in the bedroom door, and cursed Lynch for writing the letter – 'Barry had done more fucking fighting than Lynch' – and other statements to that effect.

48 P.J. Ruttledge, interview in O'Malley, *Mayo Interviews*, p. 276.

49 Macardle, *The Irish Republic*, p. 858.

50 Ó Murthuile, *History*, pp. 220–3; Seán Ó Murthuile, 'Statement to the Committee of Inquiry into Army Mutiny, 29 April 1924' (UCD, Richard Mulcahy papers, P7/C/I3); Éamon de Valera, 'Report' (UCD, Éamon de Valera papers, P150/1763): on 7 May 1923 de Valera received a report that Thomas Barry 'is ... discussing peace with certain people, mostly members of the I.R.B. amongst whom is Sean Hegarty [*sic*] of Cork'.

51 Richard Mulcahy, 'Statement to the Committee of Inquiry into Army Mutiny, 29 April 1924' (UCD, Richard Mulcahy papers, P7/C/10); Richard Mulcahy to Seán MacMahon and Seán Ó Murthuile, 4 June 1923 (UCD, Richard Mulcahy papers, P7/B/322); Army Committee of Inquiry, 'Transcript of evidence of General Sean MacMahon, 16 May 1924' (UCD, Richard Mulcahy papers, P7/C/33).

52 Richard Mulcahy, 'Statement to the Committee of Inquiry into Army Mutiny, 29 April 1924' (UCD, Richard Mulcahy papers, P7/C/10); Army Committee of Inquiry, 'Transcript of evidence of General Sean MacMahon, 16 May 1924' (UCD, Richard Mulcahy papers, P7/C/33).

53 Seán Ó Murthuile, 'Statement to the Committee of Inquiry into Army Mutiny, 29 April 1924' (UCD, Richard Mulcahy papers, P7/C/I3).

29. 1923 CONSTITUTION

1 Mulcahy, conversation with Kevin O'Higgins (UCD, Richard Mulcahy papers, P7/B/322).

2 Army Committee of Inquiry, 'Transcript of evidence of Gen. Sean Ó Murthuile, 16 May 1924' (UCD, Richard Mulcahy papers, P7/C/33).

3 Ó Murthuile, *History*, pp. 229–43; Army Committee of Inquiry, 'Transcript of evidence of Gen. Sean O Murthuile, 16 May 1924' (UCD, Richard Mulcahy papers, P7/C/33): 'We did not propose to reach everybody in the Organisation ... what we wanted to get were the people who would ensure the safety of the Organisation: the preservation of its traditional integrity without endangering the State.'

4 *Dáil Éireann Proceedings*, vol. vii, p. 3,124. O'Higgins claimed that he objected to the IRB revival from the outset. Mulcahy denied this (Richard Mulcahy, 'Notes on the IRA' (UCD, Richard Mulcahy papers, P7/D/99)). According to Mulcahy, O'Higgins had proposed Mulcahy to succeed Collins as chairman of the Provisional Government. Mulcahy refused on the grounds that he was the only person who could control the National Army after Collins' death.

5 Mulcahy, '1923 Constitution', clause 28(d) (UCD, Richard Mulcahy papers, P7/B/437).

6 Appendix VIII, Constitution of the Irish Republican Brotherhood, 1923, clause 13b (UCD, Michael Conlon papers, P97/14).

7 1923 Constitution, clause 2.

484   Endnotes

8   1923 Constitution, clause 13(b). There were eleven National Army Divisions, but only eight representatives (elected by and from the Divisional Centres) would be represented on the Council.

9   Mulcahy, 'Material relating to the arrest of Liam Deasy', November 1923 (UCD, Richard Mulcahy papers, P7/B/284).

10 1923 Constitution, clause 21(a). Elections to the Supreme Council were by the Executives (chairman, secretary, treasurer) of each Divisional Council.

11 1923 Constitution, clause 21(b).

12 1923 Constitution, clause 21(c).

13 1923 Constitution, clause 21(e).

14 1923 Constitution, clause 21(g).

15 1923 Constitution, clauses 22 and 23(a).

16 Diarmuid O'Hegarty, Cabinet Secretary; Eoin O'Duffy, Garda (police) Commissioner; Gearóid O'Sullivan, Adjutant General; Seán Ó Murthuile, Quartermaster-general; Seán MacEoin, Athlone Command; Michael Brennan, Limerick Command, Joseph Sweeney, Donegal Command; Seán MacMahon, Chief of Staff.

17 Michael Joseph Costello, interview, 19 August 1973; MacMahon probably joined the Supreme Council in April 1923. His election as president mirrored the intention of the 1923 Constitution to ally the IRB exactly with the National Army. Dan Bryan, interview, 1 March 1974: there was a rumour that Seán MacEoin was president with Ó Murthuile as secretary and Eoin O'Duffy as treasurer. If this was the case, MacMahon must have stepped down in 1923.

30. MUTINY

1   James Russell Lowell, 'Sixty-eighth birthday', *Heartsease and Rue* (Boston, 1888).

2   Tobin (foreword), *The Truth About the Army Crisis*, foreword; Bowyer Bell, *The Secret Army*, pp. 46–7; Terence de Vere White, *Kevin O'Higgins* (Dublin, 1966), pp. 157–8, 161.

3   Tobin (foreword), *The Truth About the Army Crisis*, foreword.

4   Michael Brennan to Richard Mulcahy, 15 May 1923 (UCD, Richard Mulcahy papers, P7/C/42).

5   Lyons, *Ireland Since the Famine*, pp. 483–5.

6   Thomas Ryan to Richard Mulcahy, 7 August 1963 (UCD, Richard Mulcahy papers, P7/D/108a).

7   Mulcahy, 'Tobin Mutiny File' (UCD, Richard Mulcahy papers, P7/B/195). There was no 'commander-in-chief' at this point. Tobin and his colleagues were inaccurately using Mulcahy's rank as commander-in-chief after he had left the position. Mulcahy succeeded Collins as Minister for Defence and Commander-in-Chief in August 1922 and stepped down as Commander-in-Chief in May 1923 after the Republican ceasefire. Seán MacMahon was Chief of Staff, never Commander-in-Chief.

8   Mulcahy, 'Tobin Mutiny File' (UCD, Richard Mulcahy papers, P7/B/195).

9   Ernest Blythe, interview, 13 December 1971.

10 Department of the General Staff, *Staff Duties: Appointments and Discharges*, memorandum no. 12, February 1924; Michael Joseph Costello, interview, 19 August 1973. Costello went through the list of officers named: 'Sean MacMahon was confirmed as chief of staff: he was an IRB member (and the nominal president of the Supreme Council). Major General Reynolds was appointed deputy chief of staff: he was not a member of the IRB and had only joined the IRA in 1921. The IRA organisation had complained about his rapid promotion and lack of IRA experience. Colonel James McGuinness was appointed head of the Inspection branch: he had been a member of the IRB but was not involved in the 1923–4 reorganisation. McGuinness' deputy, Patrick McClea, who was a member of the IRB who had taken part in the attempt to

Endnotes

rescue Sean MacEoin from Mountjoy Gaol in 1921, was reduced in rank to major. Colonel M.J. Costello himself had never been a member of the IRB; he was appointed head of the Intelligence branch. Colonel Padraig O'Connor was confirmed as head of the Operations branch: he had been a member of the IRB, but like McGuinness had not been involved in the 1923–4 reorganisation. Colonel Éamonn O'Carroll was appointed head of the Training branch: he had never been a member of the IRB. In the Staff Duties branch, responsible for appointments and promotions, Major General Sean Guilfoyle was confirmed as head of the branch but reduced in rank to colonel: he was not a member of the IRB. Colonel Martin Ryan was confirmed as Guilfoyle's deputy but reduced in rank to major: he had never been a member of the IRB. In fact, the only senior member of this branch who may have been a member of the IRB in 1924 was Commandant Joseph Guilfoyle, Sean's brother. If there had been an IRB conspiracy to control the National Army, IRB members would doubtless have secured control of this branch. In the Adjutant General's department, Lieutenant General Gearóid O'Sullivan was confirmed as adjutant general, a position he had held since the formation of the National Army in February 1922. O'Sullivan took part in the 1923–4 IRB reorganisation. Commandant Richard J. Feely was appointed head of the adjutant general's personal staff: he was not an IRB member and came to the National Army from the British Army. His deputy, Captain James Johnston, was not a member of the IRB and had been in the British Army with Feely. Colonel Hugo MacNeill was appointed head of the Personnel branch: he had never been in the IRB and had joined the National Army shortly after its formation. Colonel Michael Dunphy, appointed head of the Administration branch, was never a member of the IRB and had joined the army almost straight from the British Army. The head of the Discipline branch, Colonel Frederick Henry, was never in the IRB. Nor was Major General Cahir Davitt: he was confirmed as Judge Advocate General but reduced in rank to colonel. Colonel Thomas O'Higgin was confirmed as head of the Medical branch: he was never in the IRB. Lieutenant General Sean Ó Murthuile was confirmed as quartermaster general. Major General Joseph Vize, an IRB member, was appointed deputy quartermaster general: his sympathies lay with the IRA organisation in 1924. Colonel Frank Bennett was appointed head of the quartermaster general's personal staff: he had never been a member of the IRB and was disliked by the IRA organisation because of his lack of IRA service. In the Supply branch, Colonel James Shiels was appointed head, and Colonel Daniel Brophy was appointed his deputy while being reduced in rank to major: both had been members of the IRB but did not take part in the 1923–4 reorganisation. Colonel Éamonn Morcan was appointed head of the Accounting branch: he had been a member of the IRB and may have been active in 1923–4. Colonel Sean Cusack was appointed head of the Quartering branch: he was a member of the IRB. Colonel Joseph Dunne was appointed head of the Munitions branch: he was never a member of the IRB. Colonel Felix Cronin was appointed head of the Contracts and Disposals branch: he was an IRB member. Major General Sean MacEoin was appointed O/C Western Command: he had been a member of the Supreme Council since 1921. Three more IRB members were appointed to important commands: Major General Michael Brennan was appointed O/C Southern Command; Major General Peadar MacMahon, O/C Curragh Training Camp; Major General Daniel Hogan, O/C Eastern Command.'

11 Note by James O'Beirne, n.d., in possession of the author: 'Early January 1924 [I] met Charlie (Comm. Charles Byrne, Cork Command, Free State army) ... he told me that the I.R.A. men who had joined the Free State army had realised their mistake – that the Government had jettisoned the stepping-stone plan of Collins – and that because of this a mutiny was being planned and would I help. On my assuring him of this ... he asked me to meet Colonel Ben Byrne (his brother) QM Southern Command Free State army ... In answer to his question as to

Endnotes

what support could be expected from the I.R.A. I replied "none whatever" and explained that the "Ceasefire – dump arms order" of April 1923 was in fact the disbanding of the I.R.A. and that the Executive then functioning with Frank Aiken as Chief of Staff was nothing more than a sham created by de Valera to assist him in regaining power in the political field of the new state and so could not be trusted. On the other hand, I asked him (he clearly understood that I was representing no other person or body and spoke only for myself) to get me permission from his associates to place the matter before a select few of the brothers. This was done and I was given a list of men in the Free State army who claimed to have been members of the Brotherhood in either Munster or Connaught – the purpose to have it checked for authenticity. (The checked list was duly returned – Sandow [Daniel O'Donovan] arranged for the Munster area and Éamon Corbett, Craughwell, Co. Galway, arranged for Connaught) ... It was decided to co-operate. [We planned] a direct attack on the British forces still in occupation of the country and manning the Ports and Coastal defences. Such attack should be of prime importance and should synchronise with the opening of the mutiny arranged for 9.00 pm March 19, 1924 ... It was imperative that such action should be seen to be that of mutineers and we, who knowing the area and the surrounding country had undertaken this operation, were supplied with the uniforms necessary.'

12   'Karl' in John Dorney, 'The Army Mutiny of 1924 and the opening of the Army Inquiry Papers', *The Irish Story*, 17 December 2019: Liam Devlin 'was a Derry man, emigrated to Scotland and active in IRB there, returned and opened the pub in Parnell St and made it available to Collins and GHQ in the war.' 'He was an army contractor after the Truce, held close ties to Joe McGrath, and his pub was chosen as the scene of the mutiny (having been Joint No. 2 for GHQ in the war of Independence).'

13   Joseph Sweeney, interview, 2 September 1973, remembered Major General Daniel Hogan being in charge of the operation and that McGrath arrived with a letter from Cosgrave in the nick of time to stop Hogan attacking.

14   De Vere White, *Kevin O'Higgins*, pp. 163–5; Bowyer Bell, *The Secret Army*, p. 47.

15   Lyons, *Ireland Since the Famine*, pp. 484–5; de Vere White, *Kevin O'Higgins*, pp. 157–61.

16   MacMahon was reinstated in the army and kept his rank, but not as chief of the general staff. He was succeeded by Eoin O'Duffy as general officer commanding National Army. Ó Murthuile was not reinstated.

17   Peadar MacMahon to Richard Mulcahy, 19 August 1963, transcript of tape-recorded conversation (UCD, Richard Mulcahy papers, P7/B/51). Present were Martin Conlon, Peadar MacMahon, Daniel Hogan, Eoin O'Duffy, Gearóid O'Sullivan, Seán Ó Murthuile, Michael Brennan and Seán MacEoin. New members had been elected and appointed under the 1923 (Free State) IRB constitution.

18   Seán MacEoin, interview, 22 February 1973.

19   Notes of a discussion with Peadar MacMahon, 26 February 1974. MacMahon, promoted to lieutenant general after the Mutiny in 1924, was acting chief of staff of the National Army and was also present.

20   UCD, Michael Conlon papers, P97/3(2); Dan Bryan, interview, 15 January 1975: it was rumoured that £13,000 had been in O'Duffy's care, but that only £3,000 was handed over.

21   NLI, Florence O'Donoghue papers, Ms 31,258/6: McGarry, *Eoin O'Duffy*, p. 377.

22   Daniel Murray, 'Career conspirators', gives an overview of the Free State IRB: www.theirishstory.com/2015/06/29/career-conspirators-the-misadventures-of-sean-o-muirthile-and-the-irish-republican-brotherhood-in-the-free-state-army-1923-4/.

Endnotes 487

31. 'THAT'S THAT'

1 Séamus O'Doherty to Patrick McCartan, 11 June 1917 (NLI, Joseph McGarrity papers, Ms 17,676).

2 1925–61. In his book, *The Wretched of the Earth* (1961), he argued *inter alia* that subjugated people need not be bound by moral or humane principles while struggling for freedom.

3 Foster, *Modern Ireland*, p. 506: 'What had the republicans got from [the Treaty] which was not on offer before? Twenty-six counties had achieved dominion status ... Bonar Law had originally, and correctly, argued that this would enable Sinn Féin in the fullness of time to declare a secessionist republic ... But the realists, notably Collins, saw that it contained the germ of radical future developments. In a private memorandum at the time he wrote: "the only association which it will be satisfactory for Ireland to enter will be based, not on the present technical legal status of the Dominions, but on the real position they claim, and have in fact secured". He was right. But whether the bloody catalogue of assassination and war from 1919–21 was necessary in order to negotiate thus far may fairly be questioned ... in the end the Anglophobic obsession with "the Crown" outranked everything.'

4 Nicholas Mansergh, *The Commonwealth Experience: The Durham Report to the Anglo-Irish Treaty*, vol. i (London, 1982), pp. 237–43. Initial Conservative and Unionist opposition to Dominion status for Ireland was because it could lead to a republic. 'Bonar Law, leader of the Unionist Party in the Coalition and well-remembered for his pre-war assault on the third Home Rule Bill, gave the most telling reason for this. The connection of the dominions with the Empire, he warned the House of Commons in 1920, depended upon themselves ... "to say 'We will no longer make a part of the British Empire' we would not try to force them." Dominion status for Ireland therefore might and probably would mean first secession, then an independent republic.' Jan Smuts broke the deadlock and voiced the support of the other Dominions for Dominion status for Ireland. Rejecting that then became a threat to the Dominions' freedom, forcing Conservatives and Unionists to back down.

5 Foster, *Modern Ireland*, p. 509.

6 Peadar O'Donnell, interview, 22 March 1972.

7 Lloyd George, *War Memoirs*, vol. i, p. 418.

8 Ibid., p. 425.

9 Ó Ruairc, *Truce*, p. 58.

10 Patrick Mullaney, interview, 24 February 1973.

11 Garvin, *Nationalist Revolutionaries in Ireland 1858–1928*, p. 162.

12 Newfoundland was a Dominion, but preferred equivalence with Canada rather than independence. Newfoundlanders voted to become a Canadian province in 1949.

13 Ernest Blythe, interview, 13 December 1971.

14 Robert Barton, interview, 3 September 1973.

15 The 'British Commonwealth' was ended in 1949 days after Ireland withdrew. Since a republic could not be a member, a new 'Commonwealth' (dropping 'British') was created in its place so that India and Pakistan could be members, but Ireland chose not to join the new voluntary association (I am grateful to Terence Dormer for explaining this sequence).

16 Pro-Treaty votes were 484,277 (including 46,638 for Independents); anti-Treaty 135,310; spoilt ballots 19,684.

17 Emmet Dalton, interview, 7 March 1973: 'Collins was a very humane man ... he never did anything without a reason. He was always able to justify any action he did. He would never authorise or countenance the taking of life without good and sufficient warning being given.' Most of the men killed on Bloody Sunday 1920 were not given specific warning but

488 Endnotes

may be considered to have understood the danger of assassination that they were facing.

18 Ernest Blythe, interview, 4 December 1971.

19 Michael Joseph Costello, note of a discussion with the author, *c.* September 1973.

20 John de Courcy Ireland, note of a discussion with the author, 17 August 1974.

21 Patrick O'Hanlon, letter to the author, January 1973. The chief engineer whom O'Hanlon refers to was probably Assistant Chief Engineer William E. McLaughlin. The chief engineer was Vernon S. Moon.

22 Seán MacEoin, interview, 9 November 1972; UCD, Martin Conlon papers P97/3; Leon Ó Broin, *Revolutionary Underground*, p. 221, gives 1964 as the date of the transfer of funds based on Seán MacEoin's diary, and £2,835 as the amount. On the 1923 Supreme Council were: Seán Ó Murthuile (d. 1941); Eoin O'Duffy (d. 1944); Daniel Hogan (disappeared in United States, probably d. 1941); Gearóid O'Sullivan (d. 1948); Seán MacMahon (d. 1955); Martin Conlon (d. 1966); Seán MacEoin (d. 1973); Peadar MacMahon (d. 1975); Michael Brennan (d. 1986). Conlon, MacEoin and Noyk gave the money to Kathleen Clarke for the Wolfe Tone Memorial Committee, itself the creation of the IRB. Clarke used the money to help fund a statue of Wolfe Tone erected in Stephen's Green, Dublin. On 8 February 1971 Northern Irish Loyalists blew it up. Delaney re-cast and re-erected the statue within months.

APPENDIX I: INTERVIEWS

1 Maurice Twomey, interview, 11 December 1972.

2 See for example Richard Mulcahy's interview with Peadar MacMahon (UCD, Richard Mulcahy papers P7/B/181).

3 Ted O'Sullivan, interview in O'Malley, *West Cork Interviews*, pp. 160, 165: O'Sullivan, a brigade O/C in West Cork, noted that Barry 'hated Liam [Deasy] like hell'. O'Sullivan didn't care for Barry, calling him a 'bastard', and did not trust him (probably because, as James O'Beirne told me, when Barry demobbed in 1919 he returned to his home in Bandon looking for 'Shinners' to beat up and only later converted to the national cause). 'Tom Barry was watched day and night whilst he was helping training during the Tan War. That is at the beginning of his training … whilst [I] interviewed him I kept gunmen at the door of the hotel with 2 revolvers.'

4 Dan Bryan, interview, 12 December 1972. Richard Mulcahy, who had personally reprieved Deasy in 1923, met him for the first time since then in 1961. This led to a conversation. 'He started off in the readiest and most open way … He is very detached … He brings out his tremendous admiration for Collins … Deasy says that in relation to the Civil War period that what wants to be done about that is not that the people on one side would list the mistakes made by people on the other, but that the people on each side would list the mistakes they made themselves and proceed to any discussions in the light of matters so set out' (UCD, Richard Mulcahy papers, P7/D/45).

5 Patrick Mulcahy, interview, 31 August 1973. In the *Dictionary of Irish Biography*, a different account of Costello's rise is given: 'On one occasion early in the Civil War he and four other men were ambushed; although two of the men were killed and a third injured, Costello and the fifth man went after the twenty-three attackers and forced them to surrender. His action led to Costello's sudden promotion to the rank of colonel commandant by Michael Collins, of which Costello himself later said: "It was a serious mistake on Collins's part. I was surprised he did it".' Mulcahy's version is more probable since there was no reason that Costello should have been picked for intelligence because of his successful counterattack.

6 Peadar O'Donnell, interview, 22 March 1972.

Endnotes 489

7 Ernest Blythe, interview, 4 December 1971.

8 Vincent Byrne, interview, 19 April 1979. Detective Sergeant John Barton, killed on 29 November 1919, was the third DMP detective killed by the Squad.

APPENDIX II: IRB CONSTITUTION 1869–73

1 The layout and punctuation of the following constitutions are as in the original documents. Several spellings have been corrected: 'superintendance' in Appendix II, clause I; 'secresy' in Appendix II, clauses I and XIII; 'inadvertantly' in Appendix VII, clause 26(a) and in Appendix IX, clause 27(a); 'honourary' in Appendix IV subsection 'Amended Constitution' clause I, and 'reguisite' in Appendix V, clause 5. The American spelling 'Centers' in Appendix II, clauses I, XIV and XVIII, has been kept, as has 'An Saor Stait' in Appendix VII, clause 27(a). Each 'new' constitution superseded previous rules, regulations and constitutions.

APPENDIX VI: IRB CONSTITUTION AMENDMENTS 1919–21

1 This clause was in addition to clause 20 of the 1917 Constitution.

APPENDIX VII: IRB CONSTITUTION 1922

1 Michael Collins, representing the South of England Division on the Supreme Council, was not affected by this requirement.

APPENDIX X: MICHAEL COLLINS' NOTE OF THE MARCH 1922 IRB MEETING WITH COUNTY CENTRES AND SUPREME COUNCIL MEMBERS ON 'THE POST-TREATY SITUATION'

1 UCD, Martin Conlon papers, P97.

2 Whether or not to hold IRB elections in 1922 – a year earlier than planned.

3 This is almost certainly a reference to the 1873 Constitution.

4 Charlie Daly was Donegal County Centre.

5 Presumably the Louth County Centre.

6 These '1's' are unexplained. They could indicate the number of Circles being represented by each person.

7 Given the immediate context of these notes – Northern Ireland – 'Dick' probably refers to Dick Barrett.

APPENDIX XI: IRB SUPREME COUNCIL MEMBERS 1907–22

1 P.S. O'Hegarty to D. Lynch, 3 November 1936 (NLI, Florence O'Donoghue papers, Ms 31,409/1); P.S. O'Hegarty, BMH WS 26.

2 President (1907–10). Resigned. Replaced by Denis McCullough as Ulster representative and by John Mulholland as president.

3 Patrick McCormack, BMH WS 339, states that 'John McGarrity' of Hamilton was the Scottish representative at this time. P.S. O'Hegarty correctly gives the name as 'Geraghty'.

4 1870–1943. Patrick Thomas Daly, known as 'P.T.'. Printer. Socialist. Irish language activist. Elected to Dublin Corporation (1903–10). Expelled from the IRB in 1911.

490 Endnotes

5   Diarmuid Lynch, BMH WS 4: 'My predecessor as Divisional Centre for Munster was, I believe, Michael Crowe of Dublin.'

6   1868–1916. Raised an Irish Brigade for the Boers. Married and divorced Maud Gonne. Executed in 1916.

7   1879–1955. Patrick Sarsfield O'Hegarty. Author and historian (Patrick McCormack, BMH WS 339).

8   1861–1937. Methodist. Political activist. As secretary to the Lord Mayor of Dublin, he was responsible for a reception of school children for Queen Victoria on her visit to Dublin in 1900 and was criticised for this within the IRB.

9   Denis McCullough, BMH WS 914.

10 Patrick McCormack, BMH WS 339.

11 O'Hegarty, *A History of Ireland*, p. 738.

12 P.S. O'Hegarty to Diarmuid Lynch, 3 November 1936 (NLI, Florence O'Donoghue papers, Ms 31,409/1); P.S. O'Hegarty, BMH WS 26.

13 Denis McCullough, BMH WS 914: 'I was elected a member of the Supreme Council, representing Ulster, at the following election, in succession to Neal John O'Boyle of Staffordstown, Co. Antrim, who had represented Ulster on the Supreme Council for many years. He either retired or died about this time, hence my election. I retained the positions of Chairman of the Belfast Centres Board and representative for Ulster, on the Supreme Council, until the Rising in 1916.' P.S. O'Hegarty, BMH WS 26: 'Neil John O'Boyle had now retired and he died soon afterwards.'

14 P.S. O'Hegarty to Diarmuid Lynch, 3 November 1936 (NLI, Diarmuid Lynch papers, Ms 31,409/1). O'Connor was secretary of the Dublin Fintan Lawlor Circle when MacDermott was Centre (Charles Donnelly, BMH WS 824).

15 From January 1912.

16 Lynch, *The I.R.B. and the 1916 Insurrection*, p. 21.

17 P.S. O'Hegarty to Diarmuid Lynch, 3 November 1936 (NLI, Florence O'Donoghue papers, Ms 31,409/1): Seán Barrett may have come back on as a stop gap between Murphy and Gleeson.

18 Hobson, *Ireland Yesterday and Tomorrow*, p. 36, indicates that he succeeded O'Connor; P.S. O'Hegarty to Diarmuid Lynch, 3 November 1936 (NLI, Florence O'Donoghue papers, 31,409/1), states that Deakin replaced O'Connor.

19 P.S. O'Hegarty to Diarmuid Lynch, 3 November 1936 (NLI, Florence O'Donoghue papers, 31,409/1); Joseph Gleeson, BMH WS 367, said that he succeeded Murphy directly.

20 Patrick McCormack, BMH WS 339; P.S. O'Hegarty, BMH WS 26: Mulholland resigned in early 1914 and was succeeded by Deakin.

21 Denis McCullough, interview with Mr and Mrs Richard Mulcahy and Mrs McCullough, 1961 (UCD Richard Mulcahy papers, P7/D/14); Richard Connolly, BMH WS 523; Seán McGarry, BMH WS 368; P.S. O'Hegarty, BMH WS 26: Deakin resigned in late 1914 or early 1915 and was succeeded by McCullough.

22 MacDermott certainly represented Connacht in 1915 when Alec McCabe was elected (Lynch, *The I.R.B. and the 1916 Insurrection*, p. 25). In 1911 MacDermott organised arms distribution in the West. He also was acting as a general organiser. In the course of a visit to Clonmel he arranged the grouping of local IRB Circles under the Munster Divisional Board which he also formed at that time (Padraig Tobin, 'The Third Tipperary Brigade', *The Nationalist*, 9 November 1957).

23 Lynch, *The I.R.B. and the 1916 Insurrection*, p. 35. The paucity of Ulster members, as with Connacht, meant effective appointment/co-option rather than election. McCullough was Centre of the only proper Circle in Belfast: 'there were no active Circles of the organisation in Belfast, outside our group   In the half-dozen years before 1916, I was in continuous control

Endnotes

491

of the I.R.B. in Belfast and indeed in Ulster, which I represented on the Supreme Council, in so far as it existed in Ulster, outside Belfast' (Denis McCullough, BMH WS 914).

24 George Irvine, BMH WS 265: 'I was a member of the Gaelic League which I joined in the year 1905. I was approached by Seamus O'Connor, in or about the year 1907, to join the I.R.B. I refused at that time to do so. A few months later I was again approached, this time by Seamus Deakin, and I then joined and was attached to the Teeling Circle which met at 41 Parnell Square, Dublin. Later I became Centre of the Clarence Mangan Circle, an offshoot of the Teeling Circle. Sometime before 1913 I was appointed Secretary to the Dublin Centres Board and a member of the Leinster Council of the I.R.B. Bulmer Hobson was at this time Chairman of the Leinster Council and also Chairman of the Dublin Centres' Board. He remained Chairman and I remained Secretary of the Dublin Centres' Board up to the Rising in 1916. I remember the following Dublin Centres – Bulmer Hobson, George Lyons, Tom Hunter, Con Colbert, Frank Gaskin, Sean Murphy, Séamus O'Connor, P.J. Farrell, Peadar Kearney, Sean Tobin, Seamus Deakin, Greg Murphy, Cathal Kickham, Val Jackson, Martin Conlan [sic], Seán Farrelly and Sean McDermott.' Valentine Johnson, BMH WS 409: 'When I went to the Centres Board I found that Hobson was the Chairman, a position which he held until Easter Week. Other members of the Board then were Cathal Kickham, Gregg Murphy, George Irvine, George Lyons, Sean Milroy, Seamus O'Connor, Tom Hunter, Sean Murphy, Seamus Deakin, Luke Kennedy, Michael Flanagan (of the Typographical Union), Peadar Kearney, Frank Lawless of Swords, and a man by the name of Buggy, I think, but I am not quite sure. These may not be all of them, but they are all I can now recall. There were, of course in time, some changes. Buggy, for instance (if I am right in thinking he was ever a member) disappeared early. Deakin was replaced, I think, by Sean Tobin, while P.J. Farrell came on in mid-1914. The Board met monthly, at 8 p.m., and invariably at 41 Parnell [Rutland] Square.'

25 Mulholland resigned in early 1914 and Carrigan was elected to succeed him as representative for Scotland (Patrick McCormack, BMH WS 339). Patrick Mills, BMH WS 777: Mills was a member of the Motherwell Circle in Scotland. He had a different and almost certainly incorrect memory that does not accord with other members of the Supreme Council: 'After the Rising Mr Mulholland was asked to resign and Mr Andy Fegan became the representative to the Supreme Council.'

26 P.S. O'Hegarty to Diarmuid Lynch, 3 November 1936 (NLI, Florence O'Donoghue papers, Ms 31,409/1), gives Thomas Craven as possibly the member in 1913, not Gleeson. Gleeson was the member for the North of England in 1913 (Joseph Gleeson, BMH WS 367; Richard Connolly, BMH WS 523) and 1915 (Patrick McCormack, BMH WS 339) and 1916 (Lynch, *The I.R.B. and the 1916 Insurrection*, p. 28). It is possible that Craven was a co-opted member for a short time in 1912–13. He was O/C Liverpool Volunteers and was in the GPO during the Rising. In 1917–18 he was a Volunteer and IRB organiser in Mayo, Derry, Down, Antrim and Armagh. He was one of the men chosen by Cathal Brugha for the plot to assassinate the British Cabinet during the 1918 conscription crisis. In 1919–20 he was in the United States with Harry Boland raising money to equip the Volunteers/IRA.

27 Dan Braniff, BMH WS 222: 'I represented Scotland on the Supreme Council of the Irish Republican Brotherhood between the years 1912 and 1914/15. My appointment on the Supreme Council covered at least two years in all, pre-1916. I was a co-opted member of the S.C. during this period.' P.S. O'Hegarty, BMH WS 26: Braniff was co-opted in June or early July 1914.

28 Richard Connolly, BMH WS 523: 'when P.S. O'Hegarty returned to Ireland in August 1913, I was elected representative for London on the Supreme Council of the I.R.B. and O'Hegarty was co-opted at the meeting of the Council in October 1913'.

29 Richard Connolly, BMH WS 523.

492   Endnotes

30   Le Roux, *Life of Thomas Clarke*, p. 175; Patrick McCormack, BMH WS 339; Seán T. O'Kelly,
     BMH WS 1765. 'At the start of the Great War Deakin got "cold feet" and resigned' (Joseph
     Gleeson, BMH WS 367). Deakin and Mulholland were probably in sympathy with Hobson.
     Mulholland was asked to resign by Seán T. O'Kelly on behalf of Thomas Clarke. This was
     unconstitutional, but Clarke was only interested in fomenting a rising and was happy to ignore
     IRB rules when he considered it necessary.

31   Denis McCullough, interview with Richard Mulcahy, 1961 (UCD Richard Mulcahy papers,
     Ms P7/D/14); Denis McCullough, BMH WS 915: 'I believe it was in December, 1915, I was
     summoned to a special meeting of the Supreme Council of the IRB for the purpose of electing
     a new executive. This election took place every two years. I cannot remember who succeeded
     Seamus Deakin as Chairman of the Supreme Council, but when the meeting assembled and
     I had looked around those present I told Sean McDermott, who was seated beside me, that I
     intended to propose Pearse as Chairman for the coming term. He asked me "for God's sake"
     to do nothing of the kind, as "we don't know Pearse well enough, and couldn't control him" –
     an important factor then. He told me that they – I presumed Thomas Clarke and himself, in
     whom I had absolute trust – would propose a name in due course. When the matter came up,
     McDermott proposed and Thomas Clarke seconded my name for the position. I protested that I
     did not think I was a suitable man for the position; I did not wish the responsibility and in any
     event I resided in Belfast, whereas the time and the circumstances required a man resident in
     Dublin who would be available for consultation at any time and in any emergency. My protests
     were overborne and, despite them, I was elected unanimously as Chairman and occupied the
     position up to the Rising.'

32   Ó Ceallaigh, *Seán T.*, p. 149.

33   Patrick McCormack, BMH WS 339. He held the position representing Scotland until 1917
     when he resigned following the death of Thomas Ashe.

34   Patrick McCormack, BMH WS 339. Conscription was introduced in Britain in January 1916,
     but its inevitability was apparent by mid-1915 and many Irishmen of conscription age began to
     return to Ireland where there were then no plans for conscription.

35   Greaves, *Liam Mellows*, pp. 75–6. He was arrested under the Defence of the Realm Act 1914 for
     giving a speech against enlisting in the army during the war.

36   Alec McCabe, BMH WS 277. McCabe thought that Patrick Pearse was co-opted to the Supreme
     Council at this May meeting; that Patrick McCartan was present as a Clan representative rather
     than as a co-opted member, and that Neil Kerr was present. Tom Clarke presided since Denis
     McCullough, the President, was in prison. 'A Military Committee was established at this
     meeting consisting of Pearse, Ceannt and Plunkett. The purpose of this Committee was to look
     after military organisation. I understood the appointments were to be in the nature of a Military
     Staff.' McCabe was probably referring to the September 1915 Supreme Council meeting. The
     Council usually met four times: in December/January, in the spring (March/April), in summer
     (June/July) and autumn (nearly always September). Elections were held every two years, often in
     May.

37   Patrick McCormack, BMH WS 339, gives the date of the first meeting of the new Council as
     Sunday, 1 August 1915: 'all the elected members were not present, as some of them were in jail at
     the time. Alec McCabe was one and I don't remember seeing Denis McCullough and Seán Tobin
     being present.' Lynch, *The I.R.B. and the 1916 Insurrection*, pp. 28–9, thought this meeting
     might have been in September and was not certain that all eleven elected members were there,
     but thought they were.

38   Richard Connolly, BMH WS 523; Patrick McCormack, BMH WS 339.

39   Diarmuid Lynch was acting secretary until MacDermott's return in mid-September 1915. Lynch

Endnotes 493

proposed Pearse for co-option: 'it was my privilege to move the co-option of a man not hitherto a member of the "S.C." – Padraic Pearse. He was so chosen' (Diarmuid Lynch, BMH WS 4).

40 'When Hobson was expelled, his place was taken by Tom Hunter, representing Leinster, but he resigned, and a man called Seán Tobin took over. Tom Hunter only attended one meeting. He handed in £80 in cash. Leinster was the principal paying district' (Joseph Gleeson, BMH WS 367). Hobson was clear that Hunter resigned; had he not he probably would have been expelled from the Council, if not from the IRB. The remark about Leinster illustrates the importance of its representative on the Council.

41 Joseph Gleeson, BMH WS 367.

42 'In the summer Elections of 1915 … Carrigan was elected for Scotland, but only came on for a short time. He was killed in 1916 in the Rising. Pat McCormack succeeded Carrigan' (Joseph Gleeson, BMH WS 367). It may be that Carrigan's 'short time' on the Council in 1915 was for the period between John Mulholland's resignation and Patrick McCormack's election. James Byrne, BMH WS 828, gave a confusing account of Mulholland's actions in 1916, preventing the Glasgow IRB men from going to Dublin to take part in the Rising: 'On the Saturday before Easter Week 1916, I was called to an Executive meeting at London Hall, Glasgow. I was Centre for my Circle at the time. We were told at that meeting that John Mulholland, who was our representative on the Supreme Council of the Irish Republican Brotherhood, had a letter containing information regarding the date of the Rising in Dublin. John Mulholland did not turn up at the meeting and the District Centre, Mr Canavan announced that as Mulholland had not delivered this letter, it was now too late to send any men over from Scotland to take part in the Rising. John Mulholland did not deliver this letter until late on Saturday. Canavan said: "If any of you people want to go to Dublin on your own, you are free to do so, but in any case it would not be possible to get there in time." The Rising was discussed at the meeting and all present were led to believe that it was due to take place on Easter Sunday morning. I cannot say why John Mulholland did not divulge the information he had regarding the Rising sooner. We can only assume that he did not want us to take part in it. I heard afterwards that he was totally against any military action when he attended a meeting of the Supreme Council in Dublin.' Mulholland had resigned from the Supreme Council in January 1915, so this account smacks of Canavan ducking responsibility by blaming Mulholland who was most unlikely to have been given any such letter, taking advantage of James Byrne being unaware of Mulholland's resignation which, given the secrecy of the organisation, was possible.

43 Diarmuid Lynch, BMH WS 4: 'Tom Clarke, Sean MacDiarmada, Padraig Pearse and Dr. MacCartan were co-opted.' Patrick McCormack, BMH WS 339: 'The co-options were as follows: Thomas Clarke, Sean McDermott, Patrick Pearse and Dr Patrick McCartan.'

44 Dr Feargus de Burca, BMH WS 105: 'I had a son at St Enda's, and, by this circumstance, got to know Padraig Pearse. Pearse informed me that he knew that the I.R.B. existed; that he made speeches that should have attracted the I.R.B. to him. Pearse was too big a man to be only a member of the I.R.B., and the approach between Pearse and the I.R.B. should come from the I.R.B.'

45 Patrick McCartan, BMH WS 766: 'Amongst those present at that last meeting of the Supreme Council were Dinny McCullough, Sean McDermott, Thomas Clarke, Patrick Pearse, myself. The representative of Leinster was absent. I think his name was Sean Tobin. He used to work in some garage – Thompson's. The rest were all present, as far as I remember, though I forget some of their names. Joe Gleeson from Liverpool was one of them. There was Pat McCormack from Scotland, but I am not sure whether he was at the meeting or not. I knew him afterwards and I must have met him on the Supreme Council. He was representative of Glasgow or Scotland. I don't remember who was from London. I have heard his name since, but personally I can't vouch for it, whoever he was [Richard Connolly]. Diarmuid Lynch, of course, was there

Endnotes

representing Munster. Dinny McCullough represented Ulster and Sean McDermott was there as the representative of Connacht.'

46   Patrick McCartan, BMH WS 766, places O'Doherty as secretary of the Council in May 1917.

47   Diarmuid Lynch seems to have been treasurer in 1917 (Mulcahy, 'Notes to a background on talk on Collins', 21 October 1963 (UCD, Richard Mulcahy papers, P7/D/66)); Liam Gaynor, BMH WS 183: 'Dermot Hegarty, Harry Boland and Gearóid O'Sullivan were co-opted members as was also, I think, Sean McGarry ... The Supreme Council agreed, about 1918, to my proposal to increase the Irish Provincial representation from one to two, thus increasing the Council from eleven to fifteen members.' Gaynor conflates various elections and co-options and refers to Collins as secretary from 1917 when that position was held by Ó Murthuile and Collins was, in fact, treasurer. Collins may have acted as secretary when Ó Murthuile was not present.

48   Gregory Murphy, BMH WS 150. Member of the Dublin Bartholomew Teeling Circle 1903/4–11; Centre of the Terenure Circle from 1911 and Secretary of the Leinster Board; member of the 'unofficial' 1916 Supreme Council and member of the Supreme Council 1917–19.

49   Liam Gaynor, BMH WS 183: 'Sean McGarry was President during my term of office from 1916 to the Summer of 1921.' This was not correct. McGarry joined the Supreme Council in 1917 and was not president after 1919. McCartan was soon travelling to England and the United States on IRB missions, and Gaynor probably took his place.

50   Diarmuid Lynch, BMH WS 4.

51   Liam Gaynor, BMH WS 183, recalled that Larry Lardner was 'later superseded by Alec McCabe and still later by Andrew Lavin'. It is difficult to fit Lardner into the Connacht chronology unless he was appointed to the provisional Council in 1916 before Alec McCabe was re-enlisted. Tom Breen may have represented Connacht in place of McCabe (Joseph Gleeson, BMH WS 367).

52   Ashe died on hunger strike in September 1917. He was succeeded by Seán McGarry who was arrested in May 1918. Harry Boland was then co-opted to replace him and was elected president. Boland went to the United States in May 1919 as an IRB and Dáil 'envoy'. Michael Collins was then elected president in 1919.

53   Ó Murthuile, *History*, pp. 59, 64, notes that Collins served as secretary until Ó Murthuile was elected as secretary in 1919. Séamus Dobbyn, BMH WS 279, remembered Collins as treasurer in 1919. Patrick McCormack remembered Ó Murthuile as secretary in 1917 and Collins or Diarmuid Lynch as treasurer. Lynch, *The I.R.B. and the 1916 Insurrection*, p. 32, names Collins as secretary in 1917.

54   Initially, O'Hegarty may have been treasurer, but after Kathleen Clarke gave Collins control of the funds, John Devoy sent to her as well as those of the INAVDF, which makes the likelihood of O'Hegarty being treasurer nominal at best. Diarmuid Lynch was briefly treasurer of the 1917 Council until arrested in February 1918 (Mulcahy, 'Notes to a background on talk on Collins', 21 October 1963 (UCD, Richard Mulcahy papers, P7/D/66)); Liam Gaynor, BMH WS 183: 'Dermot [*sic*] Hegarty, Harry Boland and Gearoid O'Sullivan were co-opted members as was also, I think, Sean McGarry.' As mentioned above, Gaynor conflates various elections and co-options and refers to Collins as secretary from 1917 when that position was held by Ó Murthuile and Collins was treasurer.

55   Luke Kennedy, BMH WS 165: 'Some time later [after May 1917] I was elected to the Supreme Council at a meeting held at 41 Rutland Square. I cannot remember who was there, except that the whole Central Board was there. I attended meetings of the Supreme Council after that and remained in it until the dissolution in 1922.' The 'Central Board' was probably the Leinster Divisional Council.

56   Liam Gaynor, BMH WS 183: 'At my first meeting of the Supreme Council in the autumn of 1916 Leinster was represented by Greg Murphy; Munster by Seán Ua Murthuile, who acted

Endnotes   495

as Treasurer; Connacht by Larry Lardner, who was later superseded by Alec McCabe and still later by Andrew Lavin; North England by Neil Kerr and Scotland by Pat McCormack. In 1917 London was represented by Michael Collins who acted as Secretary to the Supreme Council. Seán McGarry was President during my term of office from 1916 to the Summer of 1921 [McGarry was not president after 1919]. Dermot Hegarty, Harry Boland and Gearoid O'Sullivan were co-opted members as was also, I think, Sean McGarry.' As we have seen, Gaynor confused names and dates.

57　Alec McCabe, interview, 6 December 1971: This was 'my last meeting in the IRB'. He also names Gearóid O'Sullivan as being present at this Council. It may be that McCabe was present to provide an element of continuity, as he says, and was replaced afterwards by Andrew Lavin (Liam Gaynor, BMH WS 183; Séamus Dobbyn, BMH WS 279).

58　Patrick McCormack, BMH WS 339.

59　'The man who took over after me in Liverpool was Pat Lively, a baker, he died in 1917. He succeeded me in 1916, I think, as the representative for North East England on the Supreme Council … In 1917 after being released, Sean O Murthille and I were sent to England to conduct an election for the Supreme Council of the I.R.B. At that election Neil Kerr was made Centre for the North of England. Subsequently Neil Kerr was arrested and Patrick O'Daly from Tullamore was sent over to replace him as Centre from the North of England' (Joseph Gleeson, BMH WS 367).

60　Kitty O'Doherty, BMH WS 355: Séamus O'Doherty was sent to America in 1919.

61　Gregory Murphy, BMH WS 150: 'As I had been Secretary of the I.R.B. for Leinster, I became a member of the Council of the I.R.B. in 1917 and remained a member until 1919. The other members whom I can recollect were Sean McGarry, Martin Conlon, Harry Boland, Liam Gaynor and Sean O'Murthuile.' Murphy had stepped down from the Volunteers' Provisional Committee to make way for younger men, and he probably ceased being a Centre and the Leinster representative for the same reason and was co-opted in 1917.

62　Liam Gaynor, BMH WS 183.

63　Ibid.; Séamus Dobbyn, BMH WS 279. Lynch, an American citizen, was expelled from Ireland to the United States in 1918.

64　Séamus Dobbyn, BMH WS 279. Dobbyn probably was co-opted in 1918.

65　Diarmuid Lynch, BMH WS 4. Con Collins (1881–1937), born in Newcastle West, Co. Limerick. Arrested in Kerry with Austin Stack in 1916. Had been a clerk in the civil service in London where he met Michael Collins. Elected Sinn Féin TD for Limerick West in the 1918 general election.

66　Séamus Dobbyn, BMH WS 279. Dobbyn thought Seán McGarry was president in May 1919. It may be that McGarry, imprisoned in 1918–19, preceded and succeeded Boland, with Collins being elected president in 1919. Collins was President by September 1919 (Fitzpatrick, *Harry Boland's Irish Revolution*, p. 228).

67　Liam Gaynor, BMH WS 183. Dobbyn was arrested in mid-1920 (Séamus Dobbyn, BMH WS 279). Liam Deasy, interview in O'Malley, *West Cork Interviews*, p. 189: 'Charlie Daly represented Tyrone, Donegal.' Deasy was never on the Supreme Council himself, and Daly never claimed to have been on it. More likely Eoin O'Duffy replaced Dobbyn after his arrest. 'Charlie Daly told me that he had been at a Supreme Council meeting by accident' (Jack Fitzgerald, interview in O'Malley, *West Cork Interviews*, p. 93).

68　Dr Patrick O'Daly, BMH WS 814: 'On Collins' directions I assumed control of the I.R.B. immediately I returned to Liverpool. There was no controversial arrangement about it. I just assumed control, principally in connection with the buying and dispatching of munitions … I was appointed to represent the North of England on the Supreme Council. Subsequent to

496 Endnotes

this election I had a certain amount of friction with some of the older leading members of the I.R.B. Without going into details the principal complaint was that I was not taking them into my confidence ... However, later on some of them decided, probably amongst themselves, that my election was irregular. They apparently now regretted their choice. About this time I was summoned to a meeting of the I.R.B. Supreme Council in Barry's Hotel. Before the meeting I sought an interview with Collins and put the situation before him. I told him that I would prefer not to attend the meeting under the circumstances. I was rather over-conscientious then and my abstention was I think unnecessary. Collins agreed with my line of action.' See also Joseph Gleeson, BMH WS 367.

69   Patrick McCormack, BMH WS 339.

70   Martin Conlon, BMH WS 798: 'In 1916 I was the Centre of an I.R.B. Circle – one of the Dublin Circles. It was not until much later that I became a member of the Supreme Council of the I.R.B.' This suggests that Conlon joined in 1919, not 1917.

71   Thomas Hales to Florence O'Donoghue, 30 April 1953 (NLI, Florence O'Donoghue papers, f.72); Richard Mulcahy, 'Commentary', vol. ii, p. 121; Seán MacEoin to Richard Mulcahy, 15 June 1967 (UCD, Richard Mulcahy papers, P7/D/87); Liam Gaynor, BMH WS 183. P.J. Ruttledge, not a member of the Supreme Council, in the late 1940s gave Ernie O'Malley an improbable account of the Council's membership in 1921: Seán Ó Murthuile, Fionan Lynch, Diarmuid O'Hegarty, J.J. 'Sceilig' O'Kelly, Michael Collins and Bulmer Hobson (O'Malley, *Mayo Interviews*, p. 271).

72   Replaced Liam Gaynor in 1921 (Liam Gaynor, BMH WS 183).

73   Joined in 1921, replacing Thomas Hales who had joined the Council in 1919 but had been arrested in 1920. Marie Coleman in her *Dictionary of Irish Biography* article on Florence O'Donoghue incorrectly states that O'Donoghue was a member of the Supreme Council.

74   Seán MacMahon probably replaced Kennedy. According to Mulcahy, MacMahon joined the Council in 1921 (Richard Mulcahy, 'Notes on GHQ Staff', UCD, Richard Mulcahy papers, P7/D/102). Kennedy stated that he left the Council in 1922 (Luke Kennedy, BMH WS 165). Elections were held in 1921, suggesting that Mulcahy's record was accurate.

75   Florence O'Donoghue, 'Present at IRB SC & County Centre Meetings' (NLI, O'Donoghue papers, f.72).

APPENDIX XII: IRB MEMBERS IN SENIOR POSITIONS 1916–22

1   Mulcahy, 'Commentary', vol. ii, p. 50. Pearse was Commandant until Holy Week 1916, when he relinquished this post to MacDonagh. Heuston, *Headquarters Battalion*, p. 3: James Connolly became Commandant of the 'Dublin Division' in Easter week. Macardle, *The Irish Republic*, p. 172.

2   Gerry Boland, interview with Michael McInerney, *The Irish Times*, 9 October 1968.

3   Longford and O'Neill, *Eamon de Valera*, pp. 24–5.

4   Mulcahy, 'Note' (UCD, Richard Mulcahy papers, P7/D/67).

5   Piaras Béaslaí, *Irish Independent*, 4 February 1953.

6   Ó Snodaigh, *Comhghuaillithe na Reabhloide*, p. 94.

7   Royal Irish Academy, *Dictionary of Irish Biography*.

8   With three exceptions, all were members of the IRB in 1921. Comdt Padraic Kennedy, 'Key appointments and the transition of the Irish Volunteers, the Irish Republican Army and the National Army (1913–23)' in *Defence Forces Review 2016* (Dublin, 2016).

9   Left the IRB in 1919 when the Dáil was established.

10 Never a member of the IRB.

Endnotes 497

11 Never a member of the IRB.

12 Macardle, *The Irish Republic*, pp. 1,001–2; Mulcahy, 'Commentary', vol. ii, p. 118. UCD, Ernie O'Malley papers, P17a/4.

13 Eoin O'Duffy acted temporarily.

14 Dan Hogan, O/C Fifth Northern Division, was never a member of the IRB (UCD, Richard Mulcahy papers, P7/C/24).

15 Probably a member of the IRB.

16 Probably not a member of the IRB.

17 Military Service Pensions Collection 34REF8926.

18 Military Service Pensions Collection 24SP3250; General Seán MacMahon, 'Statement to Army Inquiry', 6 May 1924 (UCD, Richard Mulcahy papers, P7/C/14): The second in command, Austin McCurtin, was anti-Treaty and 'being a local man, he had a bigger following in the area than the Divisional Officer Commanding.' McCurtin probably replaced McCormack after the Treaty.

APPENDIX XIII: IRB PARTICIPATION IN THE 1916 RISING

1 B. Mac Giolla Choille (ed.), *Intelligence Notes*, pp. 258–69; The Irish Times, *Sinn Féin Rebellion Handbook* (Dublin, 1917), pp. 69–86.

2 This list is drawn from the information given in the official list of those court-martialled in 1916. B. Mac Giolla Choille (ed.), *Intelligence Notes*, pp. 69–86.

3 These include both the 1,162 from the *Sinn Féin Rebellion Handbook*, and the 171 court-martialled and found guilty from the official list.

4 This percentage is calculated by taking the 110 farmers arrested in the countryside as a percentage of all those whose occupation was known, whether court-martialled or not.

SOURCES AND SELECT BIBLIOGRAPHY

Archives

British Library (BL)
British Newspaper Archive
Churchill College Archives Centre, Cambridge (CCAC)
Bureau of Military History (BMH) (Ireland)
Military Service Pensions Collection (Ireland)
National Archives (UK)
National Archives (Ireland)
National Library of Ireland (NLI)
National Museum of Ireland (NMI)
New York Public Library (NYPL)
Parliamentary Archives (London)
Trinity College, Dublin, Library (TCD)
University College, Dublin, Archives Department (UCD)

Particular Collections

Frank Aiken papers, UCD
C.S. (Todd) Andrews papers, UCD
Piaras Béaslaí papers, NLI
Caitlín Bean/Cathal Brugha papers, UCD
Gertrude Bloomer papers, NLI
Ernest Blythe papers, UCD
Col. Daniel Bryan papers, UCD
Sir Roger Casement papers, NLI
Éamon and Áine Ceannt papers, NLI
Erskine Childers papers, NLI
Sir Winston Churchill papers, CCAC
Michael Collins papers, UCD
Martin Conlon papers, UCD

Sources and Select Bibliography

W.T. Cosgrave papers, UCD
John A. Costello papers, UCD
Éamon de Valera papers, UCD
John Devoy papers, NLI
Geraldine Plunkett Dillon papers, NLI
John Dillon papers, TCD
George Gavan Duffy papers, NLI
George Fitzharding Berkeley papers, NLI
Desmond FitzGerald papers, NLI
Liam Gaynor papers, UCD
Oliver St John Gogarty papers, NLI
Arthur Griffith papers, NLI
Michael Hayes papers, UCD
Sean Heuston papers, NLI
Bulmer Hobson papers, NLI
Sighle Humphries papers, UCD
Douglas Hyde papers, NLI
Irish Republican Brotherhood papers, UCD
Peadar Kearney papers, TCD
Seán Lemass papers, UCD
Diarmuid Lynch papers, NLI
Thomas MacDonagh papers, NLI
Seán MacEntee papers, UCD
Seán MacEoin papers, UCD
Eoin MacNeill papers, NLI and UCD
Mary and Terence MacSwiney papers, NLI and UCD
Patrick J. Madden papers, NLI
William Maloney papers, NYPL
Constance Markievicz papers, NLI
Denis McCullough papers, UCD
Joseph McGarrity papers, NLI
Patrick McGilligan papers, UCD
Kathleen McKenna Napoli papers, NLI
Liam Mellows papers, NLI
Colonel Maurice Moore papers, NLI
Patrick Moylett papers, UCD
Richard Mulcahy papers, UCD

500 Sources and Select Bibliography

Art Ó Briain papers, NLI
William O'Brien papers, NLI
León Ó Broin papers, NLI
Patrick O'Daly papers, NLI
Florence O'Donoghue papers, NLI
Diarmuid O'Hegarty papers, UCD
Seán T. O'Kelly papers, NLI
Ernie O'Malley papers, UCD
Patrick Pearse papers, NLI
William Pearse papers, NLI
Joseph Mary Plunkett papers, NLI
John Redmond papers, NLI
Austin Stack papers, NLI and UCD
Maurice Twomey papers, UCD
Frank P. Walsh papers, NYPL

Publications

Andrews, C.S., *Dublin Made Me: An Autobiography* (Dublin, 1979)

Augusteijn, Joost, *From Public Defiance to Guerrilla Warfare: Experience of Ordinary Volunteers in the Irish War of Independence* (Dublin, 1996)

— (ed.), *The Irish Revolution 1913–23* (Basingstoke, 2002)

— (ed.), *Memoirs of John M. Regan, a Catholic Officer in the RIC and RUC 1909–48* (Dublin, 2007)

Barry, Tom, *Guerilla Days in Ireland* (Dublin, 1949)

— *The Reality of the Anglo-Irish War 1920–21 in West Cork: Refutations, Corrections and Comments on Liam Deasy's 'Towards Ireland Free'* (Tralee, 1974)

Bartlett, Thomas, *Ireland: A History* (Cambridge 2010)

— (ed.), *The Cambridge History of Ireland*, vol. iv (Cambridge, 2018)

— and Keith Jeffrey (eds), *A Military History of Ireland* (Cambridge, 1996)

Béaslaí, Piaras, *Michael Collins and the Making of a New Ireland* (Dublin, 1926)

— *Michael Collins: Soldier and Statesman* (Dublin, 1937)

Bell, J. Bowyer, *The Gun in Politics: Analysis of Irish Political Conflict, 1916–86* (London, 1987)

— *The Irish Troubles Since 1916* (New York, 2002)

— *The Secret Army: The IRA* (London, 2017)

Bew, Paul, *Ireland: The Politics of Enmity 1789–2006* (Oxford, 2007)

Sources and Select Bibliography

Biagini, Eugenio F., and Daniel Mulhall (eds), *The Shaping of Modern Ireland* (Dublin, 2016)

Biagini, Eugenio F., and Mary E. Daly (eds), *The Cambridge Social History of Modern Ireland* (Cambridge, 2017)

Borgonovo, John (ed.), *Florence and Josephine O'Donoghue's War of Independence* (Dublin, 2006)

— *Spies, Informers and the 'Anti-Sinn Féin Society': The Intelligence War in Cork City, 1920–1921* (Dublin, 2006)

— *The Dynamics of War and Revolution: Cork City 1916–1918* (Cork, 2013)

Bourke, Marcus, *John O'Leary* (Dublin, 2009)

Bourke, Richard and Ian McBride (eds), *The Princeton History of Modern Ireland* (Princeton and Oxford, 2016)

Bowman, Timothy, William Butler and Michael Wheatley, *The Disparity of Sacrifice: Irish Recruitment to the British Armed Forces, 1914–1918* (Liverpool, 2020)

Boyce, D. George, *Englishmen and Irish Troubles: British Public Opinion and the Making of Irish Policy, 1918–22* (London, 1972)

— (ed.), *The Revolution in Ireland, 1879–1923* (Basingstoke, 1988)

— *Nationalism in Ireland* (London, 1995)

— *The Irish Question and British Politics, 1868–1996* (Basingstoke, 1996)

— and Alan O'Day (eds), *The Making of Modern Irish History: Revisionism and the Revisionist Controversy* (London and New York, 1996)

Boyne, Sean, *Emmet Dalton: Somme Soldier, Irish General, Film Pioneer* (Dublin, 2014)

Breen, Dan, *My Fight for Irish Freedom* (Dublin, 1933)

Brendon, Piers, *The Decline and Fall of the British Empire, 1781–1997* (New York, 2008)

Brennan, Michael, *The War in Clare, 1911–21: Personal Memoirs of the Irish War of Independence* (Dublin, 1980)

Brennan, Robert, *Allegiance: An Account of the Author's Experiences in the Struggle for Irish Independence* (Dublin, 1950)

Brennan-Whitmore, W.J., *Dublin Burning: The Easter Rising from Behind the Barricades* (Dublin, 2013)

Breslin, John, and Sarah Anne Buckley, *Old Ireland in Colour* (Dublin, 2020)

Brown, Judith M., and Wm Roger Louis (eds), *The Oxford History of the British Empire: The Twentieth Century* (Oxford, 1999)

Browne, Noël, *Against the Tide* (Dublin, 2007)

Bowyer Bell, J., *The Secret Army: The IRA, 1916–70* (London, 2017)

502 Sources and Select Bibliography

Burnell, Tom, *26 County Casualties of the Great War* (Create Space Independent Publishing Platform, 2017)

Carden, Sheila, *The Alderman: Alderman Tom Kelly (1868–1942) and Dublin Corporation* (Dublin, 2007)

Carroll, F.M., *American Opinion on the Irish Question, 1910–1923. A Study in Opinion and Policy* (Dublin, 1978)

— *America and the Making of an Independent Ireland: A History* (New York, 2021)

Churchill, Winston S., *The World Crisis: The Aftermath*, vol. iv (London, 1923)

Clarke, Kathleen (ed. Helen Litton), *Revolutionary Woman* (Dublin, 2008)

Coleman, Marie, *County Longford and the Irish Revolution, 1910–1923* (Dublin, 2006)

Collins, Lorcan, *1916: The Rising Handbook* (Dublin, 2016)

— *Ireland's War of Independence 1919–21: The IRA's Guerrilla Campaign* (Dublin, 2019)

Collins, M.E., *Ireland, 1868–1966* (Dublin, 1993)

Collins, Michael (ed. Francis Costello), *In His Own Words* (Dublin, 1997)

— *The Path to Freedom* (Cork, 2018)

Collins, Peter, *Nationalism and Unionism: Conflict in Ireland in the Late Nineteenth and Early Twentieth Centuries* (Belfast, 1994)

Comerford, James J., *My Kilkenny IRA Days* (Kilkenny, 1978)

Comerford, Máire (ed. Hilary Dully), *On Dangerous Ground: A Memoir of the Irish Revolution* (Dublin, 2021)

Connell Jnr, Joseph E.A., *The Terror War: The Uncomfortable Realities of the War of Independence* (Dublin, 2021)

Connolly, James (ed. Desmond Ryan), *Labour and Easter Week* (Dublin, 1949)

Coogan, Tim Pat, *Michael Collins: A Biography* (London, 1991)

— *De Valera: Long Fellow, Long Shadow* (London, 1995)

— *Eamon de Valera, The Man Who Was Ireland* (New York, 1996)

Costello, Francis, *The Irish Revolution and its Aftermath, 1916–1923* (Dublin, 2003)

Costigan, Giovanni, *A History of Modern Ireland* (New York, 1969)

Cottrell, Peter, *The War for Ireland, 1913–1923* (Oxford, 2009)

Coulter, Carol, *The Hidden Tradition: Feminism Women and Nationalism in Ireland* (Cork, 1993)

Cronin, Seán, *The McGarrity Papers* (Tralee, 1972)

— *Our Own Red Blood; The Story of the 1916 Rising* (Dublin, 1976)

— *Frank Ryan: The Search for the Republic* (Dublin, 1977)

Sources and Select Bibliography

— *Irish Nationalism: A History of its Roots and Ideology* (Dublin, 1980)

Crowe, Catriona (ed.), *Guide to the Military Service (1916–1923) Pensions Collection* (Dublin, 2012)

Crowley, John, Donal Ó Drisceoil, Mike Murphy (eds) and John Borgonovo (ass. ed.), *Atlas of the Irish Revolution* (Cork, 2017)

Crozier, Frank, *Ireland Forever* (London, 1932)

Curran, Joseph M., *The Birth of the Irish Free State 1921–1923* (Alabama, 1980)

Czira, Sydney (John Brennan), *The Years Flew By* (Dublin, 1974)

Dáil Éireann Proceedings (1919–24)

Dalton, Charles, *With the Dublin Brigade* (London, 1929)

Dangerfield, George, *Damnable Question: Study in Anglo-Irish Relations* (London, 1977)

Davis, Richard P., *Arthur Griffith and Non-Violent Sinn Féin* (Tralee, 1974)

de Blaghd, Earnán (Ernest Blythe), *Trasna na Bóinne* (Dublin, 1957)

— *Slán le hUltaibh* (Dublin, 1970)

— *Gaeil à múscailt: Imleabhar III de chuimhní cinn* (Dublin, 1973)

de Lamartine, Alphonse, *Histoire de la Révolution de 1848* (Paris, 1849)

de Vere White, Terence, *Kevin O'Higgins* (Dublin, 1966)

Deasy, Liam (ed. John E. Chisholm), *Towards Ireland Free: The West Cork Brigade in the War of Independence 1917–1921* (Cork, 1973)

— *Brother Against Brother* (Cork, 1998)

Denieffe, Joseph, *Recollections of the Irish Revolutionary Brotherhood* (New York, 1906)

Department of Defence, *Chronology, 1913–21* (Dublin, 1952)

Devoy, John, *Recollections of an Irish Rebel* (New York, 1929)

— (eds William O'Brien, Desmond Ryan), *Devoy's Postbag, 1871–1928* (Toronto, 1979)

Dillon, Geraldine Plunkett (ed. Honor Ó Brolcháin), *All in the Blood* (Dublin, 2006)

Doherty, Gabriel, and Dermot Keogh (eds), *Michael Collins and the Making of the Irish State* (Cork, 1998)

— *1916: The Long Revolution* (Cork, 2007)

Dolan, Anne, *Commemorating the Irish Civil War: History and Memory 1923–2000* (Cambridge, 2003)

— and William Murphy, *Michael Collins: The Man and the Revolution* (Cork, 2018)

— *Days in the Life: Reading the Michael Collins Diaries 1918–1922* (Dublin, 2022)

Dooley, Terence, *The Irish Revolution 1912–23: Monaghan* (Dublin, 2017)

504 Sources and Select Bibliography

Dorney, John, *'Peace After the Final Battle': The Story of the Irish Revolution 1912–1924* (Dublin, 2013)

— *The Civil War in Dublin: The Fight for the Irish Capital, 1922–1924* (Dublin, 2017)

Dublin's Fighting Story: Told by the Men Who Made It (Cork, 2009)

Dudley Edwards, Owen, *Eamon de Valera* (Cardiff, 1987)

Dudley Edwards, Ruth, *Patrick Pearse: The Triumph of Failure* (London, 1977)

Dwyer, T. Ryle, *Michael Collins, 'The Man Who Won the War'* (Cork, 1990)

— *The Squad and the Intelligence Operations of Michael Collins* (Cork, 2005)

— *Big Fellow, Long Fellow: A Joint Biography of Collins and de Valera* (Dublin, 2006)

— *I Signed My Death Warrant: Michael Collins and the Treaty* (Cork, 2006)

Elliott, Marianne, *Wolfe Tone: Prophet of Irish Independence* (New Haven, 1992)

English, Richard, *Ernie O'Malley: IRA Intellectual* (Oxford, 1998)

— *Armed Struggle: The Story of the IRA* (Basingstoke, 2003)

— *Irish Freedom: The History of Nationalism in Ireland* (Basingstoke and Oxford, 2007)

Fanning, Ronan, *The Department of Finance, 1922–1958* (Dublin, 1978)

— *Fatal Path: British Government and Irish Revolution 1910–1922* (London, 2013)

— *A Will to Power* (London, 2015)

— and Michael Kennedy (eds), *Documents of Irish Foreign Policy, 1919–22* (Dublin, 1998)

Farrell, Brian (ed.), *The Creation of the Dáil* (Dublin, 1994)

Faught, C. Brad, *Cairo 1921: Ten Days That Made the Middle East* (Yale, 2022)

Feeney, Brian, *Seán MacDiarmada* (Dublin, 2014)

Ferriter, Diarmuid, *The Transformation of Ireland 1900–2000* (London, 2005)

— *Judging Dev: A Reassessment of the Life and Legacy of Eamon De Valera* (Dublin, 2007)

— *A Nation and Not a Rabble: The Irish Revolution 1913–1923* (London, 2015)

— *Between Two Hells: The Irish Civil War* (London, 2021)

Figgis, Darrell, *Recollections of the Irish War* (New York, 1927)

Fingall, Countess, *Seventy Years Young* (London, 1937)

FitzGerald, Desmond, *The Memoirs of Desmond FitzGerald* (London, 1968)

Fitzgerald, W.G. (ed.), *The Voice of Ireland, A Survey of the Race and Nation from All Angles* (Dublin, 1922)

Fitzpatrick, David, *Politics and Irish Life 1913–21: Provincial Experience of War and Revolution* (Dublin, 1977)

(ed.), *Revolution? Ireland 1917–1923* (Dublin, 1990)

Sources and Select Bibliography

— *The Two Irelands, 1912–1939* (Oxford, 1998)

— *Harry Boland's Irish Revolution* (Cork, 2004)

— (ed.), *Terror in Ireland 1916–23* (Dublin, 2012)

Foot, M.R.D., *SOE: The Special Operations Executive 1940–46* (London, 1984)

Forester, Margery, *Michael Collins* (London, 1971)

Foster, Roy, *Modern Ireland 1600–1972* (London, 1989)

— (ed.), *The Oxford History of Ireland* (Oxford, 2001)

— *Vivid Faces: The Revolutionary Generation in Ireland, 1890–1923* (London, 2015)

Foy, Michael T., *Michael Collins's Intelligence War: The Struggle Between the British and the IRA 1919–1921* (Stroud, 2006)

— *Thomas Clarke: The True Leader of the Easter Rising* (Dublin, 2014)

— *The Fenian Rising: James Stephens and the Irish Republican Brotherhood* (Cheltenham, 2023)

Friemann, Gretchen, *The Treaty: The Gripping Story of the Negotiations that Brought About Irish Independence and Led to the Civil War* (Dublin, 2021)

Gallagher, Niamh, *Ireland and the Great War: A Social and Political History* (London, 2020)

Gannon, Darragh, Brian Hanley, Tommy Graham, and Grace O'Keeffe (eds), *The Split: From Treaty to Civil War, 1921–23* (Dublin, 2022)

Garvin, Tom, *Nationalist Revolutionaries in Ireland 1858–1928* (Oxford, 1987)

— *1922: The Birth of Irish Democracy* (Dublin, 1996)

— *Preventing the Future: Why Was Ireland So Poor For So Long?* (Dublin, 2004)

— *The Evolution of Irish Nationalist Politics* (Dublin, 2005)

— Maurice Manning and Richard Sinnott (eds), *Dissecting Irish Politics: Essays in Honour of Brian Farrell* (Dublin, 2004)

Gaughan, J. Anthony, *The Memoirs of Constable Jeremiah Mee, RIC* (Dublin, 1975)

— *Austin Stack: Portrait of a Separatist* (Dublin, 1977)

Gillis, Liz, *The Hales Brothers and the Irish Revolution* (Cork, 2016)

Girvin, Kevin, *Seán O'Hegarty: Officer Commanding, First Cork Brigade, Irish Republican Army* (Cork, 2007)

Gleeson, James, *Bloody Sunday* (London, 1962)

Golway, Terry, *Irish Rebel: John Devoy and America's Fight for Ireland's Freedom* (London, 1998)

Gray, David (ed. Paul Bew), *A Yankee in de Valera's Ireland: The Memoir of David Gray* (Dublin, 2012)

Grayson, Richard S., *Dublin's Great Wars: The First World War, The Easter Rising and the Irish Revolution* (Cambridge, 2018)

506 Sources and Select Bibliography

Greaves, C. Desmond, *The Life and Times of James Connolly* (Dagenham, 1961)

— *Liam Mellows and the Irish Revolution* (London, 1971)

— *Theobald Wolfe Tone and the Irish Nation* (Colorado, 1992)

Gregory, Adrian, and Senia Pašeta (eds), *Ireland and the Great War: 'A War to Unite Us All'?* (Manchester, 2002)

Griffith, Arthur, *The Resurrection of Hungary: A Parallel for Ireland* (Dublin, 1918)

Griffith, Kenneth, and Timothy E. O'Grady, *Curious Journey: An Oral History of Ireland's Unfinished Revolution* (London, 1982)

Gwynn, Denis, *De Valera* (London, 1933)

Hanley, Brian, *The IRA: A Documentary History 1916–2005* (Dublin, 2010)

Hansard (1910–22), Parliament of the United Kingdom

Hart, Peter, *The IRA and its Enemies: Violence and Community in Cork 1916–1923* (Oxford, 1999)

— *British Intelligence in Ireland 1920–21: The Final Reports* (Cork, 2002)

— *Mick: The Real Michael Collins* (London, 2005)

Haydon, Anthony P., *Sir Matthew Nathan: British Colonial Governor and Civil Servant* (Queensland, 1976)

Herlihy, Jim, *The Black & Tans 1920–1921: A Complete Alphabetical List, Short History and Genealogical Guide* (Dublin, 2021)

Heuston, John M., *Headquarters Battalion* (Dublin, 1966)

Hill, J.R. (ed.), *A New History of Ireland, Volume VII: Ireland, 1921–84* (Oxford, 2010)

Hittle, J.B.E., *Michael Collins and the Anglo-Irish War: Britain's Counterinsurgency Failure* (Washington, D.C., 2012)

Hobson, Bulmer, *Defensive Warfare: A Handbook for Irish Nationalists* (Belfast, 1909)

— *A Short History of the Irish Volunteers* (Dublin, 1918)

— *Ireland Yesterday and Tomorrow* (Tralee, 1968)

Hogan, David, *The Four Glorious Years* (Dublin, 1971)

Holt, Edgar, *Protest in Arms: The Irish Troubles, 1916–23* (Dublin, 1960)

Hopkinson, Michael, *Green Against Green: The Irish Civil War* (Dublin, 1988)

— (ed.), *The Last Days of Dublin Castle: The Mark Sturgis Diaries* (Dublin, 1999)

— *The Irish War of Independence* (Dublin, 2004)

Horne, John (ed.), *Our War: Ireland and the Great War* (Dublin, 2008)

Hull, Eleanor, *A History of Ireland and Her People* (Oxford, 2010)

Jackson, Alvin, *Home Rule: An Irish History* (Oxford, 2003)

— *Ireland 1798–1998: War, Peace and Beyond* (Oxford, 2010)

Sources and Select Bibliography

— *The Oxford Handbook of Modern Irish History* (Oxford, 2014)

Jackson, Daniel M., *Popular Opposition to Irish Home Rule in Edwardian Britain* (Liverpool, 2009)

Jackson, T.A. (ed. C. Desmond Greaves), *Ireland Her Own: An Outline History of the Irish Struggle* (London, 1976)

James, Robert Rhodes (ed.), *Winston S. Churchill: His Complete Speeches* (New York, 1974)

Janis, E.M., *A Greater Ireland: The Land League and Transatlantic Nationalism in Gilded Age America* (Wisconsin, 2015)

Jeffery, Keith (ed.), *An Irish Empire? Aspects of Ireland and the British Empire* (Manchester, 1996)

— (ed.), *The Sinn Féin Rebellion as They Saw It* (Dublin, 1999)

— *Ireland and the Great War* (Cambridge, 2000)

— *Field Marshal Sir Henry Wilson: A Political Soldier* (Oxford, 2006)

— *1916 A Global History* (London, 2015)

Jones, Francis P., *History of the Sinn Féin Movement and the Irish Rebellion of 1916* (New York, 1917)

Jones, Thomas (ed. Keith Middlemass), *Whitehall Diary: Ireland 1918–1925*, vol. iii (Oxford, 1971)

Jordan, A.J., *Major John MacBride 1865–1916* (Westport, 1991)

Joyce, James, *Ulysses* (London, 2000)

Kautt, W.H., *Ambushes and Armour: The Irish Rebellion 1919–1921* (Dublin, 2010)

— *Ground Truths: British Army Operations in the Irish War of Independence* (Dublin, 2014)

— *Arming the Irish Revolution: Gunrunning and Arms Smuggling 1911–1922* (Kansas, 2021)

Kee, Robert, *The Green Flag* (London, 1972)

Kelly, M.J., *The Fenian Ideal and Irish Nationalism, 1882–1916* (Woodbridge, 2006)

Kenneally, Ian, *The Paper Wall: Newspapers and Propaganda in Ireland 1919–1921* (Cork, 2008)

Kenny, Colum, *The Enigma of Arthur Griffith, 'Father of Us All'* (Dublin, 2020)

Kiberd, Declan, *Inventing Ireland: The Literature of the Modern Nation* (London, 1995)

Kissane, Bill, *The Politics of the Irish Civil War* (Oxford, 2005)

Klieman, Aaron S., *Foundations of British Policy in the Arab World: the Cairo Conference of 1921* (Baltimore, 1970)

508 Sources and Select Bibliography

Kostick, Conor, *Revolution in Ireland: Popular Militancy, 1917–1922* (London, 1996)

Laffan, Michael, *The Partition of Ireland 1911–1925* (Dundalk, 1983)

— *The Resurrection of Ireland: The Sinn Féin Party, 1916–1923* (Cambridge, 1999)

— *Judging W.T. Cosgrave: The Foundation of the Irish State* (Dublin, 2014)

Larkin, Emmet, *The Roman Catholic Church and the Creation of the Modern Irish State, 1878–86* (Dublin, 1975)

Le Roux, Louis N., *Life of Thomas Clarke: Thomas Clarke and the Irish Freedom Movement* (Dublin, 1936)

Lecky, W.E.H., 'Ireland in the light of history', *Historical and Political Essays* (London, 1908)

Lee, Joseph J., *Ireland 1912–1985: Politics and Society* (Cambridge, 1989)

— *The Modernisation of Irish Society 1848–1918* (Dublin, 2008)

Leeson, D.M., *The Black & Tans: British Police and Auxiliaries in the Irish War of Independence* (Oxford, 2011)

Lewis, Matthew, *Frank Aiken's War: The Irish Revolution 1916–23* (Dublin, 2014)

Litton, Helen, *The Irish Civil War: An Illustrated History* (Dublin, 1995)

Lloyd George, David, *War Memoirs of David Lloyd George* (London, 1938)

Longford, The Earl of, and Thomas P. O'Neill, *Eamon de Valera* (Dublin, 1970)

Lynch, Diarmuid, *The I.R.B. and the 1916 Insurrection* (Cork, 1957)

Lynch, Robert, *The Northern IRA and the Early Years of Partition: 1920–1922* (Dublin, 2006)

— *Revolutionary Ireland, 1912–25* (London, 2015)

— *The Partition of Ireland 1918–1925* (Cambridge, 2019)

Lyons, F.S.L., *The Fall of Parnell 1890–1* (London, 1960)

— *John Dillon: a Biography* (London, 1968)

— *Ireland Since the Famine* (London, 1971)

Macardle, Dorothy, *The Irish Republic* (London, 1937)

MacCarthy, J.M. (ed.), *Limerick's Fighting Story* (Tralee, n.d.)

MacDonagh, Oliver, *Ireland: The Union and its Aftermath* (London, 1977)

MacEntee, Seán, *Episode at Easter* (Dublin, 1966)

MacEoin, Uinseann, *Survivors* (Dublin, 1980)

Mac Giolla Choille, B. (ed.), *Intelligence Notes, 1913–16* (Dublin, 1966)

Mackay, James A., *Michael Collins: A Life* (Edinburgh, 1996)

Macready, Sir Nevil, *Annals of an Active Life* (London, 1925)

Maher, Jim, *Harry Boland: A Biography* (Cork, 2020)

Mahon, Tom, *The Ballycotton Job* (Cork, 2022)

Sources and Select Bibliography

Mansergh, Nicholas, *The Irish Question, 1840–1921* (London, 1975)

— *The Commonwealth Experience: The Durham Report to the Anglo-Irish Treaty*, vol. i (London, 1982)

Martin, F.X. (ed.), *Leaders and Men of the Easter Uprising: Dublin 1916* (London, 1967)

— *The Irish Volunteers 1913–15: Recollections & Documents* (Dublin, 1963)

Martin, Harry F., and Cormac O'Malley, *Ernie O'Malley: A Life* (Dublin, 2021)

Matthew, H.C.G., and Brian Harrison (eds), *Oxford Dictionary of National Biography* (Oxford, 2004)

Matthews, Ann, *Renegades: Irish Republican Women 1900–1922* (Cork, 2010)

McAuliffe, Mary, and Liz Gillis, *Richmond Barracks 1916: We Were There, 77 Women of the Easter Rising* (Dublin, 2016)

McCartan, Patrick, *With de Valera in America* (New York, 1932)

McCarthy, Cal, *Cumann na mBan and the Irish Revolution* (Cork, 2014)

McColgan, John, *British Policy and the Irish Administration 1920–22* (London, 1983)

McCoole, Sinéad, *No Ordinary Women: Irish Female Activists in the Revolutionary Years 1900–1923* (Dublin, 2015)

McCracken, J.L., *Representative Government in Ireland, 1919–48* (Dublin, 1958)

McCullagh, David, *De Valera: Rise 1882–1932* (Dublin, 2017)

McElligott, Richard (ed.), *A Social and Cultural History of Sport in Ireland* (London, 2018)

McGarry, Fearghal, *Eoin O'Duffy: A Self-Made Hero* (Oxford, 2005)

— *Rebels: Voices from the Easter Rising* (Dublin, 2011)

— *The Rising: Ireland Easter 1916* (Oxford, 2016)

— and James McConnel (eds), *The Black Hand of Republicanism: Fenianism in Modern Ireland* (Dublin, 2009)

McGee, Owen, *The IRB: The Irish Republican Brotherhood from the Land League to Sinn Féin* (Dublin, 2007)

McGough, Eileen, *Diarmuid Lynch: A Forgotten Irish Patriot* (Cork, 2013)

McGreevy, Ronan, *Great Hatred: The Assassination of Field Marshal Sir Henry Wilson MP* (London, 2022)

McGuire, James, and James Quinn (eds), *Dictionary of Irish Biography* (Cambridge, 2018)

McKenna, Joseph, *Guerrilla Warfare in the Irish War of Independence, 1919–1921* (Jefferson, 2010)

McMahon, Paul, *British Spies and Irish Rebels: British Intelligence and Ireland, 1916–1945* (Woodbridge, 2008)

510 Sources and Select Bibliography

McNamara, Conor, *War and Revolution in the West of Ireland: Galway 1913–1922* (Dublin, 2018)

McNulty, Liam, *James Connolly: Socialist, Nationalist and Internationalist* (London, 2023)

Meleady, Dermot, *John Redmond: The National Leader* (Dublin, 2013)

— (ed.), *John Redmond: Selected Letters and Memoranda, 1880–1918* (Dublin, 2018)

Miller, David W., *Church, State and Nation in Ireland* (Dublin, 1973)

Miller, Kerby, *Emigrants and Exiles: Ireland and the Irish Exodus to North America* (Oxford, 1985)

Mitchell, Arthur, *Labour in Irish Politics, 1890–1930* (Dublin, 1973)

— *Revolutionary Government in Ireland: Dáil Éireann 1919–22* (Dublin, 1995)

— and Padraig Ó Snodaigh (eds), *Irish Political Documents, 1916–1949* (Dublin, 1985)

Molyneux, Derek, and Darren Kelly, *Killing at Its Very Extreme. Dublin: October 1917–November 1920* (Cork, 2020)

— *Someone Has to Die for This – Dublin: November 1920–July 1921* (Cork, 2021)

Moody, T.W. (ed.), *The Fenian Movement* (Cork, 1978)

— and F.X. Martin (eds), *The Course of Irish History* (Cork, 1967)

Moynihan, Maurice (ed.), *Speeches and Statements by Éamon de Valera, 1917–1973* (Dublin, 1980)

Mulcahy, Risteárd, *Richard Mulcahy (1886–1971): A Family Memoir* (Dublin, 1999)

— *My Father, the General: Richard Mulcahy and the Military History of the Revolution* (Dublin, 2009)

Murphy, Brian P., *John Chartres: Mystery Man of the Treaty* (Cambridge, 1995)

Murphy, John A., *Ireland in the Twentieth Century* (Dublin, 1975)

— and J.P. O'Carroll (eds), *De Valera and His Times* (Cork, 1983)

Neeson, Eoin, *The Life and Death of Michael Collins* (Cork, 1968)

— *The Civil War 1922–23* (Dublin, 1989)

Nicholson, David, *Crisis of the British Empire: Turning Points After 1880* (Somerset, 2017)

Noonan, Gerard, *The IRA in Britain, 1919–1923* (Liverpool, 2014)

Norman, Edward R., *The Catholic Church and Ireland in The Age of Rebellion, 1859–73* (London, 1965)

Nowlan, Kevin B. (ed.), *The Making of 1916: Studies in the History of the Rising* (Dublin, 1969)

Sources and Select Bibliography 511

O'Beirne Ranelagh, John, *A Short History of Ireland* (Cambridge, 2012)

O'Brien, Conor Cruise (ed.), *The Shaping of Modern Ireland* (London, 1960)

O'Brien, William (ed. Edward MacLysaght), *Forth the Banners Go* (Dublin, 1969)

Ó Broin, Leon, *Dublin Castle and the 1916 Rising* (London, 1970)

— *Revolutionary Underground: The Story of the Irish Republican Brotherhood, 1858–1924* (Dublin, 1976)

— *Michael Collins* (Dublin, 1991)

Ó Caoimh, Pádraig, *Richard Mulcahy: From the Politics of War to the Politics of Peace, 1913–1924* (Dublin, 2019)

Ó Ceallaigh, Seán T. (ed. Proinsias Ó Conluain; trans. Pádraig Ó Fiannachta), *Seán T.* (Dublin, 1972)

O'Connor, Batt, *With Michael Collins in the Fight for Irish Independence* (London, 1929)

O'Connor, Frank (Michael O'Donovan), *The Big Fellow* (Dublin, 1965)

— *An Only Child* (London, 1968)

O'Connor, Ulick, *Michael Collins and the Troubles: The Struggle for Irish Freedom 1912–1922* (Edinburgh, 2001)

Ó Corráin, Daithí, and Gerard Hanley, *Cathal Brugha: 'An Indomitable Spirit'* (Dublin, 2022)

O'Donnell, Peadar, *The Gates Flew Open* (Cork, 1965)

— *Not Yet Emmet: A Wreath on the Grave of Seán Murray* (Belfast, 2009)

O'Donoghue, Florence, *No Other Law* (Dublin, 1954)

— *Tomás MacCurtain* (Tralee, 1958)

O'Farrell, Padraic, *Who's Who in the Irish War of Independence and Civil War 1916–1923* (Dublin, 1997)

Ó Fathaigh, Pádraig (ed. Timothy G. McMahon), *Pádraig Ó Fathaigh's War of Independence: Recollections of a Galway Gaelic Leaguer* (Cork, 2000)

Ó Fathartaigh, Mícheál, and Liam Weeks, *Birth of a State: The Anglo-Irish Treaty* (Dublin, 2021)

O'Gadhra, Nollaig, *Civil War in Connacht, 1922–23* (Cork, 1999)

Ó Gaora, Colm (trans. Mícheál Ó hAodha; eds Ruán O'Donnell and Mícheál Ó hAodha), *On the Run: The Story of an Irish Freedom Fighter* (Cork, 2011)

O'Halpin, Eunan, *Decline of the Union: British Government Ireland* (Syracuse, 1989)

— *Head of the Civil Service: Biography of Sir Warren Fisher* (London, 1989)

— *Defending Ireland: The Irish State and Its Enemies Since 1922* (Oxford, 1999)

— *Kevin Barry: An Irish Rebel in Life and Death* (Dublin, 2020)

512   Sources and Select Bibliography

— and Daithí Ó Corráin, *The Dead of the Irish Revolution* (New Haven, 2020)

O'Hegarty, P.S., *Victory of Sinn Féin: How It Won It and How It Used It* (Dublin, 1924)

— *A History of Ireland under the Union* (London, 1952)

O'Mahony, Seán, *Frongoch: University of Revolution* (Dublin, 1995)

O'Malley, Cormac, *Modern Ireland and Revolution: Ernie O'Malley in Context* (Dublin, 2016)

O'Malley, Ernie (ed. Cormac O'Malley), *Rising Out: Seán Connolly of Longford (1890–1921)* (Dublin, 2007)

— *The Singing Flame* (Cork, 2012)

— (eds Cormac O'Malley and Tim Horan), *The Men Will Talk to Me: Kerry Interviews by Ernie O'Malley* (Cork, 2012)

— *On Another Man's Wound* (Cork, 2013)

— (ed. Cormac O'Malley), *The Men Will Talk to Me: Galway Interviews by Ernie O'Malley* (Cork, 2013)

— (eds Cormac O'Malley and Vincent Keogh), *The Men Will Talk to Me: Mayo Interviews by Ernie O'Malley* (Cork, 2014)

— (ed. Andy Bielenberg, John Borgonovo and Pádraig Óg Ó Ruairc), *The Men Will Talk to Me: West Cork Interviews by Ernie O'Malley* (Cork, 2015)

— (ed. Pádraig Óg Ó Ruairc), *The Men Will Talk to Me: Clare Interviews by Ernie O'Malley* (Cork, 2016)

— (eds Síobhra Aiken, Fearghal Mac Bhloscaidh, Liam Ó Duibhir and Diarmuid Ó Tuama), *The Men Will Talk to Me: Ernie O'Malley's Interviews with the Northern Divisions* (Dublin, 2018)

Ó Maoileoin, Séamas, *B'fhiú an Braon Fola* (Dublin, 1958)

Ó Riain, Seán, *Provos: Patriots or Terrorists?* (Dublin, 1974)

Ó Ruairc, Pádraig Óg, *Truce: Murder, Myths and the Last Days of the Irish War of Independence* (Cork, 2016)

Ó Snodaigh, Pádraig (Oliver Snoddy), *Comhghuaillithe na Reabhloide, 1913–1916* (Dublin, 1966)

O'Sullivan Greene, Patrick, *Crowdfunding the Revolution: The First Dáil Loan and the Battle for Irish Independence* (Dublin, 2020)

— *Revolution at the Waldorf: America and the Irish War of Independence* (Dublin, 2022)

Ó Tuathaigh, Gearóid (ed.), *The GAA and Revolution in Ireland 1913–1923* (Cork, 2015)

Pašeta, Senia, *Irish Nationalist Women, 1900–1918* (Cambridge, 2016)

Sources and Select Bibliography

— (ed.), *Uncertain Futures: Essays About the Irish Past for Roy Foster* (Oxford, 2016)

Pakenham, Frank, *Peace by Ordeal: The Negotiation of the Anglo-Irish Treaty, 1921* (London, 1967)

Pearse, Patrick H., *Political Writings and Speeches* (Dublin, 1924)

Picture Souvenir, 1916: The Sinn Féin Rebellion (Belfast, 1916)

Pollard, H.B.C., *The Secret Societies of Ireland* (London, 1922)

Price, Dominic, *We Bled Together: Michael Collins, The Squad and the Dublin Brigade* (Cork, 2017)

Pritchett, Georgia, *My Mess is a Bit of a Life* (London, 2021)

Rast, M.C., *Shaping Ireland's Independence: Nationalist, Unionist and British Solutions to the Irish Question, 1909–1925* (London, 2019)

Reid, B.L., *The Lives of Roger Casement* (New Haven and London, 1976)

Regan, John M., *The Irish Counter-Revolution 1921–36: Treatyite Politics and Settlement in Independent Ireland* (Dublin, 1999)

— *Myth and the Irish State* (Dublin, 2013)

Report of the Commission on Emigration and other Population Problems, 1948–54 (Dublin, 1954)

Richardson, Neil, *According to their Lights: Stories of Irishmen in the British Army, Easter 1916* (Cork, 2015)

Ryan, Desmond, *Michael Collins* (Dublin, 1932)

— *Remembering Zion* (London, 1934)

— *Seán Treacy and the Third Tipperary Brigade I.R.A.* (Tralee, 1946)

— *The Rising* (Dublin, 1949)

— *The Fenian Chief: A Biography of James Stephens* (Dublin, 1967)

Ryan, Louise, *Irish Women and Nationalism: Soldiers, New Women and Wicked Hags* (Dublin, 2019)

Ryan, Meda, *Michael Collins and the Women Who Spied for Ireland* (Cork, 2006)

Searle, G.R., *A New England? Peace and War 1886–1918* (Oxford, 2004)

Sheehan, William, *British Voices, From the Irish War of Independence 1918–1921: The Words of British Servicemen Who Were There* (Cork, 2005)

Sinn Féin Minute Book (NLI, 1919)

Sisley, Logan, R.F. Foster, Michael Laffan, Margarita Cappock, Barbara Dawson and P.J. Mathews, *Revolutionary States: Home Rule and Modern Ireland* (Dublin, 2012)

Smith, Jeremy, *The Tories and Ireland 1910–1914: Conservative Party Politics and the Home Rule Crisis* (Dublin, 2001)

Speake, Jennifer (ed.), *Oxford Dictionary of Proverbs* (Oxford, 2015)

514 Sources and Select Bibliography

Stephens, James, *The Insurrection in Dublin* (Dublin and London, 1916)

Stewart, A.T.Q. (ed.), *Michael Collins: The Secret File* (Belfast, 1998)

Street, C.J.C., *Ireland in 1921* (London, 1922)

Sylvester, A.J., *The Real Lloyd George* (London, 1947)

Taillon, Ruth, *The Women of 1916: When History Was Made* (Dublin, 2018)

Taylor, A.J.P., *English History 1914–1945* (Oxford, 1965)

— (ed.), *Lloyd George: Twelve Essays* (New York, 1971)

Taylor, Rex, *Michael Collins* (Dublin, 1961)

The Irish Times, *Sinn Féin Rebellion Handbook* (Dublin, 1917)

The Oxford Dictionary of Proverbs (Oxford, 2008)

Tobin, Liam (foreword), *The Truth About the Army Crisis* (Dublin, 1924)

Tone, Theobald Wolfe (ed. Thomas Bartlett), *Life of Theobald Wolfe Tone* (Dublin, 1998)

Townshend, Charles, *The British Campaign in Ireland 1919–1921: The Development of Political and Military Policies* (Oxford, 1975)

— *Political Violence in Ireland: Government and Resistance Since 1848* (Oxford, 1983)

— *Ireland: The 20th Century* (London, 1999)

— *Easter 1916: The Irish Rebellion* (London, 2005)

— *The Republic: The Fight for Irish Independence* (London, 2013)

— *The Partition: Ireland Divided, 1885–1925* (London, 2021)

Toye, Richard, *Lloyd George and Churchill: Rivals for Greatness* (London, 2007)

Travers, Rev. Charles J., *Sean MacDiarmada 1883–1916* (Cavan, 1966)

Turner, John, *Lloyd George's Secretariat* (Cambridge, 1980)

Twohig, Patrick J., *Blood on the Flag: Autobiography of a Freedom Fighter* (Cork, 1996)

Valiulis, Maryann Gialanella, *Portrait of a Revolutionary: General Richard Mulcahy and the Founding of the Irish Free State* (Dublin, 1992)

— *Almost a Rebellion: Irish Army Mutiny of 1924* (Cork, 1985)

— *Gender and Power in Irish History* (Dublin, 2008)

Van Voris, J., *Constance de Markievicz: In the Cause of Ireland* (Amherst, 1967)

Vaughan, W.E. (ed.), *A New History of Ireland: Volume VI: Ireland under the Union, II: 1870–1921* (Oxford, 1996)

Walker, Brian M., *Irish History Matters* (Stroud, 2019)

Walsh, Maurice, *The News from Ireland: Foreign Correspondents and the Irish Revolution* (London, 2008)

Ward, Alan J., *Ireland and Anglo-American Relations* (London, 1969)

Sources and Select Bibliography 515

Whyte, John Henry, *Church and State in Modern Ireland 1923–70* (New York, 1971)

Williams, T. Desmond (ed.), *The Irish Struggle, 1916–1926* (London, 1966)

— (ed.), *Secret Societies in Ireland* (Dublin, 1973)

Wilson, David. A. (ed.), *The Orange Order in Canada* (Dublin, 2007)

Woodward, David R., *Lloyd George and the Generals* (London, 2004)

Younger, Calton, *Ireland's Civil War* (London, 1968)

— *A State of Disunion: Arthur Griffith, Michael Collins, James Craig, Eamon de Valera* (London, 1972)

Articles and Other Sources

Akenson, D.H., and J.F. Fallin, 'The Irish Civil War and the drafting of the Free State constitution', *Éire-Ireland* (Winter 1970)

Béaslaí, Piaras, 'A nation in revolt', *Irish Independent*, 8 and 12–16 January, 4–5 February, 7 June 1953

— 'Memoirs', *Irish Independent*, 13–15 May 1957

Biagini, Eugenio F., 'The Protestant minority in Southern Ireland', *The Historical Journal*, vol. 55, iss. 4 (December 2012)

Bielenberg, Andy, 'Exodus: The emigration of Southern Irish Protestants during the Irish War of Independence and the Civil War', *Past and Present*, no. 218 (February 2013)

Callinan, Elaine Marie, 'Electioneering and propaganda in Ireland, 1917–1920', Dissertation for the degree of Doctor in Philosophy (TCD, 2017)

Capuchin Annual, 1966

Carey, Tim, and Marcus de Búrca, 'Bloody Sunday 1920: new evidence', *History Ireland*, vol. 11, iss. 2 (Summer 2003)

Choi, Seokmoo, 'Joyce's representation of Ireland as a partner in the British Empire', *The Wenshan Review of Literature and Culture*, vol. 12, no. 2 (June 2019)

Cusack, Michael, 'A word about Irish athletics', *The Irishman*, 11 October 1884

Devoy, Fiona, 'The Mansion House conference: Ireland's "First National Cabinet"', *University of Limerick History Society Journal*, vol. 9 (2008)

Dore, Éamonn, 'An Easter Rising memoir by Éamonn de hÓir', *The Old Limerick Journal*, vol. 50 (2016)

Dorney, John, 'The Army Mutiny of 1924 and the opening of the Army inquiry papers', *The Irish Story*, 17 December 2019, www.theirishstory.com/2019/12/17

Evans, Gary, 'The raising of the First Internal Dáil Éireann Loan and the British responses to it, 1919–21', M. Litt. thesis (National University of Ireland, Maynooth, 2012)

Farrell, Brian, 'A note on the Dáil Constitution, 1919', *Irish Jurist*, vol. iv, new series, part 1 (Summer 1969)

Farrell, Liam, 'The Tommy Gun – the Irish connection', *History Ireland*, vol. 8, iss. 4 (Winter 2000)

Fitzpatrick, David, 'The geography of Irish nationalism', *Past and Present*, vol. 78 (February 1978)

Fitzpatrick, Seán, 'The Third Tipperary Brigade', *The Nationalist*, 16 November 1957

Ferriter, Diarmaid, 'Drink and society in twentieth-century Ireland', *Proceedings of the Royal Irish Academy*, vol. 115C (2015)

— 'Black and Tans: "Half-drunk, whole-mad" and one-fifth Irish', *The Irish Times*, 4 January 2020

Glennon, Kieran, 'The dead of the Belfast Pogrom – counting the cost of the revolutionary period, 1920–22', *The Irish Story*, 20 October 2020, www.theirishstory.com/2020/10/27

Hanley, Brian, '"Moderates and peacemakers": Irish historians in the revolutionary century', *Irish Economic and Social History*, vol. 43(1) (2016)

Hart, Peter, 'Michael Collins and the assassination of Sir Henry Wilson', *Irish Historical Studies*, vol. 28, no. 110 (November 1992)

Hay, Marnie, 'The foundation and development of Na Fianna Éireann, 1909–16', *Irish Historical Studies*, vol. xxxvi, no. 141 (May 2008)

— 'Kidnapped: Bulmer Hobson, the IRB and the 1916 Insurrection', *The Canadian Journal of Irish Studies*, vol. 35, no. 1 (Spring 2009)

Hennessy, P.J., and Jim Maher, from notes left by Thomas Treacy, Jim DeLoughry, Jim Byrne V.E.C. and Peter DeLoughry, 'The Irish Volunteers in Kilkenny in 1916', https://kec1916project.files.wordpress.com/2015/01/the-irish-volunteers-in-kilkenny-in-1916.pdf

Hogan, David, 'Books from my shelves', *Sunday Press*, 17 January 1960

Kennedy, Dennis, 'An "Independence Day" for Ireland?', *History Ireland*, vol. 26, iss. 3 (May–June 2018)

Kennedy, Cmdt Padraic, 'Key appointments and the transition of the Irish Volunteers, the Irish Republican Army and the National Army (1913–23)', *Defence Forces Review 2016* (Dublin, 2016)

Kenny, Mary, 'Michael Collins' religious faith', *Irish Historical Studies*, vol. 96, no. 334 (Winter 2007)

Sources and Select Bibliography

Kline, Benjamin, 'Churchill and Collins 1919–22: Admirers or adversaries?', *History Ireland*, vol. 1, iss. 3 (Autumn 1993)

Laffan, Michael, 'The unification of Sinn Féin in 1917', *Irish Historical Studies*, vol. xvii, no. 67 (March 1971)

Leeson, David, 'Death in the afternoon: The Croke Park massacre, 21 November 1920', *Canadian Journal of History*, vol. 38, iss. 1 (Spring 2003)

Lowe, W.J., 'The Lancashire Irish and the Catholic Church, 1846–71: The social dimension', *Irish Historical Studies*, vol. 20, no. 78 (September 1976)

MacMahon, Deirdre, 'A worthy monument to a great man: Piaras Béaslaí's *Life of Michael Collins*', *Bullán: An Irish Studies Journal* (Spring–Summer 1996)

Mandle, W.F., 'The IRB and the beginnings of the Gaelic Athletic Association', *Irish Historical Studies*, vol. 20, no. 80 (September 1977)

Martin, F.X., 'The 1916 Rising: A "coup d'état" or a "bloody protest"?', *Studia Hibernica*, no. 8 (1968)

— and Eoin MacNeill, 'Eoin MacNeill on the 1916 Rising', *Irish Historical Studies*, vol. 12, no. 47 (March 1961)

Martin, Gabriel, 'North Leitrim Sinn Féin election', *Leitrim Guardian* (Christmas 1968)

McCartney, Donal, 'The Church and the Fenians', *University Review*, vol. 4, no. 3, Special Fenian Issue (Winter 1967)

McInerney, Michael, 'Gerry Boland's story', *The Irish Times*, 9 October 1968

Meehan, Niall, 'Top people', *Dublin Review of Books* (May 2010)

Moody, T.W., and Leon Ó Broin, 'The I.R.B. Supreme Council, 1868–78', *Irish Historical Studies*, vol. 19, no. 75 (March 1975)

Morris, Richard Knowles, 'John P. Holland and the Fenians', *Journal of the Galway Archaeological and Historical Society*, vol. 31, no. 1/2 (1964/1965)

Mulcahy, Risteárd, 'Mulcahy and Collins – a conjunction of opposites', *History Ireland*, vol. 16, iss. 6 (November–December 2008)

Murray, Daniel, 'To not fade away: The Irish Republican Brotherhood, post-1916', https://erinascendantwordpress.wordpress.com/2016/01/13/to-not-fade-away-the-irish-republican-brotherhood-post-1916/

— '"This splendid historic organisation": The Irish Republican Brotherhood among the Anti-Treatyites, 1921–4', https://erinascendantwordpress.wordpress.com/2016/01/19/this-splendid-historic-organisation-the-irish-republican-brotherhood-among-the-anti-treatyites-1921-4/

— 'Career conspirators: The (mis)adventures of Seán Ó Muirthile and the Irish Republican Brotherhood in the Free State Army, 1923–4', https://

518 Sources and Select Bibliography

erinascendantwordpress.wordpress.com/2016/02/13/career-conspirators-the-misadventures-of-sean-o-muirthile-and-the-irish-republican-brotherhood-in-the-free-state-army-1923-4/

— 'The elephant in the revolutionary room: The Irish Republican Brotherhood and its (maybe, perhaps, possible) role in the Irish struggle, 1917–24', https://erinascendantwordpress.wordpress.com/2021/10/15/the-elephant-in-the-revolutionary-room-the-irish-republican-brotherhood-and-its-maybe-perhaps-possible-role-in-the-irish-struggle-1917-24/

Novak, Rose, '"Keepers of important secrets": The Ladies' Committee of the IRB', *History Ireland*, vol. 16, iss. 6 (November–December 2008)

Ó Beacháin, Donnacha, 'From guns to government: The IRA in Context', *Studies of Transition States and Societies*, vol. 6, iss. 1 (2014)

O'Beirne Ranelagh, John, 'The I.R.B. from the Treaty to 1924', *Irish Historical Studies*, vol. 20, no. 77 (March 1976)

Ó Drisceoil, Donal, 'The victory of Sinn Féin: The 1920 local elections', www.ucc.ie/en/theirishrevolution/collections/mapping-the-irishrevolution/the victory-of-sinn-fein-the-1920-local-elections/

O'Halloran, Michael, 'Perilous days', *Sunday Press*, 17 January 1960

O'Kelly, Séamus G., 'Memoirs', *The Nationalist*, 24 March 1956

— 'Memoirs', *The Kerryman*, 8 April 1961

O'Kelly, Seán T., 'Memoirs', *The Irish Press*, 7–14 July 1961

Ó Lúing, Seán, 'Bulmer Hobson', *The Irish Times*, 6 May 1971

Regan, John M., 'Southern Irish nationalism as a historical problem', *The Historical Journal*, vol. 50, no. 1 (2007)

— 'Michael Collins, General Commanding-in-Chief, as a historiographical problem', *History*, vol. 92, no. 3 (2007)

Sloan, Geoffrey, 'Hide seek and negotiate: Alfred Cope and counter intelligence', *Intelligence and National Security*, vol. 33, no. 2 (2018)

Staunton, Enda, 'Reassessing Michael Collins's Northern policy', *Irish Studies Review*, 20 (Autumn 1997)

Thomas, Jim, 'Theory, method and the Irish Revolution', *Social Studies*, vol. iii, no. 4 (September 1974)

Tobin, Padraig, 'The Third Tipperary Brigade', *The Nationalist*, 9, 16, 23, 30 November 1957

Townshend, Charles, 'The Irish Republican Army and the development of guerrilla warfare, 1916–1921', *The English Historical Review*, vol. 94, no. 371 (April 1979)

Travers, Rev. Charles J., 'Seán Mac Diarmada, 1883–1916', *Breifne*, vol. iii, no. 9 (1966)

Yeates, Padraig, 'Michael Collins' "Secret Service Unit" in the Trade Union movement', *History Ireland*, vol. 22, no. 3 (May–June 2014)

ACKNOWLEDGEMENTS

This book began in 1970. My father was most of all responsible, sharing his contacts, enthusiasm and knowledge.

Over the decades since there are several people I wish particularly to thank, especially my wife, Elizabeth, without whose support, encouragement, forbearance and love I doubt if this book would have materialised. I owe a great debt to Michael J. Murphy who spent many hours discussing and moderating British and nationalist arguments and perceptions, and to Charles Townshend who helped shape the book and advised about organising the story. Christopher Andrew gave constant encouragement and was a stimulating sounding board. Micky Joe Costello identified documents in the Mulcahy archive and dispassionately analysed Civil War issues. Liam Deasy and Seán Fitzpatrick went to great trouble to establish facts; Seán told me where IRA documents dating from 1921–23 were hidden; Liam spent hours discussing the IRB and introduced me to many of his old colleagues. Timothy Dickinson as ever has been full of insight and analysis. Robert (Robin) Dudley Edwards gave me shelter at the UCD Archives Department while I was engaged in my research – and took me drinking at a pub across Stephen's Green where, after two or three occasions, I arranged with the barman to have ginger ale instead of whiskey but to be charged as if it was whiskey. Dudley subsequently was amazed by my consumption ability! Alexander Hawthorne, my brother-in-law, alerted me to points that needed clarification. Ronan Fanning read my PhD thesis and provided twelve pages of notes and comments. Stephen Hopkins made several points about the structure of the book that I have incorporated. Leland Lyons, my PhD supervisor, was a constant support. Risteárd Mulcahy opened his father's archive to me without which I would not have been able to complete my work. Joseph O'Doherty spent many days describing and discussing men and women of the period and his own role as a TD and member of the Volunteer/IRA Executive. Eunan O'Halpin cut through a mist of convention with clear insights, and actively helped me in research. Ivar Steen-Johnsen and Robert Tombs pointed out ways to make the complexity of the IRB story more accessible

Acknowledgements 521

Todd Andrews, despite an animosity towards my father, gave me his time, recollections and insights. Mariana Bonnouvrier identified Adrian Beatty's website. Jennifer Brady and Laura Carpenter helped track down a difficult reference. Maeve Casserly checked many of my archive references, bringing their cataloguing up to date. T. Desmond Williams' 'open house' was always stimulating. Terence Dormer explained the nature of the Commonwealth and Ireland's place in it. Síle Dudley Edwards translated Irish texts for me and added valuable comments. Niamh Gallagher kindly gave me a number of periodical sources that otherwise I might have missed. Ben Hanly, Jonathan King, Andrew Park, Mark Robinson and Norman Stone discussed Irish themes – Mark introduced me to Terence Dormer. Maurice Hussey painstakingly transcribed several of my recorded interviews. Joe Lee told me the most important word in an historian's lexicon: 'about'. David Leeson gave guidance on Black and Tan and Auxiliary data. Peter Martland recommended sources and clarifications. Deirdre McMahon over several decades encouraged me to write this book. F.X. Martin gave me transcripts of interviews he had conducted with IRB members. Eve Morrison shared thoughts about Kilmichael, Tom Barry and Liam Deasy. Allen Packwood introduced me to the 1921 Cairo Conference and Winston Churchill's thinking at the time. Geoffrey Sloan gave his time and knowledge over an afternoon discussing Alfred Cope and British Intelligence. Pádraig Ó Snodaigh generously translated his work and shared his research. A.T.Q. Stewart was similarly generous and insightful about unionism and sectarian differences. Rod Stoneman encouraged my opening sentence and commented on various assertions. Marcus Sweeney tried to discover more information about Noel Keating who designed the stone surround of the Wolfe Tone statue in Dublin's Stephen's Green, meeting with as little success as I did. Peter Will contributed design ideas.

More generally, I thank the staff at Cambridge University Library who fetched books and journals during the Covid lockdown years, making researching this book easier and swifter. And Mary Feehan, officer commanding Mercier Press, Cork, for her generosity and for determinedly publishing – among many other books – seventy of Ernie O'Malley's invaluable interviews, making accessible transcriptions by the man himself that are almost indecipherable.

The assembled team at Irish Academic Press – Conor Graham, Patrick O'Donoghue (who survived my attempts to give him a heart attack) and Wendy Logue, and editors Jennifer Brady and Heidi Houlihan, proofreader Sean Farrell and indexer Fiachra McCarthy – were straightforward, knowledgeable,

522 Acknowledgements

supportive and helpful with clarifications and suggestions – and correcting all those tetchy things that get in the way of a good story. The speed with which the Press went into action was stunning. I am honoured that this book is among its extensive range of publications.

My conclusions are my own.

Several teachers at the Cambridgeshire College of Arts and Technology (now Anglia Ruskin University) – a most remarkable and excellent institution shaped and maintained by Derek Mumford – set me on this path: Maurice Hussey, George James, Sidney Bolt, Bill Greenwell, John Tyler, Stephanie Plackett, John Wilkinson, Harry Browne, Robert Murray, Tom Sharpe and Hubert Webb. Their enthusiasm – and Tom's languid approach – I remember with fondness and appreciation.

INDEX

Abbey Theatre, xv, 205
abstentionism, ix, xxiv
Ackerman, Carl, 246
Active Service Unit, 156, 168, 199, 215
Aiken, Frank, 268, 299, 324, 390
Allgood, Sara, 205
All in the Blood, xxv
Allan, Fred, 64, 155, 382, 383
Allen, William, 23, 67
An t-Óglách, 218
Ancient Order of Hibernians, ix, 23, 61, 76
Andrews, Todd, 322, 324
arms shipments (*see also* Clan na Gael),
    106–8, 230–1, 237–8
Army Mutiny: British Army officers, 306,
    307; causes, 20, 306–7; Charles Dalton,
    308–9; Dáil inquiry, 309; demobilisation,
    307, 308; description, ix; Frank Thornton,
    306–7; Kevin O'Higgins, 308; Liam
    Tobin, 306–9; naval bases, 315; Sam
    Maguire, xxii; Seán McGarry, xxiii; Tom
    Barry, 306
Asgard, 108, 236
Ashbourne, xxiii
Ashe, Thomas, 55, 79, 185, 386
Asquith, Herbert, 12, 25, 109, 132–3
Assassination Squad, *see* Squad
Aud, 119, 122, 124
Auxiliaries, ix, xxxi–xxxii, ix

Balfour Report, x–xi
B&I Line, 74
Ballykissane, 122
Banna Strand, 122
Barrett, Joseph, 37, 47–8, 59, 86, 126–7
Barrett, Michael, 24
Barrett, Séamus, 384
Barrett, Seán, 382

Barry-Walsh, Stephen, 54
Barry, Leslie Mary, 324
Barry, Thomas, 54, 57
Barry, Tom, 161, 267, 299, 320
Bartholomew Teeling Circle, xxi, 54, 55, 59
Barton, Detective Sergeant John, 323
Barton, Robert, 161, 215, 315, 322, 324
Béal na mBláth, 296
Béaslaí, Piaras, 54, 79, 390
Beggars Bush Barracks, 293
Begley, Florence, 324
Belgian Congo, xvi
Belle Vue Prison, 23
Benedict XV, Pope, 12, 32
Birrell, Augustine, 130
Black and Tans, ix, xxxi–xxxii, 15
Bloody Sunday 1920, 215, 247
Blueshirts, xv
Blythe, Ernest: biography, xv; Church bans
    IRB, 38; interviewee, 324; joins IRB,
    55–6; on Collins, 167–8, 295; prisoner
    executions, 316, 323; recruiter, 61
Boland, Gerry, 158
Boland, Harry: arms shipments, 230–1;
    conflict with Clan na Gael, 231; demands
    more Clan support, 232; friendship with
    Collins, 198; Supreme Council member,
    386–8; visits US, 209, 230
Booth, Frank, 110
Boundary Commission, 17, 266
Bowyer Bell, J., xvii
Boyce, D.G., 11
Boylan, Seán, 252, 391
Braniff, Dan, 384, 387
Breen, Dan: arms raids, 212; election of
    1918, 206; isolation, 213; Soloheadbeg,
    201; war policy disagreements, 194–5
Breen, Myles, 324, 390

524 Index

Breen, Tom, 386
Brennan-Whitmore, William, 128, 173, 324
Brennan, John, 221
Brennan, Michael: Army Mutiny, 306;
  changed IRB role, 150; Church support,
  39; IRA Division Commander, 390;
  potential IRB members scrutinised,
  59; reprove by Mulcahy, 218; Rising
  preparations, 118–19;
Brennan, Robert, xv, 77, 188–9
Brennan, Una, xv, 3,
Brett, Sergeant, 23
British evacuation, 283
Browne, Charles, 324
Browne, Margaret, 121
Broy, Eamon, 7–8
Brugha, Cathal: accuses Collins of
  corruption, 238–9, 257; biography, xv–
  xvi, 236; character, 235; criticises IRB,
  139–41, 143, 236–7; drafts allegiance
  oath, 223–4; fanatic, 235; gives salary
  to Mulcahy, 238; Howth gunrunning,
  107–8, 236; joins IRB, 54, 236; opposes
  attacks on RIC, military, 218; opposes
  Treaty, xvi; resentment of Collins, 140,
  146, 159, 169, 237–9; shot in Civil War,
  294; wounded in Rising, 139, 236
Bryan, Dan, 320, 324
Bureau of Military History, ix, 20; 45, 322
Burke, Thomas, 24
Buswell's Hotel, Dublin, 107
Byrne, Ben, 324
Byrne, Christopher, 43
Byrne, Gerry, 86
Byrne, James, 251
Byrne, Vinnie, xxxi, 292, 323, 324
Byrnes, John, 17

Carleton, Peter, 161
Carrigan, Charles, 384, 385, 386
Casement, Roger: arms imports, 107; arrest,
  122; biography, xvi; execution, xvi, 172;
  role with Volunteers, 90; tries to recruit
  POWs, 113
Castle Document, 120, 122
Catholic Church: ambivalence to rebels, 39;

condemns Fenians, 34; condemns IRA,
  32, 41; condemns secret societies, 32;
  opposes conscription, 206; opposes IRB,
  2, 31, 34–8, 40
Cavendish, Lord Frederick, 24
Ceannt, Áine, 130
Ceannt, Éamonn: 111; critic of Hobson,
  120–1; HQ staff, 112, 390; Military
  Committee, 111; occupies South Dublin
  Union, 236; proposes Hyde for election,
  80; Volunteers Executive, 389
Centre: IRB Circle head, x;
Chamberlain, Neville, 315
Chartres, John, 8
Chester Castle, 23
Childers, Erskine, 107
Chotah, 108
Civil War: attempts to prevent, 285; birth of
  modern Ireland, 316; ceasefire, 299, 302;
  executions, 297, 316; execution records
  destroyed, 324; Four Courts occupation,
  286; Liam Lynch key player, 269;
  motivations, 10
Clan na Gael: description, x; Fenians, 22–3;
  funds IRB and Rising, 231; officers, 35;
  supports a rising, 72–3
Clancy, Peadar, 215
Clancy, Seán, 324
Clarence Mangan Circle, 74, 149
Clarke, Dr Emmet, xxxi, 7, 323, 324
Clarke, James, 29
Clarke, Joe, 324
Clarke, Kathleen: biography, xvi–xvii; chooses
  Collins for INAVDF, 155–6; INAVDF
  President, xii, xvii, 155; IRPDF President,
  xii, xvii, 155; memoirs, 323; on de Valera's
  illusions, 280–1; opposes Treaty, 278;
  revives IRB, 134–5; Rising and Sinn Féin,
  133
Clarke, Liam, 135, 187
Clarke, Thomas, 323
Clarke, Tom: biography xvi, 97; bombing
  campaign, 98; Catholicism, 32; concerns
  about Casement, 113; controls IRB,
  71; critical of Hobson, 92–4; driving

Index

525

force for Rising, 99; IRB Treasurer, 385; opinion on Pearse, 105; personality, 96; plans Rising, 108–9; President, 127–8; reads Proclamation at GPO, 128; revives IRB, 57, 63, 98–100; royal visit, 19; self–government, 7; Supreme Council member, 383, 384; transfers to IRB, 74; tried by IRB, 68–9

Clerkenwell Prison, 24

Cloonan, Patrick, 324

Clune, Archbishop Patrick, 229, 247, 248

Cobh attack, 309

Cohalan, Bishop Daniel, 40

Cohalan, Judge Daniel, 232

Coleman, Bessie, 12

Colgan, Patrick, 139

Collins, Con, 55, 387

Collins, Michael: ADC to Plunkett, 160; Albert Sylvester's impressions, 260; Ashe oration, 186; biography, xvii; Brugha's hostility, xvii, 140, 146, 159, 161; colleagues' opinion, xiii, 161–2, 166–8; controls the Squad, 216–7, 323; Cork loyalties, 160, 215; dominates IRB, 14, 157–8, 198; drafts new IRB constitution, 287–8; energy, 155–6; excessive drinking, 59; financial skills, 163–4, 194, 228; Four Courts attack, 286; GHQ staff, 390; governs autocratically, 295–6; guerilla mastermind, 163, 214–5; Henry Wilson killing, 290–2; influences Jewish terrorists, 21; inside 10 Downing St, 260; intelligence achievements, 5, 26; IRB collapse, 21; IRB key to his success, 5; IRB loyalty, xvii, xviii; IRB offices, 99, 168; joins GAA, 78; killed at Béal na mBláth, 296; Lloyd George's opinion, 152; major figure in Frongoch, 152–4; makes Micky Joe Costello IO, 321–2; NAF secretary, 155; National Loan, 220, 223; Note of March 1922 IRB meeting, 379–81; on Brugha, 235; personality, 160–3, 167; positions held, 165–7; pranks, 162–3, 320; realises a republic unobtainable, 248; released from

Frongoch, 151; reluctance to join Treaty negotiations, 259–60, 273; Rising failure, 15; social progressive, xxxix; stepping stone to a republic, 261; suggests shooting Bishop Cohalan, 41; Supreme Council member, 386–7; tactical skills, 16–17; tells Liam Lynch a republic unlikely, 260; tries to avoid/end Civil War, 290, 293, 294, 296; tries to heal rift with Clan, 231; urged to visit US, 233–4; weapons swapping, 292; works closely with Seán MacDermott, 121, 156

Comer, Madge, 325

Comerford, Máire, xxix, 121, 168

Comerford, Vincent, 128, 206

Constitutions of IRB: 1869–1873: 328–32; 1873–1917: 340–5; 1917–1922: 346–56; Amendments 1919–1921: 357; 1922: 358–65; 1923: 366–74

Conlon, Martin, 221–2, 253, 297, 321, 386–7

Connell, Joseph, xxix

Connolly, James, xviii, 84, 109

Connolly, Neilus, 324

Connolly, Richard: frustrated at meetings, 64; Hobson and Clarke's hostility 93; military committee, 111; need for Rising during the war, 99; role of Volunteers, 72; Supreme Council member, 384, 386, 388

conscription: act of war, 200; election of 1918, 205–6; justifies Rising, 72, 109, 115; Lloyd George bill, 195; war of independence roots, 6, 25, 126, 173

Cope, Sir Alfred: biography, xviii; 17; distorted narrative, 20; peace efforts, 245; releases Arthur Griffith and Eoin MacNeill, 314; secret negotiations with Collins, 312, 314

Cork Young Ireland Society, 57

Cosgrave, William, 176, 281

Costello, John A., 325

Costello, Micky Joe, 163–4, 279, 321–2, 325

Cowley, Michael, 54, 70, 382–3

Croke Park, 77, 188

Croke, Archbishop, 76–7

526 Index

Crowe, Michael, 382, 383
Crowley, Michael, 325
Cullen, Cardinal Paul xviii, 33
Cumann na mBan, x, xxi, xxxi, 128
Cunningham, James, 251
Curragh Mutiny, 13
Cusack, Michael, 76–7
Customs House attack, 244

Dáil courts, 220
Dalton, Colonel Charles, 308
Dalton, Emmet: biography, xxxi; Brugha's
    fanaticism, 235; death of Collins, 322;
    First World War medal, 322; interviewee,
    325; on Collins' abilities, 166; Treaty
    negotiations, 262
Dalton, Hugh, 193
Daly, Charlie, 390
Daly, Dinny, 161
Daly, Edward, xvi, 112,
Daly, Francis, 36, 274–5, 325
Daly, James, 38, 46
Daly, John, xvi
Daly, Paddy, 117
Daly, Patrick (P.T.), 64, 65, 67–8, 382, 386
Daly, Séamus, 106
de Barra, Éamonn, 278, 325
de Lacey, Larry, xxxi, 3, 61, 96, 322, 325
de Lamartine, Alphonse, 22
de Loughrey, Peter, 102
de Valera, Éamon: accepts compromise on a
    republic, 232, 259; ambiguous political
    views, 183–4; biography, xviii, 185;
    Brugha's jealousy of Collins, 239; claims
    presidency, 209–10; Civil War ceasefire,
    299; Clare election, 175–6; complexity,
    185; concessions to Lloyd George, 257;
    de Valera Papers, 319; Dublin Brigade,
    389; evades execution, 133; government
    options, 220; HQ staff, 112; interviewee,
    xxxi, 325; joins IRB, 113; Lloyd George's
    impressions, 256–7; opposes IRB, 40;
    presses Collins to go to London, 259–60;
    President of Ireland, 324; religious views
    on the Rising, 182–3; resentment of
    Collins, 166; resents IRA independence,

293; RIC ostracisation, 217; rift with
    Clan na Gael, 231–3; romantic views,
    xxix; tries to prevent Civil War, 293;
    undemocratic approach, 295; undermines
    plenipotentiaries, 262; US visit, 222,
    231–3; vacillation re IRA, 229–30
Deakin, Séamus, 72, 383, 384
Deasy, Liam, 242–3, 253–4, 267, 320, 325
Deasy, Séamus, 82
declaration of the Republic 1949, 315
Delaney, Edward, 2
Dennehy, Dan, 59
Devlin, Joseph, 101, 107
Devlin's pub, 309
Devoy, John: biography, xix; conflict with de
    Valera and Boland, 231, 276; IRB funding,
    73, 135, 136; IRB structures, 65; supports
    a rising, 72–3; supports Treaty, 277
Dillon, John, 132, 172
Dillon, Luke, 233
Dillon, Thomas, xxv
Dobbyn, Séamus, 144–5, 189, 387
Dolan, Anne, 159, 163
Dolan, Charles, 103
Dolan, Joe, 292
Dominion status, x–xi
Donovan, Dan, 325
Donovan, Jim, 325
Dore, Éamonn, 117, 153–4, 175–6
Dowling, James, 196
Dowling, Seán, 325
Doyle, Gerald, 135, 174
Doyle, Thomas, 325
Drohan, Frank, 87, 144
Dublin Castle, xi, xxx, 7
Dublin Co-op Clothing Company, x
Dublin Metropolitan Police, xi, xvii
Duggan, Éamonn, 55, 390
Dunbar, Martin, 276, 325
Dungannon Clubs, xx
Dunne, Reginald, 290, 292
Dunne, Seán, 325

Easter Rising: civilian deaths, 6, 132; Cork–
    Kerry non–participation, 141–2; death
    sentences, 133; deception of MacNeill,

118; disorganisation, 116–23; executions, 132–3; female involvement, 129–30; flawed planning, 125–6; IRB participants, 392–5; justification, 6–7; military casualties, 184; participant analysis, 141; participant occupations, 392–5; Proclamation, 8; secrecy, 117; Sinn Féin misnomer, 132; unsupported, 15; ultimate failure, 125–6; women couriers, 121

Edward VII, King, 47

Ellis, John, hangman, 292

Ellwood, John, 54

enlistment in British forces, 184–5, 206–7

Evans, Robert, 5

excessive drinking, 57, 58–9

excommunication, 19, 33, 40, 41

Fahy, Frank, 55

Fahy, Padraic, 325

Fanning, John, 325

Fanon, Frantz, 310

Fenian Ram submarine, 24

Fenians: bombing campaigns, xxiv; Brotherhood, xi; description, xi; motivate 1916 leaders, 8; US groups, 22, 23

Ferriter, Diarmuid, 9, 58

Fianna Éireann, xi, xxii, 101

Fianna Fáil, xviii, xxvi

Figgis, Darrell, 164–5, 189, 197, 209

First Dáil: allegiance oath, 223–6; condemns Soloheadbeg ambush, 217; ministers, 208; one party parliament, 208; second meeting, 221; unclear relationship with IRA, 225

Fitzgerald, P.N., 57

Fitzgibbon, Seán, 83, 90, 102, 108

Fitzpatrick, Michael, 325

Fitzpatrick, Seán, 320, 325

Fleming, Mick, 87

Fleming, Patrick, 391

Flood, Matt, 325

Fogarty, Bishop Michael, 185–6, 245

Foster, Roy, 10

Four Courts: attack ordered, 286, 287; seizure, 267, 292, 293; shelling, 293; surrender, 294

Foxe, Elizabeth, 20

Free State constitution, 284–5, 286

French Foreign Legion, xix

French Revolution, 7

French, Field Marshal Sir John, 196, 221

Frongoch, 39, 151, 152–4

Furlong, Joseph, 47

Furlong, Thomas, 102

G Division RIC, 215

Gaelic American, xix

Gaelic Athletic Association: description, xi, 76–7; IRB initiative, 76–7; IRB takeover, 80–1; manifesto, 77; nationalism, 77; RIC ban, 77

Gaelic League, xi, xx, 78–9

Gallagher, Frank, 146

Gandhi, Mahatma, 11

Garrett, J.J., 325

Garvin, Tom, 290

Gaynor, Liam, 139, 190, 242, 386–7

General Post Office, xxi

George V, King, 19, 47, 241

Geraghty, John, 65, 382

German Plot, xi, xvii, 196–7

Gibbons, Seán, 28

Gleeson, James, xviii

Gleeson, Joseph, 129, 134, 158, 383, 384, 385

Glynn, Peadar, 325

Gogan, Liam, 93, 325

Government of Ireland Act, 241

governance of IRB, 48–53

Gray, Ambassador David, 132

Greene, Arthur, 26

Gresham Hotel, Dublin, 266

Griffith, Arthur: abandons abstentionism, 171–2; biography, xix; Joyce's opinion, xix; monarchist, xiv, 10, 88, 189; rejects absolutism, xix; pacifism, 87, 172; separatism, xiv; signs Treaty, 264; wins Cavan election, 196

Hackett, Dan, 36

Hales, Seán, 278

Hales, Tom, 142, 146, 157, 213, 387

528   Index

Harris, Tom, 29

Hart, Peter, 129

Harty, Arhbishop, 217

Haskins, Rory, 26

Hayes, Michael: 206, 238; Collins' ability, 163; conscription, 206; interviewee, 325; low opinion of IRB, 27; middle-class IRB, 54; on Treaty, 281

Henderson, Frank, 147–8

Henderson, Leo, 293, 295

Hobson, Bulmer: arms imports, 106; biography, xx, 90; Clan na Gael's support, 73; cowardice accusations, 96; extent of IRB, 57; formation of Volunteers, 83; HQ staff, 112, 389; IRB constitution on a rising, 89; opposes a rising, xx, 95, 119–20; personality, 90; revives IRB, 5, 55; rift with Clarke and McDermott, 91–3, 104; Supreme Council member, 383–4; Volunteers Executive, 389

Hoey, Detective, 215

Hogan, Dan, 390

Hogan, Liam, 248, 325

Holland, John, 24

Holloway Prison, xvii

Holohan, Garry, 59, 148–9, 162

Homan, John F., 294

Home Rule: and IPP, 25, 56, 63, 133, 172, 173, 195; and Parnell, 32; and partition, 246; and republicans, 92, 106, 206, and UVF, 70, 82, 83, 106; delay in implementation, 16, 25, 134; enactment, 20–1; unionist opposition to, 12, 13, 14

Howth gunrunning, xvi, xx, 107–8

Humphries, Sighle, xxxi, 325

Hyde, Douglas: biography, xx; excludes extreme nationalists, 79–80; Gaelic League founder, 78; leaves Gaelic League, 80; supports enlistment, 80

influenza, 219

informers, 22, 62, 184

Innishannon, 213, 217, 226

International Court of Justice, 12

Invincibles, 24

Irish Citizen Army xi, xviii, 84

Irish Convention, xi

Irish Engineering Union, 222

Irish Freedom, xvii, xxi, 36, 65–7

Irish Hospitals Sweepstakes, 318

Irish Hospitals Trust, xxiii

Irish Military Service Pensions Collection, 121

Irish Nation, xix

Irish National Aid and Volunteers' Dependants' Fund (INAVDF), xii, xiii, xviii, 155–6, 163, 166, 173, 176

Irish Parliamentary Party (IPP): AOH, ix; collapse, 16; collaborates with IRB, 5; description, xii; gains control of Volunteers, 91

Irish People, xx, xxiii, 33,

Irish Relief Fund of America, 155

Irish Republican Prisoners' Dependants' Fund (IRPDF), xii, xiii, xvii, 155

Irish Revolutionary Brotherhood, 1

Irish Volunteer Executive, xii

Irish Volunteer Provisional Committee, xii, xvi

Irish War News, 127

Irvine, George, xv, 82–3, 149, 252

Irwin, Sam, 124, 325

Isaacs, Jeremy, 319

Jackson, Val, 27, 45, 46, 48, 69, 136–7

James Fintan Lawlor Circle, 46

Joachim Prince, 10

Jones, Tom, 256, 257

Jordan, Stephen, 325

Joyce, James, xix, 12

Kavanagh, Seán, 325

Kearney, Patrick, 68

Kearney, Peadar, 386

Keating Circle, 79

Keating, Noel, 2

Keaveney, Andrew, 60–1, 226

Kee, Robert, 319

Kelly, Billy, 97

Kelly, Daniel, 35, 189

Kelly, Dr Seán, 125

Kelly, Henry, 325

Index

Kelly, Paddy, x
Kelly, Robert, 77, 110
Kelly, Tom, 54, 127
Kelly's Hotel, Portlaoise, 38
Kennedy, Ben, 291–2
Kennedy, Luke, 222, 386–8
Kennedy, Tadhg, 163, 168, 186
Keogh, Seán, 135–6
Kerr, Neil, 74, 386–8
Kettle, Laurence, 85
Keyes, Raphael, 325
Kickham, Cathal, 137
Kickham, Charles, xx, 34, 83
Kilcoole gunrunning, 108, 236
Kilroy, Michael, 19, 163, 390
Kimmage Garrison, xxiv
Knocklong, 201

Lalor & Co., xvi
Lalor, James Fintan, 47
Lardner, Laurence, 121
Larkfield Manor, 129
Larkin, James, 46
Larkin, Michael, 23
Lavin, Andrew, 387
Lawless, Joseph, 78–9, 118
League of Nations, 12
Leitrim Guardian, 103
Liberty Clubs, xii, xxiv, 170–1
Lincoln Prison escapes, 219
Lindsay, Maria, 29
Lively, Patrick, 386
Lloyd George, David: accepts Home Rule, 12–13, 25; biography, xx; delayed US entry into war, 14; demands suppression of Four Courts garrison, 293; Free State constitution, 286; meets de Valera, 256–7; negotiating stance, 245, 313–4; on Collins, 314; on de Valera, 314; partition flexibility, 246; reliance on unionists, 247; replaces Asquith, 174; rules out a republic, 257, 259; secret negotiations, 17; threats to resume war, 264–5, 267; Treaty and, 264; Wales Home Rule, 313
Loughran, Eugene, 237
Lowell, James Russell, 306

Lowry, Donal, 14
Luby, Thomas Clarke, 44
Lynch, Diarmuid: biography, xx–xxi; Connacht membership, 58; Dublin membership, 61–2; envoy to Clan na Gael, 87; insurrection plans, 111; IRA Division Commander, 391; IRB organisation, 53, 55, 57, 75; on Collins, 164; recruitment, 46; religious obstacles, 34–5, 37; sent to Cork, 142; Supreme Council member, 70, 383, 384, 385–7
Lynch, Fionan, 87
Lynch, Liam: biography, xxi, 269; efforts to avoid Civil War, 286; killed by National Army, 299; rejects Treaty, 270, 275–6; resigns commission, 240; Supreme Council member, 388
Lynch, Robert, 166
Lynn, Dr Kathleen, 129–30
Lyons, F.S.L., 56
Lyons, George, 177, 182

Macardle, Dorothy, 228–9
MacBride, Major John, xxi, 8
MacBride, Maud Gonne, xxi, xxi, 3
MacBride, Seán: biography, xxi; de Valera's secretary, 293; Dublin Brigade, 389; Four Courts attack, 293; interviewee, 325; opinion of IRB, 27; peace prizes, xxi; Supreme Council member, 382, 383; Treaty negotiations and Collins, 263
MacCurtain, Tomás, 31–2
MacDermott, Seán: arms imports, 107–8; biography, xxi, 100–1; controls IRB, 71; critic of Church, 32; driving force for Rising, 99; Gaelic League member, 79–80; Irish Freedom manager, 66, 102; Keating Circle, 81; meets Clarke, 103; on Kathleen Clarke, 134; persists with Rising, 125; recruiting skills, 102, 103; Sinn Féin organiser, 102; Supreme Council, 65, 383, 384, 385
MacDonagh, Thomas, 107, 115, 125, 389
MacEntee, Seán, 326
MacEoin, Seán: biography, xxxi; confronts de Valera at funeral, 258; Easter Rising,

530 Index

133; first Dáil, 208; interviewee, 326; IPP election victory, 145–6; IRA Division Commander, 390; IRB wind up, 309–10, 318; Lincoln prison escapes, 219; pressed by Boland to go to US, 276; promotes IRB in Dáil, 210; secrecy, 45; Supreme Council member, 64–5, 388

MacGillian, Bernard, 119

Macken, Peadar, 94

Mackey, Dominic, 117

MacLoughlin, Seán, 212

MacMahon, Seán, 248, 267, 305, 388, 390

MacMahon, Thomas, 326

MacNeill, Eoin: biography, xxi–xxii; Boundary Commission, 17; cancels Rising, xxiv, 123–7; Gaelic League founder, 70, Gaelic League President, 81; Manifesto, 85–6; splits the Volunteers, 109–10; supports de Valera in by-election, 175; Volunteers' leader, 84–5

Macready, General Nevil, 241

MacSwiney, Mary, 8

MacSwiney, Terence, xxxii, 254

Madden, John, 146

Maguire, Sam: biography, xxii; Collins connections, xxii, 78; Cup, xxii; Henry Wilson killing, 291–2; Supreme Council member, 388

Maguire, Thomas, 222, 326, 390

Maguire, Tom, 4, 19, 29, 271

Mahon, Lt Gen. Sir Bryan, 172

Malone, James, 160, 249

Malone, Thomas, 4, 152, 261, 296, 326

Manchester Martyrs, 23, 34, 57

Mansion House Conference, xii

Mansion House Convention, xii, 188–9

Markievicz, Constance, xxii, x, xxii, 130

Martin, Éamon, 91

Mathews, Seán, 236

Matthews, John, 140

Maxwell, General Sir John, 132–3, 136, 172

McAnerney, John, 144

McArdle, Eoin, 150, 195

McArdle, Peter, 325

McCabe, Alec: arms imports via Liverpool, 74; arrest, 117; Collins dominates IRB, 158; Dáil–IRB relationship, 226–7; executions, 324; interviewee, xxxi, 326; recruited, 58; Supreme Council member, 385–7

McCann, Peadar, 127

McCartan, Patrick: approaches Russia, 138; Church's attitude to IRB, 36–7, 39; Irish Freedom editor, 66–9; opposes a rebellion, 71–2; opposes IPP dominance, 91; Rising date, 116; Supreme Council member, 386

McCarthy, Dan, 77–8, 168–9

McCormack, Patrick, 385–7

McCormick, Michael, 391

McCullough, Denis: Collins' intelligence network, 5; clerical hostility, 121–2, dream for Ireland, 11; Frongoch, 152–3; infiltration, 76; IRB President, 71–2, 382, 385; joins IRB, 56–7; lack of support for a rising, 89; Supreme Council member, 382, 383, 384

McCullough, James, 150, 216

McDonnell, Patrick, 259

McDonnell, Petie Joe, x, 266–7

McDunphy, Michael, 20

McEllistrim, Tom, 4, 326

McElligott, James, 8, 326

McGahern, John, xxix

McGallogly, John, 251

McGarrity, Joe, 35, 233, 277

McGarry, Seán: arms shortfall, 251; biography, xxiii; joins IRB, 55; Lincoln prison escape, 219; Redmond's growing influence, 91; Supreme Council member, 386–7; Volunteers' leader, 84

McGilligan, Patrick, 326

McGinley, William, 253

McGinn, Michael, 36

McGrath, Joseph, 155, 309

McGuinness, Joseph, 174

McGuinness, Martin, 312

McGuirk, Patrick, 222

McKee, Dick, 215, 390

McKenna, Kathleen, 162, 320

McKenna, Séamus, 146

McKenna, W.J., 326
McKenna, Willy, 162
McMahon, Liam, 265–6
McQuillan, Francis, 7
Meehan, Francis, 103
Mellows, Liam, 178–9, 297, 390
Miles, Sir Thomas, 108
Military Archives, ix
Military Service Pensions Collection, 121, 129
Milroy, Seán, 219
Minerva Hotel, Dublin, 136
Molony, Helena, 129
Monteith, Robert, 114
Moore, Col. Maurice, 90
Moore, John, 258
Moran, D.P., 83
Moriarty, Bishop David, xxiii, 31, 34, 42
Morning Star pub, Birkenhead, 68
Morrissey, Gilbert, 47
Mountjoy prison, 176
Moylett, Patrick, 296, 326
Mulcahy, Patrick, 249, 326
Mulcahy, Richard: biography, xxiii;
candidates in 1918 election, 204; cancels
Tipperary operation, 218; deniability,
214; describes IRB, 2–3, 5; distances
himself from IRB, 198; effect of Church
ban, 40; Frongoch, 154; General HQ
staff, 390; IRA defeat, 16; IRB–Volunteer
merge, 165; joins IRB, 55; meets Army
mutineers, 307–8; Mulcahy Papers, 319;
National Army Commander, xiii, 307;
supports Collins, 168, 198; supports
Treaty, 266; Treaty not a victory, 280
Mulholland, John, 72, 382, 383, 384, 385
Mullaney, Patrick, 4, 48, 59, 270, 285, 314
Mullins, Billy, 283
Murphy, Archdeacon John, 155
Murphy, Batt, 326
Murphy, Fintan, 176, 390
Murphy, Gregory, 100, 118, 386–7
Murphy, J., 382
Murphy, Jim, 326, 383
Murphy, Seán, 117, 137, 153, 252

Murphy, William, 159, 163
Murray, Joseph, 98
Murray, P.A., 310

Nally, Patrick, 76
Nally, Tom, 54
Nathan, Sir Matthew, 131
National Aid Fund, xii–xiii, 155
National Army, 311, 274
Neeson, Eoin, 272
Neligan, David, 3, 215, 326
New Ireland Assurance Co., 317
Nicholls, George, 55, 79, 121
Nicholls, Harry, 326
Northern Ireland parliament, 241
Norway, Arthur, xxvii, 13, 24–5,
Notting Hill Geraldines FC, 78
Noyk, Michael, 176, 318
Nunan, George, 326

Ó Briain, Liam, 8–9, 120, 132, 148, 326,
392
Ó Broin, Liam, 326
Ó Ciatháin, Seoirse, 94
Ó Drisceoil, Donal, 204
Ó Fathaig, Pádraig, 197
Ó Gaora, Colm, 210
Ó Maille, Padraic, 79–80
Ó Maoileoin, Séamus, 41
Ó Murthuile, Seán, 73, 136, 159, 249, 302,
386–7
Ó Riain, Pádraig, 389
O'Boyle, Manus, 39–40, 139
O'Boyle, Neil John, 65, 382
O'Brien, Edna, xxix
O'Brien, Henry, 38
O'Brien, Michael, 23
O'Brien, Nora Connolly, xxxi, 326
O'Brien, Patrick, 326
O'Byrne, Brendan, 326
O'Byrne, Fiach McHugh, xxx
O'Cahill, Donal, 326
O'Callaghan, Donal, 253, 254
O'Casey, Seán, 46, 55
O'Connell, Christy, 284, 326
O'Connell, J.J. (Ginger), 120, 267, 293, 390

532 Index

O'Connor, Art, 210
O'Connor, Batt: biography, xxiii; joins IRB, 55, 79; on Collins, 156–7, 198; Volunteer piety, 39
O'Connor, Fr Dominic, 41
O'Connor, Frank, xxix
O'Connor, Rory, 286, 297, 390
O'Connor, Tom, 257
O'Daly, Patrick, 5, 292, 387
O'Doherty, Joseph: 1798 memories, xxx–xxxi 4; continuity from 1916, 137; de Valera alliance, 189; duplication of control, 199–200; interviewee, 326; IRA control, 319–20; O'Hegarty's influence, 151; oral history, 7; recruitment, 4
O'Doherty, Katherine, 147
O'Doherty, Kitty, 282–3
O'Doherty, Liam, 28, 169, 326
O'Doherty, Séamus, 136, 138–9, 170, 311, 386–7
O'Donnell, Peadar: conscription threat, 173; conservative revolution, 312–3; 322; failure of Four Courts occupation, 322; interviewee, xxxi, 326; low opinion of Rory O'Connor, 286; oath loyalty, 19
O'Donnell, Red Hugh, xxx
O'Donoghue, Florence, xviii, 148, 161 226
O'Donovan Rossa, Jeremiah, xxiii–xxiv
O'Donovan, Séamus, 390
O'Driscoll, Barney, 163
O'Duffy, Eimar, 120, 389
O'Duffy, Eoin: Deputy Chief of Staff, 239–40; IRA GHQ staff, 390; offers Army jobs, 279; chief of police, 309; Supreme Council member, 168, 387–8
O'Dwyer, Éamon, 147, 202, 216
O'Dwyer, Liam, 27, 326
O'Flanagan, Fr Michael, 41, 170, 247, 255
O'Growney, Fr Eugene, 78
O'Halpin, Eunan, 184
O'Hanlon, John, 383
O'Hanlon, Patrick, 317
O'Hara, Michael, 326
O'Hegarty, Diarmuid: IRB GHQ staff, 390; IRB President, 296–7; Supreme Council

member, 386–8; released from prison, 136; reorganises IRB, 151, 252
O'Hegarty, P.S.: arranges 1922 Collins–de Valera meeting, 283; book translated into Hebrew, 21; Henry Wilson killing, 290–1; need for insurrection, 70–1, 95; rising plans, 114–5; Supreme Council member, 382, 383–4, 387; swears in Collins to IRB, 78; Treaty discussions, 273
O'Hegarty, Seán, 57, 67, 73
O'Higgins, Kevin, 256, 302, 308
O'Keefe, Seán T., 270–1, 385
O'Keeffe, Páidín, 55, 166, 204
O'Kelly, Fergus, 9, 326
O'Kelly, Phyllis, 326
O'Kelly, Seán T., 54, 64, 81
O'Leary, John, 56
O'Leary, Michael, 26
O'Mahony, John, 33
O'Mahony, Patrick, 110
O'Malley, Ernie, 9, 225, 391
O'Neill, Art, xxx
O'Neill Henry, xxx
O'Neill, Stephen, 279
O'Rahilly, Michael (The), 55, 80, 85, 90, 106, 112, 390
O'Rahilly, Nancy, 239
O'Reilly, Bridie, 197
O'Reilly, John, 87, 152, 159, 205, 326, 205
O'Reilly, M.W., 389
O'Reilly, Tom, 326
O'Rourke, Joseph, 74, 83–4, 137, 149, 157, 205
O'Sullivan, Fr Denis, 35–7
O'Sullivan, Gearóid, 248, 309, 387–8, 390
O'Sullivan, Joseph, 290, 292
O'Sullivan, Patrick, 327
oaths of allegiance, 10, 44–5, 223–7, 263–4, 272
oaths, iv, 19
Óglaigh na hÉireann: GHQ, xi; origins, xii, xiii
Old IRA, 308–9
Oman, William, 173, 326
Orange Order, xv

Paris Peace Conference, 207, 208, 217, 220

Index

Parnell, Charles Stewart, xxv, 32, 322
Pearse, Margaret, 155
Pearse, Patrick: arms imports, 106;
biography, xxiv; blood sacrifice, 9;
German monarch, 10; HQ staff, 390;
insists on Rising, 125; meets Clarke,
104; orders manoeuvres, 120; plans 1914
rebellion, 108; rejected by IRB, 56; Rossa
oration, xxiv; Supreme Council member,
386; surrenders, 130; undermines
Hobson, 93; Volunteer Executive, 389;
Volunteers' finances, 74
Pentonville Prison, xvi
Percival, Major Arthur, 28
Phoenix National Literary Society, xxiii
Pilkington, Liam, 19, 390
Pius IX, Pope, 33
Plaza Hotel, Gardiner Row, 186
Plunket, Count George, xii, xxiv–xxv, 10
Plunkett, Eoghan, 161–2
Plunkett, Geraldine, xxv, 3, 113, 161
Plunkett, Grace, 120
Plunkett, Joseph: by-election, 170; cadet
corps, 111; HQ staff, 112, 389; plans
Rising, 24; Volunteer Executive, 389
Plunkett, Philomena, 119
Pollard, Hugh, 78, 210, 212
Portobello Barracks, 162–3
Price, Éamon, 390
Proclamation of the Republic, 104, 128, 129
Provisional IRA, xiii, 6

Rathmore Circle, 59
recruitment procedures, 55–62, 72, 76–88
Redmond, John, xxv, 80
Redmond, Major William, 145, 175
Regan, John, 295
Reilly, Jack, 253
revolutionary women, 121
Reynolds, John, 155
Reynolds, Molly, 327
Reynolds, Peter, 327
Rice, John Joe, 260
Ridgeway, Harry, 327
Robbins, Frank, 178–9, 327

Robinson, Séumas, 149–50, 194, 200
Ronan, Patrick, 327
Ross, Violet, 6–7
Royal Irish Constabulary, xiii, xxix, 63, 87
Royal Ulster Constabulary, xiv
Russell, Charles, 161
Russell, Seán 390
Ruttledge, P.J., 77, 299
Ryan, Frank, 279

Shamir, Yitzhak, 21
Sheehan, Donagh, 250
Sheehan, Donal, 54
Sheehan, Michael, 250
Sheehan, T., 389
Sheehy Skeffington, Francis, 172
Sheehy Skeffington, Hanna, 130, 209
Shields, Jack, 143, 144, 145
Shortt, Edward, 170, 213
Shouldice, Frank, 154
Sinn Féin, xiv, xii, 10, 133
Siubhlaigh, Máire Ní, 206
Skinnider, Margaret, 129
Slater, Thomas, 86
Slattery, Jim, 27, 327
Smith, Detective Patrick, 215
Smuts, Jan, 266
Soloheadbeg, 201, 217, 219, 226
Somerville, Edith, 6–7
Special Irish Branch, 24
Squad, Army Mutiny and, 306; Bloody
Sunday and, xxxi, 215; Collins and, xxix,
168, 215–17, 292, 294; Paddy Daly and,
117; formation of, 323; IRB and, xxvii;
Dick McKee and, 215
St Flannan's College, 39
Stack, Austin, 122, 167, 238, 390
Stack, Liam, 390
Staines, Michael, 139, 389
Stephens, James, 22–3, 24, 184–5
Stern Gang, 21
Stern, Avraham, 21
Stonyhurst College, 111
Supreme Council IRB Circular, March 2021,
375–8

534   Index

Supreme Council Members IRB, 1907–1922, 382–8

Sweeney, Joe, 154, 161, 327, 390

Sweetman TD, Roger, 247

Sylvester, Albert, 256, 264, 327

T & C Martin, 74

Taylor, A.J.P., 195

Taylor, Thomas, 25, 160, 327

Teeling Circle, xv

Terror, British and Irish xxix; Civil War and, xxix; Collins and, xxix; Fenian, 24, 32; IRA and, xxix; IRB legacy of, 3; Provisional Government and, 316

Terrorism, 1970s, xxxi; Collins and, xxix, xxxi; definition, xxviii

Thomson, Sir Basil, 246

Thornton, Frank, 306

Thornton, Michael, 387, 388

Tobin, Liam, 117, 267, 306–7, 385

Tobin, Seán, 120

Tomney, James, 87

Tone, Wolfe, 1–2

Townshend, Charles, 10, 29, 127

trade unions, 221–2

Traynor, Oscar, 391

Treacy, Seán, 144, 200, 218, 219

Treaty, Anglo–Irish: Cabinet backing, 266; Dáil debates, 278–81; Dáil ratifies, 278–9; Dominion status, 315; implementation, 18–9; Lloyd George, xx; night of the signing, 264; pressures on plenipotentiaries, 264–5; pro–Treaty election majority, 290; Republic excluded, 17–18, 265, 312; stepping stone to a republic, 261; Supreme Council accepts, 269–72; tactical Dáil voting, 279; terms, xiv

Trotsky, Leon, xxxi

Truce: agreed, 242, 248; Collins on its value, 251; described, xiv; IRA recognition, 248; mixed views, 238–9; negotiations, 229; secret discussions, 234, 242, 245

Twelve Apostles, *see* Squad

Twomey, Moss: xviii, 27, 60, 246, 327

UCD Archives, 319, 320, 321

Ulster Volunteer Force, xiv, 70, 106

United Irishman, xix, xxiv

Valentia radio station, 122

Vaughan's Hotel, Dublin, 278, 308

Victoria Cross, ix

Vize, Joe, 390

Voluntary Aid Detachment, 130

von Bernstorff, Ambassador Graf, 108

Walsh, Richard: allegiance oath, 226; Cabinet assassinations, 196; interviewee, 327; low opinion of Collins, 167; movement divisions, 171; opinion of IRB, 60; opposes armed operations, 218; Soloheadbeg, 217; sought by Collins, 164

Walton, Martin, 327

Ward, Alan, 53

Whelan, Patrick, 327

Whyte, John, 31

Willis, William, hangman, 292

Wilson, Sir Henry, xxii, 290–2

Wilson, Woodrow, 11, 174

Woodenbridge, xxv, 80, 109, 110

Woods, Séamus, 267, 327

Wylie, Evelyn, 132–3

Wynn's Hotel, Dublin, 85

Young Irelanders: rebellion 1848, xiv, 22